JPS

THE AMERICANIZATION
OF JEWISH CULTURE

1888-1988

Philip and Muriel Berman Edition

University of Nebraska Press | Lincoln

JPS

THE AMERICANIZATION
OF JEWISH CULTURE

1888–1988

JONATHAN D. SARNA

The Jewish Publication Society
Philadelphia

Library of Congress Cataloging-in-Publication Data
Sarna, Jonathan D.
JPS: the Americanization of Jewish culture, 1888–1988
Bibliography: p. Includes index.
1. Jewish Publication Society—History. 2. Jews—
United States—Publishing—History. 3. Jews—
United States—Intellectual life. I. Title.
z473.J46S27 1989 070.5'089924073 88–13696
ISBN 0–8276–0318–5 (hardback)
ISBN 978–0-8276–1550–2 (paperback)

Designed by Adrianne Onderdonk Dudden

T O   R U T H

Happy is the husband of an intelligent wife

Ben Sira 25:8

CONTENTS

PREFACE

When the Jewish Publication Society first approached me to write its centennial history I turned the job down. I was then engaged in another project and felt sure that what I was doing was more important than a "mere" institutional history could ever be. As I investigated further, however, I changed my mind. I came to realize that the story of JPS could shed light on a centrally important theme: the development and shaping of American Jewish culture. JPS agreed to let me write its history in this vein; as a history of its activities and books in the broader context of their times. My official mandate, approved by the Society's board of trustees, could scarcely have been more explicit: "[to] approach JPS as a microcosm of Jewish history and not as a 'back-slapping in-house chronology.' "

Carrying out this mission proved a considerable challenge. There were, I quickly discovered, no "giants" in this field on whose shoulders I could safely stand. Not a single book-length survey of American Jewish culture existed, much less one that placed Jewish literature and scholarship within a historical context. On a whole range of significant subjects I found no secondary literature at all. I have therefore frequently blazed my own trail. I hope that others retracing my steps will widen these paths and secure them, even as they move on into other frontiers of American Jewish culture that still stand in need of exploration.

A second challenge proved no less daunting. When it came to primary sources, I found myself faced with an embarrassment of riches. Over the course of one hundred years, JPS has published or co-published over seven hundred titles (many in multiple volumes), and produced minutes, reports, and correspondence occupying hundreds of thousands of yellowing pages. However much I might aspire to write the "definitive history," I concluded that if this volume were to remain within reasonable limits I had no choice but to be selective. So I have concentrated, especially in the more recent periods, on those themes that seem to me to have been especially significant. I have also placed far more stress on the books JPS has published than on the many dedicated people who over the years have served as its trustees, publication committee members, and officers. Admittedly, this has resulted in some measure of subjectivity, but I consider that to be an inescapable part of the historian's task. My aim, here and elsewhere, is to understand and interpret the past, not merely to recount it. That, to my mind, is what distinguishes my job from that of the ordinary chronicler.

In carrying out my task, I have tried to avoid simplistic judgments. Many important personalities march through the pages of this volume and I have endeavored to give all of them their due. But I am concerned here less with the search for heroes and villains than with the place of JPS within the larger developments in American, American Jewish, and modern Jewish life. I have been primarily interested in the themes that make JPS history broadly significant: the relationship between European Jewry and American Jewry; evolving attitudes toward America, modernity, Christianity, world Jewry, Reform Judaism, Zionism, the Holocaust, and modern Israel; the clash of interests between rabbis, scholars, and laymen; debates over cultural aims, purposes, responsibilities, and standards; and perennial tensions over such issues as assimilation and identity, tradition and change, unity and diversity, timelessness and relevance, caution and risk.

Several features of this narrative deserve special mention. First, I assume from the outset that American Jewish culture exists and can be characterized. Culture is a notoriously difficult term to define, but I am here concerned with its narrowest meaning—what Raymond Williams defines as "works and practices of intellectual and especially artistic activity." Many, to be sure, have bemoaned the dearth of Jewish cultural activity in America, and just recently a respected cultural historian has written that American Jewry's "*least* impressive feature . . . is its contribution to Jewish culture itself." Having now read so much of what JPS produced over the past century, however, I am inclined to disagree. The problem, as I have come to understand it, lies not with the production of Jewish culture in America, of which there is a great deal, but rather with its distribution and consumption. Too much of what *is* produced lies unsold, unread, and unappreciated.

Second, I argue here that American Jewish cultural and religious history should be understood and periodized differently than heretofore. Where others have mapped out progress along straight lines, I have tried to chart a more difficult, but I believe a more accurate, graph that rises through periods of awakening and revival, cascades into pools of cultural stagnation and decline, and then, like the proverbial phoenix, rises anew. Such cycles are, of course, well known to students of American history and religion but generally have not been applied to the experience of American Jews. This is particularly unfortunate, since the remarkable late-nineteenth- and early-twentieth-century revival that created JPS and breathed life into so many other manifestations of American Jewish culture bears many similarities to the Jewish cultural revival of our own times.

Finally, a word must be said about the sections of this narrative that deal with recent JPS history, specifically the years since long-time editor Solomon Grayzel retired in 1966. Unlike the rest of this book, these sections are based almost entirely on the public record; much of the private correspondence from this period remains closed. We are, moreover, too close to these memorable events to view them with proper historical perspective. For the sake of completeness, I have nevertheless recounted recent developments, albeit briefly, and I have also attempted to place them within some meaningful framework, tentative as it may be. At the same time, I am quite certain that, in another hundred years, the bicentennial historian of JPS will view these events quite differently. By then they will form part of a larger historical pattern, one whose outlines we cannot clearly fathom, but must continuously work to shape.

Writers of institutional histories, in thanking those who assist them, customarily comment on the "free hand" they were accorded in pursuing their work. In my case, this is more than a mere formality since the documents on which most of this work rests are now in the public domain, deeded by JPS to the Philadelphia Jewish Archives Center housed in the Balch Institute. In addition, I have a legal contract with the Society, drawn up by a prominent Cincinnati attorney, guaranteeing my scholarly independence. This does not mean that I have indiscreetly "told all" about every JPS secret from 1888 to 1988. In matters concerning the recent past, and in dealing with private correspondence involving individuals who remain among the living, and in these cases only, I have weighed my responsibilities as a historian against my other ethical obligations and composed my narrative accordingly. In the end, the only significant changes requested by JPS concerned material in the final chapters, where, as I have indicated, my account is necessarily more tentative. Otherwise, my relationship with JPS throughout this long process has been entirely cordial. Indeed, present and former members of the staff—including Nathan Barnett, Emily Biederman, Amy M. Gewirtzman, Dorothy Harman, Bernard I. Levinson, Richard Malina, Chaim Potok, Joanne C. Pullman, Harold Rabinowitz, and Sheila F. Segal—have all proved unfailingly helpful whenever I turned to them for assistance. A special word of thanks must also go to Adrianne Onderdonk Dudden for adding her creative touch to the design of this book, her 202nd for JPS. I am also grateful to Philip and Muriel Berman, friends of the Society over many years, for their encouragement, and to Professor Yosef H. Yerushalmi, former chairman of the publication committee, who is in large measure responsible for my agreeing to undertake this project in the first place.

In the course of the five years that I devoted to this volume, I have accumulated numerous scholarly obligations that I am pleased to be able to acknowledge here, even if final responsibility in all cases rests with me. First and foremost, I am indebted to friends and colleagues who read and commented on these chapters as they were being written: Professors Benny Kraut, Robert Liberles, Jacob R. Marcus, Michael A. Meyer, and Edwin Wolf 2nd. President Alfred Gottschalk of the Hebrew Union College-Jewish Institute of Religion, and my many colleagues at the College-Institute, the Center for the Study of the American Jewish Experience, and the American Jewish Archives assisted me in numerous ways during the course of my work. While I am especially grateful to Mrs. Nurit Bowman, Professor Alexandra S. Korros, Dr. Abraham J. Peck, Dr. Ida Cohen Selevan, and Mrs. Fanny Zelcer, I have probably called on every member of the Archives, Klau Library, and American Jewish Periodical Center staffs, and I am pleased to report that all of them pretended not to mind. A special word of thanks must go to Mr. Lee B. Leopold and Mrs. Lily G. Schwartz of the Philadelphia Jewish Archives Center. I spent almost three months in their midst, reading the Society's papers, and then burdened them with a long list of documents that I needed to have photocopied. Without their help this book could not have been written. In addition I am grateful to Professor Menahem Schmelzer of the Jewish Theological Seminary, Dr. Nathan Kaganoff of the American Jewish Historical Society, Dr. Frederic Miller of Temple University's Urban Archives Center, and Dr. Larry D. Geller of the Hadassah Archives who all received me warmly when I pursued research at their respective institutions; to Mrs. Helen S-C Sax, who permitted me to examine fascinating materials in the Solomon Solis-Cohen Archives; and to Mr. Maxwell Whiteman, who made available to me copies of newspaper clippings from his own collection and alerted me to the existence of valuable documents that I would not otherwise have found.

Much of this volume was written in Jerusalem where I served as Lady Davis Visiting Associate Professor at the Hebrew University's Institute of Contemporary Jewry and as Visiting Associate Professor of American Jewish History at the Jerusalem Campus of Hebrew Union College-Jewish Institute of Religion. I am grateful to my colleagues at both institutions for their support, and especially to Professors Moshe Davis, Yisrael Gutman, Michael Klein, and Dr. Menahem Kaufman, as well as to Mrs. Tova Wilk of the Lady Davis Foundation, who did so much to make my year in Israel a productive one. I must especially thank Mrs. Nadia Kahan, librarian at the Klau Library of Hebrew Union College in Jerusalem, for service above and beyond the call of duty. For other assistance I am indebted to Dr. David Dalin, Mr. William Fishman, Dr. Leonard Greenspoon, the late Dr. Maurice Jacobs, Professor Jacob Kabakoff, Rabbi Douglas Kohn, Rabbi Charisse Kranes, Mrs. Alexandra Lee Levin, Rabbi Simeon J. Maslin, Dr. George Savran, Mr. Robert Singerman, Rabbi Malcolm Stern, and Professor Lance Sussman.

An especially warm acknowledgment goes to my family. My parents, Nahum M. and Helen H. Sarna, both read every word of this volume, made innumerable helpful suggestions, and saved me from many embarrassing errors and pitfalls. My other relatives—Sarnas, Horowitzes, Langers, Aarons, and beyond—maintained a lively interest in this project, even if (as I suspect) they had trouble understanding my enthusiasm for it. My extended *mishpoche* in Israel made the year there that much more enjoyable and ensured that I saw more of the Holy Land than just its libraries.

Finally, and most important of all, I thank my wife, Ruth. Our courtship, engagement, and first years of marriage were all consumed by this book. She has never known a time (except for our honeymoon) when I was not working on it, and many an hour that should have been spent with her were spent with my computer instead. Ruth has always understood, given me patient encouragement, and rushed to read every chapter as soon as it was finished. My dedication of this book to her is but a small token of my love, affection, and respect.

Jonathan D. Sarna
Cincinnati, Ohio
Rosh Hodesh Heshvan, 5749
Columbus Day, 1988

1

FALSE STARTS

From a Jewish point of view, pre-Civil War America was a cultural wasteland. True, the American Jewish population had only recently attained the fifty thousand mark, and Jews formed less than one-quarter of one percent of the overall population. True also that American Jews, led by the indefatigable Isaac Leeser, *chazan* (reader) of Congregation Mikveh Israel in Philadelphia, were beginning to produce basic-level Jewish books: prayerbooks, textbooks, sermons, polemics, and most important of all an English translation of the Bible (1853). But these achievements—even including those of such secular Jewish notables as Mordecai M. Noah (1785–1851) and Isaac Harby (1788–1828), both of them journalists, dramatists, and politicians—scarcely compared with Jewish literary productivity in Europe. According to the nation's leading Reform rabbi, Isaac Mayer Wise, among American Jews "ignorance swayed the scepter and darkness ruled."[1] According to the nation's best-known Orthodox rabbi, Abraham Rice, "in this country . . . the wisdom of the ages goes stale, the pious are scorned, truth is lacking, and there is none on whom to depend save our Father in Heaven."[2]

The First Jewish Publication Society

The first national Jewish effort to combat this sorry situation emerged in the 1840s. The immediate stimulus came from the outside: in this case, the threat posed by

Christian missionaries, who concentrated their efforts on the "weak links" in the Jewish community—the needy, the isolated, and the ill-educated who could not defend their faith when challenged. Ignorance and cultural stagnation, Jewish leaders realized, threatened their survival as a community.[3] An 1845 manifesto addressed to the "Israelites of America" laid the problem bare. "The time for action," it declared, "has arrived."

The action advocated was the creation of a "Jewish publication society." In the nineteenth century, Americans formed new organizations and societies whenever a new problem confronted them, believing optimistically that if a society existed a problem must at least be on the road to solution. Although the need for a Jewish publication society was not really new—Isaac Leeser had been advocating the idea for some years in his monthly, *The Occident*—the need had suddenly taken on fresh urgency. Leeser's proposed solution was for those "zealous for Israel" to learn from "the plan adopted by our opponents" and "prepare suitable publications to be circulated among all classes of our people." The desired result would have Jews "become Israelites in knowledge" and not just "Israelites merely in name."[4]

The Jewish Publication Society was thus established. Organized in 1845, its underlying aims were twofold: self-defense against Christian proselytization and the furtherance of Jewish literature.[5] Pursuing both at once, it issued a series of fourteen booklets entitled The Jewish Miscellany, about 125 pages each, modeled on Christian tracts and on the Cheap Jewish Library series in England. Over half the booklets contained stories based on the Bible and Midrash. Several offered "affecting tales," heavily Victorian in tone, designed to combat conversionism, prevent intermarriage, and foster observance of the Sabbath. Only a few—Isaac Leeser's *The Jews and Their Religion*, Moses Samuel's biography of Moses Mendelssohn, and Grace Aguilar's *The Spirit of Judaism*—plunged into more academic pursuits.

Except for Leeser's own essay, everything else published in The Jewish Miscellany series was originally composed abroad. Several of the volumes were foreign works reprinted verbatim: others were re-edited or freshly translated into English.[6] Clearly, American Jews still lacked the cultural resources to produce suitable works of their own.

The corresponding secretary and real workhorse of the Jewish Publication Society—he sometimes called it the *American* Jewish Publication Society—was Isaac Leeser. He had long championed the society's ideals, and his experience as an author and editor made him the logical man for the job. Given that Leeser lived and worked in Philadelphia, it became the home of the new publication society. Fortunately, Philadelphia also happened to be a publishing center. In the late-eighteenth century, Mathew Carey had established in "Quaker City," what became the prototype for all American publishing houses, a firm known today as Lea & Febiger. A few decades later, Joshua B. Lippincott established a publishing company there as well. By Leeser's day, publishers of religious books, including the American Sunday School Union and the Presbyterian Board of Publication, had also located in Philadelphia. But more important, from a Jewish point of view, was the fact that the most prominent Jew in the field of publishing at the time, Abraham Hart,[7] also lived in Philadelphia. His firm, Carey & Hart, issued the first edition of Davy Crockett and the first novel of William Thackeray. Hart played an active role in Jewish communal affairs and agreed to serve as the Jewish Publication Society's president.

The board of managers of the Jewish Publication Society, almost a "Who Was Who" of Philadelphia Jewry, included such men as Louis Bomeisler, Henry Cohen, Hyman Gratz, Leon Hyneman, Alfred T. Jones, Joseph L. Moss, Solomon Solis-Cohen, and Abraham S. Wolf. Most of these men were native English speakers, several were exceedingly young (Alfred T. Jones, destined for a brilliant career in printing and journalism, was only twenty-three), and all played active roles in a variety of communal affairs, demonstrating a stalwart commitment to furthering Jewish education and culture. As we shall see, several of these men later inspired their children to follow in their footsteps.[8]

From the start, the Jewish Publication Society viewed itself as an association of Jews interested in encouraging Jewish literature rather than as a commercial publisher. The board of managers expressed "not the least doubt" that "if from twelve to fifteen hundred subscribers can be obtained, at but *one dollar* each per annum," it would be enabled "to issue eight numbers of the [Jewish] Miscellany every year, distribute them to the subscribers, set apart a considerable number for distribution among the poor, and have a surplus to be sold for the benefit of the general fund...."[9] Thus the society would realize a surplus through contributions, while every member would receive its books at a discount.

The plan sounded too good to be true, and so in fact it was. No more than four booklets were ever issued in any one year, only a single auxiliary to support the Philadelphia parent society was ever set up (the Auxiliary American Jewish Publication Society of Virginia, founded in Leeser's old hometown of Richmond[10]), and, as Mayer Sulzberger delicately put it, "the energy of the founders could not be infused into the public." Only 450 people enlisted as members.[11] On the night of December 27, 1851, after more than a year in which nothing was published—perhaps because of Leeser's resignation from his position at Congregation Mikveh Israel following an ugly dispute—a fire destroyed Abraham Hart's building where most of the society's stock was stored. America's first Jewish Publication Society went up in smoke.[12]

Why did the society fail? One answer is lack of Jewish community support. Its membership was pitifully small, its funding limited, and its sales woefully insufficient. Viewed from another perspective, however, the society failed because of its own internal problems. Anticipating a mistake later made by many Jewish publishers, it never adequately balanced its lofty cultural aims with down-to-earth commercial realities. Its publications may have filled a vital need, but they lacked widespread appeal. While profitable publishers had popular books to compensate for losses sustained on unpopular ones, the Jewish Publication Society depended on memberships and charity. Furthermore, the society never solved what has been called "the most difficult problem in publishing"[13]—namely, distribution. Members received everything the society published whether they wanted it or not. But nonmembers, unless they happened to read Leeser's *Occident*, would have been unlikely even to have heard of the society's books. Given the small size and diffuse nature of the American Jewish population in the mid-nineteenth century, it may be that no solution to this problem would have worked. The fact, however, remains that the society's objective—to circulate its books among "all classes of our people"—fell far short of success.

American Jewish Culture, 1850–75

The demise of the Jewish Publication Society did not mean the end of Jewish book publishing in America. Jewish books had been published before the society existed—subsidized, in most cases, by their authors—and they continued to appear. A popular textbook like Simha C. Peixotto's *Elementary Introduction to the Scriptures for the Use of Hebrew Children* even ran through numerous editions. But a survey of American Jewish literary output from 1850–75[14] reveals that it consisted mainly of liturgies, textbooks, and sermons; original works of Jewish scholarship had to be imported from Europe. To be sure, a Jewish publisher would occasionally strive to interest the public in more scholarly works. Abraham Hart, for example, published Rabbi Joseph Schwarz's *A Descriptive Geography and Brief Historical Sketch of Palestine* (1850), translated by Isaac Leeser. Meyer (Moritz) Thalmessinger, later president of the Mechanics' and Traders' Bank in New York, published a translation of Reform leader Abraham Geiger's *Judaism and Its History* (1866) and several original works by Rabbi Samuel Adler. Henry Frank and his son Leopold, the leading American Hebrew publishers of the day,[15] issued Elijah Holzman's anti-Reform polemic entitled *Emek Refaim* (1865)—one of the first original Hebrew books published in America—as well as Bernhard Felsenthal's *A Practical Grammar of the Hebrew Language* (1868). Bloch Publishing Company, founded by Isaac Mayer Wise's brother-in-law Edward Bloch in 1854, and the oldest Jewish publisher still in existence, published most of Wise's works and a translation of Isidor Kalisch's learned *A Guide for Rational Inquiries into the Biblical Writings* (1857).[16] In addition, non-Jewish publishers made available the works of such better-known European Jewish authors as Grace Aguilar, Berthold Auerbach, Emanuel Deutsch, and Heinrich Heine. But the literature produced by the Jews in America was still minimal, and the increasing number of well-educated Jewish immigrants knew it.

The character of American Jewry was indeed changing. By the end of the Civil War, the community had ballooned to more than 150,000, many of them recent immigrants from Central Europe. By 1870, at least twenty German rabbis (or "ministers") had assumed positions in American synagogues and temples,[17] and cultured Jewish laymen could be found in every major American city. Of course, the culture cherished by most of these immigrants—in common with other German immigrants and many American intellectuals of the day—was German culture, then at the peak of its influence. This infatuation, in the case of some German Jews, proved almost religious in its intensity. German for them was nothing less than a "sacred language": They spoke German at home, read German books and newspapers, heard German in the synagogue, and insisted that their children study German in school.[18]

For years, many German Jewish immigrants maintained ties to their old homeland. They subscribed to its Jewish newspapers, returned periodically to visit relatives, and sent their children there to study. Rabbis schooled in the methods of German Jewish scholarship—*Wissenschaft des Judentums*—remained in contact with their old teachers and wrote articles for German Jewish scholarly periodicals.[19] Not surprisingly, when Ludwig Philippson, editor of the great German Jewish newspaper *Allgemeine Zeitung des Judentums*, established a society for the promotion of Jewish literature (*Institut zur Foerderung der israelitischen Literatur*) in 1855, German Jews in America were among those who joined up.[20] The lessons they learned from the German society served them in good stead when, in later years, they turned their attention to promoting Jewish literature in the United States.

The *Institut zur Foerderung der israelitischen Literatur*, one of numerous Jewish learned societies to be founded in Europe in the second half of the nineteenth century, sought to carry forward the scientific study of Judaism by encouraging the writing and distribution of high-quality German-language Jewish books. Ludwig Philippson, filling the functions that Isaac Leeser performed in the United States, did most of the society's ongoing work, but his success was never overwhelming. Within twelve months the society could boast of only two thousand members, and it peaked at three thousand. Its cultural importance, however, was vast. Each member, for an annual subscription fee of two thalers, received everything published by the society during the year. This amounted, over the eighteen years of the society's existence, to some eighty volumes covering a wide range of Jewish subjects, particularly history. Novels were also published, including translations of works by Benjamin Disraeli and Grace Aguilar. Heinrich Graetz published seven heavy tomes of his *History of the Jews* with the society, and almost every important German Jewish scholar of the day was represented on the society's list with at least one book. Somewhat uncharacteristically, the society also published an unflattering anonymous sketch of American Jewish life, which earned it a stinging rebuke from Rabbi Isaac Mayer Wise in Cincinnati.[21] Wise's criticisms, however, only underscore the attention that leading American Jews paid to the German society. Rabbi Bernhard Felsenthal of Chicago, still a Germanophile (the love affair abated considerably as the decades wore on) and one of the most important conduits between European Jewish scholarship and American soil, was, according to Adolf Kober, "vitally interested"[22] in the society's work. Others, equally interested, saw to it that selections from the society's books were reprinted in America's German Jewish newspapers and translated for the country's Anglo-Jewish press.[23]

Much as cultured American Jews may have envied the German Jewish publication society, they knew that it was no substitute for a society of their own. Like leading Americans of the day, they demanded cultural autonomy. Increasingly, they called for a Jewish literature rooted in American soil and written in the language that Americans spoke. Immigrant rabbis may have continued to insist on the importance of German, but the longer they lived in America the more committed they became to its destiny. They grew impatient with German Jewish leaders who treated American Jews with pompous paternalism. Just before the Philadelphia Conference of Reform Rabbis in 1869, for example, *The Jewish Times*, published by Moritz Ellinger and reflecting the views of David Einhorn (a Germanophile if ever there was one), declared it "high time" for American Judaism to "assume the lead" and spell out on its own "the principles by which it is to be guided."[24] A few years later, Rabbi Gustav Gottheil, speaking in German, went a step further and, as Isaac Mayer Wise had done years before, called on his fellow German-trained rabbis to adopt the language of their new homeland: "As long as we have to preach and pray in a foreign tongue," he insisted, "that long can we not speak of or hope for an American Judaism. Our hope is the youth, and it has a right to be American."[25]

The children of German immigrants *were* insisting on being American. In fact, as alarmists saw it, they were abandoning not only German but Judaism too—and in both cases with alacrity. Given the burgeoning spirit of cultural independence, growing concern for Judaism's future, old fears about the poverty of American Jewish educational efforts, and the dearth of books setting forth Jewish history and religion in an acceptable manner, it comes as no surprise that calls for a Jewish publication society in America rang out anew.

The American Jewish Publication Society

The first call emanated from the Board of Delegates of American Israelites,[26] an organization formed in 1859 to defend Jewish rights at home and abroad and to deal with the American Jewish community's burgeoning needs and problems.

Jewish education stood high on its list of priorities, and in 1867 a special committee composed of three rabbis (Isaac Leeser, Marcus Jastrow, and Samuel M. Isaacs) was formed "to draft and submit a plan for a Hebrew [i.e. Jewish] Publication Society."[27] The committee met, and in its final report proposed a plan based on the one "adopted with so much success in Germany." It urged membership "at a moderate rate," with each subscriber "entitled to a copy of the annual publications," a formal publication committee to make selections, and, most important of all, avoidance of any work "of pronounced party [i.e., partisan] character."[28] But the plan never got off the ground. Isaac Leeser soon fell ill. When he died, his special committee became defunct, and the plan was shelved. (When a new Jewish Publication Society did come into existence a few years later, these suggestions, dusted off and recast, all won ready acceptance.)

Yet another call for a Jewish publication society burst forth in 1868 in a lead editorial in the *Occident*. Its author, Mayer Sulzberger, was born in Germany and reared in the United States. Though not yet twenty-five, he was wise beyond his years; what he lacked in experience, he made up for in learning and *chutzpa*. Even Isaac Mayer Wise, who had felt the sting of his pen, called him a "young and promising genius."[29]

Sulzberger, whose father had served as *chazan* in the small German town of Heidelsheim, received a fine Jewish education and as a youth became deeply attached to Isaac Leeser, who took him under his wing. Leeser wanted him to become a rabbi, but Sulzberger settled on a legal career. He obtained his start in the office of Moses Dropsie, one of Philadelphia's leading Jewish lawyers and, like Leeser, a man deeply committed to traditional Judaism. Before long he rose to fame as well as to modest fortune. For twenty years, Sulzberger served as a judge on the Philadelphia Court of Common Pleas, seven of them as presiding judge. Near the end of his life he helped to revise the Pennsylvania state constitution. He was also a leading Jewish Republican and a personal friend of William Howard Taft.

Sulzberger, like Leeser and Dropsie, was one of Philadelphia's most prominent Jewish bachelors. He was scornful of those he referred to as "damned society ladies," and suspicious of those who married them.[30] Enjoyment to him meant a fine imported cigar, hobnobbing with fellow members of Philadelphia's prestigious Union League, and browsing the shelves of his own exquisitely fine library, then perhaps the most impressive private collection of Jewish books and manuscripts in America. He devoted the rest of his free time to scholarship (his own and others'), to civic causes, and to Jewish institutions—of which he personally helped to found at least half a dozen. He also took an active role in reorganizing the Jewish Theological Seminary of America, which became the beneficiary of most of his library, and served as the first president (his detractors called him "Czar"[31]) of the American Jewish Committee. At the Jewish Publication Society, where he came to play a central role, Sulzberger was years later remembered, somewhat unkindly, as "a mean old cuss with a tongue as sharp as a dagger, and a degree of conceit that would break all records."[32] But he was nonetheless brilliant, awe inspiring, and charitable—according to some, "the most eminent Jew in America."[33]

Back in 1868, of course, all this lay far ahead in the future. Sulzberger was editing the *Occident*, thereby fulfilling a vow he had made to Isaac Leeser before his death, and was busy upholding his mentor's platform in advocating Jewish education, Jewish unity, and adherence to Jewish tradition. Since nothing had been dearer to Leeser's heart than the books he published (over 100 different volumes), Sulzberger's very first editorial after introducing himself to the public dealt with the need for a Jewish publication society.

Sulzberger began by pointing to the profound ignorance of modern Jews, the widespread decline in Jewish cultural creativity brought on by their "wild longing to rush into those professions and positions from which they had been debarred," and the sorry consequences of this collective ignorance felt in many quarters. Since "our religion cannot be properly comprehended without a familiarity with the works teaching it," the need for a publication organization seemed to him obvious. Given the right kind of books, he felt certain that American Jews would combat "innovations" (by which he meant religious reforms), as well as "cultivate and improve those to whom instruction has never been properly imparted." With the radiant optimism that would characterize his lifelong efforts on behalf of American Jewry, he predicted a day when the country would boast of a truly great Jewish publication society:

> whose ramifications shall extend over all this continent, whose presses shall teem with the wealth of Jewish learning, whose activity shall foster native talent, and whose munificence shall enable all to drink draughts of wisdom at its fountain, so that in all the land it shall be said of us: "Behold, Israel is a wise and an understanding people."[34]

Sulzberger's lyrical prose failed to rouse the necessary enthusiasm, much less the wherewithal, to breathe life into a society for publishing Jewish books. Isaac Mayer Wise's call in 1869 for an even more ambitious publication society designed to translate Jewish classics into English met with no greater success.[35] Still, Jewish publication societies were being trumpeted in Europe—France's Société Scientifique Littéraire Israélite arose in 1868, and England's Society of Hebrew Literature followed soon thereafter—and though neither lasted long, American Jewish leaders hardly wanted to be left behind, or to remain beholden to the centers of Jewish life abroad. They had created their own Board of Delegates, were working to form an American Jewish rabbinical college, and were striving to participate as equals in international Jewish affairs.[36] An *American* Jewish publication society, besides being of obvious value domestically, would be an additional symbol of the independence they craved.

The American Jewish Publication Society was established at last on June 5, 1871. A few weeks earlier, Philadelphia's Rabbi Marcus Jastrow, chairman of a new Board of Delegates committee "for the purpose of considering the necessity and practicability of a Hebrew Publication Society," had rendered his report and won its acceptance. The Board voted to make the society an independent body (under its auspices), and Abraham Hart, president of Leeser's original Jewish Publication Society, symbolically donated the first $100 to the new society's treasury.[37] Within days, a conference of Reform rabbis in Cincinnati hailed the society "with joy and intense gratification." Rabbi Max Lilienthal, speaking at the conference, set forth four reasons why the society was of "great need": (1) Jewish literature in English "is almost a blank"; (2) suitable books in German are "closed to our American Jewish youth, who prefer to read books written in their vernacular"; (3) "our Christian brethren ... wish to be instructed on religious topics of the Israelite," but have no books to guide them; and (4) the books published "will be of the highest use and value to the pupils of our future rabbinical seminaries."[38]

As a first step, the new society decided to translate from the German "generally accepted standard works" that it (quite wrongly) supposed to be "unaffected by preconceived notions or polemical tendencies." For the long term, it promised to publish volumes on "Jewish Life, History, and Literature," and it piously pledged to be independent, to avoid religious squabbling, and to endeavor "to unite on a broad and liberal platform all shades of opinion." It set for itself the ultimate goal of bringing Jewish books "within the reach of every one." Its dues were a modest three dollars per year (which entitled the subscriber to "one copy of all the publications of the current year issued by the Society.") It also wisely resolved to avoid books of "controversial character," as well as prayerbooks, rituals, and specific school textbooks—all of which would have brought it into competition with existing Jewish publishers and threatened the unity platform on which the society staked its existence.[39]

Unlike its predecessor, the American Jewish Publication Society was largely a New York affair. Although it included a few Philadelphians—Abraham Hart served for a time as vice president; William B. Hackenburg, head of a large silk manufacturing company, served as a director; and Rabbi Marcus Jastrow sat on the publication committee—the other officers, with the exception of Simon Wolf of Washington, were all New York Jews, most of whom also sat on the Board of Delegates. Of course, the Publication Society, like the Board of Delegates, always saw itself as being national in scope. It even attempted to give itself a national aura by appointing more than one hundred rabbis and laymen from around the country—two-thirds of them from smaller Jewish settlements—to be listed on its board as "honorary vice-presidents."[40] But though the intention was good, the society had neither the leadership nor the money to be a national organization. Its reach exceeded its grasp.

From early on, New York's Temple Emanu-El took an interest in the American Jewish Publication Society.[41] Its rabbi, James K. Gutheim, wrote the society's first major public statement and was responsible for its first book, a translation of the fourth volume of Heinrich Graetz's *History of the Jews*. With this, the society anticipated by two decades one of the most successful undertakings in all of Anglo-Jewish publishing: the full English-language publication of this remarkable work, based on the German original issued in eleven volumes. Volume 4, which the American Jewish Publication Society produced in 1873, was the volume of his history that Graetz actually wrote first (in 1853; revised in 1865), dealing with the period "from the downfall of the Jewish state to the conclusion of the Talmud" and covering the development of Christianity under Saul of Tarsus. It held forth the possibility of considerable popular interest.[42] What most Americans knew of this period came from the writings of Christian historians, whom Jewish scholars easily faulted for being "unable to consult the Hebrew sources," with the result that they "in many instances" produced "erroneous, defective or perverted accounts of the prominent events and characters in Jewish history."[43] By making Graetz available to speakers of English, the American Jewish Publication Society presumably sought to correct some of these errors, and at the same time to align itself with the "scientific" spirit of German Jewish scholarship.

Gutheim's translation did no credit to Graetz's original. Although Gutheim himself may have been "the first product of German rearing to achieve wide reputation as an English orator,"[44] his style in the translation was riddled with infelicities, and betrayed evidence of haste. His work needed a good editor, and the society had none to offer. Someone, probably Gutheim himself, did decide to exclude Graetz's thirty-eight critical notes and appendices from the translation. Since the society sought to appeal to the "general reader," and to keep expenses down, it merely retained references in the text to these learned asides, and referred the interested reader back to the German original. In so doing it demonstrated anew American Jews' continuing dependence on scholarship produced abroad.

One thousand copies of Gutheim's translation were printed, but after thirty months in existence the society boasted no more than one hundred members. Only the managers' willingness to advance money to the printers permitted the book to appear at all. The exertions of a new president, Leopold Bamberger, who brought to the job considerable experience in Jewish communal work, coupled with the efforts of a diligent canvasser, brought the society's membership up to nearly eight hundred in 1875.[45] As if to celebrate, the society unveiled an elegant new logo: its initials encased in a six-pointed Jewish star with the Hebrew words "for Torah" on the right and "for testimony" on the left (after Isaiah 8:20). Two new books soon appeared under this new logo with the promise of many more to come.

Jewish Family Papers; or Letters of a Missionary, the first of these books to appear, was Rabbi Frederic de Sola Mendes's translation (with notes) of what has been called "the most brilliant vindication of Judaism published in the nineteenth century." Written by Wilhelm Herzberg, later the superintendent of the Jewish orphans asylum in Jerusalem, the book was first issued in Germany in 1868, was highly praised by Zacharias Frankel, president of the Breslau Rabbinical Seminary, and enjoyed many years of popularity. Its appearance in Mendes's thoroughly readable translation was timely, coinciding with a resurgence of Christian missionary activities in New York.[46]

Hebrew Characteristics: Miscellaneous Papers from the German was an interesting complement to *Jewish Family Papers* for it was apologetic in tone where the earlier book was a gentle polemic. The volume consisted of "Extracts from Jewish Moralists" collected by the man known as the founder of the "Scientific Study of Judaism," Leopold Zunz, as well as articles on marriage and internment of the dead, written (when he was but twenty-five) by Joseph Perles, later rabbi of Munich. Once again, the publication committee of the American Jewish Publication Society geared its work to "the general reader" and deleted scholarly apparatus.[47] Again, the critical reception was positive.[48]

The American Jewish Publication Society had ambitious future publication plans, including a projected edition of Abraham Geiger's lectures on the history of Judaism. Yet its membership still remained small—because, according to Bamberger, there were simply too few people willing to make "personal sacrifice" or "material offering" on the altar of literature.[49]

Want of people and money, however, formed only part of the problem. The society had no central leader committed enough to undertake the manifold tasks that successful publishing demanded, and it remained, therefore, a neglected stepchild of the Board of Delegates—itself in the last throes of life. Furthermore, the society was too local to serve national needs, even as its national pretensions blocked it from building an adequate local base of support. The economic downturn of the mid-1870s, coupled with the diversion of Jewish energies into other projects aimed at furthering American Jewish cultural independence—the Union of American Hebrew Congregations and the Cincinnati and New York rabbinical seminaries—diminished still further the society's meager funding. When the volunteers who composed the American Jewish Publication Society's rabbinic and lay leadership turned their attention elsewhere, no one stepped in to fill the void. The society died of neglect.

"As a literary people we are no success in America,"[50] Isaac Mayer Wise sadly admitted in 1876, yet he refused to be discouraged. The failure of the first two American Jewish publication societies, like the failure of America's first rabbinical colleges,[51] only underscored the need to keep on trying. In 1878, Wise himself called for a new plan, "a practical scheme ... for the benefit of the people."[52] In 1879, the Union of American Hebrew Congregations rejected a proposal to form a Jewish publication society but voted to help subsidize books of particular value.[53]

Two years later Max Lilienthal called on the newly formed (and short-lived) Rabbinic Literary Association to further the cause. He spelled out the books most urgently needed: "an impartial Jewish history, an introduction to the Bible, an exegesis of the various biblical books, a history of Jewish literature . . . even a new *Shulchan Aruch*, or religious code."[54] One of Lilienthal's students, Rabbi Henry Berkowitz, broadened this call to one for "books of every kind on Jewish subjects in the English language" when he addressed the need for a publication society in 1885.[55] That same year, the famed Pittsburgh Rabbinical Conference heard Rabbi Kaufmann Kohler describe "a Jewish American Publication Society . . . supported and backed by our wealthy laymen and conducted by a staff of able and competent scholarly writers," as the community's "first requisite." [56] By then, one small-scale effort aimed at creating a Jewish publication society had already been made in Philadelphia, and plans for the formation of a Jewish "Sunday School Publication Society" had been announced in New York.[57] There was talk of a new spirit in the American Jewish community, a Jewish awakening. Suddenly the prospects for a new and vigorous Jewish publication society seemed brighter than ever.

2

A REAL BEGINNING

Religious Revival

The late-nineteenth-century religious revival in American Jewish life began, as most such movements do, with a core group of young, idealistic, and highly motivated men and women who banded together to work for change. Fired with the enthusiasm of youth, these young people vowed to uplift American Jews from their spiritual malaise. They marked assimilation as their enemy and threw themselves into battle against it.

Inevitably, different people involved themselves in the movement for different reasons—some altruistic, some personal, in most cases both at once. The Social Gospel movement in American Protestantism influenced some Jews; others felt the currents of Jewish enlightenment in Europe. More immediately, however, the late-nineteenth-century revival sprang from a cultural crisis in American Jewish life born of thwarted expectations. The heady optimism that suffused American Jewry after the Civil War had been tested and found wanting.[1]

"Anti-Semitism"—a word coined in Germany at the end of the 1870s to describe and justify ("scientifically") anti-Jewish propaganda and discrimination—explains part of what happened in America.[2] The rise of racially based anti-Jewish hatred in Germany, a land that many young American Jews (and their parents) had previously revered for its liberal spirit and cultural advancement, challenged a host of Jewish assumptions about emancipation, universalism, and future religious rapprochement. Anti-Jewish pogroms in Russia, where conditions under Alexander II seemed to be moving toward liberalization, compounded this first shock and raised the specter of large-scale Russian Jewish immigration to the United States. Those who believed confidently in progress had expected the condition of worldwide Jewry to improve over time; but in fact, it was steadily deteriorating. Many Jews felt betrayed.

Even the American dream seemed to lose some of its luster during this period. Social discrimination against American Jews grew noticeably in the late-nineteenth century, heightened by two well-publicized cases of prejudice: Judge Hilton's exclusion of banker Joseph Seligman from the Grand Union Hotel in 1877 and financier-banker Austin Corbin's public announcement that "Jews as a class"—he privately labeled them a "detestable and vulgar people"—would be unwelcome at Coney Island.[3] Visions of a liberal religious alliance and of close cooperation with Unitarians were also evaporating. Although interfaith exchanges continued, Jews came to realize that many of their Christian friends privately continued to harbor hopes that one day Jews would "see the light." Much to the embarrassment of Jewish leaders, some Christian liberals looked to Felix Adler's deJudaized Ethical Culture movement as a harbinger of Judaism's future course.[4]

Finally, the end of the nineteenth century saw a considerable turn back toward religion in America. Many discovered that notwithstanding what scientific experts said about evolution and the authorship of the Bible, ritual and tradition still filled a void in their lives that intellectually oriented liberal religions could not. In Jewish terms, this led to the claim that Reform Judaism had gone too far. "Genuine Orthodox views are now becoming fashionable among Jewish young America," the *Jewish Advance* reported in 1879.[5] Commenting on the same trend, Rabbi David Stern (whose religious confusion probably contributed to his subsequent suicide) wrote to Rabbi Bernhard Felsenthal that he found the religious agenda of the day "entirely different" from what it had been before. "Then the struggle was to remove the dross; to-day it is to conserve the pearl beneath."[6]

Although religious reforms continued to win widespread approval, how to "conserve the pearl beneath" became an increasingly important concern to Jews. The solutions they devised were a host of new Jewish institutions and undertakings, the Jewish Publication Society (1888) among them. Others, likewise aimed at improving the state of Jewish knowledge and culture, included the Jewish Theological Seminary Association (1886), the American Jewish Historical Society (1892), Gratz College (1893), the Jewish Chautauqua Society (1893), the National Council of Jewish Women (1893), and the ambitious plan to produce a full-scale Jewish encyclopedia in America, on which work began in earnest in 1898.[7]

Characteristic of the major new thrust of Jewish activism in this period was the importance attached to education, an emphasis not found in older Jewish fraternal orders such as B'nai B'rith.[8] The new Young Men's Hebrew Associations, founded in 1874 (New York) and 1875 (Philadelphia)—the prototypes for more than 120 "Jewish Y's" founded by 1890—set the new pattern. Without neglecting their members' social needs,[9] they underscored the importance of Jewish cultural activities (lectures, literary discussions, and formal classes), opened free Jewish libraries, and laid plans to issue other Jewish publications, perhaps through a publication society. One of their most notable achievements in the late 1870s was the "Grand Revival of the Jewish National Holiday of Chanucka," complete with appropriate pageants and publicity—an effort both "to rescue this national festival from the oblivion into which it seemed rapidly falling" and presumably, to counteract the evident allure of Christmas.[10] The triumphant success of the 1879 celebration overwhelmed even the organizers: "Every worker in the cause of a revived Judaism," one of them wrote, "must have felt the inspiration exuded from the enthusiastic interest evinced by such a mass of Israel's people."[11]

Seeking to widen their sphere, some of the leaders of the YMHA in Philadelphia and New York initiated in 1879 a lively New York-based Jewish newspaper called the *American Hebrew*. Edited by nine precocious young men ranging in age from twenty-one to twenty-nine, the *"A.H."* gave voice to the great changes taking place in the American Jewish community even before the massive onset of Eastern European Jewish immigration. It represented the new generation of American-born Jews, those "strong for traditional Judaism"[12] yet at the same time thoroughly accommodationist. Several of its editors later played active roles in the movement that became known as Conservative Judaism—the most lasting contribution that the late-nineteenth-century revival bequeathed to American Jewish religious life.

The *American Hebrew* focused on revitalizing American Jewish life. Max Cohen, later the librarian of New York's Maimonides Library, called the newspaper "our forcible instrument for the perpetuation and elevation of Judaism."[13] Cyrus Sulzberger, a cousin of Mayer Sulzberger who went on to a notable career as a merchant and was active in civic and Jewish affairs, saw it as a harbinger of good things. On October 5, 1879, six weeks before the first issue appeared, he initiated several of his friends into a solemn covenant "for God and Judaism" called *Keyam Dishmaya*. Within a year he had "cause to be grateful to God for the successful manner in which we have begun our work." The covenant's participants could boast of all the good accomplished by the *American Hebrew*, and of a new Bible class as well—the latter a reaction to religious "indifference" and "Adlerism's success."[14]

News of the 1881 Russian pogroms propelled some of the "*A.H.* crowd"—like their young Jewish counterparts in Europe—to propose action on a broader scale. Max Cohen issued a general call for "Restoration," arguing that "the outbursts of prejudice are not spasmodic, but open manifestations of a constant prejudice which is as deep and as urgent today as ever." Cyrus Sulzberger agreed. He explained "anti-Semitism" on the basis of "religious not racial" factors, and declared "Restoration" to be "the only remedy."[15]

The Philadelphia Group and
"The Need of the Hour"

In the wake of the Russian pogroms, the immigration challenge came to dominate American Jewry's communal agenda. Over two hundred thousand Jews crossed to America's shores in the 1880s alone, nearly doubling the American Jewish population. It would be doubled again just ten years later. Efforts to raise funds and develop resources to absorb and Americanize these immigrants naturally took precedence over long-term measures to improve the quality of American Jewish life. Yet the fact that America was becoming a leading population center of world Jewry pointed up more clearly than before the need to develop American Jewry's cultural resources.

Three competing centers of nascent Jewish culture existed at this time in the United States: Cincinnati, New York, and Philadelphia. Cincinnati, the home of the Hebrew Union College, the Union of American Hebrew Congregations, and Bloch Publishing Company, had Rabbi Isaac Mayer Wise as its primary booster. He dreamed of making his "Queen City" the spiritual center of American Jewry and had wealthy congregants who supported him. By the 1880s, however, it was clear that Wise's dream would remain unrealized; the Cincinnati Jewish community was simply too small.

New York, home of the largest and most rapidly growing Jewish community in the United States, showed more cultural promise. It developed several major Jewish cultural institutions in the 1880s, notably, the Aguilar Free [Jewish] Library, with three branches that circulated some eighty thousand volumes in its very first year of existence (1886–87),[16] and the Jewish Theological Seminary of America (1886), dedicated to "the training of Rabbis and Teachers for the Jewish Congregations in North America," and "the preservation in America of the knowledge and practice of historical Judaism."[17] But New York's problem was that it was too large and diffuse; even leading Jews had yet to coalesce into a self-conscious elite. Unified efforts on behalf of shared cultural objectives carried no hope for success.

Philadelphia, the third center of American Jewish culture, continued in the 1880s to live off the spiritual legacy of Isaac Leeser, who had died in 1868. The city took pride in having been the home of the first American Jewish Publication Society and of Maimonides College—both Leeser's doing and both sadly short-lived. It also boasted an enviable community of cultured Jewish laymen, several Jewish literary societies, both a Hebrew Education Society and a Hebrew Sunday School Society, a culturally active YMHA, and a fine Jewish newspaper, the *Jewish Exponent*.[18] But where New York and Cincinnati both sought the title of "leading

Jewish city in America," Philadelphia did not. Instead, Philadelphians like Rabbi Sabato Morais, Rabbi Marcus Jastrow, Mayer Sulzberger, Solomon Solis-Cohen, and others participated actively in the work of New York's Jewish institutions, particularly the Jewish Theological Seminary.

Although they cooperated with New Yorkers, Philadelphia's Jewish leaders still remained a breed apart. Far more cohesive than their New York counterparts and conscious of their distinctiveness, they came to be known as "the Philadelphia Group,"[19] and eventually banded together in a society called "The Pharisees" (founded 1896) to discuss "questions of Jewish interest, literary, historical and practical."[20] These were not men known especially for their wealth. All certainly lived comfortably, but none (with the exception later on of Lessing Rosenwald) could boast riches that in any way rivaled those of New York's Jewish elite. Instead, members of the Philadelphia Group prided themselves on being intellectually gifted and culturally informed; several even wrote books of genuine Jewish worth. In addition, many—though by no means all—belonged to one big cousinhood with roots several generations back in America. Quite a few also adhered to traditional Judaism and worshipped at Philadelphia's prestigious Sephardic congregation, Mikveh Israel, even when, as in most cases, their Spanish heritage was largely imaginary. New York's Jewish leaders—the men of "Our Crowd"—may have entertained in grander style and succeeded more impressively in the world of business, but those in the Philadelphia Group displayed far more Jewish involvement, far more learning, and far more interest in literature, music, and art. Perhaps for this reason, Philadelphia Jewish leaders played key roles in the shaping of America's emerging Jewish cultural institutions, even those located in New York. By contrast, New York's Jewish leaders, Jacob Schiff in particular, provided the funds that kept those institutions financially afloat.

The Philadelphia Group received an unusual—and, from the point of view of the future Jewish Publication Society, a fateful—injection of new blood in 1887, when Rabbi Joseph Krauskopf arrived in town to succeed Rabbi Samuel Hirsch at Reform congregation Keneseth Israel. Born in Ostrowo, Polish Prussia, Krauskopf immigrated to America in 1872 at the age of fourteen, was admitted three years later to the first class of the Hebrew Union College, and was ordained in 1883 at its celebrated first ordination. Thanks to his oratorical gifts, his tall, handsome appearance, and his American training, he immediately secured a prestigious position at Temple B'nai Jehudah in Kansas City. Four years later, at Isaac Mayer Wise's behest, he came to Philadelphia.

The new rabbi was young, eager, energetic, and full of charisma—quite different from the other rabbis in town. At a time when so many Philadelphia Jewish leaders were involved with Jewish institutions in New York, notably the Jewish Theological Seminary, Krauskopf became a Philadelphia booster. He soon brought his adopted city to national prominence by initiating a host of projects aimed at religious, social, and cultural improvement. After just one week in office, he set off a storm of controversy by introducing Sunday services at Keneseth Israel, complete with his own specially designed ritual and featuring an English-language "Sunday Lecture," delivered to a large and usually appreciative audience of Jews and Gentiles. "Saturday Sabbath" services continued, with sermons by Krauskopf in German.[21] Other new initiatives, many of them equally controversial, followed in rapid succession, most of them aimed at improving Jewish and non-Jewish life in the city.

In late 1887, Krauskopf became involved in a nationwide Jewish controversy following publication of his article on "Half a Century of Judaism in America," which lauded Isaac Mayer Wise at the expense of many others. Traditional Jews and Reform opponents of Wise joined in criticizing Krauskopf for "falsifying history."[22] Yet they could not but respect his talents as a speaker and activist. When he called, they listened. It was only later, as his ego expanded, that Krauskopf went his own way; in 1896, after touring Russia and meeting Leo Tolstoy, he founded the National Farm School near Doylestown, Pennsylvania, which became the central focus of his energies until his death in 1923.[23]

Keneseth Israel originally hired Krauskopf to win back some of the young, native-born Jews who had deserted the congregation during its many long years without an English-speaking preacher. Being young himself—just twenty-nine— the new rabbi quickly created a rapport with young Jews, for he shared many of their concerns. Within a few months of his arrival he had gathered around him a coterie of like-minded men and women and organized them into what he called the "Society of Knowledge Seekers" for "the purpose of mutual assistance in the acquirement of the knowledge contained in the articles published in the best current magazines of America and Europe."[24] At first, members met and discussed contemporary affairs, Jewish and non-Jewish. But on December 11, 1887, the first day of Hanukkah, Krauskopf electrified his congregation with a Sunday lecture entitled "The Need of the Hour." The "need" became the Knowledge Seeker's mission.

In his lecture Krauskopf called for "some modern Judas Macabee" to rouse American Jews from their "awful lethargy" into action. "Go down your business streets, read the signs," he thundered: " 'The Episcopalian Publication Society,' 'The Methodist Book Concern,' 'The Presbyterian Tract Society,' 'The Baptist Bible Society,' and then look for the name of 'The Hebrew Publication Society,' and when you have sought for it in vain, think how true to our mission we are." The shame was bad enough, but the practical problems resulting from the situation were worse:

> Count over the Jewish publications that grace our private libraries, and remember that it takes all of $8.00 to provide our houses with the cheapest edition of

Leeser's large English Family Bibles, and $3.50 to provide ourselves with a copy of a prayer book. See whether you can think without a blush of shame of that sad incident that recently made its round in the Jewish Press, that a Rabbi about to dedicate a synagogue in a small community, asked for a copy of the Bible, and no such copy could be found in the entire Jewish community, and a Gentile had to help the Rabbi out of this disgraceful predicament, think of these facts and then of the mission of Israel, which we repeat so often and with so much gusto, and then of those words of Isaiah: "And strangers shall stand and feed your flocks."

The solution was self-evident: "We need first and foremost a Publication Society."[25]

Just eleven days passed, and Krauskopf, who saw not a little of his own reflection in the character of Judas Macabee that he painted,[26] proposed "a plan of raising money for this purpose to his friends in the Knowledge Seekers. Although his proposal easily won approval,[27] the scope of the proposed society was more controversial: Was it to be primarily congregational, local, or national? Krauskopf knew that national Jewish organizations, perhaps because they had no local constituent base, had not fared well in America. He may also have feared that a national organization would lead to a lessening of his own influence. On the other hand, his congregation alone could hardly muster sufficient resources to support an ambitious publication effort. The Knowledge Seekers had agreed to publish his lectures; more was out of the question. He therefore advocated creation of a local Philadelphia Jewish publication society and arranged meetings with leaders of Philadelphia area synagogues and YMHA officials to bring it about.

But he was immediately stymied. Solomon Solis-Cohen, a young, Jewishly learned, and native-born medical doctor who had earlier sought to organize a large-scale Jewish publication society under YMHA auspices, led other more traditional members of the Philadelphia Group (all of them opponents of Krauskopf's religious reforms) in renewing the call for a national Jewish publication society. Where Krauskopf, a rabbi, believed that congregations and YMHAs should govern the society, Solis-Cohen, a layman, wanted it to be independent—a creation of American Jews, not American Jewish institutions. When the final tally took place, Solis-Cohen's side won by a single vote—the vote of Philip Lewin, president of Reform Congregation Keneseth Israel (and twenty-two years older than his rabbi), who found himself more convinced by the tradionalists' arguments than by Krauskopf's. Bowing to the majority, Krauskopf nobly agreed to work with Solis-Cohen, and together they put out a call for a national convention to which "Jews of all shades of opinion and wherever residing" were invited.[28]

The brevity of the call to Philadelphia belied the complicated series of events that had preceded it. The awakening of interest in Judaism and Jewish culture on the part of young Jews, the challenge posed by East European Jewish immigration, the continuing desire for American Jewish cultural independence, the growing sense of American Jewry's destiny on the world Jewish stage, the heightened feeling of self-awareness on the part of the Philadelphia Jewish community, and the arrival in Philadelphia of the young, highly dynamic Rabbi Joseph Krauskopf—all these factors contributed to the process that produced the national gathering. The anticipated climax—creation by representatives of the entire American Jewish community of a new Jewish Publication Society—represented American Jewry's hope for the future.

In the heady expectation of imminent triumph, Krauskopf and Solis-Cohen committed the Jewish Publication Society to Jewish pluralism and doctrinal neutrality—"books and essays of such a tendency as shall command the support of all parties among the Jews"[29]—and they effectively repressed any lingering doubts. Along with like-minded idealists, they still cherished a belief in the commanding power of Jewish culture to weld disparate Jews together into one unified society:

> Which shall enlist the sympathy of all, even the most rigidly orthodox, and even the most wildly radical; which shall form a meeting point of intellectual kinship to those who, on religious and doctrinal grounds, are most widely and bitterly dissevered; which shall demonstrate that Judaism is a religion large enough and broad enough to grasp within its fold all the discordant elements that, contest as they may for things they hold dear or estimate cheaply, still retain a scholarly respect for that which is noble and elevating in Jewish literature.[30]

The National Convention

Sunday, June 3, 1888, was, according to contemporaries, "a great day in Philadelphia Judaism, for there was gathered there a convention which included the leading intellectual minds among the Hebrews in America." Rabbis and laymen, men and women, young and old—about one hundred persons in all—crowded into Touro Hall in the building of the Hebrew Education Society. Never in memory had American Judaism "been represented by so scholarly, thoughtful and intelligent a body of men and women coming from such diverse sections of the country and holding such various opinions on subjects apart from that which brought them together."[31] What made the national convention particularly impressive was the "immense preponderance" of young Jews among those assembled, and indeed it was they who carried the day when the Jewish Publication Society was finally gaveled into being.

By contrast, the rabbis present—more than a score of them—felt decidedly left out. Simon Rosendale, a distinguished native-born Albany lawyer (he would later serve as New York State Attorney General) and one of the most widely respected American Jews of his day, chaired the convention. It was he who announced the appointment of a committee to formally draft the constitution and bylaws of the Society. The committee, however, consisted entirely of distinguished laymen, most of them native-born: Mayer Sulzberger, Solomon Solis-Cohen, and Morris Newburger, all of Philadelphia; Aaron Friedenwald and Cyrus Adler of Baltimore; Simon Wolf, the Jewish community's chief spokesman in Washington; Adolph L. Sanger, lawyer and B'nai B'rith leader of New York; Benjamin F. Peixotto, respected diplomat and editor of the *Menorah Monthly*, also then living in New York; and Jacob Ezekiel, the veteran Jewish leader and secretary to the Board of Governors of the Hebrew Union College in Cincinnati. Allegedly, Rosendale kept clergymen off the committee "to avoid throwing too much burden on the rabbis,"—a face-saving euphemism. More likely, he wanted to prevent the kind of ugly religious in-fighting that rabbis carried on week after week on their pulpits and in newspaper columns.

The tactic misfired. Many of the rabbis present, especially Kaufmann Kohler and Gustav Gottheil, felt affronted; some even proceeded to walk out. This did not bother Sabato Morais, minister (following Sephardic custom) of Philadelphia's Sephardic Congregation Mikveh Israel and president of the Jewish Theological Seminary in New York, who tacitly advised his friends to let the rabbis "go to the devil." With "the rabbis" out of the picture, his fears that the Jewish Publication Society would follow the Union of American Hebrew Congregations into the Reform camp or Rabbi Krauskopf down the road to Sunday services might have been put to rest. Others, including several obstreperous hecklers, were equally happy to see the rabbis depart; Jewish anticlericalism had rarely been expressed in so public a forum.

In the end, however, cooler heads prevailed. David Teller, president of Rabbi Marcus Jastrow's Congregation Rodef Shalom ("pursuer of peace"), took a lesson from the name of his congregation and effectively appealed for harmony. Rabbis Jastrow, Gottheil, and Kohler agreed to have their names added to the lay committee, and Joseph Krauskopf, who deserved a place more than they did (even though it was known that "a number would not weep if he were shunted from all direction"), was added to the committee as well. After that it took only one hour under the stern guidance of Mayer Sulzberger for all the necessary documents, most of them carefully prepared in advance, to be agreed upon.[32]

In the meanwhile, a cable from Jacob Schiff, away in Berlin, brought welcome news (already known to readers of the *American Hebrew*) of the philanthropist's first major donation to the Society: $5,000 in honor of the recently deceased polymath and tireless communal worker, Michael Heilprin ("provided fifty thousand [is] raised within one year," Schiff wrote, but he later dropped the stipulation).[33] Following a well-earned supper prepared by Philadelphia's foremost Jewish caterer, Jacob Wiener,[34] a slate of officers was elected "without much loss of time." By then the hour had grown late—past ten—and tempers were wearing thin. The weary delegates, having labored all afternoon and evening, in some cases following hours of travel, clamored for adjournment. They had accomplished what they had come to Philadelphia to do. The rest would be up to the Society's new executive committee.[35]

"There seemed to be but one opinion prevailing about the rabbis," Aaron Friedenwald observed in the wake of the convention, "and it was not a very flattering one. Apparently their influence is at a low ebb."[36] This was especially true in Philadelphia, where cultured, native-born Jewish laymen faulted some rabbis for their foreign ways, others for their ignorance, most for their pomposity, and all for their inability to work together for the sake of the Jewish community.[37] Rabbi Marcus Jastrow understood that there was an "instinctive" American Jewish fear of "clerical rule"—a feeling, found also among non-Jews, that ministers "are good for any service required but otherwise should be as much as possible excluded from active representation in public affairs."[38] Yet rabbis, who thought that community leadership should rest with them, and who increasingly sought to be treated as professionals (note the title "doctor" that they coveted) so as to be distinguished from "mere laymen," found subservience to community leaders in so important a matter as Jewish culture intolerable—"an open declaration," as one of them later put it, "that your Ministry is incapacitated intellectually, and morally, and socially from participating in your public work."[39] The underlying problem, involving as it did general tensions between professionals and laymen, specific prejudices against rabbis, and the critical question of community power continued to fester.[40] It would recur periodically throughout JPS history.

The Society Takes Shape

The new twenty-one-member executive committee, elected by the convention and charged with the task of organizing and running the Jewish Publication Society, resulted from a careful selection process carried out with an eye toward prestige, balance, and commitment. The committee included businessmen, professionals (most of them lawyers), community leaders, two lay scholars, and four rabbis. It reflected theological pluralism—a full spectrum of Jewish beliefs and practices—and geographical diversity—thirteen different Jewish communities. It included one woman—Mary M. Cohen, a local Philadelphia writer and communal worker—who was appointed corresponding secretary. Most revealing of all, eight committee members were in their mid-thirties or younger (Cyrus Adler was only twenty-five), and nine were native born.[41] They represented the audience that the Society would seek to attract.

Morris Newburger, a member of Krauskopf's Knowledge Seekers and a leading Philadelphia clothing wholesaler, won unanimous election as the Jewish Publication Society's first president. Active in secular and Jewish community affairs, he was respected by all segments of the community and had the necessary time and money. He would hold his position for fifteen years and then go on to serve another fifteen as a member of the board of trustees (which assumed the functions of the executive committee when the Society incorporated in 1896). Under him served four vice-presidents: Jacob Schiff, Maecenas of American Jewish culture and one of the nation's most powerful Jews, as well as Leo N. Levi of Galveston, Bernhard Bettmann of Cincinnati, and Gustav Gottheil of New York.[42] These men were supposed to organize membership solicitations in their areas of the country. As it turned out, however, Gottheil and Bettmann never took active roles in the affairs of the Society. Gottheil was angry at the Philadelphians and soon resigned; Bettmann was presumably too busy presiding over the Board of Governors of Hebrew Union College. Even Schiff preferred to leave JPS affairs in local hands. Consequently, three new vice-presidents appeared on the slate in 1890, and thereafter the thankless position rotated frequently. In the 1896 reorganization, the Society wisely cut back to one vice-president and selected Henry Leipziger, the pioneering New York educator who had been actively interested in its work from the start.[43] He continued on in the same post, a standing monument to the link with New York Jews, until his death in 1917.

For its other officers, the Society recruited local talent so that its "Philadelphia character" would be preserved. Herman S. Friedman and Morris Dannenbaum, the first two treasurers; Joseph Krauskopf, the recording secretary; and Mary M. Cohen and Ella Jacobs, the first two corresponding secretaries (in 1896 this position was consolidated into that of the secretary and thereafter filled by a man) all lived in Philadelphia, and most had grown up there too. The twenty-six-year-old paid clerk, Ephraim Lederer, soon elevated to assistant secretary, was also born and bred in Philadelphia. His small office became the first JPS headquarters,[44] but not for long. He resigned in 1890, returning as a trustee six years later after he had made a name for himself as a communal leader. With Lederer gone, the Society moved its offices to President Morris Newburger's business, and another good Philadelphian, Charles Bernheimer, age twenty-two, became the assistant secretary. During his sixteen years at the post, Bernheimer earned his Ph.D., became increasingly involved in immigrant aid and social work, and edited his still classic study entitled *The Russian Jew in the United States* (1905). In 1906, a year after the book appeared, he resigned his post to pursue a long and distinguished career in social work.[45]

With its organization in place, the leadership of the Jewish Publication Society could move on to its next essential task: appointing a publication committee. Names were suggested, balloting accomplished by mail, and at the meeting of August 19, 1888, the results became public. The nine-member committee would consist of Marcus Jastrow, Joseph Krauskopf, Simon Stern, and Mayer Sulzberger of Philadelphia; Cyrus Adler and Henrietta Szold of Baltimore; Bernhard Felsenthal of Chicago; Charles Gross of Cambridge, Massachusetts; and Abram S. Isaacs of New York. Three of these nine also served on the executive committee, four were rabbis, three (including Isaacs, who was also a rabbi), were professional scholars, and all had themselves published books or articles in English on matters of Jewish concern. Four of the nine—Adler, Gross, Krauskopf, and Szold—were between the ages of twenty-five and thirty-one. More than four opposed Radical Reform Judaism, ensuring that Krauskopf, as one contemporary observed with joy, "has no power."[46] The man who did wield power with the committee was Mayer Sulzberger, and to nobody's surprise he was elected chairman. From this position, which he held until his death, he shaped the Jewish Publication Society's direction during its first critical decades of activity.

The publication committee's first accomplishment, apparently a joint undertaking with the executive committee, was a thirteen-page circular setting forth JPS aims and aspirations and appealing for "generous sympathy, active encouragement and liberal support."[47] It elaborated on the need for a publication society and spelled out for the first time the governing principles under which the new society would operate. As new organizations so often do, JPS endeavored to prove that it had the remedy for major communal problems of the day. It also set forth the basic arguments that it would continue to muster forever after, albeit with different emphases, in order to justify its existence.

First and foremost, the document stressed the Society's theological neutrality and its potential contribution to Jewish unity. It would show Jews how much they had in common, how they all remained bound to one culture, in spite of differences.

Second, it underscored the Society's value for improving community relations. While the need to combat anti-Semitism, later given more prominence, found no explicit mention in 1888, it was pointed out that as a minority group, Jews wherever they are, even in America, have a duty "not only to avoid being misunderstood, but to secure . . . a patient hearing and fair judgement" for themselves, especially given that so many tend "toward a certain contempt for our beliefs and our very name." The Society, through its books but without apologetics, pledged to do its part to convert "the mind of the world around us to juster conceptions of duty and fraternity."

Last but not least, the Society pointed to its role in addressing the problem of Jewish youth. "If we would inspire our youth to hopeful partisanship in our cause," it argued, "they must learn that we are the bearers of something worth preserving." Since Jewish culture could only be transmitted to the bulk of Jewish youth through books in the English language, it considered its mandate clear: to educate the coming generation of American-born Jews, and to raise their Jewish consciousness.

Yet more than just problems motivated the Society's founders; they also defended their appeal for support on the basis of American Jewry's "growing . . . prosperity and intelligence." The circular noted that "scholars are arising among us who, by their devotion to Jewish literature and their high general culture reflect honor on our community." Through their scholarship, they were realizing in America that synthesis that was the post-Emancipation Jewish ideal. With German Jewry "hampered by a revival of mediaeval prejudices," its cultural activity at a standstill, it was up to Americans to assume the mantle of Jewish culture in their stead. The Society pledged to do its part "so that Israel in America may proudly claim its literary period, as did our ancestors aforetimes in Spain, in Poland and in modern Germany." German Jewry's "valuable contributions to modern Jewish literature" provided a scholarly goal. The financial success displayed by the publication societies of "other religious denominations" in America—Methodists, Baptists, Presbyterians, and Congregationalists—suggested an appropriate financial goal: "more than $30,000 per year for publication purposes."

All that was left was to outline the criteria that would govern the selection of books. This the circular accomplished in a seven-part "declaration" setting forth for the first time the overarching JPS publishing "principles":

(1) All periods in the history of Israel, from the time of Abraham to our own, are integral portions of the life of our community.

(2) Our career in the past and our activity in the present cannot be adequately set forth either to our own community or to our neighbors without a literature.

(3) Such a literature must be free from mere aggressiveness against differing opinions, whether within or without our ranks. It must combat error by presenting truth and not by assailing adversaries.

(4) Such a literature must be in the main popular; that is, adapted for general reading rather than for scholars in special branches.

(5) It must aspire to excellence of style and tone, and, as a rule, it must be in the English language.

(6) The mechanical execution of the work must be good, and the publications should preserve such a uniformity of appearance, that subscribers will be encouraged to keep them together and thus make them a library of reference.

(7) Above all, the publication committee must have in view the sole purpose of doing the most good, and to that end must be entirely free from prejudices, for or against particular opinions or persons; since all Jews of every shade of belief are equally concerned in our work.

The new Constitution of the Jewish Publication Society of America, published as an appendix to the circular, was largely an administrative document written to conform with state requirements. It committed the Society "to publish works on the religion, literature and history of the Jews; and ... to foster original work by American scholars on these subjects." It announced three classes of membership: $3 regular members, $20 patrons, and $100 life members. It fixed benefits, assuring "every member of the Society ... a copy of each of its publications." And it set up other necessary administrative regulations. Presumably to ensure the Society's basic character, the constitution explicitly limited membership, which entailed voting rights, only to people "of the Jewish faith." Non-Jews interested in receiving the Society's publications had to apply as nonvoting "subscribers."

The Search for Members

Outwardly at least, the Jewish Publication Society looked most impressive. It already boasted, within six months of its founding, a constitution, a formidable array of officers and committee members, a circular stating its aims and principles, and a treasury filled with over $11,000, including the original $5,000 bequest from Jacob Schiff and a matching gift from Meyer Guggenheim, formerly of Philadelphia, but by then well on his way to spinning his small fortune into a large one through the alchemy of mining and smelting. (Guggenheim soon lost interest in the Society, however; he and his children lavished the bulk of their largesse on secular charities.)

What the Society still lacked—besides books, which were then in the planning stage—was members. Although it was calculated that "with a Jewish population of nearly 400,000 souls in this country, we should secure no less that 10,000 members and patrons,"[48] membership stood in fact at less than two thousand, and most of them were Philadelphians. By year's end an ambitious membership drive was underway nationwide, and leading Jews from around the country had "accepted the task of organizing their respective cities and states."[49] Like so many subsequent efforts to fatten the Society's membership rolls, however, this initial one was to prove frustrating.

Two problems hampered the quest for new members: opposition and apathy. The former came largely from rabbis. Rabbis Gottheil and Kohler of New York City, offended by the leadership and largely lay character of the Society, criticized it openly and withheld their support. Many of their colleagues followed suit. As a result, no more than 140 New Yorkers had joined the Society as late as the spring of 1889. Mayer Sulzberger, who believed that the New York rabbis "were actuated by jealousy," thought "that laymen could succeed in organizing properly even in the teeth of the most determined enmity of the clergy."[50] But no layman seems to have proved equal to the challenge. Outside of New York City various rabbis withheld their support as well.[51] What had not yet been realized was that the Society, by its very nature, bred opposition, dreams of unity notwithstanding. Since positions on the publication committee were severely limited, and since book selection carried with it the painful task of book rejection, enemies proved unavoidable. Every refused author became a potential antagonist.

Yet for all that, it was apathy, in 1888 and ever afterwards, that proved a far more serious problem. In Baltimore, a meeting called by Aaron Friedenwald to set up a committee of people interested in supporting the new Jewish Publication Society attracted just six people. Friedenwald felt "considerably disgusted." A time-consuming mail campaign to solicit memberships proved only slightly more successful. Henrietta Szold of the publication committee, aided by her mother and by Friedenwald's wife, munched on cake and drank eggnog far into the night, personally addressing eleven hundred circulars and membership blanks to the city's Jews. To their disappointment, only seventy-five people responded—and that was better than the results in many other cities.[52] By contemporary standards, the almost 7 percent rate of return seems extraordinarily high, but the vast majority who ignored the campaign spoke louder. Reasons were not far to seek, for the Society had not yet accomplished anything and could display no "tangible evidence" of its work. For the same reason, only about half of those who signed up for membership remitted their three-dollar dues in advance; given the history of past societies, they preferred to wait and see what would develop.[53] To grow beyond its committed corps of supporters, the Society clearly needed quick results; it had to publish books at once, not lose momentum as its predecessors had. The publication committee, spurred on by Mayer Sulzberger, lost no time in moving to meet this challenge.

THE GOLDEN YEARS

For most publishers, the first five years are critical ones—the years in which they set forth their aims, find their niche, establish their reputation, and seek to become financially secure. For the Jewish Publication Society these turned out to be golden years, filled with excitement and success. The books it published achieved widespread notice, won considerable critical acclaim, and secured for the Society a respected position in the field of Jewish publishing.

Outlines of Jewish History

The first JPS book, *Outlines of Jewish History* by Lady Katie Magnus, appeared in 1890. A reviewer for *The Nation* read it and liked it. "We doubt," he wrote, "whether there is in the English language a better sketch of Jewish History.... The Jewish Publication Society is to be congratulated on the successful opening of its career."[1] Congratulations were indeed in order, but strictly speaking, *Outlines* was not a new book. The Jacob Franklin Trust, a British fund set up to promote the writing of Jewish textbooks, had commissioned the volume "for use in schools and homes" back in 1884. Lady Magnus, an accomplished Anglo-Jewish writer and communal worker, wife of Sir Philip Magnus, one of England's leading authorities in technical education (knighted in 1886), completed the work just two years later. Two years after that, in 1888, a second edition appeared, revised by Michael Friedlaender.[2] In America, however, *Outlines of Jewish History* remained largely unknown, and rabbis bewailed the lack of a "popular textbook of Jewish history," especially one covering the post-Biblical period. Gustav Gottheil urged the Society to consider filling this need as one of its top priorities.[3]

How the Society decided to fill the need by issuing an American edition of Lady Magnus's work remains a mystery. Many wanted the Society's first book to be by an American author, as if further to emphasize America's arrival on the Jewish cultural scene. Mayer Sulzberger himself seems to have made the decision to go ahead with the *Outlines* regardless, realizing that this was a way for the Society to publish as its first work a volume with obvious popular appeal, that would fill an evident need, and could be brought to market rapidly.[4] The Society did not, however, merely undertake to reprint the British volume without change; that would hardly have established its own credibility and status among American Jews, particularly since reprints (or pirated editions) of Anglo-Jewish works had circulated in America for years.[5] Besides, the British volume displayed a pronounced and, in its day, quite characteristic anti-American bias. The single paragraph devoted to the New World—sandwiched in between accounts of Jews in China and Jews in Turkey—described Judaism in the United States as "not always in a very much better state of preservation than among the semi-savage sects of ancient civilization."[6] For understandable patriotic reasons then, as well as to establish its own independent identity, the Society undertook to revise and improve the Magnus volume, making it more suitable for American students.

With characteristic dispatch, Mayer Sulzberger set about looking for someone to write "an American chapter ... giving in brief outline the history of the Jews in this country from their original settlements to the present day." Isaac Markens, a journalist whose *The Hebrews in America* (1888) had won considerable praise, accepted the assignment; but, as the Society would so often find with commissioned writing, what he sent in proved disappointing. Others refused the assignment altogether. Spurred on by Sulzberger's impatience—"for heaven's sake what ever you do, do quickly"—the publication committee's two *wunderkinder,* Henrietta Szold and Cyrus Adler, agreed to assume the task themselves. It proved to be only the first of several successful collaborations between them.[7]

At twenty-nine, Henrietta Szold, the eldest child of Baltimore's Rabbi Benjamin Szold, was already an experienced author. Her father, who considered her a "disciple," had educated her like a son, and she absorbed it all—German, French, Hebrew, Judaica, the classics, botany, and much more. She had been the only Jew at Western Female High School and graduated top of her class. By eighteen she was teaching at the Misses Adams's English and French School for Girls. A year later she was writing columns in the *Jewish Messenger* under the name "Sulamith."

For the next decade she taught, studied, wrote, sat at her father's right hand for hours on end assisting him with his scholarship, played an active role in the Botany Club and the Women's Literary Club, and participated energetically in efforts to aid Russian Jewish immigrants. Just when JPS called on her, she was engaged in organizing a Russian night school for teaching immigrants English—an enormously successful undertaking that was widely emulated. She grew stout, her looks were affected, and she was usually exhausted. But when new assignments came her way she generally accepted them, for each was another challenge—and an escape from the loneliness that welled up inevitably as her sisters married and she approached thirty, single, and without prospects.[8]

Cyrus Adler, three years her junior, was one of the many fair-haired boys who frequented the Szold home while studying at Baltimore's Johns Hopkins University. Brilliant, able, determined, and thoroughly impatient, particularly with those not as gifted as himself, he was American Jewry's first great "scholar-doer"— a remarkable administrator who at the same time had first-class academic credentials. Born in Van Buren, Arkansas, he grew up in Philadelphia, and was part of the Mikveh Israel community. His father had died when he was three, and his mother, who henceforward dressed only in black and whose cold formality he inherited, came to live with her brother, David Sulzberger. Adler received a good Jewish and secular education, participated in Jewish cultural life, went to the University of Pennsylvania (where he was known as "Cyrus Aristotle Adler"), and then moved on to Hopkins to study Semitics with Paul Haupt. He later boasted of being the first American to receive a doctorate in Semitics in an American university. Appointed to the faculty of Johns Hopkins, he rose to the position of associate in Semitics. At the same time he began working at the Smithsonian Institution, where his tremendous facility for administration and organization expressed itself. He became librarian, resigned from Hopkins, moved to Washington, and later became assistant secretary of the Smithsonian. In his spare time, except on those rare occasions when his nerves gave way, he lavished his seemingly boundless energy on Jewish communal and scholarly organizations, most of which he eventually came to rule—the Jewish Publication Society, of course, as well as the American Jewish Historical Society, the Jewish Theological Seminary, and later Dropsie College and the American Jewish Committee (among others). Like Henrietta Szold, Adler was, at least outwardly, a stern Puritan. He too was single, always busy, and consumed by work, and he was as devoted to his mother as Szold was to her father. But unlike Szold, he did eventually marry. In 1905, when he was 42, he married Racie Friedenwald of Baltimore, who was nine years his junior.[9]

The new section that Szold and Adler produced in 1890 exceeded all expectations. Thirty-three pages long, it was divided into three chapters ("South America-

The West Indies," "North America," and "The Nineteenth Century"), and was in fact the first ever textbook summary of its kind covering American Jewish history.[10] Where Magnus had been negative and condescending, the revised conclusions, typifying the Society's general outlook on America, were positive and triumphant:

> From this brief summary of the early history of the American Jews, it can be gathered that the Jews and their Christian neighbors lived side by side in friendly fellowship. No spot in the land can be connected with bitter or painful reminiscences—a proud boast, which America alone, of all lands upon whose soil a scene of the world's drama has been enacted, may utter.[11]

Besides the new section on America, the JPS edition of *Outlines* boasted a new illustration and valuable chronological tables. What was really striking about the volume, however, was its outward appearance: bright red with the new JPS gold seal stamped in the middle of the front cover. The color was no accident; like so many other major and minor decisions reached over the years, it emerged only after extended controversy. The scene has been preserved:

> The first book was about to appear. The type had been selected, the format determined, the order of the paper given, the legend on the side and back arranged. There remained only the momentous question of the color of the binding-cloth, momentous because the decision might affect all future publications. The Committee was divided into the partisans of the sombre and the partisans of the gay. Doctor [Marcus] Jastrow was sitting apart, and weary of the arguments of the two sides, he engaged his nearest associate in conversation. Still the discussion on colors raged hot. "Whether red or blue, we want our books to be read," he suddenly ejaculated. The great question was decided amid laughter.[12]

But the decision was reversed within a decade. "Somber" blue (as well as dark green) came to be seen as somehow more redolent of the JPS mission. The "gay" red of the Society's first fruits reflected a more frivolous mood—appropriate to the days when the Society was young.

The first seal also proved short-lived. Presented by Moses Ezekiel, the first professional Jewish sculptor born in America,[13] the seal depicted the utopian scene described in Isaiah 11. In the background lay Jerusalem and the Star of David; in the foreground sat a child, playing with a serpent, resting on a lion, with a lamb lying contentedly nearby; and on the bottom, under a laurel and sprig of olive leaves, were the words "Israel's mission is peace." Ezekiel explained this design in a letter that associated the Society's work for "the enlightenment of our race" with "the perpetuation of the interests and objects of pure Judaism," which he defined in terms of morality and peace.[14] The unusual seal remained in use only until 1906. Then, without fanfare and probably with much relief, it was replaced by a simpler and far more conventional design: a sturdy, freestanding tree, symbol of knowledge and life.[15]

Outlines of Jewish History served its purpose. It gave "tangible evidence" of the Society's existence and made available a highly readable textbook that schoolchildren and their parents could both enjoy. Precise figures on sales are unavailable, but they number in the tens of thousands; thirty years after it was published, the book continued to sell at the rate of 1,500 copies a year. Solomon Grayzel revised the volume for a second JPS edition, published in 1929, and as late as 1958 another revised edition was published by Vallentine, Mitchell in London. The volume can still be found in many Jewish homes.

The book's enduring popularity reveals much about popular taste in Jewish history. It underscores the undiminished appeal of heroic history, filled with sentiment, homily, and romance, enjoining readers to be "loyal and steadfast witnesses"—to remain true to their faith. The challenge that history posed to the modern Jew, Lady Magnus taught, was to be "worthy . . . of these kindred of ours who loved their faith in the days when 'love was grief, and love besides.' "[16] For her, as for so many Victorian writers, history offered not just good reading but moral instruction as well.

Kaufmann Kohler, in a scathing review designed to demonstrate "that the present managers of the Publication Society are totally incompetent," correctly pointed to a great many errors and oversimplifications in the Magnus volume. Many of these errors had already been noticed by English reviewers, but the cost of resetting the plates to correct them would have confronted the Society with lengthy delays. In this case—which did not serve as a precedent for the future— it chose speed over accuracy. What none of the critics noticed, but was in fact far more serious, was the overt anti-East European bias in the volume, a bias presumably passed on to students. Years later, even Cyrus Adler was aghast to find upon rereading "a perfectly libelous statement about the Polish Jews." Lady Magnus called them "not, at any time, a very high class of Jews" and used such other choice epithets as "stagnant" and "retrogressive." If anybody read the book too carefully, Adler exclaimed, "it might cost the Society five hundred members."[17] In Lady Magnus's day, of course, this bias was common among Western Jews. The Society only became more sensitive later on.

Think and Thank

Having filled the need for a popular Jewish history, the Jewish Publication Society next turned its attention to the problem of Jewish children's literature—one of its perennial concerns. Jewish magazines for children, such as *Young Israel* and the *Sabbath Visitor*, already existed in the United States, and a few stories written expressly for Jewish children had appeared, too. Much more was needed, however, and particularly material of quality that could successfully compete with non-Jewish books for a child's attention. Making the situation particularly serious was the fact that inspirational Christian books filled Jewish Sunday School libraries, officials being careful to "run their pens through the name of Jesus" and to "write 'God' in its place." This sleight of hand may have salved guilty consciences but was hardly enough. Indeed, sensitive observers condemned the practice as being unintentionally harmful since it gave children "the idea that the words are synonymous."[18]

Mayer Sulzberger was determined to do better. Early on he turned to Lucien Wolf, the renowned Anglo-Jewish journalist and historian, hoping that he might help him find someone to write "a story for the young which has a good moral and which is nevertheless lively, capable of pictorial illustration and altogether human . . . with a slight Jewish tinge and without any lapses into Christian theology." He was even prepared to commission a suitable Jewish work from Juliana Horatia Ewing, a prominent English Christian writer of stories for children. But a competent author soon appeared closer at hand, twenty-nine-year-old Samuel Williams Cooper, a non-Jewish Philadelphia lawyer who belonged to the local branch of the Ethical Culture Society. Having found his *Think and Thank*, "a romance of the boyhood of Sir Moses Montefiore," to be "excellent . . . bright and breezy, just what boys want," the Society rushed it into press. The fact that the volume was "especially prepared for the Society by an *American* author"—that he was a non-Jew was never mentioned—made it particularly attractive to the Society's trustees. For American Jews generally, its message of obedience and self-discipline, coupled with the courage to fight off enemies, "by brains, by force of will, by calm persistency; if necessary by your animal strength; more than all, by teaching them to know you as one fearless and determined in your faith and manhood," was one that met with general approbation. It echoed secular, masculine values—Theodore Roosevelt would certainly have approved—yet preached charity and forgiveness, especially since young Moses, having beaten his enemy, later turned around and saved his life. Not surprisingly then, this volume proved a commercial success. It served as prototype for juvenile biographies of other Jewish heroes—notably Abram S. Isaacs's biographies of the young Moses Mendelssohn and Grace Aguilar—and remained in print for well over half a century.[19]

Graetz in America

While these first two books helped JPS gain needed recognition, they scarcely established its reputation as a publisher of first rank. The publication committee knew that, and so even before Lady Magnus's history appeared, it announced its intention to publish in English translation the greatest and most popular work of Jewish history to appear in the nineteenth century: Heinrich Graetz's *History of the Jews*. There was nothing particularly original about this idea. Graetz was a well-known name among educated Jews in America; his *History* had long before formed the crown jewel of the German *Institut zur Foerderung der israelitischen*

Literatur, and his fourth volume had appeared in English back in 1873 under the imprint of the old American Jewish Publication Society. Furthermore, an English translation of Graetz was already well underway in London, directed by Bella Loewy and funded by Frederic David Mocatta, one of Anglo-Jewry's leading (and most eccentric) philanthropists.[20] To publish an American edition of this translation required only that suitable arrangements be made with the British publisher, David Nutt. Charles Gross, the brilliant, young Jewish historian, successor at Harvard to the anti-Semitic Henry Adams, was in England pursuing his research into English medieval and economic history, and carried on negotiations with Nutt for the Society. He apparently agreed to buy the British edition already preprinted in sheets and prepared for binding. But Mayer Sulzberger, sensing the potential volume of sales and conscious of the Society's need to be independent, would have none of it. He offered to purchase only full North American rights for the Jewish Publication Society (including the right to make "slight modifications or additions"), and agreed to pay Nutt one shilling for every copy of each volume printed.[21]

The British edition that the Society sought was neither a translation of Graetz's eleven-volume German original nor a translation of his abbreviated popular edition. Instead, it was a "condensed reproduction of the entire eleven volumes," produced under the great historian's own direction, with an additional chapter bringing events up to 1870 (the original ended in 1848), and a new thirty-two-page interpretive "Retrospective," setting forth the master's conception of Jewish history as a whole. The detailed and erudite scholarly footnotes featured in the German were omitted, since, as Graetz put it in his preface, "historical students are usually acquainted with the German language, and can read the notes in the original." This edition was more specifically geared to lay readers, especially non-Jewish ones, and, like so many nineteenth-century works of Jewish scholarship, it had definite apologetic aims:

> It is the heartfelt aspiration of the author that this historical work, in its English garb, may attain its object by putting an end to the hostile bearing against the Jewish race, so that it may no longer be begrudged the peculiar sphere whereto it has been predestined through the events and sorrows of thousands of years, and that it may be permitted to fulfil its appointed mission without molestation.[22]

Given Graetz's international reputation as a scholar, and the popular, romantic, and highly readable style of his books—characteristic of the German historical school with its concentration on cultural and spiritual life and its passion for detail —Sulzberger had every reason to assume that his plan to bring Graetz's *History* to an American audience would win widespread support. After all, the need for a comprehensive Jewish history written in English from a Jewish perspective had long been evident, was called for early on by those working to revitalize American Judaism, and had been made a high priority by the Jewish Publication Society's founders. Yet opposition to the Graetz project arose almost at once, even from within the Society's ranks. A clamorous debate followed—they were becoming quite *de rigueur* at Society meetings—and although the rancor disgusted Sulzberger, it did in this case help to clarify both the Society's mission and its future course.

The problem with Graetz's *History* for some was simply that it was foreign, neither composed nor translated in America. The *American Hebrew*, a friend of JPS from the start, thus pointed to the "absurdity of establishing a Jewish Publication Society *of America*, in order to publish a work written by a German and translated and printed in England." Echoing other critics, it charged the Society with dereliction of duty for accentuating the inadequacies of American Jewish scholarship when it should have been encouraging native scholars to produce works of Jewish history of their own.[23] Yet even as this nativist argument was being aired, others, led by Max Cohen, then librarian of New York's Maimonides Library, vehemently insisted that the problem with Graetz was that it was too highbrow, "not of a nature to appeal to the popular taste." They wanted to commission smaller, less ambitious, and more elementary works, dealing in each case with an individual theme. What they really were saying, as Henrietta Szold pointed out with evident distaste, was that the Society's task was largely remedial: to "tone up" the American Jewish public so that it "may gradually be led on to the appreciation of what truly deserves the name literature." Although she condemned it, this view had its attractive qualities and was in line with pedagogic theory. But the opposing argument, reminiscent of Matthew Arnold's advice to read "the best which has been thought and said in the world," proved in this case to be more compelling. As Szold put it: "The mind grows by what it feeds upon. As men are prepared for liberty by the enjoyment of liberty, so for good literature by the enjoyment of good literature."[24]

The final major objection to the Graetz project came from those who feared its venturesome character and evident financial risk. They wondered aloud whether it was prudent for a Society still in its infancy to enter into "such extensive obligations," and predicted that people would hesitate to buy early individual volumes of the series for fear that the Society would not last long enough to complete the task. As the economically tremulous always do, they advised caution, even if that meant putting the project off for a later day.[25]

In the end, it was decided with only Joseph Krauskopf dissenting that publication would begin with the history's first volume, covering the period from Abraham to the Maccabees, rather than, as some had suggested, with the second.[26] With this decision, the Society had taken a firm (but by no means permanent) stand on three critical and recurring issues. It chose literary quality over the ephemeral but easily read, venturesomeness over narrow caution, and foreign works, if superior, over inferior American ones. Now it expected to move rapidly to bring out the five-volume history. As a matter of routine, the sheets sent from England went to a publication committee member, in this case Henrietta Szold, for perusal. She read them with her accustomed thoroughness, and to everyone's chagrin pointed out "dozens of inaccuracies." Her reward, not surprisingly, was a new assignment: to carry out needed revisions. Practical and contractual considerations made it impossible to carry out the "radical changes" that she proposed, but her corrections nevertheless improved the translation immeasurably. She added verse numbers to biblical citations, removed Germanisms, and touched up obvious errors.[27]

Henrietta Szold's painstaking—and of course voluntary—work on volume 1 delayed its appearance but permitted the Society to call its edition "the American edition," with the implication that it was better than the London original. Volumes 2 and 3 followed in short order, corrected (with Henrietta Szold's help) by two young men both under thirty: David Amram, a freshly minted Philadelphia lawyer who later became a leading expert in American bankruptcy law,[28] and Charles Hoffman, later a Conservative rabbi. Thereafter the work was Henrietta Szold's alone—one of the numerous tasks that fell to her when she commenced her full-time employment at the Jewish Publication Society in 1893.

In publishing Graetz, the Society made no effort to tamper with his work, not even to add sections dealing with American Jewry.[29] If it had, the historian and his heirs would probably have protested. Graetz had condescended to devote one page to America in the English edition—an improvement, but not much of one, over the single footnote to which he relegated it in the original eleven-volume German edition. But American Jewry never fit neatly into his conception of what was important in Jewish history: It had not struggled for survival or produced a significant cultural monument. In his abbreviated "popular history" (*Volkstuemliche Geschichte*), he tried to improve his American section, but only halfheartedly.[30] Graetz surely knew more than he let on, for he had read Isaak Markus Jost's substantial account of America in a history that was in many senses a forerunner of his own, and he had both a sister, Susie, and an estranged, intermarried, and apparently mentally ill son, Felix, living in the country. According to his biographer, he actually believed that "salvation would arise for Judaism out of England and America."[31] But his interpretation of modern Jewish history remained firmly rooted in Central Europe. Ironically, it was thanks to American Jews that this interpretation gained widespread currency among English-speaking peoples.

If it refused to tamper with the body of Graetz's history, the Jewish Publication Society did undertake to embellish it, adding an extra volume to the original five so as to render the work "readily available for pedagogical purposes." This is the famous "Index Volume," found in no other edition, and published in 1898 as a fitting capstone to its first great publishing achievement. A portrait and short biography of Heinrich Graetz (who had died without seeing the translation in print), chronological tables, and a pocket containing four not-very-helpful maps shared the volume. But the masterful index, anonymously compiled by Henrietta Szold, overshadowed them all. Some years earlier, Szold had written to her parents excitedly that she had "spent half the day at the Philadelphia library reading a book on 'What's an Index'" and had "rarely enjoyed anything more." This enjoyment apparently sustained her as she laboriously compiled by hand what eventually grew into an index of some 492 closely printed pages, complete with long subject entries that invited relentless pursuit of elusive facts through all five volumes of Graetz's narrative. "It must be a great pleasure to know that you have contributed an independent work to Jewish literature," an obviously overawed David Amram wrote her when he saw the magnitude of her achievement.[32] Few books in the entire history of the Society would prove to be of such enduring value.

The more than four thousand pages of Graetz's history, marketed as a six-volume boxed set and priced at nine dollars, appeared in time for Hanukkah of 1898. The set remained in print in one or another edition for over three-quarters of a century and sold tens of thousands of copies—more, probably, than any other Jewish history of its kind since Josephus, with five hundred sets a year (at $18) still being sold as late as 1957. The impact of Graetz can thus scarcely be overestimated. No modern Jewish historian has been more frequently quoted, and until new scholarship and deepening awareness of the Holocaust brought about changes in the 1960s, none had more influence on Jewish historiography and collective Jewish memory. As Rabbi Stephen S. Wise had already discovered in 1899, the history was a Jewish revivalist's dream. Many of those who read it found that it "quickened and stimulated their own love and faith and loyalty to race."[33]

Why did Graetz's history prove so enduringly popular? Certainly its epic style had something to do with it, but even more important is the fact that it offered a new historically grounded faith to modernized Jews whose religious practices and outlook had broken with the Jewish past. Graetz's history did what tradition and Jewish law no longer could: It bound the generations one to another. It did so, moreover, in ways that even non-Jewish Americans could respond to, for the histories they were most familiar with—the works of George Bancroft, Francis Parkman, and others—followed similar romantic conventions. They stressed, as it did, history's "marvelous" and seemingly providential course, marked by progress, punctuated with frequent moral lessons, and filled with hope for the future.[34]

With Graetz's history as successful as it was, it is not surprising that calls periodically arose to publish a revised Graetz: one corrected, updated, and adorned with the kinds of scholarly accompaniments found in the original. Twentieth-century American students of Jewish history, no longer fluent enough in German to read Graetz's notes, needed a history that contained references to relevant primary and secondary sources and also took account of contemporary scholarship. But ambitious plans to meet this need all eventually faltered; partly because the scholarly community could not unite behind any one proposal, partly because JPS—by then far more impecunious than in its halcyon days—had other priorities, and partly because its laymen were quite satisfied with Graetz as it was and hesitated to tamper with a work of such obvious popularity. In 1944 JPS published Ismar Elbogen's sequel to Graetz, covering the period from 1848 onward. Otherwise, it offered no new full-scale scholarly Jewish history until the first volumes of Salo Baron's massive opus appeared in 1952.[35]

Children of the Ghetto

For all of its pride in bringing a classic of Jewish history before an American audience, JPS knew that its long-term survival depended on its ability to provide its readers with more popular books, preferably fiction. The late-nineteenth and early-twentieth century saw a great fiction boom in America: "Novels were devoured as much as read," one scholar of the period writes, "and the public appetite appeared to be insatiable." American Jews shared in this obsession, but what they lacked were Jewish works of fiction, particularly those written from an American point of view. Calls rang out for "a native Jewish literature," high in quality and treating American Jewish themes sympathetically. This became one of the Society's most immediate priorities.[36]

Its first literary harvest proved disappointing. Thirty-year-old Milton Goldsmith, an active Philadelphia Jew involved in a family wholesale clothing business, cranked out a novel entitled *Rabbi and Priest*, a melodramatic and obviously didactic tale, set in Russia, and intended not only to portray "the character, life, and sufferings of the misunderstood and much-maligned Russian Jew," but also to glorify the land of the free. Henrietta Szold was opposed to publishing the book, but the Society needed novels, was desperate for American authors, and sought to focus attention on the plight of Russian Jews. When published, the novel complemented a pamphlet thoroughly documenting the Russian government's policy of anti-Jewish persecution. The pamphlet, reprinted from the British original, was the first of a new series designed to deal with "topics of timely interest."[37]

Similar moralizing characterized Louis Schnabel's *Voegele's Marriage and Other Tales*, the next and even less successful venture into literature, which was issued as a supplementary pamphlet of only eighty-three pages. But by then JPS already had the promise of better things to come. A great literary work, one of the most important that the Society would ever issue, was being rushed to the printer less than forty days after the manuscript had arrived at the Society's offices. It would appear late in the fall in two volumes entitled *Children of the Ghetto, Being Pictures of a Peculiar People*. Its author was identified as "I. Zangwill."

Israel Zangwill had burst upon the Jewish literary scene in 1889 with a brilliant analysis of "English Judaism," published in the first volume of the *Jewish Quarterly Review*. Mayer Sulzberger, Marcus Jastrow, Cyrus Adler, and Solomon Solis-Cohen all read the article and "spoke of the possibility of getting Zangwill to write for the recently born Publication Society." At about the same time, Mayer Sulzberger, having despaired of finding an American who could write a good Jewish novel, communicated with Lucien Wolf in London in hopes of finding a good Anglo-Jewish novelist there. The most widely read and extensively discussed fiction of the day was then being produced by British authors, and just a year before, in 1888, one of them, Amy Levy, had written a Jewish novel entitled *Reuben Sachs* that rocked the London Jewish establishment. Might Miss Amy Levy "be induced to write a Jewish story for us?" Sulzberger wondered. If not, was there somebody who could write for Jews a novel as powerful as Mrs. Humphry Ward's *Robert Elsmere* (a best-selling English novel dealing with the conflict between opposing religious forces, the collapse of Anglicanism, and the search for a meaningful new religion to replace the old)? Wolf recommended Zangwill, Sulzberger met him in London and liked him[38], and on February 18, 1891, Sulzberger wrote Zangwill describing the kind of novel that he wanted:

> [Why not] write a novel of about the size of Lady Magnus's "Outlines" depicting the life of your Russian immigrants in the East of London?
> Fine flowers doubtless grow on that muck-heap, and I feel convinced that no man can detect their presence or describe their beauties more competently than yourself.
> While such a story, of necessity, cannot have the hilarity of comedy, it must studiously avoid the deep distress of tragedy. It may appeal to the sympathy but must not harrow the feelings overmuch.
> You may think that this is a sparse and material way of clipping the wings of "pegasus," but I need scarcely say that fine fancy must find the market and to do that, must be in the vein of the purchaser.
> Can you do this, how long will it take you, what do you want for it-? *in money* I mean.
> Our people are somewhat restive because of the tendency of our Society to publish the works of foreigners. I regret to say that the house talent is not so plentiful as to invite on our part an exclusive literary policy. Nevertheless, as a compromise, your hero or heroine might emigrate to America—"the land of the free and the home of the brave."
> I need scarcely assure you that the remarks I make are not intended to do anything but to call your attention to the state of mind of the readers you would have to expect, and that I have not the remotest idea of trenching upon the province of the author.
> I should be glad to receive a reply at your earliest convenience.[39]

Zangwill, only twenty-seven at the time, was obviously flattered. He thanked Sulzberger, accepted the Society's terms, met his deadline, and then worried that the manuscript he submitted would be rejected because, as he wrote, "I've told the truth." He worried needlessly, for Sulzberger liked the volume and, after suggesting a few changes, predicted that it would "take."[40] He was right.

Children of the Ghetto is a realistic novel painting scenes from the lives of Jewish immigrants inside the London Jewish ghetto of Whitechapel (book one), and of native Jews outside seeking to assimilate (book two). It describes Jewish rites and customs in intimate and sentimental detail, presents a picture of religious change and generational change, conveys a generally positive and sympathetic view of immigrant life, and explicitly challenges "the conception of a Jew in the mind of the average Christian."[41] Zangwill himself summarized his major themes when he turned his novel into a play:

> Our drama shows a phase transitional
> Young loves at war with ancient ritual—
> How dead laws living, loving hearts may fetter,
> The contest of the Spirit and the Letter.
>
> Yet noble, too, that kissing of the rod,
> That stern obedience to the word of God,
> In Godless days when sweated Hebrews scout
> The faith that sunless lives are dark without.
>
> But do not deem the ghetto is all gloom!
> The comic Spirit mocks the ages' doom,
> And weaves athwart the woof of tragic drama
> The humors of the human panorama.
>
> The poet vaunts, the hypocrite goes supple,
> The marriage-broker mates the bashful couple,
> The peddler cries his wares, the player aces,
> Saint jostles sinner, fun with wisdom paces.
>
> The beggars prosper, the babes increase,
> And over all the Sabbath whispers, "Peace!"[42]

The novel's final scene, following Sulzberger's suggestion, glorified America, the land where, according to Zangwill, "Judaism is grander, larger, nobler," and "will make its last struggle to survive." As the novel closes, a vessel is gliding "with its freight of hopes and dreams across the great waters towards the New World," its passengers happily anticipating a brighter tomorrow.[43]

In its view of America, as also in its ambivalence toward ghetto life, religious tradition and rootless modernity, *Children of the Ghetto* embodied the central concerns, tensions, and hopes of its time. Its author, like the JPS, believed that Judaism needed to be revitalized: not chained to the ghetto or fully loosened from it, but inspired by its piety and virtues to fashion some new Jewish synthesis—a mixture of old and new. What precisely that new synthesis would be nobody knew, but Zangwill did believe that it would ultimately take shape in America, "amid the temples of the New World."[44] Many of those connected with the Jewish Publication Society agreed; indeed, it was the hope of forging this new American Jewish synthesis that helped spur men like Sulzberger to dedicate so much of their time to the Society's work.

Children of the Ghetto quickly became "the most talked of book of the season" and sold well on both sides of the Atlantic. Many praised its realism, the light it cast on a world that few knew anything about. It helped teach Christians about Judaism and punctured misconceptions about the Jewish immigrant ghetto not only in London, but elsewhere as well. Inevitably, some Jews censured the Society for bad judgment in publishing a book "so liable to misconstruction by the unfriendly and the ungenerous." Looking only at Zangwill's caustic comments on immigrant Orthodoxy and upper-class assimilationism, these readers feared that the book showed Jews in "a bad light to the Gentiles." They saw the Society's mission—and that of Jewish writers too—mainly in terms of public relations, apologetics, and propaganda, and conceived a good Jewish book as one that countered anti-Semitism and fashioned as favorable an image of Jews as possible. They never understood why the Society published books like Zangwill's whose commitment to "truth" might lead to its being misused by Israel's enemies.[45]

Most of those involved with the Society, however, gloried in Zangwill's success, particularly as it became clear that the Society's reputation had soared for having introduced to American readers a work of such renown. In 1895, the Society arranged with Macmillan & Co. to publish a one-volume trade edition of *Children of the Ghetto* on favorable financial terms[46]—the first of its books to be so honored by a commercial press. The book was also its first novel to be translated into foreign languages, including Hebrew. In the wake of Zangwill's success, novels about Jews won more favorable treatment from secular publishing houses—a fact that helped such struggling young writers as Abraham Cahan, but also made it more difficult for the Society to compete for good fiction. Still, Zangwill himself continued to maintain a "special relationship" with the Society. Years later he still spoke of his "indebtedness" to its "pecuniary stimulation" and "wise and understanding policy." In 1923, Zangwill returned to the roster of JPS authors with a lyrical translation of selected religious poems by Solomon Ibn Gabirol, which inaugurated the Society's Schiff Library of Jewish Classics. Fifteen years later, in honor of its golden anniversary, JPS republished three of Zangwill's works in a one-volume edition of almost fifteen hundred pages—then the largest and most expensive book in its history. It was a measure of Zangwill's enduring popularity that six thousand copies sold out within ten months.[47]

For Women and Other Readers

Had it not been for books written abroad—works by Lady Magnus, Graetz, and Zangwill—the Society's record in its formative years would have been far more meager and less successful than it was. The same might also be said of other American publishers, for they too gilded their book offerings with popular foreign imports. But the Society's mission, at least in part, was to nurture a distinctively *American* Jewish culture. Foreign works defeated its purpose. It was then with considerable relief that it was able to publish its first nonfiction work by an American resident, "Henry" (really Heinrich) Zirndorf's *Some Jewish Women*. Zirndorf, a German rabbi and poet, briefly a professor of Jewish history at Hebrew Union College and then a Cincinnati rabbi, based his book on a series of sketches he published in *The Deborah*, the Cincinnati-based German Jewish newspaper that he helped to edit. Nothing in his volume was particularly new or profound, but it appealed to the Society's large number of women readers and offered ammunition to those fighting the myth that Judaism degraded women, while Christianity elevated them to their proper estate.[48]

Liebman[n] Adler's *Sabbath Hours*, the Society's next book, was likewise homegrown and dealt with women, but it was devotional rather than historical— one of those rare devotional works that could appeal to all Jews "regardless of dogmatic differences." A posthumous translation of selected sermons by a beloved German rabbi who served for three decades in Chicago, it was "dedicated first and foremost to the use of the women in Israel." It offered them both spiritual sustenance and what it referred to as "needed knowledge." The call to educate American Jewish women about their religion sounded frequently in the late-nineteenth century, particularly in Chicago, which was a center of the nationwide women's movement and home to the National Council of Jewish Women, founded in 1893. The Society, sensing an unfilled need and a good opportunity, responded with a host of books and essays, Zirndorf and Adler being only the first, designed to elucidate "what [Jewish] women did in the past and what they are doing now."[49] Many of these volumes struck a traditional note, glorifying the Jewish "hearth and home." But a few, notably the *Papers of the Jewish Women's Congress* (1894) and the *Proceedings of the First Convention of the National Council of Jewish Women* (1897) pointed in new directions—toward greater women's concern for Jewish education, equal rights, and social welfare.[50]

In publishing the Zirndorf and Adler volumes, both originally written in German, the Society confronted for the first time the thorny problem of translation (the Graetz translation, of course, had been done in England.) It had from the start intended to translate foreign-language Jewish works, just as the earlier American Jewish Publication Society had done. But finding expert translators proved surprisingly difficult. Mayer Sulzberger was determined not to make do with a "scholarly translation" that captured meaning at the expense of style. He feared that anything less than idiomatic, tasteful English would "repel" Jewish youth and leave critics with the mistaken view that "our community are all foreigners." Late-nineteenth-century critics frequently associated culture with well-crafted writing; indeed, they were obsessed with "good form." Sulzberger wanted Jewish writing to meet these cultural standards, and he instructed translators accordingly, warning them against "too great literalness," and urging them to alter and delete as necessary for the sake of "true rendering."[51]

Unfortunately, when invited to produce specimen translations, most applicants fell far short, usually because they knew only one language well (and that language was not always English.) After several false starts, suitable translators for the Zirndorf and Adler volumes were finally found: Sylvan Drey and Wilhemina Jastrow. By far the Society's best translator of nonfiction, however, proved to be Henrietta Szold, because she possessed both a facility for language and a superb English literary style. During the years when she worked for the Society, whenever a scholarly book needed to be translated from German or French, it was she (or in a few cases one of her relatives) who did the job.

Taking Stock

At the third biennial meeting of the Jewish Publication Society held in May 1894, President Morris Newburger had every reason to be proud. Notwithstanding difficult economic times, the Society boasted some three thousand members (including one listed as living in "Indian Territory") and an endowment of over $16,000. Volunteers and paid canvassers were spreading the Society's work to every major Jewish community in the land. A dozen published volumes cast Judaism in a favorable light and were broadly educational in character, without being disagreeably polemical or forbiddingly scholarly. An occasional scholarly publication was subventioned with a small grant.[52] All of this proved that the JPS commitment to publishing was serious and backed up its claim to be "the one great central institution for the dissemination of Jewish literature and Jewish thought"—a "common ground" where all the different parties in Judaism joined together.[53] It had survived its first critical period with a strong reputation and a justified claim to being the leading American publisher of quality Judaica.

Yet there were problems. For all the talk of common ground, the Jewish Publication Society had accumulated numerous enemies—both old critics who opposed it from the start and new ones, who were annoyed at its policies. Rabbi Emanuel Schreiber, whose book on "Reformed Judaism" was one of the first that the publication committee rejected, denounced the Society for seeking to "suppress a reformatory publication" and for going "begging to England" for books instead of cultivating local talent. Naphtali Herz Imber, the cantankerous and habitually inebriated Hebrew poet remembered for his authorship of "Hatikva," complained that his book on "the ancient Jewish political and military state," written by his own admission in the space of four weeks, was rejected because of "Dr. Jastrow's ill feeling against me and Dr. Krauskopf's dislike for the Talmud ... because I do not write nonsense like [Louis] Schnabel and because I am not a Philadelphian." The Society, then, was simultaneously attacked for being too Anglophilic and too provincial, too Orthodox and too Reform. Later it would also be accused of being both too scholarly and too popular.[54] All of these accusations were partly true, and some of its books, like Schnabel's, were easy to criticize. But in its quest for a middle ground that would meet its lofty educational and cultural goals and satisfy as well the varied tastes of its diverse readership, the Society clearly courted such criticism.

The greatest danger that the Society actually faced was that its fragile community-wide coalition would break up, leaving it either the exclusive preserve of one group or totally impotent, fearful of publishing anything controversial or potentially divisive. Sulzberger, although personally far from neutral, had so far managed to prevent such a calamity, but how long he could continue to do so remained an open question. An ugly dispute in the *Jewish Exponent* over who deserved more credit for the Society's founding, Solomon Solis-Cohen or Joseph Krauskopf, boded ill for the future.[55] Could the Society remain both vibrant *and* impartial, or would it have to choose?

On the brighter side, the Jewish Publication Society could take great satisfaction in the fact that it had begun to spread Jewish books into areas where they had rarely reached before. Thanks to the diligence of Jewish communal leaders and professional solicitors, memberships from Jews in such out-of-the-way places as Demopolis (Alabama), Attica (Indiana), Terry (South Dakota), and Prairie du Chien (Wisconsin) appeared on the rolls. For these small-town Jews, who would henceforward form a disproportionate percentage of its membership, the Society served a special function: It linked them to their fellow Jews nationwide, provided them with the tools to acquire an advanced Jewish education, and gave them the opportunity even from afar to participate in American Jewry's cultural renaissance.[56]

Partly with these Jews in mind, some board members, Newburger among them, called for a monthly JPS magazine. They knew that the most important American publishers of the day produced magazines (*Harper's, Scribner's, Putnam's, Lippincott's,* and the *Atlantic Monthly,*), and that they served not only as a profitable sideline but as a training ground for developing writers and a means of publicizing forthcoming books. For the Jewish Publication Society, they argued, a magazine would also serve as a continuing tie to its far-flung members: "keeping down the number of delinquents and fallings off " while permitting the publication of popular and contemporary materials usually excluded from the Society's lists. In the end, financial problems as well as sharp differences of opinion regarding the proposed magazine's content—differences that reflected an ongoing debate regarding the Society's own mission—prevented the idea from ever getting off the ground. While it reconsidered the proposal off and on for over half a century, the board could never decide what kind of magazine it wanted: one that was lively and popular, one filled with opinion and debate, or one primarily concerned with culture and information. Inevitably, some also feared that a magazine would become controversial. Still, the fact that such a venture was even considered so early in the Society's history remains significant, underscoring the confident optimism of those involved in the early years.[57]

The same spirit of exuberance led JPS leaders to begin considering other grand projects for the future, most notably, as we shall see, a new American Jewish Bible translation. In their imagination they saw the Society's membership soaring to new heights and its achievements growing apace. In April 1893, the Society finally moved into quarters of its own, an office rented at 1015 Arch Street in the heart of the Philadelphia publishing district. This gave it a home and far greater visibility. At about the same time, "owing to the great increase of the labors of the publication committee," the board created a new full-time salaried position—Secretary of the Publication Committee—for someone who would bear responsibility for carrying out day-to-day editorial functions. Only one candidate was invited to fill this vacancy, Henrietta Szold. With her acceptance a new era in JPS history stood poised to begin.[58]

OUTLINES OF

JEWISH HISTORY

ISRAEL'S MISSION
IS PEACE

JEWISH PUBLICATION SOCIETY OF AMERICA

The first book: Outlines of Jewish History (1888) *by Lady Katie Magnus. The original JPS seal, designed by Moses Ezekiel, was stamped in gold on the cover.*

Rabbi Joseph Krauskopf (The American J *chives)*

Solomon Solis-Cohen

Rabbi Marcus Jastrow

Judge Mayer Sulzberger (The American Jewish Archives)

Morris Newburger

Simon Miller

Edwin Wolf

Henrietta Szold at the Friedenwald Cottage, Lake Placid, N.Y., June 15, 1898. The caption on the back of the photograph reads, "When is that book coming out?" (The Philadelphia Jewish Archives)

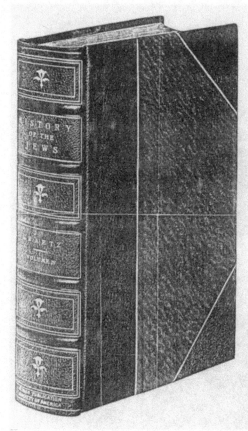

Heinrich Graetz's History of the Jews *(The American Jewish Archives)*

Subscription advertisement for "edition de luxe" (ca. 1910) (The American Jewish Archives)

4

THE HENRIETTA SZOLD ERA

The Ambivalent Editor

According to family tradition, the name Szold comes from a German word meaning "wage-earner," a name adopted by one proud family ancestor when he became the first of his faith to hold a salaried position in government.[1] Yet for Henrietta Szold, raised according to the standards of her day, being a wage-earner, especially away from home, must have been no more than a mixed blessing. It implied independence and offered the prestige that accompanies work well done, but it carried with it bleak overtones of spinsterhood, of a woman who needed to depend on a job because she could not depend on having a husband. While she lived at home, working carried less of a stigma; she was still her father's daughter. However, the 1893 invitation to become secretary of the publication committee meant moving away from her father and establishing her own identity. She greeted the offer with ambivalence, a feeling no doubt compounded by the wearisome list of responsibilities set forth in the committee's job description:

> prepare m[anuscripts] for the press, see them through the press, work over m[anuscripts], prepare circulars, keep the Society before the public in the papers and otherwise, and do such a reasonable amount of translation from time to time as the Publication Committee may direct.[2]

The compensation offered for all of this labor was $1,000 a year. The Society would have gone as high as $1,200 had Szold bargained, but, of course, a dignified woman in her position would never do that. Instead, she brooded. She considered on the one hand her roots in Baltimore, her devotion to parents and friends, and her night school for Russian immigrants. On the other hand, she recalled her sadness at home after one sister, Rachel, had married and moved away and then another, Sadie, had died tragically of rheumatic fever. Most of all, she thought of her own need, at age thirty-three, to find a satisfying and remunerative career—especially in the wake of Rabbi Benjamin Szold's forced retirement. Had her father remonstrated with her to remain at home, she undoubtedly would have listened; she always did. But since he raised no objections, and Rachel encouraged her to take the job, the lure of the new challenge, coupled with her devotion to the Society with which she had already been connected for five years, proved overwhelming. In the summer of 1893 she resigned her positions in Baltimore, dismissed her private pupils, and prepared to take up a new life in Philadelphia.[3]

As a respectable woman, Henrietta Szold did not live alone in the big city. Instead, she boarded with the family of Rabbi and Mrs. Marcus Jastrow, old friends of the Szolds and now relatives too, since Henrietta's sister Rachel had married the Jastrows' son, Joseph. A decade earlier gossipers had linked Henrietta herself with one of the Jastrow boys—the learned Morris Jastrow, then studying in Europe—but notwithstanding some proffered wishes of *mazal tov*, nothing came of it.[4] Now the Jastrows opened their Germantown home to her, and early every morning she traveled by train into town, usually returning home late at night.

There was a great deal of work for Szold to do. She began right away to meet regularly with Mayer Sulzberger, the "Grand Mogul," as she called him. She frequently came away from these meetings dejected, though, for nothing was ever accomplished as smoothly as the publication committee's impatient chairman expected. She was also learning the hard way about the manifold duties regularly connected with publication work, such as evaluating manuscripts, copyediting, proofreading, indexing, working with the printer, keeping track of manuscripts, and corresponding with authors, as well as preparing publication committee minutes.[5] Finally, she faced the inevitable day-to-day crises that beset all publishers. "I had to go to the printing office to give the foreman a blowing up," she fumed one February morning. The problem was caused by "commas in the proof. Some wrongly stupid commas have gotten mixed up with the others, and I was four hours to-day picking them out of some 40–60 pages of proof. My eyes feel queer after that hunt."[6] Yet all was not drudgery, for both editing and translating involved just the kind of reading, research, and patient scholarly absorption that she loved. There had, after all, been plenty of unhappy moments in her Baltimore work as well.

The secretary's position soon settled into its own routine. There were days when Szold was positively ebullient about her "very ladylike [and] gentle" kind of work. There were days when she would rather have done anything *but* work: "It is hot! And Philadelphia is dirty! That tells the story of a day's discomfort." There were even days when she came close to resigning: "The book is not out yet and I am afraid it may be delayed another ten days. I am receiving blame right and left for it. . . . I was on the point of giving up the whole job on Sunday, but I feel better about it now on mature reflection."[7]

No matter how she felt about the Society, however, Henrietta Szold still found it "a very unpleasant sensation" to be working for her living. She missed her parents in Baltimore, wrote to them almost daily, and visited them almost weekly; but she found herself working increasingly hard, even long into the night, because, as she admitted in one letter home, "I never trust anybody's accuracy and I am tortured by doubts every other line."[8] Yet, at the same time, she took tremendous satisfaction in her achievements. When her translations and indexes won high marks from critics, or even when she received an "appreciative letter" from an author thanking her for her "conscientious work," she felt rewarded.

Henrietta Szold felt even more rewarded, and rightly so, when she was honored at the Society's tenth anniversary celebration in 1898. Morris Newburger called her "a secretary whom the good Lord himself seems to have provided for the Society." Mayer Sulzberger, who in eight years had not permitted a word of praise for her to cross his lips, atoned by paying her an even more glowing tribute on this occasion:

> The word secretary is severely strained to describe her duties. Do you read a work in idiomatic English that originally appeared in French or German? It is the secretary who has rendered it into English. Do you find that errors in expression, in punctuation, in references, are almost non-existent in the books? It is the secretary who has read the proofs, and has spent weary hours and days and nights in verifying citations and correcting them. Do you find expressions that seem rough and uncouth? It is again the secretary who has had the trouble to suggest the corrections and the grief to have them rejected by the author. Do you look at the great index volume of Graetz, with its chronology and its maps? It is the secretary who has been the chronologer and the index-maker, and has not been without influence on the maps.[9]

The secretary felt dazed and exalted by these compliments and reacted enthusiastically: "To me it was the reward of my work, reward sufficient for two times as much work. . . . I am a very fortunate person."[10] Yet looking back years later, she realized that she received this kind of recognition all too rarely during the course of her years at the Jewish Publication Society—indeed, her contribution to the Society has always remained largely unknown. The fault, she believed, lay largely within herself, for as a woman she felt insecure about what she was doing, always more certain of her faults than her gifts. She transcended social expectations of her "womanly skills" yet still lacked the self-confidence to take credit for her achievements. So she buried her efforts in anonymity; it took years before she mustered up sufficient courage to insist on her due.[11]

Administration and Goals

Now that it had a full-time office, as well as an editor (in fact, if not in name), the Jewish Publication Society settled down into what became a regular routine. The board of trustees met quarterly to review policies and budgets and to oversee all operations. The publication committee met more frequently, usually once a month except in summer, and it decided what books to publish—usually three or four a year as well as an annual report. Interim decisions were made by the president and leading officers, who were all Philadelphians. That left day-to-day operations up to three people: Charles Bernheimer, the assistant secretary, who worried about members and carried out the orders of the trustees; Morris Dannenbaum (and later Henry Fernberger), the treasurer, who kept bills paid and creditors happy; and Henrietta Szold, the most important person in the office, who did practically everything else.

The Jewish Publication Society had three presidents during Henrietta Szold's years: Morris Newburger, Edwin Wolf, and Simon Miller. All three were successful Philadelphia businessmen who loved learning, who devoted large portions of their spare time to charitable and cultural institutions, Jewish and non-Jewish alike, and who deeply believed in the need to educate their fellow Jews to participate *as Jews* in a non-Jewish world. From a Jewish point of view these men were role models: Jews who succeeded in secular society and remained at the same time thoroughly committed to the needs of the Jewish community. As moderate Reform Jewish laymen, they tried to stand above interreligious squabbling by stressing those values, like education and charity, upon which all Jews could agree. When making decisions, all three presidents tended to rely heavily on Mayer Sulzberger, Cyrus Adler, and the rabbis and scholars of the publication committee. Even Simon Miller, Cyrus Adler's college chum and one of the few men who corresponded with him on a first-name basis, regularly deferred to him. This is not to say that Miller or his predecessors were figureheads; they were simply well-meaning, unusually cultured businessmen who saw it as their job to raise funds, manage, reconcile different factions, and oversee other affairs of the Society in a spirit of dedicated commitment.[12]

Although he never served as president, Jacob Schiff for many years wielded considerable behind-the-scenes power simply by virtue of his great wealth and largesse. His letters always received most respectful treatment at the hands of the trustees, and in practically all cases his wishes were taken as commands—Schiff usually insisted that the money he donated be spent according to his directions. In addition, the Society relied upon him for investment advice. He unofficially managed its endowment (much of which he had also funded) and advised the trustees when bonds should be bought and sold.[13]

While the president and the trustees held legal power, and Jacob Schiff looked over their shoulders, the Society's major product, its books, depended to a far greater extent on the activities of the publication committee, chaired for thirty-five years (and practically without missing a meeting) by Mayer Sulzberger. In its first twenty-five years, the committee considered for publication some five hundred books, most of them sent in unsolicited. Of these only sixty-eight titles were published—a record that bespeaks the rigor of the screening process and the tightness of money. Some proffered volumes, of course, were easier to pass upon than others. The committee rejected one heavy tome entitled "National Patriotic Societies and their Lapel Insignia" with scarcely a second thought. The many manuscripts sent in by cranks, missionaries, and fanatics—dog-eared and often handwritten chapters spouting conversionism, millennialism, pacifism, and hare-brained schemes to save the world—met with equally unenthusiastic receptions, although each as a rule was returned with polite thanks. But that still left dozens of potentially appropriate volumes that did require serious consideration, and each was accorded a respectful reading.

Monthly meetings of the publication committee, usually held at leisure on lazy Sunday afternoons, would see members gather around a long table, light up expensive cigars as the chairman described new arrivals, and then murmur a series of barely audible sighs as Sulzberger turned to one or another person asking him to read a manuscript and report on its worthiness. In an era when publishing was becoming increasingly commercialized, the atmosphere at these meetings remained amiably genteel, resembling a gentleman's club. The convivial arrangement continued with little change not only during Mayer Sulzberger's long reign as chairman but under his successor, Cyrus Adler, as well.[14]

How did the committee operate? The minutes tell mostly of decisions and bare-bones debate. Like most such documents, they are utterly lifeless, obscuring as much as they reveal. Thanks to Henrietta Szold, however, we possess a vivid insider's description of the committee's procedures. Although too long to be reprinted here in full, it deserves to be quoted at length, especially because years later she considered it "one of the best things I ever wrote."[15]

A manuscript bearing on the history of Talmudic times, let us suppose, is presented. It is referred to a subcommittee of three, consisting of a Talmudist (or *the* Talmudist), a member interested in Jewish pedagogics, and a literary man. The manuscript passes from one to another, each reader aware who his associates are. The three reports, separate and individual, are sent in writing to the Secretary. At a monthly meeting of the whole Committee, the three members of the subcommittee being present as a rule, the reports are submitted. Before a vote is taken, the non-reading members ask for explanations. They elicit illustrative proof of the criticisms, whether passed by way of censure or by way of approval. They inquire into the value of the book from the point of the Society's membership, its previous publications, and its half-developed plans. They desire to know on what grounds of expediency the manuscript is recommended, if its absolute value is not described as unassailable; or why its value for our constituency is doubted seeing that its absolute value recommends it. The subcommittee itself may be divided in its recommendations, or its reasons for condemnation or approval may not be clear. The decision is put off, and a member or two are added to the subcommittee. A new set of reports must be submitted, and the process of weighing and judging started afresh.

Or, the subcommittee may be unanimous in recommending it, but one member of the larger committee harbors misgivings, let us say about the religious bias of the book. He requests that voting shall be deferred until he has had the opportunity of reading the manuscript and forming an opinion at first hand. His intention is not obstructionist. He does not consider himself a more judicious Rabbinical scholar than the subcommittee member, or a pedagogue of wider experience, or a literary critic of greater acumen. He is exercising not a privilege, but a right and a duty, implied in the insistence of the resolution that action proposed by a subcommittee shall not be considered final. The motive that actuates him is justice, towards our reading constituency, which is entitled to the best within reach, and towards our writing clientele, which is entitled to the fairest hearing attainable. He desires to read the book in the spirit of the "gentle reader" appealed to in the prefaces of other days. At the next monthly meeting he will be qualified to tell the rest how the book is likely to affect and serve the Jew "on the street...."

The next monthly meeting: another discussion, and this time with the general non-Talmudic, non-pedagogic, non-literary public represented. Let us suppose the "gentle reader" to endorse the subcommittee's favorable recommendation. His agreement with it does not supersede a vote by the whole Committee on the question, "Shall the History of Talmudic Times be recommended to the Board of Trustees as a publication to be issued by the Society." The decision? Sometimes one way, sometimes the other.[16]

The procedures that Szold described, even as they aimed for scrupulous fairness, opened the Society up to considerable criticism. First, they were long and time-consuming, subjecting authors to endless delays and especially embittering those whose books ultimately met with rejection. Knowing this, Rosa Sonneschein, editor of the *American Jewess*, once offered to submit her stories provided the committee would pass judgment on their suitability in no more than a month. She received a hasty answer but not the one she sought; the proposition was summarily declined. Perhaps she was more fortunate than Israel Davidson, later a leading scholar of medieval Jewish poetry, who spent two years translating talmudist Isaac Hirsch Weiss's fascinating autobiography and then cooled his heels for almost another eighteen months until he learned that his translation, a poor one, was not acceptable. Davidson had immigrated from Russia only ten years earlier, and had advanced sufficiently by 1895 to win the English medal at City College, beating out the natives. This presumably brought him to the Society's notice, and since the promising student was desperate for money, the Society gave him a job. Although he was paid for his useless translation, that hardly compensated for his feelings of hurt, especially given the long delay. While the average author could expect to hear from the publication committee within six months, it was the "horror stories" that people too often remembered, and they permanently scarred the JPS image.[17]

The publication committee's procedures also meant that many books rejected as "not suited to the Society's purposes" were in fact thoroughly valuable books that other publishers signed up at once. That was fine, according to publication committee member Rabbi Samuel Schulman, since he wanted the Society to concentrate on precisely those volumes that would *not* otherwise be published, leaving the rest to commercial publishers. Rejected authors, however, thought otherwise. They could never understand why their work met with a warmer reception from Gentiles than from their own fellow Jews.[18]

On a deeper level, what is reflected here is a problem rooted in the publication committee's very marrow: its quest for consensus. Representing as it did a wide range of interests—its members included Reform, Conservative, Orthodox, and secular Jews, native Americans and immigrants, scholars, journalists, rabbis, doctors, lawyers, and professional writers—it sought to avoid books that might offend anyone. It convened in a spirit of outward harmony and tended to approve books that reinforced that harmony, even at the cost of blandness. Timely, provocative volumes advocating strong points of view on the great disputed issues of the day usually proved too threatening to win acceptance. It preferred books with broad appeal that reflected widely held values. While this certainly limited the Society's influence and cost it dearly in sales, this interpretation of the JPS mission made any other policy impossible to maintain. As a *Jewish* publication society, it felt a responsibility to represent the mainstream.

Unfortunately, personal and ideological disagreements often made consensus difficult to achieve. In the early years, for example, there were ongoing tensions between Mayer Sulzberger and Rabbi Joseph Krauskopf. Religious differences caused some of the problem: Sulzberger considered Krauskopf a puppet of "[Isaac Mayer] Wise and the Cincinnati School," and Krauskopf thought that the Society was becoming increasingly hostile to Reform Judaism. As much or more of the problem could be blamed on the virtually inevitable clash between two heavily bloated and competing egos. All might have been resolved without fanfare once Krauskopf began to devote the bulk of his time to his own National Jewish Farm School, founded in 1896. But the Society pointedly refused to donate a set of its books to Krauskopf's school, and at the JPS tenth anniversary celebration, where encomia flowed freely, Sulzberger never so much as mentioned his opponent's vital role as a founder and officer. The insult, intended or not, was deeply felt— Krauskopf conspicuously boycotted the evening banquet, notwithstanding the fact that the program scheduled him to deliver a toast. (Ironically, his prepared remarks, which survive in manuscript, heaped praise on Sulzberger for his leadership and speaking abilities, and on the Society as a whole "that kindles within us hopes of a most luminous future for Judaism.") The unpleasant episode, according to Henrietta Szold, "gave occasion for a good deal of display of feeling on the part of a clique of his [Krauskopf's] friends." As for the rabbi himself, he resigned from all posts with the Society and never attended any of its functions again.[19]

Fortunately, Rabbi Henry Berkowitz, Krauskopf's brother-in-law—likewise a Philadelphia Reform rabbi, but known for his peaceful temperament—agreed to join the publication committee at this time, heading off a schism. Yet even as outward harmony was restored, consensus was being undermined by changes in the committee's composition. At the tenth anniversary, the fourteen-man committee included six Reform rabbis of various leanings (Bernhard Felsenthal, Marcus Jastrow, Joseph Krauskopf, Max Landsberg, David Philipson, and Samuel Sale), as well as several Reform laymen (notably Henry Leipziger and Simon A. Stern). Fifteen years later the publication committee had seventeen members, only four of them Reform rabbis, while a clear majority either associated directly with the traditional-leaning Jewish Theological Seminary (Cyrus Adler, Solomon Solis-Cohen, Israel Friedlaender, Joseph Jacobs, Solomon Schechter, Mayer Sulzberger) or regularly sided with those who did (Herbert Friedenwald, Felix N. Gerson, Judah L. Magnes). In part, this change only mirrors religious changes taking place in the larger American Jewish community, particularly the rapid growth of Conservative Judaism, spurred in part by the Society's own founders. More than that, however, the change in emphasis stemmed from the growing influence of a new personality on the publicaton committee, Solomon Schechter.

Schechter, one of the great scholars of his time, was born in Rumania, trained in Vienna and Berlin, and then brought to England, where he rose to become reader in rabbinics at Cambridge University. He built his scholarly reputation as a young man with important books in the field of early rabbinic Judaism. He then greatly enhanced his fame with his much-publicized work on fragments from the Cairo Geniza. Schechter was a character: a large, lumbering man who exuded warmth with his grandfatherly white hair and beard, and who exceeded even the professorial stereotype in his absent-mindedness. Thanks in part to his wife, who wrote beautiful English, he became known for his sprightly pen, which he used both to illumine little-known facets of Judaism and to comment, often bitingly, on Jewish events of his day. He impressed all who met him with his magnetic personality and vast learning.

Members of the Philadelphia Group, who first met Schechter in England in the 1890s, tried for years to bring him permanently to America, certain that he was the man to give intellectual and spiritual leadership to the Jewish revival that they had so carefully nurtured. They invited him to deliver a series of lectures in

Philadelphia in 1895, corresponded with him regularly, and kept his name in Jewish newspapers. When Sabato Morais died in 1897, they approached him to fill the vacancy. Schechter was ambivalent at first, but soon accepted. In 1902 he arrived in America to assume the presidency of the newly reorganized Jewish Theological Seminary of America and quickly became the country's most renowned Jewish scholar. Almost at once he also began to play an active role in the work of the Jewish Publication Society. Even before he formally joined the publication committee in 1904, he was offering advice and making his presence felt.[20]

Like his friends in Philadelphia, Schechter spoke the language of consensus ("Catholic Israel") and believed in cooperation with Reform Jews in areas connected with Jewish learning, communal welfare, and social justice. At the same time, however, he vigorously opposed most of what the Reform movement stood for, to the extent that one of his colleagues warned in a private letter that "Schechter becomes a burning hell if you mention Reform rabbis." His metaphor for Jewish life was drawn from English politics, where two parties fought one another constantly, even as both agreed that "His Majesty's government, as well as His Majesty's opposition form one large community." He never doubted that his own was the majority position. Nevertheless, at least outwardly, he treated Reform Judaism with that mixture of smiling condescension and gentlemanly good manners that he thought propriety demanded.[21] The situation behind-the-scenes was different. Schechter treated Reform Judaism as a "deviation." On at least one occasion he and Cyrus Adler, who shared his sentiments, actively conspired to keep the Reform movement down. "I do not think it wise that the Reform element should have a preponderating vote upon this Board," Adler wrote privately to Schechter when the two of them planned the special committee to oversee the Society's proposed series of classics (see chapter five). "If the Classics Committee is enlarged at all it ought to be enlarged by the addition of a number of people to keep the balance just a little our way."[22] And on that principle the committee was set up.

If anti-Reform bias did affect policy on this occasion, there is no evidence that it did so on a regular basis. Indeed, the record also reveals various concessions to Reform Jewish sensitivities, for the spirit of consensus still ruled supreme. Yet, one senses over time an ongoing tension between that high-minded vision of Jewish unity that inspired the JPS founders and the more sobering reality of Jewish disunity that those connected with it later confronted every day in the community. The real-life situation of Jews engendered feelings of competition and even hostility between various religious and ideological movements, feelings that could not always be put aside by those simultaneously engaged in work supposed to appeal to Jews of all shades of opinion. This tension, of course, is endemic to consensus-based organizations; indeed, the Protestant interchurch movement was facing many of the same kinds of problems at the very same time. That the Society faced this tension, was sometimes stymied by it, and at other times conspicuously failed in its quest for neutrality is thus not surprising. Nor is it surprising that other Jewish organizations that faced this problem, notably the Union of American Hebrew Congregations, soon abandoned hopes of appealing to all Jews and concentrated on serving the needs of a far narrower constituency. But that was an option that the Society would not even have considered. The belief that Jewish learning could tie Jews together, an enduring axiom of twentieth-century American Judaism, encouraged instead renewed quests for consensus.

Emblematic of this goal was the policy, maintained throughout the early decades, of distributing every book it published to all JPS members, whether they wanted it or not (except if they selected as an alternative some previous offering). There were, of course, practical considerations here—every book published was guaranteed a minimum distribution of several thousand copies. But the main reason was that the Society, as a matter of principle, considered the books it published suitable for all Jews and consequently wanted to ensure them as wide a readership as possible. If individuals complained that one or another book failed to interest them—a problem that arose particularly in the case of children's books and narrowly conceived scholarly monographs—they were firmly reminded of the "great work" of the Society. Mayer Sulzberger insisted that "the apparent waste involved in distributing every one of our books to each member is really an incalculable gain. . . . Let them be scattered broadcast, let their recipients give them away or even sell them—they create an ever-widening zone of Jewish influence."[23]

History and Wissenschaft

The books that the Jewish Publication Society finally decided to publish during this period shed important light on its overall approach to American Jewish culture. Using the books themselves as evidence, it becomes possible to discern critical emphases and to infer from them the sorts of standards that governed all of these choices. How conscious the members of the publication committee were of the cultural values that underlay their decisions cannot be easily determined. What is clear is that these values explain far more than just what was going on at the Society itself. They reveal much about American Jewish cultural life as a whole prior to World War I—its strengths and its weaknesses.

Of all the nonfiction books published by the Jewish Publication Society, the largest category by far was history, which for many had become *the* source of ultimate truth. This, of course, continued a trend dating back to the earliest JPS offerings by Lady Magnus and Heinrich Graetz. Long before that, however, the historical approach to Judaism had been introduced by Leopold Zunz and other German Jewish scholars involved in the early-nineteenth-century cultural movement known as *Wissenschaft des Judentums* ("the Scientific Study of Judaism"). Reacting against the Enlightenment's emphasis on reason alone and influenced by ideas current in the age of Romanticism, they sought to root all doctrines in the soil of the past. Soon this became a Jewish scholarly obsession, to the extent that over half of all the nonfiction volumes published by the German *Institut zur Foerderung der israelitischen Literatur* during its decades of existence dealt with historical subjects. For many Jews, history had thus come to replace revelation as Judaism's central focus. Where their ancestors had appealed to the Holy Scriptures and the God of Sinai, they appealed to history and the God who guided Jewish destiny.[24]

The Jewish Publication Society fell heir to these currents as German historical ideas were introduced into the larger American community by scholars like Herbert Baxter Adams, professor of history at Johns Hopkins University.[25] Both Cyrus Adler, who was friendly with Adams,[26] and historian Charles Gross, also a member of the publication committee, were directly affected by these ideas, which won support elsewhere in the American Jewish community as well—particularly at the American Jewish Historical Society.[27] The happy result was a growing convergence between nineteenth-century Jewish thought and Progressive-era American thought. Publishing works of history enabled the Jewish Publication Society to approach that broad synthesis for which it so ambitiously strove. It appealed to a wide variety of Jews by showing them their common past. It linked American Jews to the prestigious tradition of German Jewish scholarship without in any way distancing them from American Progressive thought. It catered to popular tastes by providing books that its "general readers" could find edifying. Finally, it subtly inculcated ideas about tradition and change that many of its earliest founders had themselves begun to crystallize—ideas that would later become particularly characteristic of Conservative Judaism.

Many of these tendencies display themselves most clearly in the writings of Gustav Karpeles, author of three separate volumes of Jewish history published during the Henrietta Szold years, two of them issued as numbers in a special series of bound essays "on topics of timely interest." A German literary historian best remembered for his work as an editor of the prestigious *Allgemeine Zeitung des Judentums*, for his contributions to adult Jewish education, and for his numerous studies on the German Jewish poet Heinrich Heine, Karpeles believed that history had "a practical application, a moral," which he thought German Jews might profitably employ to strengthen their resolve against the onslaught of anti-Semitism.[28] The same motive clearly influenced his popular writings, including those that the Jewish Publication Society translated and prepared for its American audience.

Karpeles's apologetics, although evident, are less significant than what he had to say about the meaning and purpose of Jewish history. As a devoted student of Graetz, he stressed first and foremost Israel's belief in one God—the basis, he thought, both for Jewish unity and for Jewish continuity. He likewise highlighted change over time: the development of the God-idea as embodied in the Jewish people and expressed over "six great periods" of ongoing advancement, taking Israel "from humble, obscure beginnings to a position of prime importance in the culture and evolution of mankind."[29] This optimistic, progressive view of history, buttressed by "scientific" facts and animated by Darwinian assumptions, allowed American Jews to understand their history much the same way as their non-Jewish countrymen were understanding theirs—as the evolution of an idea (which in the American case was democracy) from its primitive origins (or "germ"), to its contemporary realization, and on to its coming worldwide triumph. Karpeles, in his first volume of essays issued by the Society, offered a particularly starry-eyed vision of a coming Utopia, one in which "all the nations of the earth, Israel in their midst," held God's ensign aloft and moved "onward and upward to a glorious goal: Humanity, Liberty, Love!"[30]

Although later essays evidenced somewhat diminished ardor, Karpeles continued to stress the uplifting idea of Israel's mission: "that Israel is called to be the witness of divine truth before all nations, and is to live as befits such a witness unto the end of all days, until the fate of the peoples of the earth shall have worked itself out."[31] This gave Jewish history its purpose and meaning, and to his mind provided the common basis upon which all Jews—Orthodox and Reform alike—still stood together. In a sense, then, here was the historical justification for the claim of the Jewish Publication Society to embrace a full spectrum of Jews.

Karpeles singled out the Talmud as a prime example of Jewish evolutionary development. He called it "Judaism's safeguard against spiritual serfdom," and characterized the rabbis of the Mishnah as "the most original expounders of the science of Judaism."[32] This view diverged markedly from the militant anti-Talmudic ideas characteristic of many early-nineteenth-century Western Jews and challenged contemporary American and Christian views of the Talmud, particularly the idea, repeated in the *Encyclopedia Americana*, that the Talmudic rabbis inculcated "a corrupt moral vision."[33] JPS offered its readers two additional European defenses of the Talmud, one by Emanuel Deutsch of England, the other by Arsène Darmesteter of France (and translated into English by Henrietta Szold), written in the same vein.[34] The Talmud, these volumes all maintained, was not only a work of which Jews could be proud; it also legitimated their entry into the modern world.[35]

Similar themes—evolutionary development, Jewish unity over time and place, principles of tradition and change, all coupled with occasional paeans to modernity and historical justifications of contemporary Jewish involvement in non-Jewish society—marked the Society's other historical offerings during these years. David Philipson, rabbi of Rockdale Temple in Cincinnati and an ordinee of the first graduating class at Hebrew Union College, authored its first historical work by an American, a volume entitled *Old European Jewries*. Originally titled "The Story of the Ghetto" and changed so as not to cause confusion with Israel Zangwill's

Children of the Ghetto, the volume surveyed the rise and fall of the ghetto as an institution, discussed the Russian Pale of Settlement (whose abolition Philipson considered "the only solution of the Russo-Jewish problem"), and assessed the ghetto as portrayed in literature. In his readable and moving prose, Philipson painted a dark picture, relieved only occasionally with warm references to such things as "that beautiful Jewish home life that has been one of the means of salvation for the Jews." He appealed to traditional values, such as family, charity, piety, and purity, insisting that they continued to maintain Jews wherever they lived. Most of all, he spoke out with characteristic optimism in praise of freedom and "the new era" introduced by emancipation. He looked forward, as Karpeles did in Germany and as the best-selling American author, Edward Bellamy, had in *Looking Backward* (1888), to a coming Utopia "when all men will be free to think, free to act, free to live anywhere and everywhere on the earth." This appealed to David Yellin, the noted Hebrew writer and educator then living in Jerusalem, who translated Philipson's book into Hebrew. Minus the chapter on Russia that was censored, the translation was published in Warsaw in 1902. Philipson believed it to be the first English-language work by an American Jew to be so honored.[36]

More enduring in value than Philipson's work was Solomon Schechter's *Studies in Judaism* (1896), a volume that was reprinted as late as 1945 and then brought out once again in a paperback abridgement that has seen a continuous life of almost thirty years. The fourteen essays on history, religion, and theology (reprinted from the *Jewish Quarterly Review* and the *Jewish Chronicle* in England) opened a window on the Judaism of Eastern Europe ("The Chassidim," "Nachman Krochmal," "Rabbi Elijah Wilna, Gaon") and presented in popular fashion, intelligible to non-specialists and non-Jews, reliable information on everything from "the dogmas of Judaism," and "the history of Jewish tradition," to Jewish mysticism, and the nature of Jewish law. They also put forward, especially in the introduction, a thinly disguised brief for what Schechter called "the historical school" of Judaism, a school he loosely associated with Jewish tradition as it evolved over time. The Historical School's attitude toward religion, Schechter explained, is "enlightened Scepticism combined with staunch conservatism which is not even wholly devoid of a certain mystical touch." *Studies in Judaism* is thus as much a scholarly volume of essays exploring Judaism in the past, as an important partisan statement regarding Judaism in the present, written from a perspective that Schechter shared with many of the Jewish Publication Society's Philadelphia founders. At least one Reform rabbi, Max Landsberg, voted against issuing the volume. But the majority chose to accept it, despite its strong point of view, on the basis of its overall quality and timeliness, and its singular ability to appeal to a wide range of readers, popular and scholarly alike. This exception to the principles of consensus and non-partisanship, although no precedent for the future, would not be the last time that the Society agreed to set aside its own guidelines to publish a work of enduring significance.[37]

Content aside, what distinguished Schechter's essays, then and today, is their unsurpassed style. An eagerness to reach beyond an academic audience led him to study the writings of such great nineteenth-century English essayists as John Ruskin, Thomas Carlyle, Thomas Macaulay, and especially Matthew Arnold, whose thought and writings influenced him greatly.[38] His own essays, ably edited by his gifted wife Mathilde, represent precisely that kind of writing—learned, popular, vigorous, lucid, timely and timeless, enlightening as well as engaging—that JPS aimed to publish all of the time.

JPS managed to offer its readers two additional volumes of studies by Schechter (one of them posthumous), and two books of the same genre by Schechter's successor at Cambridge, the Liberal Jewish leader Israel Abrahams.[39] Later on in the twentieth century it would publish some nine well-crafted volumes of Jewish history approaching this style by the Anglo-Jewish historian Cecil Roth. Outside of England, however, neither this marriage of brilliant scholarship to excellent writing, nor this model of engaged scholarship ever took hold, at least not in Jewish circles of learning. However much the Society touted the Schechter model, it found almost nobody in America who could emulate it.

The publication of Schechter's book represented a new type of arrangement for the Jewish Publication Society. The volume appeared as the first in a series entitled "The Jewish Library," commissioned by Macmillan in London, and probably the most ambitious effort to produce serious, popular Jewish books ever undertaken to that time by a major commercial house. The Society agreed to co-publish this series, with volumes appearing under its own binding and imprint. Promised future titles included Israel Abrahams's *Jewish Life in the Middle Ages*, and books by other British luminaries including Simeon Singer (who also happened to be Abrahams's father-in-law) and Morris Joseph. The arrangement ensured a steady stream of high-quality popular Jewish books. Of course, the books were not written by Americans and JPS had no hand in editing and producing them, but it put the best face on this by boasting of its own role in stimulating "the rise of a Jewish literature in the English language." "Never before," it gushed, "have general publishers ventured to issue high-class books of special Jewish interest, and it is not too much to say that our Society is one of the great, if not the greatest of the impelling forces."[40]

The Abrahams volume, a classic in terms of its style and content, was duly published soon after Schechter's and became a perennial JPS bestseller, still in print decades later as a paperback. The Macmillan agreement, however, ended there. Problems with deadlines, the fact that the Society had no control over the content of volumes it co-published, fear that the Macmillan series was excessively partisan, and a growing sense that the Jewish Publication Society should mainly publish works that "would meet with difficulty or discouragement . . . at the hands of the average publishing house," led to a reaction against all co-publications; Henrietta Szold counted a total of only four of them in twenty-five years out of a total of seventy-five proposed to the publication committee. With few exceptions, the Society in these years distributed only its own books––even if in content, style, and appeal they did not quite meet the standards that it had set for itself. Yet the tension between those who wanted to offer members the best available Jewish books no matter who published them and those who insisted that as a publication society it should distribute only books that it itself had overseen and produced, had by no means been permanently resolved. The issue would arise again and again.[41]

Having decided to stress its own commissioned books, the Society chose to encourage the publication of historical biographies, an increasingly popular genre in the nation as a whole. During this period four biographies were issued in the Jewish Worthies Series, co-sponsored by the Jewish Historical Society of England.[42] Nobody ever explicitly defined what made for a "Jewish worthy." Proposed subjects ranged from Judah Maccabee and Hillel the Elder to the German Jewish banker Gerson von Bleichroeder and the American philanthropist Judah Touro. In the end, as so often happened, only a small fraction of the original plan ever came to fruition. The result was a thoroughly miscellaneous series consisting of books on Maimonides (1898, by Israel Abrahams), Rashi (1906, by Maurice Liber), Philo (1910, by Norman Bentwich), Josephus (1914 by Norman Bentwich), and Moses Montefiore (1925, by Paul Goodman). It paralleled many late-nineteenth- and early-twentieth-century collections of short biographies, such as American Statesmen, American Worthies, American Men of Progress, and Men of Achievement and notwithstanding factual accuracy, shared many of their faults. These series, one historian of American biography concludes, "added little to the literature of biography. They were not intended to be complete lives; they were largely uncritical; and they were small in form. The majority were for popular consumption, although they are not particularly interesting or readable. They have a value, however, in that their publication indicates a growing interest in biography as a separate form."[43]

What gives these volumes interest today are the values that they sought to project, the moral and ethical lessons that readers of these books were supposed to imbibe from them. Maimonides, for example, emerges as something on the order of a medieval saint. "His gentleness, his even temper, his modesty," Israel Abrahams wrote, "were as conspicuous as his belief in himself and his mission, his giant-like intellect, his determination to make truth prevail." Like the leaders of the Jewish Publication Society, he is described as urging Jewish harmony and union. He also opposes zealotry, "adopts a modern standpoint . . . in the scientific study of religion," occasionally approaches "the modern view" (conceded to be impossible for a man of his day) that "the Bible enshrines expressions dating from different strata of religious belief," and believes that the final message of the Hebrew Scriptures is to be found in its highest and purest ideas, not in its more primitive and popular phraseology."[44]

Rashi, by Maurice Liber (translated from the French by Henrietta Szold's sister Adele), was a far better book, and truly extraordinary when one considers that the author, later France's chief rabbi, was only twenty-one years old when he completed it. But for all of its scholarship, it too followed the accepted conventions, peppering chapters with apologetic and didactic passages in praise of Jewish harmony, scientific scholarship, and domestic virtues.[45] As for Norman Bentwich's two volumes, one on Philo of Alexandria (whose work Bentwich later compared to that of the Historical School[46]) and the other on the Jewish historian Josephus,[47] it may be revealing that Bentwich devoted no more than a single sentence to the two books in his autobiography. By then he himself probably knew that the volumes were hasty and superficial; neither withstood the test of time.[48]

The last volume of the Worthies series, a biography of Moses Montefiore by Paul Goodman, secretary of London's Bevis Marks Synagogue, was actually rejected when first submitted in 1917. The six pages of detailed criticism that the publication committee (probably in the person of Cyrus Adler) sent Goodman were diplomatically phrased, but they indicate that when it came to accuracy, comprehensiveness, and the needs of the American reading public, the Society took a firm stand. It likewise displayed a patriotic insistence on stressing American involvement in history whenever possible:

> Inasmuch as the book is intended for an American audience the relationship of Sir Moses and his Palestinian work with Judah Touro and the fact that one of Touro's executors actually visited Sir Moses and went into detail about his plans ... should have a little more space. The importance of the mission of Sir Moses to Morocco would be enhanced if attention were directed to the fact that ... the American consul submitted a lengthy report to this Government which is extant and a copy of which can be furnished you.

Goodman apparently took the criticisms to heart. His revised manuscript was accepted, published in 1925, and, for all of its manifold inadequacies, remained the standard biography for many years.[49]

Given all the volumes of history that the Jewish Publication Society published, the fact that not a single work devoted to American Jewish history appeared on its lists during this period seems surprising. Interest was not lacking, and, as we have seen, an American dimension was frequently added to manuscripts that would otherwise have passed over the New World in silence. Moreover, many of the people involved in the JPS leadership, particularly the indefatigable Cyrus Adler, were simultaneously active in the work of the American Jewish Historical Society, founded in 1892. Some had even urged a merger of the two societies. Cyrus Adler opposed that idea on principle, conceiving the functions of the two societies as distinct: "It is the business of the Publication Society to publish popular works," he wrote, "it is the business of the Historical Society to publish at times dry-as-dust material."[50] But, though he opposed a merger, Adler did turn to the members of the American Jewish Historical Society in hopes of stimulating them to produce the kind of popular works that could prove appropriate for JPS readers.

As early as 1897, Adler attempted to put together an American Jewish Worthies Series to include volumes on individuals including David Einhorn, Michael Heilprin, Emma Lazarus, Isaac Leeser, Uriah P. Levy, Haym Salomon, and Gershom Mendes Seixas. None of the volumes ever materialized, perhaps because all but one of the authors he contacted were busy men of affairs who pursued research and writing only in their rare moments of spare time. American Jewish history came up again a decade later when Simon Wolf, the American Jewish community's unofficial spokesman in Washington, proposed that the Society update his bulky (and none-too-reliable) apologia designed to document American Jewry's patriotism: a volume entitled, with no effort at all at subtlety, *The American Jew as Patriot, Soldier and Citizen* (1895). Adler obligingly pushed a resolution through the publication committee supporting "a work on the Jews in the Wars of the United States . . . arranged in popular form," but that too came to nothing.[51]

For the most part, the popular works that JPS sought to issue depended on research that had not even been started. Nor were there any full-time scholars engaged in American Jewish historical research during this period; the field was filled with amateurs. The growing interest of American Jews in their own history, and the Society's desire to serve and even stimulate that interest could not, in the end, overcome the hurdle posed by the dearth of suitable manuscripts. The problem would not be resolved until the field of American Jewish history gained in age and stature, a development that took place only after World War II.

Russian Jewry, Zionism, and Divisive Contemporary Issues

While the Jewish Publication Society slighted American Jewish history, it devoted a surprising amount of attention to contemporary Jewish affairs. Of course, it continued to be wary of volumes treating issues in an openly partisan fashion and sought to project those elements that held Jews together, not what threatened to rend them asunder. There was, however, one contemporary issue that did unite all Jews and won them sympathy from non-Jews in America as well: the battle against Russian Jewish persecutions, an issue that attracted particular attention in the United States in the wake of the infamous 1903 pogrom in Kishinev. Earlier, in 1891, the Society had reprinted the Russo-Jewish Committee of London's pamphlet entitled *The Persecution of the Jews in Russia*, written by Joseph Jacobs. Several subsequent authors, notably David Philipson, referred to the Russian Jewry crisis in their volumes, but still with the hope that the problem could be resolved by new policies or a more enlightened Russian regime. This all changed in the twentieth century when remaining hopes were effectively crushed by renewed anti-Jewish persecutions. Increasingly, emigration came to be seen as the only viable long-term solution for Russian Jewry's problems. Jacob Schiff and others talked seriously of "making it possible for the Jews to leave Russia in toto."[52]

With news of the Kishinev pogrom still fresh, the Jewish Publication Society held its annual meeting on May 24, 1903. All around the country Jews were organizing, seeking ways to overcome the frustrating feeling of powerlessness that was the inevitable lot of those emotionally tied to a tragedy occurring thousands of miles away. Without dissent, JPS members added their voices to the multitude who deplored the massacre, and called on the president to do what he could "to prevent a recurrence of similar events." A second motion proposed more direct action:

> That the Publication Committee be requested to prepare from time to time and the Board of Directors to publish and distribute in such manner and in such quantity as may be most effectual, information bearing upon the condition of the Jews in Russia.[53]

For the first time, JPS had actually voted to engage in direct propaganda. Taking this as a mandate, the publication committee quickly decided to publish a series of informational pamphlets and appointed Cyrus Adler, who they knew would get the job done, to oversee the effort. Showing how rapidly action could take place when unfettered by burdensome procedures, Adler brought out two volumes in the space of one year: a special edition of Michael Davitt's *Within the Pale* and his own *The Voice of America on Kishineff.*[54]

Davitt's volume, written by a leading Irish revolutionary patriot on the basis of his own visit to Russia as a special correspondent for the Hearst papers, and first published for the mass market by A.S. Barnes, was largely geared for consumption beyond the JPS membership. The Society, having collected special funds, produced a cheap edition and sent complimentary copies to the president, the cabinet, members of Congress, the justices of the Supreme Court, the governors of the states, the three assistant secretaries of state, and to the mayors of cities "who had officially taken action in regard to the Kishineff affair." It wanted them all to be exposed to this famous non-Jew's "graphic description of almost unparalleled horrors, with the superadded value of documentary evidence," particularly since this account was not only sympathetic but firsthand.

So eager was the Society to spread this message that it overlooked Davitt's openly stated plea "for the objects of the Zionist movement." "I have come from a journey through the Jewish Pale," Davitt wrote, "[as] a convinced believer in the remedy of Zionism. I failed to see any other that can offer an equal hope of success. . . . Hope for partial or ultimate emancipation in Russia there is none. Other countries cannot be expected to relieve Russia of the unhappy victims of oppression and poverty. Where, then, are they to go?"[55] Many of the Society's leaders, Cyrus Adler among them, were far less certain than Davitt that the solution lay in Zion. But they published and distributed his book anyway, probably calculating that the good it could do in attracting support for Russian Jews far outweighed other considerations.

Adler's own book, meant to complement Davitt's, was one of those nightmarish volumes known to every publisher that seems to have been born under an unlucky star. A fire at the Baltimore printer (The Friedenwald Company, one of two Jewish printers that the Society used on a regular basis) delayed publication for seven weeks, and was followed almost at once by a general conflagration in the same city that held up the work even longer. Then there was a question of whether the book "ought to be issued during the war between Japan and Russia, lest it be taken, by the larger public, as a document intended to sway public opinion and thus perhaps react unfavorably upon the fate of the Jews living in Russia." It took a special meeting at the home of diplomat Oscar Straus to put that fear to rest. The book did finally appear, almost five hundred pages long, and it amply succeeded in documenting "the feeling engendered in the United States by the report of atrocities committed upon Jews in a far-off town." Here was proof to the world that in America all people of good faith—Christians and Jews, Orthodox and Reform—united both to protest anti-Jewish atrocities and to call out for human rights. This, in turn, helped to build up support for anti-Russian sanctions, including the abrogation of an 1832 treaty of commerce and navigation between the United States and Russia, one of the Jewish community's leading political objectives. At the same time, the volume also served internal Jewish needs. It underscored the spirit of consensus that underlay the Society's involvement in the Russian Jewry cause in the first place.[56]

Although it did not produce additional volumes of this sort—issue-oriented publications on affairs of the day soon became the domain of the newly formed American Jewish Committee (founded in 1906), whose first president was none other than Mayer Sulzberger—JPS did continue to concern itself in a more traditional way with the "Russian Jewish problem." As in many of its earlier histories, it sought to make available as much data as possible in order to stimulate sympathy and promote understanding. In 1910, for example, it published Abraham B. Rhine's appreciation of the Russian Jewish poet and critic Judah Leib ("Leon") Gordon, revised from a Hebrew Union College rabbinic thesis. Described in the preface as "a tale of the struggle between medievalism and modernity," the volume had a clearly stated communal objective: "A study of the nineteenth century Hebrew literature cannot but tend to raise the Russian Jew in the estimation of his American brother, and bring about a clearer understanding between them, which will inevitably result in closer fellowship and a firmer tie of sympathy." The fact that the study was written by a Lithuanian immigrant who was not only personally familiar with enlightenment circles in Russia, but who had himself Americanized and become rabbi of a synagogue filled with Jews of German extraction, made the volume particularly well suited to serve these ends. It offered a kind of "living proof" that the Russian Jewish "problem" could be solved.[57]

Similar considerations underlay Jacob Raisin's book *The Haskalah Movement in Russia*. Authored by a Polish-born Hebrew Union College graduate who saw himself as part of the movement he described, the volume pledged "to unfold the story of the struggle of five million ... human beings for right living and thinking, in the hope of throwing light on the ideals and aspirations and the real character of the largely prejudged and misunderstood Russian Jew." The treatment fell below the standard for JPS books, and even after considerable editing still explained historical change largely on the basis of the germ theory ("persons ... inoculated with the Haskalah virus"). But on the belief that "American writers like Mr. Raisin ought to be encouraged by the Society," and thinking that his book, despite all of its defects, "would nevertheless form a valuable means of acquainting American readers with the Russian Jew," the Society accepted it.[58] Meanwhile, it continued to cast about for something better.

Simon Dubnow, the dean of Russian Jewish historians, came closest to producing the kind of work on the Jews of Russia—at once comprehensive, scholarly, readable, and politically useful—that the Society had been grasping for. Best-known for his ten-volume *World History of the Jewish People* (1920–29), a remarkable synthesis that reconstructed Jewish history on the basis of such themes as the centrality of Jewish peoplehood, shifting autonomous centers of world Jewry, Diaspora nationalism, and the impact of external political events on internal Jewish life, Dubnow first came to the attention of American Jews with his essay entitled *Jewish History: An Essay in the Philosophy of History*, published by JPS in 1903. Henrietta Szold, who translated this essay on the basis of a German translation by Israel Friedlaender, privately described it as "one of the best things I have seen for a long time." Edwin Wolf, the Society's president, considered it a model of what JPS should be publishing on a regular basis.[59] Thereafter, Dubnow was periodically invited to submit additional volumes for consideration, including biographies for the Worthies Series on Elijah Gaon of Vilna and Jacob ben Wolf Kranz of Dubno ("The Dubner Maggid"). But Dubnow, deeply immersed in other research, always demurred.[60]

When Israel Friedlaender, Dubnow's longtime correspondent, disciple, and translator, came to America to teach at the Jewish Theological Seminary and then became active on the JPS publication committee, efforts to secure an important volume from Dubnow's pen increased. They were inspired at least in part by Friedlaender's belief that Dubnow's positive view of the Diaspora, somewhat akin to that of Ahad Ha'Am, held special relevance for American Jews and could be useful in forging new harmonious ties between Western, particularly American, Jewry and the Jews of Eastern Europe. In October 1910, at Friedlaender's urging, the publication committee invited Dubnow to take up his long-delayed "History of the Jews of Russia and Poland" arguing that it "would have in English-speaking countries, not only a literary and scientific value but also a social and practical value for his compatriots emigrating to such countries." Two months later, the Society went further, offering Dubnow "an honorarium of two thousand dollars for a book of about 175,000 words," and pleading with him, according to the minutes, to begin at once, for "such a work ... might have a distinct influence upon the welfare of the Russian Jew in the United States." Dubnow was persuaded, although he insisted that he could not begin work on the volume until 1913. "What attracts me most," he wrote to Friedlaender, "is your principal argument: the desire to connect the American branch of Jewry, which is continually developing and occupying an important place in the future of our people, to its ancient root in the east of Europe." Like Friedlaender and like the members of the Philadelphia Group years earlier, Dubnow had thus become convinced of American Jewry's emerging role as a future great center of Jewry. He viewed his assignment in much the same terms as the Society viewed its overall mission: to prepare American Jews for the task that lay before them.[61]

The first installment of the work Dubnow ultimately produced did not quite satisfy Israel Friedlaender because, as he wrote to the author, "you have dwelt at undue length upon the economic and legislative developments in the History of the Russian Jews, and have not laid sufficient stress upon their spiritual life."[62] Dubnow, who had altered his personal views on the nature of Jewish history since his earlier essay, and now, in contradistinction to Graetz, tended to subordinate culture to politics, only met Friedlaender's strictures part way. He invited his disciple, however, to take considerable editorial liberties in translating the work, and Friedlaender did so, rearranging, cutting, and adding numerous explanatory footnotes for the benefit of American readers unacquainted with the Russian situation. Correspondence between the two men flew back and forth, Russian censors and wartime conditions delayed the volume, and for a time it was feared that Dubnow's highly important section covering the period beginning with the accession of Nicholas II would never get past the Russian border.

In the end, however, the work secured "with great trouble" and published in great haste appeared in three black volumes (1916, 1918, and 1920). Mayer Sulzberger, who personally read and corrected the proofs, never ceased believing that they contained but "an arrangement of 'Annals'" from which Dubnow could yet fashion "a real History," and Cyrus Adler even years later criticized the historian for serving as no more than a "chronicler of misfortunes and pogroms."[63] Still, the work had a vast impact, remained important enough to be reprinted and updated in 1975, and, for all of its evident faults, represented precisely that kind of authoritative historical synthesis on a subject of contemporary Jewish concern that JPS often sought to produce, usually with far less success. Tragically, Israel Friedlaender, who tirelessly devoted himself to this work at the expense of his own, never lived to see it complete. On July 5, 1920, he and Rabbi Bernard Cantor were murdered in the Ukraine while on a mission for the Joint Distribution Committee.[64]

The campaign to inform Jews and non-Jews in America about Russian Jewish conditions gave the Jewish Publication Society a renewed feeling of purpose. It showed itself able to make a distinctive and highly useful contribution to what had become the preeminent political cause of American Jews and demonstrated in the process that it could serve as a useful instrument for molding public opinion. Yet there remained great questions as to whether it was wise for the Society to involve itself in issues of contemporary concern: Would this not conflict with its larger educational effort? Besides, it was only a rare issue that united American Jews the way the Kishinev pogrom did; for the most part, contemporary issues proved divisive. The Society's dilemma was clear: Disinterested aloofness from contemporary affairs rendered it lifeless; active engagement might undermine the all-encompassing nature of its mission.

The issue of Zionism brought this question to a head. Although the Zionist movement was still young during this period, it had already attracted fervent sympathizers, particularly from the ranks of young Jews committed to Judaism's revival. Heightened worldwide anti-Semitism, growing pressures to restrict immigration into the United States, the rise of nationalism in Europe, and the evident weakness of Turkey's hold on Palestine lent support to the new movement. Zionism also offered a new and absorbing ideal that filled a void left by the failure of nineteenth-century liberalism, the promises-gone-sour of the Enlightenment, and the misguided utopianism of post-Emancipation Jewish assimilationists. Zionism, however, posed a formidable challenge to Jewish modernists who viewed their Jewishness in essentially religious terms and considered Zionism reactionary. They feared that Zionism would rekindle old charges of dual loyalty, threatening the status of Jews in lands where they had just won emancipation. The question sparked loud and passionate debate throughout the American Jewish intellectual community. It soon confronted the Jewish Publication Society as well.

Henrietta Szold declared herself a Zionist in her early years at JPS, probably in 1896, and soon engrossed herself in Zionist literature, discussing its implications with such like-minded young thinkers as Joseph H. Hertz, later chief rabbi of the British Empire. She also corresponded with leading American Zionists and on at least one occasion admitted to having worked behind the scenes to try and "help the Zionist cause by having a non-Zionist agency [JPS] publish Zionist literature."[65] But Mayer Sulzberger, her boss, never came to share her enthusiasm. Recalling that many of Zionism's leaders lacked traditional religious attachments to Judaism, he questioned whether the movement would be able to grow and sustain itself. Until more evidence on that score was forthcoming, he objected to discussions of Zionism in any JPS publications.[66]

The issue, however, was not so easily dismissed, for authors wanted their views on the Zionism question to appear in print. By distributing Israel Abrahams's *Jewish Life in the Middle Ages* (1896), for example, the Society let stand an attack on Zionism as a "conception that has no roots in the past and no fruits to offer for the future." This was later balanced by Michael Davitt, whose volume, as we have seen, extolled Zionism as the only viable solution to the Russian Jewish problem. Gustav Karpeles, in a book that the Jewish Publication Society not only distributed but edited, was told to "leave out one-sided criticism of Zionism." Only nonjudgmental discussion of the subject was permitted to appear in Julius H. Greenstone's *The Messiah Idea in Jewish History*. Yet, surprisingly, only three years later, the Society published Nahum Slouschz's *The Renascence of Hebrew Literature*, translated by Henrietta Szold, even though it overflowed with sympathy for Zionism and was in fact a thinly veiled brief for modern Hebrew as a living language. According to Slouschz, the volume sold about 15,000 copies and played an important role in the development of Hebrew studies in the United States.[67]

This manifestly inconsistent policy, partly caused by uncertainty, partly by benign neglect, ended when Leon Simon, a leading Anglo-Jewish Zionist, submitted for publication his translation of selected essays by Ahad Ha'Am (Asher Ginzberg). One of the most incisive and influential of modern Jewish thinkers, Ahad Ha'am had a profound effect on European Zionist thought. Zionists in America like Henrietta Szold and especially Israel Friedlaender (who had earlier published the first collection in German of Ahad Ha'Am's essays) quoted him to show how Zionism could counter assimilation and be made compatible with Diaspora loyalties. Many at the Jewish Publication Society believed that a thinker of such renown should be made available to an English-speaking audience. Yet there remained the problem of Ahad Ha'Am's Zionism: Could JPS publish his book without seeming to endorse his views? At stormy sessions of the publication committee, David Philipson labelled the essays an *ex parte* statement and opposed their publication on that basis. His own proposed book, "The Reform Movement in Judaism," had just a year earlier met with rejection largely on these same grounds. As he saw it, nonpartisanship for better or for worse had become clear JPS policy. The fact that he personally believed Zionism to be "absolutely incompatible and irreconcilable" with Judaism was quite beside the point.[68]

Others, however, including Samuel Schulman, who shared many of Philipson's views on Judaism and Zionism, and Cyrus Adler, who attempted to distinguish *ex parte* from polemical writing, supported publication in this case because of Ahad Ha'Am's stature, the quality of his writing, and the fact that he set forth his ideas not as "partisan opinion" but as an analysis "that evokes either intelligent assent or thoughtful dissent." This view, similar to that which permitted publication of Solomon Schechter's essays, ultimately triumphed. In 1912, *Selected Essays By Ahad Ha'Am* was published to considerable acclaim. It remained in print thirty-six years later when the State of Israel was declared. But the bruising battle over the book discouraged other efforts to present controversial ideas to the JPS readership. Volumes deemed "safe" had a far easier time winning acceptance.

Trying a different approach to the problem posed by divisive contemporary issues, the Jewish Publication Society undertook in 1910 to produce a series consisting of volume-length essays describing ("on the basis of the most trustworthy scientific research") six great movements in Jewish life: Pharisaism, Hellenism, Mysticism, Rationalism, Zionism, and Reform Judaism.[69] These books would demonstrate that contemporary disputes had historical roots, and that even sharply conflicting movements could claim legitimacy from Jewish sources. By offering each movement "equal time," the Society could publish volumes advocating controversial points of view without violating its broader consensus-oriented mandate.

Zionism, the most timely of the proposed volumes, kicked off the series, and in impressive fashion. The author was Richard Gottheil, professor of Semitic languages at Columbia University, a one-time president of the Federation of American Zionists, and son of Gustav Gottheil, whose harsh words about the Society had long since been forgotten. Gottheil's volume, an expansion of the author's pioneering article on "Zionism" in the *Jewish Encyclopedia,* was the first book-length, sympathetic study of the subject in English. Because no volume expressed a contrary point of view, however, the Society's larger purpose—to forge a balanced series reflecting diverse ideological commitments without descending into polemics and without offending Jews of any persuasion—necessarily remained unfulfilled. *Hellenism,* by Norman Bentwich, a far shallower book filled with homiletical asides, did nothing to solve that problem; nor did it add to the Society's stature. As a result, when other volumes failed to come in, the series was quietly buried. A fascinating symbol of the Society's overall dream, it proved, like that dream, too visionary to be realistically attainable.

The American Jewish Year Book

If never fully attained, however, the Society's dream did achieve at least a measure of fulfillment in the *American Jewish Year Book*, first published to appear in time for Rosh Hashanah (the Jewish New Year) of the Hebrew year 5660 (1899–1900) and published annually thereafter. Because the *Year Book* concentrated on data, rather than ideology, and could therefore be scrupulously nonpartisan on controversial issues like Reform Judaism and Zionism, it could appeal to the widest range of American Jews. The long lists of national and local Jewish organizations, featured in the *Year Book* from the beginning, symbolized diversity within overarching unity. The mass of data also lent support to the new, more positive image of American Jewry that the Society's leaders were trying so hard to fashion. "A cursory examination ... will, I think, convince the most pessimistic that Jewish ideals have a strong hold upon the Jews of the United States, especially in the direction of charitable and educational work," Cyrus Adler wrote in his preface.[70] By widely distributing the *Year Book*, the Society hoped to allow the facts to speak for themselves, to better inform Jew and non-Jew alike about the American Jewish community and its growing significance.

The idea for a yearbook was hardly a new one. By the 1840s, Jewish almanacs and yearbooks of one sort or another had already appeared in such European countries as Austria-Hungary, England, France, Germany, and the Netherlands. In the United States, Judah Lyons and Abraham de Sola issued *The Jewish Calendar for Fifty Years* in 1854, a volume filled with useful data on the American Jewish community of the day. Ensuing years witnessed the publication of a slew of less important almanacs, as well as the rather more impressive *American Jews' Annual* published by Bloch Publishing Company from 1884 to 1896. All of these volumes began with one indispensable feature: a Jewish calendar listing dates according to the traditional Jewish lunar system, as well as Jewish holidays and fast days, weekly Torah portions, and in many cases the proper hour for Sabbath candle lighting. Taking their cue from almanacs and yearbooks in the general community, as well as from Catholic and Protestant denominational yearbooks, they also included additional features such as reviews of the year, lists of Jewish notables, and occasional articles designed to make the volumes more interesting and appealing.[71]

No Jewish yearbook aimed to serve as a permanent reference work, however, until Joseph Jacobs, described in his day as a combination "critic, folklorist, historian, statistician, [and] communal worker," issued in England in 1896 what he called *The Jewish Year Book*, subtitled "an annual record of matters Jewish." Jacobs believed that the British Jewish community had "been impaired" and some communal improvements "rendered nugatory" because of inadequate information. To remedy this, he sought on his own to supply the facts and figures that the community needed to know about itself. He also provided additional data—a guide to Jewish reference books, a glossary of basic Jewish terms, lists of Jewish celebrities, and the like—to serve as a basis for Jewish home education and communal self-defense.[72]

Jacobs' *Jewish Year Book* directly stimulated and also served as the model for the *American Jewish Year Book*. Cyrus Adler had proposed a plan for an American Jewish yearbook (the word "yearbook" spelled in this case in the standard American way) in 1896, even before the appearance of the British volume. But while Joseph Jacobs, working independently, moved forward, Adler's proposal, which was likely spurred by knowledge of Jacobs's plan, dawdled in a subcommittee. In 1897, the *American Hebrew* (on whose editorial board Adler sat) urged the Society to produce a yearbook on the British model, and Adler himself periodically spurred the publication committee on. But it took fully three and a half years before the proposal won complete approval.[73]

The *American Jewish Year Book* soon proved its value. Thanks to the diligence of Cyrus Adler and Henrietta Szold, it became the leading reference book of its type, and won wide recognition. But it also soon proved to be an overwhelming burden, one far greater than ever envisaged. The second volume, for example, contained long and detailed directories of national and local Jewish organizations, rosters of Jews who served in Congress and fought in the Spanish-American War, lists of American Jewish gifts and bequests during the year and of synagogues and charitable institutions dedicated during the year, plus half a dozen other features— including a long and brilliant narrative summary of the year's Jewish events, written by Henrietta Szold. The result was a volume of inestimable value, greatly superior to anything produced in England or anywhere else. All this data, however, had required hundreds of hours of editorial work (most of it Henrietta Szold's), 644 pages of small print (the first volume, by contrast, was only 290 pages long), and thousands more dollars of scarce publication funds than anyone had ever estimated. The Society recovered some costs by printing its own annual report and membership roster in the *Year Book,* instead of separately as heretofore, but that only added another 110 pages to a volume that was by all accounts already bulky enough. Volume 3 referred interested readers back to earlier volumes for some features, and could therefore be kept down to a manageable size. The underlying problem with the *Year Book,* however, admitted of no easy solution. Year after year it pitted those who counted costs against those who strove for quality, those who pressed for selectivity against those who demanded comprehensiveness.

Henrietta Szold usually came down on the side of quality, and then volunteered to do the extra work necessary to guarantee it herself—without additional compensation. But as time went on the burden became too great even for her, especially when she became the *Year Book*'s co-editor with Cyrus Adler in 1904 and then sole editor two years later. Her letters are filled with complaints about the "crazy orgy of work" and the "hated drudgery" involved in the annual labor; one evening in 1907 she "collapsed entirely" over it. In a particularly poignant letter to her then dear friend, Dr. Louis Ginzberg, she described herself as a "veritable martinet, writing to certain organizations that would not answer, and writing again, and still again, all but sending . . . the sheriff after them." But to no avail: "The stars with which I conscientiously mark unofficial information remain numerous in spite of the eighteen hundred personal letters I have dictated since July 15, not to mention circulars galore."[74] Still, individuals became angry when they found themselves or their organizations excluded from the *Year Book,* even if the exclusions resulted from their own neglect.[75]

The fundamental question the Society faced was whether all the time, effort, and money that the *Year Book* required could really be justified. Some JPS members insisted that it could not. They found the massive amounts of data contained in the *Year Book* dull and repetitive, felt annoyed that the Society produced the volume year in and year out, even when it only published three volumes total, and demanded that the *Year Book* be published, if at all, only once every few years so that it might prove less of a drain on limited resources. Community professionals, however, considered the *Year Book* essential, not only for Jews but for non-Jews. They noted that many libraries included the volume in their reference collections, and expected an updated edition annually—which, after all, is what made it a yearbook.

For a time the Society attempted to raise money for the *Year Book* by selling advertisements on inside pages and by raising the cover price to nonmembers. By 1907, however, the volume's cost, the enormous administrative burden of production, and membership dissatisfaction reached the point of crisis. Henrietta Szold, seeking to escape from the worst of the *Year Book* drudgery and eager to take a long vacation in 1908, suggested to Mayer Sulzberger that the American Jewish Committee take over the tedious statistical research. Given the new division of labor in the American Jewish community, and the Committee's strengthening hold on the area of contemporary Jewish affairs, this seemed like a sensible arrangement.

The Committee, however, went further—further, indeed, than Henrietta Szold wanted. It agreed to take responsibility for compiling the entire *Year Book*, to supply an editor from within its own ranks (as it turned out, JPS continued to supply editorial assistance and Henrietta Szold continued to devote many long hours to the work behind the scenes), and to contribute $1,500 toward publication costs. JPS, according to the agreement signed in 1907, continued as publisher, paid the cost of printing its own report in the volume, and assumed responsibility for overall distribution. The agreement came into effect in time for the 1908–1909 *Year Book*, at which point Herbert Friedenwald of the Committee, Cyrus Adler's brother-in-law, took over as editor.[76]

As time passed, the relationship between the Jewish Publication Society and the American Jewish Committee underwent numerous changes; at various times each organization believed that the other was not pulling its share of the weight. The size and cost of each *Year Book* and how those costs should be shared, whether or not the Society should take up valuable pages to print its full membership roster, and the proper balance between text and reference sections all became subjects of acrimonious discussion, especially during periods of financial belt-tightening. A revised agreement, signed in 1949, clarified roles somewhat: From then on, the American Jewish Committee prepared the *Year Book* completely and the Jewish Publication Society merely acted as co-publisher.

To most of those connected with JPS, however, the formal relationship has always meant far less than the dependable appearance of the *Year Book* in its annual catalog. Listed regularly year after year, it has in itself become a symbol of the Society's continuity, an effect heightened by the *Year Book*'s generally familiar format, revised thoroughly only once (following the publication of volume 50) since 1899. Symbolic too is the fact that each volume has embodied critical values that the Society cherishes: education, objectivity, and American Jewish communal identity. Churlish critics might add that the predictability and blandness of the *Year Book*, mitigated only somewhat by annual feature articles, also bespeak JPS characteristics; only in recent years have more controversial subjects been touched upon. Be that as it may, the contribution of the *Year Book* can scarcely be overestimated. As the premier reference work dealing with events and trends in American and world Jewish life, it has brought together facts found nowhere else, educated and informed many, and preserved for posterity a unique historical record.[77]

Religion and Controversy

With all the attention that it paid to historical and contemporary events in the life of the Jewish people, the Jewish Publication Society often seemed to overlook the religious experience of American Jews: the sacred literature, profound ideas, and elaborate ritual that defined Judaism and linked Jews to their culture. There was, to be sure, much talk of translating the Bible. Solomon Schechter had also proposed publication of a traditionally oriented Bible commentary. But critical studies of the biblical period and the ancient Near East received no encouragement at all from the publication committee; they smacked of higher criticism (Schechter called it "higher anti-Semitism"), a subject far too controversial for the JPS to handle at that time. Other volumes dealing with religion similarly met with resistance. They opened the door to precisely that kind of intra-Jewish controversy that was to be avoided.

Difficulties surrounding the first important JPS volume of a purely religious nature, *Jewish Services in Synagogue and Home* (1898), illustrate the broader problem. In 1893 Joseph Bogen, a Reform rabbi in Greenville, Mississippi, had submitted a short manuscript dealing with Jewish religious customs. Joseph Krauskopf favored publication, Marcus Jastrow and Mayer Sulzberger did not, and Bernhard Felsenthal urged acceptance of the manuscript with necessary changes. As a compromise (and also as an act of charity), Rabbi Henry Gersoni, a gifted, cantankerous, perennially impoverished, and highly embittered scholar (disliked by some on account of his having once been connected with Christian missionaries and by others on account of his difficult personality), was employed to revise the book, over the objections of several Reform members of the publication committee. When Gersoni decided not only to revise but to rewrite (his word was "reconstruct") Bogen's manuscript and then demanded to be listed as first author, the volume was cancelled. Bogen was furious.[78]

Soon afterward an analytical volume dealing with the Jewish prayer book was offered to the Society by a distinguished Louisville lawyer, politician, and versatile lay scholar named Lewis N. Dembitz, probably best remembered today as Louis Brandeis's uncle and idol. Dembitz read twelve languages, wrote voluminously, and dabbled in mathematics, astronomy, and philology, as well as Jewish studies. His father had been a follower of the sect founded by the antinomian pseudomessiah, Jacob Frank, while Dembitz himself had reverted to Orthodoxy at age thirteen as a student in Prague and later associated himself with the modernized traditional brand of Judaism (alternatively called Conservative and Orthodox) that was taught at the newly founded Jewish Theological Seminary and espoused by most members of the Philadelphia Group.[79] Sulzberger, Marcus Jastrow, and Cyrus Adler were thus predisposed to favor his work, but on Adler's recommendation they only offered him a contract with the proviso "that the [Publication] Committee shall have the power to abridge or omit controversial or other matter which, in its opinion, it would be injudicious for the Society to publish should any such occur." As further protection against controversy, they advised him to couch his analysis within a historical framework, so as to make it appear more scholarly.[80]

The volume, when it appeared, *was* scholarly, notwithstanding (or perhaps evidenced by) the over one hundred marginal notes to it published by Rabbi Wolf Willner.[81] No better English-language introduction to Jewish rituals of the synagogue and home existed anywhere. Yet, despite the Society's best efforts, including many long hours spent by Henrietta Szold and Joseph H. Hertz (who would later, as British chief rabbi, issue a work of his own on this subject), controversy could not be avoided; the same interest in liturgical reform that made Dembitz's volume timely also sparked considerable debate. The book, which barely concealed its anti-Reform bias, did nothing to promote Jewish unity, and in all likelihood only reinforced the prejudices of those who believed that books on religion only stirred up controversy and divisiveness. Nevertheless, this was far and away the most important book by an American citizen that the Society had yet published. It remained for many years the only advanced textbook of its kind in the field of Jewish liturgy.[82]

During Henrietta Szold's tenure the only other significant synthetic book about religious aspects of Judaism was Moritz Lazarus's masterwork, *The Ethics of Judaism* (2 vols., 1900–1901). Written in German and translated almost at once for the Society by its indefatigable secretary of the publication committee, these volumes were supposed "to make clear the inner life of Judaism" as a counterpoint to Graetz's history, which "portrayed the part which the Jews have played in the world."[83]

JPS took pride in having enlisted Lazarus as one of its authors. Years before he had practically invented the field of *Voelkerpsychologie* (the comparative psychology of peoples), a discipline that "sought to fathom the patterns and features of a people's national life by studying its constellation of geographic, ethnic, physiological, and historical conditions." He had then risen to become professor of philosophy at the University of Berlin (actually only honorary professor; German Jews, as Peter Gay has pointed out using Lazarus as his example, "found access to the academic ladder far easier than ascent."[84]) Unlike so many other Jews in German universities who either converted or became modern marranos, he continued to take an active role in Jewish affairs. He presided over two German Jewish synods, vigorously defended the German Jewish community against the rising tide of anti-Semitism beginning in 1879, and argued eloquently for acceptance of Jews as members of the German *Volk*. In 1883, representatives of the Jewish communities of London, Paris, Vienna, and Berlin commissioned Lazarus to undertake a comprehensive study of Jewish ethics that would counter the widely held view that Jews, on account of their ethical system, were more "primitive" than their Christian counterparts, and undeserving of legal and social equality. Lazarus, who as a scholar regarded "the entire human race as one family," and as a layman supported liberal Judaism, seemed like the ideal person to write on this subject.[85]

Given Lazarus's enormous reputation and the manifest importance of his undertaking, JPS committed to translate and publish his *Ethics* even before seeing a completed manuscript. Those who wanted to introduce American Jews to the fruits of German scholarship, and those who wanted the Society to publish more works from a Reform Jewish perspective probably joined forces on this issue. For his part, Lazarus, who was on friendly terms with several American Jews and had recently accepted an honorary degree from Hebrew Union College, raised no objections. He obligingly gave the Society permission to translate his work and told it to pay him whatever it considered appropriate.[86]

Had the Society's leaders known then what they later found out, they would not have been quite so ecstatic. First of all, the book proved to be exceedingly dry and scholarly—in that respect not at all like Graetz—and even Henrietta Szold, for all that she considered it a "great work," could not do much to enliven it.[87] When, soon after the book appeared, several JPS trustees proposed that the publication committee devote "less attention to the issuing or translation of such works as do not appeal to the Jewish public at large, on account of their scientific character,"[88] it was the Lazarus volume that they had in mind. Second, the book was never finished. Lazarus died before completing the work and the project had to be abandoned; the set as published lacks even an index. A decade later, when Jakob Winter and August Wuensche published a sequel in German based on surviving notes, the Society had lost all interest in the work and refused to translate it. Finally, and again unlike Graetz, the book itself was quickly dated; younger scholars viewed it as ahistorical, imprecise, and apologetic.[89] After sharp criticism from such philosophers as David Neumark and particularly Hermann Cohen, its influence faded. Although the reduction of Judaism to ethics may have had some impact in liberal Jewish circles, Lazarus's work taken as a whole reflected neither the dominant views of the publication committee nor the needs of most JPS members. No similar work appeared on the Society's lists again for over half a century.[90]

Textbooks for Children

Like books on religion, textbooks for children also proved troublesome for the Society. They inevitably offended the religious sensibilities of some members, and others, without children of suitable age, complained whenever such books were included among the annual selections. As time went on and JPS books became increasingly scholarly in nature, children's books also came to be seen as somewhat undignified, not in keeping with academic standards. But the demand for textbooks was great and they did prove profitable, as the success of Lady Magnus's history demonstrated.

In 1907 Solomon Schechter urged the Society to devote more attention to textbooks, and in 1913 Cyrus Adler, bowing to the need to appeal to all camps, suggested that where differences arose "instead of being neutral we might undertake to publish two sets of text books . . . one for the use of the Conservative Congregations and one for the use of the Reform Congregations." Thereafter, at least once every decade someone would raise the textbook issue anew, but to no avail.[91] JPS, committed to consensus policies and scholarly values, played no part in Jewish educational reforms pioneered in New York by Samson Benderly and his students, and never understood the new professional world of Jewish textbook publishing that emerged following World War I. Meanwhile, different branches of Judaism began to issue their own school textbooks, and other publishers moved in where the Society had feared to tread. Although individual JPS books occasionally won adoption as classroom texts and did very well, textbook publishing as such never became a priority.

During the Henrietta Szold years, the Society grudgingly managed to produce five children's textbooks, more than in any comparable period later on. All of the five were written or edited by women. Three of them were old-fashioned compilations containing selections from Jewish and non-Jewish authors, carefully balanced to appeal to all camps and designed, as the first of these volumes indicated, "to provide matter suitable for reading and recitation in Sabbath-schools and Sunday-schools, at entertainments of Jewish societies, and in the home circle."[92] In one case, Isabel E. Cohen's collection of *Legends and Tales in Prose and Verse* (1905), the Society only accepted the volume reluctantly and then warned its members that the book was only for the young, "and any comparison between it and works of real scientific merit is unfair."[93] Another volume, Marion Misch's *Selections for Homes and Schools* (1911), was accepted with equal reluctance and not before the author agreed to add selections designed to make the volume more balanced and more Jewish, and to drop selections viewed as "too closely identified with Christian hymnology," and "too polemical."[94]

The only one of these five volumes that really stood out was a charming kindergarten text, written and illustrated by Katherine Myrtilla Cohen (a Philadelphia sculptress and artist, sister of the one-time JPS corresponding secretary, Mary Cohen), and issued in cooperation with Philadelphia's Hebrew Education Society. One of the first Jewish children's books to be printed in color, *A Jewish Child's Book* (1913) focused on festivals and religious observances and was supposed to inaugurate a series of texts for Jewish kindergarten children, as well as a new era of cooperation between the JPS and Jewish educators.[95] But lack of funding, lack of enthusiasm, outdated ideas, and perhaps Cyrus Adler's personal pique at the growing Zionist emphasis in American Jewish education kept these plans from ever developing. In later years, aside from an abridged English Bible issued in 1931 in conjunction with the Hebrew Sunday School Society, JPS avoided instructional texts. Its program for American Jewish youth focused almost entirely on children's literature.

The Fiction Debate

During Henrietta Szold's tenure, JPS gradually developed a multifaceted literary publishing program including both novels for adults and fiction suitable for children. The boundaries between adult and youth fiction were never formally set forth, and they sometimes blurred completely. Just as Francis Hodgson Burnett's *Little Lord Fauntleroy* (1886) became a volume loved by Americans of all ages, so too many JPS children's books were read and enjoyed by adults who were children at heart. Thus *David the Giant Killer* (1908) by Emily Solis-Cohen, although written for young readers, was later advertised as a volume suitable for the entire family. By the same token, some of the fiction published for adults, particularly stories about Jewish life in European ghettoes, could be shared with children.[96]

Whether for children or for adults, fiction remained the most popular type of book that the Society published. The "fiction boom" in America was continuing, and it affected Jews no less than other Americans. Mayer Sulzberger was forever on the lookout for a budding American Jewish literary giant—if not an "American Israel Zangwill," then at least someone who could write about "our own time and country" and make "a welcome addition to our sadly deficient literature." Yet even as the Society attempted to heed the preferences of its members, recognizing "how much more good fiction appeals to the reader than any other sort of literature," and despite its best efforts to obtain "high class Jewish fiction," no aspect of its publication program caused more unease or generated more criticism.[97]

The problem was twofold. First there were those, including Solomon Schechter, who questioned whether fiction publications fulfilled the Society's lofty educational goals. It was all very well for commercial publishers to issue volumes—including, increasingly, American Jewish novels—on the basis of their potential mass-market popularity, but could JPS justify its actions on that basis? Was that really its mission? As early as 1901, Morris Newburger, sensitive to this criticism, pleaded with members "to try to appreciate the value of the *other* kind of literature we are sending them."[98] He seemed to be siding with those who, using a classic marketing approach, sought to capture members with books they wanted to read in the hope that they would later learn to appreciate the more scholarly offerings. A dozen years later, Rabbi Samuel Schulman rationalized fiction on different grounds, attempting to show that when written by a "great artist" Jewish fiction *did* fulfill the Society's aims:

> As, in general, the novel is to-day considered the most efficient and popular literary document for expressing the spirit of the times, so fiction treating of Jewish subjects and, above all, of contemporary Jewish life, is the truest and most efficient medium for the expression of that life. Given a great artist, and he seizes the soul of a time much better than those who theorize about it. . . . The artist gives it whole. Jewish fiction, if ideal or perfect, would give us a picture of Jewish life as it is to-day, with all the centuries living in us Jews.[99]

But many of the publication committee's members, particularly the scholars, remained unconvinced. As a result, the attitude toward fiction, far from being settled, fluctuated decade by decade, remaining a perennial subject for debate. Although fiction of one sort or another comprised 28 percent of the JPS lists during its first quarter-century, during the next twenty-five years it occupied only 15 percent (with no novels at all published from 1929 to 1937). During its third quarter-century, from 1938 to 1963, the total number of books it published more than doubled, but the volume of fiction increased far more slowly, rising to no more than about 18 percent.[100]

Whether to publish fiction at all was only one problem that the publication committee had to face; the other, no less tractable, was what kind of fiction? Should standards for selection be primarily artistic or didactic? Should authors be encouraged to strive for reality, even if sordid, or should they be encouraged to idealize Jewish life by putting the best possible face on it, in the hope that one day that would *become* reality? When, in 1909—apparently in response to New York Police Commissioner Theodore A. Bingham's allegations of Jewish criminality— some Jews called on the Society to use didactic fiction as a means of immigrant uplift, the publication committee knew that it had to protest; that was propaganda. "It is not within the province of the Jewish Publication Society to publish novels which teach morality by the one means of pointing out the evils of wrong-doing," it laid down in a rare policy pronouncement. "If we publish a book, the normal life should be represented as well as the abnormal, and the reader will then get a true picture of the Jewish community."[101]

But how to define "a true picture?" What was "normal," what was "abnormal," and whose values would ultimately govern? All of this remained subject to considerable dispute. Back in 1894 a manuscript by the budding American Jewish novelist Emma Wolf was rejected, despite favorable reports from some readers, because "some of the characters [are] immoral and the Rabbi hero impossible . . . whenever a traditional Jewish custom is discussed in the book, the Rabbi declares himself conscientiously unable to observe it."[102] Mayer Sulzberger tried to coax what he hoped would be a more appropriate novel out of journalist Abraham Cahan, whose English works, particularly "Yekl" and "The Imported Bridegroom," showed tremendous promise. He even met with the socialist writer to persuade him to write the kind of novel that the Society was seeking. But Cahan foresaw trouble ahead in Sulzberger's injunction against "selecting ugliness as the ideal," and he worried that "the gulf between the tastes and views of your organization and my own seems to be impassable." Sensing his literary potential, the Society took a chance and sent him a contract anyway, even offering to pay him a partial fee if it found his novel unsuitable. But Cahan never delivered. Instead, he published both his *The White Terror and the Red* (1905) and his great classic *The Rise of David Levinsky* (1917) with A.S. Barnes.[103]

The man some were then comparing to Cahan, twenty-eight-year-old Herman Bernstein, author of *In the Gates of Israel* and later a distinguished journalist and diplomat, submitted a manuscript as Sulzberger requested, and the Society paid him $1,000 for the rights to publish it. But in the end his *Contrite Hearts* proved no closer to the "true picture" that the Society wanted than Emma Wolf's manuscript had been, and he too received a rejection notice. Bernstein's theme— the breakdown of Jewish tradition in Russia, the rise of romantic love, and the domestic tragedies that ensued—seemed to some members of the publication committee to be "too somber." Other readers must have considered the novel unacceptably anti-Reform.[104] Yet neither criticism prevented the book from being published by a secular house. It appeared in 1905, complete with a prefatory note that sounds like it was written with the Jewish Publication Society's rejection slip in mind:

> To write of Jewish life is to handle a most delicate subject. There are so many ever-ready, though by no means ever-just fault-finders in Israel, there are so many different sections to be pleased—and to please one is to displease the others—that, I believe, if one were to adapt the treatment of his work to the

various tastes he would necessarily fail to do justice to the subject—for it is impossible to please all and yet be sincere.[105]

JPS did publish fiction, it *was* sincere, and it did not please everyone. But for the most part—Israel Zangwill's work being the most notable exception—it steered clear of the themes that secular publishers were trumpeting.[106] The shame of the cities, the problem of Jewish-Christian intermarriage, social and political reform, the struggle for economic survival, the plight of the secular intellectual—these and the related problems that stimulated American novelists schooled in realism found few echoes in the works that the Society distributed to its members. *Beating Sea and Changeless Bar* (1905), a volume of "poetic love tales," did contain a polemic against intermarriage, seeking to show that "no power can force a true Jewess to surrender her religion," but it was in a class by itself.[107] Most JPS fiction, aside from the children's literature, emphasized two themes: first, the beauties and terrors of Jewish life in the Old World, with special emphasis on the charms of Jewish tradition and the horrors of anti-Jewish attacks; and second, immigrant uplift, the successful assimilation of immigrants and their children into the new Western way of life. By no coincidence, both themes nicely complemented the social, educational, and political goals that the Society emphasized in its general nonfiction: renewal of Jewish tradition, dissemination of Jewish knowledge, fostering of better relations among Jews of different backgrounds, promoting better understanding of Jews by non-Jews, and opposition to European anti-Semitism, particularly as manifested in Russia.

The work of Samuel Gordon, a young London Jewish novelist whom Sulzberger recruited, probably at Israel Zangwill's recommendation, illustrates many of these themes. His collection of short stories, *Strangers at the Gate* (1902), endeavored to depict:

> the Russian Jew in his native surroundings as a creature possessing organs, dimensions, senses, affections, passions, actuated in his dealings both with his brother in faith as well as with his Gentile neighbor, by the same motives, good and bad and indifferent, which actuate those of his fellow beings to whom the Providence of history has been less of a step-mother.[108]

The evident sympathy Gordon showed for his subjects, his abiding love for Jewish tradition (he served as secretary to London's Great Synagogue and his father was the synagogue's cantor), as well as his opposition to all forms of Jewish ghettoization and his positive stance toward modernization, naturally appealed to the Society's Philadelphia Group founders. Gordon's novel, *The Sons of the Covenant* (1900), appealed to them no less. It focused on a scheme for a "training institute, chiefly of a technical nature," designed to equip young English Jews, children of immigrants, to leave the ghetto and enter on "new surroundings, new interests, and a mode of life contrary to all their past experiences." Americanization, immigrant distribution, and industrial training were goals that many American Jews, particularly Jacob Schiff, likewise advocated as long-term solutions to the problems posed by East European Jewish immigration, and Christian Social Gospel literature reflected similar religious action concerns. Gordon's novel therefore found a ready and appreciative audience.[109]

An even more appreciative audience was attracted to the ghetto fiction of Martha Wolfenstein, the Society's most notable literary discovery after Israel Zangwill. Daughter of Rabbi Samuel Wolfenstein, who headed the Cleveland Jewish orphanage, she began writing stories even in her youth. After the Society rejected her offer to translate Leopold Kompert's stories of Jewish life in the *Judengasse*, the Austrian ghetto, she was inspired by Kompert's work and by her father's Old World memories to produce a moving first novel entitled *Idyls of the Gass*. Henrietta Szold, who obviously identified with this talented and Jewishly knowledgeable daughter of a rabbi—also unmarried, devoted to her father, and lacking confidence in her own abilities ("I have never yet finished a bit of writing that I was not wholly depressed with," Wolfenstein admitted in one letter)— expressed great admiration for the novel. Where much of the literature of the day portrayed Jewish life in the ghetto as backward and Jewish treatment of women as bleak, Wolfenstein offered a brighter picture, full of obvious sympathy for ghetto folk and their traditional, highly ethical way of life. The publication committee, delighted to have finally discovered an American Jewish writer who was not only talented but shared its ideology, rushed the volume into press, hailing it as "a distinct literary contribution." Warm words of praise from Israel Zangwill and a bountiful harvest of favorable press reviews confirmed the correctness of this judgment.[110]

Martha Wolfenstein contracted tuberculosis soon after her novel appeared and never produced a sequel. The Society issued a volume of her early stories entitled *A Renegade and Other Tales* in 1905 and tried in various ways to interest secular publishers in her work. But though her death in 1907 was widely mourned, and her stories were occasionally reprinted in later decades, her star soon faded from the literary firmament. JPS, disappointed in its search for the great American Jewish novelist, had by then already begun to rethink its policies. In later years it would concentrate on translating literature from other languages rather than attempting to discover Anglo-Jewish writers on its own.[111]

Literature in Translation

Prior to 1906, JPS had only been willing to translate scholarly works of nonfiction, and even then it faced criticism from those who wanted it to publish works by American Jews exclusively. But the onrush of East European Jewish immigration to America, and the acknowledged flowering of Yiddish literature during this period—the era of Mendele Mokher Sforim, Sholom Aleichem, and Isaac Laybush Peretz—led many, including Henrietta Szold, to suggest that this literature be translated into English for American readers. Szold felt sure that they would greet it with as much appreciation as she had when she read it in the original. Although some continued to disdain Yiddish as a "jargon," and others were convinced that its renaissance was only of minor cultural significance ("a fiddle with one string," Mayer Sulzberger once called it[112]), she helped to persuade the publication committee that Yiddish culture would have an important role to play in American Jewish life. At her urging, the committee agreed to put translations from Yiddish literature on its agenda.

Actually, the Society had first discussed Yiddish literature back in 1898, when Mayer Sulzberger reported "that Dr. Leo Wiener was prepared to furnish the Society with a book on 'The History of the Literature of Russian Jews.'" Wiener, born in Bialystok and married to an American of German Jewish descent, was then an instructor in the department of Slavic Studies at Harvard. Aggressive and combatant by nature, he was also a secularist and assimilationist—so much so, in fact, that his son, the brilliant mathematician and inventor of cybernetics Norbert Wiener, was kept in the dark about his Judaism until he was a teenager. Wiener was thus not the kind of Jew that the Society usually dealt with, but he was undoubtedly a rare talent. He had already introduced the poet Morris Rosenfeld to an American audience, and he had done extensive research in Europe on the history of Yiddish literature, amassing in the process the books that would later form the basis of Harvard University's Yiddish collection. After considerable debate, his manuscript, including pages of translated "specimens," was duly commissioned; Wiener was paid $400.[113]

What happened next is unclear. Wiener later claimed that friction developed over the issue of whether "a Jew was a Jew before he was a man, and . . . owed inalienable allegiance to his own group before humanity itself." The publication committee minutes suggest somewhat more prosaically that Wiener showed his book to Scribner's, which published it, even though Sulzberger had already publicly announced that the Society would publish the volume (he had even gone so far as to extol Wiener as a "distinguished American"). In yet another version, offered some years later, the Society boasted that it had stimulated Wiener's study "in order to establish for political and social as well as literary purposes the claims of Yiddish as a language, [and] as a literature," but that "the purpose of the book was better served by leaving it in the hands of a regular publisher" so that non-Jews would read it.[114] Whatever the case, Wiener's *History of Yiddish Literature in the Nineteenth Century,* now recognized as a pathbreaking study of supreme importance, was never published by JPS. Anticipating a trend that would be seen more and more frequently in later decades, a recognized secular publisher produced the work, sensing that its subject matter might interest more than just the Jewish community alone.

The book that Henrietta Szold championed, and that did finally introduce JPS readers to Yiddish literature, was not nearly as ambitious as Wiener's. It was instead a hefty volume of stories by the immensely talented, and in those days not-yet-famous, Yiddish writer, I.L. Peretz.[115] The stories were translated from the Yiddish by a then unknown English translator, Helena Frank, one of Henrietta Szold's proudest discoveries. The publication committee had been on the lookout for a good Yiddish translator for some time without success when Szold chanced upon a good translation of a Peretz story in a New York Jewish newspaper. She went to the publisher, found out that the translator was Helena Frank, and convinced the publication committee to offer her a contract.[116]

Helena Frank was a "demure, cautious, gentle, refined English woman, verging on middle age," who was a cousin of the Duke of Westminster, and a believing Christian—although she admitted that her "father's father was born a Jew in Northern Germany."[117] For reasons she never revealed (Could her Jewish grandfather have been one of them?) she embarked on what she thought would be a "short excursion ... into the land of Jargon" about 1902, encouraged and aided by Leo Wiener.[118] She tarried long enough to complete several volumes of literary translations that did much to introduce Yiddish literature to the English-speaking world.

In addition to showing that a writer of the first rank had used Yiddish as his medium, the Peretz translations also had a clear political objective. Proponents of immigration restriction legislation, including Senator Henry Cabot Lodge, sought at the time to admit immigrants to America's shores only on condition that they could read and write "the language of their native country"—literacy in Yiddish would not be enough. By making the fruits of Yiddish culture available in English, the Society tried to prove that the language was not, as some charged, a dialect without a literature, and that cultural discrimination against Yiddish speakers was totally unwarranted. In 1908, as demands for a literacy bill grew, JPS commissioned a subsequent anthology by Helena Frank, *Yiddish Tales,* so as to demonstrate, according to the minutes, "that Yiddish was a full-fledged language, capable of stimulating a many-sided literary development."[119]

Yet politics was not the Society's sole motivation by any means. The high quality of Yiddish literature, the positive view of Jewish life that the literature (at least that which the Society translated) reflected, and the growing presence of Yiddish-speaking East European Jews on American soil also encouraged more attention to Yiddish. In 1909 the publication committee added a Yiddish expert to its roster, Russian-born Leon Moisseiff, hoping that he could be a conduit for more Yiddish material. Besides being an accomplished bridge engineer (responsible, among other things, for the Manhattan and Queensboro bridges) Moiseiff was also a well-known Yiddish writer, critic, publisher, and promoter. He championed a more sympathetic view of East European Jewish life and culture, even as he symbolized in his success the kind of Americanization that the Society's leaders would have happily seen all East European Jewish immigrants in America achieve.[120]

The trend toward publishing literature in translation soon spread. The following year, as if to redress the balance from Eastern Europe, two fictional volumes on German Jewish life were translated: one by Ulla Frankfurter-Wolff ("Ulrich Frank"), granddaughter of the famed Rabbi Akiba Eger, portraying contemporary German Jewish life in negative terms; the other by Salomon Hermann Mosenthal, a respected Austrian-Jewish dramatist and poet, portraying in positive terms "the beautiful simplicity of Jewish home life, as it existed in Germany half a century ago." The contrast between these volumes, unrecognized at the time, reveals much about the ambivalent attitude of German Jews in America toward their old home, and it highlights in yet another setting the tension between tradition and change that was one of the leitmotifs of this whole period in JPS history. Ironically, both volumes were translated by Henrietta Szold's sister, Adele, who was at the time anything but traditionally oriented. She used the money from her translations to help eke out a living with her idealistic new husband, Thomas Seltzer, editor of the radical *Masses* and later the controversial publisher of D.H. Lawrence.[121]

During this period the Jewish Publication Society also published translations of two Hebrew volumes by Jehudah Steinberg, a modern, enlightened, and still traditionally oriented Russian Jewish writer. His short novel, *Bayamim Hahem* (1915), translated by a Russian Jewish immigrant and Zionist named George [Gershon] Jeshurun, focused on the vicissitudes of a cantonist, a Jew impressed into the Russian army during the reign of Czar Nicholas I. The soldier's struggle to remain Jewish in the face of pressures from his patron, his peers, and even his Christian beloved—whom, significantly, he never married—countered the melting pot message found in so much of the Anglo-Jewish literature of the day.[122]

Two years later came Emily Solis-Cohen's translation of eighteen of Steinberg's popular children's stories, complete with four illustrations in color by fourteen-year-old Edith Rudin, a star student in the Boston Museum of Fine Arts class operated by Deborah Kallen, sister of the philosopher Horace Kallen. The book, *The Breakfast of the Birds*, received high praise, was loved by youngsters, and went through numerous printings. In 1955, however, one reader who purchased the book for a relative was horrified to find that it contained "stories which no child psychologist would consider putting into the hands of children of that age," such as a story about a child having his throat slit. Noting that "tastes in books change with the times," Solomon Grayzel, then the Society's editor and also a perceptive historian, wryly noted that in the 1950s gory scenes seemed shocking when found in children's books while children were left free to watch "all kinds of horror stories on television."[123]

The Search for Children's Literature

The problem of Jewish children's literature, of course, was an old one. The Jewish Publication Society had committed itself to producing works appropriate for Jewish young people soon after its founding. It published *Think and Thank*, a juvenile biography of Sir Moses Montefiore in 1890, but five years later no work of similar quality had been submitted for its consideration. In a continuing effort to remedy this situation, the publication committee announced a $1,000-prize competition, publicized in all the leading literary journals of the day, "for the best story relating to a Jewish subject suited to young readers." Some twenty-seven manuscripts arrived, more than expected. But the initial excitement drained away when the judges deadlocked between two top submissions: one by the Jewish writer Emma Wolf, the other by the non-Jewish writer Louis Beauregard Pendleton. Since no consensus could be reached, and neither story pleased everyone, the committee accepted the Solomonic suggestion of Henry Leipziger and decided in October 1897 that it would award no prize at all.[124]

With the problem of finding suitable children's literature still in mind, the board of trustees gently suggested that some of the competition manuscripts should be published anyway; a weak children's story, after all, was better than none. The publication committee took this as an order and accepted for publication Louis Pendleton's all-but-prize-winning *Lost Prince Almon*. Thereafter, through the 1920s, stories suitable for Jewish children were published with some regularity. The publication committee—not necessarily the best judge of what Jewish children's books should be—frequently expressed dissatisfaction with the volumes it felt obligated to approve, justifying them only on the basis of the "dearth of Jewish juvenile literature." The books themselves, however, did well. At least six went into multiple editions, and two—Pendleton's *Lost Prince Almon* and Sara Miller's *Under the Eagle's Wing*—were later translated into Hebrew.[125]

All of the JPS children's books published prior to Steinberg's *Breakfast of the Birds* related either to the Bible or to Jewish history. In form and style the volumes resembled their Christian counterparts, filled with romance, overt didacticism, and inspirational messages. Theirs was an uncomplicated world in which the righteous were rewarded and the wicked punished—a world far removed from the realities of twentieth-century American life. Following a common formula, the books' heroes—youthful paragons of virtue who trusted in God and minded their elders—triumphed over adversity and prejudice, and then watched as their conniving enemies received their just rewards. Pendleton's *Lost Prince Almon*, a story based on the life of Jehoash, son of Ahaziah, and Eleanor E. Harris's *The Game of Doeg*, based on the life of King David, both follow this formula and end on a similar moralistic note.[126]

Only two volumes diverged somewhat from this familiar pattern. Sara Miller, a New York elementary school teacher whose *Under the Eagle's Wing* (1899) had come close to winning the children's fiction contest, wove her story around Joseph, beloved disciple of Moses Maimonides.[127] She portrays Joseph as a courageous fighter for Judaism: "If every Jew had been less submissive, and had shown some of the fire and courage which animated our forefathers," she has him proclaim at one point, "we should not now be a despised and persecuted people." Influenced perhaps by new currents of European Jewish thought and early Zionist writings, Miller makes a surprisingly strong case for overt expressions of Jewish pride, militant self-defense if attacked, and even active retaliation in extreme cases of provocation. Yet just at the point when her hero stands ready to wreak personal vengeance on his father's murderer, she has Maimonides and his niece, Esther, intercede on the doomed man's behalf, reminding Joseph that man "shalt not harbor thoughts of revenge but trust to God, Whose ways are inscrutable, and Who, in His own time, will reward the patience of His children." The resolution is traditional, but no other Jewish children's story of the day had confronted youngsters with a moral dilemma of similar weight. [128]

The Young Champion, Abram S. Isaacs's story of one year in Grace Aguilar's childhood, was a good deal less sophisticated but unique in a different way, because it was prepared especially for girls. In selecting an appropriate female role model, Isaacs chose neither a typical biblical personage nor a medieval "woman of valor" but, rather, a highly educated nineteenth-century woman, a modern profile in courage, who despite recurrent bouts of illness had written a shelf-full of secular and Jewish books before she died, unmarried, at age thirty-one. Grace Aguilar's writings had achieved extensive popularity in America, especially among Jews. The Society itself had reprinted one of her volumes, *The Vale of Cedars,* in 1902, more than half a century after its initial publication.[129]

Having selected Aguilar as his subject, Isaacs could still include in his biography commonplace pieties about the Jewish home ("the real altar of Judaism") and women's domestic duties—subjects that Aguilar herself had addressed. What is striking, however, is the stress he also laid on the importance of properly educating girls, not only to acquaint them with Jewish and secular learning but also to help them develop their own innate capabilities. "It is one of our old traditional sayings that every mother in Israel should reflect that her son might become a Messiah, a deliverer of his people," Isaacs quotes Grace Aguilar's mother as saying. He then has her expressing precisely the same hopes for her own daughter: "May Grace be such a deliverer to champion Israel's truth and rescue the nations from prejudice and error."[130] This volume, like *Under the Eagle's Wing*, quietly hinted at new social currents without fully embracing them. Once again, the Jewish Publication Society illustrated the tension between tradition and change but did not come down forcefully on either side.

Standards, Style, and Solicitations

Taken as a whole, the publications distributed during the Henrietta Szold years (1893–1916)—even without considering the Bible translation, the *Legends of the Jews*, and the Schiff Library of Jewish Classics, which were all begun during her tenure but completed later—reveal much about American Jewish culture generally during this period. Most importantly, it was during these years that American Jewish culture really emerged; never again would the country be considered a Jewish cultural wasteland. While the Society's most important books were still not being written by authors trained in America, they at least carried the name "America" on their title page, serving as proof to the world, as David Philipson observed, "that American Jewry has literary possibilities and even literary worth."[131] General characteristics of this period—one of great social change, enormous stress, unbounded hopes, and recurring doubts—go far toward explaining this dramatic emergence. Like the nation as a whole, the American Jewish community had become aware of its own potential and was rapidly emerging as a prime mover in world affairs. The community was growing in numbers, power, and wealth, and could boast of an increasing number of rabbis and scholars. At the same time, it was being transformed by East European Jewish immigration and increasingly sundered along religious, ideological, generational, and even Old World lines. Anti-Semitism, assimilation, ignorance, widespread religious dissatisfaction, immigrant unrest, internal strife—these and other American Jewish communal problems demanded attention. Conditions in Europe, meanwhile, suggested that America would soon become the center of world Jewry, a mantle that American Jews sought eagerly to fit into but were ill prepared to wear. Faced with a host of new problems, foreign and domestic, and poised to take advantage of new opportunties, American Jews struggled to equip themselves for the challenges that lay ahead. The Jewish Publication Society was one of the organizations to which they looked.

In selecting books to meet the needs of American Jews during this period of communal transformation, the leaders of the Jewish Publication Society evolved a series of unwritten guidelines that defined its overall standards as well as its social assumptions and cultural values. These, in turn, were reflected in their decisions about what to publish. First and foremost, they insisted that all JPS volumes be broadly educational. Heirs to nineteenth-century liberal Jewish thought, to the educational ideas of European Jewish scholarship, and to Victorian didacticism, they understandably extolled education, specifically education through books, as a cure for everything from anti-Semitism to assimilation. Working hand in hand with other Jewish organizations that promoted Jewish education, like the Jewish Chautauqua Society, they sought to combat "ignorance from within and prejudice from without." More broadly, they saw themselves "laying the foundation for a Jewish renaissance in America." They expected a new and more culturally vibrant American Jewish community to be shaped by their efforts.[132]

Besides being educational, JPS books also had to be noncontroversial, acceptable to "all parties." This stipulation, set forth back in 1888, represented both an ideal of American Jewish unity and a practical objective, given the Society's broad intended audience. In 1909 Rabbi Samuel Schulman termed the Society "perhaps the only moral force in existence that is making for the unification of the Jews in America." Its leaders did not, of course, seriously believe that differences among Jews would suddenly disappear. They wanted instead to project an image of unity. They knew that only as a unified community could American Jewry assume its destined central role in the Jewish world.[133]

Fear of controversy and manifest disunity deprived the Society of many important books. Naphtali Herz Imber, author of *Hatikvah*, saw his *Autobiography of an ex-Chassid* withdrawn owing to objections from Solomon Schechter and others, even after it had been accepted and set up in galleys.[134] Pauline Wengeroff's remarkable *Memoirs of a Grandmother*, a volume that Solomon Schechter considered "a great human document," and that Jacob Schiff and his wife personally championed, never saw the light of day because Mrs. Wengeroff insisted that her brother, Ephraim M. Epstein, serve as translator. Because he was alleged to be a "notorious apostate" and a one-time Christian missionary to the Jews, several members of the publication committee opposed having anything to do with him. This controversy doomed the volume, albeit by an unusually close margin.[135] Volumes on Zionism, Reform Judaism, and Orthodox Judaism were similarly rejected when they seemed too divisive. Other books only won acceptance once their controversial sections were excised. But though the Society met frequent criticism for what Rabbi Henry Berkowitz called its "cowardly course," and though Henrietta Szold herself later lamented that her superiors had been "afraid of life,"[136] this characteristic was nevertheless a reflection of a noble ideal: "the very exalted one of making Israel in America conscious of its distinctive spirit . . . which, despite partisan differences and all centrifugal influences, makes for its unity."[137] Where others laid stress on those elements in American Jewish life that divided Jews from one another, the Jewish Publication Society was committed to showing how much American Jews still held in common. Practically alone, it championed the idea of a unified Jewish cultural tradition, rooted in history, ideas, values, and sacred texts, that linked American Jews to their spiritual ancestors in the great Jewish centers of Europe and Babylon.

The third key criterion for Society offerings was that they be dignified. This sense of propriety, of projecting a positive Jewish image, stemmed in part from the well-known post-Emancipation Jewish concern with manners and mores. American Jews, like their European counterparts and even more than middle-class Americans generally, had become self-conscious. They looked for occasions to display their new refinement, hoping thus to disprove Christian stereotypes and prove that they had arrived.[138]

What the Society meant by dignified is somewhat more difficult to define. Certainly it meant that its books had to have a fine outward appearance and be written in acceptable English. But it also meant that it would not engage in anti-Christian polemics or publish works offensive to Victorian sensibilities. "The sensational 'best-seller'. . . the polemic, the party pamphlet, the apologia"—all of these, Henrietta Szold reported at the Society's gala twenty-fifth anniversary, "were on the whole kept on the outside."[139] Beyond that, as this anonymous report on a proposed novel makes clear, the Society looked for books that were pure and elevating:

> The story seems to me unsuitable for our Society. It is very locally English. Its idea of birth control is unhealthy. Its two intermarriages are unlikely and are both spoken of without any repugnance to that idea. Excepting the hero and his mother and the old woman all his Jews are vulgar, uneducated and material to the last degree. The style itself is the poorest kind of journalese. Not only is the book unsuitable for our Society but I believe its publication will be on the whole harmful to the Jewish cause.[140]

The reference here to the "very locally English" character of the rejected novel points up yet another characteristic of the Society's style: its unabashed pro-American patriotism. Stung by early attacks on its policy of publishing books by foreigners, and eager to demonstrate America's centrality, the Society strove mightily both to find authors who lived in America and, insofar as practicable, to add "American dimensions" to the books that it published. At the annual meeting of 1900, Morris Newburger made this policy official. He issued a public call for "stories which would make our own country their scenes or background, or which would bring in features of Jewish life as developed under American conditions."[141]

This evident and sometimes exaggerated emphasis on America is easy to understand. American Jews, like Jews in other Western countries, and like many other American immigrant groups, felt compelled to go to great lengths to prove their loyalty and patriotism, particularly when these were so frequently being called into question by nativists and anti-Semites. American Jews also had the additional problem of having to earn the respect of their European cousins who viewed them as cultural barbarians. Constantly emphasizing America thus made sense on two grounds: It evidenced allegiance and it publicized American Jewish achievements. When Rabbi Samuel Schulman, at one annual meeting, associated the Society with the "patriotic component of . . . national life,"[142] he was in effect telling JPS members just what they wanted to hear—that the Society, by championing America, had helped the cause of American Jews both at home and abroad.

Finally, there remained the matter of popular appeal. Books may have been educational, noncontroversial, dignified, and patriotic, but they still had to be defended in terms of the perceived needs and demands of the general JPS membership. That "the members of the Society would not be interested" in a book could be reason enough for it to be rejected.[143] The fact that members craved fiction and sought suitable books for their children, on the other hand, resulted in some books being accepted that might not otherwise have made it through. As for nonfiction, Edwin Wolf, president of the Society from 1903 to 1913—one of those unique Philadelphia Jewish businessmen who was at heart a book-loving educator— defined the ideal JPS book as "a work that is simple in style, but backed by knowledge and scholarship, and of such a compass as to appeal to a large proportion of our constituency."[144] Henrietta Szold put forward Solomon Schechter's popular essays as the epitome of that very ideal.[145]

Yet for all this, given a choice between books that members obviously wanted and books it thought American Jews needed, the publication committee often selected the latter. It paternalistically assumed that as time went on it could educate members to appreciate Jewish books of a higher level. As JPS grew older, the debate over popular appeal grew more acute and focused on the question of how much emphasis should be placed on works of Jewish scholarship. In the end, no matter what it thought of the perceived needs of the American Jewish community, the Society learned from bitter experience that it could not completely ignore the expectations of its members. Sooner or later economic circumstances reminded those in command that popular appeal was as important as all of the other standards that a proposed manuscript had to meet; to think otherwise was to court disaster.

How well *did* the Jewish Publication Society appeal to the public? Statistics presented at its twenty-fifth anniversary celebration in 1913 paint a mixed picture. On the positive side, longtime trustee Ephraim Lederer estimated that some 550,000 volumes had been sold or distributed since its founding, a remarkable figure by any standard, and testimony to its vast cultural impact. Many of the sixty-eight JPS titles would likely not have been published at all, and certainly not in America, but for the Society's encouragement. On the other hand, membership figures fell drastically below expectations. In 1893 membership stood close to 3,000. In 1897 it reached a total of 4,101. In 1905 it crested at 5,430 and promptly fell precipitously, owing in part to demands for funds from Jewish organizations involved in receiving and settling East European Jewish immigrants. A membership drive in 1909 raised membership back up, and by 1913 it stood at better than 11,000. It would continue to grow until early 1921 when, if the published figures are correct, it reached 16,780. Yet considering the vast growth of the American Jewish population during these years, the membership, proportionately speaking, actually dropped. This is not surprising, since most of the immigrants neither knew enough English to read JPS books nor had enough money to pay for them. Still, the sad fact that after twenty-five years of productive labor fewer than one American Jew in two hundred even belonged to JPS was a bitter pill for the leadership to swallow. In 1913, even the Federation of American Zionists claimed more members, while American Jewish fraternal organizations boasted collective membership figures totalling more than 600,000—practically one American Jew in four.[146]

The Jewish Publication Society tried various means of increasing its membership. For years it employed an agent named Katherine Harris Scherman, who traveled around the country soliciting members on commission, but with only limited success. Her son Harry later became famous for inventing a better means of book distribution; he called it "The Book of the Month Club."[147] In 1903, the Society experimented with a new membership scheme centered around the creation of a New York branch office to attract more New York members (and money) and improve the Society's national image. The scheme may also have been a trial balloon to see if the Society as a whole should move to New York, which would explain why the loyal Philadelphian Mayer Sulzberger threatened to resign in protest. Whatever the case, within eighteen months the experiment was dead. Thereafter the Society did maintain a presence in New York, and all of its editors spent at least part of their time there. Yet, though that helped to keep the Society in touch with the worlds of Jewish scholarship and general publishing, it had no effect whatsoever on membership. What did help, especially in the membership drive of 1909, were the same old-fashioned techniques that the Society had employed back in 1888: circulars, solicitation by volunteer committees, and support from rabbis and communal leaders.[148]

There was, however, one highly noteworthy difference between the campaigns of 1888 and 1909. In 1888, the Society had solicited support on an optimistic platform, stressing its role in furthering an American Jewish renaissance. Later, as a surviving circular signed by Edwin Wolf reveals, the mood and the solicitation pitch had changed:

> The Jews are a minority in every land. Under the circumstances, it becomes our duty not only to avoid being misunderstood, but to secure for ourselves a patient hearing and fair judgment. The growing Jewish population of America must have a strong central organization in order to create a feeling of unity among the Jews scattered throughout the land. This can only be done by a systematic distribution of good Jewish reading matter.... The Jewish Publication Society of America is practically the only great medium for supplying the necessary literature which can centralize public opinion so that the attention of the world becomes favorably focused upon our struggle for justice.... We are engaged in a great cause—the welfare of the Jewish people—and this vital end cannot be efficiently furthered without your cordial participation.[149]

In associating itself, at least on a public relations level, with the work of communal self-defense, the Jewish Publication Society was realistically reading the times: optimism was waning, fears of anti-Semitism growing. It made sense to appeal for support on the basis of what American Jews felt to be the needs of the hour. But implicit in this approach was a decision to downplay education and culture for their own sake. The idea that American Jews needed Jewish books in English to better acquaint themselves with the tenets of their religion, to deepen the wellsprings of American Jewish culture, now took a back seat to the defense and welfare needs of Jewry as a whole. This is not to say that the JPS publishing policies themselves noticeably changed; they did not. But there developed a growing chasm between what the Society did and what members wanted and expected it to do. The old optimism, the quest for self-improvement and for communal enrichment, was giving way under the pressure of world events to a new spirit of hard-nosed realism.

This change, of course, did not happen overnight, and its full impact on the books was not felt until after World War I. Meanwhile, enriched by several thousand new members, the Society enjoyed a small-scale boom. On April 5 and 6, 1913, to celebrate the twenty-fifth anniversary of its founding, JPS staged a gala ceremony in Philadelphia that attracted nationwide attention. Many of its former authors gathered for a special evening in their honor, leaders of the Society delivered major addresses, and a banquet for 350 people took place at the Mercantile Club with Mayer Sulzberger serving as toastmaster. Nahum Sokolow, Herman Struck, Moses Hyamson, and Aaron Aaronson represented Eastern Europe, Western Europe, England, and Palestine, and a diverse group of notables from across the country attended as well (although the flooded Ohio River kept Rabbi David Philipson at home). All of the great Jewish cultural institutions, foreign and domestic, sent messages, many of them filled with praise for what the Society, Henrietta Szold specifically, and American Jewry generally, had accomplished.[150]

The ceremony symbolized in its own way what the Jewish Publication Society had come to stand for: the unity of American Jews, the centrality of American Jewry, the perpetuation of Jewish culture in America and beyond. With twenty-five years behind it, and three significant projects in the works, the Society, notwithstanding evident problems, could take pride in its accomplishments. No Jewish publication society anywhere had done as much. It was easy, then as later, to criticize the Society and point to its shortcomings. But those who looked to it from afar were understandably impressed; they saw in its achievements a portent of American Jewry's future course.

A message sent on this occasion from Jews' College in London captured the prevailing mood:

We on the other side, in the older country, watch with deepest interest the marvellous strides you have made and are making in this great and glorious land of freedom and independence, where careers and opportunities are open to talent and industry.

Your great philanthropic institutions are the admiration of all visitors to the United States. They bear witness to the munificence of their founders, the generosity of their supporters, and the efficiency of their administrators. But the Publication Society whose semi-jubilee we are to-day celebrating proves that, in this land of material progress, you recognize that man does not live by bread alone. You care for things of the spirit, you are alive to the intellectual and spiritual side of life. You provide windows for the soul of Israel....

May you advance by leaps and bounds, and when ... America will be the centre of Jewry, may this Publication Society be a world-wide organization fostering the Jewish spirit, strengthening the Jewish consciousness, giving adequate expression, and thus helping to do justice, to the Jewish life, the Jewish character, the Jewish soul.[151]

With the Bible translation, the completion of Louis Ginzberg's *Legends of the Jews*, and the Schiff Library of Jewish Classics still ahead, JPS looked forward to fulfilling all of these promises and more.

Final session of the Board of the New English Translation of the Bible, held at the Jewish Theological Seminary of America, New York, November 1915. From left: Joseph Jacobs, Solomon Schechter, Max L. Margolis, Cyrus Adler, Rev. Dr. David Philipson, Rev. Dr. Kaufmann Kohler, Rev. Dr. Samuel Schulman.

FOR OUR 60,000 AMERICAN JEWISH BOYS
IN THE GREAT WAR

The Jewish Publication Society of America has undertaken the important task of distributing, free of charge, to every Jewish lad in the United States Army and Navy, copies of an abridged

PRAYER BOOK, IN HEBREW AND ENGLISH

and a

SOLDIER'S AND SAILOR'S BIBLE

for which the text of the New Translation of the Bible was used.

The publication of One Hundred and Twenty Thousand Prayer Books and Bibles, enough to supply the Sixty Thousand Jews in the service, will cost thousands of dollars.

You, no doubt, feel that we ought to at least equal the efforts of our Christian neighbors in this regard and do as much for our Jewish boys as they are doing for their boys.

WHAT WILL YOU DO TO HELP?

If you have already contributed, will you not do so again? Make a contribution yourself on the accompanying subscription blank and get your relatives, friends and business associates to do likewise.

Let us place a Jewish Bible and Prayer Book in the kit of every Jewish Soldier and Sailor. The sacred writings of their fathers will inspire them to hallow their trust as Americans and as Jews and will cheer them in their many hours of trial.

This cause demands everything you can give. Give as much as you can and make it big—as big as the occasion requires.

Special World War I appeal. Some 100,000 volumes were eventually distributed without charge. (The American Jewish Archives)

Jacob H. Schiff

Cyrus Adler

Benzion Halper

The Committee on Jewish Classics of the Jewish Publication Society. FROM LEFT: (SEATED) *Frederic de Sola Mendes, Mayer Sulzberger, Rev. Dr. Kaufmann Kohler, Cyrus Adler, Rev. Dr. David Philipson, Samuel Schulman;* (STANDING) *Louis Ginzberg, Jacob Z. Lauterbach, Henry Malter, Alexander Marx, Israel Friedlaender, H. G. Enelow.*

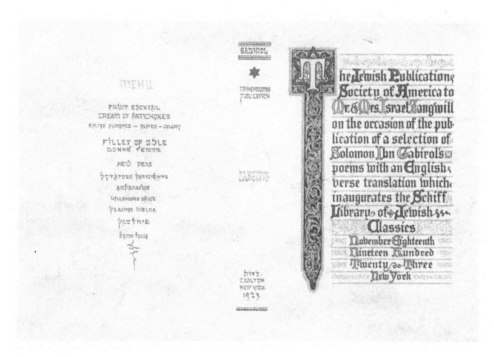

Engraved menu from the banquet honoring Israel Zangwill upon the publication of his Selected Poems of Solomon Ibn Gabirol, *the first volume of the Schiff Library of Jewish Classics (1923)*

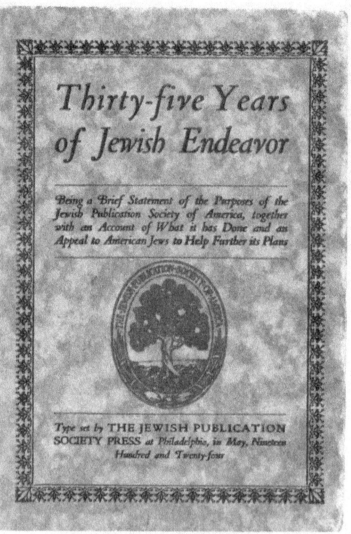

Thirty-fifth anniversary campaign for funds: a collectors' volume containing the title pages of books issued by JPS from 1888 to 1923

△
This
little
volume
of which
250 copies
have been prin-
ted especially for
the friends of the So-
ciety contains the title-
pages of over one hundred
and twenty books issued by
the Society of which over 1,500,000 copies have been
buted The following are the names of the authors of
publications [the names printed in Italics are no l
er among the living, may their memories be a bless
The living, may they be encouraged to produce mo
books to the greater glory of God and our people
I. Abrahams, C. Adler, E. Adler, *L. Adler, G.*
Aguilar, Ahad Ha'am, N. Bentwich, H. Bern-
stein, W. Canfield, I. Cohen, S. W. Cooper,
A. Darmesteter, I. Davidson, Nina Davis,
M. Davitt, L. N. Dembitz, E. Deutsch,
S. M. Dubnow, H. Friedenwald, H.
Frank, U. Frank, L. Ginzberg, M. Gold-
smith, S. Gordon, R. Gottheil, *H. Graetz,*
Julius H. Greenstone, *B. Halper*, E. Harris,
I. Husik, *H. Iliowizi, A. S. Isaacs, J. Jacobs,*
G. Karpeles, K. Kohler, I. Kraft, Jacob Lazarre,
M. Lazarus, E. Levinger, M. Liber, *K. Magnus*
Henry Malter, M. L. Margolis, S. Miller, M. Misc
S. H. Mosenthau, S. Oppenheim, Louis Pendlet
I. L. Peres, David Philipson, P. M. Raskin, M. Ra
Jacob S. Raisin, A. B. Rhine, *Esther J. Ruskay,* Sol
Schechter, L. Schnabel, Harry Schneiderman, N. Sol
Emily Solis-Cohen, *Judah*
Steinberg, Henrietta
Szold, *M. Wolfenstein,*
Yehoash, D. Yellin,
Israel Zangwill
Henry Zirndorf,
and others.

▽▽▽
▽▽
▽

Colophon from the volume above

5

THE BIBLE, THE CLASSICS, AND THE *LEGENDS*

American Jews and the Hebrew Bible

Even before the Jewish Publication Society was founded, American Jews took pride in the special relationship that they as a community maintained with the Hebrew Bible, a relationship that non-Jews both recognized and respected. Although only a small minority of American Jews could actually study the Bible in the original, Americans credited the community as a whole with perpetuating important biblical traditions and preserving God's words in their original language. Two early-nineteenth-century Jews, Jonathan (Jonas) Horwitz and Solomon Jackson, even sought to publish Hebrew texts of the Bible in America. The so-called Dobson Bible (1814), the first independently produced edition of the Hebrew Bible in the United States, was based on the Hebrew text that Horwitz had originally worked on.[1]

Given their special relationship to the Bible, it is not surprising that American Jews were dissatisfied with available Protestant translations of the text. English Bibles distributed by the American Bible Society contained the Hebrew Scriptures and New Testament in one volume, according to the Christian canon and in a thoroughly Christological format. Every page and every chapter bore a brief summary heading, and in many cases these read Christian interpretations directly into the text—for example, "The Prediction of Christ" above Psalm 110, or

"Christ's Birth and Kingdom" above Isaiah 9. The standard King James translation likewise reflected Christian understanding of Scripture, and on the basis of Jewish feeling, law, faith, and tradition, Joseph H. Hertz, Britain's chief rabbi, urged Jews as late as 1920 to avoid using it. "For Jewish purposes," he wrote, "we must have a Jewish translation."[2]

Jews might have created an English Bible of their own simply by deleting the headings, repairing offensive translations, and rearranging the order of the books so as to conform to Jewish tradition. But this did not in fact happen. Instead, Isaac Leeser, the man who had earlier founded the first American Jewish Publication Society, translated the Bible anew. His *The Twenty-Four Books of the Holy Scriptures*, translated with notes and published in 1854, was the first English Bible translation composed by an American Jew.

"Leeser's Bible," as it became known, stands as one of the foremost American Jewish cultural achievements of the pre-Civil War period. It was Jewish both in format and in content since it frequently relied on the commentary of Rashi as well as "the studies of modern German Israelites." Rather than deferring to a translation authorized by, as he later put it, "a deceased king of England, who certainly was no prophet," Leeser affirmed the independent Jewish claim to the Bible based on the original Hebrew.

Although Leeser claimed that his translation was "literal," this claim, like most such, was largely a cover for replacing one mode of interpretation with another. In fact, his translation was to a considerable degree both apologetic and polemical. It defended the Jewish understanding of Scripture and tried to refute Christian interpretations that Jews considered erroneous. Jews who knew no Hebrew could, using Leeser, now study the Bible from an English text written from a Jewish point of view. Christians who knew only their own translations of the Hebrew Bible, could now discover how Jews, who revered the same Bible, understood the text very differently.[3]

Isaac Leeser's translation won wide acceptance, especially after 1856 when it appeared in a revised quarto-size edition. It was also heavily criticized. Rabbi Isidor Kalisch, reviewing the work in the *American Israelite*, called the translation "antiquated" and pointed out numerous errors and linguistic infelicities in just the few chapters that he examined closely.[4] A special committee of the Union of American Hebrew Congregations, meeting in 1873, lamented that Leeser's volume was so expensive, "$3.00 apiece at retail, and even by the dozen at $2.50," far more than the Bible published by the American Bible Society, which as late as the twentieth century cost only twenty cents in its cheapest edition. The committee also criticized Leeser's style as "often too literal" but "sometimes not literal enough."[5]

Yet, for lack of an alternative, the Union decided to subsidize a cheap edition of the Leeser Bible priced at $1.00 a volume. Besides being still too expensive, this was only a temporary solution. The need for a new translation, one that was more up-to-date, more scholarly, and more polished had already become painfully obvious. A new Anglo-Protestant translation of the Bible (commissioned in 1870), being produced by some of the greatest Christian scholars, promised to set a new standard by which all Bible translations would thenceforward be judged. Leeser's translation looked pale by comparison.[6]

Characteristically, Rabbi Isaac Mayer Wise was the first to see the writing on the wall. As early as 1876 he proposed that a new translation be undertaken under the aegis of the Union of American Hebrew Congregations and as a cooperative effort of America's leading Jewish scholars. In 1885, the year that the new Protestant translation (known as the English Revised Version) appeared, the Jewish Literary Union, over which Wise presided, optimistically announced a new Bible translation project; it was endorsed by Kaufmann Kohler at the Reform Rabbinical Conference in Pittsburgh later that same year. The project, however, never got off the ground. Nobody, not even the redoubtable Wise, commanded the resources necessary for such a momentous undertaking.[7]

A Modern Jewish Bible Translation

The founding of the Jewish Publication Society breathed new life into the Bible translation project. At its second biennial convention, in 1892, the call was issued for the Society to furnish "a new and popular English rendition of the book which the Jews have given to the world, the Bible, that shall be the work of American Jewish scholars."[8] Much had changed since 1880, when one member of the Philadelphia Group had wondered aloud why young Jews, unlike their Christian peers, were so indifferent to Bible study, and *Keyam Dishmaya*, the Philadelphia secret society "for God and Judaism," had organized a "Bible class" to "redeem" Jews back "to the ancient faith." Now, in the mid-1890s, Jews had rediscovered the Bible: Both the Jewish Chautauqua Society and the National Council of Jewish Women placed it at the center of their adult education curricula.[9] Small wonder, then, the proposed translation was linked to the "rejuvenescence of Judaism" seemingly "at hand." "The path of duty shines before American Jewry," a JPS circular declared. "The ancient Torah gone forth from the distant East will illumine the West...."[10]

Given this revived Jewish interest in the Bible, as well as an upsurge in Bible study among American Christians, many of whom reportedly requested a translation acceptable to Jewish scholars,"[11] the decision to proceed with an American Jewish Bible translation "at the earliest possible time" was predictable. By 1893, a special subcommittee on Bible translation had set to work. It was chaired by the learned

Rabbi Marcus Jastrow, recently retired from his congregation, with Cyrus Adler serving as secretary.[12]

The first order of business was to devise a series of guiding principles designed to ensure the highest standards. Some of American Jewry's leading luminaries at the time—Cyrus Adler, Marcus Jastrow, Kaufmann Kohler, Max Landsberg, Mayer Sulzberger, and Benjamin Szold—met for two hot summer days in Atlantic City. After reviewing numerous suggestions, including some offered in absentia by committee members Gustav Gottheil, Sabato Morais, and Isaac Mayer Wise, [13] they hammered out a fifteen-point guideline that the publication committee eventually adopted.[14] Five of these provisions proved particularly significant and troublesome.

> (1) That the version be based on the translation commonly known as Leeser's Bible, and that no individual name appear on the title page.

The Society ascribed to the Leeser translation near canonical status. Just as the Protestant Revised Version was based on the King James translation, the Jewish revision would be based on Leeser. Although a great compliment to American Jewry's leading religious figure of the pre-Civil War period, this begged an important question that Rabbi Bernhard Felsenthal of Chicago noticed at once: "Why," he asked, "should the new version be based on Leeser's Bible"—especially when it had become "obsolete and insufficient"? Would it not be better to take the new Revised Version as the basis for the JPS translation?[15] English Jews, who never much respected Leeser's translation,[16] raised the same objections when approached to cooperate with the project. To prefer the translation made by a lone American Jew over that made by scholarly English Gentiles seemed to them—and to some American critics of the Society as well—provincial in the extreme. Jastrow soothingly promised that "making the Leeser Bible the working basis for our enterprise was not intended to fetter the hands of the contributors in any way."[17] Nevertheless, by the time the translation finally appeared it was based upon the scholarly Revised Version, rather than Leeser's.

> (2) That the version be a translation of the Masoretic text.

In retrospect, this guideline seems obvious: Could a Jewish translation be based on anything other than the traditionally accepted text of the Bible? Even the King James and Revised versions rested on the authoritative Hebrew Masoretic text preserved by Jews through the ages. The question that caused disagreement, then, was not whether the Masoretic text should be used, but whether a Jewish translation could *ever* diverge from it, for example, if the text seemed corrupt, or if the Greek translation suggested a superior reading. Protestant translations had permitted occasional exceptions on these grounds, and some Jews, notably Rabbis Bernhard Felsenthal and Emil Hirsch, thought to do likewise.[18] But the Society stood firm in principle: Both the translation it published in 1917 and the one it published in 1962–1985 pledged strict fidelity to the Hebrew text as traditionally accepted.

> (3) That the translation be prepared under the editorial direction of three persons to be known as the Managing Editor, the English text Editor, and the Style Editor.
> (4) That the various books be assigned to different contributors for revision in accordance with a plan to be prescribed.
> (5) That the results of the labors of the contributors be referred to a Revision Committee, to consist of two persons, and the English text Editor.

These three guidelines, quite different from those that governed the Revised Version, which was entirely the work of a committee, created difficulties and dissent from the beginning. Besides being too elaborate and burdensome, they assumed that a sufficient number of competent translators could in fact be found, that the translators would selflessly allow themselves to be revised first by Marcus Jastrow, the English text editor (later renamed editor-in-chief), and then by a style editor, and, finally, that everyone concerned would then wait patiently while still further revisions were made by the two rabbis of the revision committee (later renamed the editorial committee), the traditionalist Frederick de Sola Mendes and the liberal-minded Kaufmann Kohler. Of course, viewed in their most positive light, these complex and cumbersome procedures bespeak the concern to ensure the very highest scholarly and literary standards without offending any of Jewry's major religious wings. But it requires no great shrewdness to see that the plan as a whole was entirely unworkable. It involved too many people, too many levels of responsibility, and too little respect for individual pride of authorship. Equally unrealistic was the Society's estimate that the whole project, including a pressrun of five thousand copies, would cost only $10,000; the final budget was about ten times as high.[19]

Some at the Society sought to make the new translation a joint Anglo-American effort. A proposed list of contributors to what was then still called the "Bible Revision" included the names of eight Englishmen, but nothing ever came of the idea, even after the Society dropped its insistence on using the Leeser Bible as its basis. According to Cyrus Adler, the English Jews concluded that what they had already prepared—the Revised Version with a leaflet of Jewish corrections—"answered the needs of their community."[20]

With the English out of the picture, Marcus Jastrow set about farming books of the Bible out to thirty-two rabbis and scholars, a "who's who" of American Jewish scholarship. Given the prestige of these assignments, those invited quickly accepted them and promised to conclude their work with alacrity. But when reality dawned, the mood of urgency passed. Fully one-third of the proposed contributors never fulfilled their assignments at all. The others moved slowly: Bible translation is a painstaking and tedious art. As drafts did begin to trickle in, problems multiplied. Some contributors needed to be reminded to make their translations "readable and fluent," or to pay "more attention to the 'instructions to translators,'" or to stick to the Masoretic text and not dabble in emendations.

New problems cropped up at every turn. Rabbi Sabato Morais died just as he was finishing his translation of the Book of Jeremiah; fortunately, the work was completed by his learned daughter, Nina Morais Cohen. Rabbi Emil G. Hirsch agreed to translate the formidable book of Isaiah but never sent in a single chapter; all he did was criticize the translation effort in his newspaper. Rabbi Gustav Gottheil sent in his translation of the Book of Ecclesiastes, but he refused to accept any revisions.[21] Through all of this, the Society continued to issue rhapsodic reports of progress, complete with descriptions of editors "busily pursuing the work of revising and editing the books of the Bible as they came to them from the hands of the translators." But it also explained that "the work is necessarily slow, and . . . a considerable time must elapse before the entire Bible can be ready for publication."[22]

The first (and only) book of the Bible to emerge from this morass was Kaufmann Kohler's translation of the Book of Psalms. Its completion capped a long struggle. While the translation was still in progress, Jastrow and Kohler clashed repeatedly: "Dr. Kohler," according to Jastrow, "caring more for the beauty of the phrase, and I for the correct[ness] of rendition, being of the opinion that accuracy is the first requirement of a Bible translation."[23] New difficulties developed once the style editor was brought in. The Society first offered the job to the venerable Charles Eliot Norton, one of America's leading humanists, but he declined. It then turned to George Lyman Kittredge, professor of English at Harvard, who accepted—he needed the money—but demanded a fee of $350 for the Psalms alone. This was a fortune, considering that most of the Bible translation work was still being performed gratis, but the Society was determined to hire a man of stature and accepted the terms. Two months later it wisely decided to remunerate the translators as well. Kittredge, brought in as an "expert," proceeded to effect wholesale changes in the translation—so much so that Jastrow had to insist that he, Kohler, and Mendes, not an outside professor, would retain the final say. Kohler went further, demanding that final decisions should be his alone. The publication committee, cast in the role of peacemaker, awarded Editor-in-Chief Jastrow a vote of confidence, and accepted Kohler's resignation from the Bible editorial committee. Rabbi David Philipson was appointed to replace him.[24]

Only one final decision remained to be made before sending Kohler's *Psalms* off to the printer, and that was a decision on format. Should the Society append an explanatory headnote (or title) above each Psalm as the American Bible Society edition and most other Christian Bibles did, or should the translation be allowed to stand alone, without any explanatory notes whatsoever, as in the Bible itself? Persuasive arguments could be made on both sides. To include headnotes would be to follow in the ways of the Gentiles but would serve as an aid to readers and offset Christological interpretations. Not to include them might disappoint some readers, but it would point up the Jewish commitment to a received text and underscore the critical distinction that Jews traditionally make between text and commentary. The latter view, championed by Cyrus Adler, won out. The proposed headnotes that had already been prepared were printed in a five-page appendix, but for the future the publication committee decided that "no explanatory notes shall appear in connection with the translated text." Instead, it recommended that "the Society shall, as soon as possible, undertake the publication of a brief, popular commentary."[25]

With this decision made, the *Psalms* were at last ready for publication. All that remained was for Marcus Jastrow to complete his final reading of the proofs. Happily, Henrietta Szold was present to record the scene, for it bespeaks both the painstaking scholarship for which Jastrow is so justly remembered, and his high standard of perfection in everything connected with the Bible:

> The Psalms had been put into type. All the editors and sub-editors and style revisers and members of committees had submitted their comments and suggestions. These had been collated, digested and applied. Again and again the Hebrew and the English had been compared with each other, verse by verse, word by word, letter by letter, sign by sign. The final proof lay before the chief editor. A doubt—is this expression correct? Instantly the frail man was up and out of the armchair by the desk and across the the room with a short, energetic step. He lifted the package of papers out of the iron safe, traced the development of the expression from copy to copy of the manuscript, and satisfied himself that he was presenting the views of the translator and his advisers. Back to his desk, only to repeat the process twice and three times on every page, for the sake of a word, for a comma, for the indentation of a line. At last he uttered the "imprimatur."[26]

In 1903, the handsome pocket-sized *Psalms*, modeled on the similar-looking but more cheaply produced pocket Psalter published in 1901 by the American Bible Society, finally appeared. Tragically, Jastrow himself had died just a few months earlier on October 13, 1903. Not a single word of the translation he had spent so long editing found its way into print during his lifetime.

Kohler's *Psalms* received widespread acclaim, and was fairly described by the Society's then president, Edwin Wolf, as "a volume symbolic of the culture of the twentieth century Jew of America, a valuable stone in the monument of learning the Jewish people of the United States are rearing for themselves." Wolf personally kept a copy in his bedside table and read a Psalm from it every night before going to sleep.[27] As for the rest of the books of the Bible, seventeen in various stages of revision lay untouched when Jastrow died, while the rest had not yet even been submitted (see table below).

BIBLE TRANSLATION—STATUS REPORT[28]

Genesis	Max Landsberg	Ready for style editor
Exodus	Lewis N. Dembitz	Being revised by Dr. Mendes
Leviticus	Lewis N. Dembitz	Being revised by Dr. Mendes
Numbers	David Philipson	Being revised by Dr. Mendes
Deuteronomy	F. de Sola Mendes	Being revised by Dr. Mendes
Joshua	Joseph H. Hertz	Awaiting second revision by Jastrow
Judges	Stephen S. Wise	Not yet sent in
I Samuel	Max Heller	Not yet sent in
II Samuel	Max Heller	Undergoing second revision by Jastrow
I & II Kings	Max L. Margolis	[Status not reported]
Isaiah	Emil G. Hirsch	Not yet sent in
Jeremiah	Sabato Morais	Awaiting preparation for style editor
Ezekiel	H. W. Schneeberger	Awaiting revision by assoc. eds.
Hosea	Samuel Sale	Not yet sent in
Joel	Oscar Cohen	Awaiting revision by assoc. eds.
Amos	H. P. Mendes	Awaiting revision by assoc. eds.
Obadiah	J. Voorsanger	Awaiting second revision by Jastrow
Jonah	J. Voorsanger	Awaiting second revision by Jastrow
Micah	Maurice Harris	Ready for style editor
Nahum	Lippman Mayer	Awaiting second revision by Jastrow
Zephaniah	Max Schlesinger	Ready for style editor
Habakkuk	R. Grossman	Awaiting second revision by Jastrow
Haggai	S. Mendelsohn	Awaiting second revision by Jastrow
Zachariah	Joseph Stolz	Not yet sent in
Malachi	D. Davidson	Awaiting revision by assoc. eds.
Psalms	Kaufmann Kohler	In press
Proverbs	Louis Grossman	Not yet sent in
Job	Benjamin Szold (deceased)	No successor appointed
Song of Songs	Morris Jastrow Jr.	Not yet sent in
Ruth	Joseph Krauskopf	Not yet sent in
Lamentations	Samuel Schulman	Not yet sent in
Ecclesiastes	Gustav Gottheil	Refuses to accept Jastrow revisions
Esther	William Rosenau	Awaiting revision by Jastrow
Daniel	Richard Gottheil	Not yet sent in
Ezra	Richard Gottheil	Not yet sent in
Nehemiah	Richard Gottheil	Not yet sent in
I & II Chronicles	M. Mielziner	Awaiting revision by Jastrow

For sixteen months the Bible translation effort lay dormant, paralyzed by the loss of its editor-in-chief. The logical replacement for Jastrow, Solomon Schechter, was too busy. Besides, he expressed doubts as to the whole enterprise:

> I do not think that we have the men combining the thorough acquaintance with the Hebrew tongue with a real knowledge of archaic English indispensable for such a work.... I have never thought that we shall be able to improve upon the Revised Version, at which the flower of the great English Universities, both in their capacity as Semitic scholars and students of English, were active for a large number of years, and backed by all the wealth and the resources of the two great English Universities.[29]

Eventually, though, he gave in ("probably because he was the only one who could carry on [the] work already begun," Henrietta Szold later conjectured), agreeing to oversee the reorganized Bible translation effort that was triumphantly announced in February 1905. A newly constituted board of editors was expanded to include not only the two rabbis, Frederick de Sola Mendes and David Philipson, but also five additional full-time scholars: himself, Israel Friedlaender, Joseph Jacobs, Casper Levias, and Max Margolis. Clearly, Schechter wanted to sway the balance of power on the committee from rabbis to scholars. The scholars were also assigned to the committee's top editorial posts. Precocious young Israel Friedlaender (age twenty-nine), then only in his second year as Sabato Morais Professor of Biblical Literature and Exegesis at the Jewish Theological Seminary, took on the arduous job of secretary to the board of editors, agreeing to "perform the labor of managing editor formerly done by the late Rev. Dr. Marcus Jastrow." Joseph Jacobs consented to be the new style editor. For its part, the Society's board of trustees promised to raise $50,000 to cover the costs of the new effort, including, when funds permitted, "compensation for the members of the Board of Editors."[30]

At first, the new arrangement seemed to work well. By October, Schechter was promising "early publication of the Pentateuch," and "delivery of all manuscripts still outstanding ... within the next six months." But as time went on, promised manuscripts failed to materialize, the drive for new funds fell far short, and discouragement inevitably set in. Friedlaender resigned on March 17, 1907, probably as much on account of his other pressing obligations as from dissatisfaction with the lack of progress. Three months later, Schechter admitted that he too had lost hope: "I am afraid that the whole arrangement, translation by one person, revision by the Editor and by the Secretary, the return of the MS to the author, new revision by the Style Editor, and submission for final decision to the Chairman of the Translation Committee is too complicated to give any prospect of real results within a reasonable period," he complained in a letter to Mayer Sulzberger. And with that he joined Friedlaender in resigning, convinced that there was nothing he could do to rescue the situation.[31] The whole project seemed in danger of collapse.

The Margolis Translation

At the very moment that the Society's efforts appeared to have reached a dead end, a new and more modest plan for an American Jewish Bible translation was being hatched by the Central Conference of American Rabbis. Meeting in Frankfort, Michigan, the nation's Reform rabbis resolved to "enter into negotiations with the publishers of the Revised Version for an issue of the Old Testament exclusively."[32] The CCAR edition, to be published by Oxford Press, was to include all of the books of the Hebrew Bible, in the traditional Masoretic order, and with a sixteen-page appendix, on the Anglo-Jewish model, setting forth "the corrections and emendations of the text necessary from the Jewish standpoint." Significantly, the Reform rabbis refused to permit the proposed Bible translation to carry the CCAR imprint. "At present the revised version is the best translation obtainable," Rabbi Hyman Enelow explained, "and we want to put the Bible into the hands of our children in the best English we can give them. On the other hand, I am opposed to putting even the semblance of the sanction of this Conference on this version, because there are a number of things in it we should like to see improved in the course of time. But we cannot wait for that."[33]

Recognizing that the CCAR project was a pragmatic stop-gap measure, Mayer Sulzberger wrote a personal letter to David Philipson, then president of the CCAR but also a member of the Society's own publication committee, suggesting that it might be well for the JPS to join the CCAR "in its project of disseminating the Revised Version as widely as possible." But after meeting with CCAR representatives in New York, talking with Cyrus Adler and members of the JPS publication committee, and thinking the proposal through thoroughly, Sulzberger changed his mind, convinced that "official recognition" by Jews of the Revised Version would be inappropriate. Instead, he and Adler began formulating privately what the publication committee minutes cryptically call a "definite and practicable plan" for a new try at creating a thoroughly Jewish Bible translation: one that would be completed quickly enough to satisfy CCAR demands.[34] On February 2, 1908, Adler recommended to the JPS board a plan on the following lines:

> That the text of the Revised Version be used as the basis, and that the revision of it by this Society be primarily of such a nature that it will remove all un-Jewish and anti-Jewish phrases, expressions, renderings, and usages . . . that there shall be an Editor whose whole time shall be devoted to the work, and that his departures from the Revised Version shall be submitted to a Board of Editors (number not determined) at stated meetings.

He proposed that Dr. Max L. Margolis be invited to become the editor for a sum of $3,000 annually for two years, plus an additional $1,500 for two years for the travelling expenses and fees of the board of editors, etc.—in all $9,000 payable in the course of two years, "at the end of which time the Bible manuscript may be expected to be ready for the press."[35]

The board of trustees suggested a more modest budget—"a sum not over seven thousand dollars"—and urged that a fifteen-month deadline be adopted. The key question, though, was whether the CCAR could be persuaded to go along with this plan and abandon its arrangement with Oxford Press. Everyone knew that this would be a delicate and difficult task, especially given past history, and it was agreed that there was only one man with the diplomatic experience to be able to pull it off—Cyrus Adler. Sulzberger appointed him as a committee of one to confer with David Philipson and see what he could do.[36]

The climactic meeting took place in Adler's study in Washington on February 13, 1908. The two men, once fellow students at Johns Hopkins, spoke at length and discovered a large area of common ground. By day's end a joint memorandum of understanding had been hammered out. It endorsed cooperation, called for joint representation on the "Board of Revision"—two representatives of the CCAR, two of the publication committee, and a fifth to be mutually agreed upon—and reported the following elliptical exchange regarding Max L. Margolis:

> Doctor Adler asked Doctor Philipson specifically whether Professor Margolis was satisfactory to his body as the person to do the principal work and be chief editor. Doctor Philipson replied that he had the fullest confidence in Professor Margolis's scholarship and ability to do the work.[37]

Max L. Margolis was recognized by this time as one of American Jewry's leading scholars of Bible and Semitics. Born in Russia, he immigrated to America from Berlin in 1889, at the age of twenty-three, and two years later, under Richard Gottheil, received the first Ph.D. in Oriental Studies ever awarded by Columbia University. His subject was "an attempt to improve the damaged text of the Talmud through reference to variant readings in Rashi's Commentary ... demonstrated through the tractate Erubhin." Margolis wrote the thesis in Latin. But the difficulty of obtaining rabbinic sources in the United States, coupled with the fact that his first academic position, at Hebrew Union College, required him to teach biblical studies, soon shifted his focus to Semitics. In 1897, he was appointed assistant professor in Semitics at the University of California at Berkeley. Seven years later, Kaufmann Kohler, then president of Hebrew Union College, persuaded him to return to Cincinnati to serve as professor of biblical exegesis. Kohler thought that he had found in Margolis the kind of scholar he needed to revitalize his college faculty.[38] But it soon became clear that the two men, both of them overpowering personalities, saw eye to eye on very little. After two years of constant squabbling over what courses Margolis could teach, how he should teach them, and whether he was clandestinely seeking to introduce Zionism into his classes on the Prophets, Margolis resigned along with two other pro-Zionist members of the faculty, a move that reverberated throughout the American Jewish community. Looking to escape this academic firestorm, he and his wife of a few months departed for a year in Europe where he hoped to rededicate himself to "study and productive research."[39]

Adler and Sulzberger knew that Margolis was the man they wanted for the Bible editor's position—and Margolis, in a private letter to Solomon Schechter, had even expressed interest in the job. But Adler and Sulzberger also were anxious about whether the Society could afford Margolis, and they wondered whether his appointment "might be construed as a slap in the face by H.U.C. and backers."[40] Since no similarly qualified person was available, and since Margolis was already involved in JPS work—both as part of the 1905 reorganization of the Bible translation and as a contributor to the Bible commentary project that Solomon Schechter was editing (see below)—they took the risk and put forward his name.

Adler succeeded better than anyone could have hoped in convincing Philipson that Margolis, notwithstanding his Zionism, his ugly quarrel with Kohler, and his admitted personality defects, was the best man for the job. In fact, years later Philipson "recalled" (historians call this "deceptive retrospect") that the choice of Margolis had been originally his all along![41] In any event, Philipson undertook to sell the new collaborative scheme to his colleagues at the CCAR. The executive board voted 13–1 in favor of the plan and made only two significant changes: the board of revisers was renamed the board of editors and its number was increased from five to seven (three each from JPS and the CCAR, plus the editor-in-chief.)[42]

The semantic change is especially noteworthy. Although all agreed that the Revised Version was to be the basis of the new translation, a conscious effort was made, especially as time went on, to play down this fact so as to stress the Jewish character of the work. While Margolis would continue to point out that his was only a "revision," the publicity connected with the new translation and the introduction written for it when it was done both emphasized the many elements that made the new translation different and better.[43]

With Margolis's draft complete, only three tasks remained before the Bible translation could finally see the light of day: The board of Bible editors had to approve it, money had to be collected to help defray the cost, and the final text worried that he might have to work on a committee containing his old nemesis, Kaufmann Kohler, Margolis accepted the offer for a fee of $5,000, calculated at the rate of $250 a month for twenty months. As it turned out, the CCAR did nominate Kohler to one of its three committee spots, and Schechter, acceding to Sulzberger's entreaties, agreed that as a matter of "duty" he would serve as well (although one year Friedlaender substituted for him.) To fill the Society's other two spots, Sulzberger appointed Cyrus Adler and Joseph Jacobs, explaining that "the former has the tact, composure, discretion and large view which must be combined in some one person in order to hold the Board together," whereas Jacobs offered "expertise in English style and his phenomenally broad general culture." Perhaps as a counterweight to all of these professional scholars, the CCAR filled its two remaining places with practicing rabbis: David Philipson, rewarded for having negotiated the compromise, and Samuel Schulman, the learned and highly esteemed rabbi of Temple Beth-El in New York.[44]

Although nobody seems to have recognized the fact at the time, the new Bible translation committee reflected the growing Americanization of Jewish scholarship: A majority of the committee's members (Adler, Margolis, Philipson, and Schulman) had received at least an important part of their formal Jewish education in the United States. The committee also reflected the full spectrum of Jewish religious observance, and for much of its existence was perfectly balanced between the three leading American Jewish academic institutions (two members each from the Jewish Theological Seminary, Hebrew Union College, and Dropsie College). On the other hand, aside from Margolis himself, the committee represented much less than the best that Jewish Bible scholarship in America had to offer. Moses Buttenwieser, Jacob Hoschander, Morris Jastrow (Marcus Jastrow's son), Casper Levias, Julian Morgenstern, William Rosenau, and, the most talented of all, Arnold Bogumil Ehrlich, although recognized by their peers as qualified biblical and Semitic scholars, were conspicuously missing. In Ehrlich's case, we know the reason; Sulzberger considered him "cleverer" than Margolis, "but *too* clever. He cannot recognize the common consent of mankind as against a luring guess."[45] In other cases, although evidence is lacking, decisions were probably made on the basis of religious politics, personality, facility in the English language, and, above all, the desire to move ahead quickly without becoming bogged down in scholarly fine points.

Once Margolis and his wife settled down in Philadelphia, work on the translation revision forged ahead with what can only be termed astonishing speed. Genesis, completed on September 4, took all of a week. Working with what he called "zeal and earnestness,"—sixteen hours a day, six days a week—Margolis completed his revision of the entire Pentateuch by November 1. He revised the Book of Judges in five days flat, "allowing one day for the Song of Deborah." Other books could not have taken him much longer, for the first draft of the entire Bible revision was completed on August 1, 1909, just eleven months from the day he started. On September 21, he triumphantly informed Cyrus Adler that he had completed the translation, and that three-quarters of the work was already transcribed and ready for the editors. Since his salary had been calculated on the basis of twenty months, he received the remainder in the form of a bonus: $750 at once, $1,000 more to be paid "as soon as the Manuscript of the Bible Translation, which includes the transcribed copies as well, is duly completed," a job that took Margolis's wife (doubling as his secretary) another six months. By then, Margolis's career had taken another turn: Adler appointed him professor of biblical philology at Dropsie College.[46]

How did Margolis manage to work so quickly? Certainly his brilliant mind and boundless energy tell much of the story. But it is also significant that he took seriously the Society's instructions. Instead of beginning with the Hebrew text, he began with the text of the Revised Version—the large print edition—which his wife pasted up for him page by page into a blank workbook. In the margins, and sometimes in the text itself, he noted suggested improvements to the translation based on the five sources he was instructed by the publication committee to examine: the marginal notes printed in the Revised Version, the changes suggested by the American Committee that cooperated with the Revised Version, the list of Jewish "divergent renderings" prepared for Anglo-Jewish readers of the Revised Version, the translations already made for the Society, and the so-called "standard Commentaries," Jewish and non-Jewish alike. Margolis used his own critical judgment, and often deviated from the Revised Version on scholarly and literary, not just on religious grounds. By his own estimate, he introduced "upward of 40,000 changes" into the text, far more than anyone originally anticipated. Still, much of the work he did was mechanical and tedious, rather than creative. He made rapid progress by burning the midnight oil and adhering strictly to schedule.[47]

The Compromise Translation

With Margolis's draft complete, only three tasks remained before the Bible translation could finally see the light of day: The board of Bible editors had to approve it, money had to be collected to help defray the cost, and the final text had to be prepared for the press. From the vantage point of 1909, the money problem seemed the most intractable. A special committee chaired by Mayer Sulzberger estimated that the Bible work—the translation and a projected commentary—would require a fund of between $75,000 and $100,000 over the next decade, with $10,000 needed at once. But after twelve months the Bible Fund's coffers held a scant $3,000, not even enough to cover ongoing costs. A more narrowly focused effort to collect $50,000 in support of the Bible translation alone proved slightly more successful, especially as the proposed publication date grew near. But more than three-quarters of the goal was still unmet in 1913, when Jacob Schiff electrified the Society's twenty-fifth anniversary celebration with the announcement that he would himself donate the needed $50,000. With characteristic generosity he insisted that some of the money be distributed to the Bible translation's editors who, with the exception of Margolis, had never been compensated for their time.[48]

In fact, the work of the board of editors had taken up far more time than had been expected. The first meeting began on December 28, 1908, following receipt of Margolis's Pentateuch draft, and lasted a full week. According to Adler, the board met "in a rather strained atmosphere." By prior arrangement, Adler sat next to Margolis and Philipson next to Kohler in order to "pour oil on troubled waters." But a few months later Adler was privately describing the meetings as "very successful" precisely because men who disagreed on so much nevertheless found "that they could work together."[49]

As the work dragged on, the pleasure of the meetings ebbed. Where Margolis, working alone, could move quickly, the committee of seven, working together, debated even minor points at endless length. Unfortunately, detailed minutes of the meetings have not been preserved. A published general description, however, gives the flavor of what went on:

> A copy of the manuscript was sent in advance to the members of the Board of Editors in order to give them ample time to consider the merits of every improvement proposed by the Editor-in-Chief and to enable them to make new suggestions not included in the draft. Sixteen meetings, each lasting ten days or more, covering a period of seven years (1908–1915), were held, at which the proposals in this manuscript and many additional suggestions by the members of the Board were considered. Each point was thoroughly discussed, and the view of the majority was incorporated into the manuscript. When the Board was evenly divided, the Chairman cast the dividing vote. From time to time sub-committees were at work upon points left open, and their reports, submitted to the Board, were discussed and voted upon. Before being sent to the printer the manuscript was once more examined in order to harmonize, as far as possible, the various suggestions made in the course of seven years.[50]

The lack of unanimity displayed on so many questions resulted in a strained mood at many of the meetings. Schechter and Kohler could be particularly vituperative. A typewritten note still preserved in the files, probably from some tension-filled day when it was passed around the table, speaks volumes: "Place seven or eight men together," it reads, "and they become so many fools. The reason is that when they do not agree they are keener to argue than to decide." Still, Cyrus Adler's diplomatic skills and social charm usually managed to keep tensions down to at least a manageable level. Once he went so far as to take the scholars to the Ziegfeld follies for a diversion. He laconically reports that "opera glasses were in constant use, and after the show was over, one gentleman astonished us by saying: 'I never knew that so many girls were vaccinated on their legs.' "[51]

Two examples, both from issues left unsettled near the end of the translation process, illustrate the kinds of problems with which the board of editors continually wrestled. The first concerned Isaiah 9:5 (9:6 in Christian texts), a verse interpreted by Christians as a reference to Jesus. The Revised Version, following the King James translation, exudes Christology:

> For unto us a child is born, unto us a son is given; and the government shall be upon his shoulder: and his name shall be called Wonderful, Counsellor, Mighty God, Everlasting Father, Prince of Peace.

Jewish translators of the Bible always insisted that nothing in Isaiah's original refers to the future (Leeser's text, for example, reads "government is placed on his shoulders and his name is called"), but they had trouble with the translation of the Hebrew phrase *sar shalom*. Leeser continued to use "prince of peace" but printed it in the lower case, presumably to avoid misinterpretation. Samuel Schulman urged his colleagues on the translation committee to follow the same practice because "it calls attention to the fact that we wish to avoid any possible Christological interpretation of the phrase." Max Margolis and Cyrus Adler, by contrast, insisted that using the lower case would imply that the "prince of peace" was a human being, "exactly the thing we wished to avoid." Strongly worded letters flew back and forth.[52] The final translation, clearly influenced more by the desire to instruct Christians and defend Jews than by considerations of scholarship, banished "prince of peace" altogether:

> For a child is born unto us,
> A son is given unto us;
> And the government is upon his shoulder;
> And his name is called
> ªPele-joez-el gibbor-
> Abi-ad-sar-shalom;

ªThat is, Wonderful in counsel is God the Mighty, the everlasting Father, the Ruler of peace.*

Note that besides changing the words, the new translation also cast Isaiah's verse into poetry. The Revised Version had taken the lead here, applying the rules of poetry to such obviously poetic passages as the Song of Deborah (Judges 5). It continued, however, to translate the Prophets into prose. The new Jewish translation printed far more sections as poetry—an innovation adopted by subsequent Christian translations of the Bible as well.[53]

A dispute over the famous paean to women in Proverbs 31 suggests a different source of trouble for the translators—the changing nature of the English language. Margolis followed the Revised Version and retained what he called "the stately diction of the Elizabethan period," complete with English forms of spelling. He considered "King James" prose a language "which alone seems to fit the sacred literature," and he carefully reread "Shakespeare, Marlowe, Ben Jonson and every possible Elizabethan author" to make sure that any changes he introduced were in the linguistic spirit of the sixteenth century.[54] But in this case—"A virtuous woman who can find?"—the English neither meant what it did three hundred years before, nor conformed to the original Hebrew. Although the Revised Version

---

*The New 1985 Jewish Publication Society translation reads, "For a child has been born to us,/A son has been given us./And authority has settled on his shoulders./He has been named/"The Mighty God is planning grace;/The Eternal Father, a peaceable ruler."

had retained it, the translation was obviously most inappropriate—"a reproach to the women of Israel or indeed to all women." The problem was how to change it. The word in Hebrew, *chayil*, appears twice in the chapter, once functioning as an adjective (v. 10) and once as an adverb ("Many daughters have done virtuously," v. 29), and consistency was thought to demand that similar forms of the same English word be used in both cases. Margolis, following the American Revised Version, proposed "a woman of worth" and "worthily," but that, as Philipson pointed out, was "colorless." Adler proposed "a brave woman," and "bravely," but that was no better. The final decision—reached, as usual, only after prolonged negotiations—was to go with "valour" and "valiantly," despite fears that "valiant" was "too militant a term."[55]* With this kind of careful, painstaking consideration given to many similarly troublesome phrases, the editing of Margolis's draft took some 160 days of working sessions and seven long years of labor before it was finally complete.[56]

The last meeting of the translation committee took place on November 16, 1915. It was closed "with a prayer of thanks to God that the great task was completed and that the group . . . was still intact." The prayer, however, proved somewhat premature. Further changes in the translation continued to be made throughout the first months of 1916 on the basis of correspondence, and serious disagreements regarding the introduction remained to be reconciled. By the time the volume actually appeared in print in 1917, two members of the committee, Joseph Jacobs and Solomon Schechter, were no longer alive to see it.[57]

What made the introduction so difficult to write was the wide range of its potential readership, and the divergent views among the different translators as to its overall purpose. All agreed that the introduction, like the translation, should seek to encompass a full spectrum of Jews, from Orthodox to Reform. Beyond that, however, some wanted it to be a lengthy piece that would address the interests of both scholarly and lay readers, Jewish as well as Christian, whereas others called the very idea of an "introduction" to the Bible thoroughly absurd. They proposed a brief "preface," like that found in the Revised Version, recounting the history of the translation effort, the methods employed by the translators, and the improvements that resulted.[58] What emerged in the end was a composite five-page document that tried to satisfy everyone, artfully woven together by Cyrus Adler. It recounted the story of the translation but prudently left out technical details and justifications of specific points (including what he privately called "tacit emendations"); these were published elsewhere.[59] What the preface did stress were two themes with which no one disagreed: first, the Jewish legitimacy of the translation; second, the significance of the translation in terms of American Jewish history and culture.

* The 1985 translation reads (v. 10) "What a rare find is a capable wife!/ Her worth is far beyond that of rubies," and (v. 29) "Many women have done well,/But you surpass them all."

The first theme, legitimacy, was aimed at Jews and Christians alike. Presumably in answer to Jews who opposed any Bible translation as assimilationist, the translators justified their enterprise in terms of Jewish tradition. Even as they took note of certain rabbinic "misgivings" about vernacular translations, they still insisted "that the people at large" had awarded translation their wholehearted approval. "The Jew," the preface proclaimed in a much-quoted passage, "cannot afford to have his Bible translation prepared for him by others. He cannot have it as a gift even as he cannot borrow his soul from others."[60]

The translators certainly believed that their translation—based, as they boasted, on Jewish and non-Jewish translations, "all available Jewish commentators" and "all the important non-Jewish commentators"—was more than a match for *any* Christian version, even the most recent ones. Dignity, however, demanded that this triumphalist thrust be sensitively worded, despite what many saw as insulting comments in the prefaces of the Revised Version and the American Standard Version.[61] Still, the polemical intention of the preface showed through clearly. The times had changed and so had the tone of the theological debate with Christianity, but the need to defend Jewish understanding of Scripture in the face of divergent Christian interpretations remained as urgent as ever.

With surprising boldness, the translators proclaimed their second theme: the American Jewish community's coming of age, its emergence as a center of Jewish life and creativity. "The greatest change in the life of Israel during the last two generations," the preface announced, has taken place in the New World:

> We have grown under providence both in numbers and in importance, so that we constitute now the greatest section of Israel living in a single country outside of Russia. We are only following in the footsteps of our greatest predecessors when, with the growth of our numbers, we have applied ourselves to the sacred task of preparing a new translation of the Bible into the English language, which, unless all signs fail, is to become the current speech of the majority of the children of Israel.[62]

Along with the completion of the *Jewish Encyclopedia* in 1906, the founding of the American Jewish Committee the same year, the organization of the American Jewish Joint Distribution Committee in 1914, and other developments in the years immediately before and after World War I, the publication of a new Bible translation reflected American Jewry's changing self-image, its growing cultural independence, its quest for preeminence. The preface made clear that, in part through the Society's efforts, American Jewry had arrived.

Before the text of the preface could at last be sent off to the printer, one final hitch had to be overcome. In what sounds like a caricature of the whole translation process, it literally involved a single item in one footnote. But since this seeming pedantry resulted in reams of correspondence, concerned one of the leading

American Jews of the twentieth century, and has in recent years once again become the subject of speculation, it requires some attention.

The controversy arose over a proposal to list in a footnote those translations of individual books of the Bible commissioned by Marcus Jastrow and actually turned in. Everyone agreed that no matter how bad some of these translations were, this was the proper thing to do. But the question was raised as to whether the name of Rabbi Stephen S. Wise should be included on the list. Wise, who by this time was already a major Zionist leader and founding rabbi of New York's Free Synagogue, had been commissioned to translate the Book of Judges for the Society back in the 1890s. The translation had not yet been delivered by the time Jastrow died, but in 1908, after Margolis was appointed, Wise informed him that it was finished. Instead of following directions, Wise had created a fresh translation of his own, based on a variety of earlier translations and commentaries, and shaped by his own masterful grasp of the English language. But Margolis, working quickly and basing himself on an existing translation, had no use for it and gave it back. It thus had no impact whatsoever—one of the few activities Wise ever engaged in about which that may be said. The question to be decided in 1916 was whether the Society could honestly list the manuscript as one of the translations "presented to this committee."[63]

Margolis, who was Wise's friend and fellow Zionist, insisted that the answer was yes, especially since he admitted in retrospect that nobody else was ever asked to redo his manuscript, and that Wise's was not the only manuscript to arrive late. Kaufmann Kohler, David Philipson, and Samuel Schulman, who thought less of Wise (and opposed him on Zionism), disagreed. "In plain words," Schulman wrote angrily to Adler, "we never used Dr. Wise's manuscript, and we therefore have no right to give him any credit for it in a foot-note, because our Preface should contain only facts and not be disfigured by any misstatement." To his credit, Adler, although no great friend of Stephen Wise, managed to produce yet another Solomonic compromise. Wise handed his Judges manuscript back to the Society, and the preface included his name in a list of those who "prepared" translations for the Society to use.[64]

The whole episode was soon forgotten. But it surfaced anew in 1982, when Wise's biographer (wrongly) concluded, based on interviews he conducted, "that not only did Wise not do the translation of Judges, but none of the other luminaries [mentioned in the Preface's footnote] did their parts either." The documents now available, of course, prove otherwise. What nobody realized, however, is that the actual physical evidence of the translation, the manuscript translation of Judges written out in Wise's own inimitable hand, still exists. It rests unread in the Jewish Publication Society's safe.[65]

Even as the translators were still completing the final details of their work, the arduous task of printing and proofreading the new Bible translation was well underway. A joint committee on Bible printing, including representatives of the trustees, the publication committee, and the translation committee began meeting in December 1913, and after three highly productive sessions managed to decide both on technical points such as layout, thickness, binding, and paper, and on a printer. Several Jewish printers bid for the job, including the Friedenwald family's Lord Baltimore Press, which had worked with the Society on many books, and with which Cyrus Adler, Henrietta Szold, and other Society leaders had family ties. Yet, in the end, it was a non-Jewish press, R. R. Donnelley's Lakeside Press in Chicago, that won the contract. It provided the highest-quality specimens and had a reputation for being "the best printing establishment for thin paper"—which explains why the same company is known for printing telephone books. A contract for 20,000 copies of the Bible (at 57½ cents a copy) was signed on May 25, 1914, and first galleys were prepared shortly thereafter. Given the numerous substantive changes that the translators made in the galleys, a second galley proof was commissioned late in 1915.[66] The money given by Jacob Schiff enabled the Society's president, Simon Miller, to approve an expensive, exacting program designed to ensure letter-perfect accuracy:

> That the Printer be asked to furnish a second galley-proof; that galley-proof II be then collated with galley-proof I; that first page proof be compared with galley II and then by two persons with the Hebrew; that page-proof II be compared with page-proof I and then read by a professional proof-reader; that plate-proof be compared with page-proof II, and then read by a professional proof-reader, then once more compared by two persons with the Hebrew.[67]

Three professional proofreaders worked on the manuscript, every member of the translation committee read the proofs four times, and Henrietta Szold, with her typical compulsiveness, went through the text twelve times. No detail was too small to worry about; every punctuation mark had to be just right, every letter correctly formed. In December, after a full year of work on the text, preparations reached fever pitch. Telephone, telegraph, and special delivery rushed corrections and proofs back and forth from Chicago to Philadelphia with the aim of producing the first copy of the new translation by January 10, 1917, Jacob Schiff's seventieth birthday. The goal, much to Adler's relief, was achieved. Schiff could not have been more delighted.[68]

Twelve days later, on January 22, 1917, a gala kosher dinner, attended by over one hundred dignitaries at New York's Astor Hotel, celebrated the new Bible's formal introduction. Each guest and each member of the translation committee received a specially bound and artistically inscribed copy of the new translation. "Blessed the eye that beheld the vision of the new glory of Israel on our beloved American soil, which witnesses a revival of the study of the Torah, a renaissance of the spirit of Jewish knowledge and wisdom, as in the days of Spain and

Babylon," Kaufmann Kohler gushed, in one of half a dozen speeches delivered during the course of the evening. He and others then used the occasion to drum up support for the Jewish Publication Society's two other great projected undertakings: a full-scale Jewish Bible commentary, begun by Solomon Schechter, and a Jewish classics series, which Schiff, in celebration of the Bible translation, had just endowed.[69]

In his memoirs, Cyrus Adler recounts that during the dinner, Rabbi Charles I. Hoffman of Newark discovered two misplaced lines in the first chapter of the Book of Isaiah. The Bibles distributed to all of the notables read on page 480 (Isaiah 1:19–20), "If ye be willing and obedient,/ Ye shall eat the good of the land;/ But if ye refuse and rebel,/ Ye shall eat the good of the land." Adler, in a panic, had the edition stopped and personally spent "four days from morning to night" carefully "reexamining every page on which there were any corrections" before authorizing the printer to proceed. Nobody could explain how such a gross error escaped so many layers of proofreaders. Later, it was found that a printer's assistant caused the error when he "dropped a page of type and covered up the fact." The error had been caught early enough to correct, and only a very few copies of the original—"wicked"—Bible survive today as collectors items. Unhappily, one of those surviving copies managed to cause renewed mischief. It was later accidentally used as the basis for the Society's large-size 1919 pulpit Bible—a fact only discovered, once again, by Rabbi Charles Hoffman, in 1937.[70]

The Holy Scriptures/According to the Masoretic Text/A New Translation/With the Aid of Previous Versions and with Constant Consultation of Jewish Authorities quickly became the Society's best-selling volume. Nearly 40,000 copies were distributed within a year of publication, about 100,000 by 1925, and thereafter more than 10,000 a year, including some in the large-size pulpit (family) edition issued in 1920. The one-volume Bible commentary, edited by Joseph H. Hertz, used the Society's translation as did the multivolume Soncino Bible commentary, edited by A. Cohen. Most Jewish textbooks, as well as the leading Orthodox, Conservative, and Reform prayerbooks, also turned to the Society's translation when they came to quote Scripture. An abridged edition of the Holy Scriptures "for use in the Jewish school and home," prepared by Emily Solis-Cohen and issued by the JPS in 1931 in conjunction with the Philadelphia Hebrew Sunday School Society, meant that even young schoolchildren became familiar with this text. Increasingly, then, *whenever* Jews quoted the Bible in English they quoted "the JPS." Generations of English-speaking Jews were raised on its English and quoted its renderings as a matter of course.[71]

This is not to say that the Bible translation was without critics. Cyrus Adler himself admitted that "here and there a rendering crept in ... which I thought was unhappy," while Max Margolis, according to Solomon Grayzel, "complained bitterly that suggestions he had made" were "voted down because they did not conform to King James."[72] Some attacked the antiquated language of the translation, others lamented that, following Elizabethan tradition, it employed British rather than American orthography. One person protested that the Bible contained no table of contents (an omission that was later corrected). An Orthodox writer, Judah D. Eisenstein, complained even before the translation was complete that it could not, as claimed, be an authoritative Jewish version because it was not based upon careful study of "the best Jewish commentaries." A more modern Orthodox rabbi, David de Sola Pool, wished that other biblical scholars besides Margolis had been involved in the work so that it might have been less dependent on previous translations. Perhaps most interesting of all was the reaction of Morris Levine, professor of Hebrew literature at the Jewish Theological Seminary. Without questioning the scholarship or the approach of the translators, he worried about the implications of a "Jewish translation" of the Bible: Would American Jews use it as an excuse to stop studying the Hebrew text in the original? Could American Judaism survive if it was based on a watered-down, "translated Judaism," stripped of the original text's power, beauty, and soul? The achievement that so many interpreted as evidence of an American Jewish renaissance was to his mind a "false light," evidence of assimilation, and cause for sorrow and mourning.[73]

But this was an extreme and decidedly minority view. Most readers agreed that the translation filled an urgent need, achieved the major goals it set out for itself, and made available a Bible that benefited English-speaking Jews. Even the English scholar, Israel Abrahams, who had been so critical of Isaac Leeser's Bible and had refused to take part in the Society's translation when it was first proposed, pronounced himself thoroughly pleased with the new effort. In a widely publicized review he wrote "The new edition stands the severest tests. It is scholarly without pedantry, it is original without sensationalism, it is Jewish without bias . . . it should be widely adopted as our standard version."[74]

The Bible Commentary Project

With the successful completion of the Bible translation, plans called for the Society to move directly into the second phase of its Bible work—a projected Bible commentary. "Our translation is finished but we shall once more be at Bereshit, the beginning, in our Bible Commentary," Max Margolis announced at the dinner celebrating the translation. He characterized the new project as "the dying testament of our unforgettable colleague and master, Dr. Schechter."[75]

Schechter had begun agitating for a new Jewish Bible Commentary while he was still in England. In the mid-1890s, when the JPS Bible translation project was first getting underway, he tried to sell the commentary idea to Marcus Jastrow. In a letter to Mayer Sulzberger in 1899 he reiterated the plea for "a good commentary on the Old Testament by Jews and for Jews."[76] In 1905, as a member of the publication committee, he raised the subject anew. On January 7, 1906, he and Samuel Schulman presented a series of recommendations that became the basis for the project:

> 1. The commentary is to represent the results of sound scholarship and to be as little technical as possible. It is to be a popular commentary, and therefore should be written in simple language and in attractive style. Controverted points where discussion is indispensable might be dealt with in an appendix.
> 2. The commentary is to explain the *Masoretic Text*. Where *emendations* are obvious and unavoidable, they are to be referred to in text of commentary, after commentator has given his best interpretation of the Biblical text as traditionally accepted.
> 3. The writer is to use the Jewish Commentators, and give them credit wherever possible. He is to elucidate the Biblical text, by quotations, short and pithy, from Rabbinical sources, thus making the commentary both popular and *Jewish*.
> 4. While in explaining the text of Bible much archaeological and historical information will naturally be given, moral and religious truths are to be emphasized, so that the commentary be not only instructive, but edifying and religiously constructive.
> 5. As an aid to the appreciation of the text, the commentary should contain a table of references to contemporary events, in the history of other nations, arranged chronologically, and, when suitable, a map of the regions referred to.
> 6. The commentary of every book should have an introduction, giving a general view of historic position and contents of the book, and a brief statement of commentator's sources and methods.[77]

The key words, as far as Schechter's conception of the Bible commentary went, were "popular," "sound," and "Jewish." Like the enormously successful Cambridge Bible for Schools and Colleges, a series highly respected on both sides of the Atlantic, the new series would seek to bridge the gap between the scholar and the intelligent lay reader; Schechter disagreed with those who thought that scholarship, in order to be "scientific," had to be abstruse. Just as important but far more difficult, he hoped to blend the fruits of contemporary Christian biblical scholarship—provided it was "sound"—with traditional forms of Jewish biblical exegesis as set forth in rabbinic commentaries. To be sure, Schechter had very little use for "higher" biblical criticism, which he found to be either profoundly anti-Semitic or grossly irrelevant. As he later put it in a proposed set of instructions to contributors:

> In books where the discussion of the results of modern Biblical criticism is unavoidable, such discussion as to problems of the integrity of the book and as to arrangement of parts of it according to such criticism, should be disposed of altogether in the introduction. And such discussion should be as condensed as possible.

Schechter was willing to accommodate the historical and literary insights offered by scholars if they did no violence to the average Jew's "reading and appreciation of the Biblical material as a literary message conveying moral and religious truths."[78] His approach thus promised to solve the Society's longtime problem with biblical materials, for it steered a compromise between the scholarly and religious extremes.

Unfortunately, only one example of the kind of commentary that Schechter had in mind ever appeared. As an experiment, the Society in 1906 commissioned Max Margolis to produce a commentary on the Book of Micah. (This, of course, was while Margolis was still at Hebrew Union College, a year before he became editor-in-chief of the Bible translation. Indeed, it was in part his happy experience with the commentary that played a role in his subsequent editorial appointment.)

He produced what became the Society's model commentary, a Jewish answer to recent Christian commentaries on the book, particularly the Cambridge Bible edition of Micah, edited by Reverend Thomas Kelly Cheyne.[79] In his introduction, Margolis put Micah into historical context, mentioned Jewish and Christian scholarship, and freely discussed such issues as corruption of the biblical text and the relationship of Micah to the Prophet Isaiah. Yet, unlike Cheyne, he insisted on "unity of authorship . . . for the entire book." The six small-print pages he devoted to the approach of biblical criticism were cast wholly within a polemical context to rebut the critics' "preconceived notions," "fatal errors," and "unsubstantiated . . . reasonings." His commentary continued in a like vein: It noticed modern exegetes but referred far more frequently to traditional Jewish commentators and rabbinic literature—again with some effort to defend the Masoretic text against its detractors. His additional notes then explored in detail subjects of special interest, such as the Jewish view of the Messiah and "the Prophetic estimates of the sacrificial cult," both subjects relevant to twentieth-century Jews.

A recently published document discloses that one note in *Micah* entitled "the rich and the poor" had a revealing ulterior aim. It was insisted upon by Solomon Schechter, "who thought it very necessary" in light of allegations in his day linking Jews and Prophetic teachings to Communism with its expropriative attitude toward property. "The sacredness of property is categorically proclaimed in the Decalogue," Margolis insisted, echoing Schechter. "Theft is a crime, whether committed by the poor or by the rich." He admitted at the same time, of course, that "the Law contains a number of provisions having for their purpose the mitigation of the evils arising from an unequal distribution of wealth, as well as exhortations addressed to the conscience of the wealthy."[80]

Following the publication of *Micah*, work on the Bible commentary was temporarily suspended pending completion of the Bible translation upon which the commentary was to be based. Kaufmann Kohler urged that the suspension be made permanent; he doubted that a commentary acceptable to all wings of Jewry could be produced. Schechter, however, continued to press the issue. Israel Friedlaender agreed with him and suggested an improvement that would make the series even more distinctive and Jewish: "Print the Hebrew text side by side with the English translation." But Friedlaender was, as usual, ahead of his time, and Schechter was beginning to lose hope: "I shall probably not be blessed with seeing so blessed a thing accomplished." When he died suddenly and unexpectedly on November 19, 1915, no further volumes of the commentary had appeared, nor would they for twenty-two more years. Although Adler, Margolis, and Samuel Schulman took over the project upon Schechter's death and actually commissioned several volumes, the project was suspended, for financial reasons, in October 1921.[81]

In 1923, the ill-fated commentary project momentarily took on new life when one of the commissioned authors, Hartwig Hirschfeld, a professor both at Jews' College and at University College in London and best known for his work on Judah Halevi's *Kuzari*, submitted a manuscript on Deuteronomy. JPS deemed it both too polemical and too technical to publish and sent it back with a request for changes. When, after many years of unpleasant correspondence, Hirschfeld failed to produce an acceptable revision, it gave the volume over to Joseph Reider, Max Margolis's successor at Dropsie, for recasting. This turned out to be a mistake. Scholars rarely are able to recast one another's books; instead, they end up producing new ones of their own. That, in fact, is what Reider did, and when Hirschfeld's heirs understandably refused to allow their father's name to be attached to it, JPS published it in 1937 under Reider's name alone, supposedly as the second in the long-dormant commentary series. One glance was all that was needed to demonstrate that the similarity was in name only. Reider's book differed in style and conception from Margolis's model and was much further removed from the scholarly mainstream, given its insistence that most of Deuteronomy "originated during the last days of Moses, exactly as stated."[82] Two subsequent volumes, *Numbers* (1939) and *Proverbs* (1950), both prepared by Julius Greenstone based on courses he taught at Gratz College, were even further removed from Margolis's model. Greenstone was a popularizer, not a biblical scholar, and his work was entirely derivative. At one time, H. L. Ginsberg, one of America's leading biblical scholars, expressed interest in undertaking the Society's volume on Genesis, a move that might have enhanced the series' reputation, but he insisted on being "given a free hand to deviate from the plan for the Commentary series," and nothing further was heard.[83] Instead, in 1950, the series was quietly ended, far short of its original aims.

The goal of preparing a commentary that could appeal to scholars and lay members of the community, Reform, Conservative, and Orthodox alike, seemed for many years quite unattainable. The Soncino Press in London, to be sure, did produce a full-scale English Bible commentary (1945–52), this one complete with a Hebrew text, but it was nonscholarly and written from an avowedly Orthodox perspective.[84] The need for a Bible commentary reflecting both the latest in scholarship and a traditional Jewish outlook on Scripture remained unmet. Returning to the challenge, and recognizing the problems that the task would entail, the

Society announced in 1973 that it would make a fresh attempt. The project, under the general editorship of Nahum M. Sarna with Chaim Potok as literary editor, was slated to begin with a five-volume commentary on the Pentateuch now scheduled for publication in 1988–89.

The Schiff Library of Jewish Classics

The Bible Commentary was only one of two long-term projects that the Jewish Publication Society undertook in the wake of the Bible translation. The other, an even more ambitious one, was known as "the Jewish Classics," a series of volumes "reproducing in the original and in the vernacular" the best of post-biblical Jewish literature prior to the modern era. At the 1917 dinner celebrating completion of the Bible translation, this project, by then almost three years in the planning, was officially launched amid a great deal of fanfare. Jacob Schiff, who generously endowed the new series with a $50,000 trust fund, predicted that it would "open up to the Jew his great inheritance, of which unfortunately present Jewry knows so little."[85] The way Cyrus Adler later told the story, the original idea for the Jewish classics series was conceived in Jacob Schiff's own head:

> His brother-in-law, James Loeb, had in 1910 undertaken the great work of publishing in the original texts and English translations all of the Greek and Roman classics. One day a few of the new volumes of the Loeb Classical Library were lying upon a table in the drawing room at the Schiff home, and a number of persons present were examining them with admiration. Mrs. Schiff, turning to her husband, said: "Why couldn't you do for the Jewish classics what Jimmie is doing for the Greek and Roman?" The remark at the moment elicited no response, but soon afterward he took up this new project, with his customary ardor. At a dinner, given on February 10, 1914, to celebrate the completion of the manuscript of the Bible translation, he expressed his desire to add a second considerable fund to the Publication Society's resources, for the purpose of issuing the Jewish classics, and made a formal offer to the president of the Society, on May 4, 1914.[86]

The reality, in this case, is vastly more complicated. The phrase "Jewish classics" ("classic" defined as "a piece of writing that admits of a commentary") appears in the minutes of the publication committee as early as 1909, when it was suggested as a title for a proposed monthly forum of enduring essays dealing with noteworthy themes of Jewish interest.[87] Nothing came of this, but two years later Isidor Singer, the eccentric promoter who originated the enterprise that produced the *Jewish Encyclopedia*, issued a slick brochure trumpeting a new project, this one to produce a handsome set of the "Hebrew Classics, in 25 volumes, royal octavo," edited by the old JPS nemesis, Emil G. Hirsch. An impressive international advisory board (which by no accident excluded the Philadelphia and New York leaders of the Jewish Publication Society), as well as endorsements from a long list of rabbis, Semitic philologists, Christian theologians, and European Jewish scholars stamped the new undertaking with the seal of legitimacy and gave it an aura of definitiveness.[88]

Cyrus Adler was livid. With uncharacteristic rudeness, he had his clerk write to Singer that "under no circumstances" would he "become associated in any way" with the new enterprise, and behind the scenes he did his best to undermine it. Nor was this merely spite: Adler, after all, had been called in to rescue the *Jewish Encyclopedia* when its publication seemed in doubt, and he knew that Singer had a long history of dreaming up fantastic schemes (including one for an international Jewish loan of $500 million dollars to finance Jewish migration) that he never saw through to fruition. Singer's wild personal letters composed in a frenzied mixture of English and French (sprinkled with German, Hebrew, and Yiddish) bespoke a man possessed—one who could dream large inspiring dreams but who lacked the patience, drive, administrative ability, and scholarly convictions necessary to sustain them when faced with cold realities. His heart may have been in the right place— like Theodor Herzl, he had seen anti-Semitism close up in Vienna and Paris and was obsessed with the need to combat it—but his mercurial personality and rash promises were forever getting him into trouble.[89] Emil G. Hirsch, no less a gadfly, seems to have been able to work with Singer: each played to the other's vanity.[90] But Adler, burned by his past experiences with the man, considered him a menace. Knowing that Singer's project would in the long run need the kind of funds that only Jacob Schiff could provide (as he ultimately had done for the *Jewish Encyclopedia*), Adler privately reported to Solomon Schechter that he "told Mr. Schiff in the strongest terms possible that Singer was a promoter and that reputable scholars would not work with him." The Society, meanwhile, set up its own "Subcommittee on a Hebrew Classics Series," which, though nobody ever admitted it, was clearly designed to foil Singer. Foil him it did, for in the end it was the Society that came away with Jacob Schiff's $50,000 bounty, while Singer was left empty-handed and forgotten.[91]

With Schiff's endowment in hand, planning for the Hebrew classics series entered a new phase. At Schiff's insistence, a new committee was set up consisting of Mayer Sulzberger, still chairman of the JPS publication committee, three Reform rabbis (Hyman Enelow, David Philipson, and Samuel Schulman), three representatives of the Conservative wing in Judaism (Professors Israel Friedlaender and Alexander Marx of the Jewish Theological Seminary, and Rabbi Frederick de Sola Mendes), and all three presidents of America's Jewish colleges (Cyrus Adler, Kaufmann Kohler, and Solomon Schechter). Three additional members were added later (Louis Ginzberg, Henry Malter, and Jacob Z. Lauterbach), one from each of the same three Jewish colleges. At first glance the committee looked perfectly balanced, much like the Bible translation committee had been. Closer examination reveals, however, that Cyrus Adler and Solomon Schechter consciously shaped the committee so that it would be weighted toward the "conservative element," which they thought should "predominate." Rabbi Emil G. Hirsch, who had been involved with Singer's project, and whose appointment Kohler (his brother-in-law) repeatedly urged, was pointedly excluded.[92]

The new committee's first task was to define the scope of the "Hebrew classics." Everyone realized that $50,000 would scarcely suffice to publish all of the masterworks produced by post-Biblical Jews. Not even the Loeb series' endowment would have been sufficient for that, and the endowment Schiff provided was only about one-tenth its size. So the committee voted to create a series of twenty-five volumes, the same number that Singer had projected to publish. A "conservative estimate" suggested that Schiff's money would stretch at least that far.[93]

Preliminary correspondence among the committee members found wide agreement that the term "Hebrew classics" should be defined broadly, "to refer not to language but to mind." Since nobody wanted to exclude works written in Aramaic or Arabic, and in order to prevent misunderstanding, the series was renamed the "Jewish Classics." In 1920, when Jacob Schiff died, the board voted to name it in his memory the "Schiff Library of Jewish Classics."[94]

The far more difficult question was the basis for selections. Kohler urged that "the Benthamian principle: 'the greatest good to the greatest number'... be followed," with an eye toward acquainting general readers with various works representing "different epochs and departments of Jewish literature," meaning that the series should include "modern classics" as well. Sulzberger, who viewed the series as a whole in much more scholarly terms than Kohler did, sought to exclude anything written after 1650 ("This marks the definite separation of Spinoza from the Synagogue. With him begins the *modern unrest*, which I would totally exclude."[95]). It was, however, Schechter who in a remarkable and previously undiscovered private letter to Adler best enunciated what others too must have seen as the *central* problem, illustrating both the ambivalence of modern Jews toward their heritage and the tension between scholarship and apologetics that characterizes so much of Jewish studies in his day:

> The great question which occupies my mind and which I should like to have properly discussed with you is the following: Such an undertaking as is planned by Mr. Schiff, should, above all, result in raising the respect of Jew and Gentile for Jewish literature and the thoughts treasured up therein. It should, in brief have, besides all other results, also that of contributing to *kiddush hashem* and to the glory of Israel. Now, this literature occupied my mind all my life almost and I had my hand at translations for more than a quarter of a century, and I am convinced that there are very few books that will bring about the desired results. They may have even the very opposite results. All that we can do is to give selections, but to translate whole books would be inadvisable. Neither their style nor their contents recommend themselves to the mind of the modern man. They are always in need of an apology or explanation.... You will find that even in Germany, with all its multitude of students and able contributors, Jews never

encouraged wholesale translations of Hebrew books. As a rule, such translations did more mischief than good.[96]

In a subsequent letter, Schechter brought the point home with astonishing frankness: "The more I think about the matter the more I am convinced that it will require a good deal of discretion and good taste to make a proper selection. Somehow, the works of St. Augustine (as his 'Confessions' or his 'City of God') can be read by the modern man with more pleasure than our edifying literature."[97]

Thanks, as usual, to Cyrus Adler, a compromise plan was ultimately hammered out. The classics committee reported to the JPS trustees in January 1915 that the series would cover "the entire range of Jewish literature . . . up to some [indefinite] point in modern times," but promised that the subjects included would be "sufficiently remote to be removed from present day controversies." All classes of post-biblical Jewish literature would be represented, but "a much larger share" would be given to "works of general literary interest such as Poetry, Ethics, etc." Although most of the volumes suggested were to be translated in their entirety, a few, such as the volumes dealing with Mishnah and Talmud, would include only selections.

A list of forty-four potential contributors, three-quarters of them Americans and Canadians, and more than 50 percent of them full-time scholars, was appended to the report: evidence that the task was feasible and could largely be accomplished by talents close at hand. Over the next few months this list was pruned down, new names were added, and the masterplan for the projected twenty-five volumes was set. On November 9, 1915, Schechter, as chairman of the classics committee, sent out letters of invitation to those selected to be contributors, optimistically requesting that they submit their completed manuscripts "within twelve months or earlier." In all likelihood, he never saw their responses, for ten days later he was dead.[98]

Cyrus Adler succeeded Schechter as classics committee chairman (also as president of the Jewish Theological Seminary), and in most cases easily negotiated final contracts. Some of those invited, like Emil G. Hirsch and David Neumark, said no, rejecting committee oversight of their work, and in Hirsch's case because of personal pique.[99] Still, contributors had, for better or for worse been found for most of the volumes by 1917, and the plan was ready to be made public. What makes it interesting, especially in terms of the development of Jewish studies as a discipline, is the list of series selections (and omissions!), the overall classification scheme employed—thirteen categories in all—and the relative importance attached to different subjects:[100]

APOCRYPHA—two half volumes.
Sɪʀᴀᴄʜ with Hebrew text and translation.
Fourth book of Ezʀᴀ.

First and Second MACCABEES.
Letter of ARISTEAS—without text and with short notes.
Editor and Translator: Prof. Max L. Margolis, Dropsie College.

MISHNAH—two volumes.
Mo'ED.
NEZIKIN.
Editor and Translator: Prof. Louis Ginzberg, Jewish Theological Seminary.

TALMUD—one volume.
TA'ANIT—Babylonian Talmud.
BIKKURIM—Palestinian Talmud.
Editor and Translator: Prof. Henry Malter, Dropsie College.

ETHICS—three volumes.
HOBOT HA-LEBABOT.
WILLS.
Editor and Translator: Dr. Israel Abrahams, Cambridge University, England.
a. ABOT DE-RABBI NATHAN.
  Editor and Translator: Rabbi Louis M. Epstein, Toledo, Ohio.
b. IGGERT MUSAR OF AL-'AMMI.
  Editor and Translator: Rabbi Israel Bettan, Wheeling, W. Va.
c. DEREK EREZ RABBA AND ZUTA.
  Editor and Translator: Rabbi Jacob Minkin, Hamilton, Ohio.
d. MESILLAT YESHARIM.
  Editor and Translator: Dr. M. M. Kaplan, Jewish Theological Seminary.
  a, b, c, d, all in one volume.

MYSTICISM—one volume.
ROKEAH—first chapter.
TOMER DEBORAH, by Moses b. Jacob Cordovero.
SHA'ARE KEDUSHAH.
MAAMAR HA-GEULLAH of Moses Haim Luzzatto.
Editor and Translator: Rabbi Samuel Cohon, Chicago, Ill.
MASEKET AZILUT.
PERUSH ESER SEFIROT.
KETER SHEM TOB.
Editor and Translator: Dr. Meyer Waxman, Albany, N.Y.

MIDRASH—two volumes.
MEKILTAH.
Editor and Translator: Dr. J. Z. Lauterbach, Hebrew Union College.
PESIKTA RABBATI.
Editor and Translator: Dr. B. Halper, Dropsie College.

CODES—one volume.
First two books of Maimonides' YAD.
Editor and Translator: Dr. M. Hyamson Jewish Theological Seminary.

PHILOSOPHY—four volumes.
IKKARIM (two volumes).
OR ADONAI.
Editor and Translator: Dr. Harry Wolfson, Harvard University.
EMUNOT WE-DE'OT.
Editor and Translator: Dr. Henry Malter, Dropsie College.

HISTORY—three volumes.
1. HISTORICAL TEXTS.
   Editor and Translator: Dr. Alexander Marx, Jewish Theological Seminary.
2. EPISTLES.
3. SHEBET YEHUDAH.
   Editor and Translator: Dr. A. A. Neuman, Dropsie College.

POETRY—five volumes.
1. GABIROL.
   Editor: Dr. Israel Davidson. Jewish Theological Seminary. Translator: Mr. Israel Zangwill, England.
   KALIR.
   Editor and Translator: Dr. Israel Davidson, Jewish Theological Seminary.
   JUDAH HA-LEVI.
   Translator: Mrs. Nina Salaman, England.
   MAHBEROT 'IMMANUEL.

HOMILETICS—one volume.

RESPONSA—one volume.
Editor and Translator: Dr. Gotthard Deutsch, Hebrew Union College.

FABLES AND FOLK LORE—one volume.
MAASE BUCH.
Translator: Dr. Moses Gaster, England.

To be sure, some obvious classics, like Maimonides's *Guide of the Perplexed* and Judah ha-Levi's *Kuzari*, were omitted from the list because English translations already existed; the committee preferred to issue works "not accessible in the English language or in any other modern language." Philo and Josephus were likewise omitted as they were to be included in the Loeb Classical Library.[101] Still, the absence from the classics of any Hasidic literature, and of such indisputable masterworks as the mystical *Zohar* and the legalistic *Shulchan Aruch* (the basic code of Jewish law), and at the same time the disproportionate weight given to poetry, philosophy, and ethics indicates that scholarly criteria were far from the only considerations involved. As Solomon Schechter realized in his note to Adler, and as Isidor Singer had understood from the start, the series actually concealed a far larger agenda—one with implications of far-reaching importance to all modern Jews, and to American Jews in particular.

In order to understand the Society's larger aims in undertaking the classics series, it is necessary first to consider the series that the Society took as its model: the Loeb Classical Library. James Loeb founded the series in 1910. He stipulated that it would make available in pocket-sized form, with an introduction, a carefully edited and annotated text, and a facing English translation, the great works of Greek and Latin authors that together (some 360 volumes) constitute what is generally considered to be the classical heritage of Western civilization. Loeb was a Jew, as was the man who gave him the idea, the French Jewish scholar Salomon Reinach, yet their project, delimited as it was, accepted a standard Western Christian view of what defines "the classics." Two Jews, Philo and Josephus, gained admission into the accepted canon; the rest of post-biblical Jewish literature—in Hebrew, Aramaic, and Arabic—was left out.

For Jews this all-too-familiar scenario posed a serious problem, for it effectively excluded them from "Western civilization," and contributed to the ugly stereotype that they had contributed little to its furtherance. In response, seeking both to battle anti-Semitism and to promote Jewish self-pride, Jews began to stress what they called "the Jewish contribution to civilization." In 1919, the Jewish Publication Society itself published an apologetic little book by that title, written by Joseph Jacobs. Later, and on a more serious level, some of the greatest twentieth-century Jewish scholars, including Harry Wolfson and Saul Lieberman, worked in a different way to break down the formidable barriers between "classical" and "Jewish," documenting mutual influences between the two realms. The Schiff Classics as a whole, and many of the specific volumes selected for inclusion, must be seen as part of this same overall effort. It sought to publicize the fact that Jews *had* classics of their own; that they *had* contributed literature of undoubted value to Western civilization, and that there *was* a demonstrable corpus of Jewish post-biblical literature that Christian scholars simply ignored. Jewish classics that did not serve this purpose, or that if translated literally might actually have cast Judaism in an unfavorable light, were excluded from the series.[102]

Those involved in the classics project defended it in more than just apologetic terms; they also insisted that Jews needed to be better informed about their post-biblical heritage. The late-nineteenth-century revival of American Judaism, and most JPS publications, had focused on history and Scripture to the exclusion of post-biblical texts; the Society had offered its readers no primary documents, certainly none in translation. In 1915, the publication committee commissioned a two-volume anthology (one of original texts, one of translations) entitled *Post-Biblical Literature*, edited by Benzion Halper, a brilliant young Semitist at Dropsie, to serve as a textbook in this area. But this was seen only as a first step in helping Jews recover some eighteen hundred years of their cultural heritage.[103]

The classics series was designed to go much further. As Mayer Sulzberger reported, the goal was both to introduce "the Hebrew Classics into the world of general literature and scholarship" and to serve as "an example and incentive to renewed activity in this field by Jews." When the first volume of the series appeared in 1923, the Society reiterated the same two themes in more delicate language that could apply equally to Jews and Christians. It hoped that its series would "awaken the interest and command the support of those who feel the obligation to see to it that the Jewish Classics which, with few exceptions have been unknown to English readers, shall come into their own, and take their rightful place among the classic literatures of all peoples."[104]

On another level, the classics series was an attack on the cultural hegemony of German Jewry in the realm of Jewish scholarship. The awakening of Jewish life in America in the late-nineteenth century, and the work of the Society in particular, already had resulted in the publication of a growing number of serious Jewish books in English, works that even German Jews had to notice. Perhaps the most visible symbol of such efforts was the monumental twelve-volume *Jewish Encyclopedia*, completed in 1906 and published by Funk & Wagnalls. Relying heavily on scholars living in America and England, it showed beyond any shadow of a doubt that the English-speaking world was emerging as the center of both Jewish life and Jewish scholarship. Now, publication of the classics promised to confirm these claims. JPS president Simon Miller boasted in 1916 that "most of the authors are Americans, many having received their Jewish education in this country." Actually, almost half of the volumes finally published were edited by English Jews, but it scarcely mattered. The German language requirement for critical works of Jewish scholarship had been effectively broken.[105]

The Jewish Publication Society undertook the classics project with the clear understanding that it was to be a scholarly endeavor in the most exacting sense of the word. As in the Loeb classics, scholars would first be expected to produce a critical text based on a painstaking study of available manuscripts, employing in the process all of the usual scholarly apparatus. Translation into English was the secondary task and, for some of the contributors, far less important. This scholarly emphasis marked a startling departure from what had previously been seen as the Society's primary mission. In 1892 the Society explicitly *excluded* "works of a distinctively scientific character" from its publishing ambit, and when it published Graetz's history it unashamedly left the "cumbersome" scholarly notes out. "The Jewish Publication Society," Cyrus Adler once explained, "is dependent on popular subscriptions and is bound to publish popular works." Not even the Bible was printed with an accompanying Hebrew text.[106] Yet when it came to the classics, all of these precedents were set aside and the establishment of the correct text became the "first principle." JPS was committed not only to "making accessible to English readers some of the treasures of Jewish literature," but also to "adding to Jewish scholarship by presenting carefully edited texts" that it hoped would eventually become standard.[107]

All of this posed a difficult practical problem: There was no press in America with the capability of producing Hebrew books of such high scholarly quality. Cyrus Adler had long worried about this situation, noting that America's few existing Hebrew print shops were both too limited and too expensive to serve scholarly needs. As a result "much time and effort was wasted in sending such work to Europe." When World War I led to the destruction of several great Hebrew presses in Europe—and cut America off from quality Hebrew printing altogether—sending copy abroad simply became too risky. Unless a way was found to print the classics in America, the whole series stood in danger of being postponed.

Adler, long the proponent of American Jewish cultural independence, used the situation to agitate for the Society to acquire its own high-quality Hebrew press. The board of trustees was willing, and when Jacob Schiff and Louis Marshall saw how urgent the need was they offered to underwrite most of the costs. They clearly realized, as Adler had, that if America was to be a center of Jewish life, it would have to be a center of Jewish printing as well.[108]

Characteristically, before plunging ahead Adler made a complete study of new printing technologies, aided by the printers Maurice and Julius Weyl. They determined that a press consisting of a pair of monotype machines with Duplex keyboards was best suited to the Society's need for a mixture of English and Hebrew in all sorts of type faces. Joseph P. Abrahams, secretary of the Jewish Theological Seminary (over which Adler now presided), designed a new Hebrew type in the "American tradition" for the Society, based on a modified version of the Hebrew typeface used in the seventeenth century by Manasseh Ben Israel. Although the press was manufactured in Europe, Adler was determined that it have a distinctly American identity.[109]

In 1921, after wartime and other delays, the new Hebrew press was inaugurated. Moses Alperovich, who had formerly worked for the now destroyed Romm Press in Vilna, was appointed to manage the new operation, embodying precisely that cultural transfer from Europe to America that the press and the classics series as a whole represented. A perennial pattern in Jewish history was being reenacted: From the ruins of the Jewish cultural centers of Europe, the new Jewish center in America was arising.[110]

The first volume of the new Schiff Library of Jewish Classics was not published until 1923, and thereafter the series proceeded slowly. Difficulties in obtaining manuscripts, delays caused by the war and the new printing press, miscalculations regarding the length of different classics ("We figured . . . that the Mekilta would form one volume; it actually was published in three"), and individual personal problems were all to blame. Further delays resulted when two authors, Israel Abrahams and Henry Malter, died while their books were still in galley proof. More often, however, manuscripts were held up by the committee, which pertinaciously insisted that authors meet exacting standards of excellence. "Every book that was handed in was read and studied very carefully by at least two members of the Committee," Alexander Marx later recalled. "At the meetings of the Classics Committee very elaborate reports with all the details were given, and occasionally long discussions took place, not on general principles . . . but on the question of how to interpret a particular passage, whether the author's conception was right or whether we should correct it."[111]

Gotthard Deutsch, who submitted a somewhat idiosyncratic volume on responsa, died before his volume could be revised, and it never appeared. Moses Hyamson, frustrated by the committee's heavy-handedness, published his translations from Maimonides elsewhere. Moses Gaster carried on a long and bitter correspondence with the classics committee regarding his translation of the seventeenth-century *Maase Buch*, submitted in 1920 (among other things, the committee demanded a better introduction and the "toning down or deleting [of] such sections as may be regarded as indelicate[112]), with the result that he waited for fourteen years before it was published. Mordecai Kaplan waited two years longer than that: His edition of Moses Hayyim Luzzatto's *Mesillat Yesharim*, another volume that became mired in controversy, was not published until 1936.[113]

Without question, the volumes that emerged from these prolonged delays and endless revisions were better than would otherwise have been the case; after all, they had been subject to criticism in advance by some of America's leading Jewish scholars. But the price was high. Delays sapped the morale of authors, raised costs significantly (especially when changes were demanded in the proofs), damaged the reputation of the Society, and even led to charges of censorship. Cyrus Adler, disappointed at the slow pace, admitted that he found his committee "a little difficult to deal with," and tried hard to convince members to allow authors somewhat more autonomy. But the tension between what authors demanded as their "rights" and what the classics committee insisted upon as its standards was not easily resolved; each volume involved its own set of delicate and complex negotiations.[114]

In the end, however, it was not the classics committee that doomed the series but the Society's treasury. Schiff's endowment, large as it had seemed back in 1914, was (in part due to inflation) completely depleted by the time Mordecai Kaplan's volume was published. Since no additional funds were forthcoming, the series was concluded without fanfare. The project ended up as nine miscellaneous titles (published in 17 volumes) in six subject areas: Poetry (*Selected Religious Poems of Solomon Ibn Gabirol, Selected Poems of Jehudah Halevi, Selected Poems of Moses Ibn Ezra*); Ethics (*Hebrew Ethical Wills, Mesillat Yesharim*); Talmud (*The Treatise Ta'anit*), Midrash (*Mekilta de-Rabbi Ishmael*); Philosophy (*Sefer ha-'Ikkarim*); and Folklore (*Ma'aseh Book*). The remaining sixteen volumes were quietly forgotten.[115]

By all accounts (and by Cyrus Adler's own admission), the Schiff Classics was a less successful series than the Loeb, not only in terms of impact and comprehensiveness, but also as a commercial venture. Readers complained that many of the Society's classics were too scholarly and pedantic. They might have preferred what Cyrus Adler had suggested years before: a separately published "popular" edition of the classics in English alone.[116] But if the Schiff Classics as a series was a disappointment, each of the titles individually was a triumph: at once a noteworthy scholarly achievement, a masterpiece of Jewish bookmaking, and a highly readable translation, particularly so in the volumes of poetry. Many titles in the series are still considered definitive, and six remained in print more than half a century later, testimony to their enduring quality. Moreover, the Schiff Classics influenced subsequent American Jewish scholarship and publishing. It set a high standard of excellence that others sought to emulate and left an agenda of unfinished work that others moved in to complete.[117] It encouraged dual-language publications, which later became standard throughout the Jewish publishing world. Perhaps the greatest compliment paid to the classics series is the fact that the Society itself moved to reactivate it in honor of its seventy-fifth anniversary in 1963. This proudly proclaimed "revival of the Jewish Classics series" eventually took the form of an occasional series of books entitled "Judaica: Texts and Translations." It carried on the same high level of scholarly and literary excellence as the classics, and is responsible for some of the most significant volumes issued by the Society in its recent history.[118]

The Legends, *Louis Ginzberg, and Henrietta Szold*

The classics series was the first great project undertaken by the Society without benefit of Henrietta Szold's editorial expertise. She was still serving as secretary of the publication committee when the series took shape, and she undoubtedly made her usual behind-the-scenes contributions to it in the form of demure suggestions. But on December 1, 1915, just two weeks after Solomon Schechter's sudden death, she announced her resignation, effective as soon as a suitable replacement could be found. She was fifty-five at the time and had served in her position for more than twenty-two years. Now, she explained in a letter to the Society's president, her mother lay gravely ill, and her financial security had been assured thanks to an annuity arranged for her by Judge Julian W. Mack, so that she might be free "for Jewish communal duty of various kinds." It was, she felt, the right moment for her to move on.[119]

The reasons Henrietta Szold gave for making "so revolutionary a change"[120] in her life were honest enough. But there was also a deeper reason behind her move, one that had been gossiped about for years, strained her ties with the Society, and was without question the turning point in her life. It concerned one of the foremost American Jewish scholars of the twentieth century, a direct descendant of the great Gaon of Vilna, and a man who would publish nine luminous volumes with the Society, some of which she herself translated. His name was Louis Ginzberg.

Born in Kovno, Lithuania, and educated at the greatest Lithuanian yeshivot and the most prestigious German universities of his day, Ginzberg immigrated to America in 1899, at the age of twenty-five, to accept an appointment to Hebrew Union College. By the time he arrived in New York his appointment had been withdrawn, allegedly because it had become known that he espoused biblical criticism. When a job at the *Jewish Encyclopedia* also came to an abrupt end (only temporarily, as it turned out), there seemed no choice for him but to return to Germany. Fortunately, Mayer Sulzberger, unwilling to see any Jewish scholar of ability leave the country, convinced him to stay. He offered him $1,000 to write a volume of three hundred pages on the "Jewish Legend Relating to Biblical Matters." Ginzberg accepted, and the agreement ultimately proved beneficial to both parties: The money tided Ginzberg over until he had more secure employment as professor of Talmud at the Jewish Theological Seminary, and the proposed book yielded one of the most important studies that the Society ever issued, Ginzberg's seven-volume *Legends of the Jews*.[121]

Sulzberger's interest in a book on Jewish legends relating to the Bible probably had to do with the interest in folk legends displayed by so many Americans of his day, an interest explained by historian Jackson Lears as being in part "an effort to recover a larger mental inheritance" lost in the drive for modernity. Ginzberg's interest was surely also somewhat different: He had written his doctoral dissertation on biblical legends preserved in the Church Fathers and was eager to expand his scholarly researches in new directions.[122] In any case, Ginzberg set to work, and periodically reported back to the committee that his manuscript was growing, first to two volumes, then three, then five, and finally seven. His conception of the work in progress had grown too. He was now attempting for the first time in any language "to gather from the original sources *all* Jewish legends, insofar as they refer to Biblical personages and events, and reproduce them"—in English—"with the greatest attainable completeness and accuracy." He tracked down Jewish legends with the same assiduousness the Brothers Grimm had employed in their search for German fairytales, and he found them in the most obscure places—nestled in ancient and medieval Jewish legal texts, hidden in rare manuscripts, cloaked "in Christian garb" in the writings of churchmen. He then organized all of this literature and cast it in the popular style that the JPS liked; he promised "a readable story" and "an interesting tale." Of course, he wrote in German and was not always equal to the literary challenge that he had taken upon himself. But it hardly mattered, for Henrietta Szold, who had not then met Ginzberg, promised to translate his work into English, and *her* style could be depended upon. The publication committee, over Cyrus Adler's objections, decided that Ginzberg's extensive notes, filled with learned citations and brilliant scholarly insights, should be published later, in separate volumes geared for students.[123]

Henrietta Szold encountered Louis Ginzberg for the first time in 1903, soon after her father died, when she and her mother moved to New York so that she might, in addition to her work for the Society, take courses at the Jewish Theological Seminary. "I met him February 11–12, 1903, at the Clara de Hirsch home," she remembered years later. "Dr. Jastrow had prepared me for the scholar, Adele [her younger sister] for a conceited coxcomb, and I at once saw only the man, the idealist, the single-minded searcher for truth, the free-thinker so radical that he was conservative." Ginzberg was also handsome, brilliant, charming—and lonely. Henrietta Szold saw in him the reincarnation of her own father, and for the first time in her life, at age forty-three, she fell in love. "My whole happiness lies with you," she confessed to him in a letter composed but never sent, "you are the first to give my soul its woman's heritage, a soul that up to the time it was awakened by you—Oh! so many happy months ago—had known only filial passion." The long hours spent translating the *Legends* became now less a duty than a labor of love. And there were many more such labors, for she jumped at the chance to do even the most trivial favors for her beloved, and while he at first only acknowledged them with reluctance, he later turned to her eagerly, enjoying her intellectual company and reaping the many benefits of her friendship. After Ginzberg's father died in 1907, the relationship deepened: He needed her emotional support, she basked in what she perceived as his love, and responded with devotion. They worked together, they dined together (at her table), they walked together. And then he went off to Europe, fell passionately in love with young, lively Adele Katzenstein, and returned in October of 1908 to inform Henrietta Szold that he was engaged.[124]

The emotional blow was shattering. "Today it is four weeks since my only real happiness in life was killed by a single word," she wrote in her diary. "Since then I have hardly been conscious of living—there has been only suffering, nights and days, and days and nights of suffering." She brooded and she wrote; "perhaps," she thought, "it will help me to adjust myself to the new, cold, loveless life I must henceforth live." But she did not adjust, and her emotional distress affected her work at the Society. The fact that she could not avoid seeing Ginzberg, and was still obligated to translate and edit his manuscript, made it all the harder for her to put him out of mind. His writings were always before her, driving her back into depression. Solomon Schechter and Mayer Sulzberger tried to divert her with a scholarly project dealing with Jewish women's devotional literature. There was also talk of a long vacation. In the end, she received six-months paid leave plus an extra $500 gift from the Society that enabled her to extend her European tour on to Palestine. She was at once grateful and apologetic:

> Loyal, intelligent, conscientious and effective you call my service to the Society—your recognition of that will accompany me and sweeten a vacation forced upon me by regrettable circumstances, and perhaps be as potent as the vacation itself in restoring me to a normal degree of self-confidence and joy in living and working.[125]

The time away was therapeutic, the visit to Palestine life changing. "I am more than ever convinced," she wrote to one of her friends, "that if not Zionism, then nothing—then extinction for the Jew."[126] She returned to America determined to devote more of her life to Zionism; it gave meaning to her existence. The work at the Society, by contrast, constantly reminded her of past sorrows. Even while abroad she had dragged around uncorrected proofs of Ginzberg's second volume of *Legends*. Now, back in Philadelphia, a third volume stared up at her. It was more than she could bear.

She had complained about her work at the Society before in letters to friends, but inevitably found herself "bound by sexual limitations" from speaking out. "If I were a man," she wrote to one of her relatives, "I could make my voice heard." When she had grumbled to Ginzberg about her job dissatisfactions, he had sensibly advised her to have her "work and duties exactly defined." "If," he continued "the J.P.S. expects you to be a *Maedchen fuer alles*—secretary, translator, author and collector of statistics—then let them look for somebody else."[127] But she never gave serious thought to resigning, for hers was a prestigious job, where she met fascinating people, learned a great deal, and had the chance to serve the cause of American Jewish culture. Her complaints concerned only specifics—policy decisions she disagreed with, too heavy a burden of work, insufficient pay. The position itself, however, made her feel useful. She could no more think of abandoning it than Jane Addams could of abandoning Hull House—until now. "I must give up the position with the Publication Society because I cannot, cannot, cannot bear the handling of his book, and more than that I cannot do my duty to the Society," she wrote in her diary. She read over the list of books she had assisted with over the years and suddenly lamented that her name appeared on none of them, that she was somehow "damned to ineffectuality." She even felt "the idea of suicide becoming more and more familiar."[128] Twenty months had already passed since that terrible day in October of 1908, but still nothing had been resolved; the life-changing repercussions of the trauma had not yet shown themselves.

On June 8, 1910, Henrietta Szold finally summoned up the courage to put Ginzberg's book behind her. "My request," she wrote to Judge Sulzberger, "is that you relieve me of the work as well as the responsibility connected with seeing volumes 3 and 5 of Dr. Ginzberg's 'Legends of the Jews' through the press, and give me permission to employ some one to do it at my expense.... I admit that in setting a personal feeling over against my sense of responsibility and loyalty, I am putting a strain upon the latter. Let that be the measure of my present embarrassment. What it should indicate further is, that, being a human woman besides a proofreader, I may not be in a condition to do my literary duty to the author properly." Sulzberger gave his approval at once; he understood.[129]

When volume 3 of the *Legends* appeared, in 1911, it was distinguished from its predecessors in that it carried two names besides those of Ginzberg. Dr. Isaac Husik of Dropsie College was listed as "Reviser and Proof-Reader," a tacit announcement to those who needed to know that this usually anonymous task was *not* done by the Society's usual copy editor. As for the translation, it was done by a twenty-seven-year-old, impecunious, and about-to-be-married Ph.D. student named Paul Radin, son of Rabbi Adolph Radin. Little did the Society know that he would rise to become one of America's leading anthropologists, author of the influential book *Primitive Man as a Philosopher*.[130]

Although she was now free of Ginzberg's *Legends*, Henrietta Szold was not free of his ghost. Haunted by past memories, she threw herself into an orgy of work—editing a long issue of the *American Jewish Year Book*, preparing an elaborate index to the first ten volumes of the *Publications of the American Jewish Historical Society*, organizing the scattered records of the Federation of American Zionists. The news, early in 1911, that Mrs. Ginzberg had become pregnant only drove her to toil longer and harder; she took on more and more assignments—anything to stave off the relentless torments of life and memory. And then inevitably, she collapsed. An operation and a prolonged convalescence took her away from the Society, from New York, from Louis Ginzberg, for six wonderful months. "I am cheerful and even optimistic...," she wrote that summer to her friend Alice Seligsberg. "I realize now that I was completely brokendown—everything about me had run to seed. The elation produced by the European trip was illusory. I was trying all these three years to 'bluff' myself—first recreation was what was needed to restore me to sanity, and then hard work, but the body rebelled as the soul had before. I am determined now to blot out some of the passages of the past and leap into a new existence as soon as the elasticity of the body at least is restored."[131]

For the next four years, as her Zionist activities multiplied, she was marking time at the Society. She did her job as thoroughly as ever, but her heart was no longer in it. She took on no more extra assignments, no more translations, no more behind-the-scenes work for which others received credit. Instead, she devoted herself to a new women's organization, the Daughters of Zion, dedicated to the "promotion of Jewish institutions and enterprises in Palestine." This organization, shortly renamed Hadassah, became the new focus of her life. As for Ginzberg's *Legends*, its fourth (and last) volume of texts appeared in 1913, but publication of the notes that were meant to accompany and elucidate the volumes, as well as the comprehensive index, were both indefinitely postponed. There was only one project of the Society's that excited Henrietta Szold as of old during these years, and that was the Bible translation. Perhaps fittingly, her resignation as secretary coincided with the completion of the manuscript text of that great work, and her first voluntary assignment for the Society after her resignation was to serve as one of its proofreaders.[132]

With the Bible complete, Solomon Schechter dead, and plans already in place for the Hebrew Press and the classics series, Henrietta Szold's departure meant that a vigorous and productive era at the Society was ending. She herself was conscious of the fact: "I realize," she wrote in a personal letter to Mayer Sulzberger, "that the Jewish Publication Society is about to enter upon a new phase in its development. . . . I am inclined to view my own severance from it as an added sign that a period has closed and another will begin." The Society was, in a sense, the first-born son that she now knew she would never have. In saying farewell, she compared herself to "a mother when she stands on the threshold of her home and watches her son fare forth to mould his own career." "Her heart is full of good wishes," she explained, "even while she realizes that big things are approaching in which she will have no direct part."[133]

6

THE LEAN YEARS

Contrary to Henrietta Szold's expections, the two decades following her resignation were marked by some of the darkest years in the Society's history. Its membership declined, its financial condition deteriorated to the point of crisis, and its annual list of publications lost much of its luster. For a time the Society's very existence was threatened; even some of those closest to it doubted that it could survive. To be sure, the Society did not suffer alone. The interwar years, and especially the Great Depression, also wrought havoc on numerous other American Jewish organizations, particularly those dedicated to Jewish education and culture. Relief for Jews at home and abroad became American Jewry's number one priority. In the Society's case, however, economic difficulties formed only part of the problem. Other factors, some of them symptomatic of far-reaching changes within the American Jewish community, were at least equally to blame.

The Post-Szold Years

Henrietta Szold's replacement at the Society was thirty-two-year-old Benzion Halper, born in a suburb of Vilna, educated in England ("one of the most brilliant students Jews' College ever produced"), and already one of the most promising young Jewish scholars in America. Although he officially bore the title of "Editor," which Henrietta Szold never did, Halper actually worked at the Society only part-time, while he served as associate professor and custodian of manuscripts at Dropsie College.[1] Since he spent as much time as he could actively pursuing his own professional research, many of the duties formerly undertaken by Szold now fell to the Society's assistant secretary, George Dobsevage. He had been Szold's unofficial assistant since 1906, when, at the age of twenty-two, he replaced Charles Bernheimer as the person in charge of membership and administration. With Szold gone, he assumed various publication committee responsibilities as well. It was, as he later complained, a most difficult and wearisome assignment:

> In a general way my duties with the Society are as follows: General Secretary of the Society, Secretary to the Board of Trustees; Secretary to the Publication Committee; Secretary to the Classics Committee; Secretary to the many Sub-Committees; member of the Year Book Committee; I am in charge of the office routine; I look after preparation of circular letters, advertisements and review of books; attend to the correspondence which comes to us in many languages and covers subjects which could only be answered intelligently by one who has a knowledge of Jewish literature and the Jewish situation. Moreover, I am in charge of the manufacture of books; reader of many of the manuscripts; proof reader; look after the Hebrew Press; prepare estimates and perform many other large and small duties.[2]

George was the son of Abraham Dobsevage, a notable East Side Hebraic scholar, and one of that multitude of starving immigrant writers who failed to find the recognition they felt they deserved in the "upside down world" of New York, and lived out lives of tragedy, eking out a bare existence as they poured mind, heart, and soul into scholarly tomes that they then had to subsidize to see published.[3] George Dobsevage physically resembled his father and inherited from him many of those maddening *luftmensh* qualities that marked so many East European Jews of his type. He loved learning, fawned over scholars, and revered the printed word, but he was disorganized, forgetful, and perpetually in debt. Henrietta Szold kept him in line, but once she left authors began to complain, as they never had before, of unkept promises, unanswered letters, and even lost manuscripts. German-style efficiency, the hallmark of the Szold era, gave way to amiable disorder; but Dobsevage had been around too long to be replaced. By tradition, anyone who served more than a few years at a Jewish organization enjoyed informal tenure.[4]

During these years, more than ever, Cyrus Adler wielded the power behind the throne at JPS. He sat on every one of its critical committees, wrote letters in the Society's name, insisted that no decisions be taken without his being apprised, and gradually came to dominate the all-important publication committee, although he was not formally listed as its chairman until 1925, two years following the death of Mayer Sulzberger.[5] In truth, Adler was far more actively involved in the Society's affairs than Simon Miller, its president. Too deeply wrapped up in his own shirt manufacturing business to give the necessary time and energy, Miller only continued on in his post at Adler's insistence, always hoping for the financial independence he needed to devote full attention to the Society's affairs. Yet, he served as president for twenty years, 1913–33, longer than anyone before or since. When he finally retired from the post, past age seventy, he continued to sit on the board of trustees and the publication committee until his death in 1945.[6]

Besides Halper, Dobsevage, Adler, and Miller, the Society elected year after year a long list of officers, trustees, honorary vice-presidents, and publication committee members—a roster amounting, in 1916, to some five dozen names. Of these, only a few did any serious work. The officers, all of them Philadelphians except for the first vice-president, who traditionally came from New York, rarely did more than chair committees. The board of trustees, including the officers, met regularly for deliberations, but often business proceeded with fewer than 50 percent present. Although a majority of the trustees were Pennsylvanians (and usually Philadelphians), they were busy men of affairs who belonged to numerous organizations, lent their names and made donations, but did not otherwise involve themselves. The Society's honorary vice-presidents, a roster of thirteen rabbis and lay people from around the country, were even less active. A few solicited subscriptions and most responded favorably when called upon for help, yet without exception all were far more deeply involved in other causes. What they did do was ensure that the Philadelphia-based Society never appeared too provincial; they were a visible symbol of its claim to represent the interests of Jews nationwide.

The most active and significant of the Society's governing bodies remained the publication committee. Unlike other positions at JPS, which were filled on the basis of such standards as an individual's community prestige, net worth, and place of residence, appointments to the twenty-member publication committee still depended largely on merit. The Society's leaders also took pains to ensure that the publication committee remain fairly well balanced. Were any one group to become predominant, they knew that the Society's claim to represent the whole spectrum of American Jews would be open to question. The composition of the publication committee had changed over time to include more professional scholars, more Conservative Jews (the Orthodox went unrepresented until 1941, when Samuel Belkin was appointed, but some of the Conservative Jews were thoroughgoing traditionalists), and more Jews of East European background. By 1916, a good mix had been achieved; still, most of the time the committee operated on consensus rather than majority rule. Besides, many members were inactive. Several never attended meetings (and not just because they lived far away), others refused to read manuscripts; four, Cyrus Adler once noted with distaste, had neither been seen nor heard from at all in five years.[7]

Financially, the Society still appeared to be holding its own when Benzion

Halper took over as editor. It boasted assets of over $157,000, including about $100,000 squirreled away in various funds, and its books balanced. Upon closer inspection, however, the picture looked considerably less rosy. Expenses exceeded income by nearly $8,000 and the deficit was being made up out of the endowment. At that rate, it would not take long for the capital to be entirely eaten away. Nor were membership figures particularly bright. The 13,822 members listed meant that the Society had not kept pace at all with the growth of the American Jewish population: Only 1 American Jew in 250 now belonged. Of course, nobody expected to attract many members from the ranks of the Yiddish-speaking immigrants, but with over 1.6 million Jews in New York State, were there really only 3,182 who cared about Jewish culture? As before, the Society did best in rural areas where its books were among the few sources available to those interested in deepening their Jewish knowledge. In Indiana, for example, the Society had 201 members, proportionately almost double what the state contributed to the American Jewish population as a whole. New York, by contrast, housed 47 percent of America's Jewish population, but only 23 percent of the Society's members. True, the Society did comparatively well in the South, and had individual members stretching all the way out to Alaska (where there was one), and in twelve foreign countries, especially the English-speaking lands: Canada, South Africa, England, and Australia. Yet, the fact that the six most Jewishly populous states in the Union contributed far less than their share of the Society's membership seemed an ominous sign. Was the Society doing something wrong? Was it continuing to meet the needs of American Jews?[8]

World War I and the Postwar Decline

America's entry into World War I put these questions into temporary abeyance. Suddenly the Society had a new mission: Jewish boys in uniform, far from home and cut off from their familiar moorings, desperately needed prayerbooks, Bibles, and other Jewish reading material. The Society, experienced at meeting the needs of a full spectrum of Jews, undertook to supply them. In 1917, a committee of three—Cyrus Adler, representing the United Synagogue of America, William Rosenau, representing the Central Conference of American Rabbis, and Bernard Drachman, representing the Union of Orthodox Congregations—prepared an abridged prayerbook. Shortly thereafter, Adler and his wife, in consultation with David Philipson and Solomon Solis-Cohen, compiled *Readings from the Holy Scriptures*, "a little book of 276 pages, weighing but two ounces" and based on the newly completed translation. The Society issued both volumes in conjunction with the Jewish Welfare Board (conveniently headed by Adler), and pledged to "rush through the press as many editions as may be required." Thanks to government money and private donations, some 100,000 volumes were eventually distributed without charge.[9]

In addition to these specific efforts, JPS took part in a nationwide "Books for Soldiers" campaign, distributing its most popular titles free to Jews in uniform. It also sent full sets of all of its published works to army cantonments and military libraries. The patriotic mood of the country in general, and the special interest Jews had in demonstrating their loyalty and willingness to fight (a response to anti-Semitic charges that Jews would never fight for any country except Palestine) made this a JPS priority. Indeed, the Society not only did its part for Jews in uniform but urged all American Jews to do likewise. In language calculated to evoke religious sympathy, it called on Jews to "equal the efforts of our Christian neighbors" and encouraged them to "do as much for our Jewish boys as they are doing for their boys."[10]

Although the war demonstrated anew the Society's singular importance as an institution for the promotion and dissemination of Jewish culture, the postwar period saw no improvement in its deteriorating financial condition. Wartime paper shortages, rapid postwar inflation, and subsequent economic recession affected the entire American book industry; JPS was not spared. During just one eighteen-month period (1918–20), its book production costs actually doubled. Its total increase in production costs over prices prevailing during the prewar period exceeded 150 percent. To make matters worse, the Society, like the rest of the book trade, customarily sold books on credit. By the time customers paid for their books—if they paid—their money had substantially decreased in value.[11]

The Society, which was already operating at a deficit in 1916 and lost further sums as a consequence of its wartime generosity, suffered even more seriously than most publishers during this crisis. Although in 1919 it raised its general dues from three to five dollars, and also increased some of its books' sticker prices, it feared raising prices too much lest it drive away members and readers. As a result, it actually began to lose money on every new member it enrolled, especially when members took advantage of its liberal credit policies and stretched payments out over long periods. By 1921, when the annual report proudly announced that "a most conservative count places our membership at seventeen thousand, the largest in the history of the Society," the handwriting was already on the wall.

As the bills began to pile up and the demands of creditors grew louder, Simon Miller, admitting that "the finances of the Jewish Publication Society of America are in a rather chaotic condition," moved decisively. He ordered "that all projected work shall cease," and appealed for a sustaining fund of $200,000. Hoping to stave off disaster, the board of trustees tried to economize. It introduced a cheaper marketing system that did away with sales through agents on commission, suspended work on various projects, including the Bible commentary, and cut down on the number of books distributed annually, permitting just two to go out in 1922 (and one of them was the *American Jewish Year Book*). In the end, all of these measures were to no avail. The deficit mounted, the sustaining fund fell far short of its goal, and the new marketing system proved a failure. Although few people knew it at the time, the Society was staring at a whopping debt of $120,000, which it had no way of paying.[12]

A downward spiral took hold. Authors whose books were held up became furious. Supporters grew discouraged and turned to other organizations. Members, who received less and less for their money, resigned in growing numbers. Others, who might have been kept on the rolls in easier times, were dropped for non-payment. Membership plunged to 11,023 in 1923 and to 9,950 a year later. By 1927 the membership was down to 8,300, and it would fall still further during the Great Depression. "Shall the Jewish Publication Society of America, with its great record of service, live or die?" Simon Miller asked as the crisis continued to deepen. Thanks to small bequests, severe cutbacks, tight financial management, and special arrangements with creditors, the Society edged close to the precipice but lived on—just barely. The situation still looked so grim for the Society in 1928 that it did not even bother to celebrate its fortieth anniversary.[13]

The Larger Causes of the Decline

Economic conditions obviously account for a good deal of what happened to the Society in the postwar period, but they still leave many questions unanswered. Why, for example, was the Society already suffering from financial and membership problems even before World War I? Why didn't it recover during the "roaring twenties" as other publishers did? Why did its small fund drive in the 1920s fall so far short—this at a time when American Jewry proved able to raise over $60 million to aid Jews abroad?[14]

According to Cyrus Adler, "practically every Jewish organization of higher learning or science" in America "was broke."[15] The balmy prewar conditions that had spawned and nurtured so many different Jewish cultural initiatives gave way in postwar America to a winter of discontent. The mood of American Jews underwent another of its periodic great turnabouts, reversing the trend that had begun some four decades earlier. The heady Jewish religious revival that first led to the Society's founding and then generated so much enthusiasm for its publication program failed to survive the war. By 1920 it was dead—as dead as the American Progressive movement and the Protestant Social Gospel, which were, to some extent, its national and Christian counterparts. What one historian has called "the age of optimism" in American Jewish history, that era that saw American Jews deepen their religious commitments and initiate a broad range of cultural projects, gave way in the postwar world to what might be called an age of pessimism, characterized by burgeoning concerns over such things as immigration restriction, worldwide anti-Semitism (including anti-Semitism in America) and the perilous financial and political state of European Jewry.[16]

Back in the prewar decades one could still dream about transforming American Jewry into a great, culturally vibrant Diaspora center, and in the case of the Society, one could patiently consider what kinds of books American Jews most needed so as to properly prepare themselves for the great tasks ahead. Now, in the 1920s, America *was* a Diaspora center, and attention abruptly shifted from the realm of culture to the urgent social, political, and economic tasks at hand. Many of the Society's own key leaders, beginning with Mayer Sulzberger and Cyrus Adler, devoted increasing amounts of time to such organizations as the American Jewish Committee and the American Jewish Joint Distribution Committee. Henrietta Szold similarly turned her attention to the medical work of Hadassah. The Society's mission, by comparison, seemed decidedly less important.

Another factor was that American Jewish culture itself had become vastly more secular. Historians of American Christianity sometimes speak of the "religious depression" of the postwar era; among Jews, no less affected by this "depression" than their Christian neighbors, there was a shift from religious awakening to deepening interest in universalism, or what has been called the "cosmopolitan spirit."[17] Judged by this new standard, the Society's goals and achievements seemed decidedly parochial and behind the times. Although the publication committee was still committed, literally and figuratively, to time-tested Jewish classics, the most creative young Jewish intellectuals of the day—men like Morris Raphael Cohen, Waldo Frank, Felix Frankfurter, Joseph Freeman, Horace Kallen, Walter Lippmann, James Oppenheim, Paul Rosenfeld, and Walter Weyl—were trying to remake the world; if they had a Bible, it was, for many of them, *Das Kapital.* Had the Society followed the lead of the *Menorah Journal* (the vibrant new magazine founded in 1915 by and for young Jewish intellectuals) and agreed to publish a full range of Jewish views, perhaps it might have seemed more relevant. But since its leaders were highly disdainful of the radical ideas (not to speak of the sometimes loose morals) of young Jewish intellectuals, and since they were committed to consensus rather than to diversity of expression, they made no overtures at all to these men. And the "young radicals" proved quite capable of publishing their writings elsewhere.

The new-found ability of Jews to find other publishing outlets for their Jewish writings points to an additional cause of the Society's decline: competition. Back in 1888, the Society, along with Bloch Publishing Company, held a virtual monopoly over American Jewish publishing. By the 1920s, however, competition had sprung up on two fronts: from general publishers and from Jewish publishers. The former included for the first time serious general publishing houses founded by Jews—

firms like B. W. Huebsch, Alfred Knopf, Boni and Liveright, and Thomas Seltzer. They had learned, in part from the Society, that books (and especially novels) with Jewish themes could be profitably marketed, even to non-Jews. These firms, along with non-Jewish publishers, especially Macmillan, actively competed for the best Jewish writers, offering them book contracts and market access (to say nothing of prestige) that the Society could not begin to match. The Society was thus deprived of precisely those offerings that had once been the most popular with its members; the result in terms of declining membership was inevitable.[18]

Among Jewish commercial publishers, the much revitalized Bloch Publishing Company was JPS's main competitor, but there were also newer firms, like Hebrew Publishing Company and Behrman House. None of them could assure authors, as the Society could, that their books would be distributed to a wide audience of several thousand subscribers. But they could promise both speedier handling of manuscripts and strict editorial independence, for they had neither publication committees nor rigid limitations on the number of books that they could issue in any given year.[19] Evidence from the Society's "rejected books" file indicates that most authors still approached the Society first. Nevertheless, it seems clear that the very existence of competition for publishing Jewish books detracted from the Society's general appeal.

In short, the Society's world had changed. When it stood practically alone in the field of American Jewish publishing, it could truthfully claim that it single-handedly made possible the appearance of high-quality Jewish books in America; without its efforts some of the most important American Jewish books ever published would never have appeared. Now that claim was substantially less convincing, because it was actually publishing only a small fraction of the total number of Jewish books produced annually in America, and a minority even of those books recognized as being the "best" American Jewish books in print. Of the "One Hundred Best Available Books in English on Jewish Subjects" listed in the *American Jewish Year Book* of 1925–26, for example, only twenty-eight were titles published by JPS; the rest were issued by Bloch, Macmillan, Oxford, and more than two dozen other firms.[20] JPS was still playing an unquestionably important role—no other firm, after all, had as many as twenty-eight titles on the list—but it was obviously not *as* important as it had been in the past. A growing number of American Jews purchased JPS books in bookstores if they found them appealing but saw no reason to join its membership rolls, and even less reason to grant it extraordinary support.

The nationwide financial crisis, the collapse of the prewar religious revival, the new pragmatic agenda of American Jews, the rise of secularist cosmopolitanism, the increase in competition—these were all developments that damaged the Society's fortunes but were essentially beyond its control. Yet the Society's postwar problems cannot be blamed on external forces alone. Difficult as it may have been to admit, members' dissatisfaction also played a part in the decline. The Society's limited selection of books, increasingly scholarly publication focus, and strict membership requirements drove a growing wedge between it and those it most wanted to reach. Although it sought a large membership and a wide readership, its books and policies made it ever less popular; more and more, it became a society for Jewish scholars, Jewish professionals, and strongly committed Jewish laymen.

The increasing emphasis on scholarship has already been noted several times and was at least partly anticipated even by the Society's founders. Back in 1888, in the brochure it published to introduce itself to the public, JPS predicted that "increasing learning will demand of us works of deeper scholarship, which comparably few among us appreciate today." In private, Mayer Sulzberger likewise insisted that "the scholarly element must not be totally excluded" from the Society's list. He conceded this even though it was he who laid down the principle that "there must always be a sufficient element of popularity in a work in order to prevent dissatisfaction among our members."[21] What JPS hoped eventually to achieve was a good balance. But in fact, over time, the scales tipped ever more heavily toward the scholarly side. Already in 1910, the publication committee noted pressure from members seeking "a larger proportion of less serious works." Yet in 1913 the Society announced a bequest from the estate of Professor Morris Loeb, Jacob Schiff's brother-in-law and a brilliant chemist who died prematurely at the age of forty-five, for a fund whose income was reserved *exclusively* for books of scholarship ("distinct contributions to knowledge.") Even before the first volume was issued under the terms of this fund, the publication committee admitted that its efforts at achieving popularity had failed. The "preponderance" of "the Society's past publications," a disappointed subcommittee reported in 1915, consisted of "bulky advanced work as compared with the simple, condensed presentation." With the planned Jewish classics series it appeared likely that scholarly volumes would continue to dominate JPS offerings for many years into the future.[22]

The reasons for this increasing emphasis on the publication of scholarly works are closely tied to the growth and professionalization of Jewish studies in America during the first decades of the twentieth century. It was during this period that a distinguished group of new professors, some holding chairs in Semitic Studies at major universities, others ensconced at one or another of America's three Jewish colleges (Hebrew Union College, the Jewish Theological Seminary, and Dropsie College), as well as their students, began working in earnest to upgrade the status of their nascent field.[23] "Professionalism" was the catchword of the day all across the country, and with it came increasing specialization along career lines: Organizations were formed for everyone from doctors to lawyers to rabbis, as professionals sought to distance themselves from "mere" lay people.[24] Jewish scholars joined the bandwagon and, operating somewhat upon the German model of Jewish scholarship, worked to establish themselves on an independent footing—complete with their own scholarly journal (the *Jewish Quarterly Review*, brought over to America in 1908), and their own academic organization (the American Academy of Jewish Research, founded in 1920 after several earlier efforts had failed[25]). They also required their own scholarly publisher, and it was here, they thought, that JPS, especially given its Hebrew Press, could play a significant role. Nobody at the Society, least of all Cyrus Adler, ever dreamed that it should become exclusively scholarly; the goal was to serve popular and scholarly needs at once. But this was difficult to reconcile with the professional demand for "scholarly standards," and would have required a two-tiered system for evaluating books. In fact, with the Society's increasing turn toward scholarly volumes, many of its more popularly attuned readers simply dropped out.

Had the Society changed some of its procedures to accommodate these members, perhaps more of them might have stayed. But it continued to publish four volumes a year at most—fewer after the decline set in—and continued to insist that members accept all of them, whether they wanted them or not. Only occasionally did it publish a scholarly book in limited circulation expressly for those members who requested it. Louis Marshall sought a less rigid policy and urged the trustees to grant each member the "right to receive such intellectual provender as he desires and you can supply," but he was politely ignored. Cyrus Adler once similarly suggested ("informally") that instead of publishing three or four books a year, "the Society might issue five or six"—in more limited editions—"and members be allowed to choose three or four in which they might really be interested." But again, according to the minutes, "the committee took no action."[26]

Indeed, "no action" sometimes seemed to characterize the Society as a whole during this period of crisis. Authors complained that manuscripts they submitted lay unread and unreturned. Even the author Maurice Samuel, a JPS supporter and a personal friend of George Dobsevage, once lost his patience and called the Society "inconsiderate and unfair" in its handling of one of his submissions. Others, without personal connections, received still worse treatment. Those with manuscripts accepted for publication complained too: Delays of four years between acceptance and publication had become common, and several books lingered "in process" for over a decade.[27] To be fair, the administrative and leadership paralysis that affected all levels of the Society during this period was partly a byproduct of its overall crisis. Had JPS been financially better off, the situation might have been different. Yet the paralysis also extended and even exacerbated the crisis. Too often the very people whom it most needed to hold onto and attract—members, contributors, and authors—felt as if the Society cared nothing about them; they went away disillusioned and embittered.

Proposed Solutions

Like any sick patient, JPS received no shortage of unsolicited advice on how to get well. Some proposed that it publish one or another specific book (usually their own or a friend's), others that it concentrate on a particular genre of books (usually polemics or apologetics), still others suggested that it abandon its efforts to serve all Jews and focus on the reading needs of East European Jewish immigrants or their children. None of this well-meaning advice was ever taken seriously. Over the years, however, three insiders put forward reorganization plans that did command close attention. Although their ideas met with rejection, each proposal reflects a particular understanding of the American Jewish community and its needs. In addition, they demonstrate that, at critical moments, JPS might have been developed along quite different lines—a reminder that its history was a product of conscious leadership decisions, both good and bad.

In 1915 Israel Friedlaender put forward the first full-scale proposal for reorganizing the Society. Typically, it was bold, powerfully written, and full of insights. Friedlaender submitted his proposal when the Society still appeared to be thriving, but he, prescient as usual, knew better. "Our subscribers," he wrote, "do not read the books intended for them." In so many words, he suggested to the leadership that it had lost touch with the times. "The state of culture, the mental attitude, and the literary taste of the individual members," he observed, had become "vastly different from one another, and in that same ratio must necessarily differ the demands they make." There was, he believed, only one solution: "The time has arrived to differentiate our activities and to adapt them to the heterogeneous character of our present constituency."

Essentially, Friedlaender called for JPS to produce two categories of books, each suited to a particular group of subscribers. The first, which he called "a popular series," would consist of books containing "elementary facts of Judaism," written by good writers (not necessarily experts), in an interesting (nontechnical) style, and with sufficient brevity to appeal to "the average businessman . . . with an average intelligence and an average amount of Jewish interest." The second, "a scientific series," would be geared to the better-educated members of the Jewish community and would consist of readable "contributions to Jewish learning" of the type that the Society had been publishing for years. All members, according to the plan, would continue to receive the *American Jewish Year Book*, redesigned "to serve as a mighty agency for the dissemination of Jewish knowledge, with an equal power of appeal to the various elements of our membership."[28]

Friedlaender's plan received respectful attention. A special subcommittee, although it disagreed with some aspects of the proposal, specifically endorsed its call for "issuing two grades of publications parallel with each other." But owing to the Society's financial crisis and growing institutional paralysis under Dobsevage, none of the major changes Friedlaender recommended ever went into effect. In 1920 JPS did announce plans for a popular series of sixteen-page educational pamphlets entitled "Little Studies in Judaism," designed to "spread the knowledge of Jewish belief and practice and deepen Jewish conviction," but after the first number appeared, Samuel Schulman's *Rosh-Ha-shanah and Yom Kippur*, the series collapsed from lack of funds and a dearth of publication committee support. Scholars among the Society's leadership felt uncomfortable with popular pamphlets on religious subjects: The genre demanded generalizations and oversimplifications of the kind that they shunned, and inevitably engendered religious partisanship. Meanwhile, Friedlaender, one of the few scholars on the committee who had a feel for popular writing, lay dead, murdered while on a mission to the Ukraine. His ambitious plan for the Society died with him.[29]

A second set of proposals for revitalizing the Jewish Publication Society came from the fertile mind of Cyrus Adler. Over the years, he urged numerous changes designed to increase administrative efficiency, overall popularity, and the number of books that it could publish. At one meeting of the publication committee, after Henrietta Szold's departure, he proposed a new, streamlined committee structure designed to speed up the processing of manuscripts. At other meetings he recommended smaller pressruns even if this meant that the books would no longer be distributed automatically to every member. Most interesting of all, in 1919 he made the radical suggestion—subsequently repeated by others, down to the present day—that the Society undertake to sell Jewish books issued by publishers other than itself. "It is within our purview," he declared, "to disseminate works 'giving instruction in the principles of the Jewish religion and in Jewish history and literature' whether such works are published by ourselves or another agency. There is a reasonable profit in such sale. We have . . . a large potential clientele which at least in the smaller cities and towns has no opportunity for even learning of the existence of publications in our field issued by other agencies." When, nine years later, influenced by the success of the Book-of-the-Month Club, Adele Seltzer and others proposed that the Society form a book club of its own, Adler was clearly interested. But in spite of his prestige and power, his suggestions failed to win majority support. Had he personally lobbied for his proposals and spent time patiently convincing trustees of their far-reaching value, perhaps things might have been different. But Adler was involved in the running of so many organizations, particularly Dropsie and the Jewish Theological Seminary, that he simply lacked the time to follow through on all his proposals.[30]

Although Adler, like Friedlaender, believed that JPS needed to reach out to a larger percentage of the American Jewish reading public, others felt that the Society required a more limited mission that would remove it from competition with other publishers and give it an exclusive niche, namely, publishing professional Jewish books. Longtime trustee Julius Weyl, convinced by this argument, proposed limiting the Society to "the publication of such technical, scholarly Jewish books as would not otherwise find publication," somewhat like a university press. This view would have meant accepting the Society's decline as more or less permanent, and would also have involved a considerable retreat from the broad educational mission that its founders had originally envisaged. On the other hand, it might have made it easier to raise money on a charitable basis since its books would have been unprofitable almost by definition, and certainly would have answered the needs of Jewish Studies professionals. *New York Times* publisher Adolph Ochs, when he served on the Society's board, strongly favored the view "that the membership is really a subsidy to enable the publication of worthwhile books on Jewish subjects, which books otherwise could not be published," and his son-in-law, Arthur Hays Sulzberger, agreed with him. But a majority of the Society's leaders, especially its younger members, disagreed. Appealing both to history and to the contemporary needs of American Jews, they insisted that the Society's wider cultural mission—to educate American Jews and to stimulate the production of high-quality, broadly appealing Jewish books—remained as urgent as ever, especially because other Jewish publishers only issued books that they thought could make a profit. A host of problems may have made that mission more difficult to realize in the postwar era, and alternatives designed to help JPS realize its mission in other ways may have seemed too risky even to attempt. But abandoning the Society's historic mission was not something that these leaders were about to do. Instead, they continued to cherish the hope that one day the Society would be revitalized.[31]

Julius Grodinsky

In May 1926 a special committee of the board of trustees discovered, to its horror, certain "irregularities" in the Society's finances, which resulted in the resignation of George Dobsevage.[32] Subsequent audits revealed only "a relatively small amount of dishonesty." Much more was lost from "inefficient and uneconomical management" and from the "absence of a well conceived selling policy." The appalling situation persuaded the trustees to hire Julius Grodinsky, an instructor in economics at the Wharton School of the University of Pennsylvania, to serve as the new secretary of the Society on a part-time basis. It would require a man of his expertise, they thought, to put the Society's house back in order.[33]

Grodinsky, soon promoted to executive secretary, was American-born and a mere thirty years old. Like Adler four decades earlier, he had a reputation for being somewhat of a *Wunderkind*. In 1920, when he was only twenty-four years old, he had begun teaching at Wharton—this at a time when academic openings for Jews in any field were scarce. Five years later he received his doctorate in economics. He continued on at Wharton throughout his life, rising to become professor of finance, and authoring several important books (including a classic study of railroad magnate Jay Gould). By temperament, Grodinsky was a hard-headed business analyst with one eye always firmly fixed on the "bottom line."

His Jewish involvement, however, seems to have been virtually nil. Unlike his predecessors, he boasted no record of activity in Jewish communal life, and even after he left JPS, his only noteworthy Jewish affiliation was with the anti-Zionist American Council for Judaism.[34]

What Grodinsky represented at JPS was a turn away from the "genteel" tradition of publishing, with its family ties and "old boy" network of insiders, and a shift toward a more business-like approach, such as that taking hold across the industry as a whole.[35] This proved a mixed blessing: On the one hand, it ended many abuses and saved a great deal of money; on the other hand, it alienated many of the Society's friends and diminished its Jewish character, undercutting the traditional Jewish idea that education and culture have inherent value that cannot be measured only in terms of dollars and cents. In the interests of penny-pinching, Grodinsky quarreled with Max Margolis over minor payments to a clerk, tried (unsuccessfully) to convince Cyrus Adler that a translator was being overpaid, and complained bitterly about the cost of printing the notes to Louis Ginzberg's *Legends*. In each case he put forward cogent economic arguments, but always failed to understand that JPS was more than just a business in trouble.[36]

This basic difference in outlook is perhaps best seen in Grodinsky's dealings with the Society's part-time editor, Isaac Husik, appointed in 1924 upon the untimely death of Benzion Halper. A full professor of philosophy at the University of Pennsylvania and lauded now as "one of the most distinguished historians of philosophy [that] America... produced," Husik was twenty years older than Grodinsky and enjoyed a sparkling professional reputation. He was a modest, retiring man, meticulous and immensely learned. Both of the works he published with the Society, *A History of Medieval Jewish Philosophy* (1916) and his five-volume edition of Joseph Albo's *Sefer ha-'Ikkarim*, issued during his stint as editor, were enduring works of scholarship that remained in print for years. To Grodinsky, however, all of this was irrelevant. He considered Husik to be a staff employee and looked upon his salary as just one more bloated expense. In 1927 he suggested to Simon Miller that Husik's salary be cut. It wasn't. In 1933, when Husik took sick and was unable to work, Grodinsky stopped paying him altogether and indicated that, owing to the Depression, he would have to work at a far lower scale when he returned. Husik naturally complained—"My salary was discontinued just at a time when I needed money most"—and Grodinsky was overruled (although in the interests of economy Husik did eventually have to endure a 20 percent salary reduction). The whole episode, however, left a very bad taste.[37]

Grodinsky pointed out in his defense that he demanded no more of others than he did of himself. "In 1932," he informed one critic, "I have allowed myself only $50 for travelling expenses, at the rate of $8 per trip. I leave at 7 o'clock in the morning, and I usually return about 11:30 at night." He urged upon everyone connected with the Society "the necessity of conserving all our time, energy, and money, so that we can use whatever is left for the purpose of publishing as many books as possible." But if Grodinsky saved money and liquidated the Society's debt, he never succeeded in winning friends. Thirty years later, Solomon Grayzel still remembered him, perhaps unfairly, as the executive secretary who "did not see why the JPS was needed and always predicted that if we did not close up shop voluntarily, we would have to close in the course of a few years anyway."[38]

Where Grodinsky made a particularly important contribution to the Society's welfare was at the Hebrew Press, which had been set up from the start to operate on a commercial basis. The press published several independent volumes under the logo of the "Conat Press," named for Abraham ben Solomon Conat, one of the earliest printers of Hebrew books in Europe. But during its first years it ran up an enormous deficit, due mostly to mismanagement. Losses incurred just on the printing of the great Yiddish translation of the Bible by Solomon Bloomgarden ("Yehoash") amounted to an estimated $7,170. Other press publications, including the Reform Movement's *Union Prayer Book* and *Haggadah*, the Conservative Movement's *Festival Prayer Book*, Israel Davidson's monumental *Thesaurus of Mediaeval Hebrew Poetry*, and various scholarly journals, for all that they kept the press humming and demonstrated its enormous value to the American Jewish community, failed to keep it solvent: Too many estimates were low and too many jobs had to be redone because of shoddy workmanship.[39] Working closely with trustee Julius Weyl, a professional in the printing business, Grodinsky turned the press around. He increased its business, regularized its procedures, and made it profitable. In 1931 he oversaw the formulation and publication of "Rules for the Jewish Publication Society Press," a marvelous pamphlet that brought order where chaos had previously reigned, and improved the quality of everything the press produced.[40] By 1934 the press was characterized as being "busier than it has been for years" and its activities dominated the Society's annual report:

> The work of the Press is varied and, in addition to occasional keyboarding in English, includes composition in Hebrew, Syriac, Greek, Arabic, Latin, Spanish, German, French—9 languages in all. The list of Press customers is impressive and includes the American Philosophical Society, the American Academy for Jewish Research, Harvard University, Yale University, The Jewish Theological Seminary, Hebrew Union College, The Jewish Quarterly Review, Journal of Biblical Literature, and many others. The 4–volume *Thesaurus of Medieval Hebrew Poetry*, by Professor Israel Davidson, an extremely important work in the field of Jewish bibliographical literature, was manufactured by our Press, and at present among our jobs are *Texts and Studies in Jewish History*, volume 2, by Prof. Jacob L. Mann; a new Sephardic Daily Prayer Book, edited by Dr. D. deSola Pool of New York; the George Alexander Kohut Memorial Volume; and an important educational book sponsored by the Bureau of Jewish Education of New York.[41]

According to Julius Weyl, Grodinsky had come to know "more about Hebrew composition on the monotype machine ... probably than anybody in the United

States." The expertise redounded to the Society's benefit, for beginning in 1930 revenues from the press frequently exceeded those from the sale of books, sometimes by nearly a two-to-one margin.[42] The Society's trustees, who had heard so much bad news over the years, could feel satisfied: Their Hebrew Press had made possible "the printing of much Hebrew literature, particularly in the field of primary study, which otherwise would not have been made available in printed form."[43]

Publications, 1918–36

Although the Hebrew press had become a great communal asset, the books issued by JPS during this period declined in quantity, quality, and variety. Important volumes were still distributed to members, but most of these were volumes that the Society either had commissioned earlier for one of its series or found independent funding for outside of its regular budget. In a departure from tradition, the Society decided to distribute several of its most highly specialized publications (like most of those in the classics series) only to those members who requested them; this saved money and prevented complaints. It also issued two works paid for privately, not geared for members at all, and never passed on by the publication committee. They had the Society's name on their title page only because they had been printed and edited at its press—a potentially misleading practice that was quickly stopped.[44] In matters of fundamental publication policy, however, standards continued unchanged. The publication committee continued to seek books that were at once educational, noncontroversial, dignified, definitive, readable—and, if possible, American in authorship.

The Society's most significant achievement during this period was the publication of all seventeen volumes of the Schiff Library of Jewish Classics. Funded from the endowment set up by Jacob Schiff, the long-planned series (see chapter 5) was inaugurated in 1923 with *Selected Religious Poems of Solomon Ibn Gabirol*, translated into English verse by Israel Zangwill from a critical text edited by Professor Israel Davidson of the Jewish Theological Seminary, one of the world's leading authorities on Hebrew poetry. The volume marked a new departure for Zangwill, best known as a novelist, essayist, and playwright, and it proved a fitting capstone to his literary career. The Society justifiably touted it as "the finest product of the noblest mind of medieval Jewry rendered into English by the foremost literary figure of modern Jewry." At a gala dinner honoring Zangwill and celebrating the new publication, the air was thick with nostalgia and hope as speakers recalled *Children of the Ghetto*, Zangwill's first book for the Society, and dreamed of the great future that now lay ahead for the classics. Most of those at the dinner never saw Zangwill alive again, for he died prematurely in 1926. *Ibn Gabirol* was his last major book.[45]

The next book in the classics series, *Selected Poems of Jehudah Halevi*, also became a farewell, but this time there was no surprise: The volume was literally a race against death. Nina Salaman of England, who translated these poems of the leading religious poet of Spanish Jewry's Golden Age, had published her successful *Songs of Exile by Hebrew Poets* with the Society back in 1901, at the age of twenty-four, under her maiden name of Nina Davis. By 1916, when plans for the classics took shape, she had become a recognized literary figure in England, closely associated with Israel Abrahams and Israel Zangwill. She was delighted to be asked to participate in the classics series with them and was the only woman known to have been invited; Halevi's poetry, she understood, could be her literary monument. War caused various delays, but she submitted her manuscript in 1922, based largely on the critical text of Halevi's divan prepared by Heinrich Brody. Her neatly bundled package, representing years of effort, lay unread for months; Dobsevage and Adler were apparently too caught up in the Society's financial problems to notice it.[46]

Sadly, by the time the Society took up her manuscript, she was already in the throes of a terminal illness. Her husband, Dr. Redcliffe N. Salaman, a leading Anglo-Jewish figure in his own right, appealed to the Society: Could the book possibly appear while his wife yet lived? Cyrus Adler was determined that it would, and as usually happened when he took matters directly into his own hands, action followed. The readers read, the printers printed, and correspondence sped back and forth across the Atlantic resolving problems. The Society, for example, had altered some of Salaman's titles for Halevi's poems, and she insisted that they be changed back. "Had they been retained," her husband fumed, "it would have marked her down not only as lacking in poetic feeling and taste, but as an amateur, whereas in point of fact she is probably the least amateurish of any orientalist, being exact and accurate to a degree." A disagreement also broke out over the spelling of Halevi's first name: Salaman wanted "Yehudah," Adler wanted "Judah" and they compromised with "Jehudah."

Adler's goal, ironically, was to send out the first copy by Christmas of 1924, but the Hebrew Press did not have the volume ready in time. Furious as he was, Adler would not be stopped: "I had a few copies carried to the binder, folded by hand and mailed," he wrote, and although no fast boat was immediately available, he prayed that the book would arrive before it was too late. It did. "The Halevi volumes have arrived to-day and I must write at once and thank you for your successful efforts in getting it out sooner than we had expected," reads a letter from Redcliffe Salaman dated January 6, 1925. "My wife was very delighted to have it and to know that the work is complete." Nina Salaman died seven weeks later, on February 24.[47]

The story of Salaman's *Jehudah Halevi* reveals much about the classics series and the Society as a whole. Cyrus Adler's personal intervention (to the exclusion of both the editor and the secretary), the human concern displayed in the face of tragedy, the editorial heavy-handedness shown in attention to detail, and the obvious inefficiency of the office when Adler was not around to supervise—all reflect aspects of the Society that affected everything it did, for good and for bad. With the remaining classics the attention to detail was still there but without the same feeling of urgency, and with so much dependent on part-time employees and a committee of volunteer scholars the books proceeded much more slowly. The next title, Israel Abrahams's *Hebrew Ethical Wills* (in two volumes), suffered fully five years of delays. Adler, appalled at this sluggish pace, tried at one time to speed things up, but members of his classics committee, especially Jacob Z. Lauterbach, insisted that the work was full of errors and infelicities that needed correction. By the time everyone was satisfied, Abrahams had died; the work was published posthumously.[48]

There was, however, a bright side to all of this. When finally published in its improved form, *Hebrew Ethical Wills* was a magnificent achievement. No such collection of "testamentary directions for the religious and secular guidance of children" existed before in any language. Indeed, the very term "ethical will" was previously unknown; Professor Judah Goldin has recently suggested that Abrahams, one of the first scholars to approach the genre systematically, may actually have coined the expression himself. Furthermore, *Hebrew Ethical Wills* differed from previous volumes in the Schiff Classics in that it was also, quite overtly, a work of Jewish apologetics. In the anti-Semitic atmosphere of the "tribal twenties," it provided new data for those seeking to defend the Jewish image. Abrahams himself described the book as "a most effective vindication of the Jewish character." Later, Jews read the wills differently: as inspirational literature, as wisdom from the past, as "an audacious attempt at continuing speech from fathers in the grave to children in a reckless world." More than most of the other volumes published in the Schiff Classics, *Hebrew Ethical Wills* succeeded in speaking to a wide variety of readers, touching them in different ways, even stimulating some to write ethical wills of their own. Subsequently reprinted in a one-volume paperback edition (1976), the volume continues to inspire readers.[49]

Henry Malter's *The Treatise Ta'anit of the Babylonian Talmud*, published two years after Abrahams's volume, had far less widespread appeal. This came as no surprise, but there was no choice: A series of Jewish classics that omitted the Talmud would have been unthinkable. Wisely, then, Schechter selected for inclusion one of the most accessible of all the Talmudic tractates, and one with "great value as a source for Jewish history, liturgy, folklore, and other matters of interest." Equally wisely, he invited Henry Malter of Dropsie College to take on this assignment, for he was not only one of America's leading Jewish scholars but also one of the few men in the country whose work in rabbinics was taken seriously by European Jewish scholars.[50]

Born to a traditional household in Galicia, Malter had studied with the Jewish bibliographer and scholar Moritz Steinschneider, at the University of Heidelberg, and at the *Lehranstalt für die Wissenschaft des Judentums*. In 1900, with this *Wissenschaft* training behind him, he immigrated to the United States to assume a position at Hebrew Union College. He left there seven years later, "being at variance with the leaders of the institution as to the fundamentals of the theology of Reform Judaism...," and in 1904 was appointed professor of Talmud at Dropsie. *Ta'anit* was actually his second commission from JPS. Earlier JPS had invited him to produce a popular biography of Saadia Gaon of Babylonia for its Jewish Worthies series. Malter submitted instead a heavily footnoted work of enviable scholarship, employing for the first time evidence from the Cairo Genizah. Rather than revising so important a work, the Society published it as a "scientific volume" entitled *Saadia Gaon: His Life and Works* (1921), the first book issued under terms of the Morris Loeb bequest. According to some critics, it was "the best and most scholarly biography of a Jewish worthy ... in the English language."[51]

Now, in his *Ta'anit* volume, Malter again exceeded his mandate. Somewhat to the Society's surprise, he submitted an elaborate critical Hebrew text based on every manuscript extant, complete with a complex system of symbols designed to highlight textual variations and establish correct renderings. He saw his as a first attempt at a "scientific" edition of the Talmud employing *Wissenschaft* methodology. He urged the Society to continue his work and to take the same approach to other classic texts, such as the Mishnah, Tosefta, and the numerous halakhic and haggadic Midrashim.[52]

Nobody had ever before undertaken to do what Malter did, and everyone agreed that the task, although infinitely tedious, was of inestimable value to students of rabbinics. The Hebrew text of *Ta'anit* that Malter prepared reflected great scholarship and originality, and was a remarkable demonstration of how far Jewish studies in America had come from the days when Max Margolis abandoned the field of rabbinics for want of available resources (Malter was able to use at least twelve rare books and manuscripts found in American libraries). But the manuscript itself was far too large and complex to be included in the classics series; it needed to be printed as a folio. As a result, Adler arranged that the American Academy of Religion (he was its president, Malter its secretary) would print the full work, complete with critical apparatus, in a limited edition. The Society, having drawn the line beyond which its scholarly publications would not go, published only the final fruits of Malter's tireless research: the new improved text that he had derived from studying the full range of variants. It also published (not without grumbling) a valuable commentary of cross references and citations, as well as the full English translation—save for one paragraph, an earthy Midrash about Rahab the Harlot, that the learned Malter saw fit to translate into Latin, presumably to avoid offending readers' sensitivities. A lonely and unhappy man who suffered a great deal in his lifetime, Malter died before seeing any of his *Ta'anit* work in print. Having read the first proofs of his manuscript, and with the bulk of his life's work still unfinished, he wasted away of cancer in 1925 when he was only 61 years old.[53]

With the publication of *Ta'anit*, the classics series began to move more quickly. Grodinsky, knowing that delays were expensive, permitted fewer of them; Adler, feeling his age, sought to close the series out. As a result, between 1929 and 1936 all five of the remaining titles appeared, twelve volumes in all. First to be published was Isaac Husik's five-volume edition of *Sefer Ha-'Ikkarim: Book of Principles* (1929–30) by Joseph Albo, a translation and critical edition of a popular fifteenth-century work that attempted to answer for its day a perennial question: What are the basics of Jewish belief that distinguish Judaism from other religions? The work was a particularly good choice for inclusion in the classics series since it nicely exemplifies many characteristic features of medieval Jewish thought, sheds light on Jewish social life, covers a wide range of philosophic subjects, and deals with fundamental religious questions of continuing relevance. In addition, published texts of the work varied widely, in part owing to censorship, so the need for a critical edition and translation was apparent.

Husik originally believed that he would need only two volumes for the text including "just enough notes to explain words and phrases which might otherwise be unintelligible." As happened so often in the series, however, the assignment took on a life of its own. By the time he was done, his manuscript filled 2,692 pages, boasted hundreds of scholarly notes, and claimed acceptance as the "standard edition" of the Hebrew as well as the English—which in fact it has remained. Grodinsky understandably grumbled that the five volumes cost $28,862.45 to publish, almost 58 percent of the entire sum Schiff had allocated for the series as a whole! But since Husik was the Society's editor, scholarship triumphed over business sense, and the five volumes appeared.[54]

Jacob Z. Lauterbach's *Mekilta de-Rabbi Ishmael*, the only volume in the Schiff Classics to appear without a translation of the title, was an indication of just how scholarly the series and the Society as a whole had become. The *Mekilta*—a title that most Jews couldn't even pronounce—is a Tannaitic Midrash, a body of ancient commentary and traditional interpretation covering large sections of the book of Exodus. Lauterbach employed no fewer than twenty-seven sources in preparing his critical Hebrew text, and he devised an elaborate methodology for deciding which text to adopt in the case of variant readings. His introduction alone was more than four times longer than planned, and his final manuscript, including the English translation, biblical citations, and critical notes on facing pages, ballooned to three volumes instead of one.[55] Some of Lauterbach's material had previously appeared among the legends preserved in Louis Ginzberg's *Legends of the Jews*, but Ginzberg emphasized readability and consigned all scholarly material to separately printed notes. Following the Society's mandate back in 1909, he had catered first to his popular audience and met scholarly needs second. Twenty-four years later, by the time Lauterbach's volumes appeared, the Society's priorities had changed.

The next volume in the series, the *Ma'aseh Book*, a classic work of Jewish folktales and legends, had become mired in controversy in 1920. Louis Ginzberg charged that the introduction by Moses Gaster, chief rabbi of the Sephardic community of England, was riddled with errors. David Philipson demonstrated that the same was true of Gaster's translation. Adler, for his part, considered the text too frank and thought it "advisable to omit a few stories altogether." Gaster was too independent and too egotistic to accept criticisms lightly, and in one letter, written by his secretary, he charged Adler with entertaining "a personal animosity towards him." In the end, Isaac Husik simply re-edited large sections of the manuscript, and, after more acrimonious correspondence, JPS published it—to nobody's total satisfaction. Yet the *Ma'aseh Book* was the most accessible of all the Schiff Classics: It contained interesting, if sometimes horrifying tales with none of the burdensome scholarly trappings (and foreign language text) that made works like the *Mekilta* seem so forbidding. Alone of all the classics, it was deemed popular enough to be distributed to the membership at large.[56]

The last two titles in the Schiff Classics, *Selected Poems of Moses Ibn Ezra* and *Mesillat Yesharim: The Path of the Upright* are noteworthy as much because of the men who translated them as for the texts themselves. In the case of Ibn Ezra's poetry, the translator was seventy-seven-year-old Dr. Solomon Solis-Cohen. One of the Society's few surviving founders, Solis-Cohen was actually a medical doctor by profession; by avocation, he had long been a poet, translator, and gentleman scholar, though never before published in so professional a forum. Here he collaborated with Professor Heinrich Brody of Berlin, the world's greatest expert in Spanish poetry, whose Hebrew texts had been used as the basis for the Jehudah Halevi volume. Brody selected the examples of poetry to be included, supplied accurate Hebrew texts, wrote an introduction, and added 153 pages of small-print scholarly notes. The undaunted Solis-Cohen translated the poems into English, supplied a foreword of his own, and added yet another forty pages of "notes on translation," some of them no less scholarly. The result, not originally foreseen, is a true synthesis of German and American scholarship, yet another symbolic reminder that the days when American Jews "merely" translated the fruits of German Jewish scholarship were over; they were now making original scholarly contributions of their own.[57]

Fittingly, the final volume of the Schiff Classics was by Mordecai Kaplan, the only one of the professional scholars involved in the series to be educated and trained completely in the United States. One of the most creative figures in twentieth-century American Judaism, Kaplan served as professor of homiletics at the Jewish Theological Seminary, and when he was commissioned in 1916, he was also serving as rabbi of New York's Jewish Center. His colleagues looked down on him somewhat because he did not fully immerse himself in scholarly pursuits; but since he actively participated in community affairs and concerned himself with social ethics, he was the natural person to turn to for a translation of Moses Hayyim Luzzatto's eighteenth-century ethical treatise, *Mesillat Yesharim* ("The Path of the Upright"). Kaplan proved an excellent choice. Not only was the translation judged to be "beautiful" and "elegant," but the introduction was among the most significant written for any of the volumes—indeed, one of the most stimulating and succinct (albeit least-known) discussions of Jewish ethics in the English language.[58]

Kaplan, who always wrote for an intelligent lay readership rather than for scholars, was at the time formulating his own broad view of Judaism as a "religious civilization."[59] He saw works like Luzzatto's as serving a distinct didactic and apologetic function: They demonstrated that accusations of Judaism's narrowness and inner bankruptcy—claims "that Judaism was nothing but a formal system of practices which exacted outward conformity regardless of inner meaning or attitude of mind and heart"—were, historically speaking, "groundless." He also realized that behind a work like Luzzatto's lay relevant issues of no small interest to contemporary Jews. As a result, he set his discussion of Luzzatto's work within the widest context of Jewish ethics and in terms that lay readers could understand. He then extended his analysis to explain three specific points of divergence that distinguished traditional Jewish ethics from the secular (or "philosophic") ethics that so many Jews actually embraced:

> (1) [P]hilosophic ethics confines itself to conduct affecting our social relationships. Jewish ethics includes the entire gamut of human conduct; it gives to the cultus or religious observances at least as important a place as to social conduct.
>
> (2) [P]hilosophic ethics recognizes no authority but that of reason based on experience; all philosophic ethics is therefore humanistic. Jewish ethics does not deny the authority of reason, but subordinates it to the authority of God who has made His will known through the Torah and the Prophets. Jewish ethics is, therefore, theocentric.
>
> (3) [P]hilosophic ethics relies upon knowledge of the effect, in terms of individual and social well-being, that flows directly from the deed, as a stimulus to the good and as a deterrent from evil. Jewish ethics points to the system of rewards and punishments which, according to tradition, are meted out by God. There is no direct causal relationship between virtue and its reward, or sin and its retribution. What the reward or retribution shall be in each instance is ordained by God.[60]

In a fitting capstone to the classics series as a whole, Kaplan ended his introduction with an explanation of why the *Mesillat Yesharim*, and by inference other traditional Jewish texts of its type, should be read and studied. They will "ever serve as a true mirror," he wrote, "reflecting the inwardness and spirituality which Judaism demanded of those who lived in conformity with its laws."[61]

The Jewish Communities Series

Beside the classics, the Society had previously committed itself to publishing several other volumes that appeared during this period. Two learned volumes of notes by Louis Ginzberg to his *Legends of the Jews*, long-delayed volumes of essays by Ginzberg and Solomon Schechter (published posthumously), and Paul Goodman's *Moses Montefiore*, the last in the Jewish Worthies Series—all finally saw the light of day in the 1920s and were issued with barely concealed relief. In 1931 the Society fulfilled a long-overdue promise made to Hermann L. Strack and finally issued an English-language edition of his famous *Introduction to the Talmud and Midrash*, published in five German editions dating back to 1887, and characterized as "indispensable" by the usually hard-to-please Alexander Marx. Strack was a Christian philo-Semite who made numerous important contributions to rabbinic scholarship and courageously defended the Talmud against anti-Semitic critics. Despite his open involvement in Christian missionary activities directed toward Jews, he befriended leading Jewish scholars. His *Introduction*, in addition to being a wonderful reference work, refuted claims heard even in America in the 1920s that the Talmud was a "secret book" that Jews conspired to keep hidden from Christians. "May this Introduction to the Talmud," Strack prayed, "help to further a knowledge of truth and thereby also a just judgement." Eager to see this prayer answered, the American Jewish Committee and the Central Conference of American Rabbis helped sponsor the long-delayed revised translation, and it was carried out (anonymously) by Max Margolis, whom Strack had befriended years before. In 1969 the *Introduction* was published as a paperback, and it was still in print in 1987—a century after its first publication.[62]

The rest of the previously commissioned books that appeared during this period formed part of what was originally known as the Historical Jewish Community Series, published in eight volumes from 1929 to 1943. Like so many other projects, this one too had originated in the fertile mind of Solomon Schechter, perhaps influenced by his own personal experiences in different Jewish communities around the world as well as his scholarly studies of their characteristic features. Community studies of various sorts were in vogue early in the century—E. P. Dutton, for example, ran a series on medieval towns—and the JPS series demonstrated that Jews too played a part (indeed, no small part) in the history of the world's great cities. Whatever the reason, a committee consisting of Schechter, David Philipson, and Solomon Solis-Cohen (Alexander Marx was added in 1916) met to plan the series in 1914, and by the time Schechter died, short histories of the Jews in Rome, Cairo, and Amsterdam had already been commissioned. Under David Philipson, who succeeded Schechter as chairman, the list of communities to be included in the series grew. Renamed the Jewish Community Series, its mandate was also broadened: One plan called for soliciting a volume on at least one central community in every major country where Jews lived, including Turkey, North Africa, Palestine, and Western Asia. As usual, those who signed on with the series received a long list of instructions, including such by now familiar phrases as "popular," "sound research and information," and "interesting style." Also as usual, authors delivered their manuscripts years late. But in this case, when completed manuscripts began to arrive at the Society's headquarters, disappointment set in. The books, to quote Solomon Grayzel, "made a fetish out of dullness."[63]

To some extent, the problem was characteristic of the genre as a whole. Community histories, narrow by their very nature, easily fall prey to filiopietism and antiquarianism. Community natives, and those especially interested in a particular place, may still be drawn to them, but not the average reader—unless the histories are written with particular charm. Compounding the problem was the fact that most of the Society's volumes were composed abroad by people unacquainted with the needs of the American Jewish reading public. Some certainly included in their volumes material of great scholarly importance as well as data not otherwise available in English. But it was data that properly belonged in scholarly monographs and learned journals, not in the popular series that the Society intended.[64]

After only three volumes in the series had appeared— *Frankfort*, *London*, and *Venice*—Professor Abraham A. Neuman of Dropsie, himself a historian, recognized some of these problems and suggested that it might be wiser to replace the community series with "single volumes devoted to single countries." The publication committee also discussed changing the series; some members suggested killing it outright. But the Society had made commitments and kept them, even though volume after volume was criticized. In a devastating review of the series as a whole in the *Menorah Journal*, Cecil Roth, who had himself written the volume on Venice, was particularly merciless. He attacked everything from the Society's choice of authors, to its selection of cities, to its inadequate editing of the manuscripts submitted. He noted niggling errors and major problems (Raphael Straus's "highly specialized volume on Regensburg and Augsburg"). Most of all, he lambasted the style of the volumes he reviewed, which he somewhat immodestly contrasted to the "dramatic" and "lively" prose characteristic of his own writing. Actually, his *Venice*, although among the most important and certainly the easiest to read of the series, was itself not above criticism. Instead of documenting every fact with footnotes that could be checked, Roth "respectfully requested" readers to take it on faith that he had seen "evidence which appears to him reliable." Still, the criticisms he leveled at the other volumes in the series, much as they made his friends at the Society wince, struck a responsive chord. After his review appeared, the Society went on to publish Israel Cohen's *Vilna* (1943)—by then, alas, a memorial to a community that was no more—and thereafter it quietly let the Jewish Communities Series die.[65]

"Margolis and Marx" and Other Histories

If the community histories that it published during this period were not successful, the Society did commission and publish historical volumes of enduring significance during these years, especially when it found adequate funding for them. History continued to be the members' favorite genre, and because Jewish history books, unlike Jewish novels, were difficult to place with commercial publishers, the Society attracted the cream of the crop. Its greatest achievement in this realm was an authoritative one-volume history of the Jewish people, published in 1927, and co-authored by Max Margolis and Alexander Marx. The volume, less daunting than Graetz but more comprehensive and sophisticated than Lady Magnus's *Outlines*, filled a longstanding need. As early as 1901, Israel Abrahams had called for just such a semi-popular history, and in 1906 the Jewish Chautauqua Society strongly seconded the call, offering to cooperate with JPS if it could find someone to assume the task. The Society turned to Israel Friedlaender, and in 1907 he agreed to accept the commission, promising to complete the work in three years. Unfortunately, Friedlaender's manifold other obligations prevented him from carrying out his plan. In 1910, and again in 1914, he requested extensions. By the time of his tragic murder in 1920, the volume had still not materialized, although the need for it had become greater than ever.[66]

In 1923 the Society unexpectedly came into a windfall that permitted it to take up the subject of a one-volume history anew. Abraham Erlanger, a prominent New York philanthropist, heard from Cyrus Adler about the need for a one-volume history and saw in the idea great potential for fighting anti-Semitism, a major concern given the anti-Jewish propaganda disseminated by, among others, Henry Ford. Fortuitously, he was then executor of the estate of Rosetta M. Ulman of Williamsport Pennsylvania, who, according to Erlanger, "often expressed an interest in the idea of a compact History of the Jews which in simple and concise form, should not only educate the Jews themselves in the story of their past, but should also help to bring about a better understanding of them and their ideals by non-Jews." With this money, which he quietly supplemented from his own funds, he put together a $16,000 sum to cover the costs both of preparing a one-volume history and of distributing twelve thousand free copies, including a significant number to "non-Jewish institutions, societies and individuals"—the same places, surely by no coincidence, where copies of Ford's *The International Jew* were being sent at no charge. Given the immediacy of the need, and knowing the Society's past record, Erlanger made sure to stipulate that "this volume shall be completed and actually ready for distribution within two (2) years and six (6) months from the date of your acceptance of my offer."[67]

Having received the money, the Society offered a contract to Alexander Marx, who knew more about Jewish history than any other American Jewish scholar of the day. But he claimed to have too heavy a workload already, and was not up to the task. Max Margolis, who had proved that he could be trusted to finish a job on time and had authored short books on aspects of biblical history for the Society, was more interested; Margolis, however, was not at all expert in the modern and medieval periods. Collaboration was the only solution and was in fact agreed upon. Margolis would actually write the volume for a fee of $5,000; Marx would receive $3,000 for supplying his lecture notes and other data, as well as for working with Margolis to ensure the accuracy of "every fact and date and expression."[68]

Margolis began his assignment immediately and then left for a year in Jerusalem, where he taught both at the American School of Oriental Research and the newly opened Hebrew University. "I love the place, " he wrote of Jerusalem, "and am thrilled by the atmosphere. I have made a circle of friends and everybody has treated me most kindly." Even with all his boyish enthusiasm and footloose touring, he still put in seven long hours a day on the history. In September, he reported to JPS that he had made "good progress." "The whole thing," he wrote, "is shaping itself beautifully." Tragedy marred this joy when one of his two young sons took sick in Jerusalem and died; but Margolis, who never recovered from the loss, somehow managed to push on.

By the end of 1925, back in Philadelphia, Margolis had reached the year 1815 in his narrative. His early chapters, revised in long sessions with Alexander Marx, were being revised once more, thanks to suggestions from a committee of readers. Four months later, Adler happily announced to the trustees that the manuscript was finished; Margolis had worked his magic once again. The history took longer than expected to print, especially since it contained color maps and valuable chronological tables. It also cost almost twice as much as budgeted. Recognizing how much had nevertheless been accomplished in a remarkably short time, Erlanger agreeably extended his deadline for a few months and generously paid all the excess costs. The Society celebrated the handsome volume's publication in early 1927. In a year of continued financial crisis, the one-volume history was a ray of light, a reminder of what the Society could achieve with the right people and adequate funding.[69]

In its 737 pages of text, *A History of the Jewish People* reflected a fascinating combination of Jewish traditionalism, European scholarship, American patriotism, and enthusiastic Zionism. The early chapters, dealing with the Biblical period, were essentially noncontroversial. Although Margolis was certainly familiar with the radical new theories of biblical history propounded by critical scholars, he assumed, even more than in his *Micah*, what he and Marx called with delicious elusiveness "an attitude free of mistrust in the essential veracity of tradition." In other respects, the history leaned heavily on Graetz and the *Jewish Encyclopedia* but viewed Jewish history in terms of shifting centers of Jewish life, a conception borrowed from Simon Dubnow. It also devoted more attention than previous

Jewish histories did to social and economic forces, subjects that historians generally had begun to see as important.[70]

Particularly striking was the treatment of America. Not only was American Jewish history covered fully and integrated into the larger framework of the narrative, rather than left as a separate chapter, but America was actually given primacy in the modern period. Book Five, "The Age of Emancipation," opened with the chapter "Jews in America," preceding "Jewish Emancipation in France." The idea, of course, was to make the American Revolution the turning point in Jewish history rather than the French Revolution. Yet if American Jewish history received its due here, the future, as far as Margolis and Marx were concerned, lay with Zion. The two authors saw "the new exodus from Eastern Europe and the creation of the center in the ancient homeland" as the start of a new era. Their very last paragraph described "the foundation for Jewish cultural revival in Palestine" symbolized "by the creation of the Hebrew University of Jerusalem"— an event that Margolis was present to watch. Their peroration, quoted from the High Commissioner's statement on that occasion, well reflected Margolis's and Marx's own Zionist sentiments: "Blessed be He who hath kept us alive to reach this day!"[71]

JPS watched with pleasure as its one-volume history won acceptance in classrooms, achieved a wide sale, and was translated into French and Spanish. Naturally there were also criticisms: Some thought the volume too dry and encyclopedic; others disagreed with its presentation of the modern period. But everyone agreed that it was the most comprehensive, most accurate, and most effectively organized one-volume Jewish history on the market. At the same time, however, it was still very much of a textbook—not the kind of volume that most people read for pure enjoyment. From that point of view, Graetz's history was more successful. What the Society still needed, especially given the many weighty tomes among its selections, was someone who could write history effectively in a thoroughly popular style—a latter-day Solomon Schechter or Israel Abrahams.

Max Radin, who had previously written *The Jews Among the Greeks and Romans*, tried to cast himself in this role with a popular volume about Jews in biblical times, but it proved a disappointment. Although he was a significant scholar, his field was not Bible, and popular writing was not his metier.[72] Through its community series, however, the Society had discovered one serious historian who did fit the bill, a man who could produce creative, first-class scholarship in readable style. His name was Cecil Roth.

Born in England in 1899 and educated at the City of London School and at Oxford, Roth was a trained historian who had written his first major book on the Florentine Republic. He shifted into Jewish history at a young age and began a lifetime of voluminous writing, publishing over 600 items. Roth fit the stereotype of an English gentleman scholar and might easily have been mistaken for his own caricature, complete with liberal dashes of eccentricity, charm, and Anglophilia. But if his personality and temperament mocked the dry, "scientific" ideal of German Jewish scholarship, and even if he researched and wrote history, as he claimed, for the sheer pleasure of it, he nevertheless possessed an original, exacting, and creative mind. These qualities ultimately won him his appointment as reader in Jewish Studies at Oxford in 1939.[73]

Roth and JPS quickly realized that they could be of service to one another. The Society gave Roth an American outlet for his facile pen and allowed him to make far more money from his writings (and from the lucrative American lectures that so often came in their wake) than he could have done otherwise. Roth gave the Society the kind of popular scholarship that its members loved, providing an effective counterweight to those who thought that it should be publishing only dry-as-dust scholarship. During one period in the 1930s, when he was still earning his living mainly from his writing and lecturing, the Society published a book of his every other year—a fact that reportedly prompted one member of the publication committee to wonder sardonically whether the Society was becoming his "official publishers."[74] Later, from 1946 to 1948, when he was already full-time at Oxford, JPS published three books of his in three years. Even today, many of these volumes remain the most readable surveys of their subject on the market.

A History of the Marranos, published in 1932, indicates why. Characteristically, Roth begins with a captivating pronouncement: "I have the great honor to present to the Reader, in the following pages, what may fairly be described as the most romantic episode in all history." He then briefly sets forth the story's various significant aspects. ("I stand astonished at my own moderation," he wrote, "in having compressed them into chapters, or even paragraphs.") Yet he remained sensitive to the reader's point of view. Thus, although he privately opined that "the history of the Marranos in America is only a trifling aspect of the question," he devoted to the subject, by his own admission, "disproportionate space." He likewise emphasized British aspects of the story, in both cases because he knew that readers would be interested. On the other hand, he consciously downplayed the sometimes unlovely economic aspects of Marrano life that may on occasion have given rise to their persecution. "I would not dare to make [this point] in public," he privately confessed, but "it would have been possible to write this story in anything but a heroic strain." To his credit, he refused to skip over these "less pleasant aspects" altogether, as some suggested he do, but again it was the satisfaction of readers rather than the demands of scholarship that ultimately determined his course.[75] "In the books I have written for the Society," he explained:

> I have done my best to produce a dramatic story and to tell it in a lively fashion. It has not always been easy, and I may not always have been successful; but in publications that are intended for the general reader, such as yours are, it is absolutely essential for the author to make the attempt, and for the publisher to

insist on its being made.... It entails a certain amount of planning. It entails, too, a certain amount of pruning, and the sacrifice of some choice antiquarian details. But it is the least that the reader and purchaser have the right to expect.[76]

Roth's views, backed up by the success of his own volumes, certainly influenced the Society's attitude toward history. Other factors, however, also entered into the selection policies. As before, for example, it looked especially hard for books dealing with American Jewish history. These continued to be difficult to find, given the dearth of professionals in the field, but in 1929, it issued its first: David Philipson's *Letters of Rebecca Gratz*. Henry Clay, one of the great names in American history, figured indirectly in this volume, because his grandson, Thomas Hart Clay, had married Anna, the niece of Rebecca Gratz, and it was she who presented these fascinating letters of Philadelphia's best-known early American Jewish woman to Philipson. He edited them in Victorian style, omitting "such portions as are of too intimate a family nature to be paraded before the public eye," and convinced the Sisterhood of his Rockdale Temple to sponsor their publication in honor of his fortieth anniversary with the congregation. Cyrus Adler disapproved of some of Philipson's anachronistic notes on Reform Jewish practice, but pronounced the volume "interesting and valuable"; the President of the American Jewish Historical Society, A.S.W. Rosenbach, also recommended their publication. The letters appeared, thanks to the subsidy, without delay.[77]

In 1936 the Society published a more important book on American Jewish history, Isaac Goldberg's *Major Noah*. The first-ever full-scale biography of Mordecai Manuel Noah—a leading early American journalist, politician, and playwright, and the foremost American Jew of his day—brought to bear important new sources, was written in a popular style, and remained the standard work on the subject for almost half a century; it was even published in a special trade edition by Alfred A. Knopf. JPS did not manage in this period to commission a comprehensive history of American Jews, although it tried; to its credit, it passed up the chance to publish many an inferior volume of gross filiopietism. But the two volumes it did issue were enough to give it a foothold in the field and paved the way for more substantial publications in American Jewish history later on.[78]

During the 1930s, American Jewish history commanded far less attention than did events across the Atlantic in Germany. The rise of Nazism, followed by Hitler's accession to power in 1933, confronted American Jews with what many rightly saw as an even greater challenge to Jewish well-being than the Russian czar had been a generation earlier. Just as all Jewish organizations, including the Society, had involved themselves in the earlier anti-Russian campaign, protesting the Kishinev Pogrom and battling for the abrogation of America's commercial treaty with Russia, they all also, in one way or another, participated in a massive campaign against Germany. The *American Jewish Year Book*, now jointly published by JPS and the American Jewish Committee, devoted large sections of its "Review of the

Year" to German events. "The year 5693," it predicted with frightening accuracy, "will stand out in the post-Exilic history of the Jewish people as the year in which a country universally regarded as an outpost of civilization and culture permitted itself to be led astray by a malicious race mania onto a path of the most degrading mass persecution."[79]

Another book was also published with the German situation in mind: Albert Tager's *The Decay of Czarism*. A historical exposé of the notorious 1913 Mendel Beiliss "ritual murder" trial in Kiev, it was based on hitherto secret czarist documents and was translated from a volume published in Moscow in 1933. Although apparently commissioned by the Soviets to curry favor with the West by proving the anti-Semitic nature of the pre-revolutionary Russian regime, by the time it appeared in English the volume had a different lesson to teach, as the publication committee made clear in a special preface:

> The story of the book, horrible and depressing as it is, is both instructive and timely. The Jews are again the object of attack in Germany. Similar tactics are employed by their traducers, even to the ritual murder accusation. No originality is required in an autocrat who desires to influence the opinion of the masses, neither is truth an essential. Brazenness and cynicism will do the work—for a time. History moves slowly and patiently, but in the end retribution comes, "overflowing with righteousness."

Tager's was the first JPS book to be clothed in a paper jacket. A struggling young artist named Howard Alper had proposed this innovation, urging that it would help JPS compete in the marketplace. The jacket he designed aroused considerable comment, including the remark by one member "that this was the first one of the Society's publications which immediately challenged his interest when he received it." Alper subsequently designed over one hundred JPS book jackets and modernized the Society's advertising, logo, and stationery.[80]

As the situation in Germany worsened, the Society realized that it needed to produce a special book to provide in-depth information about German Jewry. The result was Marvin Lowenthal's *The Jews of Germany*, published in 1936. Like Margolis and Marx's history, this was a commissioned volume, paid out of a specific grant and demanded by a specific date. In June 1933, Philadelphia lawyer (and later judge) Louis E. Levinthal had suggested such a volume, and the idea won approval at a special joint meeting of the publication committee and the trustees on July 5. Three clear reasons for the book were articulated: "the prevailing ignorance of the subject, the fact that Jews in this country have been 'extraordinarily callous' to the existing situation . . . and the likely advantages to the Society of the publication of such a volume." As usual, the goal was a book that would be not only "accurate" but "readable as well." After much discussion, JPS turned to Marvin Lowenthal, a professional writer and lecturer with a German Jewish background, who had published several popular books of Jewish interest with non-

Jewish houses and had authored various non-Jewish books, too—in short, the kind of man whom the Society could not usually attract. Thanks to a donor, Lowenthal received a modest advance—less than his usual fee, but he conceded that this was an "emergency situation"—and he promised to return, manuscript in hand, within a few months.

The months stretched into years, for Lowenthal underestimated what the job would entail and was chronically short of money. Still, within less than thirty-six months *The Jews of Germany* was out and the Society boasted that it "has received the finest press comments of any book we have ever published." The volume sold over twelve thousand copies, including a trade edition published by Longmans, Green and Co., and even decades later remained the only one-volume German Jewish history in English. Unfortunately, Lowenthal expected to make more money from the book than he did, and he was bitter—partly at the Society for underpaying him, partly at the world for praising his book rather than buying it (although by the Society's standards, it had sold well). In the end, however, the book stood the test of time better than anything else he authored.[81]

Although *The Jews of Germany* has since become dated, the volume still commands respect for its farsightedness—especially when compared to other writings of the period. First, anticipating a theme later popularized by postwar historians, Lowenthal linked Nazi persecutions of the Jews to earlier persecutions dating back to medieval times; he did not view the Nazis as simply an aberration. Second, he understood that the Nazis were not persecuting Jews alone but others as well, and that their persecution of Jews would not be confined to Germany alone but would probably spread. Finally, and most importantly, he predicted that "nothing can be reckoned upon to divert or soften the effort toward extermination." More commonly, American Jewish writers in this period offered words of consolation, a sense, found even in the Society's preface to Alexander Tager's book, that "this too will pass." Lowenthal put forward a picture that most Americans needed to hear yet were still unwilling to accept. The book ended with the word "death" still ringing in its readers' ears.[82]

Light Reading

For all of its interest in history and the classics, to say nothing of contemporary affairs, the publication committee did not totally forget that members enjoyed books of light reading—novels, stories, travel accounts, and the like. In 1930, to be sure, a report to the board of trustees insisted that "our present membership is not interested ... in fiction, and they have turned more nearly to what we might call serious books on Jewish subjects,"[83] but most of the Society's experience suggested otherwise. The real problem was twofold: first, that commercial publishers snapped up the kind of high-quality popular books that members wanted because JPS lacked the resources to compete. For example, Ludwig Lewisohn's brilliant anti-assimilationist novel, *The Island Within* (1928), seems not to have been offered to the publication committee at all but went instead to Harper and Brothers. Second, most Jewish fiction from this period was either too sexually explicit or too frankly assimilationist for the Society's taste; the books could never pass its "dignity" test. What we see here again is that the Society's leadership consisted more and more of people at odds with contemporary culture. This made it difficult to meet persistent demands from members for books of light reading, but not, of course, impossible.

There was, for example, the one great novel that the Society did issue during this period: Sholom Asch's *Kiddush Ha-Shem*, translated from Yiddish and published in 1926. Born in 1880 in Kutno, Russian Poland, Asch[84] had settled in New York in 1917. He was introduced to the Society by the well-known East Side journalist and New York Alderman (at the time, Asch's agent), Charney Vladeck, who urged the Society to translate Asch's historical opus about the life of Polish Jews during the Cossack massacres of 1648. "It is full of ardor for the Jewish faith and Jewish capacity for self-sacrifice," Vladeck wrote. "Besides being artistic from a technical and a literary standpoint, it is inspiring as a work of a Jew who managed to understand and express a tragic period in the history of the Jews."

Cyrus Adler, who at one time or another seems to have met almost everybody, knew and respected Asch ("both as a man and as an artist"), and the Society, recognizing the importance of East European Jews, was pleased to have another Yiddish volume to translate. After the usual delays, it issued *Kiddush Ha-Shem* to considerable acclaim. What made the novel particularly valuable from the Society's point of view was the fact that it highlighted a historical period—Poland at the time of the Cossack massacres in 1648—yet shed light on Jewish heroism and martyrdom in more recent memory as well. The book's values were traditional, and it was good history too. Members liked it so well that the Society followed it up with a translation of Asch's *Sabbatai Zevi*—one of the few plays it ever issued— a dramatic account, based on the life of the mystical seventeenth-century false Messiah and the movement he spawned. That, however, was the last of Asch's work to appear on its list. Once he became known in America, Asch found more lucrative commercial publishers for his books; at the same time his novels, from a Jewish point of view, became much more controversial.[85]

The Society published no other adult fiction during this period, although it rejected many submissions. Instead, it sought to capture the imagination of its members through richly evocative tales of Jewish life around the world, as recounted by travelers and old-time residents—all of them, significantly, East European Jews by birth. In 1927 it published Nahum Slouschz's *Travels in North Africa*, a historically as well as anthropologically important volume dealing with Jewish communities that most American Jews knew little about—Libya, Morocco, and Tunisia. With a novelist's flair, Slouschz described in rich detail unusual customs and out-of-the-way places. Some of his data were not his own, for we now know that he gave less than due credit to his native guide, Mordechai Hakohen. He also shaped his facts to make them agree with his wrongheaded nineteenth-century theories of history and culture. But his book, reprinted in 1944 with the more sober title, *The Jews of North Africa*, was sufficiently exotic to please readers of every sort. Even in translation from the original French, it preserved all the excitement of a first-person narrative account.[86]

Worlds That Passed, by A. S. Sachs, editor of the New York Yiddish daily *The Tog*, appeared a year after Slouschz's book and described Jewish life as he remembered it in Europe before the ravages of World War I. Translated from the author's highly acclaimed Yiddish memoir, the account is a moving but obviously romantic tribute to the "many truly beautiful customs and practices associated with the Jewish life of Lithuania and Samut that are now gone forever." What made it unique was its emphasis on class analysis: "There were," Sachs wrote "always two opposing factions; the aristocratic and the democratic factions." As a dyed-in-the-wool Socialist, Sachs found economic motivations in everything, even in small-town squabbles. For the most part, however, and certainly in his depiction of the masses, he portrayed an idyllic East European world, at once democratic, learned, and charitable. If that was not the Old World that most of the Society's members personally recalled, they could certainly agree with its values and, along with the author, "heave a sigh of regret at their loss."[87]

Perhaps the most evocative of all the books of this type was *The Feet of the Messenger*, a lyrical and gently humorous account by Yehoash (Solomon Bloomgarden) of his sojourn in Palestine during 1914–15. Written originally in Yiddish in three volumes and later translated into Hebrew, the work was seen at the time as having "succeeded in introducing to the reader the real atmosphere of Palestine," particularly in its sympathetic portrayal of "the quaint life and customs of the immigrant Jews." Yehoash described as an eyewitness the tragic effects brought on by the war, which forced him to return to New York. As the Society proudly pointed out, he also gave "a very complimentary account . . . of the conduct of American sailors towards poor refugees who were transported to safety." But more than anything else, he won praise for the beauty and poetry of his language—qualities that the translation preserved and that later won Yehoash a wide following when he put them to work in his Yiddish translation of the Bible.[88]

In addition to being a valuable memoir in its own right, *The Feet of the Messenger* reflected growing interest in Palestine among American Jews during the interwar years, particularly as refugees from persecution found homes in Zion, and romantic pioneers began to make the desert bloom. Although the Society tried to steer clear of controversial questions connected with political Zionism, it did seek to meet the hunger for books dealing with Palestine, preferably with popular works, written from a nonpartisan point of view that both Zionists and non-Zionists could embrace.

Zev Vilnay's Hebrew volume of Holy Land legends, published in London in 1929, filled the bill. The volume contained Hebrew and Arabic legends from different periods and relied on written and oral sources, but it was politically neutral. This seemed safe enough, so in 1932 the Society published an English edition of Vilnay entitled *Legends of Palestine*, a translation "with additions and re-arrangements," complete with sixty-nine illustrations of Holy Land sites. A special preface expressed the hope of the publication committee that the book might "bring from Palestine a message to those who see in the tales of simple folk the real spirit of the land"—as distinct, presumably, from the militant spirit stimulated by the Hebron riots of 1929. Thirty-eight years later, Vilnay published in Hebrew a two-volume enlarged edition of his legends, including eight times as much material. Subsequently, JPS prepared a new translation, with new illustrations, which it published in three volumes. Vilnay's own preface to this edition made no reference at all to "the spirit of the land." Instead, he held up his legends as something much more powerful: "The creation and product of the country which is cherished by Israel and all humanity."[89]

Children's Literature

During this period the Society continued to publish children's literature, a genre that the publication committee saw as important but did not fully understand. Even more than before, the books that it published in this category dripped with syrupy didacticism: They told children what the Society's authors, in good parental fashion, thought they should know and do, rather than appealing to children's own sense of fantasy and imagination. Elma Ehrlich Levinger authored instructive children's stories for Jewish holidays as well as moralistic Bible legends for children, the latter based on Louis Ginzberg's *Legends of the Jews*. Israel Goldberg, in a book geared for older children, produced a nostalgic and somewhat self-righteous volume of childhood memories from New York's Lower East Side. In 1928, the Society even published posthumously a children's book by the most time-worn children's book writer of them all, Abram S. Isaacs. His subject, appropriately enough, was "a Jewish school whose atmosphere was undoubtedly old-fashioned," and his book, predictably, was a failure. But its preface, written for parents, is highly revealing, for it sets forth the ideology that underlay not only his own writing but the Society's didactic view of children's literature as well:

In the education of our young people in this stirring era, a more earnest, inspiring note must be sounded. Our Jewish boys and girls must be fitted for our day, it is true, but not for our day alone. Past, present, and future can never be separated in Israel, nor can solemn obligations be lightly blown aside as empty bubbles. Reverence and knowledge must go hand in hand. The old fashions which developed faith and joyousness, modest living and resolute character have still their potency and cannot be abandoned without the gravest peril, as history so unerringly proves. Methods may change, but the foundations cannot be moved.[90]

Winds of change were, in fact, blowing through the field of Jewish children's literature during this period, but the Society, which lacked the benefit of professional guidance in this area, never felt them. Nothing resembling the charming *Judische Jugendbucher* (1920) series appearing in Germany was discussed by the publication committee, nor did anyone pay attention to the important call issued in 1924 for a new style of Jewish children's writing that would "dispel the illusion with which our children are growing up, that Jewish life has always been too austere to lend itself to fairies, too confined to the ghetto to dream of green fields and sunny skies, too oppressed to produce real heroes, and too much absorbed with grim reality to be conscious of a magic world."[91] When Sadie Rose Weilerstein approached JPS in 1933 with her magical "K'tonton" manuscript, it could not appreciate the book's pathbreaking character and immense value. The volume was rejected.

K'tonton was born, according to Weilerstein's own account, when her husband, a Conservative rabbi, read aloud to her S.Y. Agnon's fabulous tale of Rabbi Gadiel Hatinok, a tiny rabbi, finger-sized but adult, who saves the Jewish people from a blood accusation. When her son asked what his father was reading, she answered him "about a tiny person, so high," sticking up her thumb. He insisted on hearing the story, but she didn't want to tell a five-year-old about a blood accusation. "So I turned the tiny person into a thumb-sized boy much like himself, except for size, who took a ride on a chopping knife and wished he hadn't. It was my husband who gave him his name, meaning 'very tiny' in Hebrew." Stories about K'tonton, an impish combination "of mischief and morality, of Jewish observance and universal values" made their popular debut in the first issue (September 1930) of the Women's League *Outlook*, the journal of the national organizations of Conservative sisterhoods.

By 1933 Sadie Rose Weilerstein had accumulated enough material for a book. Submitted to the Society, it went, in the usual fashion, to three readers. The first, Rabbi Max Klein, disliked it but suggested sending it to somebody else. The second, Bernard Frankel, a prominent lawyer, disapproved of its style and did "not think the story would interest the members of the Jewish Publication Society or their children." The last and most distinguished reader, David Blondheim, a pioneering scholar and linguist (who at the time had no children but had once written a school textbook for teaching French), found the story "unreadable," "without probability," "without charm," and (most revealingly of all) "without fact." On this basis, having apparently consulted neither children nor their teachers, nor anybody at all boasting fewer than two college degrees, the publication committee made its decision, and sent the volume back.[92]

Happily, K'tonton survived. The Women's League published *The Adventures of K'tonton* in 1935, and it became an instant classic, helped along by Professor Israel Davidson, a clandestine fan of children's literature, who in a widely read anonymous review fashioned a brilliant imaginary conversation between K'tonton and Alice in Wonderland. In later years, as we shall see, the Society published other successful books by Sadie Rose Weilerstein and changed its procedures so that books like *K'tonton* would not likely be rejected again. But *K'tonton* itself did not appear on its lists for four decades—until it published *K'tonton on an Island in the Sea* in 1976. Four years later, in honor of K'tonton's fiftieth birthday, all was forgiven. The Society suitably feted what had by now become the most beloved character in all of Jewish children's literature with a sumptuous volume entitled *The Best of K'tonton*, complete with an appreciative introduction by Francine Klagsbrun.[93]

Winds of Change

The Society's years of crisis coincided with a dramatic new development in the American book business: the success of the Book-of-the-Month Club, founded in 1926.[94] Where JPS marketed only its own books, advertised them on the basis of their inherent value ("Jewish Books in Every Jewish Home"[95]), and offered members a fixed number of books per year, the Book-of-the-Month Club was independent, sold books of different publishers preselected by a panel of experts, advertised books on the basis of their therapeutic value, and offered members both a wide array of choices and maximum convenience. Clearly, the new formula worked: Within a decade the club boasted 200,000 satisfied members.

The Society's leaders noticed the Book-of-the-Month Club's success. They even investigated several proposals aimed at starting a Jewish book club along similar lines (one of which resulted in the establishment of the Jewish Book Club, founded in 1930).[96] But with little money and a small membership, they held back. Rooted in the ideals of an earlier age, they expressed less interest in sales figures and profits than in the traditional functions of JPS: "education of its subscribers and readers," "conservation of Jewish cultural and spiritual resources," and "preservation of the self-respect and independence of the Jewish scholar and man of letters."[97]

If the Society did not completely restructure itself in response to its problems, it did begin a process that eventually resulted in significant changes and considerable growth. Clearing the way was Simon Miller's announcement on March 26, 1933, that after serving two consecutive decades as president he would not accept another term. A few months later, Cyrus Adler, Miller's friend and college classmate, resigned as chairman of the publication committee. He remained a member and continued to offer advice from afar, but no longer felt strong enough to wield the gavel. Both Adler and Miller were in their seventies, had devoted significant portions of their lives to the Society, and now were weary; they professed a desire to give some "younger man" a chance.[98] In fact, they both had a specific "younger man" in mind. He was a Philadelphian, a nephew of one of the Society's founders, and a person with all the right family connections. His name was Jacob Da Silva Solis-Cohen, Jr.

Solis-Cohen was forty-three when he became the Society's fourth president, and he had already spent many active years in Jewish communal life. By profession he was a real estate consultant and appraiser, which seems to have been his avocation as well. He had neither the specific literary interests of his uncle Solomon nor the broad cultural commitments that characterized the first generation of the Society's leaders. What he did have was the Solis-Cohen character—a rough, sometimes brash exterior. Yet he listened well, was full of enthusiasm, and refused to be bound by old conventions. He knew nothing about publishing (which he admitted), and very little even about the Society (which he did not admit). But within a few months he had concentrated in his own hands both the presidency of the Society and the chairmanship of the publication committee. Then, possibly taking his cue from the New Deal, he began work on a "five-year plan," and started to effect changes.[99]

First off, Solis-Cohen altered the Society's governing boards. He retired several inactive members of the publication committee, replaced them with two lawyers to "balance between the professors and the rabbis" around the table, and did away completely with the post of first vice-president, formerly reserved for a resident of New York. Next he tackled the Society's dilapidated offices. Not only did he have the rent reduced, but he forced the landlord to completely renovate the offices, "making them more attractive in every way." Finally, he inaugurated a long overdue reexamination of the Society's objectives, policies, and procedures.[100]

Personally, Solis-Cohen made known that he felt the Society should become more popular. He wanted at least one of its books each year to be a "readable book on a Jewish subject that would appeal to the laymen." But as a good businessman, he did not just rely on his own prejudices. He also consulted with outside experts and listened to them. The result was a comprehensive ten-point program that called, among other things, for a new effort at soliciting members by mail, a return to the use of traveling sales representatives, increased use of wholesale distributors and retail book stores, better public relations (including the publication of a bulletin), an improved physical appearance of new books, and most importantly, "development of plans to cooperate with commercial publishers for trade editions of the Society's books and for special offers of other publishers' books to our members at substantial discounts."[101]

In a further move to increase popularity, Solis-Cohen also initiated a reevaluation of the Society's policy on fiction. A five-point memo advised the Society on how to attract good fiction. A $2,500 prize novel contest, named for the Society's second and recently deceased president, Edwin Wolf, and funded by his children, sought to encourage first-rate submissions. There were even suggestions that the Society contact Henry Roth, whose *Call It Sleep* had just been published to rave reviews, to see if he would grace the Society's list ("some people say this boy is a genius," Cyrus Adler wrote, "I have not seen the book"). Through all of this Julius Grodinsky clucked negatively, certain that the "market for Jewish books" was "extremely limited," and that the spending of money "for advertising, circularization, etc." was actually "highly dangerous," given the low rate of return that could be expected. In 1936, however, he resigned "so that he might devote more of his time to his work as a member of the faculty of the Wharton School." To replace him, Jacob Solis-Cohen turned to a very different kind of man, one who shared his own youthful enthusiasm, viewed American Jewish life as positively as he did, and would be willing to lead the Society along the new path that he and his associates had begun to map out. The man he found was Maurice Jacobs, and with his appointment a new era in the history of JPS began.[102]

Jacob De Silva Solis-Cohen, Jr.

Isaac Husik (The American Jewish Archives)

Jacob R. Marcus (Portrait by Carlson)

Maurice Jacobs (The American Jewish Archives)

The JPS headquarters at 222 North 15th Street, Philadelphia, Pa. 19102

Advertising brochure for the Hebrew Press

Three denominations of American Judaism at a JPS meeting: Rev. Dr. David Philipson, Alexander Marx, and David de Sola Pool

Judge Louis E. Levinthal
(The Jewish Exponent)

Salo Baron, Solomon Grayzel, and Edwin Wolf 2nd (Alan D. Hewitt)

A meeting of the Advisory Editorial Committee, working on the new Bible translation. FROM LEFT (SEATED): *Bernard J. Bamberger, E. A. Speiser, Committee Chairman Harry M. Orlinsky, Harry Freedman, Max Arzt;* (STANDING): *Edwin Wolf 2nd, Judge Louis E. Levinthal, Lesser Zussman, Solomon Grayzel. Wolf, Levinthal, and Grayzel were* ex-officio *members of the committee. One member, H. L. Ginsberg, was not present when this picture was taken. (Shull Photo Service)*

The translators of The Torah *presenting a first edition to Supreme Court Juctice Arthur J. Goldberg:* (FROM LEFT) *Solomon Grayzel, Rabbi Max Arzt, Harry M. Orlinsky, Justice Arthur J. Goldberg, H. L. Ginsberg, Rabbi Harry Freedman, Bernard J. Bamberger. E. A. Speiser was unable to attend. (Abe Fried)*

THE MAURICE JACOBS YEARS

Maurice Jacobs came to the Society at a critical moment in American Jewish history. Caught in the throes of the Great Depression and stunned by ever-worsening news from Germany, American Jews had grown increasingly anxious and insecure:

> Young people went to college but with faint prospect of employment....The economic future of the Jews in the United States seemed in question.... Father Charles E. Coughlin broadcast nationally from Detroit, and his anti-Semitism became more explicit with each weekly talk. At street-corner meetings in upper Manhattan hatred of Jews was spewed and in subway stations beneath they could be assaulted. The Nazis of the German-American Bund sought to carry on like their mentors in Germany. There was a plethora of anti-Semitic organizations. All the time American Jews had in mind the ravaging of the Jews in Germany, like themselves educated, acculturated, patriotic, economically successful.[1]

Against this background, many American Jews sought to increase their knowledge of Judaism and Jewish history. They wanted to be able to counter the blatant misinformation believed by some of their neighbors, as well as the malicious disinformation spread by the German Bund and professional Jew-haters. They sought to know more about what was going on in the Jewish world and hungered for books that could somehow fortify them against the abuse that the Jewish people had to endure on a daily basis. At a deeper level, this effort was also a form of cultural resistance, a resolve to maintain Judaism in the face of opposition and danger. Many came to espouse Zionism, convinced that only a Jewish state could ensure the security of the Jewish people worldwide. This atmosphere of burgeoning Jewish consciousness created new opportunities for JPS. Its challenge was to supply the kind of literature that American Jews of the day were searching for.

The Maurice Jacobs Revolution

Maurice Jacobs was well-suited to help JPS rise to the occasion and meet this challenge. A short man with a quick mind, boundless energy, and abiding self-confidence, he came to the Society in 1936 at the prime of his career. At forty, he personally knew many of Jewry's leading figures and had already spent twenty years as a professional and lay worker for Jewish causes, including nine as executive secretary of Phi Epsilon Pi, a Jewish college fraternity organization. As a volunteer, he had founded the University Lodge of B'nai B'rith, chaired the publication committee of the National Federation of Temple Brotherhoods, and played an active role at Philadelphia's Congregation Keneseth Israel, his home congregation. He revered Joseph Krauskopf and believed passionately in Reform Judaism and its future. He also cultivated friends in other circles, people he met in the course of his work or in the community, and he brought to JPS an ambitious personal vision of how it could best contribute to the Jewish community. He had Jacob Solis-Cohen's full confidence and carte blanche to effect changes. Before long, he was making his presence felt.[2]

Jacobs made clear from the outset that, in his mind, JPS fell far short of its potential. Its activities "were not generally enough known," the format of its books "could be improved," its membership "could be substantially increased," and it had "merchandise that could be sold." As a result, he began concentrating on publicity, membership, and sales. He recommended to his friends that they join the "Society's family," initiated a program to place the Society's books in Jewish fraternities, and offered existing members bonus books for every new member they signed up. He advertised books in Jewish (and sometimes Christian) magazines, ran around to book fairs, and experimented with all manner of sales techniques from agents-on-commission to mail order. The results, in terms of new members and increased sales, showed at once, and sales continued to accelerate throughout the next decade. Jacobs also took an important step aimed at upgrading the Society's communal image. In late 1937, he convinced the trustees to move the JPS offices to a more central Philadelphia location at the corner of Fifteenth and Locust

Streets, opened up a reading room, and extended a warm invitation to members and customers to "pay us a visit." He wanted those belonging to the Society's family to know that under his administration they would not be taken for granted.[3]

Under Jacobs, JPS introduced more far-reaching changes in conjunction with its fiftieth anniversary in 1938. First, it published eight volumes (seven titles) in a year, more than ever before and double the number of the previous year. Following an old suggestion of Cyrus Adler's (which Jacobs may or may not have known about), the trustees offered members the freedom to choose any three books that they liked as part of their membership and the chance to buy other volumes at a discount. The scheme worked, members were pleased, and the new plan, which permitted a greatly enhanced publication program, became the norm. Within a few years, many members were paying double the regular membership fee to ensure that they received every book published.

With more books issued annually, JPS could also enhance the mix of books that it offered. Of the seven titles on its 1938 list, for example, there were three works of fiction, including the massive *Selected Works of Israel Zangwill*; two scholarly volumes, including Louis Finkelstein's two-volume *The Pharisees*; Norman Bentwich's semipopular biography of Solomon Schechter; and the *American Jewish Year Book*—at least one book to satisfy every taste. Equally important, although members did not know it, was the fact that many of these books had been published promptly, without the interminable delays that had plagued volumes issued under previous administrations. Jacobs knew that the Society would only be able to attract quality manuscripts if it could promise to bring them out in timely fashion. Except when war intervened, he managed to issue most books within a year or two of their acceptance, and in unusual cases even more quickly.[4]

To Jacobs, the 1938 jubilee served almost as a rite of passage, symbolically ushering in a new era in JPS history. The modest ceremony held to celebrate the occasion, if not as lavish as the festivities of twenty-five years before, showed that the Society had turned the corner and was on the road to recovery. The mood was upbeat, the leadership seemed hopeful, and the future looked bright.[5]

Another indication of the change that had taken place was the publication in 1938 of the index volume to Louis Ginzberg's *Legends of the Jews*. This settled a long-festering dispute, closed out the Society's oldest unfinished project, and restored amicable relations with the Jewish scholarly community, a group that no Jewish publisher could afford to antagonize. Bad feelings and controversy surrounding the *Legends* index went all the way back to 1924, when Ginzberg himself had called for this volume, pointing out that without "an exhaustive and thorough index" his great work could never live up to its full potential; it would be akin to a treasure-trove without a key. To further enhance the value of the index, he offered to write for it three scholarly excursuses promised in the body of the notes but never completed, and a one-hundred-page bibliography surveying the entire

Midrashic field. After several false starts, Rabbi Benjamin (Boaz) Cohen of the Jewish Theological Seminary agreed to undertake the massive indexing assignment for $1,250; 70,000 cards later, in 1931, he submitted it. But for years it lay unpublished—partly because Cohen's penmanship was difficult for the printers to read, partly because Grodinsky believed "that the cost of printing the index under the most favorable circumstances will be high and hardly one hundred copies will ever be sold." Heart-rending letters from Cohen and his wife, the daughter of Israel Friedlaender, failed to advance the project, nor did the poverty-stricken Cohen receive most of the money he was due. Worst of all, boxes of cards stowed away in the office began to disappear; they were taking up too much room. The whole unhappy story created a great deal of bitterness toward the Society in circles where it formerly had many friends.

Learning of this situation within days of his appointment, Jacobs agreed at once that the volume should appear no matter what the cost. This proved an expensive decision, for the painstaking work of typesetting and proofreading required hundreds of hours of tedious work and consumed thousands of dollars. To his mind, however, the Society's reputation, the scholarly contribution of the index, and the need to open a fresh page in the Society's history were far more important. Besides, he predicted that sales of the *Legends* would improve considerably once the index was in place. As it turned out, he was quite right. Although Ginzberg never wrote the excursuses and bibliography he promised, the *Legends* in seven volumes, including the index, gained fame as one of the greatest works of original Jewish scholarship ever published in America. It sold thousands of copies, still remains in print, and repaid the Society's initial investment many times over.[6]

With the jubilee and the index behind him, Jacobs proceeded to initiate important personnel changes. In 1939, he convinced Jacob Solis-Cohen that the Society's ailing editor, Isaac Husik, needed an assistant. Husik agreed that the best man for the job was Solomon Grayzel, a member of the publication committee who was at the time instructor and registrar at Gratz College. Grayzel was appointed, part-time, for $1,500. But he did not remain assistant for very long. "Within a matter of weeks," Grayzel later recalled, "Dr. Husik fell very seriously ill, and exactly one month after I had been selected to be his assistant, he passed away. So, on April the first, I became the editor of the Jewish Publication Society, something which I had not hoped for, had not looked forward to, and which I was sorry to have so soon. Dr. Husik had given me absolutely no instructions about what I was to do or what I was to deal with. I came into the situation cold, and I must admit a little bit frightened."[7]

Born in 1896 in Minsk, Russia, and educated in America, Grayzel was the son of an enlightened and Jewishly learned Hebrew teacher. He received his first lessons in editing as a youngster when he worked as a printer's devil and errand boy at a Yiddish newspaper. He went on to City College and Columbia University, as well as to rabbinical school at the Jewish Theological Seminary, and he had the good fortune to marry the daughter of one of the leading Conservative rabbis of the day, Elias Solomon. After five unhappy years in the active rabbinate he set his sights on academia. In 1927 Grayzel earned his doctorate in history from Dropsie College with a dissertation on the subject that would occupy him for most of his scholarly career—the relationship between the Catholic Church and the Jews. When he became the Society's fourth editor, he was forty-three years old. He would serve in the post for the next twenty-seven years, longer than anyone before or since. Indeed, he was the first editor since Henrietta Szold to be totally identified with the Society. After 1945 when the editor's post again became a full-time position, he gave it nights and vacations as well as eight hours a day. Also like Henrietta Szold, one senses that he always felt somewhat ambivalent about his job. He enjoyed working with authors and took pride in his achievements, but he missed teaching and scholarship, and never felt fully secure in what he was doing. Over and over, he privately lamented that he lacked the confidence to assert himself more vigorously on behalf of policies that he believed in, or books that he wanted to see accepted, or even for such benefits as a qualified secretary and a raise. Friends knew him as a "gentleman and scholar, modest, soft-spoken, erudite, articulate, and above all dedicated"—all of which he certainly was. But he was also an easy man to take for granted. He never mastered the politics of the Society, played down his own successes, and brooded aloud over his failures. "Counting up my experiences," he wrote when he was sixty, "I know that I have been wrong more often than right." In fact, as the books published by the Society bear witness, this was far from true. Yet he believed it, and others, as a result, did not always give him the credit that he was due.[8]

Grayzel was far from the only new appointment at the Society in 1939. That year also witnessed important changes on the publication committee. Its acting chairman, Jacob Solis-Cohen, who was never suited to the post, finally vacated it (he continued on as president), and was succeeded by Louis Levinthal. This brought renewed status to the committee, for it was now once again headed, as in Mayer Sulzberger's day, by a highly respected, traditional-minded Jewish judge, a member of Philadelphia's Court of Common Pleas. Levinthal, in fact, resembled his predecessor in many ways and consciously followed in his illustrious footsteps, even writing an important monograph on his judicial opinions. He also acquired, as Sulzberger had, all the proper Philadelphia Jewish credentials: He studied at the University of Pennsylvania, appreciated high culture, displayed wide-ranging Jewish and secular learning, and served as a trustee of Gratz College. But while he possessed many characteristics of the old Philadelphia Group whose members had founded the Society, he was also distinguished from them in one critical respect: He was an East European Jew, the son of Philadelphia's leading Orthodox rabbi,

Bernard Levinthal. His appointment thus symbolized the coming of age of second-generation East European Jews in America. It serves as another indication that the barriers dividing "old" and "new" Jews were steadily breaking down in the interwar years, as the nation's Jews slowly "ethnicized" into a single American Jewish community.[9]

In his new position, Levinthal worked closely with Maurice Jacobs and Jacob Solis-Cohen to reinvigorate the publication committee by adding to it the men—still no women—who represented the rising new generation of American Jewish cultural leaders. These included Louis Finkelstein, Cyrus Adler's successor as president of the Jewish Theological Seminary; Jacob R. Marcus, professor of Jewish history at Hebrew Union College, who came to play an increasingly important role on the committee, especially in the realm of American Jewish history; and Harry A. Wolfson, professor of Jewish literature and philosophy at Harvard. Many Jews of East European background were appointed to the publication committee during the next few years, including, for the first time, several leading figures in Orthodox Jewry: Samuel Belkin, Oscar Z. Fasman, Joseph H. Lookstein, and David de Sola Pool. Of course, the Society also appointed powerful Reform and Conservative Jews to the committee, and important anti-Zionists too; indeed, even more than before, it reflected a full spectrum of American Jewish life. As the committee became more representative, however, it also became larger, growing first to twenty-nine members and then gradually bulging out in annual increments until in 1950, when it reached a membership of forty-nine—an unmanageable size.

For efficiency's sake, Levinthal and Jacobs decided to divide the publication committee into various specialized subcommittees. They also conducted more and more business by mail; the pleasurable monthly meetings at Dropsie College became a thing of the past. Still, over time, the committee's influence as a whole waned considerably. Quite a few members did no work at all during their tenure, while there were others who did work but proved themselves incompetent to judge whether books should be published. After some unhappy experiences, Grayzel stopped consulting some members altogether: "They were not the kind of people," he explained, "whose judgement I valued or would trust." As a result, a small coterie of publication committee leaders ended up making most of the major decisions. Other members served either as occasional advisors and readers, or simply as yea-sayers at annual meetings.[10]

The same process of centralization—a trend in management seen throughout the country at the time—took place at other levels of the Society as well. At one point, Jacobs had the inspired idea of inviting heads of all major American Jewish organizations (including women's organizations) to join the Society as "honorary vice-presidents" so as to associate them with its work. He and Jacob Solis-Cohen also reshaped the composition of the board of trustees, whose size was constitutionally delimited, to include some of the wealthiest and most important figures in American

Jewish life (Jacobs repeatedly urged that "certain outstanding women" be included in this group, but made no specific recommendations, so none were selected.) This greatly embellished the Society's "official family," translated into new credibility, and offered the security that always comes from having friends in high places. Yet while the Society's governing body was now a gallery of stars (such as Walter H. Annenberg, Samuel Bronfman, Murray Seasongood, and Stephen S. Wise) fewer and fewer of these busy VIPs ever attended meetings. Unofficially, at least, they left decisions up to a central executive board consisting of major officers, and they, in turn, frequently deferred to Jacobs, Solis-Cohen, Levinthal, and Grayzel. Beginning in 1942, when war impinged on the Society's operations, this policy was institutionalized. The board of trustees and the publication committee now met in joint session perhaps once or twice a year, with much of that time spent yawning through endless reports, for everything had essentially been decided in advance. Substantive meetings to debate policy or financial questions took place far more rarely, and then only at moments of crisis.[11]

Along with the new structure, Jacobs introduced a new emphasis into the Society's work. Where his predecessors had stressed book publishing and membership growth, he made clear that his first priority was book distribution, the sale of as many volumes as possible to members and nonmembers alike. Having convinced even the publication committee that "our main purpose is the distribution of books of Jewish nature," he received the green light from them, and more importantly, from the officers, to try all sorts of creative merchandising schemes. His announced goal, which he more than surpassed, was for the Society to distribute at least 100,000 Jewish books a year, more than double the number distributed in the banner year of 1938.[12]

In 1936, his first full year at the Society, Jacobs introduced a Spring Book Festival timed to coincide with what was then known as Jewish Book Week. This was the Society's first book sale of its kind, and it moved 4,000 books. Thanks to its success, it became an annual event, and was later shifted to Hanukkah-time in the winter. A year later, probably influenced by a successful book club promotion, Jacobs announced a "Dollar Book Shelf." "Our experience indicates," Solis-Cohen explained in the annual report, "that many young people desirous of having a group of books on Jewish subjects in their homes, cannot afford to pay $2 to $4 per book, and we are now working on a plan to dispose of our older books on hand, as well as reprints of those out of print at a special price within the reach of all." By 1940 the plan was in place and Jacobs boasted that "we have helped to carry through our slogan of 'more Jewish books in Jewish homes' by making many titles available at low prices. Thus 3,435 books were sold at $1.00, 1,011 at 75 cents and 508 at 50 cents."[13]

The key to these low-priced books and, indeed, to much of the distribution effort, was an ambitious, and later quite controversial, reprint program designed to restore to print titles from the Society's backlist. Years had passed since most of these books had first appeared, and few American Jews had them in their homes. By making the volumes available anew, Jacobs claimed that he gave these volumes a second life, enhanced the Society's reputation, satisfied customers, and made the Society a profit besides. Reprinting a book cost no more than the price of printing and storage, because like most publishers of the day JPS owned its books outright and did not pay royalties. Furthermore, Jacobs claimed that he held down the production cost of reprints by utilizing slack-time at the Society's own press. But others at the Society came to believe that the reprint policy was an outrageous waste of money and merely an excuse for keeping the press busy. For a time, Jacobs managed to confound critics by turning the stock rapidly enough to justify increasing the volume of reprints year by year. During World War II, owing to periodic manufacturing delays, he built up large inventories "to make certain that orders could be filled promptly." In 1945 alone thirty-nine books were reprinted, and the Society boasted more titles available for sale than at any previous time in its history. But in the late 1940s publishing slumped and the Society found itself overstocked and deeply in debt. Jacobs's critics never forgave him.[14]

The second key to Jacobs's program of book distribution involved marketing. He studied the ins and outs of the book trade and determined that the Society should sell its books the way that most major publishers sold theirs—in bookstores, by mail, even in mass-market racks. He offered trade discounts, struck up deals with leading book distributors, and offered greater incentives to agents. He advertised, experimented with mail order (which worked better than the agents did), and often co-published books with trade publishers. For a few years, he even toyed with a farfetched idea for distributing books via big city Jewish Federations in exchange for allocations to the Society on a dollar for dollar basis. Most any scheme, he thought, was worth a try so long as it promised to place Jewish books in more Jewish homes. In the 1930s and 1940s, a period of great economic and business experimentation in America, this "try anything" spirit, akin to the "try anything" economic policies of Franklin Roosevelt, was the hallmark of a good business executive, someone not stuck in his ways. This spirit certainly characterized Jacobs, and for the Society it was a welcome breath of fresh air. So long as Jacobs continued to avoid a deficit and kept the business honorable, the officers and the board were pleased and left him alone.[15]

Jacobs's achievements with the Society's Hebrew press proved especially significant. This partly reflects the legacy from Grodinsky who had brought the press up to some $25,000 in sales, a highly respectable figure. But it was under Jacobs's direction that the operation developed from a Hebrew press into an almost universal foreign-language press. "From a small staff of five men working part time five years ago," he boasted in 1941, "we now have a staff of fifteen full-time workers, most of whom we have trained ourselves. From two typesetting machines we have expanded to eight. From two typemaking machines we have expanded to five. Jewish scholarship will not find the Press of the Society wanting when books are submitted to us for printing."[16]

Just as the Society's press was expanding, World War II was bringing down the curtain on the last remaining Jewish presses in continental Europe; only those in Palestine, England, and the Americas continued to operate. Jacobs took this as a challenge: "Our Press," he declared "is ready to assume its greater responsibility.... The record of the scholarly presses of Europe can and will be duplicated and perhaps surpassed in the scholarly Press of Philadelphia." Under David Skaraton, who immigrated to America as a youth after roving bands in the Ukraine murdered his father and found a home at the Society's press from 1929 onward, the operation improved to the point that it could advertise itself as "the finest foreign-language press in the country." In addition to Hebrew and English, it offered all of the Latin languages, all of the Cyrillic languages, as well as Greek, Syriac, Arabic, Babylonian, Judeo-Arabic, and Yiddish. It had at least five journals and a dozen institutions as regular customers, did work for Jews and Christians alike, proudly printed a Bible and New Testament in Russian for the American Bible Society, and in 1941 had sales that exceeded what it and the Society together grossed in 1935—all of this before the great boom in business following America's entry into World War II. Indeed, with its new technical capabilities and its growing list of customers, the press was rapidly outrunning the Society's main business, the publication and distribution of Jewish books. This certainly did wonders for the annual financial report, and made for good publicity as well. Given the Society's traditional priorities, however, it was not a situation that could continue indefinitely without some serious rethinking of goals.[17]

During Jacobs's first decade on the job such problems did not worry him. He summed up his mission in one word—"forward"—and he marched the Society smartly ahead. Looking back, the decade stands as the most successful in the Society's whole history; never before or since did it grow so quickly. By 1945, total income (including war work) stood close to $300,000, fully five times what it had been ten years earlier. Income from book sales and from the Hebrew Press increased at an even greater rate. Indeed, the Society progressed in every department and by every standard of measure, as the following table (page 184) demonstrates.[18]

A close look at these figures shows that the Society progressed more slowly in the areas of membership and new books than in others. Jacobs, as we have seen, thought that the largest potential for growth lay in book distribution and the Hebrew Press, and he concentrated his efforts there—recklessly so, his critics would later charge. Still, Jacobs demonstrated that JPS could grow even in a competitive

Year	Mem-bers	Dues	Book Sales	Books Distrib-uted	New Books	Reprints	Press Sales	Total Income[19]
1935	3,343	$19,795	$14,725	na	3	0	$ 24,717	$ 60,419
1936	4,212	23,593	19,224	na	4	8	22,296	71,203
1937	5,504	29,924	22,560	na	6	6	24,099	80,587
1938	6,989	37,264	22,672	46,000	8	8	24,713	98,191
1939	6,297	36,838	22,455	47,000	6	14	32,723	92,673
1940	6,357	37,027	28,993	52,844	6	18	38,997	106,796
1941	6,228	37,039	30,960	58,358	7	11	60,605	131,307
1942	6,335	39,823	29,149	55,736	8	12	87,203	159,597
1943	8,216	56,069	43,748	107,317	6	24	154,039	260,634
1944	8,864	61,918	75,683	110,673	7	22	148,302	296,233
1945	9,775	71,487	83,278	112,780	7	39	131,537	297,866

publishing environment and transformed what had once been a small and struggling business into what he now proudly described as "the largest publishers of Jewish books in English in the world." The trustees, appropriately impressed by these developments, repeatedly promoted him, each time with a hefty raise in salary. They sought to keep him happy, hoping that he would carry through with his dream to "build our Society to the point where it will do approximately a million dollars' worth of business a year"—if not more.[20]

World War II

War, the threat of war, and the aftermath of war characterized practically the entire period of Maurice Jacobs's tenure. He carried on his activities against the background of the deteriorating Jewish situation in Europe. The Society itself did not actively work to save European Jewry, nor did it overtly propagandize; these were not its functions. However, it did not sit on the sidelines and do nothing either. JPS leaders, remembering all they did following the Kishinev pogrom, would have been thoroughly horrified at the thought. Instead, the Society undertook activities that helped: (1) to assist Jewish refugees on an individual basis, (2) to provide information and shape public opinion through timely books, (3) to meet the wartime needs of Jewish soldiers, and (4) to prepare American Jews for the responsibilities and challenges of the postwar world.

The refugee challenge was the first to be met. It began to be felt early in the 1930s and demanded ongoing but quiet action for the next decade as increasing numbers of Jews left Germany or sought to leave and needed support. To offset charges that the newcomers would "steal" the scarce jobs of native Americans or remain unemployed and a "burden" on the country, numerous Jewish organizations strove to create jobs for them within the "Jewish subeconomy," particularly as teachers and ritual functionaries and in the kosher food industry. The Society did its part—a small part, to be sure—by employing English-speaking refugees as solicitors and agents. It sent them, armed with an "Agents Sales Manual," sample volumes, and membership blanks, to knock on doors in Jewish neighborhoods offering to sign people up to receive the Society's books. "The violent wave of anti-Semitism which is sweeping Germany...," it instructed them as part of their training, "is something upon which you may dwell as eloquently as you are able in advocating membership." The program brought in few subscribers, and Jacobs eventually had to cut it back: The renewal rate was too low to justify its continuance. In a program that had more impact, however, he put as many refugees as he could to work at the Society's press. David Skaraton trained them to set type and some remained on with the press for years.[21]

On a different level, the Society sought to help refugee scholars and writers. It sent Adolf Kober, Cologne's *Gemeinderabbiner* (communal rabbi) who was "very much in need of funds," a large advance on his book on Cologne, and then tried to help him resettle in America. It also sent an affidavit and other assistance to Max L. Berges, founder of the Union of Jewish Artists in Hamburg, who at the time was managing a five-and-ten-cent store in Manila, the only place where he and his wife could find safety after war routed them from their first refuge in Shanghai. The Society had accepted Berges's novel, *Cold Pogrom*, for publication, and the advance he received for the book helped pay for the couple's passage to the United States in December 1938. Three months later, when Berges and his wife were at wits end—"We didn't pay our rent ... and we can't buy ourselves something to eat.... I don't know anymore what to do"—Jacobs immediately sent him an extra advance on his honorarium ("This is contrary to our contract but I appreciate your needs at the present time and this may help a little bit") and a long letter of encouragement. He then enlisted a personal friend of his to try and help the Bergeses out.

In yet another example of charity, the Society heeded a plea from Hebrew Union College President Julian Morgenstern, a leader in the effort to help refugees, and purchased English rights to three German stories by Dr. Emil Bernhard Cohn for $150. It promised the rabbi, remembered as the biographer of Zionist leader David Wolffsohn, an additional $350 if he came up with seven more stories, enough for a book. Privately, Jacobs admitted that this was a "charity case" for the book would never pay for itself. Still, Cohn desperately needed the money, so contrary to its usual policy the Society paid him after each group of stories was accepted, even before the full manuscript was done. Cohn finally did finish his assignment, but unfortunately the volume itself, entitled *Stories and Fantasies* and translated by

Charles Reznikoff, did not appear until 1951. Three years earlier, Cohn had been killed by a speeding automobile in Los Angeles.[22]

Besides helping these and other individuals, the Society also worked in a more general way to focus public attention on the plight of European Jewry as a whole. Marvin Lowenthal's *The Jews of Germany* and well-documented articles in the *American Jewish Year Book* spearheaded this effort, but as the situation continued to deteriorate still more was called for. In response, the publication committee ordered translated and rushed into print the novel *Cold Pogrom* (1939), written in Shanghai by Max Berges, the man whom Jacobs later assisted. Published with a definite publicistic aim, the gripping novel told the story of "a middle-class, comfortable, well-intentioned, hard-working Jewish family," with longstanding roots in Germany, that was eventually destroyed by the Nazis through indirect forms of murder. Berges, long-active in German liberal circles, used his novel to settle accounts with Jews who ignored his warnings and deluded themselves into thinking that all would "end well" so long as everyone kept quiet and attended scrupulously to his "own affairs." He also took the opportunity to extol the heroism of those (like himself), "who struggled against the blight of the Nazis before they came to power and ... continued to stand up against them even afterward." Yet far more important from the Society's point of view was *Cold Pogrom*'s convincing portrait of the overall Jewish situation in Germany, "showing more graphically than ... in any newspaper report or historical treatise the terrible repercussion of the Hitlerian tragedy." Benjamin Epstein of the Anti-Defamation League of B'nai B'rith translated the volume, and the ADL reprinted an extract from one of its most effective sections in pamphlet form for wide distribution. Much to the Society's regret, however, it proved unable to find a co-publisher willing to market the novel to the trade. A representative of Henry Holt and Company explained that "the outbreak of the war has changed conditions considerably and ... interest in books dealing with Jewish persecution in Germany has been side-tracked."[23]

Although it continued its efforts to keep American Jews informed, JPS, too, shifted the mood of its books somewhat once war began. The news from Europe was so bad that the Society worried lest Jews despair of their situation—a not unjustified fear considering the wave of well-publicized suicides among Jewish intellectuals of the period. "I think the time has come when a responsible organization like ours must call a halt to terrorizing the Jewish population in this country—the last Jewish population which still retains its self-confidence," Solomon Grayzel wrote in early 1941. He admitted that he was worried about the "psychological effect" of too much bad news on the American Jewish community's morale. As a result, he used his prerogative as editor to reject both a personal account of experiences in the concentration camps of Dachau and Buchenwald and a manuscript entitled "The Massacre of the Jews in Vienna." Although he found both "gripping" and was certain that they would make effective anti-Nazi propaganda, he encouraged both writers to try to publish their work elsewhere, where non-Jews might have a greater chance of reading them.[24]

Grayzel and the publication committee preferred to publish more upbeat volumes. They recommended Ruben Rothgiesser's *The Ship of Hope*, a story about the capture and liberation of fifteenth-century Spanish Jewish children imprisoned by pirates, as "a ray of hope to those of our faith who saw nothing but darkness ahead." Significantly, the captives in the story retained their Jewish consciousness in the face of adversity, never abandoning their belief in divine intervention. On the basis of a similar argument—"in difficult times like those we are passing through, a book of Jewish humor might be considered escapist literature, and necessary"—they also approved S. Felix Mendelsohn's *Let Laughter Ring*. This was the only book of its kind that ever appeared on the Society's list, telling proof of how much had changed from the days when it only published weighty tomes that others wouldn't touch. Mendelsohn's collection contained a full chapter of "laughs" devoted to the Third Reich, including such revealing examples of gallows humor as the following:

> A German Jew said that he would like to see Hitler converted into a candelabrum.
> When asked to explain the meaning of this peculiar wish, the German Jew said:
> If Hitler were a candelabrum, I would see him hang during the day, burn at night, and be extinguished in the morning.
>
> During the early days of the Brown Terror, a Jewish father residing in Frankfort sent the following postcard to his son in the U.S.:
> "You realize of course that, since the Germans are a civilized people, we have nothing to worry about under the new regime. We continue to enjoy peace and security and what you read in the newspapers is only a heap of atrocity and lies. P.S. We have just buried Uncle Max who had expressed a contrary opinion."

In publishing *Let Laughter Ring*—and without an essay on "the philosophy of Jewish humor" that some scholarly members proposed—the Society apparently read the needs of American Jews accurately. The volume sold over four thousand copies in two months, became its biggest seller in 1941, and eventually went through at least six printings.[25]

Rabbi Joseph L. Baron's two books, *Candles in the Night* and *Stars and Sand* represented a different effort by the Society to meet the needs of American Jews in wartime. Given the vast outpouring of anti-Jewish hatred during this period, these volumes, the first a collection of "Jewish tales by non-Jewish authors," the second a collection of pro-Jewish statements by distinguished non-Jews, held aloft the banner of interfaith harmony, seeking to remind Jews and Gentiles alike of the "critical moments" when "Gentile friends have . . . carried the torch in the struggle for equal rights, and espoused valiantly the cause of liberty and justice for the Jew." Later, the Society was somewhat embarrassed when some of the people quoted in *Stars and Sand* turned out to be anything but paragons of tolerance; indeed, one of those quoted was Josef Stalin![26]

As the United States prepared to enter World War II, JPS moved into a new phase of its wartime activities. It worked with the Jewish Welfare Board in meeting the religious and cultural needs of Jews in uniform. As in World War I, it undertook to print prayerbooks for Jewish soldiers. Rabbis Solomon Freehof, Eugene Kohn, and David de Sola Pool—representing Reform, Conservative, and Orthodox Judaism—revised the soldiers' prayerbook, and the Society's press printed hundreds of thousands of copies. It also issued, with less than one month's notice, an abbreviated high holiday prayerbook and later a soldier's Passover Haggadah. In 1944 it was even commissioned to print a French-Hebrew prayerbook for the use of Jewish soldiers in the French army. All told, the Society printed under contract to the Jewish Welfare Board an astonishing (and lucrative) total of 2,545,085 copies of prayerbooks and Haggadahs during World War II, almost seven times the number of volumes it published for the military in the previous war. In addition, it aided in the publication of a new abridged Bible for Jewish soldiers, based on its 1917 translation. Because of stringent government regulations, however, it did not print the volume itself; instead, the War Department contracted the job out.[27]

Late in the war, the military asked the Society's press to undertake a secret mission, not revealed by Jacob Solis-Cohen until after hostilities had ceased. The Press agreed to set type in Greek, Russian, Serbian, Croatian, and Rumanian for pamphlets "to be dropped from airplanes behind the enemy lines." Although seriously understaffed at the time, it successfully completed this assignment, as well as its other military work, for employees worked sixty and seventy hours a week. The Society's own books, however, were somewhat delayed on this account, as well as by war-related shortages of paper, cloth, and binding materials. In 1945, the worst year, it issued only two of the seven books it projected, and had to defer less pressing commercial work. Normal operations did not resume until 1946–47, when it also returned to its schedule of annual meetings for, like most other American organizations of its type, it suspended regular meetings during the war years.[28]

Even as it met the special wartime needs of American Jews, JPS also kept in mind its larger cultural responsibilities to the Jewish world at large. With the destruction of European Jewry, it became, as Jacob Rader Marcus put it at the time, "the only surviving literary medium of mass instruction west of Jerusalem." In what became the last JPS annual meeting before America's entry into war, Marcus, at the time chairman of the Committee on Contemporaneous History and

Literature of the Central Conference of American Rabbis, underscored these new responsibilities in emphatic terms:

> There was never a time in our American life that the work of this press was more vital and necessary than it is today. Almost everywhere Jewish books are being destroyed. Almost nowhere outside the United States are they being printed .... The burden is solely ours to carry: Jewish culture and civilization are shifting rapidly to these shores.

Pointing to Germany's worldwide campaign of "lies" and "halftruths" about Jews and Judaism, he challenged the Society to respond with books, "both popular and technical, the scientific integrity of which is beyond the shadow of suspicion." "Every volume that comes forth from Munich," he cried, "must be countered by a volume from the City of Brotherly Love."[29]

The Society took this responsibility seriously. It increased the number and variety of books it published and undertook new efforts aimed at distributing them widely, especially abroad. In a particularly important move, it permitted foreign students of Judaism, as well as its own members overseas, to purchase books without payment, simply with the understanding that payment could be made when European currency restrictions were lifted.[30]

Largely through Marcus's own efforts, the Society also committed itself to publish volumes on American Jewish history. With the rise of a generation of native-born Jews and the country's emergence as the unquestioned center of diaspora Jewish life, the need to bring American Jewry into the mainstream of Jewish history had become more urgent than ever. This was important not only for its own sake and for the sake of American Jewish patriotism, but also as an effective antidote to the lachrymose conception of Jewish life that had become increasingly prevalent in the wake of the European Jewish persecutions. As part of its effort to uplift Jewish spirits during those dark days, JPS published more books dealing with American Jewry than during all of its previous decades combined.[31]

As before, many of these volumes were produced by antiquarians and non-professionals; American Jewish history had not yet become a recognized scholarly field. Lee M. Friedman, a Boston lawyer who published numerous valuable and highly readable articles in American Jewish history, thus issued two well-received collections: *Jewish Pioneers and Patriots* (1942) and *Pilgrims in a New Land* (1948). Abram Vossen Goodman, a rabbi, published *American Overture: Jewish Rights in Colonial Times* (1947). The titles of all three of these books reveal much about their aims. They underscore the theme of American exceptionalism, the idea, especially common in postwar American Jewish historiography, that the country represented a break from past Jewish experience—something new, different, indubitably better.

Goodman made the point explicit in his concluding pages: "The glory of this land," he wrote, "is in the moral force of its political philosophy which today represents a new sign of hope to a world wearied by the shibboleths of fascism and reaction."[32] Leon Huhner's biography of philanthropist Judah Touro, also published during this period, added a note of apologetics, but the overall themes of Jewish pride and American greatness remained the same. "Touro was one of the finest characters in American Jewish history," Huhner explained in a private letter to Solomon Grayzel, "a man of whose career all American Jews may justly be proud; and a truthful presentation of his life would do much to disarm anti-Jewish prejudice."[33]

The importance of fostering these ideals became the hidden agenda for most books of American Jewish history published at this time. Yet the Society also realized, perhaps earlier than others did, that the American Jewish community in the postwar era also demanded serious histories of its own. To this end, it solicited, nurtured, and eventually published Hyman B. Grinstein's *The Rise of the Jewish Community of New York, 1654–1860,* its most scholarly volume to date in American Jewish history, and in many respects a turning point in the field. The volume began as an exhaustively researched and highly detailed doctoral dissertation at Columbia University, directed by its versatile Jewish historian, Salo Baron. Reflecting Baron's own interests at the time, it dealt with the inner life of the Jewish community—religion, charity, society, culture—and sought to understand how Jewish life in New York developed against the background of the traditional Jewish community's structure as well as evolving American conditions. Heroes and villains, patriotism and pietism are only featured indirectly here; designed as a scholarly volume, it contained instead well-documented facts, important analyses, and "the groundwork for an understanding of the later development of the community, its structure, its institutions, and its movements." Unfortunately, like many a doctoral dissertation, when Grinstein's manuscript arrived at the Society it desperately needed a stylist, and some of its more evident anti-Reform bias (Grinstein was Orthodox) had to be toned down. Still, Solomon Grayzel knew that the work was important and guided Joseph L. Blau—later a well-known professor at Columbia University—in helping to rewrite the manuscript to make it "interesting and readable" enough for publication. The effort paid off: The 607-page volume (including fourteen appendixes) set a new standard in American Jewish history and remains a classic. Appearing just as the war ended, it served as yet another indication that American Jewry had matured and would demand its rightful place in the history of the Jewish people.[34]

JPS planned to produce two other important works in American Jewish history: Emily Solis-Cohen's biography of Isaac Leeser, and a big one-volume history of American Jews written by a team of scholars. It also had plans for a host of lesser works: a volume of short biographies, several community studies, a history of German Jews in America, and more. For the most part, however, these all came to naught: Some were never completed; others, when submitted, did not live up to expectations. Still, with the war ending and the realization growing that American Jewry had become, in Jacobs's words, "the largest, the freest and the wealthiest Jewish community the world has ever seen," the Society redoubled its commitment to the subject. In the years that followed, books on American Jewish history and life would always rank high whenever the publication committee planned for the future.[35]

The Society also projected an imposing list of other plans. The ever-ambitious Maurice Jacobs called for "the publication of a Philadelphia *Schass* ... edited by a scholar like Louis Ginzberg." He believed that such a new edition of the Talmud was essential after the destruction of Vilna's great Romm Press, and he promised that such an undertaking "would bring the Society more fame than it has ever had in its history." Somewhat more modestly, Solomon Grayzel urged publication of a new edition of the *Shulchan Aruch*, the basic code of Jewish law, with an English translation. In this case, the idea became mired in controversy, for, as Jacob Marcus explained: "The Reform Jews wanted the entire Shulchan Aruch published in a scholarly edition *in toto*, because the average American Jew would find it ridiculous and burdensome, and the Orthodox Jews, on the other hand, insisted on its publication in part; they wanted to choose only those items which would leave a good impression upon the American public." Needless to say, that idea was dropped.

For his part, Marcus himself, as chairman of an eight-member postwar planning committee, produced a bold agenda for the Society's future. It called, among other goals, for the publication of at least twelve volumes a year and listed better than fifty volumes (some out of print, some not yet translated, some not yet written) that it urged the Society to publish within five years, in some cases to ensure that the best of European Jewish literature would be saved from extinction. With the war over, the Society thriving, and America the predominant Jewish community in the world, many things suddenly seemed possible. The Society dreamed great dreams and looked expectantly ahead.[36]

The Explosive Debate over Zionism

JPS leaders were not the only dreamers in this period. The rise of Nazism, the spread of worldwide anti-Semitism, and the tragic plight of Jews barred from America's shores and unable to find safe refuge anywhere in the world, all gave new stimulus to the Zionist dream, the longing for a Jewish homeland. Only a state of their own, more and more Jews came to believe, could solve the problems of diaspora Jewish life once and for all. Opposition to Zionism still remained strong, especially on the part of those who saw Judaism as a religion rather than a nationality. As before, the opponents raised the specter of dual loyalty and perceived Zionism as a threat to American Jewry's welfare. Nevertheless, Zionism gained more and more adherents during the 1930s and 1940s, so much so that ideological polarization set in. The issue divided not only American Jews, but also a good many American Jewish organizations, JPS among them.

Since the days of Henrietta Szold and the battle over Ahad Ha'Am's essays, the Zionism question had rarely arisen. The Society left partisan books for others to publish, preferring dispassionate works around which all Jews could unite. But when Jacob Solis-Cohen and Maurice Jacobs returned to publication of more popular volumes, the Zionism issue could scarcely be avoided; it was *the* central question of the day. Among the publication committee's members sat leading American Zionists, chief among them Louis Levinthal, who in 1941 became president of the Zionist Organization of America, as well as such leading non-Zionists as Jacob Solis-Cohen and Rabbi William Fineshriber, both members of the anti-Zionist American Council for Judaism. All trod carefully for a time, knowing how divisive the issue could be, but a clash, sooner or later, seemed inevitable.

The volatile question first arose in connection with a small volume of poems submitted to the Society by Jessie Sampter back in 1934 and published three years later under the title *Brand Plucked from the Fire*. Sampter, disabled by polio as a child, was one of several prominent and highly cultured American Jewish women of her day, including Alice Seligsberg and Louise Waterman Wise, who belonged to Felix Adler's Ethical Culture Movement in their youth (for a time Sampter even identified as a Unitarian), and later found their way back to Judaism by way of the Zionist movement. She was specifically influenced, as Seligsberg had been, by Henrietta Szold and first visited Palestine under her auspices in 1919, at the age of thirty-six. She was enthralled, returned to settle permanently in 1922, and in 1934, after publishing her first work in Hebrew, determined (a decision she later went back on) that all of her future poetry would be in her newly acquired tongue. She asked the Society to publish the collection of her English-language poetry, which she had been writing from the age of nine, partly as a consequence of this decision; the volume would symbolize a historic turning point in her life.[37]

Why the publication committee accepted her manuscript is not clear, but it was only with the proviso that Solomon Solis-Cohen, its resident poet and by then a confirmed non-Zionist, could select for the volume just those poems that he considered most suitable. In the end, he cut out a good many verses dealing with Zionism, and Cyrus Adler vetoed some additional lines that were particularly anti-British. What remained were largely inspirational poems reflecting, in Mortimer Cohen's words, "the struggles of a sensitive Jewish spirit in these tumultuous, uncertain times for a faith by which to live." The volume still breathed love of

Zion, but it was now more "tactful"—non-Zionists could accept it. Members, as it turned out, were less accommodating, and neither sales nor reviews were particularly flattering. "Poetry," Jacob Solis-Cohen sadly concluded, "does not seem to be the Society's strong point."[38]

"Tactful" volumes, sympathetic to Zionism in a muted and always non-polemical way, appeared on the Society's list with increasing frequency after the Sampter volume was published. Levinthal supported them as chairman of the publication committee, and Jacobs discovered that so long as they were not poetry they even sold well. Nor did non-Zionists object to these volumes provided they remained free of politics. In 1939, the Society thus published in translation (a somewhat error-prone translation, in fact) three stories by the great Jewish poet Hayyim Nahman Bialik, including his "Aftergrowth" ("*Safiach*"), which some consider "a key to all his verses." A year later, with the unanimous agreement of the publication committee, it published an abridged translation, without notes, of Alex Bein's masterly biography of Theodor Herzl. In the original, this was a thoroughly scholarly work, not a paean of praise—which is probably why it won approval. Louis Levinthal, however, in seeking to persuade Maurice Samuel to undertake the translation of the work, gave him extraordinary latitude to make changes:

> It is my desire to have the Society publish a popular and a dramatic life of Herzl. I do not want to have an ordinary translation of Bein's book. I feel that you could do a creative piece of work in using Bein's material and transforming it into a fascinating story.

Samuel, who as an ardent Zionist had a personal interest in the book's success, produced a translation that was not only readable and interesting but also thoroughly sympathetic. In addition, the book came close to setting a sales record. Both the Zionist Organization of America and Hadassah purchased numerous copies, and the abnormally large first printing of eight thousand copies was rapidly exhausted. Non-Zionists were understandably displeased.[39]

Having enjoyed such great success with Samuel's translation, it is not surprising that Jacobs jumped at the opportunity to publish Samuel's own book on Zionism, a lyrical and highly personal history of Palestine's rebirth entitled *Harvest in the Desert* (1944). The volume was submitted by Abram L. Sachar, then national director of the B'nai B'rith Hillel Foundations, and he and Jacobs, old friends, worked out a mutually profitable arrangement: If the Society agreed to publish the book, Hillel promised to purchase three thousand copies at a special price for sale to Jewish college students. Jacobs soon arranged a trade edition with Alfred A. Knopf for a sale of two thousand copies, and he lined up other orders from the Zionist Organization and Hadassah. Even before the publication committee formally accepted the volume, it was clear that it would have the largest advance sale of any JPS book. There was only one catch: Samuel was known to be impatient and the Society had to move fast. If it could not decide on the book quickly, the whole deal would be off.[40]

Three readers known to be sympathetic to Zionism—Sachar, Levinthal, and Dropsie College President Abraham A. Neuman—agreed to report on the book at once, and all three, in addition to Solomon Grayzel, responded with accolades. Levinthal was particularly exuberant:

> Maurice Samuel's "Harvest in the Desert" is, in my opinion, the best work of its kind that I have had the pleasure of reading. . . . Fortunately, it is completely lacking in offensive argumentation. It is a good-humored book by a man who has such a profound faith in Jewish Palestine that he lets the facts, the events, speak for themselves, supremely confident that the unbiased reader will be charmed by the story he tells. . . . I am convinced that despite his own devotion to the Zionist cause, Samuel has been scrupulously truthful and fair in his presentation. There is not the slightest doubt as to the accuracy of his every statement, the validity of his every premise, the soundness of his every conclusion. . . . Particularly in these times where there is so much confusion as to Zionism, its achievements and its aspirations, our Society will be rendering a significant service by publishing this book.

On this basis, Jacobs wrote members of the publication committee asking them, in the usual *pro forma* way, to vote on whether the book should be accepted. Twenty-five members, as he anticipated, never bothered to respond, and twelve voted yes. To his surprise, however, three distinguished Philadelphia members—Rabbi William Fineshriber of Keneseth Israel, Bernard Frankel, the Society's attorney, and its president, Jacob Solis-Cohen—voted no. The board of trustees still had to confirm the decision of the publication committee, and given the nature of the opposition a battle loomed for certain. The stage was thus set for the most tumultuous and portentous meeting of the board of trustees since JPS was founded.[41]

The meeting held on January 27, 1944, was long and bitter. A full thirty-two-page transcript survives, complete with sharp, angry exchanges between two distinguished judges, Louis Levinthal and Horace Stern, as well as between various officers of the Society, and even at one point between Maurice Jacobs and Jacob Solis-Cohen. Procedures, standards, and long-term policies were all featured in this debate, which raised substantive and difficult questions. Should, for example, Grayzel have sent Samuel's manuscript to known anti-Zionists for review, or was he right to have sent it only to basically sympathetic readers? Fairness, Simon Miller thought, demanded that a range of views be solicited in advance; Grayzel, on the other hand, feared that this procedure could easily result in prior censorship. An even more basic question: Should the Society agree to publish a work that was, by all accounts, partisan (opponents called it "propaganda"), or should it confine itself to impartial analyses, for fear of offending some of its members? Stern believed that "a propaganda book that would very much infuriate people . . .

should not be published by the Jewish Publication Society." Jacobs countered that "to limit itself to colorless books" would not justify the Society's existence. Levinthal, unable to restrain himself, pointed out that even "the Bible was a propaganda book." Yet historically, as Jacob Solis-Cohen reminded everyone, the Society had avoided controversy, a policy that had served it well. Finally, the most important question of all came up: Should the Society as a matter of policy publish books bearing on divisive issues of contemporary concern, or should it go back to issuing only intrinsically nonthreatening works, books of history, learning, and scholarship? Levinthal's position was clear: "I think it is unfair to the Jewish community of America to say that because Zionism is a controversial subject the Society should not publish this book if it is a valuable contribution to Jewish literature." Stern maintained his contrary view unswervingly: "It is not the function of the Society to enter into present-day political or economic subjects."[42]

The Society's dilemma, rooted in the fundamental tension between unity and diversity that characterizes so much of American Jewish life, was in the final analysis irresolvable. What was new in this case was the issue: Zionism and all that it represented. True, the publication committee had argued about the subject before, but now the context was entirely different. Almost every Jewish religious and communal organization debated this question in the 1940s—some, like the Central Conference of American Rabbis, directly; others, like JPS, indirectly—and not a few came close to schism. "It is," Horace Stern sadly admitted at one point in the Society's debate, "almost unbelievable the bitterness that prevails on this subject. I have seen what is going on in the [American Jewish] Conference, the American Jewish Committee, the Union of American Hebrew Congregations, in synagogue meetings. Feeling is very tense—there is a great deal of hysteria." Given the stresses and fears of wartime, the special frustrations of American Jews watching helplessly as so much of European Jewry was marched off to its death, and the frightening specter of a world out of control, being transformed in ways that could neither be predicted nor understood, the Zionism controversy took on a special edge; it became, in a sense, the focus for a larger debate over tradition and change in which the future of American Jewry seemed to hang in the balance. *Harvest in the Desert*, in and of itself, was unimportant; even Levinthal admitted that it was "not great literature." What was important, as well as deeply revealing, were the passions unleashed by the debate over the book. They bespoke the hopes and fears that underlay the whole Zionism question.[43]

When the shouting died down, however, both pro- and anti-Zionists on the board of trustees agreed on one point: "that the Jewish Publication Society should not have a cleavage." A painfully hammered out compromise, unanimously agreed to, resolved that Levinthal would formally appoint three additional readers for *Harvest in the Desert*, Solis-Cohen, Frankel, and Fineshriber; that their reports, the original reports, and any supplementary reports by the original readers would be circulated to all members of the publication committee for a second vote; and that the trustees would reconsider the book as soon as the new vote was in. Jacobs interpreted this decision as a personal affront and immediately handed in his resignation. But he worried needlessly, for the publication committee quickly voted twenty-one to ten in favor of publication, and the trustees unanimously went along, adding a proviso that the book be carefully edited and carry a disclaimer. A letter by Edwin Wolf 2nd, one of the board's youngest members, and the third generation of his family to be involved in JPS, helped carry the day. Sent from the Army Specialized Training Program at the University of Missouri where he was serving, it set forth an ideological middle ground, couched in staunchly American terms, that all sides found themselves able to accept:

> As the only major Jewish publishing house we should betray our trust if we deny publication to a book because it reflects views, not subversive, irreligious nor undignified, but merely contrary to those which some of us hold. One of the basic tenets of a free country is freedom of opinion, and it is not for a group of men, presumably interested in "the publication and dissemination of literary, scientific, and religious works, giving instructions in the principles of the Jewish religion and in Jewish history and literature" to set themselves up as the censors of Jewish opinion in America.... I hope that were an equally good anti-Zionist book to be written the same view would be taken.

This broad-minded approach essentially vindicated the policy enunciated by Levinthal and gave the green light to additional volumes of the same sort. As for Maurice Jacobs, the trustees refused to accept his resignation, and instead promoted him to executive vice-president. In addition, "in view of the splendid results in membership and in other business of the Society in 1943," they voted him a substantial raise.[44]

Harvest in the Desert sold every bit as well as Jacobs had projected. It commanded the largest first printing in the history of the Society, 21,500 copies, and went through at least four more printings within the next four years. Copies distributed by JPS (but not other editions) carried a carefully written statement by Louis Levinthal, explaining that "every Jewish work of literary value, offering positive, constructive help in understanding Jewish life and culture" fell within the Society's scope. "To discharge its obligation," it continued, "the Society, without necessarily endorsing the opinions of this or any author, publishes books of diversified subject-matter and points of view." The old consensus-oriented policy, at least on paper, was no longer in effect.[45]

Soon after, the Society published two additional pro-Zionist books, each carrying the same protective disclaimer. The first, Solomon Liptzin's *Germany's Stepchildren*, a study of Jewish involvement in German literature, was a thinly veiled brief against the inherent "duality" of Jewish life in the Diaspora. A pioneering attempt to derive "lessons" from the German Jewish tragedy, it advocated an idealistic form of cultural Zionism, the hope that the Jewish people "might soon begin to betake itself to the land of its glorious past and resume its long interrupted creative activity."[46] The second and better-known work was Marie Syrkin's *Blessed Is the Match: The Story of Jewish Resistance*, the first full-length account in English of how courageous Jewish parachutists from Palestine, along with underground Jewish fighters in various parts of Europe, resisted the Nazis even in the face of insuperable odds. A popular, avowedly pro-Zionist book, it followed in the tradition of Samuel's volume, complete with a large advanced sale. Yet in this case, it passed without fireworks: Jacobs and Levinthal simply repeated the procedures agreed upon earlier.[47]

Opponents of Zionism reminded the Society that freedom of expression meant a fair hearing for their side too. In 1945, they submitted a pair of anti-Zionist volumes for JPS consideration: Israel I. Mattuck's *What Are the Jews?* and Elmer Berger's *The Jewish Dilemma*. Both volumes had significant insider support, and both were sent out for evaluation in the usual fashion. Yet, much to Levinthal's relief, neither won final approval. In the case of Mattuck, a leader of British Liberal Judaism, his volume was secretly doomed by eighty-year-old Samuel Schulman, a longtime opponent of Jewish nationalism, and one of Mattuck's friends and admirers. "I feel like the father who, having thrashed his son, said that it hurt him more to give the thrashing than for the boy to take it," Schulman wrote after finishing his lengthy critique of the work. Nevertheless, he recommended "that the Committee decline to accept the manuscript as inadequate"—which it did.

Berger's manuscript, reflecting the views of one of America's leading anti-Zionists, the moving force behind the American Council for Judaism, proved a more difficult problem. Rabbis Sidney S. Tedesche and William Fineshriber both heartily recommended it for publication. Grayzel compiled a long list of its purported "distortions"; but, of course, he was a Zionist. Partisans on both sides sharpened their knives for a renewed confrontation. By the time the publication committee met to make its decision, however, *The Jewish Dilemma* was on the market, published by Devin-Adair. As a matter of policy, the Society routinely rejected books already in print, and so Levinthal sent it straight back to the board of trustees. Solis-Cohen and Frankel were chagrined, but there was nothing that they could do. By a five-to-two vote, the trustees agreed "that the Society maintain its established precedent and that the request of Elmer Berger to publish his book *The Jewish Dilemma* be declined."[48] Several trustees urged the publication committee to renew its efforts "to obtain a suitable manuscript written from a non-Zionist point of view." But later in the postwar period, as American Jews mourned the loss of six million in Europe and then watched proudly as the State of Israel was born, these last gasps of anti-Zionism faded away. The Society, along with the bulk of American Jews, formed close ties to the new state, and came to support Israel as a matter of course.[49]

Many at JPS viewed with dismay the angry, exhausting battles over Zionism. They cherished the memory of those days when divisiveness and rancor rarely intruded upon the gentlemanly atmosphere of its deliberations, and consensus ruled supreme. Yet in numerous ways, this stormy debate actually proved salutary, for it confirmed the Society's emergence as a modern publisher. It already looked like a modern publisher, employing up-to-date methods of administration and book distribution. Now, at last, it had modern publishing policies to match. Henceforward, it could address controversial issues head on, publish responsible books without necessarily endorsing their message, and invite popular authors writing on timely subjects to appear under its imprint, much like trade publishers did. Of course, the Society did not fully cast off the traditions of the past, and continued to move cautiously in many areas. But in its view of itself and of its responsibilities to the Jewish community, it had entered a new era.

The Search for New Literary Standards

The Society's new look was not confined to books on controversial subjects. Its publishing policy in general underwent a perceptible change. Beginning in the late 1930s, books appearing under its imprint became more diverse, popular, timely, readable, and interesting—not surprisingly, for they had to satisfy a growing and variegated membership and to contend in an ever-widening Anglo-Jewish literary marketplace. By now, the Society had largely made peace with the fact that it faced competition. It joined with other Jewish publishers in the Jewish Book Council, founded in 1940, and it participated in Jewish Book Week, inaugurated by librarian Fanny Goldstein, "to call attention to the large amount of literature of and about the Jews that has accumulated and that is still accumulating." With more manuscripts being submitted to it for publication than it could possibly issue—over fifteen hundred from 1936 to 1945—it no longer felt threatened by the entrance of others into the Jewish publishing field. Knowing that its competitors would gladly publish what it did not, it concentrated on supplying members and potential members with the best and most appropriate books that it could find for them to read.[50]

Now that it published six books a year instead of three, JPS sought to diversify its annual offerings "so that both the layman and the scholar could have their choice." As always, the publication committee was pulled in numerous directions:

> Shall we ... give precedence to biography or to history, to poetry or to fiction? What proportion of our publications should be devoted to juvenile and adolescent needs? Shall we seek manuscripts only in English, or shall we translate works already written or published in foreign languages? Shall we wait for manuscripts to be submitted, or shall we commission authors to write on specially assigned

topics? Shall we publish apologetic literature aimed solely to combat anti-Semitism? Then too there is the constant problem of choosing between the popular and the erudite volume.

What was new in this period, even before the debate over Zionism arose, was that relevance became a prime factor in making decisions. Rabbi Mortimer Cohen of Philadelphia, a member of the publication committee and Grayzel's closest friend, explained that the Society needed to place greater stress on the "literature of power," "those books that, rooted in the finest scholarship, are so written as to utilize that scholarship to interpret the present, and to make knowledge of the past meaningful in the searchings, perplexities and struggles of our own times." Many of his colleagues seem to have agreed.[51]

This emphasis soon showed up on the Society's list of new and forthcoming books. Timely and popular volumes predominated; books thought to have "no connection with present-day Jewish life" were rejected for that reason alone. Thus Montagu F. Modder's *The Jew in the Literature of England*, a volume bearing on anti-Semitism and written by a Gentile, won acceptance, despite its inadequacies, because it had important contemporary implications. In addition, works of nineteenth- and twentieth-century history showed up on the list more frequently than ever before—a reflection, perhaps, of heightened interest in the recent past among Americans generally, as they realized how quickly their world was changing. On the other hand, once the Schiff Classics series ended, new critical editions of Jewish texts as well as other volumes written for scholars alone practically vanished from the list; the Society's broader membership did not find them appealing.[52]

The trend is easily visible in the Society's offerings in the area of biography, which still featured prominently on its list, but now dealt largely with modern figures. There was Bein's massive biography of Theodor Herzl and Solomon Poesner's valuable study of the French Jewish leader Adolph Cremieux, both translations of works that first appeared abroad, as well as Norman Bentwich's somewhat uncritical biography of Solomon Schechter, a volume carefully edited by Schechter's surviving friends. When Cyrus Adler died in 1940, he left a chatty autobiography that the Society also published, its first venture into that genre. Two other collections that it published during this period, Alexander Marx's, *Essays in Jewish Biography* and Leo Schwarz's fascinating collection entitled *Memoirs of My People* contained an abundance of contemporary material as well. Without it, the books would probably not have passed muster.[53]

Two volumes issued in the 1940s focused on the contemporary period as a whole. Mark Wischnitzer, in a pioneering and penetratingly insightful work (originally prepared for the American Jewish Committee) entitled *To Dwell in Safety*, detailed the history of a central, but at the time surprisingly little studied aspect of contemporary Jewish life—the story of Jewish migrations since 1800.

James G. McDonald, onetime chairman of President Roosevelt's Advisory Committee on Political Refugees, was impressed with the volume and agreed to recommend it in a preface. "Nowhere else, in any other volume or group of volumes," he wrote admiringly, "can one find the facts so clearly portrayed or the causes and results of this modern exodus so searchingly analyzed." The volume is particularly remarkable for its prescient critique of Allied refugee policy during and after World War II, and of British policy toward refugees seeking entry into Palestine. Without equivocating, it charged—this in 1948—that "many more Jews could have been brought out from Nazi Europe and the post-war detention camps had the democratic governments shown a genuine will to help the victims of totalitarianism." It continued with a prediction: "If history condemns, as it surely will, the Nazi-fascist states which had persecuted, expelled, and slaughtered the Jews it will also point an accusing finger at those states which refused entry to the survivors of the holocaust. Exceptions were few." Unfortunately, the volume quickly fell victim to the bane of all contemporary history—the onrushing tide of human events. The founding of the State of Israel and changes in American immigration policy dated the volume, while its indictment of Allied policy was buried as interest shifted to happier subjects. When the bleak story was rediscovered two decades later, Wischnitzer was long forgotten.[54]

Events had an opposite effect on the Society's other, and even more ambitious work in contemporary history—Ismar Elbogen's *A Century of Jewish Life*—which actually gained in stature as time went along. This was a commissioned volume designed to bring Graetz's history up to date, and the man originally selected for the task was Cecil Roth. But the trustees failed to approve him, notwithstanding even Alexander Marx's recommendation, on the grounds that "if possible an American scholar should be employed to do this work." Elbogen, professor since 1902 at Germany's famed liberal seminary, the *Lehranstalt* (1922–33, *Hochschule*) *für die Wissenschaft des Judentums*, hardly qualified on this score, but in 1939 he at least had the advantage of living in the country, and at age 65 he was recognized as a senior scholar who had contributed mightily to German Jewish life and culture. Under a unique arrangement among America's leading institutions of higher Jewish learning, he had been brought to New York as a refugee scholar and appointed Research Professor in the Fields of Jewish and Hebrew Research based at the Jewish Theological Seminary. Contemporary history was not really his major field—he is best remembered for his path-breaking work in Jewish liturgy—but he nevertheless accepted the assignment "with enthusiasm": partly because he needed the money, partly because it allowed him to reevaluate the world in which he himself had lived and worked. In just under two years he completed an enormous manuscript (almost eight hundred pages of printed text), and Moses Hadas of Columbia University promptly translated it into English. JPS was preparing to invite Elbogen to undertake a new project when, only a few days after submitting his final revisions to the history, he suddenly died. It was left to Grayzel to see the volume through the press.[55]

Elbogen's first draft proved a disappointment to some readers. It overemphasized events in Germany and worldwide anti-Semitism, underemphasized cultural developments and American Jewry's contributions—even though JPS had included in its commission the usual stipulation that American Jewish history "receive generous treatment"—and, "while smooth-flowing," some complained that the whole narrative "lacked drama." Elbogen, Hadas, and Grayzel corrected some of these problems before publication, and those that remained were not so serious as to detract from the history's many virtues. Nor did Elbogen's unconcealed enthusiasm for Zionism cause much of a stir. Although the American Council for Judaism issued a ritualistic condemnation, most who read it sympathized with its moderate stance, which rejected "any thought of a double allegiance," while supporting unity, good will, and compromise.[56]

What did cause a major controversy, unforeseen by any of the book's advance readers, was Elbogen's hostile treatment of the Soviet Union. His belief, which history has vindicated, was that the Communists ("Bolshevists") on the extreme left were no better than the Fascists on the extreme right, and he tarred both with the same brush, accusing the Communists of fomenting revolution and engaging in anti-Semitism. This may have been somewhat impolitic, because by the time the book appeared Russia had broken with Hitler to become America's wartime ally, and thousands of Jews were fleeing to Russia seeking refuge from Hitler's advancing armies. Elbogen's most persistent critics, however, were less concerned with his timing than with his ideology in general. Although reports of Stalin's anti-Semitism had surfaced, they vehemently denied them, certain that all criticism of the Communist regime was propaganda. Rabbi John Tepfer, then on the faculty of the Jewish Institute of Religion, for example, characterized Elbogen's allegations as "downright vicious" and charged that he wrote "like a real Fascist." Jacob B. Aronoff, the lawyer who spearheaded the anti-Elbogen drive, demanded that all copies of the history be recalled (another reviewer urged that they be burned) and proposed that a new "positive" volume be issued demonstrating that "the Soviet Union is a powerful state which has set an example to the nations of the world in showing that a state and people determined to eradicate anti-Semitism can do it."[57]

In the end, after various experts agreed that the history contained some factual errors in its treatment of Russia, Grayzel introduced "a number of changes and corrections" into the second printing. To take the most controversial example, Elbogen had charged that "the Bolshevist Red Army " in the Ukraine (1919) "was also responsible for more than a hundred pogroms, but with them plunder rather than murder was the main objective." Grayzel changed this to read that "undisciplined elements, whose shifting allegiances sometimes brought them under the Bolshevist flag, were also responsible for many pogroms. Such elements were, however, sternly reproved by the Bolshevist government." He also wrote into the text a new paragraph praising Russia both for recognizing "the principle of national self-determination for all" and for declaring anti-Semitism "punishable as a counter-revolutionary crime." Yet as time went on, Elbogen's interpretation, not just of Russia's treatment of Jews but of contemporary developments generally, was borne out. His periodization scheme, his belief that World War II marked a turning point in Jewish history, and his sense that postwar Jewish history would be concerned with the rise of a Jewish state (or commonwealth) and the need to maintain Jewish identity intact were right on target, anticipating themes that would dominate all postwar Jewish historiography.[58]

Even as he brought Elbogen's work to press, Solomon Grayzel was completing his own contribution to this new historiography: a one-volume Jewish history covering the entire period from the Babylonian exile (not the Biblical period, "I was afraid to deal with that") to the end of World War II. He developed it out of his teaching at Gratz College and geared it "for the confirmation age level, from fifteen up." Rather than taking the encyclopedic approach of Margolis and Marx, he planned his as a readable interpretive narrative, akin to Abram Sachar's best-selling *History of the Jews*, but with different emphases and more attention to social and economic developments. In the wake of World War II, Grayzel, as we have seen, believed that Jews needed reassurance as to their future. "One of my reasons for writing *A History of the Jews*," he confided, "has been my desire to fortify the spirit and strengthen the determination of my fellow Jews to persevere in the path of our ancestors, and patiently and hopefully to labor for the welfare of mankind." Although he followed Elbogen's lead in stressing Zion and what he called "the responsibility to carry high the banner of Jewish hope and idealism through the ages yet to come," his analysis of the contemporary period was much more centered on America. "It is in America," he firmly believed, "that the opportunity of living the Jewish life in freedom has the brightest hopes of realization."[59]

Fearing conflict of interest, Grayzel sought to publish his history with a commercial house. He worked on his manuscript at home and, always sensitive to criticism, tried hard to ensure that nobody could ever accuse him of writing his history on "company time." But Maurice Jacobs, seeing the volume's potential as a textbook, convinced him to submit the work anonymously to the publication committee, and it was accepted. The volume appeared in 1947, it was revised in 1952 to include the establishment of the State of Israel, and with several additional updatings it continues in print. It still remains one of the leading textbooks in the field.[60]

For all of its emphasis on the contemporary, the Society also published some half-dozen other works of history during this period. They covered different eras and spanned the spectrum from popular to scholarly. What was common to all of them, however, was an abiding concern for timeliness; they related events in the past to the needs of the present. Cecil Roth, who authored fully half of these volumes and was the Society's most popular historian during these years, made this one of his indispensable keys to success.

Roth's ambitious *History of the Jews of Italy* is a case in point. First proposed to JPS back in 1938 but published only after the war, it covered "over twenty centuries and half a dozen successive civilizations" and traced the history of Jews all the way through the end of the Nazi occupation. Given Italy's prominence in the news, this was obviously a timely volume, but it was also more. For Roth loved Italy ("I have ... known more happiness there than in any other land"), and felt a special responsibility to make his history, the first of its kind in any language, as thorough and accurate as possible. As a result the book is one of his best; even his perennial critic, Professor Isaiah Sonne of Hebrew Union College, praised its "vast erudition." In this case, however, Sonne's comments in the *Jewish Quarterly Review* are more often remembered as the stimulus for one of the great literary exchanges in the history of book reviewing. Noting that Roth cited no sources, Sonne wrote that "one should like to know the basis or source" for some of his statements about an obscure ninth-century liturgical poet named Menahem Corizzi. The answer appeared in the very next issue. "My authority for this," Roth wrote, was a scholarly article in Italian, which he then cited by title. "And the name of the Author?" he continued, savoring the moment. *"None other than Dr. I. Sonne!"*[61]

Unfortunately, Roth's other two volumes, biographies of Doña Gracia Nasi and her nephew Joseph Nasi, Duke of Naxos, were far less successful, at least from the historian's point of view. Although the former may be remembered as one of the first books in English on any Jewish woman of the medieval period, it was patronizing and uncritical. If his history was faulty, however, his message, filled with contemporary allusions, reveals much about the mood of Jews in the immediate postwar period; for both volumes were nothing less than briefs for Jewish power and self-determination. Interestingly, Roth compared Doña Gracia to Henrietta Szold, and Joseph Nasi to Theodor Herzl.[62]

Though admittedly to a lesser extent, the same powerful sense that the Jewish past carries important lessons for those living in the present also animated the historical works produced during this period by Louis Finkelstein, Salo Baron, and Abraham A. Neuman—all three published as part of the scholarly Morris Loeb series. Finkelstein's two-volume *The Pharisees* sought to prove that "the prophetic, Pharisaic and rabbinic traditions were the products of a persistent cultural battle carried on in Palestine for fifteen centuries, between the submerged, unlanded groups, and their oppressors, the great landowners." This was more than just another Marxist analysis, for it also dealt learnedly with urban-rural tensions and even with the environmental basis of some Talmudic disputes. But the volume nevertheless had a contemporary ring. For, although Finkelstein claimed that a

1925 visit to Palestine inspired the major themes of his study, it also seems likely that his views were influenced by the Great Depression, which highlighted some of the very same social, cultural, and class tensions within American society. In his preface Finkelstein himself noted "the widespread fear that political antagonisms are moving toward the destruction of our inherited civilization." He worried about economic uprootedness in America and what he perceived as a weakened sense of communal responsibility, especially on the part of intellectuals. "Perhaps at such a time," he concluded significantly, "the ancient amalgam of urbanity and rusticity . . . which formulated itself successively in the profoundly spiritual movements of Prophecy and Pharisaism may be studied not only out of curiosity or historical interest, but also for guidance."[63]

Salo Baron's remarkable three-volume study, *The Jewish Community: Its History and Structure to the American Revolution*, had similar pedagogic goals. Its opening pages both rebutted the Nazi definition of Jewish community and promised "to promote clarity" about a subject that Zionists and Reform Jews, philo-Semites and anti-Semites all lustily debated, more out of ignorance, usually, than fact. As a broad synthetic work, covering everything from "the Palestinian municipality" to the Jewish community as "crucible of capitalism and enlightenment," the study stood in stark contrast to the narrowly conceived volumes of the earlier Jewish Community series. It exemplified instead what may be seen as the Society's new ideal for what scholarship published under its imprint should be: big books on big subjects. Indirectly, it also reinforced the theory, first propounded in Margolis and Marx's history, that the modern period in Jewish history should begin with the American Revolution, a patriotic stance that the Society did not insist upon but certainly endorsed. Yet, what made *The Jewish Community* particularly significant, as *Chicago Jewish Forum* reviewer Samuel M. Blumenfield recognized at the time, was that it "ushered in a new era in Jewish historiography." With it, Jewish social history finally came into its own. "Such a study of the Jewish community in its totality," Blumenfield continued, echoing the Society's own thinking, "is particularly valuable at this stage of Jewish history when Jewish life is shaken to its very foundations and there is need for sounder knowledge and better understanding of the Jewish Community of yesterday—to help evolve the Jewish community of today and of tomorrow."[64]

The same sense that the past could help guide both present and future is found again in Abraham A. Neuman's two-volume social, cultural, and political history of the Jews of medieval Spain. His claim, however, took in more than the other books, for he saw his history as not only timely but also prophetic. Like many before him, he read a moral lesson into Spanish Jewish history, the idea that those who persecuted the Jews would ultimately suffer dire consequences. This was a message of hope in the dark days of 1942, and it infused his reading of Spanish Jewish history with contemporary meaning: "Were the historian to turn prophet," he wrote, "he would be tempted to forecast for a Gestapo Germany the social decline and the intellectual and spiritual deterioration of an Inquisition-ridden Spain."[65]

"A Hunger for Affirmations"

Surveying the Jewish literary scene immediately after the war, Joshua Bloch, chief of the Jewish division of the New York Public Library, wrote of a "general change of mood which has taken place in Jewry." He described the new mood in critic Van Wyck Brooks's phrase as "a hunger for affirmations, for a world without confusions, waste, or groping, a world that is full of order and purpose." "Quite inevitably," he concluded, "a time of national and world disaster has turned multitudes to a search for something by which the spirit can live, to positive affirmations."[66] JPS, which understood the popular mood very well, stood in the forefront of those who sought to meet this new need. More than ever before, it now welcomed popular books designed to promote "Jewish enrichment," such as its new series of Jewish holiday anthologies. The first three volumes of the series, the only ones to appear during this period, covered three joyous days: *Hanukkah* (1937), *Sabbath: the Day of Delight* (1944), and *The Purim Anthology* (1949), the latter specifically aimed at "conveying to its readers a feeling of optimism concerning the Jewish future." Naturally, all three volumes avoided religious controversy, which was one advantage of the anthology format. They also addressed the specific needs of Jews in America and overflowed with material for families with youngsters, an appropriate bow to the increasingly child-centered nature of American Judaism in general. Philip Goodman, whose *Purim Anthology* was the most skillfully arranged and successful of these volumes, later carried the series forward with books about the other major holidays, completing the Jewish festival cycle.[67]

The Society's other books of Jewish enrichment focused on the Bible. It published popular commentaries to the Books of Numbers and Deuteronomy and co-published with Harper and Brothers the first two volumes of Rabbi Solomon Goldman's *Book of Human Destiny*, a projected large-scale introduction and survey of the Bible left incomplete at the author's untimely death. Most important of all, it issued Mortimer Cohen's *Pathways Through the Bible*, a volume that sold over two hundred thousand copies and became one of its all-time bestsellers. Known as the "Junior Bible" during its years in preparation, *Pathways* began as a modest project designed to produce "an abbreviated Bible for boys and girls of about fifteen," who were not yet ready to read the Bible in Victorian English, much less in the original Hebrew. By the time it was ready to appear, however, the Society realized that this "simplified version of *The Holy Scriptures*," rewritten and edited with introductions and subheadings so as to be "readable, easy to comprehend and even enjoyable," and endorsed by a special group "of rabbis, scholars and educators, representing various shades of American Judaism," might, given the mood of the day, have broader commercial possibilities. So it marketed the volume exuberantly as an aid to any "unskilled traveller," young and old, Jew and Gentile, seeking "to hew out pathways through the richly luxuriant and forestlike complexities of the Bible literature." It tried particularly to win its acceptance into Jewish confirmation and high school classes, a market Jacobs had long wanted the Society to break into.[68]

One of *Pathways*'s unusual features was its generous use of artistic illustrations. Comparable books by Christians always included "Bible portraits" as teaching aids, and educational theorists had concluded that, at least for children, "pictures are an essential method of grasping ideas." Because Cohen sought to make his volume as competitive and alluring as possible, he decided that his volume should include illustrations too—but not, of course, the standard Christian ones. Instead, he looked for genuinely Jewish Bible pictures. In a fascinating and highly revealing memo that speaks volumes about his whole attitude toward the Bible and its affirmative message for Jews, he spelled out just what he wanted these pictures to convey:

> 1. Biblical pictures should not express a warlike spirit, nor should they be scenes of violence and cruelty. The famous artists of the past in the Bible pictures they painted, often glorified the military rather than the peaceful virtues of the ancient Jews. In large measure, they are responsible for the false notion that the Bible is a book of violence and the God of Israel is a harsh and cruel God. . . .
> 2. Biblical pictures should not mislead the modern reader into believing that the Bible is concerned only with persons and events of the dead past. Such pictures create the feeling that the Bible has only an antiquarian interest for the present generation. . . . The clothes on the figures in the pictures, therefore, should be of a universal character—drapes rather than exact reproductions of the ancient garments. They will not then emphasize too much the difference in time between the past and the present.[69]

When the Society decided to commission the illustrations, Columbia University's great art critic, Meyer Shapiro, strongly recommended to Grayzel that before doing anything rash he consider an unpublished series of works by the then fairly obscure artist, Marc Chagall. Grayzel, when he saw the paintings, was impressed. But the Society's laymen, who had never heard of Chagall, did not agree (Grayzel thought that they found the paintings "too Jewish.") At a much higher fee and a royalty besides (indeed, his contract was worth more than Cohen's), they contracted with the better-known Arthur Szyk, whose anti-Nazi cartoons had won him a vast following in American Jewish circles. Time, however, proved them wrong. Szyk's agent and later his heirs caused no end of problems, always believing that the artist had been underpaid and underpromoted, while his somewhat controversial illustrations neither lived up to Cohen's hopes, nor to the Society's. Chagall's Bible paintings, by contrast, won worldwide fame. Still, Szyk may have contributed to the popularity of *Pathways Through the Bible*, and his chilling dedication, printed in the front of the volume on a separate page, received considerable notice:

> In March 1943 my beloved seventy-year-old mother, Eugenia Szyk, was taken from the ghetto of Lodz to the Nazi furnaces of Maidanek. With her, voluntarily went her faithful servant, the good Christian, Josefa, a Polish peasant. Together, hand in hand, they were burned alive. In memory of the two noble martyrs I dedicate my pictures of the Bible as an eternal Kaddish for these great souls.[70]

While books on the Bible and Jewish practice may have helped answer the "hunger for affirmations" that American Jews felt on a popular level, the Society privately admitted that it had done nothing to satisfy "a hunger on the part of our intellectuals for an approach to Jewish theology." The postwar period witnessed a theological renaissance among Jewish intellectuals, but the thinkers that some of the best minds were drawn to were Christians, particularly existentialists and so-called crisis-theologians. Their answers to the perplexities of the day, born of war and the failed social vision of the 1930s, were anything but Jewish. Solomon Grayzel, "horrified" by this trend, thought "that type of non-Jewish thinking should have been far from the mind of a thinking Jew." He believed that the Society, now a major force in American Jewish cultural life, had a responsibility to come up with something better. He called on Rabbi Milton Steinberg, one of the most gifted Jewish thinkers of the day and a highly influential writer, to help out.

Steinberg pronounced himself "deeply interested" and agreed with Grayzel that new ideas denying "man's ability to attain the good either in his individual or his collective life," were "a prime heresy," even an "affront to the Jewish spirit." "I think," he declared, "that we ought to go out and do battle against this new notion . . . as our forefathers went out and fought Gnostic dualism."[71] Unfortunately, ill health ultimately prevented him from personally leading the theological countercrusade that he believed necessary. But this exchange still reveals much about the Society's outlook during these years, its strivings as well as its limitations. Although understanding the cultural needs of American Jews, it could not always meet them. Although watching out for new cultural developments, it often ended up opposing them.

The same ambivalence characterized the Society's approach to fiction. On the one hand it understood that fiction was a prime vehicle for reaching out to a broad popular audience; it therefore searched eagerly "for a second Zangwill." On the other hand, it continued to find most of American Jewish fiction utterly distasteful, filled with immorality, intermarriage, and Jewish self-hatred. Back in 1935, when it offered the Edwin Wolf award "for the best novel of Jewish interest submitted to the Society," it was disappointed. After admitting that most of the submissions were poor, the judges—novelists Fannie Hurst and Dorothy Canfield Fisher, as well as trustee Edwin Wolf 2nd—awarded the prize to Beatrice Bisno for her novel entitled *Tomorrow's Bread*, a reluctant choice. This was a realistic radical novel based on the rise to power of a Chicago Jewish labor leader—clearly Sidney Hillman, whom Bisno had worked under for eight years—and it portrayed the humble tailors of the garment industry, whose lot the protagonist sought with single-minded devotion to improve. The story proved too strong for JPS members, some of whom protested, and Grayzel considered it unsympathetic and without charm. Worst of all, it failed to convey the "positive Jewish point of view" that the Society looked for in all of its books. No novel of this type ever found its way onto the Society's list again.[72]

What JPS published instead were novels of affirmation: tales of courage, of Jews who, having strayed from their faith, found it anew, and historical allegories filled with contemporary meaning, many of them written by immigrants and refugees. Its leading novelist during this period was Soma Morgenstern, a highly cultured refugee from Vienna, who published a trilogy centered around the return to Judaism of "the son of the lost son," the child of a convert to Christianity. Maurice Samuel recommended the first in the series, actually entitled *The Son of the Lost Son,* as "a brilliant and sophisticated novel, filled with charming and moving incidents, keen characterization, vivid description and tense situations." Freshness of theme and literary merit were not all that recommended it. One member of the publication committee approved the novel in the hope that it would also "warm the cockles of many a Jewish heart and awaken a longing to return to those old and matter-of-course practices of daily orthodox living from which many of the children of Israel have become estranged." There is, however, no evidence that Morgenstern himself had any such revivalistic aims in mind.

Novels of return to Judaism, if not necessarily to Orthodoxy, were becoming increasingly common in European Jewish fiction, particularly under the "back-to-the-ghetto movement," as well as in American Jewish fiction. This was an understandable trend, given the world Jewish situation. Ludwig Lewisohn wrote several books along this line, including *Renegade* (1942), which JPS co-published, and in 1946, the very year that Morgenstern's first novel appeared, Harper and Brothers published *Wasteland* by Ruth Seid (Jo Sinclair), an account of a Jew who denied his heritage and, as a result, suffered serious psychological consequences. "Today," Elliot E. Cohen observed in 1947, summing up Jewish cultural trends in America, "Jewish reaffirmation is the watchword."[73]

The rest of the Society's fiction consisted of two genres. First, there were tales woven from biblical materials, like the Anglo-Jewish novelist Louis Golding's *In the Steps of Moses* and the Viennese playwright, Richard Beer-Hoffmann's *Jacob's Dream*. These underscored the timelessness of the Bible, the idea, common also in Christian circles, that Scripture speaks to modern man. Beer-Hoffmann's play, for example, was praised as a work "that seems to have been written especially for our times, when the Jewish people need encouragement and enlightenment in facing the sorrows and tragedies of our world." Neither his nor Golding's work, however, secured much of a following.[74]

Second, there were historical novels centered around episodes from the Jewish past. Although perhaps less religious than the first group, these still were far safer than fiction depicting the contemporary scene, and they provided readers with background in Jewish history besides. They also proved popular with members. Of the four such works published, three came from Europe where the tradition of Jewish historical fiction was firmly established. The only exception, Charles Reznikoff's *The Lionhearted*, based on the York massacre in the twelfth century, is noteworthy as being among the first Jewish historical novels of its type written by an American Jewish author. Of the European works themselves, Joseph Opatashu's *In Polish Woods*, a rich Yiddish novel dealing with the clash between Hasidim and the Maskilim (enlightened Jews) in mid-nineteenth-century Poland, and filled with true-to-life depictions of Jewish involvement in the timber trade, was, by the time the Society published it, already recognized as a literary masterpiece, and had been translated into half a dozen languages. In making it available in English, the Society helped introduce Opatashu, who by then lived in New York, to a wider American audience, and added to its already impressive roster of Yiddish classics in translation.[75]

Selma Stern's *The Spirit Returneth*, set in fourteenth-century Germany, dealt with persecutions of Jews at the time of the Black Death. Written by a noted German Jewish historian who was a refugee living in Cincinnati, the novel was obviously composed with the contemporary situation of German Jewry in mind. It reminded readers of Germany's long history of anti-Jewish persecutions, and echoed with the crisis of faith that tormented so many who lived through the Nazi atrocities. Yet the story ended on an uplifting note, reflecting the very sentiments that JPS at the time was seeking to encourage. "The remnant remains," it concluded, in a solemn testimony to abiding trust in God, "And that remnant of the House of Judah will shoot roots below and bear fruit above."[76]

The Society's most important historical novel, a difficult work that many members disliked at the time but that today is considered a classic, was written by a social philosopher. Published in 1945, it was entitled *For the Sake of Heaven*, and its author was Martin Buber. Already a figure of considerable intellectual renown in the Jewish world, Buber was scarcely known in the United States since few of his works had yet been translated. Clearly seeking to be better known, he approached JPS in 1941 with a plan for "a book about Judaism and Christianity." With obvious regret, the Society turned him down. "The subject, under present circumstances," Grayzel explained, "is likely to cause a certain amount of irritation in this country, especially if it were to appear under our imprint."

Yet even before he received this rejection, Buber had dispatched to the Society the manuscript of his novel, in German, which he called "Gog and Magog": a novel of ideas, set against the background of the Napoleonic era, that explored the world of the Hasidim, depicting their conflicting attitudes toward the French conqueror, as well as the tension between opposing types of religious figures, different approaches to the problem of evil, and, at the deepest level, disagreements over the meaning of Israel, redemption, and human existence itself. Taking no chances with the Society's usual crew of readers, Grayzel sent the manuscript for review to Professor Shalom Spiegel, then of the Jewish Institute of Religion, who knew Buber, and to Abraham Joshua Heschel, one of the refugee scholars brought over by Hebrew Union College, who knew Hasidism. Both responded with enthusiasm, the book was accepted, Ludwig Lewisohn translated it, and it was published. By then the title had been changed. Nobody much liked "Gog and Magog," and everybody was much amused at Buber's alternate suggestion, ' ɔr God's Sake." *For the Sake of Heaven*, however, nicely captured his central idea. The novel, which, according to his biographer, Buber personally considered "his most important book," appeared in paperback in 1953 and spawned a considerable critical literature. It stands alone in Buber's vast oeuvre: "A book of this kind," he himself admitted, "I have never written before . . . and even if God grants me a long life, I shall never write such again."[77]

A Positive Jewish Point of View

"There is no business which demands more constant adherence to a high standard than that of publishing books," B.W. Huebsch of Viking Books, one of the most distinguished Jews in the publishing industry, reminded those assembled at the Society's annual meeting in 1936. He was warning them away from the kind of "inferior thinking and writing that offends the cultivated mind and degrades our taste." Although everyone presumably nodded in agreement, this standard, from the Society's point of view, did not go far enough. To bear its imprint, books also had to be, as Solomon Grayzel once put it in a letter to Lionel Trilling, "on a subject of Jewish interest with a positive Jewish point of view." This naturally meant different things at different times, but for the most part Grayzel and members of the publication committee, heirs to past Society policies, conservative by nature, and fearful of criticism, preferred to err on the side of caution. They understood a "positive Jewish point of view" to mean one that conformed to Jewish tradition, adhered to Victorian standards of morality, and portrayed Judaism in as favorable a light as possible. In the wake of the debate over *Harvest in the Desert*, some spoke of the need to "give up the paternalistic attitude which tries to mould and fails to recognize the possibility of differences," and the Society did relax its demands for ideological conformity. Still, the general contours of what defined a "J.P.S. book" changed little: The Society basically wanted its books to be a credit to Jews in general and to the American Jew in particular.[78]

The Society's standards are easily seen in the realm of children's books. Under Jacobs it issued more of these than ever before, and in a sharp break from the previous era they were now modern, fantasy-filled volumes, complete with fabulous illustrations, large type, and other features especially designed to appeal to youngsters. Sadie Weilerstein, who helped precipitate this change, forgot her hurt over the rejection of *K'tonton* and wrote two charming books for JPS during this period, *What the Moon Brought* (1942) and *Little New Angel* (1947), both classics that a whole generation of young Jews was raised on. Deborah Pessin created the ever-popular *Aleph-Bet Story Book* (1946), an inspired volume that wove memorable tales around each letter of the Hebrew alphabet.[79] Henry J. Berkowitz took time off from his rabbinical duties to author two thrilling teenage adventure stories for Jewish boys, *The Fire Eater* (1941) and *Boot Camp* (1948), possibly the first examples of this particular genre in all of Anglo-Jewish fiction.[80]

Each of these juvenile books conformed to what librarian Fanny Goldstein set forth as the central aims of all good Jewish children's literature: "the development of an appreciation for ethics, the distinction between right and wrong, an awareness of the intrinsic value of virtue and morals, a perception of beauty, the development of normal emotions and responses, and finally an integration with the world at large." JPS subscribed wholeheartedly to these values, even in literature not directly intended for children. Beyond these virtues, JPS also made special efforts to foster patriotism by shifting the focus of Jewish children's literature away from the distant past ("playmates in Egypt") and toward the American present. It therefore urged Berkowitz to make his own world the setting for his fiction; he previously had written mostly about Eastern Europe.

JPS published Dorothy Alofsin's *The Nightingale's Song,* despite no more than lukewarm praise from advance readers, because it thought that another book teaching Jewish and American values was urgently needed. A description of this story about an Americn Jewish girl on a "humble farm" and "her triumph over all obstacles," stressed how the heroine's "four-thousand-year-old Jewish tradition and her ennobling American background have become blended in her spirit. She draws strength out of each separately and from the two together." Similarly, JPS emphasized in advertising Sadie Weilerstein's *What the Moon Brought*, that the holiday stories are "always told from the point of view of an American Jewish child"—they were different indeed from holiday stories for Jewish children passed down through tradition.[81]

Otherwise, however, the Society's approach was idealistic rather than realistic.

When, for example, Grayzel read a scene in one manuscript in which a father justified his son's violations of the Sabbath based on American conditions, he was appalled. Although this reflected reality, he urged that the message be reversed:

> If you could turn this incident into one in which his desire for fun gets the better of his sense of duty to his parents in their desire to see him attend the synagogue on the Sabbath, you would be making the boy much more human and at the same time put yourself on record as one who does not excuse the violation of the Sabbath by a child, or for that matter by an adult.

When, in another case, he thought that author Deborah Pessin was associating Jewish life "with suffering, exile and all the rest of it," he urged her to make her stories "pleasanter." When, in still other cases, he found language or depictions that seemed to him "vulgar" (like the phrase "kick in the pants") or unseemly (like a sharply drawn contrast between a Jewish boy and the son of a Baptist minister), he insisted that they be "washed" and rewritten. "Literature for children," he explained, summing up the Society's philosophy as well as his own, "must be elevated rather than realistic."[82]

The same applied to literature for adults. In this case, the Society's files preserve a revealing example of how its standards were applied even to the most serious of literature—the poetry of A.M. Klein, now recognized as one of the most distinguished Canadian poets of the twentieth century. Born in Ratno, Russia, in 1909 and brought to Canada as a child, Klein obtained a traditional education, trained as a lawyer, and began to publish poetry dealing with secular and Jewish themes as early as 1927. He formed part of what Leon Edel has called the Montreal Group, a miniature Canadian Bloomsbury of young, alert, politically engaged and rebellious cultural figures. In 1940, Behrman House published Klein's first volume of poetry entitled *Hath Not a Jew*. It featured a memorable foreword by Ludwig Lewisohn, who pronounced Klein "the first contributor of authentic Jewish poetry to the English language," and "the only Jew who has ever contributed a new note of style, of expression, of creative enlargement to the poetry of that tongue." This was high praise indeed, especially coming from Lewisohn, and the Society, which had earlier rejected Klein's poetry (apparently, an earlier version of his first book) soon sat up and took notice.[83]

Louis Levinthal who, like Klein, was an Orthodox Jew of East European background, a Zionist, and a lawyer by profession, made the initial overture to the poet (perhaps introduced by Lewisohn), and in 1942 he was rewarded with a 116-page manuscript that he gladly recommended for publication. Far less happily, the publication committee and the trustees went along. "While the Society does not expect a large sale of a book of poetry," Jacobs explained, "we feel it necessary to occasionally print such a book in order to encourage Jewish poets." Yet before the volume, entitled simply *Poems*, could finally be published in 1944, Klein had to agree to accept revisions. One reader, for example, found "too much biology . . . mostly feminine," in the poetry. Others found some of the language crude, at least by the Society's standards. As a result, six love sonnets ("Assurance") were deleted completely. A malediction on Hitler, that he "be remembered if remembered at all, / In the name of some newly found, particularly disgusting fly, / Or in the writing on a privy wall," was also removed; the word "privy" proved objectionable. In addition, "gutter" was changed to "pavement," "ugly filth" became "ugly words," and at least one reader sought to tone down a "steamy" reference to pregnancy—"nine months"—in a poem about the birth of a first-born child. In this case, Klein put his foot down: "I am informed by my wife and by the Civil Code of the Province of Quebec," he wrote, "that the period of gestation is nine months." The offending reference remained in place—but one notes that both the Reform and Reconstructionist Passover Haggadot censored references to these unseemly "nine months" from their translations of the song "Who Knows One" (*"Echad Mi Yodea"*).[84]

Readers criticized another group of Klein's poems for being either "blasphemous," or for sounding too "hopeless a cry in a day when nearly the only thing left to the Jew is hope." Thus the poem "Rabbi Yom-Tob of Mayence Harangues His God" was criticized for its title. Klein gave in, and replaced "harangues" with "petitions." "A Psalm of Resignation," with its plaintive cry, "For who indeed can keep his quarrel hot / And vigorous his cries, / When he who is blasphemed, He answers not, / Replies no word, not even a small sharp word?" had to be excluded altogether; it seemed too heretical. "Kalman Rhapsodizes," with its uncomplimentary reference to angels, met the same fate, as did "Psalm 173," a frightening evocation of inner madness that could easily be interpreted in a negative Jewish way. In each case, the Society made its changes not on a literary basis, to improve the manuscript's quality—although by mutual agreement other poems were excluded for this reason—but rather on the basis of its larger need to project a positive Jewish image to the world. Klein, who himself occupied a responsible position in the Jewish community, understood. "The J.P.S., which knows not who its evesdroppers [*sic*] are," he wrote in a letter to Judge Levinthal, "cannot afford to give its imprimatur to something which the enemies of Israel might use against us." On second thought, however, he was not so certain. "We have indeed come to a sorry pass," he mused, "when we cannot even afford the luxury of self-criticism, lest the foe seek to confound us out of our own mouths."[85]

Although Klein's poetry, albeit in somewhat expurgated form, won final publication, perhaps because Levinthal took so personal an interest in it, a great many other manuscripts considered excessively critical of Jewish life, "too negative," "insufficiently dignified," "too controversial," or the like met with speedy rejections, often even before they were sent out to readers. Censorship was not the question here, for JPS had no monopoly on publishing: Books that it turned down could still be issued elsewhere. These rejections do shed light, however, on the Society's overall cultural standards. They show how insistence on a "positive Jewish point of view" resulted in a policy that kept some highly significant books from appearing under its imprint. When, for example, a learned neurologist proposed writing a psychobiography "from the pathological point of view" about the mystical Rabbi Joseph Karo, author of the legal code known as the *Shulchan Aruch*, Grayzel gave him no encouragement. "We are, after all, an organization with a positive Jewish consciousness," he pointed out. "I wonder whether we would not lay ourselves open to a great deal of criticism if we take one of the saints and heroes of rabbinic life and present him from that point of view." Fear of criticism similarly prompted him to reject the Hebrew novelist Aaron Kabak's work on Jesus. "The translation is excellent," he wrote approvingly, "I really enjoyed reading it. Still, it is Jesus, and I have an ineradicable feeling that it is a subject which is best left alone." Fiction dealing with intermarriage generally fell under the same taboo. "It is not a question of shutting our eyes to what is going on about us," Grayzel explained. "Heaven knows, there is too much intermarriage both in this country and elsewhere. The Jewish Publication Society, however, is dedicated to the presentation of material which tends to strengthen Jewish loyalties." It did so, moreover, through positive books, not polemics. Grayzel, like his predecessors, believed that "it would not be right for the Jewish Publication Society to engage in theological discussions."[86]

In fact, for all the manifold changes that he, Solis-Cohen, Jacobs, and Levinthal had made, and notwithstanding the disclaimers that had been introduced into some books, JPS still adhered to standards remarkably similar to those that applied under Henrietta Szold. It sought educational, noncontroversial, dignified, and patriotic works that it felt members liked, and remained nervous about anything that smacked of divisiveness. Thus, it hesitated to invite the philosopher Horace Kallen to submit a volume of his essays because it considered him too inclined "to the heretical." It refused to publish Jacob Klatzkin's *Crisis and Decision in Judaism*, despite its "learning" and "provocative thought," because the book expressed hopelessness about the chances for diaspora Jewish survival, an idea that in 1944 seemed too hot to handle. It rejected Emanuel Velikovsky's wide-ranging reinterpretation of ancient history that sought to explain events described in the Book of Exodus on the basis of Egyptian documents and natural causes, "lest it turn out to be be a lot of nonsense and the Society be made a laughing stock." It turned down Rabbi Bernard Drachman's autobiography, and many similar volumes, because they included criticism of individuals and organizations. "We are a public institution supported by all sorts of people," Grayzel explained to Drachman's son, spelling out the policy that explains why the other books were rejected as well, "and we have to be careful that we do not take sides in matters of religious or social controversy." Yet a noncontroversial and perfectly harmless book like Harold Ribalow's *Jews in Sports* met with rejection too. "The book ought to sell," Grayzel rightly predicted, "but it just does not fit in with the *dignified* policy of the Jewish Publication Society."[87]

Oral tradition adds one more volume to the list of books that the Society rejected: Gershom Scholem's magisterial *Major Trends in Jewish Mysticism* (1942), one of the seminal works of twentieth-century Jewish scholarship. Scholem himself seems to have believed that the Society rejected him, and he nurtured a grudge against it for many years. Surviving records, however, cast grave doubt on whether his memory of what happened was in fact correct. The first significant mention of this subject appears in the minutes in 1940, when a subcommittee on "Movements in Jewish Life" suggested that Scholem "be asked to write a volume for the Society . . . on the subject of mysticism." The publication committee endorsed the idea, a letter was dispatched to Jerusalem, and nothing more was heard, for the letter went astray. Six months later, Grayzel wrote a second time, and finally in June 1942 Scholem replied that he would have difficulty accepting the assignment because his *Major Trends* had just appeared in English. "I am sure you will see a copy yourself and will be able to best judge yourself whether there will be room for a second publication on similar lines," he wrote. "In my modest opinion such a book would prove derogatory to the first one, and my publisher might think so too."

As a substitute, Scholem offered to sell the Society English rights to the volume he was then writing on the "History of Sabbathianism." No doubt to his disappointment—and this may be the root of the subsequent misunderstanding—Grayzel promised only to consider that volume when it was completed. Meanwhile, the subcommittee on movements in Jewish life continued to hold out for a popularized version of *Major Trends*. "Your volume," Grayzel wrote to him in its name, "is far too scientific for our purpose. What we want is a popularization of the entire movement . . . a book which an intelligent lay reader moderately interested in history could read and profit from." But Scholem did not even bother to reply. "Our correspondence with Professor Gershom Scholem," the minutes of December 6, 1944, read, "has not led to any satisfactory result."[88]

Postwar Decline

Close readers of the Society's annual reports may have noticed something unusual about the one issued in 1946. For the first time in five years the Society operated at a loss. A loss of $10,720.62 on an annual budget that totaled close to $300,000 hardly aroused much concern, especially because an accumulated past surplus more than covered it. But in 1947 the Society lost money again, this time $11,091.36, and the year after that the loss ballooned to $30,432.96. Something had clearly gone wrong.[89]

What had happened was similar in many respects to the situation that JPS had faced following World War I. Once again, inflation drove up costs much faster than the Society was able to raise its prices, and the book business nationwide fell into a tailspin as the national economy contracted in a steep postwar recession. According to a 1949 study, book production costs nationwide rose by 55 to 65 percent in a decade, whereas book prices themselves increased only 25 percent. Publishers all over the country were suffering; Schocken Books, to take one example, was reported to be near bankruptcy.[90]

Yet, these external factors were only part of the problem. For his part, Jacobs met the crisis the only way he knew how: by continuing to forge ahead. He was certain that the economy would pick up and besides, as Jacob Marcus recalls, he "believed that his first duty was to print and distribute good books, to raise the cultural standards of American Jewry." He was far less concerned about debts, and repeatedly urged the trustees to cover the annual deficit by setting up an endowment for the Society and by raising money through donations. In 1946, when others cut back, he took advantage of a downturn in property prices and convinced the trustees to purchase for the Society its first permanent home: a building on North 15th Street that it acquired from the *Legal Intelligencer* for only $50,000. This gave the Society the space it needed and ultimately proved a magnificent investment, but it also added to already burgeoning costs at a time when the Society was having more and more trouble making ends meet. Two years later, in honor of JPS's sixtieth anniversary, Jacobs, although he knew that "finances were limited," announced a "special program" of ten titles, more than ever before published in a single year. He also reprinted thirty-three titles to make up for the depletion of the Society's stock of books during the war, and spoke of publishing twelve books a year—a book a month—by 1950. It was, he later admitted, a serious mistake. "With inadequate working capital" and "funds tied up in inventory, stock, and plant," the Society could not pay its bills, was forced to take on new bank loans, and at one point had even to borrow $49,500 from some of its "friends" to meet immediate expenses.[91]

Jacobs himself was not entirely to blame. Near the end of 1947, the trustees undertook to raise a quarter of a million dollars for working capital and told Jacobs, as he related it in a letter to Abram Sachar, "not to worry about money any more," for "they would see me through." He took this as a green light to move full steam ahead and wrote that he could "face life much pleasanter." In fact, he began "planning bigger and better things than ever before." The promised money, however, never materialized. Instead, on December 6, 1948, for the second time in its history, the officers reported that "the affairs of the Jewish Publication Society are in a desperate state. There is a serious question of whether the Society. . . shall continue or not."[92]

Jacobs never forgave those responsible for putting out this report. He insisted that JPS was not in the same desperate situation as a quarter-century before, because it had hundreds of thousands of dollars in fixed assets, including a thriving press, a new building, and innumerable books in the warehouse, as well as accounts receivable, that together far exceeded the value of bills unpaid. "It seems to me," he wrote bitterly, "that irreparable harm has been done, not alone to the Society, but to me personally." Still, the officers realized that only a crisis atmosphere would permit much-needed cost-cutting and bring in new funds. In 1949, at their insistence, the Society cut back to five the number of new titles it issued, and all but one of them, Julian Morgenstern's collected essays entitled *As a Mighty Stream*, were inexpensive co-publications that other companies printed and that JPS merely marketed to its members. In addition, it slashed its employment rolls, raised new income by adding a small postage charge to each book, changed its marketing procedures, sought donations more aggressively, and ended the controversial program of reprints that kept books available but tied up large sums of money in slow-moving stock. Even Jacobs, who described the tension in the office as "terrific" and pronounced himself "far from satisfied," admitted that the organization had become "more compact and more efficient."[93]

One additional change of far-reaching importance took place in 1949: the introduction of a new slate of officers. After sixteen years of shepherding the Society through its greatest period of growth, Jacob Solis-Cohen asked to be relieved of his duties. The sudden downturn may have persuaded him that the time had come for somebody new. Lester Hano, who had been treasurer for only three years, also resigned; he too was clearly unhappy with all the red ink. A more dynamic and strong-willed group of officers was elected to replace them. Judge Louis Levinthal became the new president, the first person of East European stock ever to hold the position. Justice Horace Stern still continued on as vice-president—after thirty-eight years in the post, he practically owned it—but now he shared it with young Edwin Wolf 2nd, who was determined to put the Society's house in order, and was elected to the newly reestablished position of second vice-president. Sol Satinsky, a modest, cultured, and highly intelligent businessman, was elected the new treasurer; Jacobs described him as "very active and very much on the job." Finally, Jacob R. Marcus succeeded Levinthal as chairman of the publication committee, the first time that position had ever gone to someone outside of Philadelphia. When the dust settled after all of these changes, Jacobs's independence had been considerably reduced. Where Solis-Cohen had believed in him and had given him enormous freedom of action, Levinthal, Wolf, and Satinsky, their faith shaken by the Society's deficit, kept close watch over everything he did. They took a "practical" view of the Society's affairs, in contrast to what he considered his own "more idealistic" viewpoint. They also expressed growing dissatisfaction with what they saw as his excessive devotion to the Society's press. According to them, it only thrived at the expense of the publication end of the business.[94]

Clearly, Jacobs and the Society's new leaders were on a collision course. He was unhappy, they were unhappy, and each side was suspicious of the other's intentions. When the 1949 figures revealed that the Society had sustained yet another loss—$3,835 on a total income of $331,733—the two sides came to a parting of the ways. On December 9, 1949, Jacobs announced that he would resign on the following March 15 after fourteen years on the job. They had been, he wrote, "the most fruitful years of my life." He had seen JPS grow from an operation of $60,000 to a business worth nearly $350,000, from a staff of 8 people to 50 (including the press), and he had moved JPS into its first permanent home in 60 years. He felt that he had "helped place the Society in its proper place in American Jewish life." He was leaving, he admitted, with "a feeling of great sadness," and the sadness was not his alone.[95]

Yet, at age 54, Jacobs had no intention of fading away. He needed to work, he was somewhat bitter, and he was eager to prove that his own ideas about the press and the Jewish book trade had been right all along. So, in a move calculated to make waves, he soon announced the establishment of a new firm, Maurice Jacobs, Inc., which would "publish and print magazines and books for scholars and scholarly institutions in all languages," and was "contemplating also the establishment of a new Jewish book club." The challenge to JPS was clear, especially because many of the people who had formerly worked with him at the press, like David Skaraton, announced their readiness to follow him into his new venture. Meanwhile, Jacob Marcus and Solomon Grayzel also considered resigning. "Those were," Grayzel later remembered, no doubt understating the case, "rather exciting days."[96]

Thanks to the skillful mediation of Sol Satinsky, a man whom both sides respected, disaster was averted and a compromise achieved. The Society, without Jacobs, had already begun to lose money on the press, and on June 15, 1950, abandoned the printing business entirely. It leased its facilities and equipment to Maurice Jacobs, Inc., which subsequently purchased the press outright for $20,500. For its part, the new company, which now occupied the second floor of the JPS headquarters, agreed to be a printing establishment alone: It neither published new books nor formed a competing book club. Instead, within a few years, it became one of the leading specialty printers in the United States, and one of the foremost printers of Judaica anywhere in the world. Meanwhile, the Society, now smaller and more manageable, resolved to concentrate all its energies on the task for which it had originally been established: the publication and dissemination of high-quality Jewish books.[97]

THE CHALLENGES OF
POSTWAR AMERICAN
JEWISH LIFE

In the wake of Maurice Jacobs's departure, the Jewish Publication Society faced two enormous challenges. Most pressing was the need to put its financial house in order. This was no easy task given what was widely described as a crisis in the American book industry: "Greatly increased costs for material and labor since the end of the war have virtually wiped out profit margins . . . nine companies with volume ranging from \$250,000 to \$10,000,000 showed an average operating loss before taxes averaging 20.1 per cent." The Society's creditors were growing impatient, and its officers were embarrassed. To stop the flow of red ink, they called for "drastic economies and retrenchments" and prepared to cut expenses to the bone.[1]

The second challenge, even more daunting, was to continue trying to reorient the Society to meet the changing needs and conditions of postwar American Jewish life. The mass murder of six million Jews in Europe, the rise of the State of Israel, the great migration of American Jews out to suburbia, the explosion of the atom bomb, America's emergence as the leader of the free world—all this and more led to a much touted "American Jewish revival." Parallel to the Christian revival that added "under God" to the Pledge of Allegiance, the Jewish revival was evidenced by massive synagogue building, new interest in the Bible and Jewish theology, and deepening communitywide Jewish commitments. "There are incontestable signs," Salo Baron wrote, "not only of a general cultural awakening, but of a certain eagerness of the Jewish public to pioneer in the unexplored realms of a modern culture which would be both Jewish and American, and to find some new and unprecedented spiritual and intellectual approaches to the Jewish position in the modern world." Unfortunately, this eagerness did not automatically translate into new support for the Society's publishing efforts. To the contrary, it found itself beset by a host of new competitors—trade publishers, Jewish publishers, and university presses. With the changing cultural climate, JPS now more than ever had to justify its existence by demonstrating that it still had a vital role.[2]

"Consolidating the Position"

The man tapped to face these problems was Lesser Zussman, who had just resigned as assistant to the executive director of the Philadelphia Allied Jewish Appeal. A big, jovial man with two degrees from the University of Pennsylvania, Zussman was a social worker by training and he boasted considerable experience in Jewish philanthropy. In selecting him to succeed Maurice Jacobs, the Society's inner circle—Levinthal, Wolf, Satinsky, and Stern—expressed their sense that the Society needed somebody who understood charity and social service to guide its affairs in the postwar era—a Federation man and not a businessman like Jacobs. Zussman also was a knowledgeable Jew who had spent time studying at the Hebrew University, a loyal Philadelphian (although not a native), and an unabashed American patriot who had distinguished himself in wartime service and remained on after the war as a lieutenant colonel in the army reserves. True, he was a "slow worker"—especially by comparison to his dynamic predecessor—but JPS was a much smaller operation without the press. Far more important over the years was the fact that he "kept his nose to the grindstone," befriended the right people, avoided risks, followed time-tested Society practices, maintained a low profile, and proved reliable and stable. He remained on the job for twenty-three years, longer than anyone had before. Even when he retired to the position of executive director emeritus, he maintained an active interest in the Society's welfare.[3]

Zussman's top priority when he assumed his post in 1950 was to balance the budget: "It is essential," he wrote, "that we see our way clear so far as our present heavy indebtedness is concerned before we make any definite plans for substantial expenditures." Where Jacobs, even when money was tight, spoke of "marching forward," Zussman summed up his attitude with the military metaphor of "consolidating the position." In effect, as many at the time understood, that was practically a synonym for retreat. Publication committee chairman Jacob Marcus vigorously dissented, fearing that the Society's "pet projects" were "being taken over by others, one by one." "Merely to survive," he warned, "is not enough." But the cost-conscious Philadelphians who appointed Zussman, and who served consecutively as president for the next sixteen years, backed him to the hilt. They insisted on what Saul Satinsky—at various times treasurer, vice-president, president, and, until his death in 1966, chairman of the finance committee—described as a "pay as you go policy."[4]

Working closely with Saul Satinsky, Zussman initiated a series of measures aimed at cutting costs and raising additional funds. In 1950, at their behest, JPS raised its membership dues, campaigned for financial contributions, and published only five books (including the *Year Book*), four of them with a first printing of less than five thousand copies. It also held an extensive remainder sale aimed at converting its thousands of warehoused volumes into cash. The sight of so many important Jewish books stacked up on department store remainder shelves and priced at only pennies on the dollar distressed authors and members alike. Ten years later Jacobs, whose policy of reprints created the surplus, was still fuming about the books "disposed of in 1950 for next to nothing," which he believed not only disgraced the Society but also "killed the market." Fully 56,217 volumes were sold in this fashion, however, and, at least according to Louis Levinthal, "the sale ... constituted favorable advertisement for the Society and its publications." Most important of all, from Zussman and Satinsky's point of view, the sale saved money by freeing up expensive storage space and generating immediate funds. The Society for the year turned a small profit, putting it back on the road to financial recovery.[5]

In the years that followed, Zussman and Satinsky directed what they referred to as a "three-phase program" for the rehabilitation of the Society's financial structure. In the first phase the officers and trustees announced a determined fund-raising effort with a goal of $150,000. They hired a professional fundraiser—the first in a series, all of them young novices whose rates the Society could afford—and hoped that money thus collected would pay off the accumulated deficit and establish an endowment from which the Society could draw. Next, using Zussman's experience and connections, they made new applications to Jewish Federation and Welfare Funds across the country "for allocations which would assure the Society the funds needed for a modest annual subvention." In a break from past tradition, they frankly admitted that membership dues and book sales could only be expected to account for 85 percent of the Society's needs. The rising costs of publishing, they explained, made a 15 percent shortfall in the operating budget almost inevitable; donations would henceforward be needed to cover it. Finally, in the third stage of the recovery effort, JPS announced "a program of membership recruitment." Membership had fallen to 8,712 in 1951, probably because dues had risen while members were offered fewer books to choose from. Even though experience had taught the officers not to expect a large membership, they sought to turn this trend around.

Two small-scale recruitment drives took place in 1954. One, undertaken on familiar turf, was directed by the newly appointed first woman trustee, Evelyn Margolis (widow of Max Margolis), who set up a women's committee in Philadelphia and held "membership teas." The other, initiated in the fast-emerging Jewish center of Los Angeles, saw the formation of a Southern California chapter of the Jewish Publication Society, whose members pledged to do "everything possible to bring the Society's program to the attention of their community." A year later both efforts expanded, thanks to the Society's first full-time membership secretary, Mrs. Allen G. Diamond. Her job, a demanding one, was to initiate and coordinate membership recruitment and advertising programs all across the country.[6]

Slowly but surely these efforts, coupled with some unusually good luck, paid off. In 1955 the treasurer, Myer Feinstein, reported that "the Society is in a stronger financial condition . . . but that there is much room for improvement." A year later, those attending the annual meeting witnessed "the burning of the mortgage on the Society's national headquarters." Three years after that, in 1959, the trustees heard the best news of all: The Society was completely free of debt, and membership enrollment had reached the goal of 10,000.[7] In part, of course, this was a tribute to prudent management. But a great deal of credit for this recovery also rests with a name familiar from the past—Jacob Schiff.

To be sure, this Jacob Schiff—Jacob R. Schiff rather than Jacob H.—was not even a relative of his famous namesake. He was a notable New York lawyer, quite unknown to the Society's officers, who died on January 10, 1949 (by coincidence, Jacob H. Schiff's birthday), and directed in his will that a committee of three— the presidents of Columbia University, City College, and the Jewish Publication Society—dispense funds from his multimillion-dollar residuary estate in order to help nonprofit institutions "further the ideals of American democracy." After several years of probate, the money was distributed. The executors of the trust, Louis Levinthal among them, voted large sums to Columbia and City, and $150,000 to JPS for establishment of the Jacob R. Schiff Library of Jewish Contributions to American Democracy. The series was based on a plan submitted by Jacob R. Marcus and eventually encompassed twenty-two books (fifteen titles) on American Jewish history and life. Subsequently, the estate's executors voted the JPS two additional grants: $100,000 in 1956 for improvements to its headquarters, and the identical amount in 1963 for "general purposes." A final $20,000 was paid to the Society in 1973 when the trust wound up its affairs.[8]

With these grants and other smaller bequests from deceased friends, the Society not only stabilized itself financially but also managed to achieve some noteworthy gains, especially in the halcyon days of the early 1960s when there was a substantial influx of new funds. Progress came in measured, steady steps, and caution remained the byword. Remembering the financial crisis of the late 1940s, the trustees viewed innovations with a wary eye; they liked to be reassured, as they were in 1961, that "the inventory is in good condition, with reprints controlled carefully and new books printed in conservative quantities."

For the Society's seventy-fifth anniversary in 1963, even the trustees loosened up; it was an occasion for celebrating. To mark the event, the Society published twelve books, two more than it usually offered its members, as well as several new paperbacks. It also announced the revival of its long-dormant classics series, and it formally issued *The Torah*, its new translation of the Pentateuch. In addition, thanks to the Schiff Fund, it completed renovations on its Fifteenth Street building, which the Maurice Jacobs Press had obligingly vacated, and which stood in desperate need of repair. In place of what had formerly been cramped offices, it now unveiled a handsome two-story headquarters and "cultural center," complete with a 200-seat auditorium, a bookstore, and a library.[9]

Statistics collected at five-year intervals beginning in 1950, when Lesser Zussman was appointed, and ending in 1965, Solomon Grayzel's last full year as editor, put the Society's recovery and subsequent progress into sharper focus. Although some of these gains were undoubtedly due to inflation, real growth, especially in terms of total income and books distributed, was still undeniably impressive:[10]

Year	Members	Books Distributed	New Books	Reprints	Total Income
1935	3,343	na	3	0	$ 60,419
1950	9,479	137,710*	5	4	203,172
1955	8,874	114,064	9	10	324,008
1960	11,321	160,403	10	12	439,094
1965	13,394	192,000	11	14	520,614

* Includes 56,217 books distributed as "remainders."

To the JPS board of trustees, the conservative management style and steady growth policy that Zussman pursued was only right; it was, in fact, almost the same prescription that President Eisenhower was administering to the nation as a whole. Zussman may thus have displayed little in the way of flamboyance, brilliance, or unusual creativity, and he certainly put forward no bold new initiatives. But thanks to him and Grayzel, the Society did its work, paid its bills, progressed from year to year, and published volumes of indubitable significance and worth. There was only one problem: The world of Jewish publishing was rapidly changing, and the Society was not.

The Challenge of Competition

The new world of Jewish publishing came up for discussion at the Society's annual meeting in 1953. Louis Levinthal, in his presidential address, politely hailed the new developments: "We seek," he declared, "to stimulate Jewish literary productivity, not to monopolize it. We do not claim sole guardianship of American Jewish culture. We welcome the development of meritorious publication enterprises in our area of service. We regard them as complementary to, and not competitive with our own." Levinthal was referring not so much to Jewish publishers as to the trade and university presses that responded to growing popular interest in Jews and Judaism by greatly enhancing their Judaica lists. In the realm of nonfiction alone the previous decade and a half had witnessed publication of a spate of important Jewish books that the Society would undoubtedly have liked to see on its list but in fact appeared under other auspices—books by such important Jewish writers and scholars as Martin Buber, Louis Finkelstein, Mordecai M. Kaplan, Joseph Klausner, Alfred Kazin, Frederic Morton, Koppel S. Pinson, Maurice Samuel, Milton Steinberg, Harry Wolfson, and Solomon Zeitlin. A recent statistical study shows that of more than one thousand nonfiction Jewish books published in America in the 1940s, only thirty-four (3.4 percent) were issued by JPS while upward of 70 percent were issued under non-Jewish auspices. University presses alone during this decade accounted for twice as many Jewish books as JPS did. Later, during the 1960s, the Society published only 2.26 percent of the 2,870 nonfiction Jewish books listed in the *Jewish Book Annual*; by contrast, 11.53 percent of the books were issued by university presses—over five times as many.[11]

Solomon Grayzel certainly understood the problem. A former president of the Jewish Book Council, which collected data on Jewish books issued in America, he kept abreast of trends in the general publishing field. What's more, with Jacobs's departure and the growing popularity of his own history textbook, he had become the Society's principal liaison to the larger community, delivering lectures, writing articles, and representing its interests in scholarly circles. He thus labored under no illusions: He recognized the new situation and tried to convince the trustees of the need to respond to it. As early as 1950, he urged the Society to formulate "a supplementary list" of recommended Judaica by other publishers that it would sell to members "at an attractive discount." "In this way," he argued, "we would be expanding our activity, attracting more members, fulfilling our objective of spreading Jewish books, and helping the publication of such books as are worthwhile but which we cannot undertake to publish." In 1962, in a special memorandum to the board, he repeated this idea, along with other suggestions designed to meet what he correctly saw as "our new challenge." But he always met resistance from those who feared that a supplementary list would detract from JPS's own publications. Increasingly the Society's two stated functions—to publish Jewish books and to disseminate them—conflicted with one another.[12]

What the trustees did sanction was the publication of *The JPS Bookmark*, a "house organ" designed to publicize the Society's books and activities, and to "discuss the literary needs of the Jewish community in the United States and how these needs are being filled by us and by others." Calls for the Society to publish a literary magazine had been heard for decades and always voted down, but *Bookmark*, an eight-page newsletter sent out four times a year, was nothing so grandiose. It did include occasional cultural pieces—such as Gerson Cohen on "Jewish Prayer Books of the Middle Ages" and Jacob Neusner on the "Crucial Role of Jewish Libraries,"—and it regularly published addresses delivered at Society functions.

Bookmark also listed from time to time "such reading matter, not published by the Jewish Publication Society, as deserves special attention." Solomon Grayzel explained that "we want our people to read as widely as possible. We know that a person of deep Jewish interests cannot be content with the ten titles published annually by the JPS." Yet *Bookmark* never succeeded in positioning the Society above its competition. At best, it kept the leadership more closely in touch with the membership, evidencing an honest desire to serve members better.[13]

Another strategy JPS employed to serve members better was its system of co-publications. Typically, it purchased at the publisher's discount a few thousand copies of a book that the publication committee considered to be exceptionally worthwhile, and then offered it to members under its own imprint as a regular selection. In some cases, for example Abraham J. Heschel's *Man Is Not Alone* and Will Herberg's *Judaism and Modern Man*, it actually initiated volumes that eventually appeared under joint imprints. Roger Straus of the firm of Farrar, Straus and Cudahy, a good friend, was particularly amenable to these kinds of arrangements, which from a financial point of view could be mutually advantageous. In the case of Salo Baron's revision of his *Social and Religious History of the Jews*, an outside publisher brought JPS into negotiations at an early date in hopes of increasing potential sales. Little did anyone suspect that the agreement for a "five-volume history" to be co-published with Columbia University would stretch out over more than three decades and yield what is already recognized as one of the greatest and most erudite presentations of Jewish history ever written—a work now projected at twenty volumes reaching through the end of the seventeenth century.[14]

Most co-publications, however, were more mundane affairs, similar to standard book-club contracts. Grayzel, who took an increasingly dim view of these arrangements, once complained that they relegated the Society to serving as "merely a distributing agency for the books of Jewish interest published by other organizations." In the case of Nelson Glueck's best-selling *Rivers in the Desert*, the Society went so far as to warn readers—some of whom had objected to Glueck's *The River Jordan*, which it had likewise co-published—that the work, important as it was for Jews to read, was intended for non-Jews, and that "a Jewish reader will occasionally find a phrase or a sentence not put in our usual form." Co-publishing thus posed a clear dilemma: On the one hand, JPS sought to foster the widest possible dissemination of Jewish books and wanted its own list to include works of the highest quality, no matter who originally published them. On the other hand, it primarily was interested in *initiating* the publication of such works, and was not content merely to distribute them. The compromise solution remained, as it had been under Jacobs, a mixed list composed of original works and co-publications alike.[15]

During the presidency of Edwin Wolf 2nd (1954–59), the Society twice concluded open-ended co-publishing agreements that covered whole series of volumes and moved it into areas where it had not been active before. Both were essentially agreements with Jewish friends in the publishing field, undertaken with an eye toward mutual benefit. By sharing costs and appealing to broader audiences, JPS sought to accomplish with others what it could not risk doing alone.

The first was an arrangement with Roger Straus (by then a JPS trustee) involving children's books geared toward pre-adolescents and young teenagers. Outside of Henry Berkowitz's books, the Society had produced little for these ages. With growing concern about assimilation ("the greatest tendency to turn away from Jewishness...," Grayzel pointed out, "occurs during the adolescent years"), as well as new demands from parents themselves, calls for books of this type had been heard with increasing frequency. Philip Seman, for many years director of the Jewish People's Institute in Chicago, for example, spent his retirement in California soliciting support for a "Jewish Youth Book Club." The Zionist Organization of America, through its youth division, resolved to commission a series of teenage books. The Society, eager to do its part, asked Azriel Eisenberg to chair a committee on the subject and laid plans (which it later abandoned) for a nationwide joint conference on "Youth, Books and Publishing" in the hope of stimulating a cooperative approach to the problem. Yet, for at least two very good reasons, all the talking, planning, and hand wringing yielded only very meager results. First, Jewish books for young adults, unless issued under a trade imprint, had a sad history of poor sales, especially in comparison to secular books geared to the same level. Second, there was a dearth of capable authors who could create interesting books for young adolescents, and those who could preferred to write for the general trade where pecuniary rewards were much greater.[16]

Roger Straus's proposal to the Society appeared to solve both problems. He called for a biography series to be known as Covenant Books, jointly published by the Society and his own company, Farrar, Straus and Cudahy. The books would be distributed not only to the trade and to the Society's regular membership, but also through a new Covenant Club for Jews eleven to fifteen years old—four books a year for $7.50. Wolf and the trustees were impressed, and both sides easily reached an agreement in 1956. Grayzel and Straus would serve as co-editors of the new series, both publishers would make money available for author advances, and each side retained the right to veto manuscript selections. Two years later the handsomely produced volumes began to appear. Well-illustrated and richly detailed, these "story-biographies," many by authors who had successfully written juveniles for general audiences, tackled subjects that were carefully chosen to reflect a wide range of Jewish heroes from different walks of life. There were men and women, rabbis and prophets, artists and poets, scientists and scholars, statesmen and sportsmen, pioneers and merchants, doctors and nurses—in short, positive Jewish role models, not martyrs whose lives reflected Jewish tragedies. Quite intentionally, American Jewish heroes made up a majority of the subjects, and they usually were portrayed as people devoted to their faith and loyal to their country.[17]

Reviewers in the Jewish press hailed the new books as a "genuine achievement in Jewish juvenile literature . . . a new and exciting expedition into the realms of Jewish experience, created to delight and to instruct." Sales, however, ran far below expectations. Perhaps the demand had been exaggerated; perhaps too many of the biographies dealt with unfamiliar figures, like Jo Davidson and Louis Fleischner, rather than with well-known heroes who commanded a natural following. Whatever the case, many of the books lost money, and the Covenant Book Club failed completely. To make matters worse, some members of the Society complained that the four books annually devoted to the Covenant Series (later reduced to two) crowded out the adult books. As a result, the Society had no choice but to cut back the series, especially after Farrar Straus and Cudahy withdrew from its agreement in 1962. Still, it continued to produce Covenant books on its own sporadically for over a decade, and some of its volumes—especially William Wise's *Albert Einstein: Citizen of the World*—are now seen as minor classics. Later, the Society would see the wisdom of a more varied approach to the young adult field, including fiction. But the Covenant series as a whole, twenty-five volumes long, had a significance that far transcends the sum of its parts: It set a new and ambitious standard in American Jewish children's literature that JPS would henceforward seek to uphold.[18]

The second agreement signed by the Society during this era involved a whole new style of book—the paperback—geared for use in college classrooms and adult education programs. By the 1950s the revolution that had made these cheaply produced volumes available to a mass-market audience at a fraction of their original cost was some two decades old. Yet the Society, like many small specialty publishers, remained wary. How, it wondered, would it market softcovers? Could it sell them in sufficient numbers to make a profit? Would they tarnish its dignified image? Might they destroy the market for its hardcover books?

Arthur Cohen, president of Meridian Books, a house that specialized in quality paperbacks, undertook to answer these questions and reassure the Society that its fears were groundless. He was a trusted friend from the days when he was a student at the Jewish Theological Seminary, and though still only twenty-nine, he had already made a name for himself as an innovative pioneer in the publishing field. Now, in 1957, he proposed a cooperative agreement whereby Meridian would produce and help market selected volumes from the JPS backlist in return for some advance payment and a share in the royalties. Some of the trustees, conservative as ever, had misgivings about the scheme, but Edwin Wolf 2nd was exuberant. He praised Cohen's "interest and restless intelligence," gave a tongue-in-cheek reassurance that the covers of the proposed books would "not seduce buyers by a colorful display of Marilyn Monroe playing Bathsheba in her bath," and signed a one-year renewable contract covering six titles.[19]

Twenty-four months later, after the books had been out for a year, the Society knew that Wolf's decision had been right. Its investment was more than repaid, it experienced a 25 percent increase in its general sale of books, largely due to the new paperbacks (which, it turned out, did not diminish hardback sales at all), and it had the satisfaction of seeing some 60,000 inexpensive copies of its books distributed, mostly by Meridian. Over the next six years many additional titles were reprinted, including several originally published by university presses that were now brought under the Society's imprint for the first time. Then, much to everyone's disappointment, the agreement with Meridian was ended, apparently because of problems that occurred after Cohen sold the firm to World Publishing Company and left the enterprise. Having itself in the interim learned much about the paperback field, JPS was soon able come up with a new co-publishing agreement, this time with Harper and Row's Torchbook series. But that too proved short-lived. Thereafter, following the general trend in publishing, it undertook to independently publish and distribute its own paperbacks, which it continues to market to members and nonmembers alike.[20]

Meridian paperbacks and Covenant books represented important new departures in the effort to redirect JPS to meet its competitive challenges. They scarcely altered the fact, however, that the Society's role in the overall field of American Jewish publishing was rapidly diminishing. The number of Jewish books published elsewhere proliferated, major trade publishers entered the market, and both Schocken Books and Ktav Publishing Company began to nudge their way into JPS's traditional areas of specialization. The Society also noticed an ominous decline in the number of new manuscripts it was receiving annually, an indication that it was no longer the publisher of choice for many Jewish authors. Given this situation, questions regarding the Society's role and purpose—whether in fact it had outlived its usefulness—began to recur with nagging persistence. In response, for the first time in its history, it embarked on an extensive self-study.

Actually, the Society commissioned two studies: an in-depth examination of its membership by an independent research firm (Research, Inc.), and a survey of the publication committee's works and aims with the object of evolving a plan for the future, undertaken by publication committee member Eli Ginzberg, son of Louis Ginzberg and himself a respected economist and manpower expert, and author of the widely read *Agenda for American Jews.* In the context of the 1950s, there was nothing particularly unusual about the Society's having undertaken these studies. Sociology was all the rage—witness the popularity of *The Lonely Crowd* and *The Organization Man*—and even in Jewish circles self-studies were being undertaken with increasing frequency. As early as 1945, the National Jewish Welfare Board undertook a highly influential study of its activities, published as the *JWB Survey.* Four years later, Ginzberg's *Agenda,* sponsored by the American Palestine Institute, argued that "the social sciences can make an important, if limited, contribution to the effective solution of the complex problems that confront American Jews." The National Community Relations Advisory Council, in 1951, commissioned Professor Robert MacIver to study duplication and competition in the overall operation of Jewish organizations, a report that was much discussed but never implemented. In 1958, the Council of Jewish Federations undertook an important study of Jewish cultural organizations that led to the establishment of the National Foundation for Jewish Culture. In commissioning studies of its own membership and operations, the Society only marched in step with the times. It hoped that the results would more than justify all the trouble and expense.[21]

The membership survey, the first to appear, was generally upbeat. Over one-half of the fourteen hundred randomly selected members surveyed took the trouble to respond to the four-page questionnaire—a remarkable return rate. Based on the results, Research, Inc. painted an enviable profile of the "typical" JPS member:

> A member in the Jewish Publication Society is usually the head of the household and past middle age [62% are over forty-five]. He is well educated having received college training [over 80%] and often [about 50%] gone on to advanced studies. Some profession is the main source of his income and he is a member of a Conservative synagogue [47%; more than Orthodox and Reform members combined].
>
> The Jewish Publication Society is very important to him. He has been a member for over ten years [over 50%] and believes that the society is doing important work in the Jewish Cultural Field. Because of this work he thinks he would continue to support the society at his present level of dues even if he had to pay extra for any books he might select that were issued by the society [56%].
>
> It is his belief that the Society must continue to publish books. These books should be both scholarly and of general interest [87%]. He reasons that though he himself may be primarily interested in one type or another, none-the-less he believes that taste in books vary with the individual. He also believes it is important to enlist a great number of people into the society. And, that this can best be accomplished by catering to a variety of preferences. Thus the need for both types of books.

When he selects a book he usually reads it. On the whole, he likes the book he selects and thinks the subject matter is very good. There is no doubt in his mind that he likes the work the society is doing and believes it should continue its existence.[22]

The Society's inner circle was naturally pleased by this optimistic assessment, although the survey covered only members and said nothing about the vast multitude of Jews who were not. But closer analysis revealed two areas of potential concern. First, the Society's membership was generally elderly; "younger people," the leadership realized, "are not being attracted to our lists." Second, the membership had a disproportionately high number of professionals, even relative to the Jewish occupational pattern. Business people and the less well-educated members of the community found the Society far less attractive. Both of these situations held important implications for the future and raised disturbing questions as to how well JPS was fulfilling its broad overall mandate. Before recommending action, however, the leadership decided to wait until Eli Ginzberg submitted his final report.[23]

Ginzberg's report appeared in two stages. The first, a thoughtful preliminary analysis, was distributed to the leaders before the membership survey became available. Unlike the survey, it stressed the need to effect changes. The conditions under which the Society operated, it emphasized, had been transformed:

> The current position of the Society can be briefly delineated. With a membership of approximately 10,000 who contribute on the average a little more than $8.00 per annum, the Society is able to publish, co-publish or distribute books published by others totaling about 10 titles. The Society loses about a fifth of its membership annually and gains approximately a like number....
>
> In its early years the Society had what amounted to a near monopoly in the United States in publishing books in English of Jewish interest. Today it faces intensive competition from three sources: commercial publishers, university presses, and specialized Jewish agencies....
>
> The Society has been caught between the need to publish a sufficient number and variety of titles to hold its membership and the paucity of good manuscripts which it has been able to secure in the face of ever greater competition.

Based on this new situation, Ginzberg recommended that the Society reorganize itself, seeking "substantial support from the Welfare Funds," and that it "take the risks involved in declaring itself to be a cultural and educational agency concerned with the production and distribution of *quality* books"—nothing less. "Cease publishing novels and nonfiction of indifferent quality," as well as the Covenant series of juvenile books, he urged, even if that meant issuing fewer books annually. He also called for administrative changes, including restructuring of the publication committee, so as to create a new system "with adequate strength and flexibility to operate what is at once a highly technical and at the same time competitive enterprise."[24]

Ginzberg's final report, issued in April 1959, incorporated replies to this analysis, and formulated a consensus statement on the Society's future along with eight specific policy recommendations. In response to criticism, the section on the publication committee was modified, and a few other recommendations were toned down. But the overall message, especially the insistence that the Society "reorganize itself" and "reshape its program" remained unaltered. The concluding summary, which exerted considerable influence on subsequent policy, offered a prescription for change:

a. That the JPS cease publishing or co-publishing novels. The Society might on occasion offer outstanding novels of special Jewish interest to its members.
b. That at an appropriate early date the JPS seek to divest itself of a direct interest in Covenant Books.
c. That the JPS seek to increase the quality of its list and if necessary cut back the number of its titles.
d. That the JPS seek to accelerate recent trends in broadening the membership of its Board of Trustees to make it more truly representative of the country at large.
e. That the Publication Committee be restructured to accomplish the following:
1. Remove inactive members.
2. Establish a series of standing Subcommittees in major fields—Bible, Rabbinics, History, etc.
3. The Chairmen of the Subcommittees together with the President and Editor would form the Executive Committee which will have power to act on all matters under broad policies laid down by the Trustees and guided by the recommendations of the Publication Committee and its several Subcommittees.
4. Major responsibilities of the several Subcommittees will be to develop long-range programs of important works that the Society should publish as its resources permit.
f. That these long-range publishing programs, individually or jointly, when approved by the Trustees, form the basis for requests for subventions from Welfare Funds, foundations, and other potential sources of support.
g. That the JPS energetically explore how it can increase its contribution to Jewish literacy along such lines as the reprinting of its back titles (Meridian); by providing encouragement to new writers; and by other appropriate means.
h. That the JPS strive to find its appropriate place among near and distant competitors, including commercial publishers, specialized Jewish publishers, university presses, so as to make its optimal contribution in terms of its specialized background and resources.[25]

Not since Israel Friedlaender had submitted his reorganization proposals forty years before had the Society been forced to rethink its aims so carefully. This time the challenge was particularly daunting, because the experts themselves were in disagreement. Ginzberg called for higher-quality offerings and scholarly books that would "add to the educational and cultural development of American Jewry," even at the risk of losing members. The membership survey, by contrast, saw a need to attract the young and less well educated, and therefore advocated popular, nonscholarly books, the very kind that Ginzberg wanted to banish from the list altogether. Neither suggestion was new, of course, and both had roots deeply embedded in JPS tradition. Only one direction, however, could reasonably be followed; a choice had to be made.

Given Ginzberg's prestige, the availability of popular Jewish books elsewhere, a continuing reaction to the direction in which Jacobs had steered the Society, and a nationwide emphasis on education and intellect spurred by the success of the Russian *Sputnik*, "quality" won. For the second time in its history, the publication committee voted "to cease publishing or co-publishing novels,"[26] except under extraordinary circumstances—a decision, Grayzel wrote, "which leaves us free to turn our attention to more basic tasks." As in the 1920s and early 1930s, the Society began to describe its mission in terms of "works which deserve publication and might not otherwise be published," "books of reference for generations to come," "the desirable rather than the desired," and "books geared primarily for the intellectual elite of the American Jewish community." At one point, the Society stressed that it was "a creative communal publisher and not a book club," making clear that it stressed the goal of "enhancing our Jewish culture through the publication of good books," rather than "membership retention and enrollment." Grayzel himself admitted in his oral history that he sought books that served to "increase knowledge" and "foster loyalties." "What interested the people themselves," he recalled, "was to me secondary. What they needed in order to enhance their Jewishness was to me primary."[27]

Over the years, JPS adopted a good many of Ginzberg's other ideas as well. It experimented with yet another subcommittee system for the publication committee (a failure like all such plans proved to be[28]), it appealed to the community for more liberal donations, it undertook to translate Jewish scholarly and literary works from Hebrew (or other foreign languages) into English, and it occasionally agreed to commission books, rather than always depending on manuscripts that fortuitously "arrived." This latter innovation, which Grayzel had long advocated as both a competitive necessity and a valuable inducement to scholarship, was furthered in 1963 when a $100,000 bequest from insurance executive Adolf Amram enabled the Society "to provide ... subventions to qualified author-scholars to prepare books of scholarly quality and of scholarly interest which cannot be financed on a commercial basis." The thrice-repeated emphasis on "scholarship" in the bequest's terms nicely harmonized with the Society's current priorities. Not that all of its members were scholars, of course, but each was now expected to be a "serious minded person, the sort of person who, while not necessarily a scholar, sets the tone and sets the climate for Jewish life in our day." "Our foremost challenge," Grayzel declared, "is to influence these people and help them create a more profoundly Jewish attitude to Jewish life."[29]

Back to the Bible

In the midst of this period of competition, revival, and reappraisal of goals, the Society renewed its historic emphasis on the Bible—its single greatest bestseller and the book that, more than any other, justified its existence in the eyes of many American Jews. Here it faced no competition, for it held exclusive rights to its 1917 translation. It also felt a special communal responsibility, because American Jewish pride was at stake. The Bible, after all, was the one Jewish book that non-Jewish Americans revered.

What made renewed emphasis on the Bible particularly important was the religious atmosphere of the day. A great wave of interest in the Bible accompanied the postwar religious revival in America, affecting Jews and Christians alike, and resulting in a tremendous upsurge in the sale of Bibles and books about it; even a spate of Bible novels and films. For the most part, this was the Bible offered within a Christian framework that Jews found thoroughly alienating. They looked, therefore, for a respectable Jewish alternative, some way of expressing their own reverence for the "Book of Books" in a positive yet nonassimilative manner. One proposal, put forward by Trude Weiss-Rosmarin, editor of the *Jewish Spectator*, called for a concerted campaign to place JPS Bibles in the rooms of all Jewish (kosher) hotels, an obvious response to the Gideons. Others called for synagogue Bible classes and home study programs. In each case, the underlying goal was the same: "To reclaim the Bible for the Jews."[30]

This back-to-the-Bible movement redounded so much to the benefit of the Society that, according to Solomon Grayzel, Bible sales virtually "kept the Society going." Recognizing that this was a marvelous way of furthering the interests of the Jewish community even as it furthered its own, the Society throughout the 1950s laid special emphasis on its Bible work, seeking to make its Bible as widely available as possible. In 1951, it published a quarto-size pulpit Bible, designed for use by Jewish chaplains in the armed forces. At the suggestion of Edwin Wolf 2nd, Lesser Zussman had 750 copies bound in expensive leather for synagogues, collectors, and "special occasion" gifts—a highly profitable venture. Lewis Strauss used one of these Bibles when he was sworn in as Secretary of Commerce. In 1955, responding to an unsolicited request, JPS signed a contract with Consolidated Book Publishers to issue an illustrated large-size edition of its Bible for sale door-to-door. The volumes were apparently much in demand, but after a number of salesmen were caught breaching the contract, it had to be terminated. Also in 1955, JPS issued its long-promised Hebrew-English Bible in two volumes. Menahem Polak Press, Feldheim Publishers, and Soncino Press cooperated in producing the edition, which required sophisticated photoreproduction techniques to match the 1917 English text to the Soncino Hebrew. The investment paid off; thousands of copies were distributed. A year later, in a much bigger investment, the Society came out with a whole new edition of its basic English translation with enlarged type, a better binding, and a more elegant, up-to-date appearance. The edition, championed by Wolf and Zussman, again proved popular; indeed, sales exceeded expectations. The end result of all of these diligent efforts may be seen in the Society's book distribution figures. Bible sales spurted ahead, with 47,232 distributed in 1956 alone, plus 12,683 copies of *Pathways Through the Bible*—almost half of the total number of volumes (124,571) that the Society distributed during the course of the entire year.[31]

In addition to these staples, the Society enhanced its Bible offerings with collectors' items related to the Bible. As an alternative to Christian Bible art, it published magnificent editions of *The Book of Jonah* (1953) and *The Book of Ruth* (1957), both with woodcut illustrations by Jacob Steinhardt and hand-lettered texts by Franzisca Baruch. It also published a new edition of Franz Landsberger's *Rembrandt, the Jews, and the Bible* (1961), a large-size volume whose very title linked Jews not only to the greatest book that Western culture had ever produced, but also to one of its greatest painters. With somewhat less success, it tried to interest its readers in the Koren "Jerusalem Bible Pentateuch," a large-size all-Hebrew edition of the Torah, printed in Israel. Apparently the high cost of the volume and the absence of a translation inhibited sales. In a decade when almost every text of the Bible sold well, it was the only major disappointment.[32]

Bible-related books proved more of a problem, because they almost inevitably engendered controversy, no matter how innocuous they seemed. Thus a one-volume edition of Louis Ginzberg's *Legends of the Jews* (co-published with Simon and Schuster), masterfully introduced by Shalom Spiegel, and retitled significantly *Legends of the Bible*, raised howls of protest from those who insisted that the Bible has no legends, only divine truth. Grace Goldin's lyrical *Come Under the Wings* (1958), a poetic retelling of the Book of Ruth as elaborated upon by the rabbis, faced criticism from the same corner. One ultra-Orthodox reader found its passionate descriptions of Ruth's relationship to Boaz offensive to "the Jewish conception of . . . Modesty, Decency, Chastity, Personal Hollines [*sic*], and Purity." Such essentially fundamentalist attacks reminded everyone of just how sensitive some Jews were when it came to Judaism's holiest book. With the Society just beginning a new translation of the Bible, the lesson was timely indeed.[33]

When JPS completed its first translation of the Bible back in 1917, Jacob Schiff had predicted that the work would "not be done again for several centuries." The King James version had lasted that long, and the Jewish translation, he thought, was even better. Not more than eight years passed, however, before calls for revision arose. The traditionalist Henry Pereira Mendes, rabbi of the Spanish and Portuguese Congregation in New York, spoke of "hundreds of questionable renderings" and "queer-ities of English" that detracted from the translation's "majesty of expression." The secularist philosopher Horace Kallen lambasted the whole production as "disingenuous . . . far behind the conventional American version in the candor, sincerity and courage of the scholarship." Both criticisms found receptive ears, but no revision was seriously considered until the 1940s when Mortimer Cohen raised the issue in connection with his *Pathways Through the Bible*. Everyone agreed with him that the English of the Society's translation was inappropriate for a volume geared for young people, and Cohen therefore received permission to employ a "modernized English idiom," the first time the Society had conceded that its translation did not serve the needs of all readers. In 1946, the publication committee followed this decision up with a general discussion on the merits and faults of the 1917 translation, including a recommendation that the English "be slightly revised." In the end, it appointed a subcommittee to "study the problem." Little did anyone suspect that "the problem," in one form or another, would continue to occupy the Society for most of the next forty years.[34]

Solomon Grayzel staunchly supported the idea that the Society's translation of the Bible should be modernized. What he had in mind, however, was merely a linguistic revision. King James's English, which a previous generation considered essential to any Bible translation, no longer inspired Americans the way it once had—indeed, some of its archaic forms were no longer even understood. Grayzel thought that "a good stylist," taking "our own translation of the Bible as the basis" could "easily turn it into fluent, intelligible and dignified English," without great cost.[35]

On October 31, 1949, the Society brought together a group of scholars and "others interested in the subject" to discuss in a more formal way the need for a Bible translation. Plans were afoot for a Hebrew-English Bible, and some thought that a new translation could be prepared in conjunction with it. The meeting, however, ended inconclusively; "some wanted basic revision, others only superficial revision, still others objected to any revision at all."[36] Jacob Marcus, ever the realist, put forward a simple proposal designed to cut the Gordian knot: securing the services of one or two competent scholars who would point out the most obvious errors as indicated by mistranslations or by new discoveries in the field of biblical science, and a skilled writer who would modernize the 1917 version and incorporate the necessary changes. Marcus knew that leaders of the Central Conference of American Rabbis were talking about the need for a modernized translation of the Bible, and he feared that if the Society did not act soon, the initative would pass out of its hands altogether. As a result, he and Grayzel suggested a number of "competent writers"—including Mortimer J. Cohen, Maurice Samuel, Charles Reznikoff, and Marvin Lowenthal—and even made preliminary contacts to see if any of them would be interested in the job. But he found no takers. Nor was there any assurance that the cost-conscious trustees would ever grant the project approval.[37]

Meanwhile, in 1952, the Protestant Revised Standard Version of the Old

Testament appeared, representing eight years of intensive effort by some of America's leading biblical scholars, including one Jew, Professor Harry Orlinsky of the Jewish Institute of Religion in New York. This was an avowedly modern Bible translation that moved away from King James English, incorporated the fruits of recent biblical scholarship, and set a new standard against which other translations had now to be measured. Catholics too had a new Bible translation in progress, the so-called Confraternity Bible, later published as the New American Bible. The Jewish community, as a matter of pride, felt compelled to act. Sixty years before, the appearance of the Protestant Revised Version had put the Leeser Bible to shame, spurring efforts to create what became the 1917 translation. Now, in much the same way, the new Revised Standard Version was putting the 1917 translation to shame, and the Catholic Bible threatened to do the same. Harry Orlinsky, in a much-publicized address at the Society's annual meeting on May 10, 1953, challenged the Society to respond vigorously. His title summed up his proposal: "Wanted: A New English Translation of the Bible for the Jewish People."[38]

Orlinsky delivered his address at the behest of Grayzel and Zussman, and with the explicit aim of influencing "some reluctant members of the Society" to support the Bible translation project. To this end, he traced the long history of Jewish Bible translations, including the Society's own, and spelled out the two reasons why he considered the 1917 translation inadequate: "Firstly, the English language itself has undergone rapid change, far more since the days of World War I than it did through the entire 19th century preceding; and secondly, our knowledge of the background and text of the Hebrew Bible has increased since World War I by such enormous leaps and bounds that scores of passages in the older translations are now to be understood differently and more correctly than previously." He reminded the audience that American Protestants and Catholics had new translations of the Bible, and that both "rejected the English of the King James." "We Jews," he sadly observed, "are in the anomalous position of clinging to that English." He enumerated various inaccuracies in the 1917 translation, and explained why the Revised Standard Version, which retained numerous Christological readings, could not serve Jewish needs, just as the Protestant Revised Version had proved unacceptable a generation before. "The Jew," he exclaimed, echoing the very words of the preface to the 1917 translation, "cannot afford to have his Bible translation prepared for him by others." To Orlinsky, there was but one acceptable option: for JPS to undertake the kind of revision "which is already long overdue."[39]

Orlinsky was "far from optimistic" that he had "persuaded the key men that a revision is really necessary." He had received a respectful hearing, but he knew from earlier discussions that some, like Justice Horace Stern, still questioned the whole undertaking on the argument that "the emotional, as well as cultural, overtones" inherent in the familiar biblical text should be preserved. Others, like Jacob Marcus, wanted something far less than a full-scale revision, fearing (not without reason, as it turned out) that under Orlinsky's proposal, "we would have to call in scholars from all fields, spend years, spend a huge sum of money and come up with a compromise translation."

In the end, the trustees approved a plan modeled on the one that Max Margolis had worked under fifty years before. It called for one scholar, hired to serve as "revisor," to draft a new translation on his own, much as Margolis had done. This text, in turn, would be reviewed by a committee consisting of rabbis affiliated with each of the three major Jewish rabbinic bodies: the Rabbinical Council (Modern Orthodox), the Rabbinical Assembly (Conservative), and the Central Conference of American Rabbis (Reform). The inclusion here of a Modern Orthodox rabbi, not represented on the earlier committee, signifies that movement's new-found status, as well as its recognized willingness to cooperate with non-Orthodox Jews for the sake of the Jewish people. Although none of the rabbis involved officially represented their respective rabbinic bodies—this would have compromised their independence—the intent was clear. In fact, all three rabbinic organizations had privately agreed in advance "to urge the support of the project" upon their members.[40]

Selecting the members of the Committee of Consultants to the Revision of the JPS Bible Translation proved no easy task. American Jewry by this time boasted a comparatively large number of Jewish scholars and learned rabbis, many of them friends of JPS. Deciding whom to include and exclude required a great deal of diplomacy, forethought, and tact. One decision was foregone: Harry Orlinsky, who had campaigned for the translation, worked on the Revised Standard Version, and had written important scholarly studies on ancient Jewish translations of the Bible was both Grayzel's and the trustees' choice for the position of "reviser" (later renamed editor-in-chief). The publication committee, however, thought that to ensure credibility at least one additional scholar should be involved in the translation process; neither the 1917 translation nor the Revised Standard Version, after all, had been the work of one scholar alone. So despite well-grounded fears that this would slow down the process, it appointed Ephraim A. Speiser, professor of Semitic languages at the University of Pennsylvania, as its "official representative" to the translation committee. Significantly, both he and Orlinsky had received the bulk of their professional training in the United States, further indication of the country's emergence as a Jewish cultural center. Later, an additional scholar was added to the committee: Harold Louis ("H.L.") Ginsberg, professor of Bible at the Jewish Theological Seminary of America and one of the most highly respected Jewish biblical scholars in the country. The Society had come to realize that its new translation would inevitably be compared to its Christian counterparts, and would be considered the authoritative Jewish view of what the Bible meant. It therefore strived to assemble a committee that would pursue the highest degree of scholarly excellence—a decision that would cost it dearly in terms of money and time.[41]

Excellence, in a scholarly sense, was not the most important consideration behind the selection of the committee's rabbis. With the growth of American Jewish scholarship, friction had developed between "active scholars" and "active rabbis," with the former, proud of their newly acquired professional status, increasingly dismissing the latter as amateurs or dilettantes. Appointing both on an equal basis would thus have been a recipe for disaster. Instead, the Society looked for men who could work well together, lived on the East Coast, and were sufficiently esteemed by their colleagues "to have influence ... in their individual respective groups." Bernard Bamberger, a noted Reform rabbi who served at Temple Shaaray Tefila in New York, fit the bill ideally. He had just published a scholarly book with the Society, was a respected voice in the Central Conference of American Rabbis, and was deservedly known as a masterful diplomat—so much so that he was eventually chosen to preside over most of the committee's meetings. Choosing the representative Conservative rabbi proved more difficult, because there were several obvious candidates, including Mortimer J. Cohen and Robert Gordis. For the sake of peace, therefore, no congregational rabbi was selected, and Grayzel turned instead to Rabbi Max Arzt, assistant chancellor of the Jewish Theological Seminary, who was deeply interested in Jewish scholarship, highly influential in the Conservative movement, and, most important of all, "was a practical man and easy to work with." Rabbi Harry Freedman, the Orthodox representative, possessed similar qualities. He had edited Jeremiah in the Soncino commentary on the Bible, was known as a moderate, and enjoyed a fine personal and scholarly reputation within the Orthodox community. Unfortunately for the Society, in 1956 he left his congregation in Brooklyn and returned to Australia where he had previously served. He continued, however, to participate in the committee's work from afar.[42]

"The first meeting of the Committee of Consultants to the revision of the JPS Bible translation, took place on Monday, January 24 [1955] at 4 P.M., at the Jewish Students' House (Hillel Foundation) of the University of Pennsylvania." Judge Levinthal himself came for the occasion, and he heard an extended discussion of the five translation principles that he and leaders of the three American rabbinical organizations had personally formulated in advance:

(1) That the entire Bible be undertaken, experience in other countries and at other times having proved that the publication of a Pentateuch translation frequently stands in the way of completing the task.

(2) The revision is to retain, as far as possible, the flavor of the King James English and the existing J.P.S. version.

(3) Obscure passages are to be translated for intelligibility, with a note indicating that this was "a conjectural translation."

(4) The Masorah is not to be tampered with.

(5) The present J.P.S. Version is to be reviewed entirely, but is to form the basis of the revision. Some such statement is to be made on the title-page as "Holy Scriptures based on the Masoretic text, originally published in 1917, revised 19—."[43]

Three of these principles did not last through the first two meetings. On the question of English, the committee (soon renamed the Advisory Editorial Committee) insisted on having greater freedom, and decided "to see how the translation works out." That was the last heard of King James English. The question of the Masorah—the extent to which the translation might benefit from textual emendations—was similarly held in abeyance. "Each case," the committee ruled, would "be decided on its own merits, and perhaps a general principle will emerge in the course of the work." Finally, with regard to the 1917 translation, the committee refused to be bound: It decided that wherever the English could "be improved upon, be it ever so slightly, the change be made." For a time it did give the existing translation "the deciding vote" when committee members themselves were "divided and uncertain"—an idea borrowed from the Revised Standard Version, which awarded the same privilege to the American Standard Version of 1901. Before long, however, even this was abandoned. What began as "the revision of the Bible Translation" became a more self-confident entirely new translation—billed as "the first entirely new English version of the Scriptures based on the original Hebrew text," and the "best and most accurate translation of the original Hebrew into any language."[44]

The slow, painstaking work of translation began in earnest in the late spring of 1955. At first the committee met sporadically and at various places, sometimes in Philadelphia, sometimes New York. Before long, however, a routine settled in: Meetings generally took place every other Thursday, all day, at Orlinsky's office in the Jewish Institute of Religion in Manhattan. Orlinsky himself has described the process:

> I prepared the draft of the entire *Chumash* [Pentateuch]. I hardly ever would prepare more than two or three chapters ahead of the committee so that I would be able to benefit from the decisions that the committee members reached. Unlike the Revised Standard Version, I would prepare a draft of a chapter or part of a chapter with a tremendous amount of commentary culled from the readings and translations from sources going back to the ancient Near East, the Septuagint, Targum, Vulgate, Syriac translation, Talmud, the medieval commentators, medieval grammarians, Sa'adia's translation, the rationalist Protestant translation of the 16th century, the Catholic, and of course, the modern translations.... I would send that off to the JPS where it would be run off and sent out to my colleagues. They in turn would react, verse by verse or word by word, with counter suggestions. They would type that up and send that into JPS where, again, it would be run off and sent out, so that when we got together to do Genesis, and then all the way through, we would have the draft, we would have the comments of each of the committee members, as many as had reacted. We had it all before us, and we could all study it before we came. On the other hand, however, once we got together, the argument and the discussion pro and con would go far beyond what anybody had on any sheet of paper. We were very stimulated by the oral arguments back and forth. Not infrequently what came out as our final draft was something that none of us had envisaged to begin with.[45]

To support this exacting process, JPS undertook the largest fundraising effort in its history. It realized early on that this was going to be the most expensive project that it had ever undertaken, and this time there was no Jacob Schiff willing to fund the project on his own. The rules of Jewish philanthropy, however, had changed considerably since Schiff's day: Mass appeals for local, national, and international causes had now become the fashion. So, in what proved to be a brilliant stroke, the Society decided to capitalize on communitywide interest in the Bible by providing "every American Jew with a chance to share in the undertaking." In an almost populist vein—quite appropriate to an era that saw Jews heavily involved in liberal politics and movements for social change—the Society's president, Edwin Wolf 2nd, declared that "the Jewish Publication Society does not want to limit participation in this sacred work of revision to a few men of wealth, but prefers to extend the privilege to all Jews who may seek to share in it." Having estimated that the whole translation would cost $150,000, JPS called "for the support of one thousand persons, each of whom will contribute $25 a year for each of the six years required to prepare the new translation." As a bonus (and in a less populist vein), it promised each sponsor "a copy of the first edition of the new Bible, numbered and limited, bound in gilded and tooled morocco with the sponsor's name on the cover, which will signify his participation in the historic undertaking, and which will unquestionably become a valuable collector's item."[46]

Wolf and Zussman took to the road and spoke to an endless array of parlor groups and community meetings. They also managed an active campaign of mail solicitations. "The Catholics have done it; the Protestants have done it; AND NOW THE JEWS ARE GOING TO DO IT," one solicitation letter began. The overt appeal to Jewish "team spirit" and religious pride evidently paid off. By the end of 1961, the Bible Fund listed 1,719 sponsors and almost $247,000 in pledges, far more than the original goal. Unfortunately, rising costs had more than kept pace with donations, so after the first volume of the translation, *The Torah*, was published in 1962, a Second Bible Fund became necessary, and was set up on the same basis as the first. By early 1967, when fundraising for the Bible was suspended, a combined total of just over $507,000 had been raised from 3,451 contributors. In the Society's whole history, no fundraising effort had ever achieved such resounding success. Because Zussman prudently funded as much of the Bible translation as possible from general operating capital, the Bible money was never totally used up. What remained laid the basis for the Society's increasingly important Endowment Fund.[47]

Meanwhile, the translation itself inched forward at a discouragingly slow pace. There were, in Grayzel's words, "endless, interminable discussions" sometimes over what seemed like the most trivial of points. There were debates over what a particular Hebrew word or phrase meant "to the writer," debates over whether or not individual English words properly conveyed the sense of the Hebrew "to the reader," debates over form and over style, debates between supporters of connotative language ("man knew his wife Eve") and supporters of denotative language ("man had intercourse with his wife Eve"), and perhaps most difficult of all, debates over limits—just how far away from the "literal" and "familiar" meaning of the text could the translation move without giving offense?[48] Had the translators been content merely to revise the 1917 translation through "the updating of the language, the correction of serious errors, and the substitution of new interpretations for old when made necessary by the discovery of new data and analysis," progress would doubtless have been more rapid. The translators were convinced, however, that the American Jewish community, "in keeping with its new status and verve," wanted something better—"a complete break with the past history of Bible translation." They therefore rejected the philosophy of literal, mechanical translation, the so-called word-for-word method, in favor of an idiomatic translation, an effort to transmit faithfully "what the writer ... meant to convey to his reader." This gave them a great deal more freedom and resulted in a far more readable translation, but it also generated innumerable time-consuming delays.[49]

Ephraim Speiser, in some ways the radical of the group, prided himself on his original English renderings; "... most of the new insights and much of the bolder phraseology," he claimed at one point, "can be traced back to me." It was, for example, at his insistence that Gen. 1:26 was originally translated "I will make man in my image, after my likeness," although the Hebrew clearly indicates a plural form ("Let us make man in our image after our likeness"). The "emphatically singular rendition" of the following verse, Speiser argued, meant that the singular best captured both the sense of the verse and the intent of the writer, even if the words themselves (which he believed to be "plurals of majesty") read otherwise. Yet some of his colleagues, even if they personally understood the verse no less monotheistically than Speiser did, wondered if it should be translated that way. Here as elsewhere, what he considered idiomatic, they considered an emendation; what he considered bold, they considered reckless.

Similar arguments, sometimes sparked by Speiser, sometimes by somebody else, took place meeting after meeting, sapping morale, and leading in a few cases to personal acrimony and threats of resignation by those who could not abide being out-voted by men whom they considered their inferiors. Rubbing salt into the wounds was the fact that even after having been decided by majority vote, old questions were often reopened when drafts underwent revision—Genesis alone was revised thirteen times! Grayzel, as secretary of the committee, along with Louis Levinthal, Sol Satinsky, Edwin Wolf 2nd, and Lesser Zussman tried to pour oil on troubled waters, even as they prodded the translators to move along faster. In 1959, in response to demands from Ginsberg and Speiser, they agreed to grant each of them the title "editor" (Orlinsky remained "editor-in-chief," but only of the Pentateuch), a status that elevated them above the committee's rabbis. Concessions, cajoling, and expressions of the trustees' concern, however, only succeeded to a limited extent. It was 1962, seven long years after the translation began, before the first fruits appeared (actually 1963; the volume was "held up until the New York newspaper strike was over"), and what was published then was only *The Torah*—translations of the Prophets and the Writings still lay ahead.[50]

Harry Orlinsky has characterized the new translation* that appeared beginning with *The Torah* as "a revolutionary breakthrough in Bible translation." It set a new tone right from its first words: "When God began to create." Throughout its text, it "avoided obsolete words and phrases and, whenever possible, rendered Hebrew idioms by means of their normal [and most accurate] English equivalents," no matter how familiar the "standard" English of earlier translations may have become. In the Ten Commandments, for example, it translated the third commandment as "You shall not *swear falsely* by the name of the LORD your God" (Exodus 20:7). The more familiar "take in vain," like other familiar but now discarded renderings, appeared only in a footnote. The same was true of the affirmation of faith known as the *Sh'ma* (Deuteronomy 6:4), translated as "Hear O Israel! The LORD is our God, the LORD Alone." The translation that generations of schoolchildren have memorized, "The Lord our God, the Lord is one" was relegated to footnote "b." The new translation also banished, this time completely, mechanical renderings of Hebrew particles, and archaicisms like "thou" and "thy." In keeping with the linguistic spirit of the original Hebrew as well as contemporary usage, even God became a "You."

What was most important to the translators was not slavish consistency or literal word accuracy, but the larger meaning of phrases and expressions, what "the sense required." The same philosophy lay behind the new system of paragraphs, arranged according to "logical units of meaning even when they did not coincide with conventional chapters and verses," as well as the special form employed to indicate poetry. The translators never deviated, however, from the traditional Hebrew (Masoretic) text itself. Although they debated this point frequently early on, particularly when changes in vocalization alone made a difficult word clear (e.g., Gen. 10:10), they decided in the end that on this subject there could be no compromise. They occasionally admitted in a footnote that they could not fully understand a particular Hebrew word or phrase because it was "obscure"—a much criticized term, changed in later editions to the more humble "Meaning of Hebrew uncertain"—but they did not presume to amend the text at all, not even when

---

* Orlinsky generally referred to the new translation as the "New Jewish Version" (NJV), emphasizing its "newness," as distinguished from the Protestant "Revised *Standard* Version." But others involved in the translation objected to the word "version," because it implied that the Jewish translation bore official sanction, which, unlike the Protestant and Catholic versions, it did not presume to have. The official title of the Bible published in 1985 strikes a middle ground: *TANAKH: A New Translation of The Holy Scriptures According to the Traditional Hebrew Text* (revised in the third printing to *TANAKH: The Holy Scriptures: The New JPS Translation According to the Traditional Hebrew Text.*)

alternative readings were available in ancient manuscripts, the Greek Septuagint, or the Aramaic Targum. "Important textual variants," when noticed at all, appeared only in the footnotes.[51]

This deeply reverential attitude toward the traditional Hebrew text—far beyond anything found in recent Protestant or Catholic versions of the Bible—is one of the features that identifies the new JPS translation as *intrinsically* Jewish, not just a new translation made by people who happened to be Jews. The "Jewishness" of the translation is similarly revealed in the language of the translation, especially in sensitive verses that Jews and Christians traditionally understand differently. In Gen. 49:10, for example, the new translation reads "The scepter shall not depart from Judah. . . . So that tribute shall come to him"—a far cry indeed from the King James translation of "until Shiloh comes," understood by Christians as a reference to Jesus. Similarly, in Zechariah 12:10, which Christians have understood to mean ". . . and they shall look up to Me whom they have pierced," the reading here is totally different: "and they shall lament to Me about those who are slain." The new translation even steps gingerly around words connecting God to "salvation," and forms of the verb "to save." Given Christian associations with these words, the translators usually preferred "deliverance" and forms of the verb "to deliver," so as to prevent misunderstanding.[52]

Of course, the Jewish translation still made full use of Christian scholarship. Indeed, Orlinsky's *Notes on the New Translation of the Torah* cites Christian scholars repeatedly. As part of their mission, however, the translators strived whenever possible to draw on Jewish tradition: the work of "Jewish commentators, grammarians, and philologians." This, as it turned out, became more than just a religious duty or a statement of ideology; it had important scholarly implications as well. "A major consequence" of the new translation, Orlinsky reports, "is the realization that Jewish interpretation of the Bible, beginning with the earliest rabbinic literature . . . should command in vastly increased measure the respect and gratitude of modern critical scholarship."[53]

The new translation's Jewish character did not prevent it from being criticized in some ultrareligious quarters. "No one, even a prophet can reinterpret anything in the Torah," warned a telegram from Rabbi Pinchas M. Teitz, a member of the presidium of the Union of Orthodox Rabbis. "No Torah scholar has ever recognized or will recognize any translation but the Targum and the Septuaginta as authentic." The participation of a modern Orthodox rabbi in the work made no difference: "We were," Grayzel recalled, "all but put in *herem* [excommunicated]."[54]

Otherwise, beside debates about religious authenticity and recognition, the translation met with a generally positive response, tempered with expected caveats. Some missed the stately (if unintelligible) English of the King James, others found fault with particular renderings that they considered wrong, awkward, or too colloquial. Professor Theodore Gaster of Columbia University, in a significant review printed in *Commentary*, called the translation a "notable and important achievement," but lamented that "with all its excellences and clarifications" it lacked "the magic of the Bible . . . the verbal tact, the economy of statement, the pregnancy of phrase, the ability to catch a scene in a sentence and a situation in a word, the tints and shades." Still, leading Jewish, Catholic, and Protestant scholars warmly welcomed the new volume, and it was selected as an Alternate Choice by the Book-of-the-Month Club. At a "Dedication Dinner" held at the Waldorf-Astoria Hotel in New York, Justice Arthur J. Goldberg, then newly appointed to the United States Supreme Court, pronounced the new translation "excellent," commended JPS for publishing it, and characterized the work as an exercise in religious freedom. Most important of all, from the Society's point of view, *The Torah* achieved wide sales, estimated at one point at "7,000 a month, or 230 a day"—a quarter of a million copies were in print within a decade. Given this demand, the Society looked forward with understandable anticipation "to the completion of the rest of Scriptures," confident that a "major contribution" was being made.[55]

A myriad of difficulties, however, soon intervened. In 1962, Ephraim Speiser resigned from the translation committee. He was by then a sick man, dying of cancer, and he found the work of the committee increasingly frustrating and burdensome; he was not replaced. After he left, an ugly dispute erupted over who would write up the notes to the new translation of the Torah. Once that was settled, several years were spent translating the *haftarot* (the special Prophetic portions read in conjunction with the weekly Pentateuchal reading), as well as the Five *Megilloth* (scrolls) read on different Jewish holidays, with the aim of publishing them in a one-volume Hebrew-English edition of the Torah designed for synagogue use. The volume was prepared and announced, but because of financial constraints and technical problems that arose in finding a suitable Hebrew text, only the *Five Megilloth and Jonah* appeared in a Hebrew-English edition, and that was years later (1969). The one-volume Torah with the *haftarot* never appeared at all.[56]

Through all of this, the committee continued to work on a regular basis, but it refused to be hurried; every word was too important. After years of effort, *Isaiah: A New Translation* appeared in a special artistic edition in 1973, followed twelve months later by *Jeremiah*. *The Prophets* as a whole, with H.L. Ginsberg as editor-in-chief, finally came out in 1978. In most respects, the translation of the Prophets closely adhered to the model of *The Torah*. Its footnotes, however, diverged: They were replete with suggested emendations designed to explain difficult passages. The preface piously warned those who disapproved "either on scholarly or on religious grounds" to disregard these notes, but the fact that they were printed at all signified an important change in the committee's thinking. Earlier, it permitted no conjectural emendations whatsoever, following the precedent of the 1917 translation. Now, given many passages that were difficult to understand in the

Prophets, and seeing the heavy emphasis on emendations in other scholarly translations, the committee refused to be similarly confined. Instead, it charted a new compromise course, which it held up as a model for others to follow: In its text it followed a conservative posture, translating idiomatically directly from the traditional Hebrew; in its footnotes it permitted "all kinds of emendations" to explain passages where "the text probably is corrupt."[57]

Having monitored the pace of the Bible translation for a full decade, the Society's trustees realized, in 1965, that the undertaking would be more arduous and more time-consuming than anyone had originally envisaged. Determined that the translation should nevertheless appear "within five years," they decided to create a new committee, charged with the task of translating the third division of the Bible, the *Kethubim* (The Writings), leaving aside the Five Megilloth already completed.[58]

In 1966, the new committee, overwhelmingly American trained and younger by a full generation than the earlier one ("all Bible committees age rapidly," Orlinsky has observed) came into being. Like the earlier committee, it consisted of three scholars (Moshe Greenberg, Jonas C. Greenfield, and Nahum M. Sarna), three rabbis, one Conservative, one Reform, one Orthodox (Saul Leeman, Martin Rozenberg, and David Shapiro), and the then editor of the Society, Chaim Potok, who offered literary guidance and also served as secretary. Revealingly, all of the scholars selected taught at secular universities, a fact that reflected both the growing acceptance of Jewish studies as a legitimate academic discipline, and the increased willingness on the part of universities to permit biblical studies to be taught by Jews. Also revealingly, two of the three scholars on the committee (Greenberg and Greenfield) eventually assumed positions at the Hebrew University in Jerusalem, an indication of American Jewish scholarship's increasingly close ties to Israel on social, intellectual, and scholarly levels. Numerous meetings of the committee actually took place in Jerusalem; the rest were held in Philadelphia or at the Sarna home in Brookline, Massachusetts.[59]

In its procedures, the *Kethubim* translation committee generally adhered to the practices established for *The Torah* and *The Prophets*. Each professional scholar undertook to prepare an annotated draft, which was circulated to all concerned. Everyone then had an opportunity to criticize the rendering and to offer detailed suggestions when the committee met. In its style, however, the new committee struck a decidedly more cautious and conservative stance, in harmony with the new mood that overtook Americans generally in the 1970s and 1980s, a mood at once both more hesitant and less self-confident than before. Unlike the older committee, it stressed the inherent difficulties in translating the Hebrew, and the "as yet imperfect understanding of the language of the Bible." It refused to hazard emendations, even in the notes, and its favorite footnote read "meaning of Hebrew uncertain." Instead of exuding confidence, it admitted in its preface that its translation had "not conveyed the fullness of the Hebrew, with its ambiguities, its overtones, and the richness that it carries from centuries of use."[60]

The *Kethubim* committee's translation of the *Psalms* appeared in 1973, followed in 1980 by its *Book of Job*, and then at long last by the *Writings* as a whole in 1982. On May 26, 1982, a gala dinner, modeled on the one held sixty-five years before, feted the new translation, and honored at the same time the descendants of those involved in the 1917 Bible project. Perhaps appropriately, given how long the translation had taken, the theme of the evening was "Hope." Elie Wiesel, later to win the Nobel Peace Prize, spoke on the meaning of the Bible for Jews, Jewish history, and mankind generally—a reminder that the translation was for Jews and Christians alike; anyone, indeed, who valued the Bible and sought to understand it from a Jewish point of view.[61]

In 1985, all three parts of the Bible translation, with revisions, were brought together in one volume entitled *Tanakh*—from the Hebrew acronym for *Torah* (Pentateuch), *Nevi'im* (Prophets), and *Kethuvim* (Writings). The title of the new volume, carefully chosen, underscored yet again the Jewishness of the new translation: A "Judeo-Christian" title like "The Holy Scriptures" was consciously rejected. *Tanakh* thus encapsulated an important message of the translation as a whole: that Jews, even as they share the Hebrew Bible in common with their Christian neighbors, understand much of it differently, and even call it by a different name.[62]

While the Society's translation of the Bible was finished, its effort to explicate the text for contemporary Jews was not. A new JPS Commentary to the Bible, launched back in 1973 and successor to the commentary called for decades earlier by Solomon Schechter (see Chapter Five), was already well underway. Several noteworthy Christian commentaries utilizing new Bible translations had begun to appear during this period, notably the Cambridge Bible Commentary, based on the New English Bible. In addition, Doubleday had launched its very successful nondenominational Bible commentary, the Anchor Bible, edited by William Foxwell Albright and David Noel Freedman. American Jews, however, still had no up-to-date English Bible commentary of their own. Moreover, the most familiar Anglo-Jewish commentary on the Pentateuch, the one-volume Soncino Press edition of *The Pentateuch and Haftorahs* edited by Joseph H. Hertz, was fifty years old and its scholarship antiquated. The time had come for a major new American Jewish Bible commentary, making use of the most current archeological, historical, and linguistic discoveries. Like the Anchor Bible, the JPS commentary would be aimed at the general reader with no special formal training in biblical studies; yet it would still represent the highest standards of scholarship. Unlike the Anchor and Christian commentaries, however, the new JPS commentary would also include the traditional Hebrew text and the new JPS translation; it would also utilize the 2,000-year-old tradition of Jewish exegesis.

In August 1973, JPS president Jerome J. Shestack met in Jerusalem with Nahum M. Sarna, Moshe Greenberg, Jonas Greenfield, Yosef Yerushalmi, and Chaim Potok. Together they formulated guidelines for the new commentary. A few months later, Shestack announced the appointment of Sarna as general editor of the project and Potok as literary editor. He also undertook to establish "a modern 'Septuagint' of 70 donors" who would each contribute $5,000 to help defray the project's costs. Technical problems connected with complexities of producing an English-Hebrew text with commentary delayed the project somewhat, but it was planned to have the first volumes ready in time for the Society's Centennial in 1988. Scheduled for release in the 1990s was a one-volume synagogue Pentateuch, abridged from the five-volume commentary but with the addition of the traditional Prophetic readings (*haftarot*) and a commentary to them by Michael Fishbane.

Thinking about Judaism

The JPS Bible translation reflected in two important ways the Jewish cultural agenda of the postwar period. First, it offered a Jewish response to those of the "postmodern generation" who looked to "return to religion" but found, as philosopher Will Herberg put it, that "we have lost our direction and all but lost the ability to read the map that might show us how to regain it." Second, it distinguished this Jewish answer from contemporary Christian answers, however similar they may at first glance have appeared.[64] This same two-fold agenda—reconciling Judaism and modernity and distinguishing Judaism from Christianity—lay behind numerous other books that the Society issued during this period, including four volumes in which one of these two themes actually received title billing: Herberg's *Judaism and Modern Man* (1951), Abba Hillel Silver's *Where Judaism Differed* (1956), Leo Baeck's *Judaism and Christianity* (1960), and Mordecai Kaplan's *The Purpose and Meaning of Jewish Existence* (1964).

JPS would once have eschewed such volumes as too intellectual and controversial; for years it scarcely published any books on Jewish thought at all. Now—given its new mandate to produce serious books, the sense that American Judaism was undergoing a "revival," the growing number of young Jewish theologians dissatisfied with the optimistic liberalism of prewar Jewish religious philosophy, the fears expressed about "the assembly-line sameness of American suburbia" becoming a threat to Jewish survival, and Grayzel's personal dismay at what he considered to be non-Jewish trends in contemporary Jewish thought—this policy was reversed. From 1951 to 1965, as if to make up for past inattention, JPS published (or more often co-published) a score of books on Jewish philosophy and theology, including works by or about almost all of the leading Jewish thinkers of the day: Leo Baeck, Martin Buber, Hermann Cohen, Will Herberg, Abraham Joshua Heschel, Mordecai Kaplan, and Franz Rosenzweig.[65]

Departing from past policy, Solomon Grayzel stated that when it came to Jewish thinkers it was the duty of JPS "to publish all points of view provided they are properly presented." This was never more apparent than in 1951 when two seminal yet utterly divergent philosophic volumes that it had initiated at different times appeared within a few months of one another, both co-published by Farrar Straus and Young: Will Herberg's *Judaism and Modern Man* and Abraham Joshua Heschel's *Man Is Not Alone*.[66]

In a letter to Mortimer Cohen, Grayzel explained why he had commissioned Herberg's volume in 1948:

> Realizing the urgent need for a defense of Judaism against Jewish indifference, I looked about for someone who could prepare a volume—interesting, well written, and based on modern attitudes—presenting the case for Judaism from the Sociological-Psychological viewpoint—a sort of counterpart of the books written by [Jacques] Maritain. We have no Maritains in our midst. The closest I could think of was Will Herberg.[67]

Herberg was in fact the obvious choice. In January 1947 he had published a much discussed article in *Commentary* entitled "From Marxism to Judaism." The piece traced his disaffection with and break from the Communist "religion" of his past and spelled out his gradual discovery, through what he called "essential Judaism," of the religious truths he was searching for. His odyssey, if not quite that of the French neo-Thomist Catholic philosopher Maritain (a convert from Protestantism), did parallel that of several other well-known former Jewish Communists, and even bore some similarity to the story, then little known, of the German Jewish philosopher Franz Rosenzweig's return to Judaism (Herberg too had thought of converting to Christianity, but Reinhold Niebuhr told him that he could not become a good Christian until he was first a good Jew). What was most striking about Herberg's article, however, was its "appeal for a renewal of Jewish theology":

> Throughout the world, even in America, there is a widespread hunger for metaphysics, engendered by disillusionment with the shallow formulas and plausible half-truths of positivism. Throughout the world, there is a renewed concern with theology, amounting to a renaissance. Catholicism has its neo-Thomism, Protestantism has its new and vital neo-orthodoxy associated, in various forms, with the names of Karl Barth, Emil Brunner, and Reinhold Niebuhr. What Judaism needs today, in my sincere opinion, is a great theological reconstruction in the spirit of a neo-orthodoxy distant alike from sterile fundamentalism and secularized modernism.[68]

When approached by Solomon Grayzel, Herberg felt ripe to assume this task of "theological reconstruction" himself. Milton Steinberg, who had previously expressed interest but was unable personally to take on the job, encouraged him in this effort, and, apparently, urged Grayzel to offer Herberg a contract. When the manuscript was ready, however, Grayzel read it and pronounced himself "really concerned" and "uncomfortable." Herberg's Judaism, he found, contained heavy doses of Christian neo-Orthodoxy—the influence of Reinhold Niebuhr and Karl Barth—including such ideas as the "Leap of Faith" and "Original Sin." He turned to Steinberg for advice. "At first it was my notion that the manuscript ought to be toned so as to cease to represent Herberg and become more expressive of normative Judaism," Steinberg replied, writing just two months before his death. "But when I worked over the manuscript with Herberg, I came to realize that that would do violence to the man and to his writing and, what was more, would deprive us of a fresh and original expression of Jewish outlook, affected, to be sure, by non-Jewish thought-currents, but not the less interesting and valuable by virtue of that fact." Steinberg concluded that "we ought not attempt to twist Herberg into a conventional model, but should give him publication, making it altogether clear that this represents a distinctive and idiosyncratic view of the Jewish tradition. The book will have greater meaning and is more likely to evoke interest in that fashion." Grayzel took the advice, and *Judaism and Modern Man*, significantly subtitled *An Interpretation of Jewish Religion,* appeared a year later. It has since been characterized as "one of the few genuine synthetic works of Jewish theology written against the background of the American experience." Its influence, especially on "postwar college students and young adults," was considerable.[69]

Abraham Joshua Heschel's *Man Is Not Alone*, published a few months before Herberg's volume appeared, shared its neo-Orthodox critique of the idea that religion and reason are synonymous and was likewise directed toward the predicament of modern man. But where Herberg's theology was largely derivative, heavily influenced by the great Jewish and Christian religious minds of the twentieth century, Heschel's was, at least to Americans, entirely new. "In the face of the tragic failure of the modern mind, incapable of preventing its own destruction," Heschel recalled in 1962, "it became clear to me that the most important philosophical problem of the twentieth century was to find a new set of presuppositions or premises, a different way of thinking." *Man Is Not Alone* was his first major English-language work directed toward meeting this goal.[70]

Heschel submitted what he imagined would be the major part of his book on Jewish theology to JPS in 1949, four years after he had become professor of Jewish Ethics and Mysticism at the Jewish Theological Seminary. "In view of contemporary intellectual and religious currents," and recalling that it had produced practically nothing in a like vein since the work of Solomon Schechter, it accepted the manuscript at once and scheduled it for publication the next year. In the meantime, Heschel, in completing his work, discovered that it was "impossible to set forth his ideas and apply them to actual Jewish living" in less than six hundred pages—more than the Society could afford to print. So the volume was divided into two, and Farrar Straus and Young came in as co-publisher, easing the financial burden. With this hurdle overcome, the first volume, issued under the original title but with only half of the original subject matter included, was hurried into print. It immediately attracted attention.[71]

Reinhold Niebuhr, hardly a man given to easy praise, pronounced the book "a masterpiece." "Not the least of this really profound and creative study," he explained in a prominent review in the *New York Herald Tribune*, "is a distinguished literary style which combines qualities of precision and poetry which are not frequently joined." Heschel, he predicted, would "not long remain unknown after the publication of this volume." He was right. Heschel's novel emphasis on wonder ("radical astonishment"), awe, transcendence, holiness, the "need to be needed," and on the dialectical interaction between God and Man, all deeply influenced by his background in Hasidic piety and classical Jewish texts, had a pronounced influence on Jews and Christians alike. No Jewish religious thinker living in America has ever made so great an impact. Furthermore, from the Society's point of view, Heschel represented precisely the right response to the cultural crisis of the day: He was traditional yet modern; endorsed by Orthodox, Conservative, and Reform rabbis; devoted to Judaism yet open-minded enough to speak to Christians; and he offered a Jewish answer to Christian neo-Orthodoxy that Christians themselves found persuasive. Unsurprisingly, then, Heschel became the Society's favorite Jewish thinker. It offered its members more works by him than by any other Jewish theologian living or dead.[72]

While Heschel sought to validate neo-traditional Judaism, other Jewish thinkers of this period adopted a more basic, survivalist goal: to preserve Judaism's ideological distinctiveness in an age when "Judeo-Christian," a syncretistic term, had become a watchword. As American Jews moved out to the suburbs, drew closer to their Christian neighbors, became familiar with the works of Christian writers and thinkers, and began to engage in interfaith dialogue, the idea that Judaism and Christianity were fundamentally congruent gained considerable currency. "How intimate are the relations of the two religions," Hebrew Union College president Julius Morgenstern gushed in 1943, "so intimate and insoluble that they are truly, basically one, that they have a common descent, a common vision, hope, mission, face a common foe and a common fate." As a growing number of Jews and Christians expressed similar sentiments, emphasizing consensus and "common faith," the threat to Jewish identity seemed increasingly serious.[73]

The demand of the day was for books that would quite specifically explain what Trude Weiss-Rosmarin, in a book *not* published by the Society, bluntly referred to as "Judaism and Christianity: The Differences." Grayzel, who spent his scholarly career studying the enmity between the Church and the Jews, considered this need to be particularly acute. Having published Herberg, whose interpretation of Judaism reflected some of the very tendencies he found most disturbing, he was eager for books that would set the record straight. *Fallen Angels* (1952) by Bernard Bamberger, a study of the belief in Satan and other malevolent divine beings, did just that. "Following the fortunes of the belief in fallen angels," Bamberger explained, "we shall gain a deeper insight into the character of Judaism and the character of Christianity, *and into their divergences*." He concluded that "belief in a malignant devil" formed "one of the basic differences between Judaism and Christianity," and charged that "the new Christian theology" that was bringing back the devil in a different guise was not only "extremely dangerous" but also far from the "ancient Jewish message."[74]

Five years later, Rabbi Abba Hillel Silver, one of the leading pro-Zionist Reform rabbis of his day, presented a far more wide ranging polemic against contemporary efforts to blunt Jewish-Christian differences. In *Where Judaism Differed* (co-published with Macmillan) he declared:

> The attempt to gloss over these differences as a gesture of goodwill is a superficial act which serves neither the purposes of scholarship nor the realities of the situation. It is far better and more practical to look for ways of working together on the basis of a forthright recognition of dissimilarities rather than on a fictitious assumption of identity. Indifference to one's own faith is no proof of tolerance. Loyalty to one's own is part of a larger loyalty to faith generally.

Silver, in line with the demands of pluralism and America's religious tradition, emphasized that he was *not* claiming Judaism's superiority over other systems of belief. "Qualitative differences," he pointed out, "are not necessarily competitive assessments."[75]

The claim of Jewish superiority, however, was quite definitely maintained in Leo Baeck's *Judaism and Christianity*. Baeck, a leading figure in Liberal Judaism and a respected scholar and thinker, served as rabbi of Berlin from 1912, and from 1933 was president of the *Reichsvertretung*, the representative body of German Jews. Deported to Theresienstadt in 1943, he continued to serve as a "witness of his faith" as he held classes and 'kept up morale. In the postwar years he was an esteemed personage, hailed "as one of the most saintly men of our time." JPS therefore decided in 1951 to offer its members a selection of Baeck's writings, specifically five of his essays on Judaism and Christianity—a significant choice given his well-known belief that Judaism was superior, and that the Apostle Paul substituted "faith in Jesus for the faith of Jesus." Abraham Heschel recommended the essays, and philosopher Walter Kaufmann, Baeck's personal choice, agreed to translate them.[76]

By the time the essays appeared in 1958, Baeck had died. His ideas, however, remained timely. "Serious Christians should care to know in what respects one of the outstanding Jewish thinkers of our time considered their religion to be open to objections," Walter Kaufmann wrote in his hard-hitting introduction. And in case anyone missed the underlying message of Baeck's essay on "Romantic Religion," Kaufmann summarized it, drawing contemporary polemical implications that the Society would probably not have permitted into print decades before:

> Baeck's point was not that Judaism was not inferior to Christianity but rather that Judaism was distinctly superior. It is one of the oddities of our time that this view is scarcely ever discussed in public.... Most Christians are convinced of the immeasurable superiority of Christianity over all religions, and quite especially over Judaism; but it is polite to grant that the Jew, of course, considers his religion the equal of Christianity; and it is the acme of liberalism to grant that, theoretically at least, he might be right. The view, however, that Christianity is inferior to Judaism is simply ignored.[77]

Although the Society did not pursue this polemical theme further, in 1961 it reissued two volumes in paperback (both originally published elsewhere) that underscored historical Jewish claims against Christianity and stressed anew important interreligious differences. James Parkes's *The Conflict of the Church and the Synagogue*, an examination of the origins of anti-Semitism, was written by a leading Christian philo-Semite on the eve of World War II. Joshua Trachtenberg's *The Devil and the Jews*, a study of medieval anti-Semitism, showed how Christians had portrayed Jews as allies of Satan—with disastrous results. Implicitly at least, both volumes made the same point: that those who spoke of Judeo-Christian harmony and engaged in rapprochement needed to recall Christianity's long history of anti-Jewish enmity, a legacy of hatred that might be overcome but could not safely be forgotten.[78]

In an effort to do justice to a full range of Jewish thinkers, especially those who exercised a major influence, JPS hoped to publish a whole series of biographies of contemporary Jewish thinkers along with excerpts of their writings. Later, it gave serious consideration to an ambitious plan advanced by Mordecai Kaplan for a Jewish "Great Books Project," covering Jewish thought throughout the ages, and modeled on the American series of the same name.[79] Although neither idea was carried out, owing to lack of funds, seven additional volumes dealing with Jewish thinkers and their work did appear during this period. In more than half the cases, the subjects were, like Leo Baeck, highly cultured German Jews, a measure of German Jewry's impact on all contemporary American thought, secular and Jewish alike.

First and most significant was *Franz Rosenzweig: His Life and Thought*, by Nahum Glatzer, a follower of Rosenzweig in his youth and himself a distinguished scholar, then serving as an editor at Schocken Books. Solomon Grayzel had long been looking for someone to write a book on Rosenzweig, a heroic thinker who founded the famous *Freies Juedisches Lehrhaus* (Free Jewish House of Learning) in

Frankfurt and broke new ground in Jewish philosophy with his *Star of Redemption*, one of the few truly seminal works of Jewish thought written in the twentieth century. Now Glatzer had gone and done the work on his own. "I confess that I envy Schocken the publication of this book," Grayzel wrote when he saw the manuscript. "Rosenzweig along with Buber laid the foundations for the revival of Judaism among the European intellectuals, and a book on him should have been in our list." Soon, thanks to his prodding, the book *was* on the Society's list, as part of a carefully worked out co-publication arrangement. It sold well and sparked considerable interest in Rosenzweig within American Jewish intellectual circles. By 1966, when *Commentary* published its symposium on the "Condition of Jewish Belief," Rosenzweig ranked as the most influential Jewish thinker among those polled, ahead of Martin Buber and Mordecai Kaplan.[80]

The rest of the Society's list reads like a who's who of Jewish scholars and intellectuals, most of them German: Hugo Bieber on Heinrich Heine, Max Wiener on Abraham Geiger, Hans Lewy on Philo, Alexander Altmann on Saadya Gaon, Isaak Heinemann on Jehudah Halevi, Mordecai M. Kaplan on Hermann Cohen (actually on Reconstructionism, but Cohen's *Rational Religion* provided the foil for his argument), and Julius Guttmann on *The History of Jewish Philosophy from Biblical Times to Franz Rosenzweig*. Kaplan, in his volume, expressed a practical aim that the Society shared: "to put a stop to the stampede of our Jewish intellectuals from Jewish life." To that end, JPS offered a philosophical smorgasbord: classical thinkers and modern ones, traditionalists and innovators alike. It did not always succeed in securing precisely the books that it wanted, and its own predilections certainly affected its selection policies. But in terms of quality, quantity, and range, the list of books that it issued was enviable. Readers seeking to understand Jewish ideas had a broad selection of thinkers to choose from.[81]

America and Israel

The "foundation for our survival," Louis Levinthal told the Society's annual meeting in 1952, "must rest on our cultural and spiritual heritage which all Jews—in Israel and in the Diaspora—share in common. We are convinced that unless the children of Israel—not only in the State of Israel but throughout the world—remain the *Am ha-Sefer*, the 'People of the Book,' there is little likelihood that we shall find the spiritual energy so essential to guide and sustain us and give significance and meaning to our life as Jews." Levinthal's cultural Zionist perspective, his stress on the need both for Israel and the Diaspora to be culturally vibrant, reflected the thinking of many at JPS. With the rise of the State of Israel, earlier debates regarding Zionism had become moot and were replaced by a sense of common identity. Levinthal's belief that Israel's growing spiritual creativity required "a concomitant development of learning, culture and spirit in American Jewish life" found many echoes. Although Israeli scholarship and Israel itself became more prominent in the Society's publications, JPS leadership, along with American Jewish leaders generally, strongly resisted the idea that American Jewry should play second fiddle to Israel. The communally funded National Jewish Cultural Study (1958–59) expressed the prevailing mood: "An American Jewry that has rejected so firmly the role of second class citizenship on the American scene," it declared, "will not docilely accept a role of second class cultural citizenship on the world Jewish scene."[82]

The 300th anniversary of Jewish settlement in America, observed in 1954, provided the occasion for American Jews to reemphasize their primacy even as they celebrated their success. "It is obvious to all of us," Jacob Marcus wrote that year in *Bookmark*, "that American Jewry is the most important Jewish group in the world today." Correspondingly, the Society published more books than ever dealing with American Jewish history and life, many of them funded by the grant for "the Jacob R. Schiff Library of Jewish Contributions to American Democracy." Others also jumped on the American Jewish history bandwagon at this time: *Judaism*, the *Jewish Quarterly Review*, and *Jewish Social Studies* published special "Americana" issues, the National American Jewish Tercentenary Committee sponsored activities around the country, and commercial publishers issued an array of books to take advantage of the unprecedented interest in American Jewish history and life that the anniversary called forth.[83]

In evaluating books on American Jewry, Solomon Grayzel was openly scornful of the field's "usual stereotype material" and looked for volumes on a level with Grinstein's *Rise of the Jewish Community of New York*.[84] Sometimes he was fortunate. In 1951, for example, the Society published Jacob Marcus's *Early American Jewry* (volume 1) and his student, Bertram W. Korn's *American Jewry and the Civil War*. Both volumes exploited available primary sources, utilized critical methodologies, and filled major lacunae.[85] Most of the manuscripts in American Jewish history that arrived on his desk, however, failed to meet these standards: They were filiopietistic and poorly researched. The Society had therefore to decide whether it was better to stand on its stated principles and reject these volumes, or to follow instead the more lenient policy that Jacob Marcus propounded:

> I have always maintained the point of view that a poor book is better than no book. Under the circumstances, I have always asked that we be more liberal in the publication of Americana.... We have a large sum of money from the Schiff Fund, and we have a moral obligation to use it for Americana. Consequently I would always look with favor upon the publication or republication of any book that deals with American Jewish history—unless it is absolutely unreadable or is trash.[86]

When it could, the Society simply side-stepped this problem by publishing primary sources: documents, letters, memoirs, even travel accounts—such titles as Jacob R. Marcus's *Memoirs of American Jews* (1955–56); Israel Benjamin's (Benjamin II) *Three Years in America* (1955); and Charles Reznikoff's *Louis Marshall* (1957), two volumes of selected papers and addresses. In all, twelve volumes of primary source material in American Jewish history were issued during this period, more than in any other. Although most were edited for general readers rather than for scholars, taken together they represented a major contribution of unquestionable value.[87]

Where the problem of standards could not so easily be sidestepped was in the area of community studies, one of the oldest genres of American Jewish historical writing, and the most criticized. JPS had consciously shunned these volumes (indeed, it published Grinstein's book as an example of a different approach), for most had no national interest whatsoever. Like American local histories in general, the community studies were, with few exceptions, thoroughly filiopietistic and tendentious. Still, they provided raw data from which a synthetic history could eventually be written and instilled local Jewish residents with a sense of community pride. Furthermore, from a practical point of view, they offered a successful vehicle for attracting local funds to support scholarly work. Given the Society's increasing commitment to American Jewish history, the question of whether community studies should be admitted onto its list was inevitable.[88]

The question first arose in 1949 in connection with *The Jews of Charleston*, which the novelist-poet Charles Reznikoff had been commissioned to write in collaboration with Professor Uriah Z. Engelman. Charleston's Jewish community played a highly important role in antebellum American Jewish life, and Grayzel confidently expected a volume of significance. "I cannot tell you how disappointed I am," he wrote when he read it, "I am convinced that it will not add to the glory of the JPS." Instead of rejecting the work outright, however, the Society helped convene a meeting of scholars, including distinguished American historians and social scientists, non-Jews among them, to review the volume and help bring it up to standards. Their criticisms—which might as well have been applied to most Jewish community histories of the period—were blunt: The work, they charged, lacked a point of departure and a theme, was unintegrated, inadequately portrayed the integration of Jews in the general society, and was both insufficiently interpretive and unnecessarily apologetic. Reznikoff rewrote the volume somewhat taking these criticisms into account, and the Society published it the following year. The experience, however, was not a happy one.[89]

The Society did not publish another community history until 1956 when it issued one of the best of the genre: Edwin Wolf 2nd and Maxwell Whiteman's *History of the Jews of Philadelphia from Colonial Times to the Age of Jackson.* It did not go unnoticed that Wolf was the Society's president when the book appeared, the first time that had ever happened, but in this case there was no question about the volume's acceptance; it was richly researched, beautifully written, and had significance that went far beyond Philadelphia's confines. At the same time, the history held obvious appeal to the Society's many Philadelphia supporters, reminding them of an earlier, happier day, prior to the community's twentieth-century decline. Subsequent community histories failed to elicit the same interest. One of them, indicative of the problems inherent in community history, was actually returned by a disgruntled reader because it failed to give due credit to the achievements of his own family![90]

Grayzel, recalling the ill-fated Jewish Community Series of the 1930s, sought as early as 1957 to steer the Society in other directions: "There is no hope of doing anything worthwhile in the field of local histories," he complained in a letter to Jacob Marcus. "The Jewish community of Ash-Kash started in practically the same fashion as the Jewish community of Windbag. It is a waste of time and paper to repeat the same events ad nauseam." Grayzel sought to encourage instead more chronological histories, biographies, and histories of institutions.[91] But JPS leaders, perhaps swayed by Marcus's arguments, were not entirely convinced. The availability of manuscripts in local Jewish history, coupled with internal pressure to make the subject of American Jewish history a central priority, meant that the question of whether to publish such volumes arose repeatedly. It was 1978 before the Society decided that it had issued its last community history, and by then it had published a total of seven: a small fraction of the two hundred in existence, but more, certainly, than some felt were warranted.[92]

A principal, if rarely stated, aim of the Society's offerings in American Jewish history was to make the case for American exceptionalism, the idea that "American Jewish life differs from European Jewish life." This view, by no means unique to the Society, took on special significance in light of the debate over whether America was *galut* (exile) and properly belonged in the same category as other lands included under this heading.[93] Although the Society took no overt stance on this ideologically explosive question, its books tacitly furthered the exceptionalist posture. Moshe Davis's *The Emergence of Conservative Judaism* (1963), for example, stressed the fact that "few parallel situations" to that of American Jewry could "be found in the whole range of the Jewish experience." The bulk of Davis's study, an updated adaptation of his *Yahadut Amerika Be-Hitpathutah*, carefully reworked so as to be more appropriate for an American audience, concerned itself with nineteenth-century American Jewish religious life, and the activities of what he called "The Historical School"—a label that covered various approaches to Judaism that combined to influence the Conservative movement. Still, the theme of American exceptionalism ("the ancient religion's quest for expression in its new and free environment") underlay the entire book; indeed, one of the functions of the original Hebrew volume was to explain American Jewry's uniqueness to Israelis.[94]

The same sense of uniqueness emerged from Rachel Wischnitzer's *Synagogue Architecture in the United States* (1955). Written in the midst of the building boom that created the "suburban synagogue," the volume demonstrated that even Judaism's most sacred institutions had, over time, taken on a distinctively American cast ("It is obvious that what the Jews believe and the manner in which Judaism functions in this country are reflected in the form of the buildings they erect.") As if to underscore the importance of the distinction, the architecture of the European synagogue was treated in a separate companion volume published a decade later.[95]

During this period, the cultural emergence of American Jewry, a perennial JPS theme, was emphasized more than before—both because American Jewish culture was beginning to achieve outside recognition, and as a response to Israel's claims to cultural centrality. In just one year, 1964, the Society issued Irwin Malin's and Irwin Stark's *Breakthrough*, a co-published volume that celebrated the emergence of contemporary American Jewish literature onto the national scene; *The Menorah Treasury*, a collection of the best articles from the *Menorah Journal*, for several decades the most important Jewish cultural journal in America; and, most important of all, Oscar Janowsky's *The American Jew: A Reappraisal*, containing a comprehensive cultural evaluation of where the American Jewish community stood.[96]

Janowsky's volume formed a sequel to his *The American Jew* (1942), published by Harper and Brothers, sponsored by Hadassah, and designed as a wartime effort "to discern the character, trends and values" that American Jewish life displayed. This time JPS sponsored the volume, backing it with an unprecedented grant from the Schiff Fund of $6,000, and Janowsky focused more directly on the "the Jewish community and its institutions," with special emphasis on religion and culture. The results, although far from celebratory, were very much in line with the theme of cultural emergence. Jacob Marcus, in the volume's first essay, predicted a coming "Golden Age" of American Jewish life. Judah J. Shapiro, discussing the nature of American Jewish culture, quoted Solomon Grayzel on "evidence or improvement . . . seen in the establishment of the National Foundation for Jewish Culture," the very organization that he along with Edwin Wolf 2nd and others had helped to found. Finally, in the volume's peroration, Janowsky sought to drive the message home: "American Jewry is not disintegrating. It is in the process of becoming."[97]

Janowsky by no means ignored the existence of the State of Israel. Although one contributor considered it "much too early for categorical assertions about the effects of the existence of the State of Israel on American Jews," preliminary observations were not discouraged. Two revealingly different notes were sounded. On the one hand, C. Bezalel Sherman, former cultural director of the Labor Zionist Organization, castigated those who "at times leave the impression that they regard Israel as of secondary importance in the creative survival of the Jewish people." On the other hand, Judah J. Shapiro, perhaps because of his position as secretary of the National Foundation for Jewish Culture, was scornful of those who viewed Israel "as the surrogate of Jewish culture." He argued strongly *against* the idea that Israel alone bore "responsibility for defining Jewishness," and emphasized the need for a viable domestic Jewish culture in the United States.[98]

Both of these views found strong echoes in the Society's books. Grayzel himself seems to have been torn, wanting neither to slight Israel's cultural significance nor to overemphasize it at the expense of Jewish culture in America. As a result, JPS walked a fine line: It kept up on Israeli culture, published books about Israel, and translated important Israeli works into English for Americans to read; yet it proudly maintained its independence, stressed volumes dealing with America, and sought ways to market its own volumes in Israel for people there to read. In 1954, when Zalman Shazar, representing the Jewish Agency, proposed to JPS a "standing agreement" to publish selected Israeli books in America, the idea was rejected because of concern that the Society's independence would be undermined. At Shazar's suggestion, however, the Society did publish in English *The Exiled and the Redeemed* (1957), a revised translation of *Nidche Yisrael*, by the then president of Israel, Itzhak Ben-Zvi.[99]

Louis Levinthal saw the Ben Zvi volume as an opening. He had long hoped that the Society would make available in English "the best of present-day Hebrew literature in the State of Israel," and now that hope was beginning to be realized. At the 1957 annual meeting, he called special attention to the book's "dramatic portrayal of those Jewish oriental communities lost to our people, most of which the State of Israel has reclaimed and redeemed," and hailed the volume as "a significant contribution to the cultural bond between the Israel and American Jewish communities." Over the next four years, thanks in part to his prodding, JPS translated and published two additional works of Israeli scholarship: Victor Tcherikover's *Hellenistic Civilization and the Jews* and Yitzhak (Fritz) Baer's *History of the Jews in Christian Spain*—both recognized as classics in their field. Subsequently, there were many more such translations from Hebrew—too many, according to some of those concerned about domestic Jewish culture. The volumes both enriched the literature of Jewish scholarship available in English, and served as "cultural bridges" making the fruits of Israeli research available to American audiences.[100]

In addition to books *from* Israel, the Society also published during this period an increasing number of books *about* Israel. Israel was very much in the news, and American Jews sought reliable information about what was going on in the country and what implications those developments had for them. Israel's War for Independence formed the theme for the first JPS volume dealing with modern Israel, *Unambo*, a novel by Max Brod, co-published with Farrar, Straus, and Young. "*Unambo* is no simple tale," the Society assured its readers in a revealing blurb. "Battle scenes are in it and accounts of heroism. But there are in it also all the strangenesses and maladies of the modern soul . . . the end is hope—a daring hope—for Israel and for all men." A similar sense of hope pervaded Raphael Patai's *Israel Between East and West* (1953), a study of the problems "created by the presence in Israel of two major groups of population elements basically different in cultural characteristics"—Western Jews and Oriental Jews. Although others gloomily predicted the growing "Orientalization" of Israel, due to the large number of immigrants from Arab lands, Patai foresaw a "process of amalgamation which is to lead eventually to the cultural synthesis between East and West." Subsequent books did not hesitate to point out problems in Israeli society—religious problems, educational problems, social problems—but always in a warmhearted, optimistic fashion, leaving readers with an appreciation of the challenges that faced modern Israel, yet confident that somehow they would be overcome.[101]

Patai dealt in passing with one of the central questions that American Jewish leaders worried about: the Jewish State's impact on American Jewish life. His own view was definitely that of the cultural Zionist: "Israel will become the main factor in preventing the total engulfment of American Jewry within the magnetic field of the great Western civilization." How it would accomplish this feat he did not say, but in several subsequent volumes, the Society offered its readers formulations clearly influenced by the teachings of Ahad Ha'Am. In *Hebrew: The Eternal Language,* a "history of the development of the Hebrew language from its beginning to this day," William Chomsky of Gratz College hoisted aloft the banner of Hebrew as the "medium for revitalizing the Jewish community of America, for rendering it dynamic and creative." This idea, of course, had roots that went back much earlier in the century, and thanks to Samson Benderly had already influenced a generation of students. Chomsky adapted Hebraist thinking to the new post-1948 situation in America, and envisioned a hopeful future for the Diaspora as a whole:

> Young people, and adults too, who possess the proper Hebraic orientation will be not only the builders of Israel, but also the backbone of a meaningful Judaism in the Diaspora, which will integrate itself with the revitalized Judaism of Israel and model itself to some degree on the ideal patterns evolved there, while evolving and creating at the same time values and life patterns indigenous to their particular locale.[102]

Subsequently, JPS published Leon Simon's biography of Ahad Ha'Am, *Selected Essays of Ahad Ha'Am* in paperback reprint, and additional volumes setting forth cultural Zionist ideas in a variety of different contexts.[103]

Believing that American Jews, and JPS in particular, had produced books and ideas of value to Israel, Judge Levinthal proposed in 1954 a program to translate some of those books into Hebrew. The publication committee never followed up on the idea, but over the years, even before 1948, others had made such translations, and several of them were marketed by Israeli firms—evidence that the "cultural bridge" was a two-way affair. To help those who could read its books in English, the Society in 1953 presented a complete set of its publications to the Hebrew University, replacing those lost during the War of Independence. Later, it negotiated with Shoshana Rosenberg-Elbogen, daughter of Ismar Elbogen, to see if she could help arrange for its books to be sold in Israel, a task made difficult by import and export laws. As further evidence of cultural ties, it occasionally employed Israeli translators, and in the case of Gerson Cohen's edition of the *Sefer HaQabbalah*, it commissioned an Israeli printer to set the Hebrew type—an unhappy experience that delayed the book for years.[104]

Perhaps most interesting of all was the advice that some of the authors imparted to Israeli leaders. As a rule, the editor red-penciled divisive contemporary politics, but revealing comments sometimes slipped through. William Chomsky, foreshadowing the better-known thoughts of his son, Noam, thus urged Jews in the Diaspora to "safeguard the State of Israel from turning in the direction of narrow nationalism." "There is," he warned, "a strong temptation for a small people that has regained power, after having suffered for a long time from oppression and persecution, to become over-aggressive and chauvinistic. A strong international-minded Diaspora," he believed, "would serve as a brake and would induce Israel to resist such temptation." Solomon Zeitlin, in the introduction to his *magnum opus, The Rise and Fall of the Judean State: A Political, Social and Religious History of the Second Commonwealth*, offered Israel an equally controversial historical lesson. Long before such comparisons became fashionable, he likened the ultimately vanquished Second Jewish Commonwealth to the still young Third, urging Israelis to draw the appropriate conclusions:

> Then, as now, the restoration of the state was begun with a proclamation by an outside power. Then, as now, the secular and the religious viewpoints were in conflict. Then, as now, the neighbors of the new state resented its appearance. For centuries the Judaean state served as buffer between its powerful neighbors. Israel should take cognizance of this fact and in shaping her diplomacy should look to the history of the Second Commonwealth as a guide.

Zeitlin stressed one lesson above all: "History clearly demonstrates that religious leaders should not interfere in political matters, and magistrates and secular leaders should not interfere in religion."[105]

All told, the Society's attitude toward Israel, as reflected in its activities and publications, reveals the ambivalences and ambiguities that beset the relationship between Israel and American Jewry as a whole during this period: the hopes and the fears, the simultaneous wish to see Israel develop and to see American Jewry retain its own preeminent position. Characteristically, JPS was neither as Israel-centered as some wanted it to be, nor as America-centered as others desired. It saw itself, increasingly, as a cultural mediator, a bridge-builder, an interpreter of each community to the other. In 1966 the trustees made this policy official. "The Jewish Publication Society," *Bookmark* reported, "has undertaken the task of serving as the link between the world of Israel publishing and the American Jewish community." Under the new plan, the Society agreed to translate and publish Israeli books "of significant interest to American Jews."[106]

Time for a Change

Israel, America, Jewish Thought, the Bible, and other new publication emphases introduced by Grayzel could not overcome the mood of depression that increasingly gripped the Society in the 1960s. Finances were in better shape than before, and the seventy-fifth anniversary provided an occasion to celebrate, but everyone realized that the competition was gaining: It outpublished and outsold JPS, carried off more awards, and nurtured more fledgling writers. The Society, by contrast, seemed old, stodgy, uncertain of its goals and purposes, and out of touch with the youthful spirit of the day, exemplified by John F. Kennedy. At the May 1962 annual meeting, Sol Satinsky in his presidential report, and Edwin Wolf 2nd reporting on publication committee activities, both gave voice to these painful feelings of malaise. Satinsky spoke of "failure to progress," of the frustrating need "to move along very fast in order to stand still—not to fall back." He frankly admitted that the previous year had seen more activity than achievement; he had hoped for better. Wolf was even more frustrated: "The hard facts of our present existence," he gloomily reported, "are not that good Jewish books are not being written or not being published. They are—by others. We are finding it increasingly difficult to secure manuscripts of worth ... even the quality books of erudite scholarship are beginning to elude us." The reasons were clear enough: competition from trade and university presses, the desire of many Jewish authors to be published by "secular" rather than "sectarian" presses, and an increasing number of Jewish publishers crowding the market. Grayzel also realized "that a new generation of American Jews had arisen, which wanted less scholarship, more spirituality, and a more lively approach to Jewish books." With only 11,000 members and but ten new books (plus paperback reprints) published each year, several of them children's books or co-publications, JPS—notwithstanding the significant books it still issued—had greatly declined in status. To make matters worse, the personal relationship between Grayzel and Zussman had deteriorated with Grayzel's advancing age: "The atmosphere in the office of the JPS became very strained."[107]

Clearly it was time for a change. In 1964, Grayzel was 68 years old and celebrating his twenty-fifth year as editor. Sol Satinsky was 64, Louis Levinthal was 72, Jacob Marcus was 68, some of the other officers and trustees were even older. Now, in the Society as in the country at large, the moment had come for the older generation to step aside. Grayzel announced his intention to retire as soon as a successor was found. A year later, the trustees proposed far-reaching changes to the Society's constitution, to bring it more in line with the corporate model, and "to afford more individuals . . . an opportunity to serve . . . thereby insuring the constant infusion of new ideas." The new bylaws, to take effect in 1966, limited trustees to four consecutive three-year terms (except for former presidents, who were automatically appointed life trustees), and barred elected officers from serving in the same position for more than three consecutive years. This meant that all but two of the officers were ineligible to be reelected.[108]

Meanwhile, the search was on for a successor to Solomon Grayzel. A galaxy of scholars, intellectuals, and professional editors, covering a span of ages and religious orientations, either applied for or were proposed for the job. For its part, the search committee, headed by Edwin Wolf 2nd, had before it a long list of suggested qualifications, everything from linguistic, literary, and scholarly credentials, to "a strong commitment to Jewish life, ability to rise above religious institutionalism, ability to work with people—and an awful lot of patience." Most of the proposed candidates, when they learned what the job entailed, understandably removed themselves from consideration; others, for various reasons, were disqualified. The man who remained in the running was a Conservative rabbi who was then managing editor of the magazine *Conservative Judaism* and a member of the faculty of the Teachers Institute of the Jewish Theological Seminary. His name was Herman Potok, but he was known as Chaim. On June 23, 1965, the trustees offered him a contract "as Associate Editor for a period up to one year and then as Editor for a period to be determined." His tenure as Associate Editor lasted until May 31, 1966, at which time Solomon Grayzel formally retired.[109]

Grayzel's retirement brought to a close a long and productive era in the Society's history. After twenty-seven years, Grayzel had come almost to personify JPS, so much of what it did bore his stamp. Single-handedly, he had edited over two hundred books, many of them distinguished contributions. He had also commented on hundreds of other manuscripts that for one reason or another were rejected, and had written countless letters and delivered innumerable talks on the Society's behalf. More than anyone else during these years, he defined the distinctive JPS style and was responsible for maintaining its high standards. The fact that JPS still commanded a position of respect in the literary marketplace, notwithstanding all the changes that had taken place over the years, was in no small measure a tribute to his tireless efforts.

Now, in addition to a new editor, JPS was to be governed by an entirely new slate of officers. The president, five vice-presidents, treasurer, and secretary all were serving their first terms in office. The talk at Grayzel's retirement was thus of "experimentation," "new approaches," and "new frontiers." Grayzel rejoiced:

"With a new editor—young, eager, and full of ideas—the Society is certain to make its mark on Jewish life." His concluding charge before introducing Chaim Potok captured the mood of the hour: "May his tenure be long; may his achievements be high; may his influence be wide; may his success be spectacular. He has all our good wishes."[110]

Changing of the Guard: the Publication Committee meeting of 1965 introducing Chaim Potok as the new editor. FROM LEFT (FRONT ROW): *Lesser Zussman, Judge Louis E. Levinthal, Chaim Potok, Sol Satinsky, Edwin Wolf 2nd, Solomon Grayzel, Jacob R. Marcus;* (BACK ROW): *Sam Daroff, unidentified, Nahum Glatzer, Stanley Chyet, Oscar Janowsky, Saul Viener, Maxwell Raab, Jerome J. Shestack, unidentified, Eli Ginzberg, Louis Kaplan, Moshe Greenberg, Samuel Ajl, Isidor Twersky, Paul Sloane, Harry Starr, Abram L. Sachar. (Mike Zwerling)*

A joint meeting of the Bible Translation Committee at the Hebrew Union College-Hebrew Institute of Religion, New York: FROM LEFT (FRONT ROW): *Bernard J. Bamberger, H. L. Ginsberg, Harry Orlinsky;* (BACK ROW): *Martin S. Rozenberg, Moshe Greenberg, Saul Leeman, Solomon Grayzel, Jonas C. Greenfield, Nahum M. Sarna, Max Arzt, Chaim Potok. (Mike Zwerling)*

Chaim Potok (2nd from left) and Lesser Zussman (right) inspecting proofs of Tully Filmus: Selected Drawings *with the artist (2nd from right)*

Gerson Cohen

Lewis H. Weinstein and Maier Deshell celebrating the publication of Wolfson of Harvard *(1978)*

Publication Committee, 1976. FROM LEFT (FRONT ROW): *Jerome J. Shestack, Bernard Segal, A. Leo Levin, Yosef Yerushalmi, Francine Klagsbrun, Nahum M. Sarna;* (SECOND ROW): *Marvin Wachsman, Howard Sachar, Solomon Grayzel, Leo Guzik, Bernard Frankel;* (THIRD ROW): *Robert Abrams, Maxwell Whiteman, Irwin Holtzman, Maier Deshell, Abraham Karp, Abraham Katsh;* (FOURTH ROW): *Edward Shils, Koch (?), Louis L. Kaplan, Bernard I. Levinson, Jerome Cramer.*

rnard I. Levinson
a JPS exhibition

9

CONTINUITY AND CHANGE

Chaim Potok assumed the editorship of the Society during one of the most tumultuous periods in American history. The war in Vietnam, the civil rights struggle, the counterculture, the revolution on college campuses, the radical turn in religion and morals, the social changes attendant upon the New Frontier and the Great Society—these were only some of the many great upheavals that characterized the era. The period also marked a watershed in American Jewish history. More than ever before, American Jews, many of them young and native born, participated in the great movements of the day and translated them into Jewish terms. The antiwar movement, the civil rights struggle, and the counter-culture all developed Jewish offshoots. In addition, many began to confront the memory of the Holocaust, repressed for almost a full generation, and some awakened for the first time to the plight of Jews in the Soviet Union, struggling for the opportunity to live freely in the religion of their ancestors. Most important of all, in mid-1967, American Jews experienced the frantic desperation and boundless exhilaration that distinguished the period before and after the Six-Day War, a war that brought home to American Jews just how closely intertwined their fate and that of the State of Israel had become.

For the Jewish Publication Society, this tumultuous era represented both a challenge and a threat. There was, on the one hand, a growing demand for Jewish books, a restless search for answers, Jewish answers, to the gnawing questions of the day. On the other hand, there was also a potentially dangerous infatuation with newness, an iconoclastic spurning of tradition, a sense that the "Jewish Establishment" and its institutions were dated, out of touch with the times. "This is a period of confrontation and turmoil," JPS President William Fishman warned those attending the 1970 annual meeting, "and it just doesn't feel right to me that the Society go blithely on its way, publishing its books and Bibles, receiving enough in contributions from its members and other donors to pay its bills, and in a way standing somewhat apart from today's dynamics in the Jewish and other religious communities." What he called for, and what the Society under Chaim Potok and his successors looked for, was a new balance, a moderate "view toward changing our course—not abruptly and not impulsively, but steadily and firmly."[1]

Charting A New Course

Chaim Potok was the ideal man to shape this new balance. Preoccupied by the tension between tradition and modernity even as a teenager, he had spent the better part of two decades not only wrestling with that tension but writing about it. He was young, fashionably bearded, brimming with ideas, and convinced of the power of the written word. Within a year of his becoming editor, *The Chosen* (1967), his first novel, concerned as all his other novels would be with "the interplay of the Jewish tradition with the secular twentieth century," surged to the top of the best-seller list. Jews and non-Jews alike saw in him a writer who spoke to their personal concerns. His rising popularity attested to how well he sensed the tenor of the times.[2]

"What new ideas and goals ought the Society to set for itself in consonance with the reality of today and without in any way at all impinging upon the spirit and framework of its charter?" Potok asked in his first major address to the board. The question had been asked many times before, especially as the number of major publishers and university presses issuing Jewish books had multiplied. But the answer he supplied—he called it his "dream"—was new:

> There is absolutely nothing intrinsically wrong with other publishing houses putting out Jewish books. It is a healthy, welcome development. But a non-profit-motivated Jewish house must set the Socratic standard. It is not only a matter of our publishing quality books that no other house would publish, though that is very important. It is a matter of setting a tone that others will want to emulate. It is a matter not only of filling gaps, but also of creating new demands, new standards, new needs—so that when a publishing house is considering a Jewish book, it is what *our* house has published that will serve as the standard of comparison. And the standard ought to be one not only for the publishing world but for the reading world as well.[3]

Potok suggested three initial measures aimed at realizing this dream: (1) greater cooperation with Israeli publishers on a reciprocal basis; (2) "increased emphasis upon publication by JPS of current and topical books—particularly for college students"; and (3) "development of new authors for the purpose of revitalizing the JPS list."[4] More important than all of these, however, was the innovation he announced in a front-page editorial in the *Bookmark* of December 1966 under the title "The Literature of Encounter":

> We are in the midst of an overwhelming encounter with western civilization. We are not only agonizing over the *private* problem of how best to be Jewish and yet remain a part of and a contributor to the mainstream of contemporary twentieth-century civilization, we are also interested in the *public* problem of how best to remain human in a world that has b⸱⸱⸱n witness to an Auschwitz and a Bergen-Belsen. How to live as a Jew in a free   ty, how to have Jewish concepts compete successfully in the open marketplac⸱   ⸱ ideas, how to make our tradition vibrant and alive, how to enable Juda⸱   to make a viable contribution to twentieth-century culture—these are the ⸱ ⸱ blems born of our encounter with western civilization....
>
> We are interested in books that speak to our time. W⸱ ⸱re interested in books that address themselves to the problem of our day,   our own harsh realities. We are, in brief, interested in what, for lack of a better term, might be called *Jewish encounter literature.*... The criterion of encounter will henceforth operate as a basic yardstick for the works we publish under our imprint.[5]

The Society's list of publications slowly shifted to reflect this new "encounter" theme. It published books on the clash between tradition and modernity in Eastern Europe, books on the plight of Jews and Judaism in the Soviet Union, books on Israel and the Diaspora, books on the Holocaust. A new series, known as JPS Extras, permitted the Society to make timely books available after its year's list had been set, avoiding "a full year's delay in publication." Another new series, the Library of Contemporary Jewish Fiction, returned selected high-quality literature to its list, beginning with Ludwig Lewisohn's epic novel on the clash between assimilation and tradition, *The Island Within*, originally published in 1928. Two new administrative policies facilitated this change in emphasis. First, to attract the best books published in Israel, JPS agreed under extraordinary circumstances to waive the requirement that authors absorb some translation costs out of their own royalties. When it wanted a book badly, it now would offer to cover translation expenses itself. Second, it streamlined procedures to permit rapid acceptance of sought-after manuscripts. Although this reduced still further the publication committee's role, it enhanced the Society's power to compete and gave the editor additional power.[6]

Despite all of these changes, however, dissatisfaction continued, for compared to the pace of social change in the late 1960s, JPS appeared to be standing still. Even Edwin Wolf 2nd was impatient: "If we were a university," he exclaimed in 1969, "we would long ago have been invaded and forced to change ... let us get going." When it came to deciding on where to go, however, nobody could agree. One publication committee member sought specific future goals and a carefully conceived multiyear program. Another insisted that the Society needed to change not so much its books as its sales techniques: "As a first step, consideration should be given to the employment of a 'Director of Marketing' who would assist the Executive Director in the development of new resources for the distribution of present JPS books as well as new publishing ventures which may be developed in the future."

In 1969, a planning committee under the direction of Professor Edward B. Shils of the University of Pennsylvania listened to a variety of proposals, and decided as a first step to hammer out a new statement of JPS goals. The two-point statement that resulted, and subsequently won adoption from the trustees, reflected a careful compromise:

> 1. The JPS should publish works of Jewish interest in the English language of importance to broad segments of the Jewish community that fulfill one or more of the following conditions:
>   a) It is a work of quality.
>   b) It is a creative work.
>   c) It might not be published otherwise.
> 2. The JPS should commission specific types of works to fill the needs of the Jewish community to provide for a balanced publishing program.[7]

This mission statement confirmed the "mixed-list" philosophy under which the Society had operated for years, encouraged the "encounter" literature that Potok wanted "to fill the needs of the Jewish community," and still left the door open to future shifts of emphasis. It also continued the policy of communitywide consensus that JPS had cherished since its founding. But it came as a blow to those like Professor Daniel Greenberg, a young Jewish scientist on the publication committee, who sought changes on a massive scale. He and his like-minded friends felt defeated.

Nor was this their only defeat. During this period plans for large-scale transformation were put forward time and again, but opposition always arose from the same two sources: the guardians of tradition and the guardians of the purse. The former alone might have been overcome given the mood of the day, but the latter, the tough-minded businessmen who demanded fiscal responsibility and scrutinized every figure to ensure that JPS could still pay its bills, usually had their way. Greenberg, impatient with the businessmen-trustees, urged that "money-making considerations ought to be secondary . . . we would be failing our charter and our deepest purposes if we let considerations of profitability govern our course." Those with longer memories, however, recalled that the Society's continuing existence could not be taken for granted; it had come close to failing more than once for financial reasons. Given the high failure rate of other American publishing houses, they deemed prudence to be the better part of wisdom.[8]

In 1972 proponents of change at JPS momentarily had their way. President Jerome J. Shestack, working closely with David C. Gross, Lesser Zussman's then newly appointed successor, announced a doubling of the publication list in 1973 ("This year more than thirty books will be available to our members"), with increased emphasis on "popular books by noted authors," and an enlarged advertising budget—the kind of program not seen since the days of Maurice Jacobs. At a stormy meeting of the board of trustees, a majority endorsed the proposal over the objections of a vociferous minority. Six months later, however, when the bills came in and JPS found itself face to face with a whopping deficit of $130,000, support for the new program evaporated. At the insistence of the trustees, the plan was "reduced drastically" and it was agreed that "a more modest publishing program be planned for 1974."[9] The episode served to confirm past wisdom and vindicated the guardians of the purse. Henceforward, the Society developed not through sharp breaks from the past or massive year-to-year changes, but rather through slow, steady evolution. Major new projects like the Bible commentary, new publishing initiatives in literature or poetry, even new advertising initiatives—all these required long periods of gestation, and lasted only so long as they could find support from donors or prove themselves financially viable.

Edward Shils, echoing an observation made by Frank Schechter fifty years before, noted in 1980 that the tension between fiscal conservatism and teeming activism was built into the Society's very structure. "As Trustees . . . it is our traditional duty to conserve our funds with as niggardly an outlay as possible. As members of the Publication Committee it is our privilege to recommend to the Trustees a generous and perhaps even reckless expenditure in the cause of Jewish literature." These contradictory responsibilities, "often somewhat difficult to reconcile," had been the source of many a debate over the years. "The dilemma," Shils observed, "is still with us." There was, however, a welcome middle ground that began in this period to open up—a way of being both venturesome and fiscally responsible. It was the endowment, the Society's long-sought reserve fund that, thanks to generous donations and bequests, finally achieved modest proportions. By 1975 it amounted to $1,375,000—not a large sum as endowments of Jewish institutions go, but enough to provide annual income and to ensure that small deficits (large ones still caused concern) and low-budget new projects could be internally funded. Tending the endowment became an increasingly important part of the trustees' work in the 1970s and a special committee sought to increase its size through prudent investments and new donations. In 1978 the endowment was enriched by $377,317 from the estate of Abraham M. Wolfman of Los Angeles. Two years later Philip and Muriel Berman of Philadelphia, in what was the largest such gift in JPS history, donated $500,000 to a special endowment in their name.

Coupled with other donations and annual subventions from the Joint Cultural Appeal funded by Jewish Federations around the country, this meant that JPS for the first time had the confidence of knowing that it rested on a financial cushion. If its income and expenses did not quite balance, income from the endowment could make up the difference. The Society's financial situation, then, if not robust, had definitely become healthy. The annual treasurer's report, glum reading some years back, now routinely ended with good news.[10]

The annual statistics, shown here in five-year increments, bear out this picture. For the most part, the figures point to slow, steady improvement. Income rose substantially in the early 1970s, mostly due to inflation, rising membership fees, higher book prices, and the success of both the new Bible translation and the *Jewish Catalog* (see below), but the growth is deceptive; expenses rose just as fast. The only decline, an admittedly disturbing one, was in book distribution figures. JPS, like most publishers, especially academic ones, found itself issuing more books than ever, but selling them in fewer numbers. Endowment fund figures, although not included in this chart, also rose during this period, reaching close to $2 million.[11]

Year	Members	Books Distributed	New Books	Reprints	Income*
1965	13,394	192,000	11	14	$520,614
1970	13,364	na	12	12	537,726
1975	14,132	190,000	17	11	926,993
1980	15,356	181,385	15	18	1,012,614

* Membership and sales figures only for 1975–80

In 1974, with the Society enjoying financial stability, Chaim Potok resigned to spend much of his year in Israel, staying on as special projects editor, and was replaced by Maier Deshell, then serving as an associate editor of *Commentary* magazine, and formerly an editor for the American Jewish Congress. Deshell, an ordained conservative rabbi, was interested in Jewish scholarship and felt that JPS could make its most significant contribution in this realm. The chairman of the publication committee, Professor Yosef Hayim Yerushalmi, then of Harvard (he replaced Professor Gerson Cohen in 1973 when Cohen became chancellor of the Jewish Theological Seminary) was of like mind. As a result, during the decade that Deshell served as editor (1974–83) JPS edged away from the literature of encounter that Potok had favored and published a series of more scholarly tomes, several of them books on the cutting edge of Jewish scholarship that explored new subjects and employed innovative methodologies. Popular books continued to appear on the list—some initiated by JPS, others co-published with commercial presses—but the emphasis clearly had shifted.[12]

Shifts in two other realms also left their imprint during this period. First, thanks to the 1965 by-laws, the Society's leadership became much more fluid; a new president had now to be elected every three years. Those who served from the mid-1960s into the 1980s—Joseph M. First, William S. Fishman, Jerome J. Shestack, A. Leo Levin, Edward B. Shils, and Muriel M. Berman—brought with them new ideas and represented a cross-section of the Philadelphia area and vicinity Jewish elite. They were almost evenly divided between the two occupational groups that provided the leadership cadre of most contemporary American Jewish organizations: professionals and businesspeople. Dr. Muriel M. Berman, an optometrist, was not only the Society's first woman president but also, along with her husband, Philip, its most generous benefactor since the Schiffs. Berman played a particularly active role in JPS affairs, forbade the trustees from meeting at their usual club, which barred women from membership, and was also the first JPS president who, upon retirement, was elected honorary president and chairman of the board. Several of the new publishing initiatives undertaken by JPS in the 1980s stemmed from ideas that she personally had championed.[13]

The other major shift at JPS had to do with the location of its headquarters. In 1967 the trustees learned that the existing building at 222 North 15th Street lay in a redevelopment area and was scheduled for demolition. The historic mansion owned by the Women's City Club of Philadelphia (1622 Locust Street) soon became available, and in 1968 the Society bought it for $175,000. But renovations proved far more expensive and legally complex than originally foreseen, so nobody minded when it was sold—especially since the transaction yielded a handsome profit. Meanwhile, the Society stayed put, awaiting further developments. When the slow-moving state officials finally served a notice to vacate in 1974—sweetened by $369,500 in compensation funds plus moving expenses—there was nowhere to go but into temporary rented quarters at 1528 Walnut Street while the building committee searched for a new location. Nothing suitable turned up within an acceptable price range, however, so in 1977 the Society moved into rented quarters at 117 South 17th Street, the Architects Building. This space was cramped and unsuitable, so in 1982 JPS, like the proverbial wandering Jew, picked up and moved into yet another rented home, this one at 1930 Chestnut Street.[14]

Holocaust and Redemption

Jerome Shestack, in his presidential address at the annual JPS meeting in 1975, discussed two themes from the Society's past that he found "particularly remarkable." "The first," he observed, "is that the Society has always represented *K'lal Yisrael*, by seeking to preserve and enrich the total Jewish spiritual and cultural heritage. ... The second chord is the strong bond of continuity that marks the course of the

Society's history." In the era that began when Chaim Potok assumed the editorship in 1966 and ended with Maier Deshell's resignation in 1983, both themes were in evidence. Despite abundant competition from university and commercial presses and despite changes in personnel, JPS remained committed, as President Muriel M. Berman put it in 1983, "to publishing quality, authoritative books on every Jewish subject that requires attention." Scholarly books, popular books, children's books, translations, co-publications, books covering all aspects of the Jewish experience, especially in America, continued to feature on its list dependably year after year.[15]

Yet the Society was also committed to moving in new directions. Shestack himself spoke of the need to "experiment and explore," and during this period many new initiatives were undertaken. Their impact cannot yet be fully assessed. What is clear is that JPS now reached out to a young generation of Jews to whom it had not previously spoken, and confronted issues that it had rarely, if ever, addressed before. As Chaim Potok proclaimed in 1967, the Society's books were exploring "new frontiers" and tackling "vital issues born of Judaism's many encounters with forces outside itself." Three of these issues were particularly critical: the Holocaust, the Six-Day War, and the changing contemporary Jewish scene.[16]

The Holocaust, the Nazi mass-murder of more than six million Jews during World War II, was, of the three, unquestionably the most painful. A generation was growing up without first-hand knowledge of what had happened in Europe, and there were few books to which it could turn. JPS was itself partly to blame for this ignorance. From 1950 until 1965, only one book concerning the Nazi atrocities appeared under its auspices, Leon Poliakov's *Harvest of Hate* (1954), and it was a co-publication. In presenting it to JPS readers, Grayzel, who knew that the book would not be popular, felt constrained to half-apologize:

> This is admittedly not a pleasant subject, yet it is one that, in all self-respect, we ought not to forget. One cannot simply dismiss the six million martyrs from one's mind. Consequently, the Society felt it to be its duty to help in the publication of the documents for those who may want to refer to them.[17]

To be sure, volumes from the 1930s and 1940s dealing with Nazi persecutions and the accompanying refugee crisis remained available for those JPS members who wanted them, and interested students could also read the appropriate chapter in Grayzel's *History of the Jews*. But when it came to new books, the publication committee looked for more upbeat themes, such as American Jewry's success or the achievements of pioneers in Israel. Gerald Reitlinger's *The Final Solution* (1953), and Raul Hilberg's *The Destruction of the European Jews* (1961), the two most important English-language Holocaust surveys published during these years, were not among the Society's offerings, nor for that matter were any other Holocaust books. The subject was not one that seemed to interest most of the members. The realization that one-third of the Jewish people had been wiped out in the greatest single tragedy in all of Jewish history was too recent, too horrible, too numbing for most American Jews to contemplate rationally.

American Jewish attitudes toward the Holocaust began to show signs of change in 1960. In that year, Elie Wiesel issued his Holocaust memoir entitled *Night,* the first of his many books written to keep the memory of the Holocaust alive. The same year, on a more scholarly level, Jacob Robinson and Philip Friedman issued in English their *Guide to Jewish History Under Nazi Impact,* summing up research to date on the "Catastrophe" and setting forth an agenda for further research. Salo Baron, in his foreword, pointed to the rise of a new generation, ignorant of the Holocaust, and experiencing "great difficulty in even remotely envisaging the complex nature of that profound tragedy." He complained that "the Nazi barbarities already had been so forgotten that the Jews and the democratic forces of the world were lulled into a false sense of security," and held up as evidence the "wave of synagogue desecrations and other half-baked Nazi imitations in Europe and the United States." The time was ripe, he concluded, for scholars "to come to grips" with the Holocaust by placing it "within the total framework of world history and Jewish history in the twentieth century."

Baron's call, like Wiesel's, initially went unheeded. Participants in symposia on "Jewishness" and "Jewish Affirmation," sponsored in 1961 by *Commentary* and *Judaism* magazines, still made almost no reference at all to the death of six million Jews. "It is striking," Stephen Whitfield writes after surveying the writings of American Jewish intellectuals during this period, "how rarely the memory of the Holocaust elicited direct concern and contemplation." What turned the tide was yet a third development that took place in 1960: the dramatic capture of Adolf Eichmann followed by his well-publicized trial in 1961, and the ensuing fierce debate that climaxed with the publication of Hannah Arendt's *Eichmann in Jerusalem* two years later. Arendt's provocative analysis of the "banality of evil," her controversial effort to understand Eichmann, her merciless attacks on Eichmann's prosecutors, her oft-quoted allegation that Jews went to their death "like sheep to the slaughter," and her scathing portrait of Jewish leaders cooperating with their enemies—all this sparked not only rivers of criticism but also a torrent of new research, much of it designed to disprove her various theses. Within a decade, Holocaust studies, its agenda considerably broadened, had emerged as a recognized scholarly discipline of its own, complete with journals, a burgeoning literature, professional conferences, and full-scale courses offered at major universities around the country.[18]

JPS played only a minor role in these developments. It long before had rejected the idea that tragedy and persecution should lie at the center of Jewish life, and had instead emphasized such themes as cultural vibrance and communal creativity.

It could hardly ignore the lachrymose elements in Jewish history, and certainly devoted a great deal of attention to European persecutions while they were actually taking place. But it sought to project a positive vision of Judaism, a sense of Jews as contributors to civilization rather than as victims. It therefore published books with such titles as *Breakthrough*, *Vision*, and *The Purpose and Meaning of Jewish Existence*, to take just three titles from the 1964 list. Books dealing with death, destruction, catastrophe, and the "final solution" conveyed a message that was precisely the opposite of what it believed American Jews needed to hear.

Still, the Holocaust had become timely, and beginning in 1965 JPS published and co-published a series of books dealing with the theme—sometimes as many as two or three a year. In making its selections, it continued to emphasize those aspects that it considered to be of particular significance to American Jews living in the Holocaust's wake. The volumes it published were designed, with a few exceptions, not only to impart information, but also to put forward definite views on how American Jews should respond to the Holocaust—and how they should not.

Jacob Robinson's *And the Crooked Shall Be Made Straight*, the first Holocaust book that JPS offered its readers after *Harvest of Hate*, set the pattern. A devastating critique of Hannah Arendt's work, it sought to refute Arendt's "historical falsities," especially with regard to "Jewish behavior in the face of disaster." Given the widespread publicity that Arendt's views on Jewish leaders and Jewish "passivity" during the Holocaust had received, the Society believed that Robinson's message— "Miss Arendt does not convey reliable information"—was one that American Jews needed to hear. His alternative reading of the Holocaust provided a more sympathetic understanding of the Jewish position and offered many more examples of Jewish heroism; it was, in short, a "usable past" from which American Jews could draw meaning and inspiration.[19]

A similar quest, this time labeled "the search for meanings in Judaism, Jewish existence, and the Jewish people," lay behind the decision to co-publish Arthur Cohen's *Arguments and Doctrines: A Reader of Jewish Thinking in the Aftermath of the Holocaust* (1970). Four years earlier, Richard Rubenstein had published *After Auschwitz*, a much-discussed and highly controversial work that set forth in stark terms what became known as the "Death of God" theology. Without explicitly saying so, Cohen's volume offered a response, one "intended to exhibit to the reader something of the dynamics and vitality of contemporary, post-Holocaust Jewish thought." Dismissing the "Death of God" theology as either uninteresting or "psychopathological," Cohen left Rubenstein out of his reader altogether. What he put forward instead was a neo-Orthodox theology of the Holocaust that, like Robinson's response to Arendt, was more sympathetic, more inspiring, and more usable:

I believe in the coming of the Messiah. . . . I must believe that that silence of

God—for reasons I cannot fathom, but which I am obliged to honor in dismay— is not gratuitous. . . . I must conclude that his silence is maintained in the face of an awesome future, that God, like we who believe in his promises, is turned toward the future, toward the *eschaton*. The *eschaton* cannot be less magnificent than the brutalities that anticipate its achievement. What we await cannot be less than what we have endured. In the order of feeling I await what God has promised and believe what he has revealed.[20]

The search for meaning in the Holocaust—the idea that American Jews could learn from the events if they understood them correctly—comes through even more clearly in two books that JPS commissioned and published on its own. The first, Jacob Glatstein, Israel Knox and Samuel Margoshes's *Anthology of Holocaust Literature* (1968), stressed that the Holocaust was not simply a history of unrelieved evil. "There is here goodness also," the introduction insisted, and beyond that it spoke of "an epic of courage, a kind of courage that our civilization is not always willing to grasp." The anthology proceeded to mete out yet another flogging to the theories of Hannah Arendt, devoting over eighty pages to tales of Jewish resistance. Even more significantly, however, it included a whole section on "the non-Jews" in which it pointed to "shining examples of humaneness, idealism, and even self-sacrifice by Polish intellectuals, priests, laborers, and plain people." The message here, a challenge to those who learned from the Holocaust that the whole world wanted the Jews dead, was that there were in fact righteous Gentiles too, that liberal values had not completely perished in the fires of Auschwitz.[21]

A related and, from an American point of view, even more significant message emerged from the second major Holocaust volume that the Society published on its own: Leni Yahil's *The Rescue of Danish Jewry* (1969), translated from the original Hebrew, complete with a revealing subtitle, "Test of a Democracy." Denmark, although occupied by the Germans in 1940, never succumbed to the Reich's anti-Jewish laws. Indeed, in 1943, under the eyes of the Nazis, heroic Danes evacuated seven to eight thousand Jews to safety in Sweden. As a result, most Danish Jews were not exterminated. No Nazi-occupied country saw a higher percentage of its Jewish community survive. In recounting this dramatic—and sadly atypical— Holocaust chapter, Yahil stressed the importance of "the Danish national culture, as reflected in the country's free social structure and democratic form of government." She paid tribute to the triumph of "humane values." Without mentioning America at all, she concluded with words that could not but prove meaningful to an American readership: "Humane democracy stood its test."[22]

Although these volumes were only the first of the Society's many offerings in the Holocaust field, one is struck when looking at the complete list by how many of these books dealt with "rescue," "resistance," "survival," and "humane values," at least to some degree. Haim Avni's *Spain, the Jews and Franco*, translated from the original Hebrew, detailed the rescue of Jews from Nazi-occupied countries by Spain's dictator, Francisco Franco. Charles Goldstein's *The Bunker*, translated from the original French, was billed as "a study of man under virtually unendurable stress, of the conflicts bred by such stress, as well as the loftiest ethical and humane responses conceivable." Marie Syrkin's *Blessed Is the Match*, newly reprinted in paperback, had as its subtitle "the story of Jewish resistance." *Spiritual Resistance: Art from Concentration Camps, 1940–1945*, prepared by the Union of American Hebrew Congregations, presented itself as "a moving testament to the human spirit."[23] By continually emphasizing these themes, rather than the more repulsive aspects of the tragedy, JPS presented American Jews with a Holocaust message that would be meaningful to *their* lives—so greatly removed from the world of the death camps and the anti-Semitic culture that created them. Its authors refused to be seduced by slogans like "never forget" and "never again." The real lesson of the Holocaust, they implied, lay in a reassertion of old truths—the importance of human lives, human rights, and humane values.

If these were the universal truths learned from the Holocaust, there was, in addition, a special lesson for Jews alone—the importance of having a homeland. The relationship between Holocaust and Redemption, the link drawn between the fall of six million Jews and the rise of the State of Israel, found numerous echoes in books issued by JPS—especially in works by Israeli authors. Leon Poliakov, not an Israeli, had made the point back in 1954: "Jewish reality was affirmed in Palestine just when the Jews of Europe were breathing their last." Yehuda Bauer, in his *Flight and Rescue*, co-published by JPS in 1970, made the same point recounting the exciting story of the *Bricha* ("flight"), the mass-movement of Palestine-bound Holocaust survivors that became "one of the most significant, if indeed not *the* most significant, of the factors leading up to Israel's establishment." Hanoch Bartov and Dahn Ben Amotz, in two Hebrew novels that the Society offered its readers in translation, probed deeper, exploring the ambivalent attitudes and emotions underlying the Holocaust and Redemption theme, particularly in terms of Israel's identity, relationship to Jewish history, and ties to the outside world.[24]

What brought the relationship between Israel and the Holocaust home with special force to American Jews, even before many of these books were published, was the Six-Day War in June 1967. The interminable weeks of crisis in May— graves dug in Jerusalem, threats uttered at the United Nations, prayers said by Jews around the world—raised the specter of "another Holocaust." This time, the Arabs warned, "the Jews" would be driven into the sea. Then with astonishing swiftness came redemption, the six days that changed the course of Jewish history. Nothing, it seemed, would ever be the same again. Writing in a front-page editorial in the *Bookmark*, Chaim Potok, who visited Jerusalem within months of its reunification, gave voice to the feelings many American Jews experienced in the afterglow of miraculous deliverance:

It is clear that we have just lived through a hinge period of Jewish history; it is clear that May and June 1967 was a time when the future of our people hung on a thin thread of hope and anguish and stubborn, trembling defiance; it is clear that the War of Six Days was a watershed of awesome dimensions, separating a dark, blood-ridden past from a future which we cannot even begin to discern; and it is clear that the configuration of this future will be a sort that few of us dared to contemplate prior to the morning of June 5, 1967.

What is not clear, what remains unknown and unexplored because many of us are only now beginning to recover from the outcome of the War of Six Days, are the implications of the victory.[25]

One implication became evident almost at once: an increased awareness of Israel on the part of American Jewry, an identification with its aspirations and destiny that was far greater than ever apparent before. In the years that followed, Israel became the dominant focus of American Jewish life. Philanthropy, political activity, education, religious life, and culture all became "Israel-centered"—so much so, in fact, that critics charged that American Jews used Israel for "vicarious fulfillment of their Jewish identity."[26]

The trend showed itself at JPS as well. It, of course, had published books about Israel and by Israelis long before 1967, and we have seen that already in 1966 it announced a new program aimed at translating and publishing selected Israeli books of "significant interest to American Jews." But after the Six-Day War, Israel-related books became the single largest component of its list, outstripping every other major category of books, including Americana. It also opened an office in Jerusalem (1974) to facilitate cross-cultural exchange (see Epilogue). In the decade from 1968–77, fully twenty-eight of its offerings focused directly on Israel (either books about Israel and Zionism or volumes of Israeli literature in translation), more than in the previous two decades combined. Seven additional titles were either translations of books by Israeli scholars or co-publications with Israel's Keter Publishing House. By contrast, twenty-four titles dealt with America and seventeen covered Jewish history in other times and places. Naturally, the kinds of Israel-related works that JPS issued covered a broad range, everything from full-length histories and major works of literature to art books, volumes of legends, sociological studies and children's books. It brought to English readers major literary works by some of Israel's best writers and poets—books by, among others, S. Y. Agnon, Yehuda Amichai, Hanoch Bartov, Yosef Chaim Brenner, T. Carmi, Rachel Eytan, Haim Hazaz, Dan Pagis, Nathan Shaham, and Yaakov Shabtai. Thanks to co-publication arrangements, widely discussed commercial books relating to Israel also appeared on its list, including Saul Bellow's *To Jerusalem and Back* (1976), Howard M. Sachar's *A History of Israel* (1976), and, later, Amos Oz's *In the Land of Israel* (1983). To the Society's credit, however, the most insightful and provocative of all the Israel-related titles that it issued was not from a commercial house but one that JPS had commissioned: Hillel Halkin's *Letters to an American Jewish Friend: A Zionist's Polemic* (1977).

The very title of Halkin's book distinguished it from the Society's usual fare. It was, unabashedly, "a Zionist's polemic," a *cri de coeur*, not the kind of objective, dispassionate analysis that members usually expected. Having made *aliyah* in 1970, Halkin was convinced that this was in fact the only viable alternative for American Jews: "Diaspora Jewry," he wrote, "is doomed; Jewish life has a future, if at all, only in Israel." In six brilliantly written hypothetical letters to a Jewish friend in New York, he carefully built his case. He was fervidly *for* Israel, warts and all (and he admitted to many a wart). He was just as impassioned *against* "a Diaspora Jewry shrinking in numbers and resources, fighting a losing battle with its environment, increasingly resigned to the fact that it is historically played out." Religion, ideology, culture—in each instance Halkin subjected American Jewry to searching analysis and found it wanting. To live as a Jew, he concluded, there was but one choice: "coming from the Diaspora to here."[27]

JPS had earlier published more muted critiques along some of these same lines. Sociologist Charles Liebman, for example, argued in *The Ambivalent American Jew* (1973) that American Jews were threatened by contemporary currents in American life, and by their own "integrationist" (as distinct from "survivalist") values. Israeli philosopher Eliezer Schweid, in *Israel at the Crossroads* (1973), pronounced settling in Israel "the supreme test" of diaspora Jews' "loyalty to themselves."[28] But these were primarily the works of scholars: written aloofly in the third person, couched in the forbidding language of the academy, and defended with learned citations. Halkin, by contrast, wrote engagingly in the first person, correspondence style, speaking as one intellectual to another. He challenged, confronted, polemicized, demanded a response. No JPS book in years evoked so much discussion, not only in Jewish journals but also in the *New York Times Book Review*, the *New York Review of Books*, and the *New Republic*. The most searching questions of contemporary Jewish life—the future of the Diaspora, the relationship between American Jews and Israel, the obligation to make *aliyah*—had never before been so openly and forthrightly debated. "If there has been a more significant Jewish book published in this decade," one reviewer wrote, "I haven't read it."[29]

In the 1980s, the Society somewhat broadened its focus and moved into new subject areas. It published more books about Jewish culture, Jews in the Diaspora, and Jewish issues in the United States. It also inaugurated the Jewish Poetry Series (1980–   ), under the general editorship of Yehuda Amichai and Allen Mandelbaum, "to foster perceptive, poetic translations from the vast and various range of the works of Jewish poets—medieval, Renaissance, and modern—in Hebrew, Yiddish, and the many other languages in which Jews have created." Each of the eight volumes in the series presents the work of a single poet with facing texts in the case of translations. Those poets published in the series between 1980 and 1987 were Pamela White Hadas, Avoth Yeshurun, Else Lasker-Schuler, Moyshe-Leyb Halpern, Dan Pagis, T. Carmi, Gabriel Preil, and Yankev Glatshteyn (see Appendix, "JPS Authors," for titles).

Books on Israel continued to feature prominently in the semi-annual members catalog, as did books on the Holocaust; both still rated full sections of their own. This is not surprising, for as Jacob Neusner and Jonathan Woocher have shown, the Holocaust-Redemption theme became the central "generative myth" through which the American Jewish community understood itself. By recalling the destruction of European Jewry, the community linked itself up with the Jewish past, appropriating in the process a myriad of lessons relevant to its own minority situation in the United States. By identifying with the State of Israel, the community also expressed faith in the Jewish future, the vitality and creativity of the Jewish people in its homeland.[30]

Are We To Be "With It"?

In his annual report for 1969, President William Fishman posed three pressing questions for the Society's leaders to ponder:

> Should we not be publishing and distributing more books on the current scene? Should we not be commissioning authors to write on subjects which are of direct and stimulating interest to the college youth and their teachers? In general, are we to be "with it" or are we really as stodgy and complacent as we are occasionally accused of being?

His own position was clear. He called for more "timely and original books," and urged the Society to update its image "so that the American Jew will know that we do not publish for dusty library bookshelves, but for the alert reader who wants to learn more about himself through reading about his religious heritage and environment."[31]

Actually, JPS under Chaim Potok had already made important strides in this direction. In 1967, for example, it offered its readers two volumes on the plight of Soviet Jewry, then a problem just beginning to emerge onto the community's agenda. One of the volumes was Elie Wiesel's passionate and moving *The Jews of Silence*, published several months before by Holt, Rinehart and Winston. The second, which JPS translated and published itself, was entitled *Between Hammer and Sickle*, and had caused a sensation when it first appeared in Israel. Its author, who wrote under the pseudonym Ben Ami—later revealed to be Arie Lova Eliav— was an Israeli, born in Russia, who later served in Israel's embassy there and then in the Knesset. His was the most complete account of Soviet Jewish life then in print, and pulled no punches: It quoted Russian Jews as asking "Why have you forgotten us," and called on Jews everywhere to engage in "loud protest." Unfortunately, the outbreak of the Six-Day War wrought havoc on the Society's plans to promote *Between Hammer and Sickle*, but the book was not forgotten. Two years later, Signet Publishers returned it to print in an updated mass-market paperback edition that made a wide impact.[32]

Timely volumes of this sort remained highly unusual. Most of the "relevant" volumes on the JPS list came closer to the model exemplified by Marvin Lowenthal's *The Jews of Germany* (1936): well-researched background studies shedding historical light on contemporary issues. In 1968, just as Soviet troops rumbled into Czechoslovakia, the Society (by a happy coincidence) came out with *The Jews of Czechoslovakia: Historical Studies and Surveys*. It became its best-selling new book of the season.[33] That same year, with left-wing anti-Semitism becoming an issue in America, Arthur Hertzberg's *The French Enlightenment and the Jews* appeared. It demonstrated, among other things, that the phenomenon was nothing new for the left; indeed, hatred of the Jews had prevailed even among the radical intellectuals of the French Revolution. In 1979, the Society published no fewer than three "relevant" volumes of this sort: Robert Weisbrot's *The Jews of Argentina: From the Inquisition to Peron*, a volume that figured in the contemporary debate over anti-Semitism in that country; Norman A. Stillman's *The Jews of Arab Lands*, which had important implications for the contemporary Middle East; and a volume edited by David Sidorsky entitled *Essays On Human Rights: Contemporary Issues and Jewish Perspectives*.

Being "with it," of course, meant more than just being *au courant* with international affairs. JPS also strove to keep abreast of literary fashions. When, for example, American Jews developed an absorbing interest in the world of their East European forebears, the Society responded with a spate of appropriate books including memoirs, anthologies, a history of the Yiddish theater, and, of course, Irving Howe's *World of Our Fathers*, which it co-published with Harcourt Brace Jovanovich.[34] When books about women came into demand, it found fewer available books to supply; still it co-published a biography of Henrietta Szold, reprinted Cecil Roth's *Doña Gracia*, and published *On Women and Judaism: A View from Tradition*, by Blu Greenberg, one of the most widely discussed Jewish books of 1982. JPS even published a book on China when, in the wake of renewed Sino-American relations, Chinese culture came into vogue. Michael Pollak's *Mandarins, Jews, and Missionaries*, the fascinating story of the exotic Jews of Kaifeng, received considerable notice even in the secular press, sold far more copies than expected, and was eventually issued as a paperback.[35]

Another fashion that JPS sought to address was American Jewry's growing appreciation for Jewish art. The rising price of Jewish art objects, the growth of private Judaica collections, and the proliferation of Jewish museums all gave evidence of this new trend. Art, during this period, became one more vehicle through which Jews generally, and American Jews in particular, expressed their religious and ethnic identity. JPS was quick to pick up on the new trend. Some of its own trustees, after all, were leading art collectors; and, besides, art books (especially when they were also gift books) had a much larger potential audience than the Society's regular fare. With the onset of the 1970s, JPS began to cultivate this market in a more vigorous way. Where previously it had published no more than three such books a decade, now it published three in only four years (1971–74). The next year, in 1975, it issued what it advertised as "the most splendid volume" that it had ever produced: Yosef Hayim Yerushalmi's *Haggadah and History*, a panoramic survey covering 500 years of the evolution of the Passover Haggadah (1486–1972), complete with 200 facsimile reproductions, interpretive comments, and an introduction—all printed coffee-table size, in "deluxe format" and using only the "highest craftsmanship." "For the Society," Jerome Shestack later admitted, this "was a pioneering venture. The projected cost was huge; our experience in the field was small; the market for such a book was precarious; there was much to conspire against the publication." In the end, though, the gamble paid off handsomely. The *New York Times*, the *Washington Post*, the *Philadelphia Inquirer*, and *Newsweek* all featured *Haggadah and History*, and sales exceeded expectations. The Society even issued an expensive, limited edition of the work for bibliophiles.[36]

In the wake of this success, further ventures into the art and gift book market became inevitable. The Society was pleased to be able to promote various forms of Jewish artistic expression and felt encouraged to do more by members, who responded enthusiastically to its new volumes. As a result, an increasing number of such volumes appeared on its list of new offerings. Furthermore, as the titles (or subtitles) reveal, these volumes covered a wide range of subjects: *The Contemporary Jewish Experience in Photographs, A Book of Hebrew Letters, Jewish Experience in the Art of the Twentieth Century, Art from Concentration Camps, A Jewish Bestiary, The Jewish Heritage in American Folk Art*, and more. Taken together, these volumes bear witness to a cultural fact of no mean importance: the involvement of Jews, as Jews, and especially as American Jews, in a wide range of art forms, traditional and contemporary alike.[37]

The Jewish Catalog

Of all the many contemporary books published during the Potok and Deshell years one—*The Jewish Catalog*—stands out as a symbol of the Society's new course, putting to rest all doubts as to whether it really was "with it," and demonstrating anew its commanding presence within American Jewish cultural life. Few books in all of American Jewish history have ever been as influential, and only one JPS book—its translation of the Bible—ever sold more copies on an annual basis. Indeed, the *Catalog* and its sequels actually *became* a kind of bible to many young people; they turned to it for answers to all of their difficult questions about Judaism. But otherwise, the book bore little resemblance to the Bible, or even to the *Shulchan*

Arukh, the code of Jewish law. It was in fact *sui generis*, unlike any Jewish reference book ever written.

The *Jewish Catalog* began improbably in 1971 with a chance conversation that took place in a Sukkah. Admiring the novel way that the traditional booth had been constructed, George Savran and Richard Siegel, students in their early twenties enrolled in the Department of Contemporary Jewish Studies at Brandeis University, talked of how useful it would be to compile a loose-leaf collection of such practical Jewish wisdom. *The Whole Earth Catalogue* had just appeared—an American countercultural phenomenon, a massive compendium of information and resources designed to allow anyone to "conduct his own education, find his own inspiration, shape his own environment, and share his adventure with whomever is interested"— and Savran and Siegel developed their idea into something of a Jewish equivalent. Aided by a small grant from the Boston Combined Jewish Philanthropies' Jewish Student Projects Fund, and later one from the Institute for Jewish Life, they set about accumulating suitable material. At the same time, they developed their idea into a Master's thesis entitled "The Jewish Whole Earth Catalogue: Theory and Development." In fifty-three pages of dissertation prose, the thesis made the case for "a compendium of tools and resources for use in Jewish education and Jewish living in the fullest sense." "It is," the two authors argued, "the individual himself who must feel responsibility for his Jewish environment; it has been left too long to 'experts' who have failed at their tasks." They hypothesized that a catalog, "by giving people a sense of responsibility for their Jewish lives," might help Jews "recapture the personal power of a given symbol or action within the Tradition."[38]

To transform this lofty idea into a book, Savran and Siegel turned to young committed Jews like themselves who belonged to what was then known as the "Jewish Counter Culture," a movement of socially active, politically liberal students concerned with "the quality of Jewish living and the desire for an integrated life-style." Members of this group shared much in common: They were influenced by the same values that characterized the general counterculture; they were children of the civil rights movement, the New Left, and the Six-Day War; they were associated with the nascent Havurah movement, especially Havurat Shalom in Somerville, Massachusetts, where many of them, as they put it, "daven and study, ...eat together, argue and love"; and they wrote for *Response Magazine*, a contemporary Jewish review dedicated to "the continuing attempt of a group of Jewish college students to examine the vitality and relevance of Judaism to personal development and community progress." The catalog, these young people came to believe, would be their "compendium of tools and resources," a reflection of their values, concerns, and religious practices:

> All of us who see Jewish Education as active and physical, as part of total Jewish living, also feel the need to transcend supermarket *challah* and factory-made

talleism [prayer shawls]. In order to combat these depersonal, commercializing trends in Jewish life, we must personally involve ourselves and our students in the *physical* aspects of tradition. We propose, then, an experiment in communal self-help: the compilation and publication of what, for want of a better term, we now might call: *A Jewish Whole Earth Catalogue*.

The new volume, they hoped, would do for the Jewish counterculture what the *Whole Earth Catalogue* had done for its secular counterpart.[39]

The hope was not disappointed. The effort required to transform the idea into a publishable book, however, proved vastly more time consuming than anybody initially imagined. George Savran soon withdrew from the project. He grew tired of all the administrative work and went on to pursue a Ph.D. in Bible. Sharon Strassfeld, originally the project's secretary, now became co-editor, and it was she who provided the dynamo that the undertaking required. Her husband, Michael, a Brandeis graduate student, soon joined her as co-editor, and they, along with Richard Siegel, organized the volume, solicited articles from potential contributors, edited (heavy handedly, some charged) what came in, wrote from scratch various sections that did not, and saw the volume through the press. They estimated that 90 percent of the total effort was theirs. The volume as a whole was two years in the making.[40]

Early on, the editors discovered that the model of the *Whole Earth Catalogue* could not be sustained. "What was needed," they decided, as they cast about for a new name (proposals included "Bayit," "L'Olam," "A Do-It-Yourself Jewish Kit" and even "The Jew-It-Yourself-Kit") was "not so much a cataloging of already existing resources" as "a guide or manual to the range of contemporary Jewish life." Wisely, they decided to offer readers something of both:

> Basically our intentions are (1) to give enough information to be immediately useful; (2) to direct those interested to additional resources; (3) to present the traditional dimensions of the subjects covered; and (4) to open options for personal creativity and contemporary utilization of these directives.

There was, in addition, a political agenda here—an American Jewish version of "power to the people," fully in line with the pervasive anti-establishment rhetoric of the day. All of this, however, remained firmly in the background. "We do not feel that the catalogue . . . should reflect a general contrariness toward institutions in the community," Savran and Siegel had written. "It is, indeed, many of these people in the 'Jewish Establishment' whom we wish to reach."[41]

In 1972 Richard Siegel and the Strassfelds brought the manuscript of the "Jewish Whole Earth Catalogue" to Chaim Potok. Schocken Books had already turned the project down and they were dejected. Would the Society, they wondered, consider so untraditional a volume for publication? Or would it find it too popular, too subjective, too undignified? Fifteen years earlier the publication committee had vetoed an idea for a book on "how to live Jewishly" because "the entire idea is beneath our standards." But now, given the new mood, the success of the *Whole Earth Catalogue*, and the Society's own revised policies, the decision was different; a contract was signed. Potok soon became the *Catalog*'s godfather: He recognized its potential, personally took it under his wing, and made innumerable practical suggestions, particularly in terms of organization, form, style, and appearance. The revised manuscript, illustrated by Stuart Copans, adopted throughout a lighthearted, joyous tone—a happy mixture of law and lore, apt quotations, well-chosen photographs, whimsical cartoons, and general irreverence. This tone, enhanced by the volume's 8½ × 11-inch format, careful design, and aesthetic appeal, reinforced the message that the *Catalog*'s originators sought to convey: "Judaism's beauty, vitality, and strength lies in . . . manifold forms of expression—if only particularism, dogmatics, paranoia, and self-righteousness can be put aside so as to perceive the whole."[42]

Adrianne Onderdonk Dudden, the Society's primary book designer since 1970, lavished concern on the volume. She took pains with every marginal note, every photograph, every line of Hebrew; no page went to press until she found it visually pleasing. She also worked quickly. By summer 1973, *The Jewish Catalog*—the title finally agreed upon—was already in production, planned for release in time for Hanukkah. Potok, who alone foresaw the volume's impact, warned the editors to be prepared: "Your days of quiet anonymity will come to a shrieking halt."[43]

Potok was right. The *Catalog* became an overnight success, selling over 50,000 copies in only three months, over 130,000 in eighteen months, and then continuing to sell at a steady pace. The success improved the Society's financial position, sparked an ugly controversy among the contributors over how royalties should be distributed, propelled the *Catalog*'s editors into temporary fame, and spawned numerous imitations—including a "Catholic catalog," designed along the same lines. There was criticism too, especially from those who pointed out that the *Catalog* was woefully incomplete. Although its four parts ("Space," "Time," "Word," and "Man/Woman") and thirty-one chapters covered a wealth of subjects, some readers found it strange to find a whole chapter on "candles and candle-making" but no section on Israel, the Holocaust, children, charity, or ethics. The editors explained that much depended on the contributors: "what came in was what went into the book, and what didn't come in didn't go into the book." Precisely for this reason, Savran and Siegel originally proposed a loose-leaf format, with room for frequent updates. As for the absence of material on children, one of the editors admitted that "we hadn't thought about it because we don't have children!"[44]

In fact, however, the selections well reflected the Jewish counterculture's central priorities. Where the mainstream American Jewish community was obsessed with Israel and the Holocaust, and observed a Judaism consisting largely of ceremonies for children and ethical ideals for adults, young counterculture Jews looked inward, stressing the fundamental importance of ritual and tradition and seeking to live meaningful Jewish lives. "The *Catalog* is an affirmation, bordering on a celebration, of the possibilities for creative and authentic Jewish life in the Diaspora," William Novak observed, and the Society quoted his words approvingly.[45] Still, everyone knew that the critics had a point, especially since so many were using the *Catalog* as a basic primer. So in editing and compiling two sequels, *The Second Jewish Catalog* (1976) and *The Third Jewish Catalog* (1980), Sharon and Michael Strassfeld—Richard Siegel, following a dispute with his co-editors, had gone his own way—attempted to fill in the gaps. They rectified all of the major omissions in the first *Catalog*, devoted a whole volume to "the people Israel and its responsibility to itself and the world," and, in response to several complaints, changed their language to reflect "nonsexist forms."[46]

Taken together, the three volumes of the *Jewish Catalog* represent what may prove to be the Jewish counterculture's most significant and lasting legacy. The widespread return to ritual evident across the spectrum of American Jewish life, the renewed interest throughout the community in neglected forms of Jewish music and art, the proliferation of *havurot*, the awakening of record numbers of Jews to the wellsprings of their tradition—these and other manifestations of Jewish religious revival in America all received significant impetus from the *Jewish Catalog*. It served as the vehicle for transmitting the innovations pioneered by pockets of creative students, chiefly in Boston and New York, to Jews throughout North America, and beyond. It helped transform the Jewish counterculture from a peripheral movement to one that very much influenced the mainstream. It spawned a whole library of competitors and sequels and a whole network of faithful adherents.

JPS, by its role in encouraging, shaping, publishing, and distributing the three *Jewish Catalogs*, helped make all of these achievements possible. Its part in the undertaking proved its readiness to be more than just a cultural foot soldier, marching in step with the times; it showed itself capable of leading the way into uncharted cultural realms where no Jewish publisher had ever ventured before. For years it had followed and responded to important cultural trends, as for example in the 1950s when it published so many volumes of theology and Jewish thought. But only rarely through the decades had it played a pioneering role; that, it usually feared, was too risky. Now, having taken this risk, it reaped a bountiful reward. The question, as it moved toward its centennial, was what to do next.

EPILOGUE

Toward the Centennial—and Beyond

In 1983 Maier Deshell resigned, concluding a tenure marked by many important publications. Working closely with publication committee chairman Yosef H. Yerushalmi, Deshell was responsible for a long list of distinguished scholarly books by such notable authors as Robert Alter, Salo Baron, David Berger, Daniel Elazar, Philip Friedman, Simon Rawidowicz, Gershom Scholem, Joseph B. Soloveitchik, Michael Stanislawski, and Norman Stillman (see Appendix, "JPS Authors," for titles). He also guided the publication of such widely discussed popular books as the second and third *Jewish Catalogs, Haggadah and History, Letters to an American Jewish Friend*, and *On Women and Judaism*. In 1983 alone, eight volumes that he edited won prestigious awards.[1] Unfortunately, Deshell also had become the focus of considerable controversy surrounding his administrative and editorial practices. With many calling on JPS to become more popular, and Deshell eager to return to New York, it was time for a change.

The new editor, David Rosenberg, was a young writer and poet with numerous contacts in the literary and publishing worlds. The trustees hoped that he would give the Society a more popular profile by emphasizing literature, and Rosenberg set his sights on bringing in younger writers and scholars who were "now publishing with major commercial and academic publishers." Yosef H. Yerushalmi, who was not consulted about the Rosenberg appointment and considered the new editor unqualified, promptly resigned as publication committee chairman; he was replaced by Chaim Potok. Within a year, Executive Vice-President Bernard I. Levinson, unhappy with several of these changes, announced his own retirement; he was replaced by Nathan Barnett, former Director of the Delaware Jewish Federation and Senior Vice-President for Development at Albert Einstein Medical Center. At about the same time, Nahum M. Sarna, emeritus professor of Bible at Brandeis University, agreed to assume the new position of academic consultant for Judaica, which was created to ensure that the Society maintained its editorial expertise in Jewish scholarship. The result, as JPS neared its centennial, was a whole new senior staff, as well as four increasingly distinct publishing objectives: popular Judaica, belles lettres, scholarship, and children's books.[2]

David Rosenberg soon made his presence felt. Working with Chaim Potok, he revamped the publication committee to include representatives of the new generation in American Jewish scholarship, and he helped shape a small editorial committee, a working group that could meet regularly to make decisions. The enlarged publication committee now served as an advisory panel for reading manuscripts and recommending policy. With funds from the Philip and Muriel Berman endowment, Rosenberg introduced an innovative series entitled the Author's Workshop, featuring fiction by such notable Jewish writers as Isaac Bashevis Singer and Harold Brodkey. He also commissioned several important literary studies with the aim of stimulating "the definition and growth of Jewish culture in America by focusing on its imaginative writers." Rosenberg, however, never entrenched himself at JPS, and he resented the lack of support he received for his efforts to be competitive. At the end of 1985, in the face of what he referred to as "bitter rivalries" and "chronic mistreatment of authors and staff," he angrily resigned.[3]

In his place, the trustees appointed Sheila F. Segal, who was at the time serving as JPS consulting editor for *Tanakh* and *The Torah Commentary*. Segal was the Society's first female editor since Henrietta Szold, and the first woman to hold the title officially. A former Fulbright scholar in literature, she also had years of experience in writing and publishing, understood JPS traditions, and was an activist in many areas of Jewish life. She brought with her an interest in contemporary Jewish affairs that would soon be reflected in the list of publications.[4]

As all of these changes were taking place, JPS introduced a new logo and a new name. It retained the familiar tree, which in one form or another had been part of its seal since the beginning of the century, but it abandoned the confining circle surrounding the design. Now the tree stood alone, untrammeled, seemingly able to spread out in all directions. The Society's revised corporate name, "The Jewish Publication Society"—no longer "of America"—pointed to the same kind of boundlessness. Where JPS activities previously had been restricted to one country and one city, now it proudly displayed three cities on its stationery: Philadelphia, New York, and Jerusalem.[5]

In 1978 the decision "to increase the impact of JPS in the New York area" resulted in the opening of an office at 60 East 42nd Street. This was one of several initiatives undertaken during the term of JPS president A. Leo Levin, one of America's foremost jurists and a man who was himself deeply involved in both the Philadelphia and New York Jewish communities. New York had already, for many decades, been America's publishing capital, and it had during the same period also become the undisputed cultural focus of American Jewish life. Without exception, every JPS editor and executive director visited New York regularly, and a large number of the Society's authors, members, and sales came from there, too. Philadelphia, by contrast, had declined as a Jewish cultural center; many of the city's old culturally active Jewish families turned their attention elsewhere, if they did not assimilate, relocate, or simply die out. Although tradition and continuing ties to the Jews of Philadelphia prevented a full-scale relocation to New York, the new JPS office near Grand Central Station and the New York Public Library created a presence in Manhattan, and helped the Society establish a toehold in the New York literary world.[6]

The function of the New York office was soon expanded from a sales facility and meeting place to the main editorial headquarters for the new JPS juvenile book division. Maier Deshell, who recognized the need for a renewed program aimed at publishing high-quality children's books, first proposed this step, and in 1977 he hired author and editor Mae Garelick to develop a list of appropriate titles on a freelance basis. She produced several noteworthy books, including new K'tonton titles by Sadie Rose Weilerstein, Ben Aronin's *The Secret of the Sabbath Fish* (1979), Eric A. Kimmel's *Nicanor's Gate*, and Phillis Gershator's *Honi and His Magic Circle* (1980). For the first time in many years, JPS received favorable notice from children's book specialists; several of the new offerings also won national awards for excellence.

In 1979 a regular staff position was created for a juvenile book editor, and David Adler was hired. Adler, a prolific and highly respected children's book author, undertook not only to produce a well-rounded list for a broad spectrum of readers but also to make JPS "the premier publisher of Jewish juvenile books." Aided by a local advisory board of children's book writers, he moved rapidly to achieve his goals by signing up experienced authors and taking special pains to ensure that JPS volumes met the highest publishing standards.

Adler's efforts soon won recognition. *The Castle on Hester Street* (1982) by Linda Heller, a remarkable story of two loving grandparents who look back quite differently on their immigrant experiences, won the prestigious Philadelphia Book Clinic award for its design, printing, and binding, and then proceeded to win two additional awards for content: one from *Parents Choice*, the other from the Association of Jewish Librarians. A year later *The Jewish Kids Catalog*, by Chaya Burstein, captured two awards, including the coveted National Jewish Book Award. Other award winners followed in rapid succession: *Mrs. Moskowitz and the Sabbath Candlesticks* (1984) by Amy Schwartz; *Seven Good Years and Other Stories of I. L. Peretz* (1984), translated and adapted by Esther Hautzig; and *Monday in Odessa* (1986) by Eileen Bluestone Sherman. In 1987, a classic JPS children's book, *The*

Aleph-Bet Story Book by Deborah Pessin, was reissued in paperback and with an audio cassette by Judy Chernak—a JPS first. And a year later came another first: a full-color juvenile picture book, Giora Carmi's *And Shira Imagined*, that raised JPS to a level of children's publishing that it had never attained before.

By the time of the JPS Centennial, David Adler could take pride in the fact that thirty-four JPS children's books (for ages 3 and up) were in print, covering a myriad of subjects including the Holocaust, Israel, American Jewry, Russian Jewry, Jewish rituals, and Jewish lore. Moreover, better than one-third of these were prize winners! Children's book critic Marcia Posner, reviewing the JPS list in *AB Bookman's Weekly*, was fulsome in her praise: "The Jewish Publication Society," she wrote, "has the distinction of being the finest Jewish publisher of children's books. Their books have literary and artistic quality, and are beautifully designed with excellent paper and bindings." Thanks to the nationwide boom in children's books that took place in the 1980s, these volumes also became JPS sales leaders; *The Jewish Kids Catalog* alone has sold tens of thousands of copies. Whereas once the Society had lost money on juveniles and produced them only out of a sense of obligation, now the tables had turned. "It is hoped," David Adler told the publication committee with unintended irony, that "the children will stay with JPS as adults."[7]

In 1987, after nearly a decade with JPS, David Adler found that he needed to give more time to his own writing. Thus, in the summer of that year, Alice Belgray was appointed associate juvenile editor. Formerly with William Morrow and Clarion Books, Belgray added her talents to the development of juvenile titles. Adler retained his overall responsibility for shaping the JPS juvenile list.

The Jerusalem office, though not so directly involved in publishing as the stateside ones, also played an important role in the Society's effort to broaden its horizons. Founded in 1974, it aimed originally to fulfill the Society's longstanding goal of building a "cultural bridge" to Israel by marketing its books (at a significant discount) to Israeli readers. The operation was headed by Dorothy Harman, who for five years ran the sales outlet from her Jerusalem home. As Harman reported to the trustees, it soon took on a life of its own:

> In the beginning a few advertisements in the *Jerusalem Post* and *Haaretz* generated the first memberships. A bit later visits and exhibits were held on university campuses, conventions, and institutions. . . . Still later we launched our highly successful lecture and symposia series, received newspaper and radio coverage, and became well established in Israel's intellectual and belles lettres world.

An office located on tree-lined Ben Maimon Street, in Jerusalem's prestigious Rehavia section, gave the Society visibility. Its symposia, dealing with such subjects as its Bible translation and commentary, the theology of Rabbi Joseph B. Soloveitchik, contemporary Israeli literature, and the *Origins of the Kabbalah* by Gershom

Scholem, brought out Jerusalemites in the hundreds. In 1981 the office took on new responsibilities when it became the official Israeli distributor of the Harvard University Press Judaica book line and of the Jewish literary journal *Prooftexts*. A few years later it organized a book club offering Judaica titles from Princeton and Yale University presses as well. In 1984, when Harman left for an extended stay in America, Emily Biederman assumed the day-to-day management of the Jerusalem office. Biederman, who had been Chaim Potok's secretary in the Philadelphia office, then resided in Israel and was pleased to renew her JPS affiliation.[8]

"We have already embarked on a number of exciting programs," Muriel Berman reported to members as 1988 approached, and they had only to look at the Society's new name, new branch offices, attractive new catalogs, and lists of books forthcoming and in print to see what she meant. The new editor, Sheila F. Segal, revived the poetry series, launched a reprint series in American Jewish literature, brought in new fiction, and published Henry Roth's *Shifting Landscape* (1987), a much-publicized volume that brought together every story, essay, and memoir that Roth had allowed to be published since *Call It Sleep* (1934). Expressing an eagerness to recapture the momentum of *The Jewish Catalogs*, Segal also introduced a new series of books (for the "post-*Catalog* generation") on aspects of contemporary Jewish life. Michael Gold's *And Hannah Wept* (1988) set the pattern, bringing a Jewish perspective to such issues as infertility, pregnancy loss, and adoption. Other books of this type—on topics such as conversion, women and the synagogue, and the Jewish approach to terminal illness—were also signed.

In addition to the new editor, the first century moved to a close with the installation of a new JPS president in 1987, Edward E. Elson of Atlanta; a new chairman of the board, former president Charles R. Weiner of Philadelphia; and a new executive director, Richard Malina of New York, formerly the president of the publishing division at Doubleday. Malina believed that using some of the techniques employed by a large commercial publisher could help JPS improve sales, move into new markets, and build an organization that could meet the challenge of its second century. His goal was "to build on the glorious past ..." not only "by publishing the best new popular and academic writing on a wide range of topics of Jewish interest" but also by making sure "that the books are distributed widely...."[9]

Yet as the Society broadened its scope and looked ahead, it continued to debate fundamental questions that it had been wrestling with for decades, some since its founding. What, first and foremost, were its aims and objectives, especially given the new and rapidly changing world of Jewish publishing? What obligations should it feel to the American Jewish community, to Jews everywhere, to Jewish scholarship, to its members—and which of these obligations should take priority? What should be its relationship to others in the Jewish publishing field—competition, cooperation, or fallback? What types of books should it publish—should they be popular and timely or scholarly and timeless, books that members wanted or books that they should want, controversial books or those that represented a community consensus? And if the answer be "a whole range of books," how should priorities be determined, how should scarce resources be allocated, how should decisions be made, and, at the most basic level, how should JPS guarantee its own financial solvency?

A century of experience indicated that these questions did not lend themselves to easy answers, much less to resolution once and for all. Instead, these were perennial challenges. Each generation of Society leaders confronted them anew, reshaping policies to accord with changing times and fortunes.

Meanwhile, JPS could take pride in its past achievements. Over the century it had helped to stimulate, propagate, and Americanize Jewish culture; served as a medium for bringing together writers, readers, and patrons; initiated and funded a host of important literary and scholarly projects; worked to maintain high cultural standards; brought Jewish culture to bear on significant contemporary issues; and succeeded in translating some of the choicest fruits of Jewish scholarship into terms that laymen could understand and appreciate. As American Jewish culture blossomed forth, the Society's role—like that of so many other Jewish cultural organizations— necessarily changed. Cultural maturity, so beneficial to American Jewry as a whole, posed formidable difficulties for JPS—ironically so, for it had helped to bring the new situation about. The task of readjusting was, in a sense, the reward for a job well done.

If there were new challenges to overcome, there were also old responsibilities that, even after one hundred years, remained as urgent as ever. The Society's broad cultural and educational mission for American Jews, its general goal of promoting a more learned and culturally vibrant community, as well as its specific efforts to further Jewish unity, improve community relations, and stimulate the Jewish consciousness of young people—all of these were timeless concerns that no Jewish community could long afford to ignore. Others might publish Jewish books as a sideline, or to be fashionable, or to make a profit, or for prestige, but none would do so for the same community-minded reason that the Society, now with one hundred years of experience behind it, upheld as its continuing goal: "To provide significant, worthwhile, and informative books of Jewish interest in the English language, so that the Jewish religion, history, literature, and culture will be understood, and read, and known."[10]

Sheila F. Segal addressing the 100th annual meeting of JPS (The Jewish Exponent)

The JPS Centennial Convocation. On the stage are (FROM LEFT): *James O. Freedman, Sheila F. Segal, Marvin Wachsman, Edward Elson (at the podium), Charles R. Weiner, Nahum M. Sarna, Salo Baron, Elliot Shelkrot, and Saul Bellow.* (The Jewish Exponent)

Recipients of the JPS Centennial Medallion—Saul Bellow (2nd from left), Salo Baron (2nd from right), and Cynthia Ozick (right)—with Centennial Chairperson Ruth Septee, Edward Elson, and Nahum M. Sarna. (The Jewish Exponent)

Muriel M. Berman and Sheila F. Segal enjoying Henry Roth's stories at a pre-publication party for Shifting Landscape *(Joyce Culver)*

Richard Malina at the JPS Centennial Dinner (The Jewish Exponent)

The Centennial Committee. FROM LEFT (BACK ROW): *Richard Malina, Betty Cohen, and D. Walter Cohen, co-chairpersons of the Centennial Dinner;* (FRONT ROW): *Ruth Septee, centennial chairperson, Chaim Potok, Muriel M. Berman, recipient of the Henrietta Szold Award, and Edward Elson, JPS president.* (The Jewish Exponent)

David Adler (David Godlis)

David Rosenberg (Layle Silbert)

ABBREVIATIONS AND SHORT TITLES

Adler, *IHCTD*   Cyrus Adler, *I Have Considered the Days* (Philadelphia: 1941)

Adler Letters   Ira Robinson (ed.), *Cyrus Adler: Selected Letters* (2 vols., Philadelphia: 1985)

AH   *American Hebrew*

AHR   *American Historical Review*

AI   *American Israelite*

AJA   American Jewish Archives, Cincinnati, OH

AJA   *American Jewish Archives*

AJH   *American Jewish History*

AJHQ   *American Jewish Historical Quarterly*

AJHS   American Jewish Historical Society, Waltham, MA

AJPS   American Jewish Publication Society

AJSR   *AJS [Association for Jewish Studies] Review*

AJYB   *American Jewish Year Book*

Bloch, *OMMB*   Joshua Bloch, *Of Making Many Books: An Annotated List of the Books Issued by the Jewish Publication Society of America, 1890–1952* (Philadelphia: 1953)

BP   Bible Translation Papers, in the JPS vault

CCARJ   *Central Conference of American Rabbis Journal*

CCARYB   *Central Conference of American Rabbis Yearbook*

Cowen, *Memories*   Philip Cowen, *Memories of an American Jew* (New York: 1932)

Davis, *Conservative Judaism*   Moshe Davis, *The Emergence of Conservative Judaism* (Philadelphia: 1965)

EAJH   *Essays in American Jewish History* (Cincinnati: 1957)

EJ   *Encyclopaedia Judaica* (16 vols., Jerusalem: 1971)

EW2P   Edwin Wolf 2nd Papers, Philadelphia Jewish Archives Center, Philadelphia, PA

Friedman, *JLIP*   Murray Friedman (ed.), *Jewish Life in Philadelphia, 1830–1940* (Philadelphia: 1983)

Ginzberg, *KOTL*   Eli Ginzberg, *Keeper of the Law* (Philadelphia: 1966)

Ginzberg Papers   Louis Ginzberg Papers, Jewish Theological Seminary of America, NY

Grayzel, "Oral History"   Solomon Grayzel, "Oral History" (1977), typescript in author's possession

Greenspoon, *Margolis*   Leonard Greenspoon, *Max Leopold Margolis: A Scholar's Scholar* (Atlanta: 1987)

Harap, *Image*   Louis Harap, *The Image of the Jew in American Literature* (Philadelphia: 1975)

Hirshler, *Jews from Germany*   Eric E. Hirshler, *Jews from Germany in the United States* (New York: 1955)

HUCA   *Hebrew Union College Annual*

HUC–JIR   Hebrew Union College-Jewish Institute of Religion

JBA   *Jewish Book Annual*

JE   *Jewish Encyclopedia* (12 vols., New York: 1901–1906)

JExp   *Jewish Exponent*

JPS   Jewish Publication Society

JPSBM   *JPS Bookmark*

JPSP   JPS Papers, Philadelphia Jewish Archives Center, Philadelphia, PA

JQR   *Jewish Quarterly Review* (new series)

JSS   *Jewish Social Studies*

JT   *Jewish Times*

JTSA   Jewish Theological Seminary of America, New York, NY

Korn, *Eventful Years*   Bertram W. Korn, *Eventful Years and Experiences* (Cincinnati: 1954)

KS-KIP   Knowledge Seekers of Keneseth Israel Records, Keneseth Israel Papers, Reform Congregation Keneseth Israel, Philadelphia, PA

LBIYB   *Leo Baeck Institute Yearbook*

Levin, "Beginnings"   Alexandra Lee Levin, "The Beginnings of the Jewish Publication Society" (typescript, 1964), in box 14, Edwin Wolf 2nd Papers, Philadelphia Jewish Archives Center

Levin, *SOLS*   Alexandra Lee Levin, *The Szolds of Lombard Street* (Philadelphia: 1960)

Madison, *Jewish Publishing*   Charles Madison, *Jewish Publishing in America* (New York: 1976)

MJ   *Modern Judaism*

Morais, *Philadelphia*   Henry S. Morais, *The Jews of Philadelphia* (Philadelphia: 1894)

MS–LB   Mayer Sulzberger's JPS Letterbook, Philadelphia Jewish Archives Center

Orlinsky, *Essays*   Harry M. Orlinsky, *Essays in Biblical Culture and Bible Translation* (New York: 1974)

Orlinsky, *Notes*   Harry M. Orlinsky, *Notes on the New Translation of the Torah* (Philadelphia: 1970)

PAAJR   *Proceedings of the American Academy for Jewish Research*

PAJHS   *Publications of the American Jewish Historical Society*

PB   Published Books Correspondence, JPS Papers, Philadelphia Jewish Archives Center, Philadelphia, PA

PC   Publication Committee, JPS

PC–C   Publication Committee Correspondence, JPS Papers, Philadelphia Jewish Archives Center, Philadelphia, PA

PC–M   Publication Committee Minutes

Philipson, *My Life*   David Philipson, *My Life As an American Jew* (Cincinnati: 1941)

PJAC   Philadelphia Jewish Archives Center, The Balch Institute, Philadelphia, PA

PUAHC   *Proceedings of the Union of American Hebrew Congregations*

Sarna, *AJE*   Jonathan D. Sarna (ed.), *The American Jewish Experience* (New York: 1986)

Sarna, "Jewish Bible Scholarship"   Jonathan D. Sarna and Nahum M. Sarna, "Jewish Bible Scholarship and Translations in the United States," in Ernest S. Frerichs (ed.), *The Bible and Bibles in America* (Atlanta: 1988)

SBB   *Studies in Bibliography and Booklore*

Schwartz, "JE"   Shuly Rubin Schwartz, "The Emergence of Jewish Scholarship in America: The Publication of the 'Jewish Encyclopedia' " (Ph.D., The Jewish Theological Seminary of America, 1987)

Shargel, *Friedlaender*   Baila Round Shargel, *Practical Dreamer: Israel Friedlaender and the Shaping of American Judaism* (New York: 1985)

SSCA   Solomon Solis-Cohen Archives, Collection of Helen S–C Sax and Hays Solis-Cohen, Jr., Philadelphia, PA

Sulzberger Papers   Mayer Sulzberger Papers, Dropsie College, Philadelphia, PA

Szold Papers-HA   Henrietta Szold Papers, Hadassah Archives, New York, NY

Szold Papers-SL   Henrietta Szold Papers, Schlesinger Library, Radcliffe College, Cambridge, MA

TC   Trustees Correspondence, JPS Papers, Philadelphia Jewish Archives Center, Philadelphia, PA

Tebbel, *History*   John Tebbel, *A History of Book Publishing in the United States* (New York: 1975)

TJHSE   *Transactions of the Jewish Historical Society of England*

TM   Trustees Minutes

UJE   *Universal Jewish Encyclopedia* (10 vols., New York: 1948)

WSJH   *Western States Jewish History*

WSJHQ   *Western States Jewish Historical Quarterly*

YA   *YIVO Annual of Jewish Social Studies*

NOTES

1   False Starts

1. Isaac M. Wise, *Reminiscences* (New York: 1945), p. 24.

2. Abraham Rice to I.B. Kursheedt [c.1850] quoted in Moshe Davis, "Igrot Hapekidim Veha'amarchalim Meamsterdam," in *Salo Baron Jubilee Volume*, Hebrew section, eds. Saul Lieberman and Arthur Hyman (Jerusalem: 1974), p. 99 [translation mine].

3. Jonathan D. Sarna, "The Impact of Nineteenth-Century Christian Missions on American Jews," in Todd M. Endelman, *Jewish Apostasy in the Modern World* (New York: 1987), pp. 232–254.

4. "Address of the Jewish Publication Committee to the Israelites of America," in *Caleb Asher* (Philadelphia: 1845), pp. 1–4. On Leeser, see Lance J. Sussman, "The Life and Career of Isaac Leeser (1806–68): A Study of American Judaism in its Formative Period," (Ph.D., HUC–JIR, 1987); and Maxwell Whiteman, "Isaac Leeser and the Jews of Philadelphia," *PAJHS* 48 (June, 1959), pp. 207–244.

5. "Plan of a Jewish Publication Society," reprinted in Davis, *Conservative Judaism*, pp. 367–369.

6. Solomon Grayzel, "The First American Jewish Publication Society," *JBA* 3 (1944), pp. 42–45; Davis, *Conservative Judaism*, pp. 51–53. Most Jewish books published during this period are listed by A.S.W. Rosenbach in *PAJHS* 30 (1926).

7. On Hart, see *JE*; Morais, *Philadelphia*, pp. 53–58; and Louis Ginsberg, *A. Hart, Philadelphia Publisher* (Petersburg, VA: 1972).

8. Brief biographies of most of these men can be found in Morais, *Philadelphia*, and *JE*.

9. *Circular of the American Jewish Publication Society* (Philadelphia, 1845).

10. Myron Berman, *The Jews of Richmond, 1769–1976* (Charlottesville: 1979), pp. 143–144.

11. *Occident* 26 (1868), p. 54. Though small in absolute terms, 450 members still represented about 1 percent of the country's Jewish population—far more, proportionately, than joined subsequent American Jewish publication societies.

12. Grayzel, "First American Jewish Publication Society," p. 45; Korn, *Eventful Years*, pp. 45–46; Morais, *Philadelphia*, p. 176.

13. John Tebbel, *A History of Book Publishing in the United States* (New York: 1975), vol. 2, p. 102.

14. Allan E. Levine, *An American Jewish Bibliography: 1851–1875* (Cincinnati: 1959). On the problems of Jewish publishing during this period, see also remarks in *CCARYB* 3 (1893), p. 135.

15. Madeleine B. Stern, "Henry Frank: Pioneer American Hebrew Publisher," *AJA* 20 (1968), pp. 163–168.

16. Solomon Grayzel, "A Hundred Years of the Bloch Publishing Company," *JBA* 12 (1953–54), pp. 72–76.

17. For a tentative list, see Hirshler, *Jews From Germany*, p. 169.

18. Michael A. Meyer, "German-Jewish Identity in Nineteenth Century America," in Jacob Katz, *Toward Modernity: The European Jewish Model* (New Brunswick, NJ: 1987), pp. 247–267; see also on this period Naomi W. Cohen, *Encounter With Emancipation: The German Jews in the United States, 1830–1914* (Philadelphia: 1984).

19. Guido Kisch, "The Founders of 'Wissenschaft des Judentums' and America," *EAJH*, pp. 147–170; Bertram W. Korn, "German-Jewish Intellectual Influences on American Jewish Life, 1824–1972," *Tradition and Change in Jewish Experience*, ed. A. Leland Jamison (New York: 1978), pp. 106–140; Hirshler, *Jews from Germany*, pp. 42–44; 129–146.

20. A published membership list from 1867 includes some sixty American Jews, see *Alphabetische Liste der Foerderer der israelitischen Literatur als Abonnenten des Instituts zur Foerderung der israelitischen Literatur...* (Leipzig: 1867) [copy in Klau Library, HUC-JIR, Cincinnati]; see also David Philipson, "Some Unpublished Letters of Theological Importance," *HUCA* 2 (1925), p. 424.

21. See Gershon Greenberg, "A German-Jewish Immigrant's Perception of America, 1853–54," *AJHQ* 67 (June, 1978), pp. 307–341; and my "Further Notes" in Ibid., 68 (December, 1978), pp. 206–212.

22. Hirshler, *Jews From Germany*, pp. 137–138.

23. On the Institut, see *JE*, vol. 6, p. 609; *AJYB* 43 (1942), pp. 786–787; and Meyer Kayserling, *Ludwig Philippson* (Leipzig: 1898), pp. 252–258. *JT* 4 (April 5, 1872), p. 108, blamed the society's failure on the fact that Philippson and his brother authored too many of its volumes themselves, and operated "too much on the mutual-take-care-of-number-one principle."

24. *JT* August 13, 1869, as quoted in Sefton Temkin, *The New World of Reform* (Bridgeport: 1974), p. 14, cf. p. 4. For the background and aftermath of this spiritual declaration of independence, see Meyer, "German-Jewish Identity in Nineteenth Century America," pp. 259–263.

25. Richard Gottheil, *The Life of Gustav Gottheil* (Williamsport: 1936), p. 376.

26. Alan Tarshish, "The Board of Delegates of American Israelites (1859–1878)," *PAJHS* 49 (1959), pp. 16–32.

27. *Occident* 26 (1868), p. 154.

28. Ibid.

29. Ibid., p. 473.

30. On Philadelphia's Jewish bachelors, see the *Public Ledger* (June 7, 1908), p. 22; and regarding Sulzberger *AJYB* 32 (1931), p. 47. Charles Rosenberg notes that male celibacy was a Victorian ideal, see his *No Other Gods* (Baltimore: 1978), pp. 71–88. Other prominent Philadelphia Jewish bachelors included Hyman Gratz, Simon Muhr, and Samuel Elkin.

31. *AJYB* 34 (1933), p. 323.

32. Solomon Grayzel to A. Leo Levin (July 15, 1959), box 26 PB.

33. Simon Rosendale in AJYB 15 (1913–14), p. 99. For other sketches of Sulzberger, see Lloyd P. Gartner, "The Correspondence of Mayer Sulzberger and William Howard Taft," *PAAJR* 46–47 (1979–80), pp. 121–139; Jeffrey B. Morse, "The Jewish American Judge: An Appraisal on the Occasion of the Bicentennial," *JSS* 38 (1976), pp. 203–208; Davis, *Conservative Judaism*, pp. 362–365; Morais, *Philadelphia*, pp. 301–304; *Addresses Delivered in Memory of Mayer Sulzberger* (Philadelphia: 1924); Alexander Marx, *Essays in Jewish Biography* (Philadelphia: 1947), pp. 223–228; Naomi W. Cohen, *Not Free to Desist* (Philadelphia: 1972), pp. 25–26; Maxwell Whiteman, *Gentlemen in Crisis* (Philadelphia: 1975), passim.

34. *Occident*, 26 (May, 1868), pp. 49–56. A generous provision in Leeser's will granted the plates he owned of two popular books by Grace Aguilar to any viable Jewish publication society formed in New York or Philadelphia "within five years after his demise."

35. James G. Heller, *Isaac M. Wise: His Life, Work and Thought* (New York: 1965), pp. 390, 399, 414.

36. *JT* 3 (May 26, 1871), p. 201. For some sense of American Jewish aspirations in this period, see Tarshish, "The Board of Delegates of American Israelites (1859–1878)," pp. 16–32.

37. *JT* 3 (May 19, 1871), pp. 182–183.

38. *JT* 3 (June 16, 1871), p. 244.

39. *JT* 3 (July 14, 1871), p. 312; (September 29, 1871), p. 489; (October 27, 1871), pp. 550–552.

40. *JT* 3 (October 20, 1871), p. 537; (October 27, 1871), p. 551; *Hebrew Characteristics: Miscellaneous Papers From the German* (New York: 1875), pp. 97ff.

41. Emanu-El's secretary, Myer Stern, was both a founder of the society and its vice president. Later, when Rabbi Gustav Gottheil succeeded Gutheim in August 1873, he both headed the publication committee of the AJPS and controlled a fund ("the Jewish Publication Fund") that was applied to the publication of the Society's two subsequent books. During this period, Emanu-El was committed to making New York the center of all American Judaism. See Gottheil, *The Life of Gustav Gottheil,* pp. 50–59, 82–87; and *EAJH*, pp. 359–371.

42. H. Graetz, *History of the Jews* (New York: 1873), p. 54.

43. Ibid., p. iii.

44. Max Heller, "James K. Gutheim," *CCARYB* 28 (1917), p. 366.

45. *JT* 6 (February 12, 1875), p. 809.

46. William Herzberg, *Jewish Family Papers* (New York: 1875), pp. v–vi; Davis, *Conservative Judaism*, p. 191; *UJE*, vol. 5, p. 336.

47. Although the publication committee believed that the mere names of the essays' authors offered "a sufficient guarantee for the correctness of every statement contained in them," the skilled anonymous translator of *Hebrew Characteristics*, later revealed to be a literary vagabond named Alfred Henry Louis, found at least one error, which he corrected in a footnote. *Hebrew Characteristics* (New York: 1875), pp. v, 66; Gottheil, *The Life of Gustav Gottheil,* pp. 84–87.

48. The Shakespearian scholar and linguist, Richard Grant White, and the founder of the Free Religious Association, O.B. Frothingham, sent Gottheil warm letters praising the book that Gottheil reprinted in *JT* 7 (January 14, 1876), p. 730; see also Gottheil, *The Life of Gustav Gottheil*, pp. 83–84.

49. *JT* 6 (February 12, 1875), p. 809; see also *PAJHS* 29 (1925), pp. 108–109.

50. *AI* (September 15, 1876), p. 4.

51. On the failure of Maimonides and Emanu-El colleges, see Korn, *Eventful Years*, pp. 151–213; *EAJH*, pp. 359–372.

52. *AI* (August 9, 1878), p. 4.

53. *PUAHC* (1879), p. 712.

54. Max Lilienthal, "Annual Address Delivered Before the Rabbinic Literary Association (July 10, 1881)," *The Hebrew Review* 2 (1882), p. 9.

55. *PUAHC* 2 (1885), p. 1603.

56. "Authentic Report of the Proceedings of the Rabbinical Conference Held at Pittsburgh," in Walter Jacob (ed.) *The Changing World of Reform Judaism: The Pittsburgh Platform in Retrospect* (Pittsburgh: 1985), p. 97.

57. *AH* 3 (May 21, 1880), p. 4; *Jewish Conference Papers (1886) Together With Reports of the Meetings of the Jewish Ministers' Association of America* (New York: 1887), p. 41.

2   A Real Beginning

1. On the impact of revivals, see William G. McLoughlin, *Revivals, Awakenings, and Reform* (Chicago: 1978); and the "Symposium on Religious Awakenings," *Sociological Analysis* 44 (1983), pp. 81–122. For religion in this period, see Paul A. Carter, *The Spiritual Crisis of the Gilded Age* (DeKalb, IL: 1971); Naomi W. Cohen, "The Challenges of Darwinism and Biblical Criticism to American Judaism," *MJ* 4 (May, 1984) pp. 121–157.

2. Jacob Katz, *From Prejudice to Destruction* (New York: 1980), pp. 1–5, 260–272; see also Moshe Zimmerman, *Wilhelm Marr: The Patriarch of Anti-Semitism* (New York: 1986).

3. *Coney Island and the Jews* (New York: 1879), p. 21; Naomi W. Cohen, "Anti-Semitism in the Gilded Age: The Jewish View," *JSS* 41 (Summer-Fall, 1979), pp. 187–210; Nathan C. Belth, *A Promise to Keep* (New York: 1979), pp. 23–26; John Higham, *Send These to Me* (New York: 1975), pp. 116–195; Michael N. Dobkowski, *The Tarnished Dream* (Westport, CT: 1979).

4. Benny Kraut, "Judaism Triumphant: Isaac Mayer Wise on Unitarianism and Liberal Christianity," *AJSR* 7–8 (1982–83), esp. pp. 202–225; see also Kraut's other writings cited therein, and below in notes 14, 31.

5. *The Jewish Advance*, December 12, 1879, p. 4.

6. David Stern to Bernhard Felsenthal (April 24, 1884), Felsenthal Papers, AJHS.

7. Ellen Sue Levi Elwell, "The Founding and Early Programs of the National Council of Jewish Women" (Ph.D., Indiana University, 1982); Shuly Rubin Schwartz, "The Emergence of Jewish Scholarship in America: The Publication of the *Jewish Encyclopedia*" (Ph.D., JTSA, 1987).

8. Deborah Dash Moore, *B'nai B'rith and the Challenge of Ethnic Leadership* (New York: 1981), p. 48.

9. An 1878 Purim lampoon urged one member to hurry up and get married, and "thus practically carry out one of the social objects of the YMHA," see the "Purim Novelty Book" (1878) in YMHA Archive, 92nd Street YM & YWHA, New York, NY.

10. "Grand Revival," 1879 handbill in SSCA; *New York Evening Express* (1879); *Frank Leslie's Illustrated* (January 3, 1880) in YMHA scrapbook, YMHA Archives, 92nd Street YM & YWHA, New York, NY. For Isaac M. Wise's suggestion that Chanukah lights be abolished, see James G. Heller, *Isaac M. Wise: His Life, Work and Thought* (New York: 1965), p. 564.

11. Max Cohen to Solomon Solis-Cohen (December 22, 1879), SSCA. On the YMHA generally, see Benjamin Rabinowitz, "The Young Men's Hebrew Associations (1854–1913)," *PAJHS* 37 (1947), pp. 221–326, esp. 232–259; "The Union of Y.M.H.A." (1880 circular), SSCA.

12. Cowen, *Memories*, p. 50; see also Yehezkel Wyszkowski, "The *American Hebrew*: An Exercise in Ambivalence," *AJH* 76:3 (March, 1987), pp. 340–353.

13. Max Cohen to Solomon Solis-Cohen (November 10, 1879), SSCA.

14. Cyrus L. Sulzberger to Solomon Solis-Cohen (August 1, 1880; October 5, 1880), SSCA. Years later, Max Cohen described the group as consisting of "young American Jews who, although not inordinately addicted to Orthodoxy as a rigid standardization of thought and conduct, were yet opposed to the wholesale and reckless discarding of everything that was Jewish simply because it was inconvenient, oriental, or was not in conformity with Episcopalian customs." [Introduction to] Alexander Kohut, *The Ethics of the Fathers* (New York: 1920), p. 7.

15. Max Cohen to Solomon Solis-Cohen (February 18, 1881), SSCA; Cyrus Sulzberger to Solomon Solis-Cohen (August 18, 1881), SSCA. David Solis-Cohen went even further in his restorationism, promising to start an organization, travel to Jerusalem, and "to agitate the matter [restoration] as a life work." He later became one of Theodore Herzl's first U.S. supporters; see David Solis-Cohen to Solomon Solis-Cohen (June 26, 1881) SSCA; Morais, *Philadelphia*, pp. 314–316; *UJE* IX, p. 634; and William M. Kramer, "David Solis-Cohen of Portland," *WSJHQ* 14 (January, 1982), pp. 139–166. For Max Cohen's restorationist ideas, expressed in 1879, see Max Cohen to Solomon Solis-Cohen (November 10, 1879), SSCA.

16. Ruth L. Frankel, *Henry Leipziger* (New York: 1933), p. 68.

17. Davis, *Conservative Judaism*, pp. 238, 386.

18. On the founding of the *Jewish Exponent*, see Charles I. Hoffman, "Jewry Fifty Years Ago," *JExp*, May 14, 1937.

19. Solomon Solis-Cohen, "The Philadelphia Group," *Judaism and Science: With Other Addresses and Papers* (Philadelphia, 1940), pp. 246–252; Maxwell Whiteman, "The Philadelphia Group," in Friedman, *JLIP*, pp. 163–178.

20. *AJYB* 1 (1899), p. 246; Charles S. Bernheimer, *Half A Century in Community Service* (New York: 1948), pp. 6–12. In 1897 New Yorkers formed a similar but larger and more formal organization known as "The Judaeans."

21. Kerry M. Olitzky, "The Sunday-Sabbath Movement in American Reform Judaism: Strategy or Evolution?" *AJA* 34 (April, 1982), p. 79.

22. Joseph Krauskopf, "Half A Century of Judaism in America," *American Jews' Annual* (Cincinnati, 1888), pp. 65–95; Aaron Friedenwald to Harry Friedenwald (December 31, 1887), Harry Friedenwald Personal Papers, microfilm 404B, *AJA*. Earlier, in Kansas City, traditionalists praised Krauskopf for sounding "very sensible and very Orthodox," see *AH* (February 6, 1885), p. 194; (January 30, 1885), p. 178.

23. John F. Sutherland, "Rabbi Joseph Krauskopf of Philadelphia: The Urban Reformer Returns to the Land," *AJHQ* 67 (June, 1978), pp. 342–362; William W. Blood, *Apostle of Reason: A Biography of Joseph Krauskopf* (Philadelphia: 1973); Martin Beifield, "Joseph Krauskopf 1887–1903" (Ordination thesis, HUC-JIR, 1975).

24. Minutes, November 27, 1887, KS-KIP.

25. Joseph Krauskopf, "The Need of the Hour," A Sunday Lecture before Reform Congregation Keneseth Israel, December 11, 1887. See also *AJYB* 26 (1924–5), pp. 431–433. I am grateful to Rabbi Simeon J. Maslin for making a copy of this sermon available to me.

26. In later years, Krauskopf "encouraged the cult of personality by presenting each of his confirmands with an autographed photo of himself. He expected adulation." Malcolm H. Stern, "National Leaders of Their Time: Philadelphia's Reform Rabbis," in Friedman *JLIP*, p. 190.

27. Minutes, December 22, 1887, KS-KIP.

28. Ephraim Lederer, "The Origin and Growth of the Society," *AJYB* 15 (1913–14), p. 63; Abraham J. Feldman, "Joseph Krauskopf," *AJYB* 26 (1924–25), 433–36; Solomon Solis-Cohen to Editor of the *Jewish Exponent* (May 24, 1898), SSCA.

29. *AH* (April 13, 1888), p. 145. In Judaism, as in Gilded-Age Christianity, "union held the hope of redemption from the more generalized anxiety that burdened religious believers," see Carter, *The Spiritual Crisis of the Gilded Age*, p. 194.

30. *AH* (May 11, 1888), p. 2.

31. *AH* (June 8, 1888), pp. 70–71. The *AH* also pointed out that the convention was "the most emphatic refutation of the idea enunciated by Agnostic Ethical Culturalism."

32. Aaron Friedenwald to Henry Friedenwald (June, 1888) quoted in Levin, "Beginnings"; Kaufmann Kohler, "An American-Jewish Publication Society," *Menorah* 5 (July, 1888), pp. 56–62; Joseph Blumenthal to Solomon Solis-Cohen [May, 1888] in SSCA; *AH* (May 18, 1888), p. 24. For Jacob Schiff's view that it was a "serious mistake" to exclude Kohler, see Cowen, *Memories*, p. 317.

33. *AH* (June 1, 1888), p. 54; Cowen, *Memories*, pp. 314–316.

34. David W. Amram, "Random Memories of 1887," *JExp*, May 14, 1937, p. 5.

35. For fuller accounts of the national convention that created the Jewish Publication Society, see *AH* (June 8, 1888), pp. 70–71; letters of Aaron Friedenwald to Henry Friedenwald, quoted in Levin, "Beginnings"; the Philadelphia *North American*, quoted in Edward Wolf 2, "The Annual Report of the President [of the Jewish Publication Society] For the Year 1957," *AJYB* 60 (1959), pp. 377–380; Ephraim Lederer, "The Origin and Growth of the Society," *AJYB* 15 (1913–14), pp. 62–65; and Jonathan D. Sarna, "The Jewish Publication Society," *JBA* 45 (1987–88), pp. 42–53.

36. Quoted in Levin, "Beginnings," p. 4.

37. See, for example, "A Layman's Open Letter to the Rabbis," (1887) in *Leo N. Levi Memorial Volume* (Chicago: n.d.), p. 152, cf. pp. 74–77; A.S. Isaacs to Solomon Solis-Cohen (May 10, 1881), SSCA; Mayer Sulzberger to Israel Zangwill (May 3, 1892), Sulzberger-JPS Letterpress, PJAC; Isaac M. Fein, "Israel Zangwill and American Jewry: A Documentary Study," *AJHQ* 60 (September, 1970), p. 17; and Jonathan D. Sarna "Introduction" in *The American Rabbinate*, ed. J.R. Marcus and A.J. Peck (New York: 1985), p. 7. Of course, the Union of American Hebrew Congregations was also a lay body, see Steven A. Fox, "On the Road to Unity: The Union of American Hebrew Congregations and American Jewry, 1872–1903," *AJA* 32 (November, 1980), esp. p. 152.

38. "Organization of the American Jewish Historical Society... On Monday the Seventh Day of June 1892" (typescript, American Jewish Historical Society), p. 64.

39. Ibid., p. 65.

40. The "rabbi issue" would arise again at the founding of the American Jewish Historical Society in 1892, when rabbis once more found themselves excluded from leadership roles, allegedly to make room for "young blood, willing to work... for the glory of the cause, for Judaism, and the future of this society." As before, the "mistake" was rectified, and rabbis were added to the slate at the last minute; see ibid., esp. pp. 58 and 61; and Nathan M. Kaganoff, "AJHS at 90: Reflections on the History of the Oldest Ethnic Historical Society in America," *AJH* 71 (June, 1982), pp. 473–474.

41. Based on the list in *AH* (June 8, 1888), p. 71.

42. See the list of officers in *The Jewish Publication Society of America* (Philadelphia, 1881), p. 13. The list in *AJYB* 15 (1913–14), p. 65 is in error. For the most accurate listing of JPS board members 1888–1952, see Bloch, *OMMB*, pp. 283–293.

43. Frankel, *Henry M. Leipziger*, p. 75; see also Stephan F. Brumberg, *Going to America, Going to School* (New York: 1986), pp. 149–158.

44. *AJYB* 15 (1913–14), pp. 65, 69.

45. Aaron Friedenwald to Harry Friedenwald (August 20, 1888), Friedenwald Personal Papers, AJA microfilm 404b; *AJYB* 15 (1913–14), pp. 66, 80; for capsule biographies of these men, see *UJE*.

46. Aaron Friedenwald to Harry Friedenwald (July 8, 1888), Friedenwald Personal Papers, AJA microfilm 404b.

47. Executive Committee Minutes, July 8, 1888, Xerox copy in box 12, EW2P; for what follows, see *The Jewish Publication Society of America* (Philadelphia, 1888). Producing even this document was no easy task, for when the idea first arose Krauskopf suggested

that "to avoid the risk of it being consigned to the wastebasket" the circular might include a learned history of Jewish publication societies the world over. He compared what he had in mind to his own "Half A Century of Judaism in America," and pointed out that in preparing that he had consulted over three hundred books. Some agreed with Krauskopf, but not Sulzberger. "My God," he exclaimed according to one eye witness, "if you read three hundred books and wrote such an inaccurate account, it is a warning to us as to how we shall proceed in our work." When the circular appeared it contained no scholarly history at all; Levin, "Beginnings," p. 6.

48. *The Jewish Publication Society of America*, p. 9.

49. *AH* (December 21, 1888), p. 132.

50. Mayer Sulzberger to David L. Einstein (April 6, 1889), Sulzberger-JPS Letterbook, PJAC.

51. Adolph Moses of Louisville, for example, was miffed when he was neither invited to join the publication committee nor asked to contribute a manuscript for publication, see A. Moses to Joseph Krauskopf (December 31, 1888), in the personal collection of Maxwell Whiteman.

52. Levin, "Beginnings," pp. 6–8.

53. *First Biennial Report of the Jewish Publication Society of America* (Philadelphia: 1890), pp. 9–10.

3   *The Golden Years*

1. *The Nation* (July 31, 1890), p. 110.

2. Katie Magnus, *Outlines of Jewish History* (London: 1888), pp. vii; *JE* V, p. 496; VIII, p. 257; Frank Foden, *Philip Magnus* (London: 1970), esp. pp. 59–76, 84–87.

3. *AH* (May 25, 1888), p. 48.

4. Mayer Sulzberger to Jacob Voorsanger (December 11, 1889), MS–LB; *Menorah* 7 (1889), p. 219.

5. Another publisher did in fact advertise a pirated edition of the Magnus volume when it became known that the Jewish Publication Society would print an American edition, but a letter from Sulzberger seems to have put an end to the project. See Sulzberger to Bloch Publishing Company (March 4, 1890) in MS–LB.

6. Magnus, p. 313.

7. Sulzberger to Isaac Markens (November 19, 1889; November 27, 1889; January 18, 1890); Sulzberger to Cyrus Adler (December 6, 1889; January 22, 1890; January 27, 1890) all in MS–LB; Adler to Bernhard Felsenthal (October 8, 1889; March 24, 1890), Felsenthal Papers, AJHS. For praise of Markens's book, see *AH* (May 25, 1888), p. 37.

8. Joan Dash, *Summoned to Jerusalem: The Life of Henrietta Szold* (New York: 1979), esp. pp. 5–44; Alexandra Lee Levin, *The Szolds of Lombard Street* (Philadelphia: 1960); Arthur Hertzberg, "Henrietta Szold," *Notable American Women*, ed. Edward T. James (Cambridge, MA: 1971), 3, pp. 417–420, which also cites earlier sources.

9. Abraham A. Neuman, *Cyrus Adler: A Biographical Sketch* (New York: 1942); Cyrus Adler, *IHCTD*; *Adler Letters* all contain biographical information.

10. Katie Magnus, *Outlines of Jewish History* (Philadelphia: 1890), pp. 334–367.

11. Ibid., p. 346. Henrietta Szold proposed leaving out of her sketch people like Philadelphia's Radical Reform rabbi, Samuel Hirsch, whom she considered a menace to Judaism. But though Sulzberger sympathized, he gently reminded her that "what our individual views are with reference to the man ... ought to make no difference to us in writing history." In the end, Hirsch's name appeared. Following the practice of the *Encyclopaedia Britannica*, however, no living person was mentioned—which accounts for

the otherwise inexplicable omission of Isaac Mayer Wise; see Sulzberger to Cyrus Adler (March 4, 1890); Sulzberger to Henrietta Szold (March 4, 1890) in MS–LB; Magnus, *Outlines* (Philadelphia ed.), pp. 363, 366. On Hirsch, see Gershom Greenberg, "Samuel Hirsch's American Judaism," *AJHQ* 62 (June, 1973), pp. 362–382.

12. *AJYB* 6 (1904–1905), p. 404 [this anonymous sketch bears the characteristic features of Henrietta Szold's style and is almost certainly her work]; cf. 15 (1913–14), p. 67.

13. Ezekiel was the son of a Society founder, Jacob Ezekiel, and the brother of Henry, later a Society trustee and honorary vice-president.

14. *Menorah* 7 (1889), pp. 219–220; Moses Jacob Ezekiel, *Memoirs from the Baths of Diocletian*, ed. Joseph Gutmann and Stanley F. Chyet (Detroit: 1975), p. 460; cf. p. 30 for Ezekiel's reference to "the palm leaves of *peace* (Israel's mission on Earth)." See also David Yellin's interpretation of the seal in *AJYB* 15 (1913–14), p. 54.

15. For the Society's seals to 1953, see Bloch, *OMMB*, p. ii.

16. Magnus, *Outlines*, pp. 333, 334. Katie Magnus's own grandchild, son of Laurie Magnus, followed a different road. He converted, intermarried, and became Sir Philip Magnus-Allcroft.

17. *AH* (October 11, 1889), p. 168–169; Adolf Neubauer, "Review," *English Historical Review* 2 (January, 1887), pp. 161–164. Magnus, *Outlines* p. 277; Adler to Julius Grodinsky (July 12, 1929), box 28, PB. Privately, Katie Magnus was even more hostile to East Europeans. She could not bear, she wrote, to see the Land of the Bible turned into "a dumping ground for sad, soiled rubbish. I *ache* for those poor refugees—but I *can't* help put them where the prophets trod—it isn't fair to our memories nor our hopes that Zion should be repeopled except by our *best*." For this reason, among others, she opposed Zionism. See Stuart A. Cohen, *English Zionists and British Jews* (Princeton, NJ: 1982), p. 96.

18. *AH* (May 21, 1880), p. 4; see a similar account by Rosa Mordecai in Jacob R. Marcus, *Memoirs of American Jews* (Philadelphia: 1955), I, p. 283; and more generally Naomi M. Patz and Philip E. Miller, "Jewish Religious Children's Literature in America: An Analytical Survey," *Phaedrus* 7 (1980), pp. 19–29.

19. Sulzberger to Lucien Wolf (March 30, 1889); and Sulzberger to Cyrus Adler (March 4, 1890), both in MS–LB; JPS Letterbook, PJAC; *First Biennial Report of the Jewish Publication Society* (Philadelphia: 1890), p. 12 (italics added); Samuel W. Cooper, *Think and Thank* (Philadelphia: 1890), p. 15, cf. 38; Harap, *Image*, pp. 322–323. David Philipson somewhat reluctantly defended the volume as a "move in the right direction"; see his *Diary* (September 28, 1890; October 4, 1890) in AJA. More recently, Sonia Lipman has criticized the book for its historical inaccuracies; Sonia and V.D. Lipman (eds.) *The Century of Moses Montefiore* (London: 1985), p. 7. On the Isaacs volumes, *Step by Step* (1910) and *The Young Champion* (1913), see chapter 4 below.

20. See Chaim Bermant, *The Cousinhood* (New York: 1971), pp. 167–174.

21. The contract, dated July 29, 1890, may be found in the contracts file, JPSP. See also Executive Committee Minutes, 1888–1890, and *AJYB* 15 (1913–14), p. 67. Unless otherwise noted, I have relied in this section on Solomon Grayzel, "Graetz's *History* in America," in Guido Kisch (ed.) *The Breslau Seminary* (Tuebingen: 1963), pp. 223–237. For additional evidence of American familiarity with Graetz in the late-nineteenth century, see the many references to him in Emma Lazarus's 1883 series of articles brought together as *An Epistle to the Hebrews* (New York: 1900).

22. Heinrich Graetz, *History of the Jews* (Philadelphia: 1891), I, pp. v-vii. A "cursory comparison" of the German and English editions carried out in 1946 revealed that the English edition contained about two-thirds of the German original with most of the cuts involving literary and cultural history; see PC–M (March 31, 1946).

23. *AH* (October 4, 1889), p. 146, cf. 168.

24. *First Biennial Report of the Jewish Publication Society of America* (Philadelphia:

1890), p. 23; *AJYB* 15 (1913–14), pp. 67–68; Henrietta Szold, "The Jewish Publication Society of America," *Judaism at the World Parliament of Religions* (Cincinnati: 1894), p. 329; cf. Joan S. Rubin, "Self, Culture, and Self-Culture in Modern America: The Early History of the Book-of-the-Month Club," *Journal of American History* 71 (March, 1985), p. 785 for a related debate in a larger context. Henrietta Szold may also have had a personal motive in championing the Graetz project. The historian had recommended her father for his position in Baltimore. See Moses Aberbach, "The Early German Jews of Baltimore and Washington," in David Altshuler, *The Jews of Washington D.C.* (New York: 1985), p. 242.

25. *First Biennial Report*, pp. 22–23; for other arguments in favor of Graetz, see Michael A. Meyer, "Great Debate on Antisemitism," *LBIYB* 11 (1966), pp. 137–170; *First Biennial Report of the Jewish Publication Society*, p. 23; *AJYB* 6 (1904–1905), p. 403. Graetz's inaccuracies, biases, and omissions did not seem to bother his critics much, perhaps because every other Jewish history available in English was far worse. Years earlier, in 1878, Bernhard Felsenthal had privately criticized the historian's "distorted conjectures." Many had also been critical of his treatment of Reform Judaism, and serious criticisms would subsequently be levelled against his depictions of such subjects as Jewish mysticism and Hasidism. Rabbi Emanuel Schreiber of Little Rock, Arkansas, who published in Berlin an entire volume devoted to Graetz's errors and alleged incompetence, attacked the Society in print in 1892 for rejecting good books (like his own) while publishing the "charlatan"; see Ezra Spicehandler and Theodore Wiener, "Bernhard Felsenthal's Letters to Osias Schorr," *EAJH*, p. 386; Emanuel Schreiber, *Graetz's Geschichtsbauerei* (Berlin: 1881); idem, *Reformed Judaism and Its Pioneers* (Spokane: 1892), pp. xi–xii. For other views of Graetz's work, see Stephen L. Sniderman, "Bibliography of Works About Heinrich Graetz," *SBB* 14 (1982), pp. 41–49.

26. JPS Executive Committee Minutes, Nov. 24, 1890; Mayer Sulzberger to H. Montagu, Nov. 10, 1889, MS–LB. On nineteenth-century Jewish attitudes to biblical history, see Nahum M. Sarna, "Abraham Geiger and Biblical Scholarship," in *New Perspectives on Abraham Geiger*, ed. Jakob J. Petuchowski (Cincinnati: 1975), pp. 19–20.

27. Henrietta Szold, interview with Marvin Lowenthal (December 29, 1935), typescript, Hadassah Archives, N.Y., p. 41.

28. Louis E. Levinthal, "David Werner Amram," *AJYB* 43 (1941–42), pp. 375–80.

29. Grayzel, "Graetz's *History* in America," p. 229 makes a contrary claim that is unfounded, as a comparison of the English and American edition easily demonstrates.

30. Michael A. Meyer, "German-Jewish Identity in Nineteenth Century America," in Jacob Katz (ed.) *Toward Modernity: The European Jewish Model* (New Brunswick, NJ: 1987), pp. 258–259; Gotthard Deutsch, "Heinrich Graetz: A Centenary," *CCARYB* 28 (1917), pp. 354–355.

31. Joseph Jacobs noted that Jost gave a full account of American Jewry's role in the 1840 Damascus Affair, but "characteristically enough Graetz . . . entirely omits all reference to the action in America, though it is tolerably clear that he had before him Jost's account." Joseph Jacobs, "The Damascus Affair of 1840 and the Jews of America," *PAJHS* 10 (1902), p. 124. On Graetz's sister, see Ida L. Uchill, *Pioneers, Peddlers, and Tsadikim: The Story of the Jews of Colorado* (Boulder: 1957), p. 206; and on his son, see Henrietta Szold interview with Marvin Lowenthal, p. 22, and Graetz's letters to Benjamin Szold regarding his son (who lived in Baltimore) reprinted in Reuven Michael (ed.), *Heinrich Graetz: Tagebuch und Briefe* (Tuebingen: 1977). For Graetz's views on America, see Philipp Bloch's "Memoir of Heinrich Graetz," in Graetz's *History of the Jews* (Philadelphia: 1898), VI, p. 80; cf. Guido Kisch, "The Founders of 'Wissenschaft des Judentums' and America," *EAJH*, pp. 147–170.

32. Szold to "Folks" (July 12, 1894), Szold box (1); David Amram to Szold [1898], Szold box (2), JPSP; cf. Dash, *Summoned to Jerusalem*, p. 34.

33. Grayzel, "Graetz's *History* in America," pp. 231–235; Justin Wise Polier and James Waterman Wise, *The Personal Letters of Stephen Wise* (Boston: 1956), p. 22.

34. Yosef Hayim Yerushalmi, *Zakhor: Jewish History and Jewish Memory* (Seattle: 1982), p. 86; David Levin, *History As Romantic Art* (Stanford: 1959); Dorothy Ross, "Historical Consciousness in Nineteenth-Century America," *American Historical Review* 89 (October, 1984), pp. 909–928.

35. Mayer Sulzberger proposed a translation of the notes and appendices as early as 1909, PC–M May 7, 1909; Cyrus Adler repeated the call in 1916, strongly seconded by Alexander Marx, PC–M, November 5, 1916, and undated [1916] Marx memo in box 20, PB; see also PC–M December 19, 1937; December 4, 1940; May 11, 1941; October 24, 1945; March 31, 1946; February 2, 1947; "The Need of a New Edition of Graetz's History," *Journal of Jewish Bibliography* 2 (April-June, 1940), pp. 41, 66; and Ismar Elbogen's rejoinder (October, 1940), pp. 22–23. In 1946 Moses Hadas was actually commissioned and paid to retranslate Graetz, notes and all. He translated five full volumes from the German, but none were published and they remain in the Society's safe. See Unpublished Books correspondence, box 60, esp. Hadas to Grayzel (June 28, 1951).

36. Tebbel, *History* II, pp. 170–177; Harap, *Image*, p. 447, 455–471; cf. *AJYB* 3 (1901–1902), p. 198; 15 (1913–14), pp. 139–145. The only novels of any importance to appear had come from the pen of a non-Jew, Henry Harland (who wrote under the name of Simon Luska), and many found the assimilationist message in his *The Yoke of the Thora* (1887) profoundly offensive; see Susan Rieff, "Henry Harland: Philo-Semite as Anti-Semite," *Chicago Jewish Forum* 10:3 (1952), pp. 194–205.

37. Milton Goldsmith, *Rabbi and Priest* (Philadelphia: 1892), pp. 3, 310–314; PC–M (April 5, 1891); Harap, *Image*, p. 448; [Joseph Jacobs (ed.)] *The Persecution of the Jews in Russia* (Philadelphia: 1891).

38. Mayer Sulzberger to Lucien Wolf (March 30, 1889), MS–LB; Joseph Leftwich, *Israel Zangwill* (New York: 1957), pp. 45, 53, 54, 58, 63; Elsie B. Adams, *Israel Zangwill* (New York: 1971), pp. 52, 61. Accounts of the origins of *Children of the Ghetto* contradict one another. Lucien Wolf in *Transactions of the Jewish Historical Society of England* 11 (1928), p. 255 said that Sulzberger sent Krauskopf to ask him to write "a Jewish *Robert Elsmere*" and that he recommended Zangwill instead. But Sulzberger's letter and Leftwich, p. 53, show that this unduly magnifies Wolf's role. Cyrus Adler in his autobiography (*IHCTD*, p. 77), wrote that he "carried the message from Mayer Sulzberger to Israel Zangwill to ask him whether he would undertake a book for the Jewish Publication Society," but the date does not jibe with Sulzberger's letter as found in his letterbook, and in some details differs also from Adler's earlier (1926) account (where he admitted that his "recollections of those years are in a whirl") reprinted in his *Lectures, Selected Papers, Addresses* (Philadelphia: 1933), pp. 103–104. Zangwill himself [*Speeches, Articles and Letters of Israel Zangwill*, ed. Maurice Simon (London: 1937), p. 143] said that Sulzberger "was the main, if not 'the onlie begetter' " of the book—a claim that seems closest to the truth, and is backed up by Leftwich's account, esp. pp. 63–64.

39. Sulzberger to Zangwill (February 18, 1891), MS–LB.

40. Leftwich, *Israel Zangwill*, p. 34; PC–M May 24, 1891; Adler, *IHCTD*, p. 168; Sulzberger to Zangwill (May 3, 1892), MS–LB.

41. Israel Zangwill, *Children of the Ghetto* (Philadelphia, 1892) II, p. 127; for a full-length literary study see Maurice Wohlgelernter, *Israel Zangwill: A Study* (New York: 1964).

42. Prologue to the dramatic version of "Children of the Ghetto," as quoted in *AJYB* 29 (1927–28), p. 125.

43. Zangwill, *Children of the Ghetto* II, pp. 279, 324. For Zangwill's positive view of America, see Leftwich, *Israel Zangwill* p. 148; cf. Isaac M. Fein, "Israel Zangwill and American Jewry," *AJHQ* 60 (September, 1970), pp. 12–36.

44. Zangwill, *Children of the Ghetto* II, p. 279; Adams, *Israel Zangwill*, pp. 52–62.

45. Adams, *Israel Zangwill*, p. 19; Sulzberger to Zangwill (December 12, 1892), MS–

LB; Leftwich, *Israel Zangwill*, p. 43; cf. Henrietta Szold, "The Jewish Publication Society," p. 330.

46. Details of the negotiations with Macmillan may be found in box 45, PB, esp. Cyrus Adler to Julius Grodinsky (January 14, 1927). In the one-volume edition, Zangwill made several changes and added a glossary "based on one supplied to the American edition by another hand." The original British edition lacked a glossary, the Society (which probably means Henrietta Szold) added one, and Zangwill later improved it. A copy of volume 1 of the JPS edition of *Children of the Ghetto*, revised in Zangwill's own hand, may be found in the Klau Library of Hebrew Union College-Jewish Institute of Religion.

47. *AJYB* 15 (1913–14), pp. 55, 69; 40 (1938–39), p. 656; *Selected Works of Israel Zangwill* (Philadelphia: 1938); JPS Trustees Minutes (January 9, 1939).

48. Henry Zirndorf, *Some Jewish Women* (Philadelphia: 1892); Michael A. Meyer, "A Centennial History of the Hebrew Union College-Jewish Institute of Religion," in *Hebrew Union College-Jewish Institute of Religion at One Hundred Years*, ed. Samuel E. Karff (Cincinnati: 1976), p. 24; *JE* vol. XII, p. 687.

49. The most important volume of this genre, Nahida Remy's *The Jewish Woman*, published in German in 1891, was accepted for publication in English by the Society, and then rejected when the translation was found to be unacceptable. An improved and authorized translation, by Louise Mannheimer, was published by Bloch in 1895; see PC–M (May 14, 1893; October 25, 1893).

50. Liebman[n] Adler, *Sabbath Hours* (Philadelphia: 1893), pp. v–vi; *Third Biennial Report of the Jewish Publication Society of America* (Philadelphia: 1894), p. 19; *AJYB* 15 (1913–14), pp. 125–26, 137; *JE* vol. I, p. 196–7; cf. on this period Ellen Sue Levi Elwell, "The Founding and Early Programs of the National Council of Jewish Women: Study and Practice as Jewish Women's Religious Expression" (Unpublished Ph.D., Indiana University, 1982).

51. Quotes are from Sulzberger to Isaac Schwob (October 29, 1889); and Sulzberger to Edward Calisch (June 28, 1889) both in MS–LB. Problems connected with translators may be traced in PC–M.

52. In 1892, the Society voted to "set aside a sum, not exceeding five hundred dollars annually, for subventioning such scholarly publications as they see fit, preference to be given to the productions of American scholars." *Second Biennial Report of the Jewish Publication Society* (Philadelphia: 1892), p. 29. Only a few subventions were ever actually distributed, and almost half of them (a total of $1,050) went to support the biblical researches of Arnold B. Ehrlich; other subventions went to Casper Levias, Simon Wolf, and to several European scholars.

53. *Third Biennial Report of the Jewish Publication Society*, pp. 5–14.

54. Emanuel Schreiber, *Reformed Judaism and Its Pioneers* (Spokane: 1892), p. x; PC–M (June 2, 1889; August 3, 1890); N.H. Imber, "My Toast," *[Boston] Jewish Chronicle* (June 10, 1892), reprinted in Jacob Kabakoff (ed.) *Master of Hope* (New York: 1985), pp. 93–95.

55. *JExp*, May 13–27, 1892.

56. Membership statistics broken down by individual and city were printed at the back of every annual report; letters from small-town Jews may be found in miscellaneous correspondence in JPSP.

57. On the magazine proposal, see generally, Tebbel, *History*, II p. 14; and for specific proposals, *Second Biennial Report of the Jewish Publication Society of America* (Philadelphia: 1892), p. 6; *Third Biennial Report . . .*, p. 6; Executive Minutes, March 4, 1897; *AJYB* 2 (1900–1901), p. 652; 3 (1901–1902), p. 197; PC–M (December 6, 1908, January 24, 1909); *AJYB* 10 (1908–1909), p. 272; 11 (1909–1910), p. 274; 12 (1910–11), p. 369; 39 (1937–38), p. 850; 40 (1938–39), pp. 653–654; PC–M (December 4, 1940); and *Adler Letters* I, p. 147. The

Society's house organ, *JPS Bookmark*, a periodical quite different from those discussed in earlier years, began in 1954.

58. Executive Committee Minutes (June 15, 1893); *Third Biennial Report*, p. 9.

4   The Henrietta Szold Era

1. From the word "besoldeter" with the "z" added in Hungarian to maintain the "s." See Adele Szold Seltzer, unpublished biographical sketch of Henrietta Szold, box 1, Szold Papers-SL.

2. Executive Committee Minutes (June 15, 1893), p. 63; cf. Alexandra Lee Levin, "Henrietta Szold and the JPS," *JPSBM* (June, 1961), pp. 4–5.

3. Joan Dash, *Summoned to Jerusalem: The Life of Henrietta Szold* (New York: 1979), pp. 26–30; Levin, *SOLS*, pp. 321–323.

4. Isidore N. Choynski in the *American Israelite*, announced her rumored "engagement" in the issue of September 23, 1881; see also Irving Fineman, *Woman of Valor: The Story of Henrietta Szold* (New York: 1961), pp. 52, 53, 59.

5. Levin, "Henrietta Szold and the JPS," pp. 3–10; Dash, *Summoned to Jerusalem*, pp. 31–33; *AJYB* 47 (1945–46), p. 55; Szold to "Folks" (December 11, 1893), Szold box 1, JPSP.

6. Szold to "Folks" (February 20, 1894), Szold box 1, JPSP.

7. Szold to Rachel and Joseph Jastrow (November 1, 1893) in Levin, *SOLS*, p. 324; Szold to "Folks" (June 12, 1894; September 25, 1894), Szold box 1, JPSP.

8. Szold to "Folks" (April 10, 1894; April 22, 1895), Szold box 1, JPSP.

9. Szold to "Folks" (October 17, 1894), Szold box 1, JPSP; *Report of the Tenth Year of the Jewish Publication Society of America* (Philadelphia, 1898), p. 54.

10. Szold to "dear ones" (May 23, 1898), Szold box 1, JPSP.

11. See especially the quotations from Henrietta Szold's private diary in A.L. Levin to Solomon Grayzel (July 18, 1959), Szold file, PB; for similar sentiments see her correspondence with Louis Ginzberg (1905–1907) and her introspective writings from 1908, both on microfilm in AJA; and on the general phenomenon, see Mary Kelly, *Private Women, Public Stage: Literary Domesticity in Nineteenth Century America* (New York: 1984).

12. For sketches of the presidents, see *AJYB* 6 (1904–1905), p. 160; 20 (1918–19), p. 414; 37 (1935–36), pp. 55–60; 47 (1945–46), pp. 201–206. Presidential activities may be gauged through Trustees Minutes and surviving correspondence.

13. See, for example, TM (July 7, 1907), p. 277; Schiff to Simon Miller (June 8, 1916; December 13, 1918), Schiff Papers, AJA.

14. *AJYB* 15 (1913–14), pp. 78–98; "To the Members of the Publication Committee" (January 24, 1952) in box 13, EW2P; PC–M, esp. March 5, 1911.

15. Unpublished interview with Marvin Lowenthal (December 29, 1935), p. 42, Szold Papers–HA.

16. *AJYB* 15 (1913–14), pp. 83–86.

17. PC-M (March 4, 1900), p. 136; (December 2, 1900), p. 144; Manuscript Book of the Jewish Publication Society (1890–1911), esp. p. 33; cf. Carrie Davidson, *Out of Endless Yearnings* (New York: 1946), pp. 16–32.

18. *AJYB* 15 (1913–14), p. 123.

19. Sulzberger to Bernhard Felsenthal (May 22, 1893), MS-LB. Eighteen years later someone, probably Cyrus Adler, charged in a letter to Max Margolis [(November 16, 1909), Margolis Papers, Dropsie College] that Krauskopf was "trying to take his people out of the Jewish church." For other contemporary attacks on Krauskopf, see Solomon Solis-Cohen to E. Solis (September 22, 1892), SSCA; and Louis Ginzberg to Henrietta Szold (August 17, 1905), Ginzberg Papers, where Krauskopf is referred to as "a fool or a charlatan." The Society's refusal to donate books to the Farm School is discussed in

Krauskopf to Morris Newburger (September 16, 1897), Krauskopf Papers, Temple University. The tenth anniversary dinner is described in a letter from Henrietta Szold to her parents (May 24, 1898) in Szold box 1, JPSP; as well as in Horace Stern, "Memories of the Early Days" in Miscellaneous box 118, JPSP. For Krauskopf's handwritten toast, see box 3, Krauskopf Papers, AJA; and for his resignation see TM (June 15 and November 20, 1898). Although Solomon Grayzel's oral history, pp. 7–8, claims that Krauskopf was not invited to the Society's twenty-fifth anniversary celebration, there is a letter from Krauskopf to Cyrus Adler (March 10, 1913), box 120, JPSP in which he declined to attend on account of illness.

20. Norman Bentwich, *Solomon Schechter: A Biography* (Philadelphia: 1948); Abraham J. Karp, "Solomon Schechter Comes to America," *AJHQ* 53 (1963), pp. 44–62; Mel Scult, "The Baale Boste Reconsidered: The Life of Mathilde Roth Schechter (M.R.S.)," *MJ* 7:1 (February, 1987), p. 11; for Henrietta Szold's first impression of Schechter, see Levin, *SOLS*, pp. 330–331.

21. Davidson, *Out of Endless Yearnings*, p. 81. Solomon Schechter, *Seminary Addresses and Other Papers* (New York: 1959), pp. 240–241.

22. Cyrus Adler to Solomon Schechter (October 29, 1914), box 155, JPSP.

23. *Report of the Tenth Year of the Jewish Publication Society of America*, p. 36.

24. Michael A. Meyer, *Ideas of Jewish History* (New York: 1974), pp. 22–32, 152; Paul R. Mendes-Flohr and Jehuda Reinharz, *The Jew in the Modern World* (New York: 1980), p. 197; Yosef H. Yerushalmi, *Zakhor: Jewish History and Jewish Memory* (Seattle, 1982), pp. 81–101; *JE* vol. 6, p. 609.

25. Dorothy Ross, "Historical Consciousness in Nineteenth-Century America," *American Historical Review* 89:4 (October, 1984), pp. 909–928; more broadly see John Higham *et al*, *History: Humanistic Scholarship in America* (Englewood Cliffs, NJ: 1965).

26. Cyrus Adler, *IHCTD*, p. 60; *Adler Letters*, I, pp. 20, 60.

27. See Nathan M. Kaganoff, "AJHS at 90: Reflections on the History of the Oldest Ethnic Historical Society in America," *AJH* 71:4 (June, 1982), pp. 466–476; and Davis, *Conservative Judaism*, pp. 231–310.

28. Gustav Karpeles, *A Sketch of Jewish History* (Philadelphia: 1897), p. 21; Ismar Schorsch, *Jewish Reactions to German Anti-Semitism, 1870–1914*, (New York: 1972), pp. 111–113.

29. Karpeles, *A Sketch of Jewish History*, pp. 8–10.

30. Gustav Karpeles, *Jewish Literature and Other Essays* (Philadelphia: 1895), p. 105.

31. Karpeles, *A Sketch of Jewish History*, p. 91.

32. *Ibid.*, pp. 57, 59, 99, 51; cf. Karpeles, *Jewish Literature*, p. 20.

33. Quoted in E.M.F. Mielziner, *Moses Mielziner* (New York: 1931) p. 46; see Jonathan D. Sarna, *Jacksonian Jew: The Two Worlds of Mordecai Noah* (New York: 1981), pp. 139, 206; James G. Heller, *Isaac M. Wise* (New York: 1965), pp. 540–545; and for the phenomenon in Europe, Moshe Pelli, *The Age of Haskalah* (Leiden: 1979), pp. 48–72.

34. Emanuel Deutsch, *The Talmud* (Philadelphia: 1895); Arsene Darmesteter, *The Talmud* (Philadelphia: 1897), p. 49. Not surprisingly, Joseph Krauskopf, who took a decidedly more negative view of the Talmud, voted against publication of Darmesteter's book, see PC-M February 9, 1896, p. 72.

35. For other American Jewish efforts to rehabilitate the Talmud, see Isidor Kalisch, "Sketch of the Talmud" (1877) reprinted in his *Studies in Ancient and Modern Judaism* (New York: 1928), pp. 282–327, cf. 328–343; Alexander Kohut, "The Genius of Talmud," *Judaism at the World's Parliament of Religion* (Cincinnati: 1894); Moses Mielziner, *Introduction to the Talmud* (Cincinnati:1893).

36. David Philipson, *Old European Jewries* (Philadelphia: 1894), esp. pp. 193, 118, 215, 81; Philipson, *My Life*, pp. 119–120; cf. Mayer Sulzberger to Philipson (May 3, 1892), MS-LB.

37. Solomon Schechter, *Studies in Judaism* (Philadelphia: 1896), esp. p. xvii; Norman

Bentwich, *Solomon Schechter* (Philadelphia: 1948), pp. 256–257, 267; PC–M, March 22, 1896, p. 76.

38. Bentwich, *Solomon Schechter*, pp. 253–254, 258–259, 284; cf. Schechter, *Studies in Judaism*, pp. 89, 328.

39. Schechter *Studies in Judaism* (Second Series, Philadelphia: 1908; Third Series, Philadelphia: 1924); Israel Abrahams, *The Book of Delight* (Philadelphia: 1912); *By-Paths in Hebraic Bookland* (Philadelphia: 1920); on Abrahams see David G. Dalin, "Israel Abrahams: Leader of Liturgical Reforms in England," *Journal of Reform Judaism* (Winter, 1985), pp. 68–83 and works cited therein.

40. *Fourth Biennial Report of the Jewish Publication Society of America* (Philadelphia: 1896), p. 16. Executive Committee Minutes, January 8, 1895, p. 81; PC–M, April 21; October 6, 1895, pp. 59, 63.

41. Israel Abrahams, *Jewish Life in the Middle Ages* (Philadelphia: 1896; paperback reprint in 1958); *AJYB* 15, pp. 93–94, 123; cf. PC–M, June 16, 1896, p. 78. A second edition of Abrahams's book updated by Cecil Roth was published in London in 1932.

42. In this case, JPS was completely responsible for the series; the English simply reprinted each volume with new front matter. For the history of the series, see Henrietta Szold to David Philipson, April 17, 1912, box 2, file 14, Philipson Papers, AJA.

43. Edward H. O'Neill, *A History of American Biography* (Philadelphia: 1935), p. 83.

44. David Yellin and Israel Abrahams, *Maimonides* (Philadelpia: 1903), pp. 15, 48, 183, 174. The biography was written by Abrahams based on Yellin's Hebrew biography published in 1898.

45. Maurice Liber, *Rashi* (Philadelphia: 1906). Privately, Henrietta Szold lamented that the book was "about as enlivening as Moise Schwab's lucubrations" and admitted to some dislike of French Jewish scholarship in general; Henrietta Szold to "Mamma" (May 4, 1905), Szold Papers–HA.

46. Norman Bentwich, *Philo-Judaeus of Alexandria* (Philadelphia: 1910); Bentwich, *Solomon Schechter*, p. 284.

47. Norman Bentwich, *Josephus* (Philadelphia: 1914); see p. 259 for his present-oriented warning against assimilation.

48. Norman Bentwich, *My 77 Years* (Philadelphia: 1961), p. 16.

49. Adler[?] to Goodman (May 10, 1917), Goodman file, JPSP; Paul Goodman, *Moses Montefiore* (Philadelphia: 1925).

50. Quoted in Kaganoff, "AJHS at 90," p. 472.

51. PC–M (December 12, 1897), p. 108; (May 5, 1907), p. 50; cf. Shuly Rubin Schwartz, "The Emergence of Jewish Scholarship in America: The Publication of the *Jewish Encyclopedia* (Ph.D., JTSA, 1987), pp. 247–262. On Wolf's work, see Sylvan M. Dubow, "Identifying the Jewish Serviceman in the Civil War: A Reappraisal of Simon Wolf's *The American Jew As Patriot, Soldier and Citizen*," *AJHQ* 59 (March, 1970), pp. 357–369; in *AJYB* 5 (5665 = 1904–1905), p. 139, Louis Levy claimed that the book was actually based on his efforts.

52. Zosa Szajkowski, "Paul Nathan, Lucien Wolf, Jacob H. Schiff and the Jewish Revolutionary Movements in Eastern Europe 1903–1917," *JSS* 29 (January, 1967), p. 23; cf. idem, "The Impact of the Russian Revolution of 1905 on American Jewish Life," *YA* 17 (1978), pp. 54–118; Philip E. Schoenberg, "The American Reaction to the Kishinev Pogrom of 1903," *AJHQ* 63 (March, 1974), pp. 262–283.

53. *AJYB* 5 (1903–1904), p. 240.

54. PC–M (June 7, 1903), p. 193; TM (October 25, 1903), p. 218; cf. Cyrus Adler (ed.) *The Voice of America On Kishineff* (Philadelphia: 1904), pp. xiv-xv.

55. Michael Davitt, *Within the Pale* (New York: 1903), pp. v, 86; TM (October 25, 1903).

56. Adler, *Voice of America on Kishineff*, p. xxv; PC–M (March 6, 1904), p. 208; (March

20, 1904), p. 210; compare Isidor Singer, *Russia at the Bar of the American People* (New York: 1904).

57. Abraham B. Rhine, *Leon Gordon* (Philadelphia: 1910); PC–M (February 10, 1907), p. 43.

58. Jacob S. Raisin, *The Haskalah Movement in Russia* (Philadelphia: 1913), esp. pp. 202–203; PC–M (June 16, 1910), pp. 192–193.

59. S.M. Dubnow, *Jewish History* (Philadelphia: 1903); reprinted in Simon Dubnow *Nationalism and History*, edited by Koppel S. Pinson (Philadelphia: 1958), pp. 253–324; Szold to J.H. Hertz (August 29, 1901), Szold Papers–HA; *AJYB* 5 (1903–1904), p. 227.

60. See, for example, PC–M (April 5, 1903), p. 188.

61. PC–M (October 2, 1910), p. 200; (December 4, 1910), p. 209; Dubnow, *Nationalism and History* (ed. Pinson), pp. 23, 60; Moshe Davis, "Jewry, East and West: The Correspondence of Israel Friedlaender and Simon Dubnow," *YA* 9 (1954), pp. 9–62; Robert M. Seltzer, "Simon Dubnow and the Nationalist Interpretation of Jewish History," in Moses Rischin (ed.) *The Jews of North America* (Detroit: 1987), esp. p. 148.

62. Davis, "Jewry, East and West," pp. 24–25; Prof. Davis notes that Friedlaender's call for a few chapters of "Kulturgeschichte" parallel Ahad Ha'am's private critique of the first volume of Dubnow's major history.

63. Davis, "Jewry, East and West," p. 54; *Adler Letters* II, p. 140; cf. Max Vishnitzer, "Dubnov's History of the Jews in Russia and Poland," *JQR* 13 (1922–23), pp. 343–351.

64. Davis, "Jewry, East and West" traces the work's full history; cf. Israel Friedlaender to Mayer Sulzberger (November 2, 12, 1917), Sulzberger Papers, Dropsie College. On Friedlaender, see Baila R. Shargel, *Practical Dreamer: Israel Friedlaender and the Shaping of American Judaism* (New York: 1985).

65. Henrietta Szold to J.H. Hertz (November 22, 1897), Szold Papers–HA; Szold to Stephen S. Wise (February 26, 1908) JPSP; Marvin Lowenthal, *Henrietta Szold: Life and Letters* (New York: 1942) pays particular attention to her early Zionist activities and writings.

66. Mayer Sulzberger to Bernhard Felsenthal (April 7, 1901), Felsenthal Papers, AJHS.

67. Israel Abrahams, *Jewish Life in the Middle Ages* (Philadelphia: 1896), p. xxiv; PC–M (March 3, 1901), p. 148; Nahum Slouschz, *The Renascence of Hebrew Literature* (Philadelphia: 1909), esp. pp. 12, 203; "The Autobiography of Nahum Slouschz [in Hebrew]" *Genazim* 3 (1969), p. 42.

68. PC–M (April 5, 1908), p. 99; (October 25, 1908), p. 109; (April 4, 1909), p. 135; (November 6, 1910), p. 202; (March 5, 1911), p. 213. For the influence of Ahad Ha'Am, see Evyatar Friesel, "Ahad Ha-Amism in American Zionist Thought," *At the Crossroads: Essays on Ahad Ha'Am*, ed. J. Kornberg (Albany, NY: 1983), pp. 133–141, and Schechter's Hebrew letters to Ahad Ha'Am published by Norman Bentwich in *Melilah* 2 (1946), pp. 25–36. Philipson expressed his views on Zionism in an earlier controversy, see Herbert Parzen, "The Purge of the Dissidents, Hebrew Union College and Zionism, 1903–1907," *JSS* 37 (1975), p. 308; for the Society's debate over Philipson's book see PC–M (October 13, 1907), pp. 63–65.

69. PC–M (June 16, 1910), pp. 193–196.

70. *AJYB* 1 (1899), p. x.

71. *JE* s.v. "almanac," "year-book"; *UJE* s.v. "compilations, literary."

72. *The Jewish Year Book* (London: 1896), p. ix; *JE* vol. 7, p. 45; cf. on Jacobs *AJYB* 18 (1916–17), pp. 68–75.

73. PC–M (February 9, 1896), p. 73; (October 1, 1899), p. 131; *AH* (August 27, 1897), p. 487; *AJYB* 15 (1913–14), p. 91; cf. vol. 18 (1916–17), p. 71 where Sulzberger credits Jacobs for setting the standard "which has since been followed in England and in our own country."

74. Henrietta Szold to Elvira N. Solis (July 26, 1906), typescript in Szold Papers–HA;

Szold Journal, entry of July 8, 1910, in box 1, file 7 of Szold Papers-SL; Szold to Louis Ginzberg (July 22, 1907), Ginzberg Papers.

75. The original form and related correspondence are in Szold Papers, box 2, JPSP.

76. Maurice Jacobs to Harry Schneiderman (July 15, 1948), box 76, JPSP recounts the history of the *Year Book*; see also PC–M and TM (1905–1907); Henrietta Szold to Louis Ginzberg (May 20, 1907), Ginzberg Papers; Louis Levin to Henrietta Szold (October 2, 1908), Szold box 2, JPSP.

77. A full-scale history of the *Year Book* is beyond the scope of this volume; for data relating to JPS–AJC cooperation over the years, see boxes 74–76, JPSP.

78. PC–M, 1893–96; Mayer Sulzberger to Bernhard Felsenthal (April 5, 1896), Felsenthal Papers, AJHS; Joseph Bogen to Henrietta Szold (August 9, 1896; October 15, 1896), in the private possession of Maxwell Whiteman. On Gersoni, see Jacob Kabakoff, *Halutze Ha-Sifrut Ha-Ivrit Ba-Amerika* (Tel Aviv: 1966), pp. 77–130.

79. Alpheus T. Mason, *Brandeis: A Free Man's Life* (New York: 1946), 19–28, 441; Allon Gal, *Brandeis of Boston* (Cambridge: 1980), 69–70; Davis, *Conservative Judaism*, 333–335.

80. PC–M, March 14, 1897, p. 95; Lewis Dembitz to Mayer Sulzberger (November 10, 1896; June 4, 1897) in the private possession of Maxwell Whiteman; Lewis Dembitz, *Jewish Services in Synagogue and Home* (Philadelphia: 1898), p. 5.

81. W. Willner, *Judaica: Notes on Dembitz's Jewish Services* (New York: [1899]), in the Klau Library, HUC-JIR, Cincinnati [reprinted from the *Jewish Messenger*].

82. H. Szold to Joseph H. Hertz (August 3, 1898; September 22, 1898), Szold Papers-HA; Dembitz, *Jewish Services*, pp. 5, 424, 56, 244. Decades later, Prof. Louis Ginzberg was still recommending the volume to potential converts, see Eli Ginzberg, *Keeper of the Law* (Philadelphia: 1966), p. 236.

83. M. Lazarus, *The Ethics of Judaism* (Philadelphia: 1900), vol. I, p. vii.

84. Peter Gay, *Freud, Jews and Other Germans* (Oxford: 1978), pp. 114–115.

85. Ismar Schorsch, *Jewish Reactions to German Anti-Semitism* (New York: 1972), pp. 59–75; "Lazarus, Moritz," *EJ*, 10, col. 1517–19; Michael A. Meyer, "The Great Debate on Antisemitism," *LBIYB* 11 (1966), pp. 146–148; David Philipson, "Some Unpublished Letters of Theological Importance," *HUCA* 2 (1925), pp. 430–432. For the impact of ethnopsychology on American Jewish thought, see Benny Kraut, "The Ambivalent Relationship of American Reform Judaism with Unitarianism in the Last Third of the 19th Century," *Journal of Ecumenical Studies* 23 (Winter, 1986), p. 66.

86. PC–M, February 5, 1899; March 5, 1899.

87. Henrietta Szold to Bernhard Felsenthal (November 13, 1900), Felsenthal Papers, AJHS; cf. Szold to J.H. Hertz (April 1, 1899; August 8, 1900), Szold Papers–HA; Michael Meyer, "The Problematics of Jewish Ethics" *CCARJ* (June, 1968), p. 68 considers Szold's translation "rather inaccurate."

88. *AJYB* 3 (1901–1902), p. 223.

89. Samuel Schulman called it "the most convincing apologetic of Judaism in the nineteenth century," *AJYB* 15 (1913–14), pp. 133–134.

90. Nathan Rotenstreich, *From Mendelssohn to Rosenzweig: Jewish Philosophy in Modern Times* (New York: 1968), pp. 43–51; David Baumgart, "The Ethics of Lazarus and Steinthal," *LBIYB* 2 (1957), pp. 205–217; Meyer, "The Problematics of Jewish Ethics," pp. 67–74; Jakob J. Petuchowski, "On the Validity of German-Jewish Self-Definitions," *The Leo Baeck Memorial Lecture* 29 (1985), pp. 7–21; for the application of Lazarus's ideas in another setting see Hillel J. Kieval, "In the Image of Hus: Refashioning Czech Judaism in Post-Emancipatory Prague," *MJ* 5 (May, 1985), pp. 151–152.

91. PC–M (June 16, 1907), p. 58; (December 8, 1907), p. 75; Cyrus Adler to Solomon Schechter (January 8, 1913) in *Adler Letters* I, p. 223; cf. *AJYB* 36 (1934–35), p. 491; Solomon Grayzel to Ben M. Edidin (June 4, 1941), Unpublished Books Correspondence box 57,

JPSP; Jacob R. Marcus to Solomon Grayzel (December 16, 1951) uncataloged PC correspondence, PJAC.

92. Isabel E. Cohen, *Readings and Recitations for Jewish Homes and Schools* (Philadelphia: 1896), p. 3.

93. *AJYB* (1905–1906), p. *14.

94. PC–M (January 6, 1907), p. 38.

95. PC–M (March 26, 1911), pp. 220–221; (September 27, 1911), pp. 243–244.

96. Note descriptions of some of these books in Bloch, *OMMB*.

97. Mayer Sulzberger to Helen K. Weil (February 18, 1891), MS–LB; *AJYB* 3 (1901–1902), p. 198.

98. PC–M (October 30, 1904), pp. 212, 215; *AJYB* 3 (1901–1902), p. 198.

99. *AJYB* 15 (1913–14), p. 139.

100. This calculation is based on titles, excluding ephemeral publications, and counting each volume of the *American Jewish Year Book* separately. See also, Solomon Grayzel, "Two Centuries of Anglo-Jewish Book-Reading," *YA* 9 (1954), pp. 122–125.

101. PC–M (April 4, 1909), p. 134. The background is recounted in Arthur A. Goren, *New York Jews and the Quest for Community: The Kehillah Experiment, 1908–22* (New York: 1970), pp. 25–42.

102. PC–M (February 28, 1894), p. 37.

103. Abraham Cahan to Mayer Sulzberger (April 3, 1901; April 10, 1901; May 2, 1901), in the collection of Maxwell Whiteman; TM (May 19, 1901), p. 191; (October 25, 1903), p. 218; PC–M (March 1, 1903), p. 184; cf. Maxwell Whiteman, "The Fiddlers Rejected: Jewish Immigrant Expression in Philadelphia," in Friedman *JLIP*, pp. 93–94.

104. PC–M (March 6, 1904), p. 207; (January 1, 1905), p. 222.

105. Herman Bernstein, *Contrite Hearts* (New York: 1905), p. [ix].

106. For surveys of early American Jewish literature, see Carole S. Kessner, "Jewish-American Immigrant Fiction Written in English between 1867 and 1920," *Bulletin of Research in the Humanities* 81 (1978), pp. 406–430; and Harap, *Image* pp. 437–524.

107. Jacob Lazarre, *Beating Sea and Changeless Bar* (Philadelphia: 1905), esp. pp. 109, 117. "Jacob Lazarre" is a pseudonym, and the volume itself is different in terms of writing style and subject matter from other fiction published. See Bloch, *OMMB*, p. 79.

108. Montagu F. Modder, *The Jew in the Literature of England* (Philadelphia: 1939), pp. 343–346, esp. p. 345.

109. Samuel Gordon, *Strangers at the Gate* (Philadelphia: 1902); idem, *Sons of the Covenant* (Philadelphia: 1900), pp. 332–333; "Gordon, Samuel," *UJE*, vol. 5, pp. 65–66.

110. PC–M (November 8, 1891), p. 18; (October 6, 1901), p. 155; Martha Wolfenstein to Henrietta Szold (November 1, 1901, January 13, 1902), Szold box 2, JPSP; *AJYB* 3 (1902–1903), pp. 208, 218, 226, 310–311. Martha Wolfenstein, *Idyls of the Gass* (Philadelphia: 1901), esp. pp. 92–93.

111. S. Wolfenstein to Henrietta Szold (September 7, 1902), Szold box 2, JPSP; PC–M (October 5, 1902), p. 172; TM (October 13, 1902), p. 203; Mollie E. Osherman to JPS (February 26, 1922); Jane Manners to JPS (May 7, 1934), Correspondence Files, JPSP; PJAC; Samuel Wolfenstein, *Fiftieth Anniversary of the Jewish Orphan Asylum, Cleveland, Ohio* (Cleveland: 1918).

112. Mayer Sulzberger to Israel Zangwill (November 19, 1904) quoted in Isaac Fein, "Israel Zangwill and American Jewry," *AJHQ* 60 (1970), pp. 18–19; on this theme see Maxwell Whiteman, "The Fiddlers Rejected: Jewish Immigrant Expression in Philadelphia," in Friedman *JLIP*, pp. 80–98. In what follows, I take issue with some of Whiteman's conclusions.

113. PC–M (February 6, 1898), p.113; (March 6, 1898), p. 114; Norber Wiener, *Ex-Prodigy: My Childhood and Youth* (New York: 1953), esp. pp. 7–47; 143–163.

114. Wiener, *Ex-Prodigy*, p. 146; PC–M (January 1, 1899), p. 125; (May 3, 1908),

p. 103; *Report of the Tenth Year of the Jewish Publication Society* (Philadelphia: 1898), p. 50; Elias Schulman, "Introduction" to the Hermon Press reprint edition of Leo Wiener, *The History of Yiddish Literature in the Nineteenth Century* (New York: 1972). Henrietta Szold's comments on authors who "accepted commissions" from the Society, went to other publishers, and later saw their books offered back to the Society "at job lot prices" almost certainly refers to Wiener; see *AJYB* 15 (1913–14), p. 94.

115. Peretz had not given permission for the translation to be made and received no royalties. As it turned out, his works were not protected by copyright, and Helena Frank had thought that he had given her his blessing; still, the Society did give Peretz some belated compensation, and he was satisfied. See Philip Cowen to Louis Marshall (May 14, 1907), in Cyrus Adler Papers, American Jewish Historical Society; Cowen, *Memories*, p. 238; *AJYB* 15 (1913–14), p. 48.

116. See Henrietta Szold's interview with Marvin Lowenthal (December 29, 1935), p. 47, Szold Papers-HA. Henrietta Szold to Helena Frank (January 19, 1906), Szold box 1, JPSP reveals that she read the original Frank translation in the New York *Jewish Daily News*, published under the name "Golde."

117. Szold to "Family" (September 3, 1909), Szold Papers-HA; Helena Frank to Szold (January 30, 1906), Szold box 2, JPSP; cf. Israel Abrahams, "The Anglo-Jewish Yiddish Literary Society," *The Book of Delight and Other Papers* (Philadelphia: 1912), pp. 255–258; Solomon Grayzel, "A Talk With Helena Frank," *JPSBM* I (June, 1954), p. 7.

118. Helena Frank, "The Land of Jargon," *The Nineteenth Century* (October 1904), pp. 652–667.

119. PC–M (May 3, 1908), pp. 102–103; Sheldon Neuringer, *American Jewry and United States Immigration Policy, 1881–1953* (New York: 1980 [1969]), pp. 37–45; see Louis Marshall to Richard Gottheil (April 11, 1916) in *Louis Marshall: Champion of Liberty*, ed. Charles Reznikoff (Philadelphia: 1957), vol. I, pp. 153–154 where Marshall confirms this point and uses the Wiener and Peretz volumes as evidence that Yiddish is not a dialect, but "has a fine literature of its own."

120. PC–M (January 24, 1909), p. 118; Moshe Davis, *Beit Yisrael Be-Amerikah* (Jerusalem: 1970), esp. pp. 84, 123, 130; *UJE* vol. 7, p. 613.

121. *UJE* vol. 4, p. 411; *JE* vol. 9, p. 42; Bloch, *OMMB*, p. 87; Dash, *Summoned to Jerusalem*, pp. 39, 165; Alexandra Lee Levin and Lawrence L. Levin, "The Seltzers and D.H. Lawrence: A Biographical Narrative," in *D.H. Lawrence Letters to Thomas and Adele Seltzer*, ed. Gerald M. Lacy (Santa Barbara: 1976), pp. 171–201.

122. Jehudah Steinberg, *In Those Days* (Philadelphia: 1915); PC–M (1911–13); Meyer Waxman, *A History of Jewish Literature* (New York: 1960), vol. 4, pp. 62–70; Jacob Kabakoff, *Seekers and Stalwarts* (Jerusalem: 1978), p. 313.

123. Jehudah Steinberg, *The Breakfast of the Birds* (Philadelphia: 1917); Bloch, *OMMB* pp. 122–123; Deborah Kallen to Henrietta Szold (April 21, 1918), Szold Correspondence box 2, JPSP; Carolin A. Flexner to Joshua Bloch (April 13, 1955); Solomon Grayzel to Carolin A. Flexner (May 4, 1955), Miscellaneous Files, JPSP. For the information on where Deborah Kallen taught, I am indebted to Dr. Nathan M. Kaganoff.

124. *Fourth Biennial Report of the Jewish Publication Society* (Philadelphia: 1896), p. 7; PC–M (November 10, 1895), p. 65; (October 24, 1897), p. 100; (November 14, 1897), p. 104.

125. PC–M (March 6, 1898), p. 115; (January 14, 1909), p. 119. For other editions and translations of all JPS volumes, see Bloch, *OMMB*.

126. Louis Pendleton, *Lost Prince Almon* (Philadelphia: 1895), pp. 217–218; Eleanor E. Harris, *The Game of Doeg* (Philadelphia: 1914), pp. 184–186; PC–M (March 5, 1911), p. 214; cf. Louis Pendleton, *In Assyrian Tents* (Philadelphia: 1904); William W. Canfield, *The Sign Above the Door* (Philadelphia: 1912); Emily Solis-Cohen, *David the Giant Killer* (Philadelphia: 1908); and Harap, *Image*, pp. 135–188, esp. 149–150.

127. Miller called him "Joseph Ibn Assan"; in fact, he was known as "Joseph Ibn Sham'un." See *EJ* vol. 11, p. 757.

128. Sara Miller, *Under the Eagle's Wing* (Philadelphia: 1899), pp. 90, 212, 228.

129. Abram S. Isaacs, *The Young Champion* (Philadelphia: 1913), p. 6; on Aguilar, see Philip Weinberger, "The Social and Religious Thought of Grace Aguilar," (Ph.D., New York University, 1970); Beth Zion Abrahams, "Grace Aguilar: A Centenary Tribute," *TJHSE* 16 (1952), pp. 137–148; cf. James D. Hart, *The Popular Book* (New York: 1950), p. 98.

130. Isaac, *The Young Champion*, pp. 18, 30; cf. Abram S. Isaacs, *What Is Judaism?* (New York: 1912), pp. 75–85.

131. *AJYB* 15 (1913–14), p. 39.

132. *AJYB* 25 (1923–24), pp. 440, 444; 6 (1904–1905), p. 388. On Victorian didacticism, see Daniel W. Howe (ed.), *Victorian America* (Philadelphia: 1976), p. 22.

133. *AJYB* 11 (1909–10), p. 277. When, in 1913, the newly formed Intercollegiate Menorah Association committed itself to "the spirit of catholicity and non-partisanship in Judaism," it was with the Society's example in mind; see *AJYB* 15 (1913–14), pp. 167, 183–187.

134. PC–M (May 19, 1901), p. 153; (May 3, 1903), p. 189; (January 3, 1904), p. 202; (October 30, 1904), p. 216; (January 1, 1905), p. 223; (May 12, 1905), p. 232; (October 13, 1907), p. 61; Yitzhak Einav, "Naphtali Hertz Imber-Israel Zangwill: A Correspondence," *Studies in Zionism* 4 (October, 1981), pp. 185–213; Jacob Kabakoff (ed.), *Master of Hope: Selected Writings of Naphtali Herz Imber* (Cranbury, NJ: 1985), p. 13, cf. pp. 29–99. The complete manuscript of Imber's autobiography has never been located.

135. PC–M (May 31, 1909), p. 147; (March 6, 1910), p. 172; (April 10, 1910), pp. 180–184; Solomon Schechter to Therese Loeb Schiff (June 1, 1910), Solomon Schechter Papers, JTSA. Actually, Dr. Ephraim M. Epstein, Wengeroff's brother, may have been trying to return to the Jewish fold; see his letter to Israel Friedlaender (July 28, 1907), Friedlaender Papers, JTSA, as well as his donation to Hebrew Union College, *Proceedings of the Union of American Hebrew Congregations* 1 (1878), p. 491. See also Charles Freshman, *The Autobiography of the Rev. Charles Freshman* (Toronto: 1868), pp. 135–136. Mrs. Wengeroff's volume has never been translated in full, but selections of it appear in Lucy Dawidowicz, *The Golden Tradition* (Boston: 1966), pp. 160–168.

136. PC–M (October 13, 1907), p. 65; Henrietta Szold's interview with Marvin Lowenthal (December 29, 1935), Szold Papers–HA, pp. 42–43.

137. *AJYB* 11 (1909), p. 276; cf. 10 (1908–1909), p. 263.

138. See Naomi W. Cohen's discussion of "The Proper American Jew" in her *The Encounter With Emancipation: The German Jews in the United States 1830–1914* (Philadelphia: 1984), pp. 109–158.

139. *AJYB* 15 (1913–14), p. 81; cf. 19 (1917–18), p. 510.

140. "To the Chairman and members of the Publication Committee" (June 14, 1921), Miscellaneous box 120, JPSP. Although slightly later than the period we are considering in this chapter, the sentiments expressed reflect those of earlier decades as well.

141. *AJYB* 3 (1901–1902), p. 198; see also Cyrus Adler to Henrietta Szold (May 10, 1914); (July 20, 1914), Adler Letters, box 117, JPSP.

142. *AJYB* 11 (1909–10), p. 279.

143. PC–M (May 2, 1909), p. 142.

144. *AJYB* 5 (1903–1904), p. 227; Simon Miller, "Edwin Wolf," *AJYB* 37 (1935–36), pp. 55–60.

145. See Abraham Millgram and Emma Ehrlich, "Nine Letters From Solomon Schechter to Henrietta Szold," *Conservative Judaism* 32:2 (1979), p. 28.

146. *AJYB* 15 (1913–14), pp. 36, 74, 366, 384, 476. The Society published reports on its membership and financial state annually in the *American Jewish Year Book*.

147. *AJYB* 10 (1908–1909), p. 5; cf. TM (January 27, 1944) where a $10,000 contribution by Harry Scherman in his mother's memory is recorded. Scherman also served as a JPS Trustee from 1936 to 1942.

148. *AJYB* 15 (1913–14), p. 73; Executive Committee Minutes (June 8, 1904), p. 232; Circular Letter (January, 1909); Cyrus Adler to David Levy (June 9, 1909), box 168, Correspondence files, JPSP.

149. Circular Letter (January, 1909), box 168, Correspondence files, JPSP.

150. The proceedings are reprinted in *AJYB* 15 (1913–14), pp. 25–187.

151. *AJYB* 15 (1913–14), pp. 155–156.

5   *The Bible, the Classics, and the* Legends

1. This section is based on Sarna, "Jewish Bible Scholarship," pp. 83–116; cf. Harry M. Orlinsky, *Essays in Biblical Culture and Bible Translation* (New York: 1974).

2. Joseph H. Hertz, *Jewish Translations of the Bible in English* (London: 1920), pp. 4–5.

3. Sarna, "Jewish Bible Scholarship," pp. 84–92; Lance J. Sussman, "Another Look at Isaac Leeser and the First Jewish Translation of the Bible in the United States," *MJ* 5 (May, 1985), pp. 159–190; Matitiahu Tsevat, "A Retrospective View of Isaac Leeser's Biblical Work," in *EAJH*, pp. 295–313.

4. Isidor Kalisch, *Studies in Ancient and Modern Judaism* (New York: 1928), p. 266, cf. 265–281; Sussman, "Another Look at Isaac Leeser," p. 178.

5. *PUAHC* I (1873–79), p. 60, cf. pp. 40, 52, 59–62, 89–90, 125–126; Sussman, "Another Look at Isaac Leeser," p. 180; Tebbell, *History* II, p. 543.

6. Sarna, "Jewish Bible Scholarship," p. 96.

7. Davis, *Conservative Judaism*, p. 184; I.M. Wise to Bernhard Felsenthal (June 18, 1885), Felsenthal Papers, AJHS; James G. Heller, *Isaac M. Wise: His Life, Work and Thought* (New York: 1965), p. 456; *Authentic Report of the Proceedings of the Rabbinical Conference Held at Pittsburgh, November 16, 17, 18, 1885,* in Walter Jacob (ed.), *The Changing World of Reform Judaism: The Pittsburgh Platform in Retrospect* (Pittsburgh: 1985), p. 99. English Jews in the 1880s also worked for a new Jewish Bible translation; see Hertz, *Jewish Translations of the Bible in English*, p. 16.

8. *Second Biennial Report of the JPS*, p. 28.

9. Cyrus Sulzberger to Solomon Solis-Cohen (August 1, 1880; October 5, 1880), SSCA; A.S. Isaacs, "What Makes a Jew?" *The Chautauquan* 17 (1893), pp. 168–170; Isaac Hassler, "Survey of the Jewish Chautauqua Society. . . ," *Papers Presented at the Fifth Annual Session of the Summer Assembly of the Jewish Chautuaqua Society* (Philadelphia: 1902), pp. 12–27; Ellen Sue Levi Elwell, "The Founding and Early Programs of the National Council for Jewish Women: Study and Practice as Jewish Women's Religious Expression" (Ph.D., Indiana University, 1982), p. 110.

10. "The Bible for American Jews" (undated circular, [c. 1898]), BP.

11. *Report of the Ninth Year of the Jewish Publication Society of America* (Philadelphia: 1897), p. 24.

12. *Third Biennial Report of the Jewish Publication Society* (Philadelphia: 1894), p. 13.

13. The committee also included Rabbis Emil G. Hirsch and Joseph Krauskopf, but they seem to have been totally inactive. Krauskopf is recorded in the minutes as having later accepted the committee's final report. See PC–M (October 25, 1893), pp. 27–29; *AJYB* 15, p. 102.

14. PC–M (October 25, 1893), p. 28, contains the complete list of guidelines, which are reprinted in *AJYB* 15, p. 102. Compare the guidelines adopted for the Revised Version in F.F. Bruce, *The English Bible* (New York: 1970), pp. 136–137.

15. Bernhard Felsenthal to Henrietta Szold (November 7, 1893), box 168, JPSP.

16. See, for example, Israel Abrahams chapter on Leeser in his *By-Paths in Hebraic Bookland* (Philadelphia: 1920), pp. 254–259.

17. PC–M (January 13, 1895), p. 51; *Reform Advocate* 1 (June 13, 1896), p. 1; Marcus Jastrow to Mayer Sulzberger (June 17, 1896), in the collection of Maxwell Whiteman.

18. Bernhard Felsenthal to Henrietta Szold (November 7, 1893), box 168, JPSP; *Reform Advocate* 1 (June 13, 1896), p. 1.

19. Administrative difficulties can be traced directly in PC–M, or as excerpted in "The Bible Translation of the Jewish Publication Society," a typescript found in the Bible Papers at JPS headquarters. For the cost estimate, see PC–M (March 3, 1895), p. 58.

20. *AJYB* 15 (1913–14), p. 105.

21. These two paragraphs are based on letters found in Marcus Jastrow's letterbook, BP. Many of the letters are faded or illegible, but all can be dated between 1896–1900. See also PC–M (April 5, 1903), pp. 185–186. For Morais's translation of Jeremiah, see collection *P-55, AJHS.

22. *Report of the Eleventh Year of the Jewish Publication Society* (Philadelphia: 1899), p. 17.

23. Jastrow to Frederick de Sola Mendes (January 4, 1897); Jastrow to Kaufmann Kohler (n.d. [1897]), Jastrow letterbook, BP.

24. PC–M (February 2, 1902), p. 163 (quoted); (December 12, 1897), p. 107; (February 6, 1898), p. 112; (May 1, 1898), p. 117; (January 1, 1899), p. 125; (March 5, 1899), p. 129; (March 2, 1902), p. 164; (November 2, 1902), p. 174. On Kittredge, see Bartlett J. Whiting, "George Lyman Kittredge," *Dictionary of American Biography*, Supplement 3, (New York: 1973), pp. 422–424; and Clyde K. Hyder, *George Lyman Kittredge* (Lawrence, KS: 1962), esp. pp. 85, 108.

25. PC–M (April 6, 1902), p. 167; *AJYB* 15 (1913–14), p. 108. *The Book of Psalms* (Philadelphia: 1903), pp. 307–311; compare *The Psalms* (New York: 1901). Kohler's personal copy of this Protestant pocket Psalter is preserved in the Klau Library of Hebrew Union College, Cincinnati.

26. *AJYB* 6 (1904–1905), p. 402.

27. *AJYB* 6 (1904–1905), p. 385; note to the author from Edwin Wolf 2nd For a more critical appraisal, see J.D. Eisenstein, *Critical Notes on the New English Version of the Book of Psalms Published by the Jewish Publication Society* (New York: 1906).

28. Adapted from PC–M (April 5, 1903), pp. 185–186.

29. Solomon Schechter to Mayer Sulzberger (June 14, 1907), box 147, JPSP.

30. Henrietta Szold to Bernhard Felsenthal (November 9, 1907), Felsenthal Papers, AJHS; PC–M (February 5, 1905), p. 225; (March 12, 1905), p. 231; *AJYB* 7 (1905–1906), JPS Section, pp. 8–9, 15–16.

31. PC–M (October 29, 1905), p. 3; (March 17, 1907), p. 47; (December 8, 1907), pp. 71–72; Schechter to Sulzberger (June 14, 1907), box 147, JPS Papers, PJAC; cf. Bernhard Felsenthal to Henrietta Szold (October 29, 1907); Szold to Felsenthal (November 8, 1907) in Felsenthal Papers, AJHS where Felsenthal agrees with Schechter's analysis; and Adler's retrospect in *AJYB* 18 (1916–17), p. 63.

32. *CCARYB* 17 (1907), p. 35.

33. *CCARYB* 17 (1907), p. 141; 18 (1908), p. 149. For other details of the plan, see Sulzberger's report in PC–M (December 8, 1907), pp. 72–73.

34. Mayer Sulzberger to David Philipson (October 28, 1907), Philipson to Sulzberger (October 31, 1907), Sulzberger to Philipson (December 19, 1907), box 2, David Philipson Papers, AJA; Sulzberger to Adler (November 26, 1907), Cyrus Adler Papers, AJHS; PC–M (December 8, 1907), pp. 72–73. Earlier accounts by Cyrus Adler in *AJYB* 15 (1913–14), pp. 110–112, by David Philipson in his "Cyrus Adler and the Bible Translation," *AJYB* 42 (1940–41), pp. 693–697, and by Max Margolis in *The Story of Bible Translations* (Philadelphia: 1917) are incomplete, if not misleading.

35. PC–M (February 2, 1908), p. 80.

36. George Dobsevage to Henrietta Szold (February 3, 1908), BP; PC–M (February 2, 1908), p. 80, (April 5, 1908), p. 89.

37. The full text of the memorandum is in PC–M (April 5, 1908), pp. 89–90, and is reprinted in *AJYB* 15 (1913–14), pp. 110–111. Interestingly, the typescript of the April 5, 1908, publication committee minutes found in Philipson's papers (box 2/15) in AJA lack the critical paragraph dealing with Margolis. For descriptions of the Adler-Philipson meeting, see Adler, *IHCTD*, pp. 287–288; David Philipson, "Cyrus Adler and the Bible Translation," *AJYB* 42 (1940–41), p. 694. In his memoirs, Adler (p. 288) claims that Margolis was actually chosen by the board of editors after they convened. If true, this was merely a formality; Margolis was selected first.

38. Kohler described him as "a scholar of note, a man of high aims and ideals, thoroughly imbued with the spirit of Reform Judaism, no Zionist, not a one-sided man." Quoted in Michael A. Meyer, "A Centennial History of the Hebrew Union College-Jewish Institute of Religion," *Hebrew Union College-Jewish Institute of Religion at One Hundred Years*, edited by Samuel E. Karff (Cincinnati, 1976), p. 63.

39. This section is based on Greenspoon, *Margolis*, which Professor Greenspoon very kindly permitted me to read in manuscript; as well as on Meyer, "A Centennial History of the Hebrew Union College-Jewish Institute of Religion," pp. 63–68; Robert Gordis (ed.), *Max Leopold Margolis: Scholar and Teacher* (Philadelphia: 1952); and Harry M. Orlinsky, *Essays in Biblical Culture and Bible Translation* (New York: 1974), pp. 305–310.

40. Max Margolis to Solomon Schechter (April 23, 1907), Schechter Papers, JTS; Mayer Sulzberger to Cyrus Adler (November 26, 1907), Adler Papers, AJHS.

41. "When ... I suggested Margolis' name, Dr. Adler was frankly surprised and greatly pleased." David Philipson, "Cyrus Adler and the Bible Translation," *AJYB* 42 (1940–41), p. 694; idem, *My Life As An American Jew* (Cincinnati: 1941), p. 197. Philipson also errs in calling Margolis a professor at Dropsie College, which he did not become until later.

42. Full details of the CCAR deliberations are found in PC–M (April 5, 1908), pp. 91–96; cf. *CCARYB* 18 (1908), pp. 149–151.

43. For a full discussion of this issue, see Greenspoon, *Margolis*, pp. 64–71.

44. Henrietta Szold to Max Margolis (April 11, 1908; May 13, 1908); Margolis to Szold (May 27, 1908; June 22, 1908), BP; Mayer Sulzberger to David Philipson (July 31, 1908), box 2, Philipson Papers, AJA; Sulzberger to Solomon Schechter (August 2, 1908); Schechter to Sulzberger (September 11, 1908), Schechter Papers, JTS; TM (February 2, 1908), pp. 281–282, (October 17, 1909), pp. 309–310.

45. Mayer Sulzberger to Cyrus Adler (November 26, 1907), Adler Papers, AJHS. Of course, some never forgave Ehrlich for having briefly converted to Christianity; see Jacob Kabakoff, "New Light on Arnold Bogomil Ehrlich," *AJA* 36:2 (November, 1984), pp. 202–224. See also Joseph Reider's comments on Ehrlich's influence in *JQR* 14 (1923–24), p. 336. The state of Jewish Bible Scholarship in this period is surveyed in Orlinsky, *Essays in Biblical Culture and Bible Translation*.

46. Greenspoon, *Margolis*, pp. 61–64, traces Margolis's progress and careful schedule. For the letter to Adler and the financial arrangements, see Margolis to Adler (September 24, 1909), BP; TM (October 17, 1909), pp. 309–310; and Margolis to George Dobsevage (March 9, 1910), BP.

47. Margolis's workbooks can still be examined at Dropsie College. For the estimated number of changes, see TM (October 17, 1909), p. 309. A rejected draft of the preface to the 1917 translation, preserved in the Samuel Schulman Papers, AJA (box 11/4), refers to "some 40,000 new proposals, major and minor." This latter reference was deleted from the final version of the preface because Margolis realized that "the 40,000 new proposals presuppose the RV as a basis," something that the board of editors was no longer prepared to do; see Margolis to Adler (October, 1916), BP.

48. *Report of Committee on Bible Work* (1909) in BP; *AJYB* 11 (1909–10), pp. 265–269; 12 (1910–11), p. 361; "Pledges to Bible Fund" [c. April, 1913] in BP. Schiff's munificent contribution was announced in a letter to Morris Wolf (March 16, 1913), but the terms were later modified: See Wolf to Schiff (May 2, 1913); Schiff to JPS (November 18, 1913; November 20, 1913); Schiff to Simon Miller (November 26, 1913); Miller to Schiff (November 29, 1913), all in BP; TM (November 23, 1913), pp. 84–85; cf. Cyrus Adler, *Jacob H. Schiff: His Life and Letters* (New York: 1929) II, 62–64.

49. Adler, *IHCTD*, pp. 288–89; Philipson, *My Life*, p. 197; Cyrus Adler to Jacob Schiff (March 26, 1909), in *Adler Letters* I, pp. 154–155.

50. "The New English Translation of the Bible," *AJYB* 19 (1917–18), pp. 167–168.

51. Adler, *IHCTD*, p. 288; see *Adler Letters*, p. 235.

52. Samuel Schulman to Cyrus Adler (May 18, 1916); Cyrus Adler to David Philipson (June 21, 1916); Max Margolis to Samuel Schulman (June 19, 1916) in box 2, files 1, 14, Philipson Papers, AJA; Adler to Philipson (May 10, 1916); Schulman to Kohler (June 16, 1916), BP; Schulman to Adler (May 11, 1916) and copies of subsequent correspondence in box 11 file 4, Samuel Schulman Papers, AJA.

53. *AJYB* 19 (1917–18), p. 169; the best-known subsequent translation to follow this format is the Revised Standard Version of 1952.

54. *AJYB* 19 (1917–18), p. 171; Greenspoon, *Margolis*, pp. 68–71; cf. Max Margolis, *The Story of Bible Translations* (Philadelphia: 1917), pp. 78, 97, 104.

55. The correspondence is summarized in Adler to "The Members of the Board of Editors of the Bible Translation" (August 21, 1916), box 2 file 14, Philipson Papers, AJA; cf. *AJYB* 19 (1917–18), p. 189.

56. The figure is found in a discarded version of the preface in box 11 file 4 of the Samuel Schulman Papers, AJA; Margolis in *The Story of Bible Translations*, p. 102, suggests that the number of meeting days may have been even longer. According to its preface, the Revised Version consumed 792 working days spread over fourteen years.

57. "Preface," *The Holy Scriptures* (Philadelphia: 1917), p. ix; *AJYB* 18 (1916–17), p. 420; 19 (1917–18), p. 168.

58. Cyrus Adler to David Philipson (April 15, 1914), in *Adler Letters* I, p. 250, contains the first discussion I can find of the introduction. Cyrus Adler to Solomon Schechter (November 10, 1915), BP summarizes various views. Drafts of several proposed prefaces may be found in box 11 file 4 of the Samuel Schulman Papers, AJA.

59. Adler to Schechter (November 10, 1915), BP; see *AJYB* 19 (1917–18) for a lengthy and more technical discussion of the translation. A massive mimeographed volume entitled *Notes on the New Translation of the Holy Scriptures* (Philadelphia: 1921), based on notes Margolis provided to the translation committee (as edited and typewritten by H.S. Linfield) was also prepared in limited edition. It lists variants in the ancient versions and explains how different Jewish exegetes and grammarians understood a word or phrase, but does not reveal how the Society reached its own decisions. I am grateful to my father, Professor Nahum M. Sarna, for this information.

60. The translators deleted a claim found in an earlier draft that "Jews ... may be expected to have an intimate feeling for the niceties of Hebrew idiom, and are more apt for this reason to do justice to the genius of the Hebrew language." Untitled 29-page preface in box 11 file 4 of the Samuel Schulman Papers, AJA, p. 12.

61. *The Old Testament Translated ... And Revised* (London: 1905), p. v; *The Holy Bible ... Newly Edited by the American Revision Committee* (New York: 1901), p. iv; See Cyrus Adler to Solomon Schechter (November 10, 1915), BP: "I also thought in view of the maliciousness of the Revisers ... that we should not only indicate the continuity of the Jewish tradition of Biblical interpretation but also point out to them that all of their own great Versions were either dependent on a Jewish translation or was [sic] clearly influenced by Jewish exegetes and that they consciously departed from these for their theological purposes."

62. *The Holy Scriptures* (Philadelphia: 1917 [1955]), pp. vi, viii.

63. Cyrus Adler to Samuel Schulman (November 5, 1916); Samuel Schulman to Cyrus Adler (October 2, 1916), both in BP; see also Max Margolis to Cyrus Adler (n.d. [October 1916]) and Max Margolis to Stephen S. Wise (October 27, 1916), BP, as well as the 1908 correspondence between Margolis and Wise cited by Greenspoon, *Margolis*, pp. 65, 67.

64. Adler to Schulman (November 5, 1916); Schulman to Adler (October 30, 1916), BP; Adler to Margolis (November 22, 1916), box 9, PB; Adler to I. George Dobsevage (November 29, 1916), BP; *The Holy Scriptures*, p. vi.

65. Melvin I. Urofsky, *A Voice That Spoke for Justice: The Life and Times of Stephen S. Wise* (Albany: 1982), p. 15. Of course, questions remain with regard to Wise's dissertation, which Jacob Kabakoff and others have alleged to be plagiarized. In addition to the evidence put forward by Urofsky (p. 14), one might note that Henry Gersoni, the alleged ghostwriter of the work, was none-too-reliable in terms of what he took credit for—as the Society's experience with the man (see chapter 3) amply demonstrates.

66. Minutes of the conference committee on Bible printing (1913–14) interspersed with PC–M; Adler, *IHCTD*, p. 290; *AJYB* 19 (1917–18), p. 168; Hellmut Lehmann-Haupt, *The Book in America* (New York: 1951), pp. 190, 284; see also Cyrus Adler to Henrietta Szold (June 2, 1914), box 9, PB.

67. Simon Miller to Max Margolis (November 26, 1915), Margolis Papers, Dropsie College; *AJYB* 18 (1916–17), p. 420.

68. *AJYB* 18 (1916–17), p. 420; Adler, *IHCTD*, p. 290; see also Cyrus Adler to Henrietta Szold (October 25, 1916), box 9, PB; and the lengthy correspondence between Adler and the Lakeside Press in this box and in box 117. For the copy presented to Schiff, see Cyrus Adler to Isaac Landman (November 5, 1916); box 120, JPSP; R.R. Donnelley & Sons to Adler (December 19, 1916), box 9, PB; and Schiff's expression of gratitude in *JExp* (January 26, 1917), p. 2.

69. The proceedings of the dinner were published in a special commemorative issue of the *JExp* 64 (January 26, 1917); see also Adler, *IHCTD*, p. 290; and Philipson, *My Life*, p. 200. Plans for the dinner are described in Adler to Schiff (January 2, 1917), PB.

70. Surviving correspondence suggests that Adler overdramatized events. Hoffman's discovery is written in an urgent message to Adler dated one day later, and Adler wrote to Samuel Schulman that the error was discovered "within forty-eight hours after the advance copies were sent." Adler, *IHCTD*, p. 290; Charles Hoffman to Cyrus Adler (January 23, 1917); R.H. Donnelley & Sons to Adler (January 24, 1917); "Instructions & queries of Dr. Adler to the Donnelley Co. Telephone, January 25, 1917" (typewritten memo); Adler to Donnelley & Sons (January 31, 1917); Samuel Schulman to Cyrus Adler (February 7, 1917); and especially Cyrus Adler to Samuel Schulman (February 9, 1917), all in box 9, PB. Copies of the defective Bible survive in the rare book room of the Klau Library, Hebrew Union College, Cincinnati. For Hoffman's discovery of the subsequent error, see Hoffman to Adler (July 21, 1937), box 120, JPSP. In 1925, Rabbi Henry P. Mendes claimed that he "chanced to find the misprint" back in 1917 that caused the early volumes to be withdrawn. I know of no evidence to support this claim; see Mendes to Dobsevage (May 3, 1925), "Correspondence 1917–27" file, JPSP.

71. Distribution figures from *AJYB* 20 (1918–19), pp. 417–418; 27 (1925–26), p. 495; Julius Grodinsky to Cyrus Adler (January 28, 1929), box 148, JPSP. No full-scale study of the translation's spread and cultural impact exists; for the relationship with Hertz, see Cyrus Adler to J. Solis Cohen (November 5, 1935), Adler Correspondence, JPSP.

72. Adler, *IHCTD*, p. 288; Grayzel, "Oral History," p. 66.

73. A thorough survey of responses to the 1917 translation is beyond our scope; some reviews are mentioned in correspondence, others were clipped for the files. For reviews noticed here, see David Philipson to Cyrus Adler (April 2, 1917), box 9, PB; Cyrus Adler to David Philipson (May 22, 1917), BP; I.G. Dobsevage to Cyrus Adler (July 18, 1917), box

155, JPSP; Adler to Max Margolis (August 30, 1917), box 117, Adler Correspondence, JPSP; J.D. Eisenstein, *Critical Notes on the New English Version of the Book of Psalms* (New York: 1906), pp. 3–4; Morris David Levine, *Kitve Moshe Halevi* (New York: 1937), pp. 237–239. Levine's criticisms echo attacks made on Moses Mendelssohn's translation of the Bible into German.

74. Quoted in Hertz, *Jewish Translations of the Bible in English*, p. 20.

75. *JExp* 64 (January 26, 1917), p. 2.

76. He argued in the same letter that "We must save the Bible from the *goyim* if Judaism is still worth anything to us." Solomon Schechter to Mayer Sulzberger (April 5, 1899), Schechter Papers, JTS; *AJYB* 15 (1913–14), pp. 173–174.

77. PC–M (January 7, 1906), pp. 9–10; for earlier considerations see (April 6, 1902), p. 168; (October 29, 1905), p. 3; cf. Cyrus Adler, *Lectures, Selected Papers, Addresses* (Philadelphia: 1933), p. 94.

78. "Bible Commentary: Extracts from the minutes of the Jewish Publication Society of America"; "To the Publication Committee of the Jewish Publication Society" (April 1, 1914), both in box 157, JPSP; "Advertisement to the Series," bound in with Max L. Margolis, *Micah* (Philadelphia: 1908); cf. *AJYB* 15 (1913–14), pp. 173–177; Solomon Schechter, *Seminary Addresses and Other Papers* (New York: 1959), pp. 3–5, 35–39; Herbert Parzen, *Architects of Conservative Judaism* (New York: 1964), pp. 36–38.

79. *AJYB* 11 (1909–10), p. 260; Thomas K. Cheyne (ed.), *Micah* (Cambridge: 1882). Reading Cheyne and Margolis side by side reveals many points at which the latter is obviously a response to the former. Cheyne (p. 9) cites the date of Micah given in the heading (verse 1) and writes, "there is difficulty, however, in accepting this date." Margolis's *Micah* responds (p. 1), "There is no reason to doubt the accuracy of the date given in the heading." For another telling example, compare the two commentaries on "high places" in Micah 1:5.

80. Margolis, *Micah*, esp. pp. 1–16, 83–86; Cyrus Adler to Louis Finkelstein (December 27, 1934), in *Adler Letters* II, p. 289. Schechter's daughter, Amy, "was among the early converts to Communism, emigrating to Russia in the early twenties where she stayed for a few years"; Eli Ginzberg, "The Seminary Family: A View From My Parents' Home," *Perspectives on Jews and Judaism: Essays in Honor of Wolfe Kelman,* ed. Arthur A. Chiel (New York: 1978), p. 119.

81. Kohler to Cyrus Adler (March 24, 1914), Sulzberger Papers, Dropsie College; *AJYB* 15 (1913–14), pp. 173–177; Israel Friedlaender to Mayer Sulzberger (May 5, 1914), Sulzberger Papers, Dropsie College; a letter from A. Stolaroff (February 18, 1909) in box 168, JPSP also calls for a commentary with a Hebrew text. For other correspondence and minutes dealing with the Commentary after Schechter's demise, see box 157, JPSP.

82. Reider/Hirschfeld file, box 35, PB; Joseph Reider, *Deuteronomy With Commentary* (Philadelphia: 1937), p. xxvii, cf. p. vii.

83. Julius H. Greenstone, *Numbers: A Commentary* (Philadelphia: 1939); *Proverbs: With Commentary* (Philadelphia: 1950); PC–M (May 1, 1943).

84. A. Cohen (ed.), *Joshua and Judges* (London: 1950), p. v, cf. xiii–xv; *AJYB* 74 (1973), p. 641.

85. *JExp* 64 (January 26, 1917), p. 2; Philipson, *My Life*, pp. 249–250.

86. Cyrus Adler, *Jacob H. Schiff: His Life and Letters* (Garden City, NY: 1929) II, p. 64; for a similar account with Adler in a more prominent role see Adler to Mayer Sulzberger (October 27, 1920), in *Adler Letters* II, pp. 21–22.

87. PC–M (January 24, 1909), p. 120–121; (March 7, 1909), pp. 129–130. This definition of "classic" is credited to the Austrian Jewish scholar Meir Friedmann, known as "Ish Shalom."

88. The 1910 brochure announcing the "Library of Post-Biblical Hebrew Literature" may be found among the unsorted miscellaneous correspondence in JPSP. The more

comprehensive 1911 brochure entitled "The Hebrew Classics" survives in the Klau Library, Hebrew Union College, Cincinnati, OH (SC box/A-78/74); see also Schwartz,"JE," pp. 43–44.

89. On Singer, see Schwartz, "JE," pp. 37–66, 131–174 as well as his letters in the AJA.

90. Hirsch served as an editor of the Bible department in the *Jewish Encyclopedia* and wrote the introduction for Singer's *Russia at the Bar of the American People: A Memorial of Kishinef* (New York: 1904), a volume probably designed to compete with the Society's volume on the massacre, which was edited by Adler and published at about the same time; see also Schwartz, "JE," pp. 43, 190–192, 201, 204. For a typical example of Singer's flattering tactics, see his letter to Louis Ginzberg (June 19, 1914), Ginzberg Papers.

91. Adler to Schechter (February 18, 1914); Adler to Philipson (February 18, 1914); "Hebrew Classics Series" (3-page summary of deliberations 1912–14), box 155, JPSP. For Singer's angry reaction to Schiff's move, see his letter to Ginzberg (June 19, 1914), Ginzberg Papers.

92. *AJYB* 19 (1917–18), pp. 533–534; Cyrus Adler to Solomon Schechter (October 29, 1914); Schechter to Adler (October 30, 1914), box 155, JPSP; Kohler to Adler (March 24, 1914), Sulberger Papers.

93. Minutes of the Jewish Classics Committee (July 21, 1914), box 154, JPSP.

94. Mayer Sulzberger to Cyrus Adler (March 23, 1914), Sulzberger Papers; Cyrus Adler to Mayer Sulzberger (October 27, 1920), in *Adler Letters* II, p. 21.

95. Kohler to Adler (March 24, 1914), (April 8, 1914), Sulzberger Papers; Kohler to Adler (July 17, 1914), box 168, JPSP; Sulzberger to Adler (March 23, 1914), Sulzberger Papers.

96. Schechter to Adler (March 19, 1914), box 155, JPSP; cf. his quite different formal letter to Adler (March 27, 1914), Sulzberger Papers.

97. Schechter to Adler (June 25, 1914), box 155, JPSP.

98. "Report of the Committee on Jewish Classics (January 8, 1915)," box 157, JPSP; Solomon Schechter to Alexander Marx (November 9, 1915), box 155, JPSP.

99. Emil G. Hirsch to Solomon Schechter (November 11, 1915), Schechter Papers, JTS; David Neumark to Cyrus Adler (February 18, 1917), cf. David Philipson to Cyrus Adler (March 3, 1916), box 23, PB. Years later, Harry Wolfson likewise objected to the idea that he would be subject to external referees. Harvard University Press had to enact a special by-law granting him exemption from this requirement; see L.S. Feuer, "Recollections of Harry Wolfson," *AJA* 28 (April, 1976), p. 35.

100. *AJYB* 19 (1917–18), pp. 534–535. Dr. Jacob R. Marcus advises me that Israel Bettan was actually in Charleston, West Virginia, at the time, not in Wheeling.

101. Ibid., pp. 535–536.

102. "Loeb, James," *Dictionary of American Biography*, Supplement 1, (1944), pp. 503–504; Tebbel, *History* II, p. 510. Although the interpretation offered here is my own, I am indebted to Prof. Henry Shapiro who generously shared with me some of his ideas on these matters, as reflected in his study in progress of Harry Wolfson. See also Harry A. Wolfson, "The Needs of Jewish Scholarship in America," *Menorah Journal* 7 (February, 1921), pp. 32–33; and Harold S. Wechsler and Paul Ritterband, "Jewish Learning in American Universities: The Literature of a Field," *MJ* 3 (October, 1983), pp. 265–266.

103. Benzion Halper, *Post-Biblical Hebrew Literature* (2 vols., Philadelphia: 1921); see PC–M (May 2, 1915), p. 121. This was the first time that the Society issued a volume that included Hebrew texts.

104. Mayer Sulzberger to Cyrus Adler (March 23, 1914), Sulzberger Papers; "Advertisement" reprinted in Israel Davidson (ed.), *Selected Religious Poems of Solomon Ibn Gabirol* (Philadelphia: 1924), p. 5; cf. *Preliminary Announcement of a Library of Post-Biblical Hebrew Literature* (New York: 1910), p. 4.

105. Schwartz, "JE," pp. 1–35; *Preliminary Announcement of a Library of Post-Biblical*

Hebrew Literature (New York: 1910), p. 4; *AJYB* 19 (1917–18), p. 512; compare for an earlier period, Michael A. Meyer, "German-Jewish Identity in Nineteenth-Century America," in Jacob Katz (ed.), *Toward Modernity: The European-Jewish Model* (New Brunswick, NJ: 1987), pp. 247–267.

106. For a striking statement of the earlier view, see Henrietta Szold, "The Jewish Publication Society of America," *Judaism at the World Parliament of Religions* (Cincinnati: 1894), pp. 329, 331; and *Adler Letters* I, p. 70.

107. "Advertisement" in *Selected Religious Poems of Solomon Ibn Gabirol*, pp. 2–3. As a byproduct of the series, America's great Jewish libraries acquired important European manuscripts. Thus, Dropsie College obtained a manuscript of Pesikta Rabbati for Benzion Halper who was assigned this volume. The manuscript subsequently disappeared only to be rediscovered recently; see Norman Cohen in *JQR* 73 (1983), pp. 215–216. I owe this reference to Rabbi Marc Bregman.

108. Simon Miller, "Cyrus Adler and the Hebrew Press," *AJYB* 42 (1940–41), pp. 700–701; Cyrus Adler to Jacob Schiff (February 27, 1917), in *Adler Letters*, p. 325; *AJYB* 17 (1915–16), p. 403; cf. Adler to Schiff [draft] (April 17, 1918), miscellaneous box 120, JPSP; Adler, *IHCTD*, pp. 280–81; Adler, *Lectures, Selected Papers, Addresses*, pp. 146–147.

109. Cyrus Adler, "A New Hebrew Press," *Journal of the American Oriental Society*, 41 (1921), pp. 225–229; *AJYB* 21 (1919), p. 698.

110. I.G. Dobsevage to Cyrus Adler (July 18, 1917), box 155, JPSP; Miller, "Cyrus Adler and the Hebrew Press," pp. 700–701.

111. Alexander Marx, "Jacob H. Schiff and the Jewish Classics," *AJYB* 49 (1947–48), pp. 828–829.

112. "Minutes of the Classics Committee (November 29, 1922)," p. 10, in box 154, JPSP.

113. Minutes of the Classics Committee as well as related correspondence may be found in box 154, JPSP; see also Cyrus Adler to James Loeb (December 20, 1926), box 120; as well as the correpondence with Moses Gaster in box 17, PB.

114. See, in addition to items cited in previous notes, Adler to Mordecai Kaplan (October 22, 1931) and Adler to Samuel Schulman (October 22, 1931) box 24, PB.

115. Cyrus Adler to Jacob Lauterbach (May 29, 1930), box 25, JPSP, and Julius Grodinsky to Cyrus Adler (March 5, 1934), JPSP, reveal details of the financial problems; see also TM.

116. Cyrus Adler Memo (April 3, 1935), box 117; Cyrus Adler to Julius Grodinsky (December 20, 1932), box 25, JPSP; [London] *Jewish Chronicle* (December 13, 1935), p. 22.

117. See, especially, the Yale Judaica Series, established by Yale University Press in 1944, and the Jewish Classical Library, published by East and West Library beginning in 1945. Significantly, neither series printed any Hebrew texts, much less critical editions.

118. *JPSBM* 9 (December, 1962), pp. 2–3; see also on this series the correspondence between Alexander Altmann and Solomon Grayzel (December 2, 5, 11, 1963) in unsorted correspondence, JPSP. Volumes issued in the Judaica: Texts and Translations Series include Martin A. Cohen (ed.), *Samuel Usque's Consolation for the Tribulations of Israel* (1964); Morris Epstein (ed.), *Tales of Sendebar* (1967); Gerson D. Cohen (ed.), *The Book of Tradition (Sefer Ha-Qabbalah) by Abraham Ibn Daud* (1967); and David Berger (ed.), *The Jewish-Christian Debate in the High Middle Ages: A Critical Edition of the Nizzahon Vetus* (1979).

119. Henrietta Szold to Simon Miller (December 1, 1915), Sulzberger Papers. The annuity was funded by contributions from such leading American Jews as Julius Rosenwald, Louis Brandeis, Irving Lehman, Mary Fels, and, of course, Mack himself; see Harry Barnard, *The Forging of an American Jew: The Life and Times of an American Jew* (New York: 1974), p. 103.

120. Henrietta Szold to Alice L. Seligsberg (September 8, 1915) in Marvin Lowenthal, *Henrietta Szold: Life and Letters* (New York: 1942), p. 90.

121. Ginzberg, *KOTL*, pp. 59–79; *AJYB* 46 (1944–45), pp. 603–604; PC–M (October 6,

1901), p. 155; David Druck, *Rabbi Levi Ginzberg* ([in Hebrew], New York: 1933), pp. 58–72; Harry H. Mayer, "What Price Conservatism? Louis Ginzberg and the Hebrew Union College," *AJA* 10 (1958), pp. 145–150.

122. T.J. Jackson Lears: *No Place of Grace: Antimodernism and the Transformation of American Culture 1880–1920* (New York: 1981), p. 169; Ginzberg, *KOTL*, p. 57.

123. "Ginzberg, Legends of the Jews," record of PC activities, in Szold card file, JPS; Louis Ginzberg, "Preface," *Legends of the Jews* (Philadelphia: 1909–38) I, vii–xv; V, vii–xi.

124. Quotes are from Henrietta Szold's diary as cited in Alexandra Lee Levin to Solomon Grayzel (June 30, 1959), box 26, JPSP; and Irvin Fineman, *Woman of Valor: The Story of Henrietta Szold* (New York: 1961), p. 135. Fineman, pp. 119–243, is the most complete account; see also Levin, *SOLS*, pp. 372–384; Joan Dash, *Summoned to Jerusalem* (New York: 1979), pp. 47–104; Ginzberg, *KOTL*, 105–129.

125. Szold diary cited in Levin to Grayzel (July 18, 1959), Uncatalogued—"Levin File," JPSP; Solomon Schechter to Mayer Sulzberger (March 8, 1909), Schechter Papers, JTS; Henrietta Szold to Cyrus Adler (July 15, 1909) in Lowenthal, *Henrietta Szold*, p. 61.

126. Henrietta Szold to Elvira N. Solis (December 12, 1909), in Lowenthal, *Henrietta Szold*, p. 67.

127. Henrietta Szold to Louis Levin (January 13, 1905), Szold Papers, Hadassah Archives, NY; Ginzberg, *KOTL*, p. 117.

128. Quotations from Szold diary, as copied by Irving Fineman, and found in box 1 file 7 of the Henrietta Szold Papers, Schlesinger Library, Cambridge, MA.

129. Henrietta Szold to Mayer Sulzberger (June 8, 1910), Szold Correspondence, box 1, JPSP; Mayer Sulzberger to Henrietta Szold (June 10, 1910), Szold Correspondence, box 2, JPSP.

130. On Paul Radin, see *EJ* 13, col. 1498–99; *Who's Who in American Jewry* (New York: 1927), pp. 485–486. Whether Radin was also the translator of volume 4, published in 1913, is unclear. He is not listed on the title page, and Ginzberg, *KOTL*, p. 74, claims that Radin bore Ginzberg "a lifelong grudge for preventing him from translating the fourth volume—a decision over which the author had no control." But the text of volume 4 was originally included in material given to Radin to translate for inclusion in volume 3, and the minutes give no hint of another translator. Could Radin have been upset that Ginzberg failed to recommend him as translator of his notes?

131. Henrietta Szold to Alice Seligsberg (July 28, 1911), Szold Papers, Hadassah Archives, NY; Dash, *Summoned to Jerusalem*, pp. 98–100.

132. Arthur Hertzberg, "Henrietta Szold," *Notable American Women* (Cambridge: 1971), vol. 3, p. 418; Henrietta Szold to Cyrus Adler (December 1, 1915), Hadassah Archives, NY.

133. Henrietta Szold to Mayer Sulzberger (December 1, 1915), Sulzberger Papers.

6   *The Lean Years*

1. Cyrus Adler, "Benzion Halper," *AJYB* 26 (1925), pp. 459–471; Benzion Halper, "Autobiography," *Genazim*, ed. G. Kressel, (Jerusalem: 1961), vol. 1, p. 100.

2. George Dobsevage to Lionel Friedmann (November 27, 1925), PC–C.

3. Moses Rischin (ed.), *Grandma Never Lived in America: The New Journalism of Abraham Cahan* (Bloomington, IN: 1985), pp. 61–63; see also *EAJH*, p. 456; and *JE* vol. 6, p. 629. Henrietta Szold noted the similarity between Dobsevage and his father in her journal entry of April 11, 1910, file 7, Szold Papers–SL.

4. For criticisms of Dobsevage and insights into his problems at the Society, see especially Dobsevage to H.G. Friedenwald (June 14, 1921); Solomon Solis-Cohen to Simon

Miller (October 6, 1921), box 147, JPSP; Yehoash to Dobsevage (July 23, 1922; August 11, 1922), box 45, JPSP; Max Margolis to Dobsevage (May 14, 1924), box 147, JPSP; Dobsevage to Alexander Marx (April 22, 1927), Marx Papers, JTS.

5. For Adler's role in the Society, see especially *AJYB* 41 (1939–40), pp. 693–707; Adler to Solomon Schechter (January 5, 1915), box 155, JPSP; and Adler to Julius Grodinsky (October 19, 1926), unsorted correspondence, JPSP.

6. Edwin H. Schloss, "Simon Miller," *AJYB* 47 (1945–46), pp. 201–206; Simon Miller to Cyrus Adler (November 25, 1927), Adler to Miller (November 30, 1927), TC.

7. Six members of the committee were listed as "Reverend Dr.," all of them connected with the Reform movement. Seven were listed as just plain "Dr.," six of them actively associated with the Conservative movement. Jacob Kohn, the only committee member with the title "Rabbi," was also a Conservative Jew, giving that movement a slight edge. There were six practicing rabbis on the committee, five full-time scholars, and at least half a dozen members who were born in Eastern Europe. Six members of the committee either bore the title "the Hon." (Judges Mayer Sulzberger and Oscar S. Straus), or no title at all—they were "intelligent lay people," the kind who founded the Society back in 1888, and if need be they could sway the balance. See *AJYB* 17 (1915–16), pp. 413–415; and Cyrus Adler to Jacob Solis-Cohen (April 19, 1933), PC–C.

8. *AJYB* 17 (1915–16), pp. 426–429. Jewish population figures based on the 1917 estimate printed in *AJYB* 20 (1918–19), pp. 64–65.

9. *AJYB* 20 (1918–19), p. 419; TM April 1, 1917; Adler, *IHCTD*, p. 301. According to Abraham A. Neuman, Adler compiled the volume of Bible readings in a single night; *Cyrus Adler: A Biographical Sketch* (Philadelphia: 1942), p. 148.

10. *AJYB* 21 (1919–20), pp. 697–698; undated handbill in illustrations file, JPSP.

11. Tebbell, *History* II, pp. 93–96; *AJYB* 22 (1920–21), p. 466; 25 (1923–24), p. 442.

12. Simon Miller to Max Margolis (October 26, 1921), box 9 PB; TM, 1917–26; Financial data, box 113, JPSP; *AJYB* 21 (1919–20), pp. 691–692; 22 (1920–21), pp. 465–467; 23 (1921–22), p. 387; 24 (1922–23), pp. 383–386; 25 (1923–24), pp. 435–436; 28 (1926–27), p. 534. Several figures are given for the Society's debt. Simon Miller listed it as $120,000 on one occasion and remembered it as $118,000 on another; Cyrus Adler recalled it being "somewhat over $80,000"; *AJYB* 28 (1926–27), p. 534; 35 (1933–34), pp. 326–327.

13. JPS membership figures are from reports in the *AJYB*; for Miller's question, see *AJYB* 24 (1922–23), p. 385; see also Adler's comments on the 1928 anniversary, *AJYB* 30 (1928–29), p. 348.

14. Simon Miller raised precisely this question on at least three occasions, but he offered no answers; see *AJYB* 25 (1923–24), p. 436; 26 (1924–25), p. 685; 28 (1926–27), pp. 526–527.

15. Cyrus Adler to Felix Warburg (November 12, 1920) in *Adler Letters* II, p. 23; *AJYB* 23 (1921–22), p. 387.

16. Evyatar Friesel, "The Age of Optimism in American Judaism, 1900–1920," *A Bicentennial Festschrift for Jacob Rader Marcus* (New York: 1976), pp. 131–155. See Abba Hillel Silver's comments in *AJYB* 27 (1925–26), p. 497.

17. Robert T. Handy, "The American Religious Depression 1925–1935," *Church History* 29 (1960), pp. 3–16; David A. Hollinger, "Ethnic Diversity, Cosmopolitanism and the Emergence of the American Liberal Intelligentsia," *American Quarterly* (1975), pp. 133–151.

18. Madison, *Jewish Publishing*, pp. 253–285; Walker Gilmer, *Horace Liveright* (New York: 1970); and for a more recent survey of Jews in publishing, B. Krefetz, *Jews and Money* (New Haven: 1982), p. 74. For evidence of anti-Semitism directed against commercial Jewish publishers, see Tebbell, *History* II, p. 392; and Adele Seltzer to Dorothy Hoskins (January 28, 1923) in Gerald M. Lacy (ed.), *D.H. Lawrence Letters to Thomas and Adele Seltzer* (Santa Barbara, CA: 1976), p. 258: "You know, there really is a terribly strong feeling among the older publishers against the three rising Jewish firms. . . ."

19. Madison, *Jewish Publishing*, pp. 43–71, surveys the history of various Jewish publishing houses in America. For a proposal that the Society buy out Bloch Publishing Company, see Julius Grodinsky to Jacob Solis-Cohen, Jr. (May 4, 1933), PC–C.

20. *AJYB* 27 (1925–26), pp. 263–273.

21. *The Jewish Publication Society of America* (Philadelphia: 1888); Mayer Sulzberger to I. Schwob (October 22, 1889), MS–LB; Sulzberger to Bernhard Felsenthal (May 22, 1893), Felsenthal Papers, AJHS.

22. PC–M (November 6, 1910), p. 204; (November 2, 1913), pp. 25–27; (February 7, 1915), p. 106; *AJYB* 18 (1916–17), p. 418.

23. Harold Wechsler and Paul Ritterband, "Jewish Learning in American Universities: The Literature of a Field," *MJ* 3 (October, 1983), pp. 261–268.

24. Burton J. Bledstein, *The Culture of Professionalism* (New York: 1976); Theodore S. Hamerow, "The Professionalization of Historical Learning," *Reviews in American History* 14 (September, 1986), pp. 319–333; Lawrence W. Levine, "William Shakespeare and the American People: A Study in Cultural Transformation," *AHR* 89 (February, 1984), esp. pp. 62–64; Merle Curti, *American Scholarship in the Twentieth Century* (Cambridge, MA: 1953), pp. 5, 101; see Thorstein Veblen's discussion of "classics" in *The Theory of the Leisure Class* (Mentor ed., New York: 1953), pp. 254–258.

25. Adler's ideas were in part also behind the Alexander Kohut Foundation, founded in 1915, for the promotion of Jewish scholarship. Adler first advocated a Jewish academy in 1894; see *Adler Letters* I, p. 70; and reiterated his plea at the dinner honoring the publication of the Bible translation, see *JExp* 64 (January 26, 1917), p. 2. See also Ira Robinson, "Cyrus Adler, Bernard Revel, and the Prehistory of Organized Jewish Scholarship in the United States," *AJHQ* 69 (June, 1980), pp. 497–505; and Ira Robinson, "American Academy for Jewish Research," in Michael N. Dobkowski, *Jewish-American Voluntary Organizations* (New York: 1986), pp. 7–11.

26. *AJYB* 22 (1920–21), p. 475; PC–M (November 6, 1921), p. 3.

27. Maurice Samuel to George Dobsevage (July 29, 1921), PC–C; 'Yehoash' to Jewish Publication Society (August 11, 1922), box 45, JPSP; Solomon Solis-Cohen to Cyrus Adler (n.d. [April, 1918]); Adler to Solis-Cohen (April 21, 1918), box 120, JPSP; George Dobsevage to Solomon Solis Cohen (May 9, 1921), TC.

28. Israel Friedlaender, "Some Suggestions for the Differentiation of the Activities of the Jewish Publication Society" (typescript) in Sulzberger Papers; and, with minor differences, in PC–M (January 3, 1915), pp. 98–101.

29. PC–M (February 7, 1915), pp. 105–107; [Samuel Schulman], *Rosh Ha-Shanah and Yom Kippur* (Philadelphia: 1920); Cyrus Adler to Solomon Solis-Cohen (July 1, 1920), SSCA. The pamphlet series was later picked up by the Union of American Hebrew Congregations, which published a valuable series of brief popular studies on Jewish themes entitled variously "Jewish Tracts" and "Popular Studies in Judaism."

30. PC–M (January 1, 1919), pp. 1–2; (November 6, 1921), p. 3; Cyrus Adler to Julius Grodinsky [enclosing Seltzer proposal] (May 17, 1928); Julius Grodinsky, "A Project to Publish Books of a New Type ..." (typescript, May, 1928); Frank Schechter to Julius Grodinsky (June 15, 1928), all in TC.

31. Julius Weyl to Cyrus Adler (Dec. 6, 1928); Frank I. Schechter to Julius Weyl (December 18, 1928); Jacob Solis-Cohen to Adolph Ochs (March 8, 1934); Arthur Hays Sulzberger to Jacob Solis-Cohen (March 12, 1934), PC–C; cf. *AJYB* 38 (1936–37), pp. 667. Weyl may in private have supported JPS publication of more popular books under certain circumstances [see *AJYB* 38 (1936–37), pp. 24 and 667, for differing statements on this point], but in his correspondence with the Society I have not found reference to this view.

32. TM (May 28, 1926), p. 1; for additional data on this scandal see boxes 113, 117, 118, JPSP. Solomon Grayzel in his oral history, p. 3, presents a particularly unflattering portrait of Dobsevage's public and private life. After he left the Society's employment, however, Dobsevage led a life of penury, suffering one reversal after another.

33. "Memo on the Financial Status of the Society," box 113, JPSP; TM (May 28, 1926), p. 3.

34. Grodinsky file, University Archives and Records, University of Pennsylvania; see also Friedman, *JLIP*, pp. 81ff and 101.

35. Charles Madison, *Book Publishing in America* (New York: 1966), pp. 157–398.

36. Julius Grodinsky to Max Margolis (October 4, 1926), box 29; Grodinsky to Cyrus Adler (April 4, 1933), box 43; and correspondence with Louis Ginzberg, box 18, all in JPSP. See also Ginzberg's bitter comments about Grodinsky quoted in Ginzberg, *KOTL*, p. 181.

37. Julius Greenstone, "Isaac Husik," *AJYB* 41 (1939–50), pp. 57–65; Isaac Husik, *Philosophical Essays*, ed. Milton L. Nahm and Leo Strauss (Oxford: 1952), p. vii. "Isaac Husik," Miscellaneous file, box 118; Solomon Grayzel to Simon Greenberg [regarding Husik] (September 27, 1949), box 23; Grodinsky to Cyrus Adler and Simon Miller (March 31, 1927); Grodinsky to Simon Miller (February 3, 1935); Isaac Husik to "the President and the Board of Trustees" (April 16, 1933); Cyrus Adler to Julius Grodinsky (April 21, 1933), all in PC–C.

38. Julius Grodinsky to Alexander Marx (February 19, 19᠃), box 18, JPSP; Solomon Grayzel to Eli Ginzberg (May 7, 1965), unsorted PB.

39. Julius Grodinsky, [Memorandum on the] "Commercial and Financial Problems of the Society" (typescript, September 20, 1926), pp. 5–10, box 113, JPSP; on the Conat Press, see PC–M (January 5, 1919) and TM (September 11, 1921), p. 2. Louis Ginzberg's 1922 Hebrew responsum on the use of grape juice was also published by the press, which in Hebrew called itself the "New Hebrew Press," Philadelphia.

40. Julius Grodinsky to Howard Levy (October 18, 1926), TC; financial data, box 113, JPSP; *Rules for the Jewish Publication Society Press* (Philadelphia: 1931); and for Weyl's involvement, see especially *AJYB* 38 (1936–37), pp. 666–667.

41. *AJYB* 37 (1935–36), pp. 470–71. Italics added.

42. *AJYB* 36 (1934–35), pp. 480, 489; revenue figures for the press are recorded annually in the *AJYB* from vol. 33 (1931–32).

43. The anonymous report to the trustees, possibly authored by Grodinsky, is in Trustees Papers, "Annual Meetings, 1935–1942," JPSP.

44. The Classics were printed in editions of 500 copies, see Julius Grodinsky to Cyrus Adler (June 16, 1930), box 23, JPSP. The two non-JPS volumes printed were Emily Solis-Cohen, *Women in Jewish Law and Life* (Philadelphia: 1932), published for the Jewish Welfare Board; and Nehemiah S. Libowitz, *Additament to Penine Ha-Zohar* (Philadelphia: 1933).

45. *AJYB* 25 (1923–24), p. 439; 26 (1924–25), pp. 688–89; TM (January 6, 1924), p. 2; Israel Davidson (ed.), *Selected Religious Poems of Solomon Ibn Gabirol*, translated by Israel Zangwill (Philadelphia: 1924); see Heinrich Brody's favorable review in *JQR* 16 (1925–26), pp. 99–102.

46. Herbert M. Loewe, "Nina Salaman, 1877–1925," *TJHSE* 11 (1924–27), pp. 228–232; Nina Davis, *Songs of Exile by Hebrew Poets* (Philadelphia: 1901); Nina Salaman to Cyrus Adler (June 6, 1916; March 30, 1917), box 38, JPSP.

47. The full correspondence is preserved in box 38, JPSP; see also the story based on these papers in *Philadelphia Jewish Archives Center News* (February, 1983).

48. Correspondence and readers reports are preserved in box 1, PB.

49. Israel Abrahams, *Hebrew Ethical Wills*, with a new foreword by Judah Goldin (2 vols. in 1, Philadelphia: 1976), esp. pp. [7], xix, xxv–xxvi. A "modern treasury" of ethical wills, published in 1983, sought to be "a fitting continuation of the Abrahams work;" see Jack Riemer and Nathaniel Stampfer, *Ethical Wills: A Modern Treasury* (New York: 1983), p. xix.

50. Henry Malter, *The Treatise Ta'anit of the Babylonian Talmud* (Philadelphia: 1928), pp. xix–xx.

51. Alexander Marx, "Henry Malter," *Studies in Jewish History and Booklore* (New York: 1944), pp. 409–417, esp. pp. 413, 415; originally published in *AJYB* 36 (1926), pp. 261–272; cf. Henry Malter, *Saadia Gaon: His Life and Works* (Philadelphia: 1921), pp. 10–11; PC–M (February 7, 1915), p. 109; (May 2, 1915), p. 123.

52. Malter, *Treatise Ta'anit*, pp. xv–xvi.

53. Malter, *Treatise Ta'anit*, xv–xlvii, 31; cf. "advertisement," pp. 5–7; and Malter, *The Treatise Ta'anit of the Babylonian Talmud*, Publications of the American Academy of Jewish Research (New York: 1930); cf. Marx, *Studies in Jewish History and Booklore*, pp. 415–417; and Solomon Zeitlin's appreciation in *JQR* 21 (1930–31), pp. 61–73. Malter's use of Latin to translate sensitive passages followed standard Christian practice (e.g., the translation of the Church Fathers); see B. Barry Levy in *JBA* 44 (1956–57), p. 15, n. 15.

54. Isaac Husik (ed.), *Sefer Ha'Ikkarim: Book of Principles* (4 vols. in 5, Philadelphia: 1929–30); Eliezer Schweid (ed.), *Sefer Ha-Ikarim Le-Rabi Yosef Albo* (Jerusalem: 1967), pp. 27–28; Cyrus Adler to Isaac Husik (February 24, 1919); Julius Grodinsky to Cyrus Adler (June 16, 1930), box 23, JPSP.

55. Jacob Z. Lauterbach, *Mekilta de-Rabbi Ishmael* (3 vols., Philadelphia: 1933–35), esp. vol. I, pp. xiii–lxiv. For Michael Higger's favorable review, see *JQR* 27 (1936–37), pp. 419–420; compare his unfavorable review of a previous edition of the Mekilta (ed. H.S. Horowitz and Israel Rabin, Frankfurt A.M.: 1931) in *JQR* 26 (1935–36), pp. 301–305.

56. Moses Gaster, *Ma'aseh Book* (2 vols., Philadelphia: 1934); Louis Ginzberg to Cyrus Adler (May 25, 1921); Cyrus Adler to Moses Gaster (August 30, 1920); E. Grant [secretary to Moses Gaster] to Cyrus Adler (September 7, 1926); C. Omenson [secretary to Cyrus Adler] to E. Grant (September 22, 1926); Isaac Husik to Cyrus Adler (December 17, 1930); and other correspondence in box 17, JPSP.

57. Heinrich Brody (ed.), *Selected Poems of Moses Ibn Ezra*, translated into English by Solomon Solis-Cohen (Philadelphia: 1934).

58. Emanuel S. Goldsmith and Mel Scult (eds.), *Dynamic Judaism: The Essential Writings of Mordecai M. Kaplan* (New York: 1985), pp. 3–5; Samuel Schulman, "Report on Dr. Kaplan's Translation of 'Mesilat Yesharim' " (May 9, 1930), box 24, JPSP.

59. Kaplan in his *Judaism As a Civilization* (New York: 1967 [1934]), pp. 9–10, quotes Luzzatto to demonstrate "that for traditional Judaism the center of gravity of human existence lay not in this life but in the hereafter." Israel Efros, in his generally favorable review of Kaplan's *Mesillat Yesharim* in *JQR* 28 (1937–38), pp. 146–147 questioned whether Luzzatto actually stressed other-worldliness as much as Kaplan claimed.

60. Mordecai M. Kaplan (ed.), *Mesillat Yesharim by Moses Hayyim Luzzatto* (Philadelphia: 1936), pp. xiv–xv. For Kaplan's other views on Jewish ethics, see Goldsmith and Scult (eds.), *Dynamic Judaism*, pp. 172–197; and Mordecai M. Kaplan, "A Philosophy of Jewish Ethics," in Louis Finkelstein (ed.) *The Jews* (4th ed., New York: 1971), vol. 3, pp. 32–64 [orig. ed., 1949].

61. Kaplan, *Mesillat Yesharim*, pp. xi–xxxvii, esp. pp. xi, xiv–xv, xxix–xxxv. Samuel Schulman, "Report on Dr. Kaplan's Translation of 'Mesilat Yesharim'" (May 9, 1930); Mordecai Kaplan to Cyrus Adler (June 25, 1931), both in box 24, JPSP. Schulman made important suggestions that substantially improved Kaplan's draft and was hurt when the published volume did not acknowledge his assistance. Of course, by then Schulman had emerged as a strong critic of Kaplan's *Judaism As a Religious Civilization*; see Schulman to Adler (November 5, 1936), box 24, JPSP; and *AH* (September 30, 1932), p. 348.

62. Hermann L. Strack, *Introduction to the Talmud and Midrash* (Philadelphia: 1931), p. vii. Although the decision to publish Strack's volume in English was only made in 1922, Strack seems to have received an earlier commitment for an English version; see Hermann L. Strack to JPS (January 26, 1922); Cyrus Adler to Simon Miller (June 13, 1922); and other correspondence in box 42, JPSP; Alexander Marx, "Strack's Introduction to the Talmud and Midrash," *JQR* 13 (1922–23), pp. 352–365; and for the CCAR subvention,

CCARYB 30 (1920), p. 26. On Strack see *JE*, vol. 11, p. 559; and *EJ* vol. 15, pp. 418–419; and for Margolis's role, Bloch, *OMMB*, p. 176; see Greenspoon, *Margolis*, pp. 25–27.

63. Solomon Schechter to Henrietta Szold (March 25, 1914); Israel Dobsevage to David Philipson (April 24, 1918); "Historical Jewish Communities Series" (summary of activities, n.d.); and Solomon Grayzel to Charles Reznikoff (February 13, 1948) all in JPSP; PC–M (February 7, 1915), p. 1; (January 5, 1930), pp. 4–6.

64. The eight volumes published in the series are: Aron Freimann and F. Kracauer, *Frankfort* (Philadelphia: 1929); Elkin N. Adler, *London* (Philadelphia: 1930); Cecil Roth, *Venice* (Philadelphia: 1930); Max Grunwald, *Vienna* (Philadelphia: 1936); Raphael Straus, *Regensburg and Augsburg* (Philadelphia: 1939); Adolf Kober, *Cologne* (Philadelphia: 1940); Hermann Vogelstein, *Rome* (Philadelphia: 1940); and Israel Cohen, *Vilna* (Philadelphia: 1943). David S. Sassoon, *A History of the Jews in Baghdad* (Letchworth, England: 1949) was originally prepared for this series, but never won acceptance and was published separately (see p. iv).

65. *AJYB* 36 (1934–35), p. 496; PC–M (December 6, 1936), p. 5; Cecil Roth, "Advice for J.P.S.," *The Menorah Journal* 29 (1941), pp. 334–340; Cecil Roth, *Venice* (Philadelphia: 1930), p. ix. For Solomon Grayzel's response to Roth's "hutzpah," see his memo in box 119, JPSP.

66. Friedlaender's proposal regarding how the book should be written reflects his historiographical ideals:

> [I]n no part of the book should the presentation be a mere compilation, but it should be one that is based upon a critical attitude towards the material, an independent judgement of events and, though not original as regards scientific research, should be original as far as the underlying ideas are concerned. The manner of presentation should be warm-hearted, but not sentimental, didactic not apologetic. It should be subjective inasmuch as it would bring into prominence the lessons taught by Jewish history, but objective in as far as the author would scrupulously avoid distorting facts in the interest of any preconceived ideas. The book should be written in a style which would appeal to the adolescent reader and at the same time be acceptable to the average Jew of mature age, and should also prove serviceable as a manual.

Israel Friedlaender to "The Committee on Jewish History" (January 4, 1907); Charles E. Fox to Edwin Wolf (April 12, 1906); Israel Friedlaender to Henrietta Szold (May 6, 1910), (February 6, 1914); "History of the Jews, A One Volume" [summary of Society activities], all in box 29, JPSP; see also Shargel, *Friedlaender*, pp. 81–99.

67. TM (November 1, 1923), pp. 1–4; (January 13, 1924), pp. 1–2; (February 14, 1924), pp. 2–3; PC–M (December 9, 1923), pp. 1–3; *AJYB* 26 (1925), p. 686.

68. PC–M (January 13, 1924), pp. 1–3; Alexander Marx to George Dobsevage (January 7, 1924), box 29, JPSP; Max Margolis and Alexander Marx, *A History of the Jewish People* (Philadelphia, 1927), p. vi.

69. Max Margolis to George Dobsevage (July 18, 1924, August 6, 1924, September 4, 1924; December 5, 1924), PC–C; Cyrus Adler to Abraham Erlanger (January 11, 1926), box 29, JPSP; TM (1924–1927); cf. Marx, *Studies in Jewish History and Booklore* (New York: 1944), pp. 425–427.

70. TM (Feburary 14, 1924), p. 3; *AJYB* 26 (1924–25), p. 687; Margolis and Marx, *A History of the Jewish People*, esp. pp. v–xxii, 739. Abram L. Sachar's *A History of the Jews* published by Knopf in 1929 had some of the same aims as Margolis and Marx, but was a far more popular work.

71. Margolis and Marx, *A History of the Jewish People*, pp. 603, 737; cf. Robert Gordis (ed.), *Max Leopold Margolis* (Philadelphia: 1952), p. 47: "Dr. Margolis saw the forces of disintegration active everywhere in this country [America]." For an analysis of the politics

of periodization in modern Jewish historical writing, see Michael A. Meyer, "When Does the Modern Period of Jewish History Begin?" *Judaism* 24 (Summer, 1975), pp. 329–38.

72. Radin's manuscript engendered controversy among members of the publication committee for its portrayal of biblical history. When published, one snide reviewer deemed it appropriate only for "an immature group of boys and girls." See *AJYB* 30 (1928–29), pp. 345, 347; PC–M (November 16, 1927), p. 4; Radin file, box 35, JPSP; *American Jewish World* (August 30, 1929), p. 5.

73. Chaim Raphael, "In Search of Cecil Roth," *Commentary* 50:3 (September, 1970), pp. 75–81; Irene Roth, *Cecil Roth Historian Without Tears: A Memoir* (New York: 1982).

74. Grayzel, "Oral History," p. 22.

75. Cecil Roth, *A History of the Marranos* (Philadelphia: 1932), esp. pp. xi–xii; Cecil Roth to Cyrus Adler (January 2, 1932), box 36, JPSP.

76. Roth, "Advice for J.P.S.," pp. 337–338. Besides his books on Venice and the Marranos, the Society published in 1934 Roth's *A Life of Menasseh Ben Israel: Rabbi, Printer and Diplomat.*

77. David Philipson, *Letters of Rebecca Gratz* (Philadelphia: 1929), esp. pp. viii, 102; Cyrus Adler to David Philipson (January 29, 1929), box 34, JPSP.

78. Isaac Goldberg, *Major Noah* (Philadelphia: 1936); see the correspondence in box 19, JPSP; and Albert Friedenberg's favorable in *JQR* 28 (1937–38), p. 78. The book was also favorably reviewed by Richard Hofstadter. For other Society considerations of American Jewish history, see PC (March 2, 1919) and Cyrus Adler to Leon H. Rose (April 17, 1931), box 117, JPSP.

79. *AJYB* 35 (1933–34), p. iii.

80. Alexander B. Tager, *The Decay of Czarism: The Beiliss Trial* (Philadelphia: 1935), p. xvi, cf. p. 235; *AJYB* 37 (1935–36), pp. 473–474. See Hans Rogger, "The Beiliss Case: Anti-Semitism and Politics in the Reign of Nicholas II," *Slavic Review* 26 (1966), pp. 615–629; and for correspondence relating to the book, boxes 42–43, JPSP. Cecil Roth's *The Ritual Murder Libel and the Jew: The Report by Cardinal Lorenzo Ganganelli* (London: 1935) had very similar aims, see Harry Schneiderman, "The Ritual Murder Libel," *JQR* 27 (1936–37), pp. 179–187. Years later, JPS returned to this theme when it published Maurice Samuel's *Blood Accusation: The Strange History of the Beiliss Case* (Philadelphia: 1966). On book jackets, see Howard Alper to author (June 8, 1988) in author's possession.

81. Cyrus Adler to Alexander Marx (June 7, 1933), box 117, JPSP; TM (July 5, 1933); Marvin Lowenthal to Julius Grodinsky (July 22, 1933); Maurice Jacobs to "Frater" (September 1, 1936); Maurice Jacobs to Marvin Lowenthal (March 10, 1937; May 15, 1945); Marvin Lowenthal to Maurice Jacobs (July 18, 1937); Maurice Jacobs to Joseph Gitterman (December 23, 1936), all in box 28, JPSP.

82. Marvin Lowenthal, *The Jews of Germany: A Story of Sixteen Centuries* (Philadelphia: 1936), esp. pp. 417, 421. For somewhat different contemporary views published a few years earlier, see Jacob R. Marcus, *The Rise and Destiny of the German Jew* (Cincinnati: 1934), pp. 249–321, esp. p. 300; and Abraham Myerson and Isaac Goldberg, *The German Jew: His Share in Modern Culture* (New York: 1933).

83. PC–M (November 16, 1930), p. 1.

84. The Society published the book under the name "Sholom Ash," but "Sholom Asch" has become the standard spelling, and I have adopted it here.

85. Baruch Charney Vladeck to Cyrus Adler (October 6, 1920); Adler to Vladeck (October 12, 1920); and other correspondence in box 3, JPSP; Sholom Ash *Kiddush Ha-Shem: An Epic of 1648* (Philadelphia: 1926), translated by Rufus Learsi [pseudonym of Israel Goldberg]; Sholom Ash, *Sabbatai Zevi* (Philadelphia: 1930), translated by Florence Whyte and George R. Noyes; *AJYB* 36 (1934–35), p. 485.

86. Frank I. Schechter to Julius Grodinsky (April 25, 1932); Simon Miller to Cyrus Adler (April 28, 1932), both in JPSP; Nahum Slouchz, *Travels in North Africa* (Philadelphia:

1927). Although Solomon Schechter's daughter Amy is usually credited with translating this volume from French into English [see Bloch, *OMMB*, p. 158], the translation was actually jointly done by Amy Schechter and Maurice Samuel; see George Dobsevage to Isaac Husik (October 27, 1924), box 147, JPSP. On Slouschz's work in general, and his association with Mordechai Hakohen, see Harvey E. Goldberg (ed.), *The Book of Mordechai* (Philadelphia: 1980), pp. 23–26, and *Genazim* 3 (1969), pp. 40–90.

87. A.S. Sachs, *Worlds That Passed* (Philadelphia: 1928), pp. 2, 3, 52.

88. Yehoash [Solomon Bloomgarden], *The Feet of the Messenger* (Philadelphia: 1923); *AJYB* 25 (1923–24), pp. 437–8; see the correspondence in box 45, JPSP.

89. Zev Vilnay, *Legends of Palestine* (Philadelphia: 1932), p. iv; Cyrus Adler to Julius Grodinsky (April 11, 1930), box 43, JPSP; Zev Vilnay, *Legends of Jerusalem* (Philadelphia: 1973), pp. v, ix.

90. Abram S. Isaacs, *School Days in Home Town* (Philadelphia: 1928), p. 6. The earlier books are Elma Ehrlich Levinger, *Playmates in Egypt* (1920); *Wonder Tales of Bible Days* (1929); and Israel Goldberg, *Kasriel the Watchman* (1925).

91. Deborah M. Melamed, "Jewish Children's Books," *JQR* (1923–24), pp. 393–394.

92. *Jewish Post and Opinion* (October 24, 1984), p. 5; see S.Y. Agnon, "Ma'ase Rabi Gadiel Hatinok," *Elu v'Elu* (Jerusalem: 1967), pp. 416–420, and Gershom Scholem's analysis of the motif in his *Devarim Be-Go* (Tel Aviv: 1982), pp. 270–283. On K'tonton, see Francine Klagsbrun, "Introduction" to Sadie Rose Weilerstein, *The Best of K'tonton* (Philadelphia: 1980), pp. 9–12; PC–M (November 5, 1933), p. 2; Bernard Frankel to Julius Grodinsky (December 6, 1933); David Blondheim to "Publicaton Committee" (January 21, 1934), box 72 [Unpublished Books], JPSP.

93. Carrie D. Davidson, *Out of Endless Yearnings: A Memoir of Israel Davidson* (New York: 1946), pp. 183–187, reprints Davidson's review, which originally appeared in the *Menorah Journal*.

94. The discussion of the Book-of-the-Month Club that follows is indebted to Joan Shelly Rubin, "Self, Culture, and Self-Culture: The Early History of the Book-of-the-Month Club," *Journal of American History* 71 (March, 1985), pp. 782–806; as well as to Charles Lee, *The Hidden Public: The Story of the Book-of-the-Month Club* (Garden City, NY, 1958).

95. This slogan, coined by Horace Stern, appears with some variations in the sources, see *Jewish Publication Society Agents Sales Manual* (Philadelphia: [1935]), esp. pp. 7, 38; cf. *AJYB* 44 (1942–43), p. 514.

96. See, for example, the voluminous correspondence dealing with the proposed "Jewish Book-of-the-Month Club in PC–C, 1928–32,"; as well as Maurice Jacobs's report to the publication committee and board of trustees (December 6, 1944), pp. 10–11, both in JPSP.

97. *AJYB* 32 (1930–31), pp. 345–346.

98. *AJYB* 35 (1933–34), pp. 325–328; 36 (1934–35), p. 487; Grayzel, "Oral History," p. 19; Jacob Solis-Cohen to Adolph Ochs (March 8, 1934), PC–C.

99. "Jacob Solis-Cohen" in PC–C file, 1944–45; Grayzel, "Oral History," 19, 52; Jacob R. Marcus, personal conversation, July 16, 1986; *AJYB* 37 (1935–36), p. 472.

100. Cyrus Adler to Jacob Solis-Cohen (April 19, 1933); Julius Grodinsky to Jacob Solis-Cohen (March 30, 1933); Jacob Solis-Cohen to Adolph Ochs (March 8, 1934), all in PC–C; *AJYB* 36 (1934–35), p. 488.

101. Jacob Solis-Cohen to Adolph Ochs (March 8, 1934); Cyrus Adler to Jacob Solis-Cohen (October 29, 1934), both in PC–C; *AJYB* 37 (1935–36), p. 473.

102. Untitled memo on publishing fiction (1935), PC–C; press release on Edwin Wolf Prize (1935); Cyrus Adler to Jacob Solis-Cohen (February 25, 1935), Adler box; Isaac Husik to Julius Grodinsky, PC–C; Julius Grodinsky to Jacob Solis-Cohen (July 11, 1933), PC–C; *AJYB* 37 (1935–36), pp. 474–475; 38 (1936–37), p. 665.

7 *The Maurice Jacobs Years*

1. Lloyd P. Gartner, "The Midpassage of American Jewry," *The Fifth Annual Feinberg Memorial Lecture* (Cincinnati: 1982); reprinted in Sarna *AJE*, pp. 226–228.

2. "News Release: Mr. Maurice Jacobs Appointed . . ." (March 3, 1936), box 120, JPSP; *AJYB* 45 (1943–44), pp. 693–694; Solomon Grayzel, "Oral History," p. 24; J.R. Marcus, "In Memoriam: Maurice Jacobs," *AJA* 37 (November, 1985), pp. 341–342.

3. *AJYB* 45 (1943–44), pp. 693–694; 39 (1937–38), p. 857–858; 40 (1938–39), p. 653; TM (December 19, 1937), p. 6.

4. *AJYB* 39 (1937–38), p. 861; 40 (1938–39), p. 655.

5. The bibliography of JPS's books, 1890–1937, commissioned for 1938, would also have symbolized the new era. Had it been finished on time it would quite clearly have distinguished the Society's first half-century from the new era begun by Jacobs. But the author, Joshua Bloch, did not complete the book until 1952. See *AJYB* 41 (1939–40), p. 673; 48 (1946–47), p. 665; TM (January 9, 1939), p. 5; (June 28, 1937), p. 1; for correspondence regarding Bloch's *OMMB*, see box 8, JPSP.

6. Ginzberg, *KOTL*, pp. 180–181; Louis Ginzberg to Julius Grodinsky (September 16, 1926); Boaz Cohen to Julius Grodinsky (July 20, 1931, January 18, 1932); Boaz Cohen to Louis Ginzberg (March 15, 1935); Boaz Cohen to Maurice Jacobs (August 18, 1936) åd other correspondence in box 18, JPSP.

7. Grayzel, "Oral History," pp. 26–27; PC-M (March 5, 1939), p. 1; *AJYB* 41 (1939–40), p. 679.

8. A. Alan Steinbach, "Solomon Grayzel," *JBA* 28 (1970–71), pp. 110–115; Kenneth R. Stow, "Solomon Grayzel 1896–1980," *JBA* 39 (1981–82), pp. 158–163; Grayzel, "Oral History," esp. p. 36; Grayzel to Marvin Lowenthal (July 23, 1951); Grayzel to B.G. Richards (September 4, 1956), PC-C; Interview with Jacob R. Marcus (July 1, 1983); *JPSBM* 6 (March, 1959), p. 1; (June, 1959), pp. 4–5; Grayzel to S. Joshua Kohn (April 25, 1956), PC-C.

9. PC-M (March 5, 1939), p. 1; "Louis Levinthal Biographical Material," box 153, JPSP; *UJE* vol. 6, p. 637; cf. *AJYB* 41 (1939–40), p. 682 where Levinthal consciously models himself on Sulzberger. For my use of ethnicization, see Jonathan D. Sarna, "From Immigrants to Ethnics: Toward a New Theory of 'Ethnicization,'" *Ethnicity* 5 (1978).

10. *AJYB* 42 (1940–41), pp. 690–91; 48 (1946–47), p. 641; 52 (1950–51), p. 539; Grayzel, "Oral History," p. 34.

11. See *AJYB* 48 (1946–47), p. 641; TM (December 2, 1941), p. 4; (December 8, 1942), p. 5; and especially Maurice Jacobs to Jacob Solis-Cohen (September 8, 1942), unsorted correspondence, JPSP.

12. PC-M (April 4, 1937), p. 1; *AJYB* 35 (1933–34), p. 322; 41 (1939–40), p. 676; 46 (1944–45), p. 605; 48 (1946–47), p. 661; 50 (1948–49), p. 857.

13. *AJYB* 39 (1937–38), p. 856; 43 (1941–42), p. 778.

14. TM (December 8, 1942), p. 8; PC-M (December 7, 1947), p. 5; *AJYB* 47 (1945–46), pp. 649, 663; 52 (1950–51), p. 544.

15. See the annual reports in *AJYB*, especially 43 (1941–42), pp. 777, 780; 45 (1943–44), p. 605; 46 (1944–45), p. 603; 48 (1946–47), pp. 647–648.

16. *AJYB* 43 (1941–42), p. 782; cf. 42 (1941–42), p. 687.

17. *AJYB* 43 (1941–42), p. 782; 44 (1942–43), p. 510; 48 (1946–47), pp. 664–665, 668; on Skaraton see *Philadelphia Sunday Bulletin Magazine* (November 22, 1964), p. 16. I am grateful to Mr. Max Whiteman for this reference.

18. Based on data published in JPS annual reports as published in *AJYB*. All but the figures on membership and books distributed are summarized in *AJYB* 48 (1946–47), pp. 656, 663, which I have relied upon.

19. Total income includes money from dues, donations, book sales, press sales, welfare funds, "miscellaneous," and in several cases from restricted funds. For the full breakdown, see *AJYB* 48 (1946–47), p. 656.

20. Jacobs himself believed that no goal was too remote for JPS. "It is all possible," he told the trustees, echoing Theodor Herzl, "if we [but] will it." *AJYB* 48 (1946–47), pp. 657, 667; 41 (1939–40), p. 677; 46 (1944–45), p. 609; 43 (1941–42), p. 782; TM (February 10, 1944).

21. *AJYB* 38 (1936–37), p. 662; *Jewish Publication Society Agents Sales Manual*, p. 4; *Philadelphia Sunday Bulletin Magazine* (November 22, 1964), p. 16.

22. Kober file, box 24; Berges file, box 7; and Cohn file, box 13, all in JPSP; cf. Michael A. Meyer, "The Refugee Scholars Project of the Hebrew Union College," in Bertram W. Korn (ed.) *A Bicentennial Festschrift for Jacob Rader Marcus* (New York: 1976), pp. 359–75.

23. Max Berges, *Cold Pogrom* (Philadelphia: 1939); "Press Release . . . Cold Pogrom" (1939); William Fineshriber to Maurice Jacobs (April 23, 1938); Benjamin Epstein to Maurice Jacobs (February 23, 1939); Charles A. Madison [representing Henry Holt] to Maurice Jacobs (September 20, 1939), all in box 7, JPSP; *AJYB* 42 (1940–41), p. 684.

24. Solomon Liptzin, *Germany's Stepchildren* (Philadelphia: 1944), p. 285; cf. *AJYB* 47 (1945–46), p. 743: " 'fan mail' received from members indicates that this is the type of book which they want." Solomon Grayzel to Emil Gabor (September 13, 1940) Solomon Grayzel to Lester L. Riley (March 3, 1941), Rejected Manuscripts file, JPSP.

25. Ruben Rothgiesser, *The Ship of Hope* (Philadelphia: 1939); *AJYB* 42 (1940–41), p. 684; PC–M (December 19, 1937), part II, p. 3; (December 4, 1940), p. 4; S. Felix Mendelsohn, *Let Laughter Ring* (Philadelphia: 1941), pp. 131, 138; *AJYB* 44 (1942–43), p. 507; Bloch, *OMMB* p. 220.

26. Joseph L. Baron, *Candles in the Night* (Philadelphia: 1940), p. vii, cf. xix; *Stars and Sand* (Philadelphia: 1943), jacket blurb and p. xv: "its ultimate purpose [is] to help strengthen the morale of the Jew and deepen the appreciation of the non-Jew at a time when mutual understanding and friendship between peoples are needed so urgently." For the Stalin quotes, see pp. 176, 316 ("Anti-Semitism . . . is the most dangerous survival of cannibalism."). See also Solomon Grayzel to Louis Levinthal (February 22, 1943); Louis Levinthal to Solomon Grayzel (February 24, 1943), box 4, JPSP. The Zionist journalist B.G. Richards, reacting to Baron's work, pointed out that "the Jewish quest for expressions of approval and sanction on the part of Gentiles, is in a sense quite preposterous, but it is surely less crazy than the original insanity of hatred and slander which it seeks to overcome" [*JBA* 3 (1944–45), p. 35].

27. *AJYB* 44 (1942–43), p. 511; 46 (1944–45), p. 608; 48 (1946–47), p. 663.

28. *AJYB* 49 (1947–48), p. 832; 47 (1945–46), p. 744; 48 (1946–47), p. 650.

29. Maurice Jacobs expressed a similar view: "The day of German Jewry has passed, and the other Jews of communities of continental Europe have been dealt an all but fatal blow, hence our own community must exert itself more than ever before by enlarged programs in every field." *AJYB* 43 (1941–42), pp. 780–781, 789–791.

30. Bloch, *OMMB* p. 233; PC–M (December 7, 1947), p. 7. My father, Professor Nahum M. Sarna, confirms that Maurice Jacobs sent books to him and to other Jews' College students in London on precisely this delayed-payment basis.

31. See Jeffrey Gurock's discussion of "the growth of American Jewish historiography" in his *American Jewish History: A Bibliographical Guide* (New York: 1983), pp. xv–xxi. For Salo Baron's famous lament over the lachrymose conception of Jewish history, see his *History and Jewish Historians* (Philadelphia: 1966), p. 88.

32. Abram Vossen Goodman, *American Overture* (Philadelphia: 1947), p. 201; see also A.S.W. Rosenbach's introduction to Lee M. Friedman, *Jewish Pioneers and Patriots* (Philadelphia: 1943), p. xvi.

33. Leon Huhner to Solomon Grayzel (June 24, 1940), box 23, JPSP; Leon Huhner, *The Life of Judah Touro* (Philadelphia: 1946). For a more balanced assessment of Touro's life and career, see Bertram W. Korn, *The Early Jews of New Orleans* (Waltham, MA: 1969), esp. pp. 74–90.

34. Hyman B. Grinstein to Solomon Grayzel (January 1, 1943); Grayzel to Joseph L. Blau (January 27, 1943); David de Sola Pool to Maurice Jacobs (June 2, 1944), all in box 4, JPSP; Hyman B. Grinstein, *The Rise of the Jewish Community of New York* (Philadelphia: 1945), esp. pp. ix, 465. Compare Rudolf Glanz's more negative assessment reprinted in his *Studies in Judaica Americana* (New York: 1970).

35. For the largely unrealized plans of the subcommittee on American History and Biography, see PC–M (May 12, 1940), p. 11. On Emily Solis-Cohen's abortive biography, see PC–M (May 1, 1943), and Bertram W. Korn to Solomon Grayzel (June 9, 1952), PC–C. The sad history of the proposed one-volume American Jewish history volume is traced in correspondence found in box 67, unpublished books correspondence, JPSP. For Jacobs's quote, see *AJYB* 48 (1946–47), p. 654.

36. PC–M (December 10, 1944), part II, p. 11; Grayzel, "Oral History," p. 42; "Report of Planning Committee of the Jewish Publication Society," in PC–M (April 27, 1947). There was even talk in this period of working out some arrangement with the *Contemporary Jewish Record*, then published by the American Jewish Committee, so that it would become the Society's official magazine; see PC–M (December 4, 1940), p. 7; TM (December 11, 1940).

37. "Jessie E. Sampter [a biographical sketch]," box 39, JPSP; Bertha Badt-Strauss, *White Fire: The Life and Works of Jessie Sampter* (New York: 1956), esp. pp. 134–135, 160–164; Jessie Sampter, *Brand Plucked From the Fire* (Philadelphia: 1937); on Alice Seligsberg, see *AJYB* 43 (1941–42), pp. 431–436.

38. Jessie Sampter to Cyrus Adler (September 12, 1934); Isaac Husik to Cyrus Adler (February 24, 1936); Adler to Husik (February 25, 1936); *AJYB* 39 (1937–38), p. 869; 40 (1938–39), p. 649. For a positive review, see *JQR* 28 (1937–38), p. 287.

39. Hayyim Nahman Bialik, *Aftergrowth and Other Stories*, translated by I.M. Lask (Philadelphia: 1939), esp. p. 23; Grayzel, "Oral History," p. 10; PC–M (October 29, 1939), p. 4; Maurice Samuel to Louis Levinthal (May 18, 1940); Louis Levinthal to Maurice Samuel (May 28, 1940); Milton Steinberg to Solomon Grayzel (September 27, 1940), all in box 5, JPSP; *AJYB* 43 (1941–42), p. 776; cf. Alex Bein, *Theodore Herzl* (Philadelphia: 1940), p. 521.

40. Abram L. Sachar to Maurice Jacobs (June 28, 1943); Maurice Jacobs to the Members of the Publication Committee (January 11, 1944), box 39, JPSP; TM (January 27, 1944), pp. 5ff.

41. Louis E. Levinthal, "Report," included in Jacobs to Publication Committee (January 11, 1944); Maurice Jacobs to Abram L. Sachar (January 18, 1944), box 39, JPSP; TM (January 27, 1944), pp. 5–6. See Maurice Samuel, *Harvest in the Desert* (Philadelphia: 1944), p. 3, where Samuel admitted that his "fusion of research and reportage, record and impression," including his discussion of Zionism, "is all colored by my positive attitude toward the enterprise."

42. "Notes for Minutes of the Board of Trustees ... January 27, 1944," filed with TM (January 27, 1944); see also correspondence regarding this volume in box 39, JPSP.

43. "Notes for Minutes of the Board of Trustees ... January 27, 1944," pp. 15, 19. For the dispute within the Reform movement, see Howard R. Greenstein, *Turning Point: Zionism and Reform Judaism* (Chico, CA: 1981); David Polish, *Renew Our Days* (Jerusalem: 1976), pp. 115–235; and especially Michael A. Meyer, *Response to Modernity: A History of the Reform Movement in Judaism* (New York: 1988), pp. 296–334, which he kindly permitted me to read in manuscript. For the dispute within the American Jewish Committee, see Naomi W. Cohen, *Not Free to Desist* (Philadelphia: 1972), esp. p. 259.

44. "Notes for Minutes of the Board of Trustees ... January 27, 1944," pp. 25, 31, 32;

Louis I. Levinthal to Members of the Publication Committee (February 1, 1944); Louis Levinthal to Jacob Solis-Cohen (February 16, 1944), both in box 39, JPSP; "Notes of Meeting of the Board of Trustees... February 10, 1944"; Edwin Wolf to Louis Levinthal (February 5, 1944), typescript copy in the Rabbi William H. Fineshriber Records, Temple Keneseth Israel, Philadelphia, PA; TM (February 10, 1944).

45. *AJYB* 46 (1944–45), p. 608; Bloch, *OMMB* p. 233; Louis Levinthal to John B. Goldenberg (July 26, 1944), box 39, JPSP.

46. Solomon Liptzin, *Germany's Stepchildren* (Philadelphia: 1948), esp. p. 110. Professor Shalom Spiegel later claimed that he "was first to recommend L[iptzin]'s book for publication and helped to reshape it and to break down opposition to it because of an unfortunate title and unneeded political-didactic conclusion" [Spiegel to Solomon Grayzel (May 21, 1946), box 5, JPSP].

47. PC–M (October 15, 1946); *AJYB* 50 (1948–49), p. 850. Significantly, Solomon Grayzel, deeply concerned about the depressed mood of postwar American Jews, thought that the Syrkin volume would help "Jewish morale and Jewish self-respect," see Solomon Grayzel to Edwin Wolf 2nd (October 4, 1946); and other correspondence in box 42, JPSP.

48. PC–M (November 4, 1945); readers' reports for both books are reprinted in "Agenda, Joint Meeting of Publication Committee and Board of Trustees, Sunday, November 4, 1945," bound with the minutes.

49. PC–M (November 4, 1945), p. 6; cf. Maurice Jacobs to Board of Trustees (November 11, 1946) bound with PC–M (February 2, 1947).

50. *JBA* 1 (1942), p. 33; *AJYB* 48 (1946–47), p. 670.

51. *AJYB* 44 (1942–43), p. 505; 41 (1939–40), p. 683; 39 (1937–38), p. 866; Grayzel, "Oral History," p. 46.

52. PC–M (December 4, 1940), p. 3; Montagu F. Modder, *The Jew in the Literature of England* (Philadelphia: 1939); cf. Grayzel, "Oral History," pp. 28–29; Cecil Roth to Jacob Solis-Cohen (April 10, 1940), PC–C.

53. Solomon Posener, *Adolph Cremieux* (Philadelphia: 1940); Norman Bentwich, *Solomon Schechter* (Philadelphia: 1938); Cyrus Adler, *I Have Considered the Days* (Philadelphia: 1941); Alexander Marx, *Essays in Jewish Biography* (Philadelphia: 1947); Leo Schwarz, *Memoirs of My People* (Philadelphia: 1943); see the correspondence on Bentwich's biography in box 6, JPSP.

54. Mark Wischnitzer, *To Dwell in Safety: The Story of Jewish Migration Since 1800* (Philadelphia: 1948), esp. pp. vii, 286–287. This seems to be one of the earliest published references to the phrase "survivors of the holocaust"; cf. Leon A. Jick, "The Holocaust: Its Use and Abuse Within the American Public," *Yad Vashem Studies* 14 (1981), pp. 303–318.

55. Ismar Elbogen, *A Century of Jewish Life* (Philadelphia: 1944), pp. vii–xx; Maurice Jacobs to Alexander Marx *et al* (February 10, 1939); Solomon Grayzel to Maurice Jacobs (August 1, 1943), both in box 14, JPSP; cf. Meyer, "The Refugee Scholars Project of the Hebrew Union College," pp. 361–362.

56. Solomon Grayzel to Ismar Elbogen (June 12, 1939); Solomon Grayzel to Jacob R. Marcus (January 13, 1942); Louis E. Levinthal to Nahum Goldman (June 1, 1944), all in box 14, JPSP; *JBA* 3 (1944–45), p. 37; Elbogen, *A Century of Jewish Life*, p. 681.

57. Jacob B. Aronoff to Solomon Grayzel (May 15, 1944); John Tepfer to Stephen S. Wise (May 23, 1944); Jacob R. Marcus to Solomon Grayzel (May 28, 1944); Jacob B. Aronoff to Maurice Jacobs, including undated memo by John Tepfer (June 2, 1944); Maurice Jacobs to Louis Levinthal (June 6, 1944); Jacob B. Aronoff to Louis Levinthal (June 13, 1944); Nahum Goldmann to Louis E. Levinthal (June 23, 1944); Salo Baron to Solomon Grayzel (July 13, 1944); Solomon Grayzel to Salo W. Baron (July 27, 1944), all in box 14, JPSP; Mark Wischnitzer and Solomon Zeitlin in *JQR* 35 (1944–45), pp. 394–419; Grayzel, "Oral History," pp. 87–88.

58. Compare the first printing of Elbogen, *A Century of Jewish Life* (1944) with the

second (1948) and subsequent impressions, pp. ix, 471, 491, 498, and especially p. 499 (quoted) and the new pro-Soviet paragraph on p. 509 (quoted). On the question of Bolshevik participation in Ukrainian pogroms, see Salo W. Baron, *The Russian Jew Under Tsars and Soviets* (2nd ed., New York, 1976), pp. 184, as well as his review of recent literature on the subject, pp. 396–397. Elbogen's epilogue, the only part of the book that he composed in English, spells out his views on the postwar period, see esp. pp. 680–682. See also *JPSBM* 14 (September 1967), p. 7, which reports on the publication of the book in German.

59. Solomon Grayzel to Uriah Z. Engelman (May 16, 1950), box 22, JPS Papers, PJAC; PC–M (December 10, 1944), p. 12; Solomon Grayzel, *A History of the Jews* (Philadelphia: 1955 [1947]), pp. vii, 812–813; cf. p. 569 where Grayzel called on readers to "make certain that Americanism triumphs."

60. Grayzel, "Oral History," pp. 48–50, see also correspondence in box 22, JPSP.

61. PC–M (January 17, 1938); Cecil Roth, *The History of the Jews of Italy* (Philadelphia: 1946), esp. p. viii; *JQR* 38 (1947–48), pp. 469–472; 39 (1948–49), p. 217; cf. Sonne's unconvincing defense on p. 327.

62. Cecil Roth, *The House of Nasi: Doña Gracia* (Philadelphia: 1947), esp. pp. 133, 174, 184; cf. p. xiii: "any parallels with the conditions of our own day, which may be noticed in this work, are due to the irony of history and not the imagination of the author." Cecil Roth, *The House of Nasi: The Duke of Naxos* (Philadelphia: 1948), esp. pp. 108, 112, 123–124, 135. See Ellis Rivkin's scathing reviews of both books in *JQR* 39 (1948–49), pp. 309–315; 40 (1949–50), pp. 205–207.

63. Louis Finkelstein, *The Pharisees* (3rd ed., Philadelphia: 1960 [1st ed., 1938]), esp. pp. xxvi, lxi, 2.

64. Salo W. Baron, *The Jewish Community* (3 vols., Philadelphia: 1942), esp. pp. vii, 3–4; *JBA* 2 (1943–44), p. 67; for a different view, see the savage review by Baron's perennial critic, Solomon Zeitlin, in *JQR* 34 (1943–44), pp. 371–384, and Grayzel's response preserved in box 4, JPSP.

65. Abraham A. Neuman, *The Jews in Spain* (2 vols., Philadelphia: 1942), p. vii.

66. Joshua Bloch, "The Year's Bookshelf," *JBA* 5 (1946–47), pp. 3–4; see Salo Baron in Oscar I. Janowsky, *The JWB Survey* (New York, 1948), p. xiii.

67. *AJYB* 40 (1938–39), p. 650; Philip Goodman, *The Purim Anthology* (Philadelphia: 1949), p. xxiii; Abraham E. Millgram, *Sabbath: The Day of Delight* (Philadelphia: 1944); see Grayzel, "Oral History," p. 21 regarding his assistance to his friend Emily Solis-Cohen in her *Hanukkah: The Feast of Lights* (Philadelphia: 1937). Goodman's other books in this series include *The Passover Anthology* (1961); *Rosh Hashanah Anthology* (1970); *Yom Kippur Anthology* (1971); *The Sukkot and Simhat Torah Anthology* (1973); *The Shavuot Anthology* (1975); *The Hanukkah Anthology* (1976); see also Philip and Hanna Goodman, *The Jewish Marriage Anthology* (Philadelphia: 1965). On Jewish ritual observance in America, see Marshall Sklare and Joseph Greenblum, *Jewish Identity on the Suburban Frontier* (New York: 1967), pp. 45–96, esp. p. 57.

68. Solomon Grayzel to Meyer Shapiro (June 15, 1944); "Press Release: *Pathways Through the Bible*," both in box 12, JPSP; Mortimer J. Cohen, *Pathways Through the Bible* (Philadelphia: 1946), pp. ix–xi. In keeping with its American character, the volume carried an opening quotation, reminiscent of Lincoln's Gettysburg address, that read "This Bible is for the Government of the People, by the People, and for the People." Although attributed on the basis of a secondary source to John Wycliffe, Mortimer Cohen later discovered that the quote was spurious and tried unsuccessfully to have it deleted, see Mortimer Cohen to Nahum Gidal (August 14, 1952), box 12, JPSP.

69. [Mortimer J. Cohen], "General Attitudes Towards the Bible Pictures," box 12, JPSP; TM (May 12, 1940). Cohen's concern for art was later manifested in his insistence that Frank Lloyd Wright design the Elkins Park Synagogue that he moved his congregation into in 1959; see *JBA* 30 (1972–73), pp. 60–61.

70. Meyer Shapiro to Solomon Grayzel (June 20, 1944, November 21, 1944); Maurice Jacobs to Bernard Gittelson (February 28, 1947); Louis E. Levinthal to Mrs. Arthur Szyk (November 28, 1952) and other correspondence in box 12, JPSP; Grayzel, "Oral History," pp. 46–47; Cohen, *Pathways Through the Bible,* p. viii; cf. Mortimer J. Cohen, "Szyk— Illustrator of Jewish Books," *JBA* 5 (1946–47), pp. 70–77. To save money, the Society later produced a school edition of *Pathways Through the Bible* with the illustrations in black and white. Chagall's Bible scenes were not published until 1956; for an evaluation, see *New York Times,* July 26, 1987, p. 31.

71. Solomon Grayzel to Milton Steinberg (January 15, 1948); Milton Steinberg to Solomon Grayzel (February 18, 1948), PC–C; cf. Alexander Bloom, *Prodigal Sons* (New York: 1985), pp. 141ff.

72. Maurice Jacobs to Henry Hurwitz (February 27, 1941), box 19, JPSP; *AJYB* 37 (1935–36), p. 474; 38 (1936–37), p. 664; 40 (1938–39), p. 650; TM (March 9, 1936), p. 2; Grayzel "Oral History," p. 38; "Bisno file," box 7, JPSP; Beatrice Bisno, *Tomorrow's Bread* (Philadelphia: 1938). Years later, Grayzel discovered that one of the books rejected for the award was Harriet Lane Levy's *Nine Twenty O'Farrell Street,* a well-received (somewhat fictional?) memoir of a San Francisco girlhood published by Doubleday in 1947; see Solomon Grayzel to Allen Lesser (December 9, 1947), PC–C.

73. Maurice Samuel to Maurice Jacobs (December 14, 1943), box 32, JPSP; PC–M (July 6, 1944), p. 2; Grayzel, "Oral History," p. 39; Elliot E. Cohen, "Jewish Culture in America," *Commentary* 3 (May, 1947), p. 414. Soma Morgenstern, *The Son of the Lost Son* (Philadelphia: 1946); *In My Father's Pastures* (1947); *The Testament of the Lost Son* (Philadelphia: 1950); see also Alfred Hoelzel, "Soma Morgenstern 1890–1976," *Midstream* 23 (March, 1977), pp. 41–50. All three of Morgenstern's books were translated from the original German.

74. Mortimer J. Cohen "In re: Jacob's Dream," box 5, JPSP. Another edition of this play, translated from German, was published simultaneously by Johannes Press, with an introduction by Thornton Wilder. Over Prof. Shalom Spiegel's objections, the Society dropped Wilder's introduction (which spoke of the Bible in mythical terms, and was therefore deemed inappropriate) and replaced it with a new introduction by Solomon Liptzin; see Solomon Grayzel to Otto Kalir (February 18, 1946); and Shalom Spiegel to Solomon Grayzel (May 21, 1946), box 5, JPSP.

75. Joseph Opatashu, *In Polish Woods* (Philadelphia: 1938), translated by Isaac Goldberg, the last book he translated before he died; see correspondence in box 33, JPSP; and on Opatashu, *EJ* 12, pp. 1409–1410.

76. Selma Stern, *The Spirit Returneth,* translated by Ludwig Lewisohn, (Philadelphia: 1946), esp. p. 265; PC–M (December 6, 1944), p. 7; *JBA* 6 (1947–48), p. 14.

77. Martin Buber to JPS (October 26, 1941); Solomon Grayzel to Martin Buber (December 18, 1941); Buber to JPS (December 23, 1941); Grayzel to Buber (February 5, 1942); Shalom Spiegel [to Solomon Grayzel] (May 17, 1942); Abraham Heschel [to Solomon Grayzel] (May 25, 1943); Maurice Jacobs to Martin Buber (December 9, 1943); and Mortimer J. Cohen, "When Saints Wage War" [press release-review], which calls on contemporary Jews to "reach humane solutions" to world problems by learning from Buber the "spirit of *makloket le-shem shomayim,* the controversy for the sake of heaven"—all in box 8, JPSP; see also Grayzel, "Oral History," pp. 39–40; and Jacob Weinstein, *Solomon Goldman* (New York: 1973), pp. 256–258. In a letter to Shalom Spiegel, Grayzel revealed an important fact about Lewisohn's translation: "[He] gave the Shekinah a neuter pronoun whenever he had to. Buber suggested the use of a feminine pronoun. In this instance, I sided with Lewisohn, since the use of 'she' in connection with *Shekinah* gave me an inward shudder" (Grayzel to Spiegel [April 11, 1945], box 8, JPSP.) For evidence of member opposition to the book, see Grayzel to Jacobs (July 12, 1945) and Jacobs to Grayzel (July 23, 1945), PC–C. For the larger history of this novel and reactions to it, see Maurice Friedman, *Martin Buber's Life*

and Work: The Middle Years 1923–1945 (New York: 1983), pp. 309–325, esp. pp. 312–313 from where my final quotes are drawn. In addition, see *Commentary* [(March, 1946), pp. 35–38], where Harold Rosenberg lambasts the Society's presentist reading of Buber, not entirely convincingly.

78. *AJYB* 38 (1936–37), pp. 671–672; Solomon Grayzel to Lionel Trilling (June 8, 1944), PC–C; Grayzel to Salo Baron (July 27, 1944), box 14, both in JPSP.

79. Pessin composed the book based on Ashkenazic spelling ("Aleph-Bais"), but the publication committee switched it to the Sephardic mode, which both comported with its own traditions and followed the modern Zionist-Hebraist trend in Jewish education; see PC–M (December 10, 1944).

80. Berkowitz was the nephew of Rabbi Henry Berkowitz of Philadelphia, an early member of the publication committee. His *Boot Camp* (Philadelphia: 1948) was partially based on his own experiences as a chaplain at Camp Sampson. Other juveniles published in this period include Elma E. Levinger, *Pilgrims to Palestine* (Philadelphia: 1940); Dorothy Alofsin, *The Nightingale's Song* (Philadelphia: 1945); and Robert Abrahams, *Mr. Benjamin's Sword* (Philadelphia: 1948).

81. Fanny Goldstein, "The Jewish Child in Bookland," *JBA* 5 (1946–47), p. 85; Solomon Grayzel to Leon L. Berkowitz (March 26, 1940), box 6, JPSP; PC–M (December 6, 1944), pp. 4–5; "Re: The Nightingale's Song," box 2, JPSP; "Press Release: What the Moon Brought," box 44, JPSP. See generally Sophie N. Cederbaum, "American Jewish Juvenile Literature During the Last Twenty-Five Years," *JBA* 25 (1967–68), pp. 192–203.

82. Solomon Grayzel to Henry J. Berkowitz (December 20, 1940) and other correspondence in box 6, JPSP; Grayzel to Deborah Pessin (September 21, 1944), and other correspondence in box 34, JPSP; Grayzel to Dorothy Alofsin (January 31, 1945), and other correspondence in box 2, JPS Papers, PJAC.

83. Usher Caplan, *Like One That Dreamed* (Toronto: 1982); Elijah E. Palnick, "A.M. Klein: A Biographical Study" (unpublished M.H.L. thesis, Hebrew Union College, 1959); Seymour Mayne, *The A.M. Klein Symposium* (Ottawa: 1975); A.M. Klein, *Hath Not A Jew* (New York: 1940); for the Society's deliberations on an earlier version of this volume entitled "Greetings On This Day," see PC–M (February 7, 1932), p. 2 and correspondence in box 24, JPSP.

84. Louis Levinthal to Solomon Grayzel (February 24, 1942), box 24, JPSP; TM (December 8, 1942); PC–M (December 10, 1944), p. 4; Felix Gerson to JPS (May 18, 1942); Robert D. Abrahams to JPS (July 7, 1942); Mortimer J. Cohen to Solomon Grayzel (July 24, 1942); Abraham M. Klein to Louis Levinthal (August 7, 1942); Julian Feibelman to JPS (n.d.); A.M. Klein to Louis Levinthal (July 1, 1943); Solomon Grayzel to A.M. Klein (December 3, 1943); A.M. Klein to Solomon Grayzel (December 15, 1943), all in box 24, JPSP for a full discussion of changes made in the manuscript. Although Klein's original manuscript is not preserved in the files, I have been able to identify rejected poems on the basis of Miriam Waddington's edition of *The Collected Poems of A.M. Klein* (Toronto: 1974). Note that American films of this period adopted no less stringent standards of morality, see, for example, Raymond Moley, *The Hays Office* (New York: 1945), esp. the documents reprinted on pp. 240–248.

85. See previous note, and especially Klein to Levinthal (July 1, 1943). For critical reviews of *Poems*, see David Rome, *Jews in Canadian Literature: A Bibliography* (Montreal: 1964), pp. 61–62A. When Klein's novel, *The Second Scroll* was published, Grayzel reports that several members of the publication committee grumbled "about Klein's failure to take us into consideration when he had something of a more popular and acceptable nature" [Grayzel to Soma Morgenstern (October 3, 1952), box 32, JPSP.] *Poems* was reprinted in 1955 (*JPSBM* 2:4, p. 8).

86. Solomon Grayzel to Hirsch L. Gordon (June 15, 1943); Grayzel to Maurice Jacobs

(July 24, 1944); Grayzel to Ruth S. Lewis (November 17, 1947); Grayzel to Mally Dieneman (January 13, 1947), all in PC–C. Years later, the Society did issue a psychologically informed biography of Joseph Karo, see R.J. Zwi Werblowski, *Joseph Karo: Lawyer and Mystic* (Philadelphia: 1977).

87. Solomon Grayzel to Louis Levinthal (February 24, 1947); Grayzel to H.S. Latham (April 18, 1944); Grayzel to Julian Drachman (June 1, 1945); Grayzel to Harold Ribalow [italics in original] (April 1, 1947), all in PC–C; for the correspondence regarding Velikovsky's manuscript, see Unpublished Books Correspondence, box 72, JPSP.

88. See PC–M (March 5, 1939), p. 4 for the first suggestion that "Professor Sholom" might be approached; action was approved in the minutes of (May 12, 1940), p. 2. Correspondence includes Gershom Scholem to Solomon Grayzel (June 23, 1942); Grayzel to Scholem (July 22, 1942); Grayzel to Scholem (June 8, 1943), all in Unpublished Books Correspondence, box 69, JPSP; cf. PC–M (May 1, 1943), pp. 1–2; (December 6, 1944), part III, p. 6. Scholem's scholarship was praised ("despite some personal idiosyncracies") in an address to the Society by Rabbi Felix Levy reprinted in *AJYB* 47 (1945–46), p. 678. Subsequent correspondence, in which Scholem gently reminded Grayzel of their earlier dealings, includes Grayzel to "Sholem" (November 21, 1956); Scholem to Grayzel (November 23, 1956); Grayzel to Scholem (November 29, 1956), all in PC–C. Scholem's books did not appear on the Society's list until 1974 when it co-published his *Kabbalah*. A year later it co-published his *Sabbatai Sevi: The Mystical Messiah*, a new edition of the very book that Grayzel had been dubious about so many years before!

89. *AJYB* 49 (1947–48), p. 810; 50 (1948–49), p. 857; 51 (1949–50), p. 574. In *AJYB* 52 (1950–51), a new treasurer restated earlier figures, deleting "non-recurring donations" from income so as to increase the total loss over four years to $69,008.22. In *AJYB* 56 (1954–55), p. 645, Louis Levinthal reported that "at the end of 1948 our organization was burdened with a current indebtedness of $123,186.30," a figure much higher than any previously announced, but see TM (June 22, 1950) where the Society's net obligations were fixed at $97,000. Jacobs argued that "it is all a matter of how you keep your books," for if plates, goodwill, and the copyright were valued differently, losses would have been considerably less, see Jacobs to J. Solis-Cohen, Jr. et al (December 30, 1948), box 15, EW2P.

90. Maurice Jacobs to Louis Levinthal et al (December 5, 1949), box 15, EW2P; Maurice Jacobs to Jacob R. Marcus (May 9, 1949; May 23, 1949), PC–C.

91. Jacob R. Marcus, "In Memoriam: Maurice Jacobs, 1896–1984," *AJA* 37 (November 1985), p. 341; PC–M (March 34, 1946), p. 6; *AJYB* 49 (1947–48), pp. 803, 810; 50 (1948–49), pp. 851, 853; 52 (1950–51), p. 547.

92. Maurice Jacobs to Abram L. Sachar (December 11, 1947), PC–C; PC–M (November 7, 1948), p. 6; Edwin Wolf 2nd to Maurice Jacobs (December 6, 1948), box 15, EW2P.

93. Maurice Jacobs to J. Solis-Cohen et al (January 13, 1949), box 15, EW2P; PC–M (December 7, 1947), p. 10; PC–M (June 29, 1949), pp. 1–2; Maurice Jacobs to Norman Blaustein (February 11, 1949); Maurice Jacobs to Louis Levinthal (May 19, 1949); Maurice Jacobs to Jacob R. Marcus (May 9, 1949), JPSP.

94. *AJYB* 51 (1949–50), p. 563; 52 (1950–51), p. 546; Maurice Jacobs to Arthur Lelyveld (June 17, 1949).

95. *AJYB* 52 (1950–51), pp. 546–57; Maurice Jacobs to Louis Levinthal et al (December 5, 1949; December 6, 1949); Jacobs to Levinthal (December 9, 1949), all in EW2P; TM (December 21, 1949); Grayzel, "Oral History," pp. 55–57.

96. *The Reconstructionist* 15 (January 27, 1950), pp. 9, 24; for Jacobs's full plans, see the draft of his press release (January 19, 1950) in the collection of Max Whiteman; Jacob R. Marcus to Solomon Grayzel (January 3, 1950); Grayzel to Marcus (January 6, 1950), PC–C; Grayzel, "Oral History," pp. 56–57.

97. *AJYB* 53 (1951–52), p. 575; TM (June 22, 1950), p. 2; (November 28, 1952), p. 1;

Grayzel, "Oral History," pp. 56–57; Solomon Grayzel to Julian Morgenstern (May 16, 1950); Morgenstern to Grayzel (May 17, 1950), PC–C; Lesser Zussman to David de Sola Pool (July 18, 1950), box 129, JPSP.

8   *The Post-War Challenge*

1. Alan Dutscher, "The Book Business in America," reprinted in Bernard Rosenberg and David Manning White, *Mass Culture: The Popular Arts in America* (New York: 1957), pp. 126–140; *AJYB* 53 (1952), p. 574.

2. "Report by Salo W. Baron," in Oscar I. Janowsky, *The JWB Survey* (New York: 1948), p. xiii. See Nathan Glazer, *American Judaism* (Chicago: 1972), pp. 106–128 and Sydney E. Ahlstrom, *A Religious History of the American People* (New Haven: 1972), p. 980: "The postwar revival probably had a more marked effect on Judaism than on any other religious faith in America." For general trends in the period, see Paul A. Carter, *Another Part of the Fifties* (New York: 1983), esp. pp. 114–140.

3. "Bio on Lesser Zussman," box 153, JPSP; Grayzel, "Oral History," p. 59; *AJYB* 52 (1951), p. 547; 62 (1961), p. 478; 74 (1973), p. 640.

4. Jacob R. Marcus to Lesser Zussman (November 17, 1959); Zussman to Marcus (November 27, 1950), PC–C; *AJYB* 56 (1955), p. 637; 61 (1960), p. 442; For Sol Satinsky's role in the Society, see *JPSBM* 13 (December, 1966), p. 2. As if to underscore the importance of a wise financial policy, the published annual reports now gave special prominence to the treasurer's accounting; see, for example, the report of 1958.

5. *AJYB* 53 (1952), pp. 573–578; 54 (1953), p. 596; Maurice Jacobs to Sol Satinsky (November 21, 1960), unsorted correspondence, JPSP.

6. *JPSBM* 2 (September, 1955), pp. 2–3; *AJYB* 57 (1956), p. 647.

7. *AJYB* 57 (1956), p. 645; *JPSBM* 3 (March, 1956), p. 1; TM (February 26, 1959), p. 1.

8. *New York Times* (January 19, 1949), clipping in JPSP; for a slightly different account of the will see TM (February 20, 1952), and *AJYB* 55 (1954), p. 519. Marcus's memo (October 7, 1949) is in PC–C; see also the "Schiff Fund" file in EW2P; TM (October 20, 1963); and Grayzel "Oral History," p. 45. When applying for the 1956 grant, Wolf did not fail to remind the estate's other two executors of the fund's "$250,000 grants to Columbia University and the City College of New York" [Edwin Wolf 2nd to Buell G. Gallagher (September 27, 1956), EW2P.]

9. TM (December 12, 1961), p. 1; *AJYB* 66 (1965), pp. 606–608; *JPSBM* 9 (December, 1962); 11 (June, 1964).

10. Based on data supplied in the Society's annual reports as published in *AJYB*.

11. *AJYB* 55 (1954), p. 515; Charles A. Madison, "The Rise of the Jewish Book in American Publishing," *JBA* 25 (1967–68), pp. 81–86; Amnon Zipin, "Judaica from American University Presses," *JBA* 42 (1984–85), pp. 172–182. The 70 percent figure is my tabulation based on the 1949–50 listing; Zipin's figures are even higher.

12. "Report and Recommendations to the Executive Committee" [c. 1950], box 12; "Meeting Our New Challenge [1962]," box 13, both in EW2P; cf. "The Post of Editor at the J.P.S. [c. 1950]," box 118, Miscellaneous Papers, JPSP; and Jacob R. Marcus and Solomon Grayzel to Publication Committee (January 24, 1952), box 13, EW2P, where the publication committee was reported to have endorsed the idea. On rare occasions, the Society did offer members books published elsewhere, notably the *Standard Jewish Encyclopedia* and the deluxe edition of the Jerusalem (Koren) Bible, but these were extraordinary exceptions to accepted policy, and not the rule.

13. *JPSBM* 1 (February, 1954), p. 2; 2 (March, 1955), p. 6; (September, 1955), p. 4; 9

(September, 1962), pp. 3–4; 11 (December, 1964), p. 6; cf. *AJYB* 56 (1955), p. 644. *Bookmark* appeared regularly for fourteen years (February 1954 to December 1967), and then, for budgetary reasons, was cut back.

14. Solomon Grayzel to Joseph B. Soloveitchik (October 13, 1952), PC–C; "Report and Recommendations to the Executive Committee [c. 1950]," box 12, both in JPSP.

15. "The Post of Editor at the J.P.S. [c. 1950]," box 18; Solomon Grayzel to Roger W. Straus, Jr. (April 9, 1958), "Glueck file," box 19, all in JPSP; *JPSBM* 5 (September, 1958), p. 6; *AJYB* 52 (1951), p. 544. Glueck's volume used the Christian format in dating (BC, AD), translated the Bible according to the Revised Version, and occasionally referred to Jesus in ways that raised Jewish eyebrows (e.g., p. 255).

16. Grayzel to Executive Committee (April 5, 1954), PC–C; [Philip Seman], "Abstract," "A Literature for Jewish Adolescents," "Book Club for Jewish Youth," all in box 14, EW2P; on Seman cf. *JBA* 16 (1958–59), pp. 108–110.

17. Farrar, Straus and Cudahy to Edwin Wolf 2nd (May 11, 1956), PC–C; TM (June 27, 1955; December 1, 1955); *AJYB* 60 (1959), p. 381; *JPSBM* 5 (March, 1958), p. 3. Titles published include: (1) William Wise, *Silversmith of Old New York: Myer Myers* (1958); (2) Lloyd Alexander, *Border Hawk: August Bondi* (1958); (3) Lois Harris Kuhn, *The World of Jo Davidson* (1958); (4) Frieda Clark Hyman, *Jubal and the Prophet* (1958); (5) Emily Hahn, *Aboab: First Rabbi of the Americas* (1959); (6) Eve Merriam, *The Voice of Liberty: Emma Lazarus* (1959); (7) Robert D. Abrahams, *The Uncommon Soldier* (1959); (8) Sylvia Rothchild, *Keys to a Magic Door: The Life and Times of I.L. Peretz* (1959); (9) Alfred Apsler, *Northwest Pioneer: The Story of Louis Fleischner* (1960); (10) William Wise, *Albert Einstein: Citizen of the World* (1960); (11) Frieda Clark Hyman, *Builders of Jerusalem: In the Time of Nehemiah* (1960); (12) Lloyd Alexander, *The Flagship Hope: Aaron Lopez* (1960); (13) Libby M. Klaperman, *The Scholar Fighter: Saadia Gaon* (1961); (14) Robert D. Abrahams, *Sound of Bow Bells: Sir David Salomons* (1962); (15) Harold Ribalow, *Fighter from Whitechapel: Daniel Mendoza* (1962); (16) Miriam Gilbert, *The Mighty Voice: Isaiah* (1963); (17) Alfred Apsler, *Court Factor: Samson Wertheimer* (1964); (18) Lillian Freehof, *The Captive Rabbi: The Story of R. Meir of Rothenberg* (1965); (19) Sally Rogow, *Lillian Wald: Nurse in Blue* (1966); (20) Ted Berkman, *Cast a Giant Shadow* (1967); (21) Louis Falstein, *The Man Who Loved Laughter* (1968); (22) Sophie Greenspan, *Westward With Fremont* (1969); (23) Sarah Neshamit, *The Children of Mapu Street* (1970); (24) Ellen Norman Stern, *Embattled Justice* (1971); (25) Dvorah Omer, *Rebirth: The Story of Eliezer Ben Yehudah* (1972).

18. *AJYB* 62 (1961), p. 477; 65 (1964), p. 467; TM (December 9, 1958; September 13, 1962); *JPSBM* 7 (December, 1962), p. 2; see also Donna E. Norton, "Centuries of Biography for Childhood," *Vitae Scholasticae* 31 (Spring, 1984), pp. 113–127; and the criticisms of Inabeth Miller in "American Jewish Children's Literature: Narrow Perspectives and Mixed Messages," *JBA* 43 (1985–86), p. 99.

19. TM (September 11, 1957; December 9, 1958; *AJYB* 60 (1959), p. 381; *JPSBM* 5 (June, 1958), p. 3; 6 (December, 1959), p. 2; "[Draft] Contract with Meridian Books" (1957); Solomon Grayzel to Oscar I. Janowsky (October 27, 1958), both in PC–C. See Hans Schmoller, "The Paperback Revolution," in Asa Briggs (ed.) *Essays in the History of Publishing* (London, 1974), pp. 283–318.

20. TM (October 18, 1964); *AJYB* 62 (1961), p. 475.

21. PC–M (October 14, 1956); Carter, *Another Part of the Fifties,* pp. 106, 224; Janowsky, *The JWB Survey*; Eli Ginzberg, *Agenda for American Jews* (New York: 1950), p. v; Naomi W. Cohen, *Not Free to Desist* (Philadelphia: 1972), p. 339; *JPSBM* 7 (March, 1960), p. 2.

22. "Profile of Membership," *Jewish Publication Society's Membership Survey* (November, 1958), copy in box 13, EW2P; bracketed figures are taken from the "summary of findings."

23. Executive Committee minutes (February 2, 1959).

24. "Preliminary Report of the [Ginzberg] Survey" [October, 1958], box 146, JPSP.

25. "Final Report of the [Ginzberg] Survey" (April 14, 1959), box 146, JPSP.

26. Earlier, the Society published several novels including Joseph Opatashu, *The Last Revolt* (1952); Ruben Rothgiesser, *The Well of Gerar* (1953); Margaret Abrams, *Awakened* (1954); Soma Morgenstern, *The Third Pillar* (1955); Solomon Simon, *My Jewish Roots* (1956); Jacob Picard, *The Marked One, The Lottery Ticket, and Eleven Other Stories* (1956); Bernard Malamud, *The Magic Barrel* (co-published, 1958). Subsequently, it published Solomon Simon's *In the Thicket* (1963), an autobiographical novel dealing with yeshiva life in Eastern Europe.

27. PC–M (November 1, 1959), p. 4; TM (June 27, 1960); *AJYB* 61 (1960), p. 446; 62 (1961), p. 482; 63 (1962), p. 587; *JPSBM* 8 (September, 1961), p. 3; 9 (December, 1962), p. 1; Grayzel, "Oral History," p. 37.

28. Under the new procedure, the publication committee was divided into eight subcommittees and given expanded functions, especially in the area of planning. Predictably, the committees were only as good as their chairmen—most of whom were too busy to do what was needed. The system never functioned effectively and was quietly abandoned after Grayzel retired. TM (March 22, 1960), (June 27, 1960); *AJYB* 62 (1961), p. 476; Grayzel, "Oral History," pp. 50–51.

29. Amram Fund file, box 15, EW2P; Solomon Grayzel, "A Program for JPS," appended to TM (June 27, 1960).

30. See, for example, *JPSBM* 2 (March, 1955), pp. 4–7; 2 (June, 1955), p. 7.

31. Grayzel, "Oral History," p. 44; *AJYB* 54 (1953), p. 596; Lewis Strauss to JPS (January 15, 1959), PC–C; TM (June 27, 1955); "Consolidated Books file," PC–C; TM (April 6, 1954); Solomon Grayzel, "The Hebrew-English Bible [1955]," PC–C; *JPSBM* 2 (September, 1955), p. 7; (December, 1955), p. 1; *AJYB* 59 (1958), p. 531.

32. *JPSBM* 7 (March, 1960), pp. 3–5; Lesser Zussman to E. Korngold (May 8, 1962), box 15, EW2P; *AJYB* 62 (1961), p. 479.

33. Louis Ginzberg, *Legends of the Bible* (Philadelphia: 1956); Ginzberg, *KOTL*, p. 75. Grace Goldin, *Come Under the Wings: A Midrash on Ruth* (Philadelphia: 1958); Baruch Litvin to Solomon Grayzel (July 7, 1958), PC–C. Litvin was the prime Orthodox complainant in the Mt. Clemens synagogue seating dispute, see his *Sanctity of the Synagogue* (New York: 1959).

34. *JExp* 64 (January 26, 1917), p. 2; H. Pereira Mendes to "Friend" [Cyrus Adler?] (May 3, 1925), PC–C; Horace M. Kallen, "Can Judaism Survive in the United States?" *Menorah Journal* 12 (1925), p. 555; "Report of the Children's Bible" and other correspondence, box 11, JPSP; PC–M (March 31, 1946), p. 3.

35. Solomon Grayzel to Mortimer J. Cohen (April 14, 1947), box 12, JPSP; Grayzel to Maurice Samuel (June 5, 1950), PC–C; Grayzel, "Oral History," pp. 67–68.

36. Solomon Grayzel, "Memorandum: The Next Step on the Bible" [1950], box 12, JPSP; Grayzel, "Oral History," pp. 67–68. Those invited to the meeting included Bernard Bamberger, Mortimer Cohen, Abraham Feldman, Solomon Freehof, Robert Gordis, Solomon Goldman, Julian Morgenstern, Harry Orlinsky, David de Sola Pool, Oskar Rabinowitz, Joseph Reider, and Shalom Spiegel; see also "Minutes of the Meeting Held September 15, 1949 by Jacob R. Marcus, Maurice Jacobs and Solomon Grayzel," box 12, JPSP.

37. Grayzel, "Memorandum" [1950]; Grayzel to Maurice Samuel (June 5, 1950); Maurice Samuel to Grayzel (June 17, 1950), PC–C; Jacob R. Marcus to Solomon Grayzel (December 2, 1952), PC–C; "Memorandum [A meeting of the JPS Committee on Bible Revision, February 11, 1952]," box 10, JPSP.

38. See *An Introduction to the Revised Standard Version of the Old Testament* (New York: 1952); Grayzel, "Oral History," p. 68: "The RSV was helpful in persuading the authorities of the JPS to undertake a similar venture."

39. Harry M. Orlinsky, "Wanted: A New English Translation of the Bible for the Jewish People" reprinted with an illuminating introductory note in Orlinsky *Essays*, pp. 349–362; cf. Ephraim A. Speiser, *New Light On the Eternal Book* [An Address to the 69th Annual Meeting of the JPS] (Philadelphia, 1957).

40. Harry M. Orlinsky to Lesser Zussman (May 27, 1953), PC–C; "Memorandum" (February 11, 1952), box 10, JPSP; Jacob R. Marcus to Solomon Grayzel (December 2, 1952), PC–C; TM (October 27, 1953; January 27, 1954); "Minutes on the Revision of the J.P.S. Bible" (December 29, 1953) filed with TM.

41. Grayzel, "Oral History," pp. 69–71; Speiser's role is spelled out in "Minutes" (February 9, 1955), box 10, JPSP. Ginzberg's name first appears in the Minutes of January 26, 1956; he is not mentioned in the account of the Bible committee in *AJYB* 57 (1956), p. 648.

42. Grayzel, "Oral History," pp. 70–71.

43. "Minutes on the Revision of the J.P.S. Bible" (December 29, 1953), filed with TM; see *JPSBM* 2 (June, 1955), p. 1: "The principles which Dr. Orlinsky and his colleagues will follow in compiling the new revision will be the same as those asserted for the 1917 JPS Bible."

44. Translation Committee Minutes (January 24, 1955; November 13, 1955); Solomon Grayzel to Advisory Editorial Committee [c. May, 1955], all in box 10, JPSP; *AJYB* 59 (1958), p. 529; *Tanakh* (Philadelphia: 1985), jacket blurb, see p. xvii: "the idea of a modest revision of the 1917 translation met with resistance, and the concept of a completely new translation gradually took hold."

45. Harry Orlinsky, "Telling It Like It Was [an Interview]," *Moment* 8 (December, 1982), pp. 39–40, for another account see Grayzel, "Oral History," pp. 72–74.

46. *JPSBM* 3 (June, 1956), pp. 1, 7; (September, 1956), p. 2.

47. Leonard N. Simons's solicitation letter (January 24, 1956), JPSP; *AJYB* 64 (1963), p. 528; cf. 61 (1960), p. 450; TM (March 23, 1967), p. 3; Edwin Wolf 2nd, personal comment. Bible Fund activities were suspended because the Society expected to have to launch a building fund.

48. See Orlinsky, *Notes*, and Joseph First to Edwin Wolf 2nd (February 26, 1958), as well as other papers in box 10, JPSP.

49. Grayzel, "Oral History," p. 73; Orlinsky, *Notes*, pp. 10–12; Orlinsky, *Essays*, p. 402.

50. [Ephraim A. Speiser], "To the JPS Bible Committee" [n.d., 1963]; Harry Orlinsky to Sol Satinsky (July 28, 1963), both in box 10, JPSP; cf. Orlinsky, *Notes*, p. 58; Grayzel, "Oral History," pp. 73–75; Orlinsky, "Telling It Like It Was," pp. 37, 43.

51. Orlinsky, "Telling It Like It Was," p. 44; "Preface," *Tanakh* (Philadelphia: 1985), pp. xv–xxi; Orlinsky, *Notes*, pp. 3–40; Orlinsky, *Essays*, pp. 396–417; on the debate regarding Gen. 10:10, see *JPSBM* 3 (September, 1956), p. 3; and Orlinsky, *Essays*, p. 415 n. 23.

52. Exodus 15:2, which reads "salvation" in early editions is changed to "deliverance" in the 1985 version of *Tanakh*.

53. Orlinsky, *Essays*, p. 361; *Tanakh*, p. xvii; Orlinsky, *Notes*, p. 40.

54. Pinchas Teitz to Sol Satinsky (October 18, 1962); TM (November 29, 1962); Grayzel, "Oral History," p. 85.

55. Theodore Gaster, "Translating the Bible," *Commentary* 36 (1963), p. 308; *JPSBM* 9 (December, 1962); 10 (March, 1963); "Introductory remarks by Edwin Wolf 2nd [n.d., c. 1963]," JPSP.

56. TM (September 27, 1962), (December 15, 1965); E.A. Speiser to Solomon Grayzel (April 5, 1963) and other correspondence in box 10, JPSP; Grayzel, "Oral History," pp. 73–78. When Speiser died in 1965, Orlinsky was appointed to write up the notes to the new Torah translation, and the translation committee as a whole voted to reverse some of the translations that Speiser had championed. Compare the 1962 and 1966 editions of *The Torah* for Genesis 3:5, 4:7, 6:3 *et al.*

57. Grayzel, "Oral History," pp. 75–78; *The Prophets* (Philadelphia: 1978), pp. v–x; Orlinsky, "Telling It Like It Was," p. 41; for Orlinsky's earlier view on emendations see his *Essays*, p. 413, quoting Margolis: "the business of textual emendation requires a sure tact which few possess." Cf. p. 417: "The translation committee ... would like to believe

that its new version of the Torah, in its internal and external break with the past, has set a new pattern which authorized Protestant and Catholic translations of the future will tend to follow."

58. TM (May 3, 1965); Les Zussman to Sol Satinsky *et al* (November 23, 1965), EW2P. The following paragraphs are based on Nahum M. Sarna and Jonathan D. Sarna, "Jewish Bible Scholarship and Translations in the United States," in Ernest S. Frerichs (ed.), *The Bible and Bibles in America* (Atlanta: 1988), pp. 103–111.

59. Orlinsky, "Telling It Like It Was," p. 40; *The Writings* (Philadelphia: 1982), pp. v–vii.

60. *The Writings*, pp. v–vii.

61. *AJYB* 83 (1983), pp. 399–400.

62. *Tanakh*, pp. xv–xxi; *AJYB* 85 (1985), p. 460; on the revisionist view of the "Judeo-Christian tradition" that took hold in the 1970s, see Mark Silk, "Notes on the Judeo-Christian Tradition in America," *American Quarterly* 36 (Spring, 1984), pp. 79–85.

63. *AJYB* 74 (1973), p. 641; 75 (1974–75), pp. 681–682; *The Jewish Publication Society of America Bible Commentary* [undated brochure (Philadelphia: 1975)].

64. Will Herberg, *Judaism and Modern Man* (Philadelphia: 1951), p. 7; cf. *AJYB* 57 (1956), p. 649; and Orlinsky, *Essays*, p. 361.

65. Arnold Eisen, *The Chosen People in America* (Bloomington: 1983), pp. 127–148; Eugene B. Borowitz, "The Career of Jewish Existentialism," *JBA* 32 (1974–75), pp. 44–49; Nathan Glazer, *American Judaism* (Chicago: 1972), p. 114; Robert M. Seltzer, *Jewish People, Jewish Thought* (New York: 1980), pp. 720–766; *AJYB* 62 (1961), p. 483. Note that Mordecai Kaplan's *Purpose and Meaning of Jewish Existence* (Philadelphia: 1964) dealt with the thought of Hermann Cohen, and (more briefly) that of Martin Buber, as well as Kaplan's own. See also Solomon Grayzel to Joseph B. Soloveitchik (October 13, 1952), PC–C: "In response to the needs of the day, [JPS] has embarked upon the publication of a series of volumes dealing with various aspects of Judaism as a religion. I need not point out to you how important the subject is and how important it is to acquaint the Jews of the United States with current thought in this area."

66. Solomon Grayzel to Joseph B. Soloveitchik (October 13, 1952), PC–C. A full list of Society books dealing with Jewish thought and published during this period is easily culled from *A List of the Books Issued by the Jewish Publication Society of America, 1890–1978* (Philadelphia: 1979).

67. Solomon Grayzel to Mortimer J. Cohen (August 12, 1948), PC–C [the original letter is typed entirely in capital letters].

68. Will Herberg, "From Marxism to Judaism," reprinted with an introduction in Arthur Cohen (ed.) *Arguments and Doctrines* (New York: 1970), pp. 98–113; Silk, "The Judeo-Christian Tradition," pp. 74–75; cf. Eisen, *The Chosen People in America*, pp. 128–130, 138–139, 155.

69. Solomon Grayzel to Milton Steinberg (March 10, 1950); Milton Steinberg to Solomon Grayzel (March 3, 1950), PC–C. Although Steinberg is obviously replying to an earlier letter which I have not found, Grayzel's subsequent letter seems to be no more than a reiteration of earlier concerns. See Herberg, *Judaism and Modern Man*, pp. 32–41, 74–78; Cohen, *Arguments and Doctrines*, p. 98; Steven T. Katz (ed.), *Jewish Philosophers* (Jerusalem: 1975), pp. 244–245; and now Harry J. Ausmus, *Will Herberg from Right to Right* (Chapel Hill: 1987), pp. 91–107; and David G. Dalin, "Will Herberg in Retrospect." *Commentary* 86:1 (July, 1988), pp. 38–43.

70. Abraham J. Heschel, *The Prophets* (New York: 1962), p. xix. The standard one-volume interpretation of Heschel's work is Fritz A. Rothschild (ed.), *Between God and Man: An Interpretation of Judaism from the Writings of Abraham J. Heschel* (New York: 1965).

71. Solomon Grayzel to Executive Committee (June 30, 1950), Louis Levinthal to

Solomon Grayzel (August 11, 1950), both in PC–C; TM (October 9, 1950). The sequel, *God in Search of Man: A Philosophy of Judaism* (note the change in subtitle from "A Philosophy of Religion") did not actually appear until 1955, owing to revisions. Heschel called it "a continuation and application of some of the ideas in *Man Is Not Alone* (p. 427)."

72. Neibuhr's review is quoted in a Farrar Straus press release (March 28, 1951); see also the undated [September, 1951] letter signed by Rabbis Barnett Brickner [Reform], Robert Gordis [Conservative], and Leo Jung [Orthodox] recommending the volume to all rabbis, both in box 22, JPSP. The Society printed Heschel's views on the Bible in *JPSBM* 1 (October, 1954), pp. 4–5 (accompanied by a photograph of a youthful, bare-headed, and unbearded Heschel, quite different from his later image). In later years, the Society co-published Heschel's *God In Search of Man* (1955); *The Prophets* (1962); *The Earth Is the Lord's* and *The Sabbath* [two books in one volume] (1963); *The Insecurity of Freedom* (1965); and *A Passion for Truth* (1974). It also published *Prayer, Humility and Compassion* (1957), a volume influenced by Heschel and written by his disciple, Rabbi Samuel Dresner, "for all those who want religion to play a vital role in their lives"; see *AJYB* 59 (1958), p. 531.

73. Silk, "Notes on the Judeo-Christian Tradition in America," pp. 65–85; for the Morgenstern quote see p. 68.

74. Trude Weiss-Rosmarin, *Judaism and Christianity: The Differences* (New York: 1943); Bernard Bamberger, *Fallen Angels* (Philadelphia: 1952), pp. 5 (italics added), 240, 250–51. For an earlier treatment of this theme, see Leo Jung, *Fallen Angels in Jewish, Christian and Mohammedan Literature* (New York: 1926).

75. Abba Hillel Silver, *Where Judaism Differed* (New York: 1956 [Philadelphia, 1957]), pp. 287–289, but cf. pp. 74–75. Silver went even further than Bamberger in attacking existentialism and neo-Orthodoxy, see pp. 178–79.

76. Leo Baeck, *Judaism and Christianity*, translated with an introduction by Walter Kaufmann (Philadelphia: 1960), pp. 3, 260. Abraham J. Heschel to Solomon Grayzel (November 7, 1951), and other correspondence, box 3, JPSP. Originally this volume was also to include Baeck's essay entitled "Spirit and Blood." Grayzel, however, found the essay's symbolic use of blood distasteful (Kaufmann called it "unAmerican"), and the essay was dropped. In 1965 the Society co-published Baeck's *This People Israel* with Holt, Rinehart and Winston.

77. Baeck, *Judaism and Christianity*, pp. 6–7.

78. James Parkes's volume was originally published by Soncino in 1934; Trachtenberg's was published by Yale University Press in 1943. On Jewish-Christian relations during this period, see David Berger, "Jewish-Christian Relations: A Jewish Perspective," *Journal of Ecumenical Studies* 20 (1983), pp. 5–32.

79. Solomon Grayzel to Louis Levinthal and Jacob R. Marcus (August 1, 1950), PC–C; TM (November 28, 1962).

80. Grayzel to Levinthal and Marcus (August 1, 1950), PC–C; Nahum N. Glatzer (ed.), *Franz Rosenzweig: His Life and Thought* (Philadelphia: 1953); for the *Commentary* symposium, and a convincing analysis as to why Rosenzweig proved so popular, see Eisen, *Chosen People in America*, pp. 149–152.

81. Hugo Bieber (ed.) *Heinrich Heine: A Biographical Anthology*, translated by Moses Hadas (Philadelphia: 1956); Max Wiener, *Abraham Geiger and Liberal Judaism* (Philadelphia: 1962); Hans Lewy, Isaak Heinemann, and Alexander Altmann, *Three Jewish Philosophers: Philo, Jehudah Halevi and Saadya Gaon* (Philadelphia: 1960)—a paperback reprint; Mordecai M. Kaplan, *The Purpose and Meaning of Jewish Existence* (Philadelphia: 1964), pp. 285–286; Julius Guttmann, *Philosophies of Judaism*, translated by David W. Silverman (Philadelphia: 1964). Other works that the Society published in this period and that deal with Jewish thought, broadly defined, include: Louis Ginzberg, *On Jewish Law and Lore* (1954); Solomon Freehof, *The Responsa Literature* (1954); Simon Dubnow (ed.) *Nationalism and History: Essays in Old and New Judaism*, edited by Koppel S. Pinson (1958);

C.G. Montefiore and H. Loewe, *A Rabbinic Anthology* (1960)—a paperback reprint; Salo Baron, *Modern Nationalism and Religion* (1960)—a paperback reprint; Solomon B. Freehof, *A Treasury of Responsa* (1963); and Joshua Trachtenberg, *Jewish Magic and Superstition* (1963)—a paperback reprint.

82. *AJYB* 54 (1953), p. 598; cf. 56 (1955), p. 646; Sidney Z. Vincent, "Toward A Cultural Break-Through," *JPSBM* 7 (March, 1960), p. 3 [this was the cultural study that led to the formation of the National Foundation for Jewish Culture]; see also *JPSBM* 11 (September, 1964), p. 3, where Solomon Grayzel calls Israel "both a challenge to our independent efforts and an opportunity to make them yield better results." On the larger question of Israel's relationship with American and world Jewry, a much discussed subject in the 1950s, see Charles Liebman, *Pressure Without Sanctions* (Rutherford, NJ: 1977).

83. *JPSBM* 1 (February, 1954), pp. 2, 6; 2 (December, 1955), p. 3; *AJYB* 56 (1955), p. 643; *JBA* 12 (1953–55), pp. 3–66; Eisen, *The Chosen People in America*, p. 128. Two full-scale surveys of American Jewish history appeared in 1954: Oscar Handlin, *Adventure in Freedom* (McGraw Hill); and Israel Goldberg ["Rufus Learsi"], *The Jews in America* (World Publishing Co.).

84. TM (November 5, 1952); Solomon Grayzel to Joshua Trachtenberg (March 16, 1951), PC–C.

85. Revealingly, both books in different ways sought to distance themselves from the filiopietistic studies so characteristic of the field. Marcus, in his preface, expressed his desire "to understand the facts *as they really were,* to penetrate beneath the surface of accomplished events." Historian Allan Nevins, introducing Korn, praised him for displaying "the detachment of a true historian." Jacob R. Marcus, *Early American Jewry,* (Philadelphia: 1951) volume 1, p. xiv; Bertram W. Korn, *American Jewry and the Civil War* (Philadelphia: 1951), p. ix.

86. Jacob R. Marcus to Solomon Grayzel (November 22, 1957), Unpublished Books Correspondence [Gutstein], JPSP.

87. Solomon Nunes Carvalho, *Incidents of Travel and Adventure in the Far West* (1954); Jacob R. Marcus, *Memoirs of American Jews* (3 vols., 1955–56); Benjamin II, *Three Years in America*, translated by Charles Reznikoff, (2 vols., 1955); Charles Reznikoff (ed.), *Louis Marshall: Champion of Liberty* (2 vols., 1957); Joseph L. Blau and Salo W. Baron, *The Jews of the United States: A Documentary History, 1790–1840* (3 vols., 1964—co-published with Columbia University Press); Harold U. Ribalow (ed.), *Autobiographies of American Jews* (1965). Curiously, Grayzel considered Benjamin's *Three Years in America*, translated from the original nineteenth-century German, and introduced by Prof. Oscar Handlin of Harvard, to be no more than "a curiosity" ("as a source book for American Jewish history its value is exactly zero"), and saved money by not having it indexed. But those who recommended it knew better, and time has proved them correct. An unpublished index may be found in the American Jewish Archives. See Marcus to Grayzel (July 19, 1956); Grayzel to Marcus (July 23, 1956), box 5, JPSP.

88. Jeffrey Gurock, *American Jewish History: A Bibliographical Guide* (New York: 1983), p. 11; Kathleen Neils Conzen, "Community Studies, Urban History, and American Local History," in *The Past Before Us*, ed. Michael Kammen (Ithaca, NY: 1980), pp. 270–271; Jonathan D. Sarna, "Jewish Community Histories: Recent Non-Academic Contributions," *Journal of American Ethnic History* 6 (Fall, 1986), pp. 62–70.

89. Solomon Grayzel to Maurice Jacobs (July 21, 1949); "Minutes: Editorial Board on Charleston History," (September 26, 1949), box 36, JPSP. Those listed as attending the meeting were Salo Baron, Carl Bridenbaugh, Uriah Z. Engelman, Morris Fine, Hyman Grinstein, Louis Hacker, Oscar Handlin, Charles Reznikoff, Edward Saveth, Nathan Schachner, Leo Srole, and Thomas J. Tobias.

90. Solomon Grayzel to Jacob R. Marcus (April 6, 1955); S. Howard Kaufman to

Solomon Grayzel (October 27, 1964), PC–C; *AJYB* 58 (1957), p. 525; Edwin Wolf 2nd and Maxwell Whiteman, *The History of the Jews of Philadelphia From Colonial Times to the Age of Jackson* (Philadelphia: 1956), a second "bicentennial" edition was issued in 1975.

91. Solomon Grayzel to Jacob R. Marcus (April 4, 1957); Jacob R. Marcus to Solomon Grayzel (November 22, 1957), PC–C. The Society did publish three semipopular biographies during this period: Norman Bentwich, *For Zion's Sake: A Biography of Judah L. Magnes* (1954); Alexandra Lee Levin, *The Szolds of Lombard Street* (1960); Alexandra Lee Levin, *Vision: A Biography of Henry Friedenwald* (1964).

92. Solomon Grayzel to Jacob R. Marcus (April 4, 1957); Jacob R. Marcus to Solomon Grayzel (November 22, 1957), PC–C. The community histories are: Charles Reznikoff, with the collaboration of Uriah Z. Engelman, *The Jews of Charleston* (1950); Edwin Wolf 2nd and Maxwell Whiteman, *The History of the Jews of Philadelphia From Colonial Times to the Age of Jackson* (1956); Selig Adler and Thomas E. Connolly, *From Ararat to Suburbia: The History of the Jewish Community of Buffalo* (1960); Louis J. Swichkow and Lloyd P. Gartner, *The History of the Jews in Milwaukee* (1963); Lloyd P. Gartner and Max Vorspan, *History of the Jews of Los Angeles* (1970); Isaac M. Fein, *The Making of an American Jewish Community* (1971); Steven Hertzberg, *Strangers Within the Gate City: The Jews of Atlanta 1845–1915* (1978). Several of these histories were initiated by the American Jewish History Center of the Jewish Theological Seminary.

93. Grayzel to Marcus (April 4, 1957), JPSP; Eisen, *The Chosen People in America*, pp. 134–135; Ben Halpern, *The American Jew: A Zionist Analysis* (New York: 1956); *Midstream*, (Winter 1963), pp. 3–45.

94. Moshe Davis to Solomon Grayzel (October 24, 1958; May 24, 1960), PC–C; Davis, *Conservative Judaism*, pp. 15, 20, and the jacket blurb; Davis, *Yahadut Amerika Be-Hitpathutah* (New York: 1951), p. xv. Davis's analysis was not without its critics; see Charles Liebman's controversial review-essay in *Tradition* 6 (Spring-Summer, 1964), pp. 132–140.

95. *JPSBM* 2 (March, 1955), pp. 2–3; Rachel Wischnitzer, *Synagogue Architecture in the United States: An Interpretation* (Philadelphia: 1955); *idem*, *The Architecture of the European Synagogue* (Philadelphia: 1964). Two other art books published for the tercentenary served related functions: Jeanette W. Rosenbaum, *Myer Myers: Goldsmith 1723–1795* (Philadelphia: 1954); and Stephen S. Kayser and Guido Schoenberger, *Jewish Ceremonial Art* (Philadelphia: 1955).

96. Irving Malin and Irwin Stark (eds.), *Breakthrough: A Treasury of Contemporary American-Jewish Literature* (Philadelphia: 1964); Leo W. Schwarz (ed.), *The Menorah Treasury* (Philadelphia: 1964).

97. Oscar Janowsky (ed.), *The American Jew: A Composite Portrait* (New York: 1942), p. x; TM (April 30, 1961); Oscar Janowsky (ed.), *The American Jew: A Reappraisal* (Philadelphia: 1964), pp. viii, 25, 384, 399; but see Edwin Wolf 2nd's essay, esp. p. 371, for the view that the community was suffering "disintegration at the edges" and needed new kinds of leaders.

98. Janowsky, *The American Jew: A Reappraisal*, pp. 49, 382–383. "[T]he idea that Israel, once it was established, could in any serious way affect Judaism in America, or Judaism in general, appeared in the 1950s largely illusory," Nathan Glazer wrote in 1957. Whether this was true at the time is not clear, but the widely accepted view that the situation changed only after the 1967 Six Day War seems to me, in light of the evidence here, to be quite wrong; see Nathan Glazer, *American Judaism* (2nd ed., Chicago: 1972), pp. 116, 169–172.

99. Solomon Grayzel to Jacob R. Marcus (April 15, 1954); Marcus to Grayzel (April 21, 1954), PC–C; Itzhak Ben-Zvi, *The Exiled and the Redeemed*, translated by Isaac A. Abbady (Philadelphia: 1957), a second revised edition was published in 1961.

100. *AJYB* 59 (1958), p. 525; 556 (1955), p. 647; Victor Tcherikover, *Hellenistic*

Civilization and the Jews, translated by S. Applebaum (Philadelphia: 1959); Yitzhak Baer, *A History of the Jews in Christian Spain*, translated by Louis Schoffman (Philadelphia: 1961; volume 2 appeared in 1966).

101. Max Brod, *Unambo* (New York: 1952), cover blurb; Raphael Patai, *Israel Between East and West* (New York: 1953; 2nd ed., 1970), pp. xiv, 337, 340. In the second edition, published by Greenwood Press, Patai added a new postscript in which he spoke of Westernization, rather than amalgamation (pp. 383, 388). Subsequent books include Shneor Z. Cheshin, *Tears and Laughter in an Israeli Courtroom* (Philadelphia: 1959); Herbert Weiner, *The Wild Goats of Ein Gedi* (paperback reprint, 1963); and Joseph Bentwich, *Education in Israel* (co-published with Routledge & Kegan Paul, 1965).

102. Patai, *Israel Between East and West*, p. 338; William Chomsky, *Hebrew: The Eternal Language* (Philadelphia: 1964), pp. 270, 277; Ahad Ha-am is specifically discussed on p. 275.

103. Leon Simon, *Ahad Ha-am* (Philadelphia: 1960); Leon Simon (ed.), *Selected Essays of Ahad Ha-am* (paperback reprint, 1962); for other volumes that included Ahad Ha-amist perspectives see Shalom Spiegel, *Hebrew Reborn* (paperback reprint, 1962); Arthur Hertzberg, *The Zionist Idea* (paperback reprint, 1960); and Norman Bentwich, *For Zion's Sake: A Biography of Judah L. Magnes* (Philadelphia: 1954). On Ahad Ha-am's influence in America, see Evyatar Friesel, "Ahad Ha-Amism in American Zionist Thought," in Jacques Kornberg, *At the Crossroads* (Albany: 1983), pp. 133–141.

104. *AJYB* 56 (1955), p. 647; TM (December 2, 1953); Lesser Zussman to Shoshana Rosenberg-Elbogen (September 25, 1958) PC–C; Ben Zvi file, JPSP; [regarding the translation]; TM (April 13, 1964) regarding Gerson Cohen's book, which was not published until 1968. See also TM (December 9, 1958) regarding the Society's commitment to purchase Israel bonds.

105. Chomsky, *Hebrew*, p. 276; Solomon Zeitlin, *The Rise and Fall of the Judaean State* (Philadelphia: 1962), volume 1, pp. xx–xxi. Subsequent volumes appeared in 1967 and 1978. Compare the pro-Zionist epilogue of B. Netanyahu's *Don Isaac Abravanel: Statesman and Philosopher*, one of the most important scholarly volumes issued during this period, and a volume that subsequently appeared in two revised editions (1953, 1968, 1972).

106. *JPSBM* 13 (March, 1966), p. 6.

107. *AJYB* 64 (1963), pp. 523–525; Grayzel, "Oral History," pp. 20–21, 60–62.

108. Grayzel, "Oral History," pp. 60–62; *AJYB* 67 (1966), pp. 569, 577–580; see *JPSBM* 12 (June, 1965) for the proceedings of celebration honoring Grayzel on his twenty-five years as editor. Actually, 1965 was already his twenty-sixth year in the position, which he assumed in 1939.

109. Part of the search committee's correspondence may be found in box 12, EW2P; see also TM (June 23, 1965).

110. *JPSBM* 13 (March, 1966), p. 1; TM (April 24, 1966); *AJYB* 68 (1967), pp. 556–564; "SG's Retirement Speech," Miscellaneous Papers, JPSP.

9   Continuity and Change

1. *AJYB* 72 (1971), pp. 584–587.

2. S. Lillian Kremer, "An Interview with Chaim Potok," *Studies in American Jewish Literature* 4 (1985), p. 85. The entire issue of this annual is devoted to "The World of Chaim Potok"; see especially Daniel Walden, "Chaim Potok, A *Zwischenmensch* (Between Person) Adrift in the Cultures," pp. 19–25. For other information and sources see Cynthia Fagerheim's bibliographic essay (pp. 107–120) and S. Lillian Kremer, "Chaim Potok," *Dictionary of Literary Biography*, vol. 28 (Detroit: 1984), pp. 232–243.

3. *JPSBM* 12 (December, 1965), p. 5.

4. TM (June 1, 1966).

5. *JPSBM* 13 (December, 1966), pp. 1, 7. Later, Potok used a similar term—"core to core cultural encounters"—to describe his own novels; see Kremer, "An Interview with Chaim Potok," p. 86, cf. p. 104.

6. *JPSBM* 14 (March, 1967), p. 4; TM (March 22, 1967; September 21, 1967; October 22, 1967; August 24, 1970). In 1969, JPS received permission to use the Amram Fund to support its translation program (TM, June 10, 1969).

7. *AJYB* 71 (1970), p. 638; Daniel Greenberg to Lesser Zussman (June 11, 1969); "Meeting of the Planning Committee" (May 28, 1969), both in box 13, EW2P; TM (December 16, 1969).

8. TM (October 16, 1972); Greenberg to Zussman (June 11, 1969).

9. TM (October 16, 1972; July 19, 1973); *AJYB* 74 (1973), p. 641; 75 (1974–75), p. 680.

10. *AJYB* 81 (1981), p. 413; TM (February 26, 1976; December 14, 1978; September 9, 1981).

11. Figures calculated from data found in *AJYB* and the Society's minutes.

12. *AJYB* 75 (1974–75), p. 682; and personal communications.

13. TM (September 9, 1981); *AJYB* 85 (1985), p. 455.

14. TM (March 23, 1967; April 28, 1968; December 21, 1970; April 13, 1971; December 1, 1975; September 13, 1976; July 6, 1977; April 1, 1982).

15. *AJYB* 76 (1976), p. 560; 84 (1984), p. 379.

16. *JPSBM* 13 (December, 1966), p. 6.

17. *JPSBM* 1 (February, 1954), p. 7. The volume was co-published with Syracuse University Press. Compare François Mauriac's foreword to the French edition of this work (1951) translated in the 1956 British edition: "Your first impulse on opening this book may well be to close it again rather angrily. We have had our fill of these shocking stories and we want to forget them, we want to forget that we are all involved, simply because we are human beings" (p. ix).

18. Jacob Robinson and Philip Friedman, *Guide to Jewish History Under Nazi Impact* (New York: 1960), esp. p. xx; Leon A. Jick, "The Holocaust: Its Use and Abuse Within the American Public," *Yad Vashem Studies* 14 (1981), pp. 303–318; Stephen J. Whitfield, *Voices of Jacob, Hands of Esau* (Hamden, CT: 1984), pp. 31–32; Deborah E. Lipstadt, "The Holocaust: Symbol and 'Myth' in American Jewish Life," *Forum* 40 (Winter, 1980–81), pp. 73–88; Sharon Muller, "The Origins of *Eichmann in Jerusalem*: Hannah Arendt's Interpretation of Jewish History," *JSS* 43 (Summer-Fall, 1981), pp. 237–254; cf. Edward Alexander, "The Holocaust in American Jewish Fiction: A Slow Awakening," *The Resonance of Dust* (Columbus, OH: 1979), pp. 121–146. Sidra DeKoven Ezrahi convincingly argues that Arendt's narrative "was the filter through which most Americans were able to conceptualize what was otherwise a morass of indigestible, unintegrable facts"; see her *By Words Alone* (Chicago: 1980), pp. 205, 242 n. 50.

19. Jacob Robinson, *And the Crooked Shall be Made Straight* (New York: 1965), p. viii; *JPSBM* 11 (December, 1964), p. 1. Significantly, the Society did *not* co-publish *The Scroll of Agony: the Warsaw Diary of Chaim A. Kaplan* that Macmillan issued the following year. Important as the volume may have been as a text, it did not carry the same message for American Jews searching to find meaning in the Holocaust. See the listing of this volume in *JPSBM* 13 (March, 1966), p. 2.

20. Arthur Cohen, *Arguments and Doctrines* (New York: 1970), pp. xvii, 519–520, 538.

21. The *Anthology*'s concluding words, spoken by a non-Jewish Polish doctor who helped Jews survive, drove the point home, see Jacob Glatstein *et al* (eds.), *An Anthology of Holocaust Literature* (Philadelphia: 1968), pp. xiii, xix–xxiii, 360, and especially 395.

22. Leni Yahil, *The Rescue of Danish Jewry* (pb. ed., Philadelphia: 1983 [1969]), pp. x,

xix, 395. Yahil also argued that "the system has not yet been found which will insure the Jew living in the Diaspora the complete normalization of his situation as part of society and as an individual."

23. Haim Avni, *Spain, the Jews, and Franco* (Philadelphia: 1982); Charles Goldstein, *The Bunker* (Philadelphia: 1970), p. 7; Marie Syrkin, *Blessed Is the Match* (pb. ed., Philadelphia: 1976); *Spiritual Resistance* (Philadelphia: 1981); I quote descriptions of these books from the JPS Members Catalog (1986–87). For a later example, see Gila Ramras-Rauch and Joseph Michman-Melkman, *Facing the Holocaust* (Philadelphia: 1986).

24. Poliakov, *Harvest of Hate* (Philadelphia: 1954), p. 307; Yehuda Bauer, *Flight and Rescue: Brichah* (New York: 1970), p. 320; Hanoch Bartov, *The Brigade* (New York: 1968); Dahn Ben Amotz, *To Remember to Forget* (Philadelphia: 1973). Note that all of these books were co-publications. For a literary analysis of the Bartov and Ben Amotz novels, see Edward Alexander, *The Resonance of Dust* (Columbus, OH: 1979), pp. 84–91; 99–106.

25. *JPSBM* 14 (December, 1967), p. 1; cf. his earlier report from Jerusalem, *JPSBM* 14 (September, 1967), pp. 4–6.

26. Deborah Lipstadt, "From Noblesse Oblige to Personal Redemption: The Changing Profile and Agenda of American Jewish Leaders," *MJ* 4 (1984), pp. 295–309; the phrase is used on p. 306; see Jacob Neusner, *Stranger at Home: "The Holocaust," Zionism, and American Judaism* (Chicago: 1981); and Jonathan S. Woocher, *Sacred Survival: The Civil Religion of American Jews* (Bloomington, IN: 1986), pp. 76–80.

27. Hillel Halkin, *Letters to an American Jewish Friend* (Philadelphia: 1977), pp. 25, 77, 246.

28. Charles Liebman, *The Ambivalent American Jew* (Philadelphia: 1973), pp. viii, 196–197; Eliezer Schweid, *Israel at the Crossroads* (Philadelphia: 1973), p. 216.

29. William Novak in *Midstream* 23 (November, 1977), p. 91; for two of the lengthiest and most important reviews see Robert Alter in *Commentary* 64 (August, 1977), pp. 50–56; and Bernard Avishai in *New York Review of Books* (November 10, 1977).

30. Woocher, *Sacred Survival*, pp. 132–140; Neusner, *Stranger At Home*; cf. Lipstadt, "From Noblesse Oblige to Personal Redemption," esp. pp. 299–309; and for a different understanding of the meaning of the Holocaust, see Barbara S. Benavie, "The Holocaust: Something for Everybody," *Forum* 40 (Winter, 1980–81), pp. 89–92.

31. *AJYB* 72 (1971), p. 585.

32. *JPS Bookmark* 14 (March, 1967), pp. 1, 4, 5, 7; *AJYB* 70 (1969), p. 552; Arie Lova Eliav, *Between Hammer and Sickle* (pb. ed, New York: 1969), pp. 210, 224. The paperback edition, which Eliav published under his own name, included a postscript dealing with the impact of the Six-Day War on Russian Jews. For the history of the Soviet Jewry movement, see William Orbach, *The American Movement to Aid Soviet Jews* (Amherst, MA: 1979). Subsequent JPS offerings dealing with Soviet Jews include Israel Emiot, *The Birobidzhan Affair* (1981) and Martin Gilbert, *Shcharansky: Hero of Our Time* (1986).

33. *AJYB* 71 (1970), p. 638.

34. *AJYB* 70 (1969), p. 551; Zalman Shazar, *Morning Stars* (Philadelphia: 1967); Maurice Samuel (ed.), *Forward from Exile: The Autobiography of Shmarya Levin* (Philadelphia: 1967); Milton Hindus (ed.), *The Old East Side* (Philadelphia: 1969); Abraham Cahan, *The Education of Abraham Cahan*, translated by Leon Stein *et al* (Philadelphia: 1969); Joseph Brandes, *Immigrants to Freedom* (Philadelphia: 1971); Stanley Chyet, *Lives and Voices* (Philadelphia: 1972); Irving Howe, *World of Our Fathers* (New York: 1976); Nahma Sandrow, *Vagabond Stars* (New York: 1977); Irving Howe and Kenneth Libo, *How We Lived* (New York: 1979).

35. Joan Dash, *Summoned to Jerusalem* (New York: 1979); Cecil Roth, *Doña Gracia of the House of Nasi* (pb. ed., Philadelphia: 1981); Blu Greenberg, *On Women and Judaism* (Philadelphia: 1982; pb. ed., 1983); Michael Pollak, *Mandarins, Jews, and Missionaries* (Philadelphia: 1980).

36. Yosef Hayim Yerushalmi, *Haggadah and History* (Philadelphia: 1975), note Yerushalmi's awareness of "the current growing preoccupation of Jews with Jewish art." On the volume, see *Congress Monthly* 42 (March, 1975), pp. 9–12, 24; *AJYB* 76 (1976), p. 565; and Lawrence A. Hoffman's important review in the *Jewish Spectator* 41 (Spring, 1976), pp. 20–22.

37. Books published from 1978 to 1984 include Sharon Strassfeld and Arthur Kurzweil (eds.), *Behold a Great Image: The Contemporary Jewish Experience in Photographs* (Philadelphia: 1978); Mark Podwal, *A Book of Hebrew Letters* (Philadelphia: 1978); *Spiritual Resistance: Art from Concentration Camps, 1940–1945* (Philadelphia: 1981); Mark Podwal, *A Jewish Bestiary* (Philadelphia: 1984); Avram Kampf, *Jewish Experience in the Art of the Twentieth Century* (Philadelphia: 1984); and *The Jewish Heritage in American Folk Art* (Philadelphia: 1984). Later books of the same genre include: Bill Aron, *From the Corners of the Earth: Contemporary Photographs of the Jewish World* (Philadelphia: 1986); Kenneth Silver and Romy Golan, *The Circle of Montparnasse: Jewish Artists in Paris 1905–1945* (Philadelphia: 1985); and Bernard F. Stehle, *Another Kind of Witness* (Philadelphia: 1988).

38. George Savran and Richard Siegel, "The Jewish Whole Earth Catalogue: Theory and Development" (unpublished Master's essay, Brandeis University, April 1972), pp. 1, 10, 36; "A Conversation With Sharon Strassfeld," *The Eternal Light* (transcript of radio program, May 25, 1975), pp. 1–2. [I am grateful to George Savran for making the thesis he co-authored available to me, and for sharing with me some of his recollections, which are incorporated in this section. All of the conclusions, of course, are my own.]

39. Bill Novak, "The Making of a Jewish Counter Culture," *Response* 4 (Spring-Summer, 1970), pp. 5–10; Savran and Siegel, "The Jewish Whole Earth Catalogue," pp. 3–8, and appendix 1 [the original December 1971 letter soliciting contributions to the catalog]; Richard Siegel, Michael Strassfeld, and Sharon Strassfeld (eds.), *The [First] Jewish Catalog* (Philadelphia: 1973), pp. 6, 8–9; cf. "Symposium: The Havurot," *Response* 8 (Fall, 1970), pp. 11–31, and James A. Sleeper and Alan L. Mintz, *The New Jews* (New York: 1971).

40. "A Conversation With Sharon Strassfeld," pp. 2, 4–8; Sharon Strassfeld, Michael Strassfeld, and Richard Siegel to Contributors (n.d.; in the possession of George Savran). For an example of the kinds of changes in substance and tone that took place during the editing process, compare Sue Elwell and Josh Heckelman's draft of the "Baking Challah" section printed in *Response* 13 (Spring, 1972), pp. 83–92 [also in the appendix of Savran and Siegel, "The Jewish Whole Earth Catalogue"] with the section as finally published in *The [First] Jewish Catalog*, pp. 37–41.

41. *The [First] Jewish Catalog*, pp. 8–9; Savran and Siegel, "The Jewish Whole Earth Catalogue," pp. 12, 36–39; "A Conversation With Sharon Strassfeld," p. 5.

42. Solomon Grayzel to Harold Jonas (January 7, 1958), PC-C; "A Conversation with Sharon Strassfeld," pp. 8–9; Sharon Strassfeld in *Sh'ma* 16 (October 3, 1987), p. 142; Savran and Siegel, "The Jewish Whole Earth Catalogue," pp. 12, 52–53; William Novak, "The Last Word on the Jewish Catalog," *Moment* 1 (May-June, 1975), p. 81: "It was Potok who supervised its publication, turning the unformed dream into a well-designed and handsome volume."

43. Chaim Potok to Richard Siegel (July 5, 1973), PB.

44. *AJYB* 75 (1974–75), p. 680; 76 (1976), p. 564; Marshall Sklare, "The Greening of Judaism," *Commentary* 58 (December, 1974), pp. 51–57, and the subsequent exchange of letters in 59 (March, 1975), pp. 17–27; *Moment* 1 (September, 1975), pp. 9–12; Deborah Weissman, "And What of Zion?" *Jerusalem Post* (April 26, 1974); Shlomo Dinur, "Hakatalag Hayehudi," *Gesher* 21 (1975), pp. 96–100; "A Conversation with Sharon Strassfeld," p. 2.

45. Novak, "The Last Word on the Jewish Catalog," p. 84; *AJYB* 76 (1976), p. 565; cf. Sharon Strassfeld and Michael Strassfeld, *The Third Jewish Catalog* (Philadelphia: 1980), pp. 4–5. "Certainly, havurot, the *Catalogs*, and the whole 'alternative' Jewish movement are

all inner-directed and place a high value on satisfying the personal needs of their participants. Partly in reaction to much of the rest of American Jewry, which is wholly outer-directed, the havurot stand in opposition to the participation of people whose Judaism consists solely of supporting Israel, saving Soviet Jewry, or helping others to be Jewish—either physically or spiritually—but who do not spend time being Jewish themselves." For Novak's later views on havurot and Israel, see *Response* 22 (Summer, 1974), p. 111.

46. Strassfeld and Strassfeld, *The Third Jewish Catalog*, p. 5; Sharon Strassfeld and Michael Strassfeld, *The Second Jewish Catalog* (Philadelphia: 1976), p. 1.

Epilogue

1. Robert Alter, *Defenses of the Imagination: Jewish Writers and Modern Historical Crisis* (1978); Salo Baron, *Violence and Defense in the Jewish Experience* (1977); David Berger, *The Jewish-Christian Debate in the High Middle Ages* (1979); Daniel J. Elazar, *Community and Polity* (1976); Philip Friedman, *The Roads to Extinction* (1980); Simon Rawidowicz, *Studies in Jewish Thought* (1975); Gershom Scholem, *Sabbatai Sevi* (1975); idem, *Walter Benjamin: The Story of a Friendship* (1982); Joseph B. Soloveitchik, *Halakhic Man* (1984); Michael Stanislawski, *Tsar Nicholas I and the Jews* (1983); Norman A. Stillman, *The Jews of Arab Lands* (1980). Award-winning books are listed in *AJYB* 85 (1985), p. 451.

2. *AJYB* 85 (1985), p. 453; Y. H. Yerushalmi to "Members of the Publications Committee (March 29, 1984); Nathan Barnett to Members of the Association for Jewish Studies (nd [1985]), both in author's possession.

3. *JPS Members Catalog* (Spring 1986), p. 1; (Fall-Winter 1986), inside cover; David Rosenberg to "New JPS Publication Committee Members" (November 29, 1985).

4. *JPS Members Catalog* (Fall-Winter 1986), inside cover; Sheila F. Segal to Author (February 26, 1988; June 15, 1988), both in author's possession.

5. TM (October 31, 1984) contains the first suggestion that the words "of America" be deleted; the change was announced in the 1986 catalog. Of course, JPS was by no means alone in becoming multinational. The same trend was evident not only in American corporations, but in such Jewish organizations as Hadassah, B'nai B'rith, and the American Jewish Committee.

6. Executive Committee Minutes (April 10, 1978; September 15, 1978). On Philadelphia's role in American Jewish life, see Daniel Elazar, *Community and Polity* (Philadelphia: 1976), pp. 138–40, 239–41. The Society had earlier maintained small offices in New York— one of them opened as early as 1903—but none of them had the visibility or significance of the 42nd Street office. See Yosef Yerushalmi's comments on New York's "absolute primacy in the cultural and religious life of American Jewry," *Haggadah and History*, p. 57.

7. PC–M (April 20, 1986), p. 3; *AJYB* 81 (1981), p. 413; 82 (1982), p. 412; 83 (1983), p. 421; 84 (1984), p. 381; 85 (1985), p. 457; 86 (1986), p. 482; *Books for Children* [1987] (JPS catalog in author's possession); interview with David Adler (June 2, 1988; see also the 1988 Members Catalog, and *New York Times*, national edition (April 18, 1988), p. 34, on the growth of children's publishing.

8. Dorothy Harman, "Report to the Board of the Jewish Publication Society (January 25, 1985)"; see also the Jerusalem office's annual reports, and Shelly Kleiman, "Book marks," *Israel Scene* (July 1986), p. 22. I am grateful to Emily Biederman and Dorothy Harman for making this material available to me, and for filling me in on the office's activities.

9. *AJYB* 85 (1985), p. 461; Sheila F. Segal to Author (February 26, 1988), in author's

possession; *JPS Members Catalog* (Spring, 1988), p. 2; "He Brings His Skills to Jewish Publishing," *The New York Jewish Week*, August 5, 1988.

10. *A List of Books Issued by the Jewish Publication Society of America, 1890–1978* (Philadelphia: 1979), p. 1. For earlier evaluations of the Society's work, see Maurice Jacobs, "Generations of Jewish Literary Labor," *JBA* 7 (1948), pp. 89–100; and Solomon Grayzel, "Two Generations of Anglo-Jewish Book Reading," *YA* 9 (1954), pp. 109–125.

Announcement:
The Jewish Publication Society of America

The Jewish Publication Society of America appeals to the Jews of the United States for generous sympathy, active encouragement and liberal support. Organized at a National Convention of Jews, held at Philadelphia in June, 1888, it favors no special views and supports no particular party. The proud history of the past, with its glories and sufferings; the earnest striving of the present, with its ruggedness and asperity; the glorious prospect of a regenerated future, all are part of the life of Israel. The dweller in distant China, the pietist of Russia, the oppressed victim of Roumania and Morocco, equally with the learned and enlightened Jews of those countries and of Western Europe and America, are brethren of the house of Israel.

Holding these views the Society escapes the danger of sectionalism and narrowness, and cannot fail to do good work for a better understanding of the true aims and the true unity of Judaism.

The indifferent and the dull, who always fail to note the necessity of action, may say that such a society is not needed in this country; that here our political standing is exceptionally happy and our religious prosperity established and growing, but the earnest inquirer and keen observer will see manifold uses for a serious effort to create and diffuse a taste for American-Jewish literature.

No form of opinion can in our day grow without a literature, and especially true is this of a minority opinion like the Jewish religion. As we are but one in one hundred and fifty of the population of this country, all the great forces of prejudice, of party spirit, of acquiescence in the will of great majorities, of social and political power tend to favor opinions antagonistic to ours; tend even toward a certain contempt for our beliefs and our very name.

Under such circumstances it becomes our duty not only to avoid being misunderstood, but to secure for ourselves a patient hearing and fair judgment. To understand ourselves is therefore the first and most important problem. If our youth, and indeed our whole community find a certain depreciation of Jewish character and belief, subtly implied in books and papers of all kinds, such constant slights and insults must either weaken their self-respect or decrease the attraction of general culture.

The learned among us find an easy vindication against assaults in the consciousness of what we have done and suffered for the dignity of man and the betterment of conduct.

But it is precisely this position which the majority of us are not so able to assume that ought to be made easy.

We have given to the world the book, most wonderful in the effect it has produced on great masses in all climes and times—a true literature for the learned and the unlearned—a universal language of the heart and mind.

Do we feel the dignity of this our office? Are we not rather in peril of losing all share in our own inheritance?

The solemn dread with which the Scriptures were viewed in the past is yielding to another spirit. Many follow unthinking scorners who profane all reverence and deny all sanctity, while others, uncontaminated by such evil influence, are harassed by doubts and fears with which the intellectual air of our age is loaded.

Harsh utterance and disdainful silence are alike inadequate to remedy the evil.

If we would inspire our youth to hopeful partisanship in our cause, they must learn that we are the bearers of something worth preserving; that we have done and ought still to do great work for mankind, and that we hold sacred that "Hebrew truth" in whose service opposition, contempt and hostility may be incurred with honor and true glory.

Our literature illustrates this in every age and country. The true prophetic spirit is not dead within us. No people in the world has undergone so many downfalls and enjoyed so many revivals. Our neighbors know us as the people of the Bible, but only their great scholars appreciate the moral elevation of the Talmud, the tremendous Cabalistical movement, the great Spanish literature, and the enormous revival since Mendelssohn.

In the English language there are few printed works to throw light on these subjects, but there has never been a time in the history of American Judaism, when we were so able to remedy the deficiency as we are at present.

Our brethren in this country are growing in prosperity and intelligence. One by one scholars are arising among us who, by their devotion to Jewish literature and their high general culture, reflect honor on our community. They are specially fitted to become true interpreters of Judaism to us and to our neighbors.

In order to profit by their labors, organized effort is necessary. Scholars who devote their lives to literature must be supported like other workers. Hitherto we have expected our clergymen to use their spare moments by giving us literature gratuitously, forgetting that special studies are almost impossible to persons whose official duties leave them little leisure, and that authorship is in itself an honorable and useful profession.

In support of this opinion, we have the experience of other religious denominations. Our Christian neighbors have on their side all those forces which are against us, or at all events not with us, and they, it might be thought, could dispense with the aid of publication societies. But instead of taking this view, they have energetically supported such institutions.

More than a hundred years ago, the Wesleyans began this labor, and now Bible, Tract and Publication Societies do an immense and beneficent work. The Methodist Book

Concern, the Baptist Publication Society, the Congregational Publishing Society and the Presbyterian Board are all active and prosperous. A few figures will show this:

Receipts of various societies from 1881 to 1887 (seven years):

Methodist Book Concern,	$13,857,520
Baptist Publishing Board,	2,816,046
Presbyterian,	1,845,354
Congregational Board,	808,349

In order to make clear the earnestness of these denominations, we will give the number of communicants of each of these churches in the year 1886:

Methodist,	4,601,416
Baptist,	3,729,745
Presbyterian,	1,431,249
Congregational,	436,379

This would give an average of about twenty-six cents per annum for each communicant, without taking into account the million of dollars annually spent for Bible and Tract Societies. Applying these figures to our community, in the same proportion, it is found that the Jews should contribute more than $30,000 per year for publication purposes.

The history of our own efforts in the past should stir us to renewed vigor. In the year 1844, when our population was less than 50,000, Rev. Isaac Leeser organized a society, which, in the course of three years, published thirteen volumes of popular and instructive reading.

Again, in 1874, another society was organized in New York, which lived for two years and published three volumes.

Our German brethren have done better work. Some of the most valuable contributions to modern Jewish literature were published by such societies; among them Grätz's "History of the Jews," Jost's "History of Judaism," and works by Philippson, Geiger, Frankl, Hamburger, Grace Aguilar, M. A. Levy, Fürst, Kayserling, Stein, Herzfeld, Neubauer, Cassel, Munk and other eminent writers.

The efforts of our German brethren are, alas, hampered by a revival of mediæval prejudices, which must in the end give way to enlightenment and toleration, but while the work which they have so bravely assumed halts, it befits us as free citizens of the noblest of countries to take it up in their stead.

In carrying out the task entrusted to us, we desire to enlist the sympathy and obtain the aid of all the Jews of this country, without regard to their places of residence or to their special opinions, and we recognize that this end would be unattainable were we to leave doubtful the principles by which we are to be governed. We sum them up as follows:

(1) All periods in the history of Israel, from the time of Abraham to our own, are integral portions of the life of our community.

(2) Our career in the past and our activity in the present cannot be adequately set forth either to our own community or to our neighbors without a literature.

(3) Such a literature must be free from mere aggressiveness against differing opinions, whether within or without our ranks. It must combat error by presenting truth and not by assailing adversaries.

(4) Such a literature must be in the main popular; that is, adapted for general reading rather than for scholars in special branches.

(5) It must aspire to excellence of style and tone, and, as a rule, it must be in the English language.

(6) The mechanical execution of the work must be good, and the publications should preserve such a uniformity of apprearance, that subscribers will be encouraged to keep them together and thus make them a library of reference.

(7) Above all, the publication committee must have in view the sole purpose of doing the most good, and to that end must be entirely free from prejudices, for or against particular opinions or persons; since all Jews of every shade of belief are equally concerned in our work.

It cannot be expected or desired that the responsible officers and committees of the Association shall sacrifice their right to hold their opinions and beliefs, but it is imperatively demanded that they sacredly respect the opinions and beliefs of others. Our declaration of principles is not intended as any man's creed; it is a method by which many men of many minds may work harmoniously together to one common end.

The benefits of this institution, if well established and carried on, will be limited to no class among us.

Our children of all ages will be strengthened and improved by new and friendly sources of knowledge. Their native talents will be stimulated and developed. A new generation of men and women will arise, whose hunger for a larger culture will find nourishing food in this field, specially our own.

The earnestness, the emotional force and the generous enthusiasm of woman, will here find useful labors and grand rewards.

In every city, town and hamlet of this land, may we see women of Israel laboring to cement the bonds of unity, so that our organization shall become national in its extent—an organization not aiming at narrow individual advantages, but having in view the glory of our religion and our country, the elevation of our immediate brethren and all our fellow-citizens.

Nor have we achieved all that is desirable when the popular part of our work shall have become successful. As we grow stronger an ever-increasing learning will demand of us works of deeper scholarship, which comparatively few among us appreciate to-day—works whose publication will pay a debt to our country, and increase the consideration in which our neighbors hold us.

Let us hope that with our wants may grow our support, so that Israel in America may proudly claim its literary period, as did our ancestors aforetime in Spain, in Poland and in modern Germany.

Let us resolve that we, too, shall give our portion to the great structure of the world-literature, a portion ennobled by effort and suffering on the one hand, by a large love of humanity on the other.

Mere mission work or proselytism that seeks to add numbers to our ranks, we do not favor, but our whole history has been a process of converting the mind of the world around us to juster conceptions of duty and fraternity.

In this task we will not fail if our brethren in every place gather together and resolve that we shall succeed.

Our constitution, a copy of which is printed herewith, provides for members paying three dollars per year, patrons paying twenty dollars per year, and life members paying one hundred dollars. Jewish societies of any kind may become members by paying ten dollars yearly, and for every additional contribution of five dollars yearly, such society is entitled to an additional vote.

Every member is entitled to receive all the publications of the Society.

The Secretary is prepared to furnish blank subscription lists to all who take an interest in the cause. Send for these blanks and have them filled with subscriptions for memberships, and see to it that everyone who ought to subscribe does so. With a Jewish population of nearly 400,000 souls in this country, we should secure no less than 10,000 members and patrons.

A word only to those who feel doubt or discouragement. It is easy to save effort by looking with hopelessness on new movements. We can become true prophets of evil by causing the evil.

On the other hand, if all will enthusiastically hope, we cannot fail. The cause is good, the harvest is ripe, the workers are many, and success means a great step forward for Judaism and for humanity.

By order of the Executive Board,

MORRIS NEWBURGER,
President.

November 8, 1888.

Office of the Association,
714 Market Street, Philadelphia.

JPS Officers and Editors
1888–1988

PRESIDENTS

1888–1903	MORRIS NEWBURGER	1966–1969	JOSEPH M. FIRST
1903–1913	EDWIN WOLF	1969–1972	WILLIAM S. FISHMAN
1913–1933	SIMON MILLER	1972–1975	JEROME J. SHESTACK
1933–1949	JACOB SOLIS-COHEN, JR.	1975–1978	A. LEO LEVIN
1949–1954	LOUIS LEVINTHAL	1978–1981	EDWARD B. SHILS
1954–1959	EDWIN WOLF, 2ND	1981–1984	MURIEL M. BERMAN
1959–1960	HORACE STERN	1984–1987	CHARLES R. WEINER
1960–1966	SOL SATINSKY	1987–	EDWARD E. ELSON

EDITORS

1893–1916	HENRIETTA SZOLD *Secretary, Publication Committee*	1966–1974	CHAIM POTOK
1916–1924	BENZION HALPER	1974–1983	MAIER DESHELL
1924–1939	ISAAC HUSIK	1984–1985	DAVID ROSENBERG
1939–1966	SOLOMON GRAYZEL	1986–	SHEILA F. SEGAL

PUBLICATION COMMITTEE CHAIRMEN

1888–1923	MAYER SULZBERGER	1954–1961	LOUIS LEVINTHAL
1923–1934	CYRUS ADLER	1961–1969	EDWIN WOLF, 2ND
1934–1939	JACOB SOLIS-COHEN, JR. *Acting Chairman*	1969–1973	GERSON D. COHEN
		1973–1984	YOSEF HAYIM YERUSHALMI
1939–1949	LOUIS LEVINTHAL	1984–	CHAIM POTOK
1949–1954	JACOB R. MARCUS		

EXECUTIVE OFFICERS

1890–1906	CHARLES BERNHEIMER *Assistant Secretary*	1950–1960	LESSER ZUSSMAN *Executive Secretary*
1906–1926	GEORGE DOBSEVAGE *Assistant Secretary*	1960–1972	*Executive Director*
1926–1936	JULIUS GRODINSKY *Secretary*	1972–1974	DAVID C. GROSS *Executive Vice President*
1936–1950	MAURICE JACOBS *Secretary*	1974–1985	BERNARD I. LEVINSON *Executive Vice President*
1939–1944	*Executive Director*	1985–1987	NATHAN BARNETT *Executive Vice President*
1944–1950	*Executive Vice President*	1988–	RICHARD MALINA *Executive Director*

JPS Governing Boards
1888–1988

JPS Authors, Translators, and Illustrators 1888–1988

ABRAHAMS, ISRAEL
> *Jewish Life in the Middle Ages*, 1896 (with Macmillan)
> *Chapters on Jewish Literature*, 1899
> and David Yellin, *Maimonides*, 1903 (with the Jewish Historical Society of England)
> *The Book of Delight and Other Papers*, 1912
> *By-Paths in Hebrew Bookland*, 1920
> *Hebrew Ethical Wills*, 1926 (editor)

ABRAHAMS, ROBERT D.
> *Mr. Benjamin's Sword*, illustrated by Herschel Levit, 1948
> *Room for a Son*, 1951
> *The Commodore*, 1954
> *The Uncommon Soldier*, 1959 (with Farrar, Straus and Cudahy)
> *The Sound of Bow Bells: Sir David Salomons*, 1962

ABRAMS, MARGARET
> *Awakened: A Novel*, 1954

ADLER, CYRUS
> *American Jewish Year Book*, 5660–5666, 5677 / 1899–1905, 1916 (editor; co-editor with
>   Henrietta Szold on 1905 volume)
> *The Voice of America on Kishineff*, 1904 (editor)
> *The Holy Scriptures*, 1917 (editor)
> *I Have Considered the Days*, 1941
> See Robinson, Ira

ADLER, ELKAN NATHAN
> *Jews in Many Lands*, 1905
> *London*, 1930 (Jewish Communities Series)

ADLER, LIEBMAN
> *Sabbath Hours: Thoughts*, translated by Wilhemina Jastrow, 1893

ADLER, SELIG
> and Thomas E. Connolly, *From Ararat to Suburbia: The History of the Jewish Community of
>   Buffalo*, 1960

AGNON, S.Y.
Twenty-One Stories, edited by Nahum Glatzer, 1970 (with Schocken Books)

AGUILAR, GRACE
The Vale of Cedars and Other Tales, 1902

AHAD, HA'AM
See Ginzberg, Asher

ALBO, JOSEPH
Sefer Ha-ʿIkkarim: Book of Principles, edited and translated by Isaac Husik, volumes 1 and 2, 1929; volumes 3 and 4, 1930 (Schiff Library of Jewish Classics)

ALEXANDER, LLOYD
Border Hawk: August Bondi, 1958 (with Farrar, Straus and Cudahy)
Aaron Lopez: The Flagship Hope, 1960

ALOFSIN, DOROTHY
The Nightingale's Song, 1945

ALTER, ROBERT
Defenses of the Imagination: Jewish Writers and Modern Historical Crisis, 1978
The Art of Biblical Narrative, 1981

ALTMANN, ALEXANDER
Three Jewish Philosophers: Philo, Jehudah Halevi, and Saadya Gaon, translated with Isaak Heinemann and Hans Lewy, 1960
Moses Mendelssohn: A Biographical Study, 1973

AMI, BEN   (PSEUD. OF ARIE LOVA ELIAV)
Between Hammer and Sickle, 1967

AMICHAI, YEHUDA
The World is a Room, translated by Elinor Grumet, Hillel Halkin, Ada Hameirit-Sarell, Jules Harlow, and Yosef Schachter, 1984
JPS Poetry Series, co-editor with Allen Mandelbaum, 1979–

AMOTZ, DAHN BEN
To Remember, To Forget, translated by Zeva Shapiro, 1974

ANDERSON, ELLIOTT   EDITOR
Contemporary Israeli Literature, 1977

ANGEL, MARC D.
La America, 1982

APSLER, ALFRED
Louis Fleischner: Northwest Pioneer, 1960
Court Factor: Samson Wertheimer, 1964

ARKIN, MARCUS
Aspects of Jewish Economic History, 1975

ARKUSH, ALLAN   TRANSLATOR
See Scholem, Gershom S.

ARON, BILL
From the Corners of the Earth, introduction by Chaim Potok, 1985 (Philip and Muriel Berman edition)

ARONIN, BEN
The Secret of the Sabbath Fish, 1979

ARZT, MAX   BIBLE TRANSLATION COMMITTEE
  The Torah: The Five Books of Moses, 1962
  The Prophets: Nevi'im, 1978
  TANAKH: The Holy Scriptures, 1985

ASH, SHOLOM
  Kiddush Ha-Shem: An Epic of 1648, translated by Rufus Learsi (pseud. of Israel Goldberg),
    1926
  Sabbatai Zevi: A Tragedy in Three Acts and Six Scenes with a Prologue and an Epilogue,
    translated by Florence Whyte and George Rapall Noyes, 1930

ASHTOR, ELIYAHU
  The Jews of Moslem Spain, volume 1, 1979; volume 2, 1979; volume 3, 1984, translated by
    Aaron Klein and Jenny Machlowitz Klein

AVNI, HAIM
  Spain, the Jews, and Franco, translated by Emanuel Shimoni, 1982

BAECK, LEO
  Judaism and Christianity, 1958
  This People Israel, 1965 (with Holt, Rinehart and Winston)

BAER, YITZHAK
  A History of the Jews in Christian Spain, translated by Louis Schoffman, volume 1, 1961;
    volume 2, 1966; paperback in 2 volumes, 1978

BAMBERGER, BERNARD J.   BIBLE TRANSLATION COMMITTEE
  Fallen Angels, 1952
  The Torah: The Five Books of Moses, 1962
  Book of Jeremiah, foreword to, 1974
  The Prophets: Nevi'im, 1978
  TANAKH: The Holy Scriptures, 1985

BARON, JOSEPH L.   EDITOR
  Candles in the Night: Jewish Tales by Gentile Authors, 1940
  Stars and Sand: Jewish Notes by Non-Jewish Notables, 1943

BARON, SALO WITTMAYER
  The Jewish Community: Its History and Structure to the American Revolution, volumes 1, 2,
    and 3, 1942
  Modern Nationalism and Religion, 1960 (paperback reprint with Meridian Books)
  The Jews of the United States, 1790–1840, 3 volumes, 1963 (with Columbia University Press)
    (co-editor with Joseph L. Blau)
  History and Jewish Historians, 1964
  A Social and Religious History of the Jews (Ancient Times to 1650), 18 volumes, 1937–1983
    (with Columbia University Press)
  Steeled by Adversity, 1971
  Violence and Defense in the Jewish Experience, 1977 (co-editor with George S. Wise)

BARTOV, HANOCH
  The Brigade: A Novel, translated by David Segal, 1967 (with Holt, Rinehart and Winston)
  Whose Little Boy Are You?, translated by Hillel Halkin, 1979

BARUCH, FRANZISCA
  The Book of Jonah, woodcut illustrations by Jacob Steinhardt, 1953
  The Book of Ruth, woodcut illustrations by Jacob Steinhardt, 1957

BASSECHES, MAURICE   EDITOR
    American Jewish Year Book, 5708 / 1947

BAUER, YEHUDA
    From Diplomacy to Resistance, 1970
    My Brother's Keeper: A History of the American Jewish Joint Distribution Committee,
        1929–1939, 1974

BAUMANN, FRED   TRANSLATOR
    See Strauss, Leo

BAYER, LINDA
    The Blessing and the Curse, 1988

BEER-HOFMANN, RICHARD
    Jacob's Dream: A Prologue, translated by Ida Bension Wynn, 1946

BEIN, ALEX
    Theodore Herzl: A Biography, translated by Maurice Samuel, 1940
    Theodore Herzl, 1962 (paperback with Meridian Books)

BELLOW, SAUL
    To Jerusalem and Back, 1976 (with Viking Press)

BEN-ZVI, YITZHAK
    The Exiled and the Redeemed, translated by Isaac A. Abbady, 1957; new edition, 1961

BENJAMIN, I.J.
    Three Years in America, translated by Charles Reznikoff, 1955

BENTWICH, JOSEPH
    Education in Israel, 1965 (with Routledge and Kegan Paul)

BENTWICH, NORMAN
    Philo-Judaeus of Alexandria, 1910
    Josephus, 1914
    Hellenism, 1919
    Solomon Schechter: A Biography, 1938
    For Zion's Sake: A Biography of Judah L. Magnes, 1954
    My Seventy-Seven Years, 1961

BERENSTAIN, MICHAEL   ILLUSTRATOR
    K'tonton on an Island in the Sea, by Sadie Rose Weilerstein, 1976

BERGER, DAVID
    The Jewish-Christian Debate in the High Middle Ages, 1979
    History and Hate, 1986 (editor)

BERGES, MAX L.
    Cold Pogrom, translated by Benjamin R. Epstein, 1939

BERKMAN, TED
    Cast a Giant Shadow, 1967

BERKOWITZ, HENRY J.
    The Fire Eater, 1941
    Boot Camp, 1948

BERNSTEIN, HERMAN   EDITOR
    American Jewish Year Book, 5676 / 1914

BERNSTEIN, PHILIP
    To Dwell in Unity, 1984

BIALIK, HAYYIM NACHMAN
Aftergrowth and Other Stories, translated by I.M. Lask, 1939

BIBER, YEHOASH
Adventures in the Galilee, translated by Josephine Bacon, 1973

BIBLE
The Book of Psalms, translated by Kaufmann Kohler, 1903
The Holy Scriptures, 1917
The Holy Scriptures, The Pulpit and Family Bible, 1919
The Book of Psalms, 1925
The Holy Scriptures: An Abridgement for Use in the Jewish School and Home, edited by
    Emily Solis-Cohen, 1931
The Torah: The Five Books of Moses, 1962
Five Megilloth and Jonah, illustrated by Ismar David, 1969
Isaiah: A New Translation, illustrated by Chaim Gross, 1973
Psalms: A New Translation, 1973
Jeremiah: A New Translation, with woodcuts by Niko Stavroulakis, 1974
The Prophets: Nevi'im, 1978
The Writings: Kethubim, 1980
The Book of Job: A New Translation According to the Traditional Hebrew Text, 1980
TANAKH: The Holy Scriptures, 1985

BIEBER, HUGO
Heinrich Heine: A Biographical Anthology, translated by Moses Hadas, 1956

BILU, DALIA
See Shabtai, Yaakov

BIN GORION, EMANUEL   EDITOR
Mimekor Yisrael: Classical Jewish Folktales, collected by Micha Joseph Bin Gorion;
    translated by I.M. Lask, 3 volumes, 1976 (with Indiana University Press)

BIN GORION, MICHA JOSEPH
Mimekor Yisrael: Classical Jewish Folktales, translated by I.M. Lask, edited by Emanuel Bin
    Gorion, 3 volumes, 1976 (with Indiana University Press)

BISNO, BEATRICE
Tomorrow's Bread, 1938

BLAU, JOSEPH L.   EDITOR
and Salo W. Baron, *The Jews of the United States, 1790–1840,* 3 volumes, 1963 (with
    Columbia University Press)

BLOCH, JOSHUA
*Of Making Many Books: An Annotated List of the Books issued by the Jewish Publication
    Society of America, 1890–1952,* 1953

BLOOM, LLOYD   ILLUSTRATOR
Smoke Over Golan, by Uriel Ofek, translated by Israel I. Taslit, 1979

BLOOMGARDEN, SOLOMON (YEHOASH)
The Feet of the Messenger, translated by Isaac Goldberg, 1923

BRANDES, JOSEPH
and Martin Douglas, *Immigrants to Freedom,* 1971 (with University of Pennsylvania Press)

BRANDWEIN, CHAIM
In the Courtyards of Jerusalem, translated by Hillel Halkin, 1967

BRAUDE, WILLIAM G.   TRANSLATOR
  and Israel L. Kapstein, *Pesikta De-Rab Kahana: R. Kahana's Compilation of Discourses for Sabbaths and Festival Days,* 1975
  and Israel L. Kapstein, *Tanna Debe Eliyahu: The Lore of the School of Elijah,* 1981

BRENNER, YOSEF CHAIM
  Breakdown and Bereavement, translated by Hillel Halkin, 1971 (with Cornell University Press)

BROD, MAX
  Unambo: A Novel of the War in Israel, translated by Ludwig Lewisohn, 1952

BRODKEY, HAROLD
  Women and Angels, 1985 (Philip and Muriel Berman edition)

BRODY, HEINRICH   EDITOR
  Selected Poems of Jehudah Halevi, translated by Nina Salaman, 1924
  Selected Poems of Moses Ibn Ezra, translated by Solomon Solis-Cohen, 1934

BROWN, MICHAEL
  Jew or Juif?: Jews, French Canadians, and Anglo-Canadians, 1759–1914, 1986

BUBER, MARTIN
  For the Sake of Heaven, translated by Ludwig Lewisohn, 1945
  For the Sake of Heaven: A Chronicle, translated by Ludwig Lewisohn, 1953 (with Harper and Brothers)

BURSTEIN, CHAYA M.
  The Jewish Kids Catalog, 1983
  A Kid's Catalog of Israel, 1988

CAHAN, ABRAHAM
  The Education of Abraham Cahan, translated by Abraham P. Conan, Lynn Davison, and Leon Stein, 1969

CANFIELD, WILLIAM W.
  The Sign Above the Door, 1912

CARMI, GIORA
  And Shira Imagined, 1988

CARMI, T.   EDITOR
  The Penguin Book of Hebrew Verse, 1981 (with Viking Penguin)
  At the Stone of Losses, translated by Grace Schulman, 1984 (with University of California Press)
  Sunset Possibilities, by Gabriel Preil, preface to, 1986

CARVALHO, SOLOMON NUNES
  Incidents of Travel and Adventure in the Far West, introduction by Bertram Wallace Korn, 1954

CHAIKIN, MIRIAM
  Esther, illustrated by Vera Rosenberry, 1987

CHESHIN, SHNEOR Z.
  Tears and Laughter in an Israeli Courtroom, translated by Channah Kleinerman, 1959

CHOMSKY, WILLIAM
  Hebrew: The Eternal Language, 1956

CHOURAQUI, ANDRE N.
  Between East and West: A History of the Jews of North Africa, translated by Michael M.
    Bernet, 1968

CHYET, STANLEY   EDITOR
  Lives and Voices: A Collection of American Jewish Memoirs, 1972

COHEN, ARTHUR A.
  Arguments and Doctrines: A Reader of Jewish Thinking in the Aftermath of the Holocaust,
    1970 (with Harper and Row)
  The Jew, 1980

COHEN, BOAZ   INDEXER
  The Legends of the Jews, by Louis Ginzberg, volume 7, 1938

COHEN, GERSON D.   EDITOR
  Sefer HaQabbalah, by Abraham Ibn Daud, 1968

COHEN, ISABEL E.   EDITOR
  Readings and Recitations for Jewish Homes and Schools, 1895
  Legends and Tales in Prose and Verse, 1905

COHEN, ISRAEL
  Vilna (Jewish Communities Series), 1943

COHEN, KATHERINE MYRTILLA
  A Jewish Child's Book, 1913

COHEN, MARTIN A.
  Samuel Usque's Consolation for the Tribulations of Israel, 1964; paperback, 1977
  The Martyr: The Story of a Secret Jew and the Mexican Inquisition in the Sixteenth Century,
    1973

COHEN, MORTIMER J.
  Pathways Through the Bible, illustrated by Arthur Szyk, 1946; paperback, 1987

COHEN, NAOMI W.
  A Dual Heritage: The Public Career of Oscar S. Straus, 1969
  Not Free To Desist: The American Jewish Committee, 1906–1966, 1972
  Encounter with Emancipation: The German Jews in the United-States, 1830–1914, 1985

COHN, EMIL BERNHARD
  Stories and Fantasies from the Jewish Past, translated by Charles Reznikoff, 1951

COOPER, SAMUEL W.
  Think and Thank: A Tale, 1890

COPANS, STUART   ILLUSTRATOR
  The Jewish Catalog, 1973
  The Second Jewish Catalog, 1976
  The Third Jewish Catalog, 1980, by Sharon and Michael Strassfeld

COWAN, PAUL AND RACHEL
  A Torah Is Written, 1986

DAGAN, AVIGDOR   EDITOR
  See Society for the History of Czechoslovak Jews

DAN, JOSEPH
  Jewish Mysticism and Jewish Ethics, 1986 (with University of Washington Press)

DARMESTETER, ARSÈNE
The Talmud, translated by Henrietta Szold, 1897

DASH, JOAN
Summoned to Jerusalem: The Life of Henrietta Szold, 1979 (with Harper and Row)

DAUD, ABRAHAM IBN
Sefer HaQabbalah, edited and with an introduction and notes by Gerson D. Cohen, 1968

DAVID, ISMAR   ILLUSTRATOR
Five Megilloth and Jonah, edited by H.L. Ginsberg, 1969

DAVIDSON, ISRAEL   EDITOR
Selected Religious Poems of Solomon Ibn Gabirol, translated by Israel Zangwill, 1923 (Schiff Library of Jewish Classics)

DAVIS, MOSHE
The Emergence of Conservative Judaism, 1963

DAVIS, NINA   TRANSLATOR
See Salaman, Nina
Songs of Exile by Hebrew Poets, 1901

DAVITT, MICHAEL
Within the Pale: The True Story of Anti-Semitic Persecution in Russia, 1903 (with A.S. Barnes)

DAWIDOWICZ, LUCY S.
The War Against the Jews, 1933–1945, 1975 (with Holt, Rinehart and Winston)
Spiritual Resistance: Art from Concentration Camps, 1940–1945, essays by Lucy S. Dawidowicz, Tom Freudenheim, and Miriam Novitch, 1981 (with Union of American Hebrew Congregations)

DAYAN, MOSHE
Living with the Bible, 1978 (with William Morrow and Co.)

DEEM, ARIELLA
Jerusalem Plays Hide and Seek, translated by Nelly Segal, 1987

DEMBITZ, LEWIS N.
Jewish Services in Synagogue and Home, 1898

DEUTSCH, EMANUEL
The Talmud, 1895

DINUR, BEN ZION
Israel and the Diaspora, 1969

DONESON, JUDITH E.
The Holocaust in American Film, 1987

DONIACH, NAKDIMON S.
Purim or the Feast of Esther: An Historical Study, 1933

DORIAN, EMIL
The Quality of Witness: A Romanian Diary, 1937–1944, translated by Mara Soceanu Vamos; edited by Marguerite Dorian, 1983

DRESNER, SAMUEL H.
Prayer, Humility and Compassion, 1957

DUBNOW, SIMON
Jewish History: An Essay in the Philosophy of History, translated from the German of Israel Friedlaender by Henrietta Szold, 1903 (with the Jewish Historical Society of England)

History of the Jews in Russia and Poland, from the Earliest Times Until the Present Day,
 translated by Israel Friedlaender, volume 1, 1916; volume 2, 1918; volume 3, 1920
Nationalism and History: Essays on Old and New Judaism, edited by Koppel S. Pinson, 1958;
 paperback, 1961 (with Meridian Books)

DURSCHLAG, AUDRI   TRANSLATOR AND EDITOR
 with Jeanette Litman-Demeestere, *Hebrew Ballads and Other Poems,* by Else
 Lasker-Schuler, 1981 (JPS Poetry Series)

ELATH, ELIAHU
 Zionism at the U.N., translated by Michael Ben-Yitzhak, 1976

ELAZAR, DANIEL J.
 Community and Polity, 1976; paperback, 1980

ELBOGEN, ISMAR
 A Century of Jewish Life, translated by Moses Hadas, 1944

ELIAV, ARIE LOVA   (SEE AMI, BEN)
 Between Hammer and Sickle, 1967
 Land of the Hart, translated by Judith Yalon, 1974
 New Heart, New Spirit: Biblical Humanism for Modern Israel, with a foreword by Herman
 Wouk and an introduction by Amos Oz, 1988

EMIOT, ISRAEL
 The Birobidzhan Affair: A Yiddish Writer in Siberia, translated by Max Rosenfeld, 1981

ENDELMAN, TODD M.
 The Jews of Georgian England, 1714–1830: Tradition and Change in a Liberal Society, 1979

ENGELMAN, URIAH ZEVI
 and Charles Reznikoff, *The Jews of Charleston: A History of an American Jewish
 Community,* 1950

EPSTEIN, MORRIS   EDITOR
 Tales of a Sendebar (Mishle Sendebar), 1967

EPSTEIN, SEYMOUR
 Leah, 1987 (paperback, Gems of American Jewish Literature series)

EYTAN, RACHEL
 The Fifth Heaven, translated by Philip Simpson, 1986

FALSTEIN, LOUIS
 The Man Who Loved Laughter, 1968

FEIERBERG, M.Z.
 Whither? and Other Stories, translated by Hillel Halkin, 1973

FEIN, ISAAC M.
 The Making of an American Jewish Community, 1971

FEIN, RICHARD
 The Selected Poems of Yankev Glatshteyn, 1987 (JPS Poetry Series)

FEINBERG, ALFRED   ILLUSTRATOR
  David the Giant Killer, by Emily Solis-Cohen, Jr., 1908
  Step by Step, by Abram S. Isaacs, 1910
  The Game of Doeg, by Eleanor E. Harris, 1914
  The Power of Purim, by Irma Kraft, 1915
  The Breakfast of the Birds and Other Stories from the Hebrew of Judah Steinberg, by Emily
    Solis-Cohen, Jr., 1917

FELDMAN, SEYMOUR   TRANSLATOR AND EDITOR
  The Wars of the Lord, by Levi ben Gershom (Gersonides), volume 1, 1984; volume 2, 1987

FILMUS, TULLY
  Tully Filmus: Selected Drawings, 1971; paperback, 1978

FINE, MORRIS   EDITOR
  The American Jewish Year Book, volumes 49 and 50 / 1948–1949 (co-editor), volumes 51 to
    75 / 1950–1975

FINKELSTEIN, LOUIS
  The Pharisees: The Sociological Background of Their Faith, volumes 1 and 2, 1938; revised
    third edition, 1963
  The Jews: Their History, Culture, and Religion, 1949 (editor) (with Harper and Brothers)
  Akiba: Scholar, Saint and Martyr, 1962 (paperback with Meridian Books)

FISH, RICHARD   ILLUSTRATOR
  Haym Salomon: Liberty's Son, by Shirley Milgrim, 1975 (Covenant Book)

FRANK, HELENA   TRANSLATOR
  Stories and Pictures, by Isaac Loeb Perez, 1904
  Yiddish Tales, 1912

FRANK, ULRICH   (PSEUD. OF ULLA WOLFF)
  Simon Eichelkatz, The Patriarch: Two Stories of Jewish Life, translated by Adelle Szold, 1907

FREED, ELEAZAR
  The Mystery of the Silver Fish and Other Stories of Adventure, 1956

FREEDMAN, HARRY   BIBLE TRANSLATION COMMITTEE
  The Torah: The Five Books of Moses, 1962
  The Prophets: Nevi'im, 1978
  TANAKH: The Holy Scriptures, 1985

FREEHOF, LILLIAN S.
  Stories of King David, illustrated by Seymour R. Kaplan, 1952
  Stories of King Solomon, 1955
  The Captive Rabbi: The Life of Rabbi Meir of Rothenburg, 1965

FREEHOF, SOLOMON B.
  The Responsa Literature, 1954
  A Treasury of Responsa, 1963

FREIDENREICH, HARRIET PASS
  The Jews of Yugoslavia: A Quest for Community, 1980

FREIMANN, ARON
  and F. Kracauer, *Frankfort,* translated by Bertha Szold Levin, 1929 (Jewish Communities
    Series)

FREUDENHEIM, TOM L.
   Spiritual Resistance: Art from Concentration Camps, 1940–1945, essays by Tom
      Freudenheim, Lucy S. Dawidowicz, and Miriam Novitch, 1981 (with Union of
      American Hebrew Congregations)

FREUND, MICHAEL   CO-EDITOR
   with Robert Morris, *Trends and Issues in Jewish Social Welfare in the United States,* 1966

FRIEDENBERG, ALBERT MARX
   *The Sunday Laws of the United States and Leading Judicial Decisions Having Special
      Reference to the Jews,* 1908 (reprinted from the *American Jewish Year Book,*
      5669 / 1908)

FRIEDENBERG, DANIEL M.
   Jewish Minters and Medalists, 1976

FRIEDENWALD, HERBERT   EDITOR
   American Jewish Year Book, 5669–5674 / 1908–1913

FRIEDLAENDER, ISRAEL
   See Dubnow, Simon M.

FRIEDLAENDER MICHAEL
   See Magnus, Lady Katie

FRIEDMAN, ADA JUNE   EDITOR
   The Roads to Extinction: Essays on the Holocaust, by Philip Friedman, 1980 (with the
      Conference on Jewish Social Studies)

FRIEDMAN, ARTHUR   ILLUSTRATOR
   Hershel of Ostropol, by Eric A. Kimmel, 1982

FRIEDMAN, LEE M.
   Jewish Pioneers and Patriots, with a preface by A.S.W. Rosenbach, 1942
   Pilgrims in a New Land, 1948

FRIEDMAN, PHILIP
   The Roads to Extinction: Essays on the Holocaust, edited by Ada June Friedman, 1980 (with
      the Conference on Jewish Social Studies)

FRIEND, ROBERT   TRANSLATOR
   See Preil, Gabriel

FRUCHTER, NORMAN
   Coat Upon a Stick, 1987 (paperback, Gems of American Jewish Literature series)

GABIROL, SOLOMON IBN
   Selected Religious Poems, edited by Israel Davidson, translated by Israel Zangwill, 1923
      (Schiff Library of Jewish Classics)

GARTNER, LLOYD P.
   and Louis J. Swichkow, *The History of the Jews of Milwaukee,* 1963
   and Max Vorspan, *History of the Jews of Los Angeles,* 1970 (with Huntington Library)

GASTER, MOSES   TRANSLATOR
   Ma'aseh Book: Book of Jewish Tales and Legends, volumes 1 and 2, 1934 (Schiff Library of
      Jewish Classics); paperback, 1981

GAVRON, DANIEL
   The End of Days, 1970

GELLER, TODROS   ILLUSTRATOR
  Wonder Tales of Bible Days, by Elma Ehrlich Levinger, 1929

GERSHATOR, PHILLIS
  Honi and His Magic Circle, illustrated by Shay Rieger, 1980

GERSON, FELIX N.
  See Landsberger, Franz; Rothgiesser, Ruben; Straus, Raphael (translations of)

GERSONIDES
  The Wars of the Lord, translated by Seymour Feldman, volume 1, 1984; volume 2, 1987

GILBERT, MARTIN
  The Macmillan Atlas of the Holocaust, 1982 (with Macmillan Publishing Company)
  The Holocaust, 1985 (with Henry Holt and Rinehart)
  Shcharansky: Hero of Our Time, 1986 (with Viking Penguin)

GILBERT, MIRIAM
  Isaiah: The Mighty Voice, 1963

GINSBERG, H.L.   EDITOR, BIBLE TRANSLATION COMMITTEE
  The Torah: The Five Books of Moses, 1962
  Five Megilloth and Jonah, illustrated by Ismar David, 1969
  Isaiah: A New Translation, illustrated by Chaim Gross, 1973
  Jeremiah: A New Translation, with woodcuts by Niko Stavroulakis, 1974
  The Prophets: Nevi'im, 1978
  TANAKH: The Holy Scriptures, 1985

GINZBERG ASHER   (AHAD HA'AM)
  Selected Essays, translated by Leon Simon, 1912; new edition, 1936; paperback, 1962

GINZBERG, ELI
  Keeper of the Law, 1966

GINZBERG, LOUIS
  The Legends of the Jews, volume 1, translated by Henrietta Szold, 1909; volume 2,
      translated by Henrietta Szold, 1910; volume 3, translated by Paul Radin, 1911; volume
      4, 1913; volume 5, 1925; volume 6, 1928; volume 7, index by Boaz Cohen, 1938
  Students, Scholars, and Saints, 1928
  On Jewish Law and Lore, 1954
  Legends of the Bible, with an introduction by Shalom Spiegel, 1956 (with Simon and
      Schuster)

GLATSTEIN, JACOB   EDITOR
  with Israel Knox and Samuel Margoshes, *Anthology of Holocaust Literature,* 1969
  See Fein, Richard

GLATZER, NAHUM N.   EDITOR
  Franz Rosenzweig: His Life and Thought, 1953 (with Farrar, Straus and Young)

GLUECK, NELSON
  The River Jordan: Being an Illustrated Account of Earth's Most Storied River, 1946 (with
      Westminster Press)
  Rivers in the Desert: A History of the Negev, 1959 (with Farrar, Straus and Cudahy)

GOLAN, ROMY
  and Kenneth Silver, *The Circle of Montparnasse: Jewish Artists in Paris, 1905–1945,* 1985
      (with Universe Books)

GOLD, LEONARD   TRANSLATOR
  See Shaham, Nathan

GOLD, MICHAEL
And Hannah Wept: Infertility, Adoption, and the Jewish Couple, 1988

GOLDBERG, ISAAC
Major Noah: American-Jewish Pioneer, 1936
See Bloomgarden, Solomon; Opatoshu, Joseph (translator of)

GOLDBERG, ISRAEL   (RUFUS LEARSI)
Kasriel the Watchman and Other Stories, 1925
See Ash, Sholom (translator of)

GOLDIN, GRACE
Come Under the Wings: A Midrash on Ruth, introduction by Maurice Samuel, 1958;
    paperback, 1980

GOLDIN, JUDAH
Hebrew Ethical Wills, selected and edited by Israel Abrahams, 1976 (introduction)
Studies in Midrash and Related Literature, edited by Barry Eichler and Jeffrey Tigay, 1988
See Spiegel, Shalom (translator of)

GOLDING, LOUIS
In the Steps of Moses, 1943

GOLDMAN, SOLOMON
The Book of Books: An Introduction, 1948 (with Harper and Brothers)
In the Beginning, 1949 (with Harper and Brothers)

GOLDSMITH, MILTON
Rabbi and Priest: A Story, 1891

GOLDSTEIN, CHARLES
The Bunker, 1970

GOODMAN, ABRAM VOSSEN
American Overture: Jewish Rights in Colonial Times, 1947

GOODMAN, HANNA
with Philip Goodman, *The Jewish Marriage Anthology,* 1965
Jewish Cooking Around the World, 1974

GOODMAN, PAUL
Moses Montefiore, 1925

GOODMAN, PHILIP   EDITOR
The Purim Anthology, 1949; paperback, 1988
The Passover Anthology, 1961
and Hanna Goodman, *The Jewish Marriage Anthology,* 1965
The Rosh Hashanah Anthology, 1970
The Yom Kippur Anthology, 1971
The Sukkot and Simhat Torah Anthology, 1973; paperback, 1988
The Shavuot Anthology, 1975
The Hanukkah Anthology, 1976

GORDON, SAMUEL
Sons of the Covenant: A Tale of London Jewry, illustrated by Mark Zangwill, 1900
Strangers at the Gate: Tales of Russian Jewry, 1902

GOREN, ARTHUR A.
New York Jews and the Quest for Community: The Kehillah Experiment, 1908–1922, 1970
    (paperback with Columbia University Press)

GOTTHEIL, RICHARD J.H.
Zionism, 1914

GRADE, CHAIM
The Well: A Novel, translated by Ruth Wisse, 1967

GRAETZ, HEINRICH
History of the Jews, volume 1, 1891; volume 2, 1893; volume 3, 1894; volume 4, 1894; volume 5, 1895; translated by Bella Loewy; index volume, 1898, prepared by Henrietta Szold (with a memoir of the author by Phillipp Bloch)

GRATZ, REBECCA
See Philipson, David

GRAYZEL, SOLOMON   BIBLE TRANSLATION COMMITTEE
Outlines of Jewish History: From B.C.E. 586 to C.E. 1929, 1929, by Lady Magnus, revised by M. Friedlaender; revised new edition, 1929
A History of the Jews from the Babylonian Exile to the End of World War II, 1947
A History of the Contemporary Jews, 1961 (paperback reprint with Meridian Books)
The Torah: The Five Books of Moses, 1962
The Prophets: Nevi'im, 1978
TANAKH: The Holy Scriptures, 1985
See Grunwald, Max; Kober, Adolf (translator of)

GREENBERG, BLU
On Women and Judaism: A View from Tradition, 1982

GREENBERG, MOSHE   CO-EDITOR, BIBLE TRANSLATION COMMITTEE
Psalms: A New Translation, 1972, with Jonas C. Greenfield and Nahum M. Sarna,
The Writings: Kethubim, 1980
with Jonas C. Greenfield and Nahum M. Sarna, *The Book of Job: A New Translation According to the Traditional Hebrew Text,* 1980
TANAKH: The Holy Scriptures, 1985

GREENFIELD, JONAS C.   CO-EDITOR, BIBLE TRANSLATION COMMITTEE
Psalms: A New Translation, 1972 with Moshe Greenberg and Nahum M. Sarna
The Writings: Kethubim, 1980
with Moshe Greenberg and Nahum M. Sarna, *The Book of Job: A New Translation According to the Traditional Hebrew Text,* 1980
TANAKH: The Holy Scriptures, 1985

GREENSPAN, SOPHIE
Westward with Fremont, 1969
Masada Will Not Fall Again, 1973

GREENSTONE, JULIUS H.
The Messiah Idea in Jewish History, 1906
Numbers, commentary by, 1939
Proverbs, commentary by, 1950

GRINSTEIN, HYMAN B.
The Rise of the Jewish Community of New York, 1654–1860, 1945

GROSS, CHAIM   ILLUSTRATOR
The Book of Isaiah, 1972

GROSSMAN, EDWARD   TRANSLATOR
Refuge: A Novel, by Sami Michael, 1988

GRUNFELD, FREDERIC V.
Prophets Without Honor, 1979 (with Holt, Rinehart and Winston)

GRUNWALD, MAX
Vienna, translated by Solomon Grayzel, 1936 (Jewish Communities Series)

GURKO, MIRIAM
Theodor Herzl: The Road to Israel, illustrated by Erika Weihs, 1988

GUTTMAN, JULIUS
Philosophies of Judaism, translated by David W. Silverman, 1963 (with Holt, Rinehart and Winston)

HADAS, MOSES
See Bieber, Hugo; Elbogen, Ismar; Vogelstein, Hermann (translator of)

HADAS, PAMELA WHITE
In Light of Genesis, 1980 (JPS Poetry Series)

HAHN, EMILY
The First American Rabbi, 1959 (with Farrar, Straus and Cudahy)

HALKIN, ABRAHAM   TRANSLATOR
Crisis and Leadership: Epistles of Maimonides, 1985

HALKIN, HILLEL
Letters to an American Jewish Friend, 1977
See Bartov, Hanoch; Brandwein, Chaim; Brenner, Yosef Chaim; and Feierberg, M.Z. (translator of)

HALPER, BENZION
Post-Biblical Hebrew Literature: An Anthology, 1921

HALPERN, MOYSHE LEYB
In New York: A Selection, translated by Kathryn Hellerstein, 1983 (JPS Poetry Series)

HANUSCHAK, LUBA   ILLUSTRATOR
Birthday in Kishinev, by Fannie Steinberg, 1978

HARAP, LOUIS
The Image of the Jew in American Literature, 1975

HARRIS, ELEANOR E.
The Game of the Doeg: A Story of the Hebrew People, illustrated by Alfred Feinberg, 1914

HARTMAN, DAVID
Maimonides: Torah and Philosophic Quest, 1976; paperback reprint, 1986
Crisis and Leadership: Epistles of Maimonides, introduction and notes to, 1985

HAUTZIG, ESTHER
The Seven Good Years and Other Stories of I.L. Peretz, illustrated by Deborah Kogan Ray, 1984

HAZAZ, HAIM
Gates of Bronze, translated by S. Gershon Levi, 1975

HEINEMANN, ISAAK   TRANSLATOR
with Alexander Altmann and Hans Lewy, *Three Jewish Philosophers: Philo, Jehudah Halevi, and Saadya Gaon,* 1960

HELLER, LINDA
The Castle on Hester Street, 1982
Elijah's Violin and Other Jewish Fairy Tales, 1983 (with Harper and Row)

HELLERSTEIN, KATHRYN   TRANSLATOR
  See Halpern, Moyshe Leyb

HERBERG, WILL
  Judaism and Modern Man: An Interpretation of Jewish Religion, 1951; paperback, 1980

HERMAN, SIMON N.
  Israelis and Jews, 1971 (with Random House)

HERTZBERG, ARTHUR
  The Zionist Idea, 1960 (paperback reprint with Meridian Books)
  The French Enlightenment and the Jews, 1968 (with Columbia University Press)
  The Jews of the United States, introduction by, 1974 (with Keter Publishing House)
  Judaism as a Civilization: Toward a Reconstruction of American Jewish Life, by Mordecai M.
      Kaplan, introduction by, 1981 (with Reconstructionist Press)

HERTZBERG, STEVEN
  Strangers Within the Gate City: The Jews of Atlanta, 1845–1915, 1978

HESCHEL, ABRAHAM JOSHUA
  Man is Not Alone, 1951; paperback reprint, 1966 (with Harper and Row in the Torchbook
      Series)
  God in Search of Man: A Philosophy of Judaism, 1956 (with Farrar, Straus and Cudahy)
  The Prophets, 1962 (with Harper and Row)
  The Earth is the Lord's, 1963 (paperback reprint with Meridian Books)
  The Sabbath, 1963 (paperback reprint with Meridian Books)
  Insecurity of Freedom, 1966 (with Farrar, Straus and Giroux)
  A Passion for Truth, 1974 (with Farrar, Straus and Giroux)

HIMMELFARB, MILTON   CO-EDITOR
  The American Jewish Year Book, with Morris Fine, volumes 61 to 78 / 1960–1978; with
      David Singer, volumes 79 to 86 / 1979–1986

HINDUS, MILTON   EDITOR
  The Old East Side, 1969
  The Worlds of Maurice Samuel, 1977

HIRSCHLER, GERTRUDE   EDITOR
  See Society for the History of Czechoslovak Jews

HIRSH, MARILYN
  The Best of K'tonton, by Sadie Rose Weilerstein, 1980 (illustrator)
  K'tonton in the Circus, by Sadie Rose Weilerstein, 1981 (illustrator)
  Potato Pancakes All Around, 1982 (author and illustrator)

HOLTZ, BARRY W.   EDITOR
  Back to the Sources: Reading the Classic Jewish Texts, 1984 (with Summit Books)

HORWITZ, RIVKA
  *Buber's Way to "I and Thou": The Development of Martin Buber's Thought and His "Religion
      as Presence" Lectures,* 1988

HOWE, IRVING
  World of Our Fathers, 1976 (with Harcourt Brace Jovanovich)
  with Kenneth Libo, *How We Lived: A Documentary History of the Immigrant Jews in
      America, 1880–1930,* 1979 (with Richard Marek Publishers)
  with Ruth Wisse, *The Best of Sholom Aleichem,* 1979 (editor) (with New Republic Books)

HUHNER, LEON
  The Life of Judah Touro (1775–1854), 1946

HURWITZ, JOHANNA
   Anne Frank: Life in Hiding, illustrated by Vera Rosenberry, 1988

HUSIK, ISAAC
   A History of Medieval Jewish Philosophy, 1916
   Sefer Ha-'Ikkarim: Book of Principles, by Joseph Albo, 5 volumes, 1929–1930 (editor and
      translator)

HYMAN, FRIEDA CLARK
   Jubal and the Prophet, 1958 (with Farrar, Straus and Cudahy)
   In the Time of Nehemiah: Builders of Jerusalem, 1960

ILIOWIZI, HENRY
   In the Pale: Stories and Legends of the Russian Jews, 1897

ISAACMAN, CLARA
   Clara's Story, as told to Joan Adess Grossman, 1984

ISAACS, ABRAM S.
   Step by Step: A Story of the Early Days of Moses Mendelsohn, 1910
   The Young Champion: One Year in Grace Aguilar's Girlhood, 1913
   Under the Sabbath Lamp: Stories of Our Time for Old and Young, 1919
   School Days in Home Town, 1928

JACOBS, JOSEPH
   The Persecution of the Jews in Russia, 1891 (editor)
   American Jewish Year Book, 5676 / 1915 (editor)
   The Holy Scriptures, 1917 (editor)
   Jewish Contributions to Civilization: An Estimate, 1919

JANOWSKY, OSCAR I.   EDITOR
   The American Jew: A Reappraisal, 1964

JEHUDAH HALEVI
   See Salaman, Nina

JELENKO, MARTHA   EXECUTIVE EDITOR
   American Jewish Year Book, volumes 73 to 78 / 1972–1977 (with the American Jewish
      Committee)

JEWISH CHAUTAUQUA SOCIETY
   Papers Presented at the Fifth Annual Session, 1902

THE JEWISH PUBLICATION SOCIETY
   The Jewish Publication Society of America Twenty-fifth Anniversary, 1913
   Abridged Prayer Book for Jews in the Army and Navy of the United States, 1917
   Readings from the Holy Scriptures for Jewish Soldiers and Sailors, prepared and issued for the
      Jewish Welfare Board, United States Army and Navy, 1918
   Thirty-five Years of Jewish Endeavor, 1924
   The Rise of a New and Cultural American Jewry, 1929
   Rules for the Jewish Publication Society Press, 1931
   See Bible

JEWISH WOMEN'S CONGRESS
   Papers, 1894

JOYNER, JERRY   ILLUSTRATOR
Nicanor's Gate, by Eric A. Kimmel, 1980

KAMPF, AVRAM
Contemporary Synagogue Art, 1966 (with the Union of American Hebrew Congregations)
The Jewish Experience in the Art of the Twentieth Century, 1984 (with Bergin and Gurvey Publishers)

KAPLAN, MORDECAI M.
Mesillat Yesharim: The Path of the Upright, by Moses Hayyim Luzzatto, 1936 (translator) (Schiff Library of Jewish Classics); reprinted 1966
The Purpose and Meaning of Jewish Existence, 1964
Judaism as a Civilization: Toward a Reconstruction of American-Jewish Life, 1981 (with Reconstructionist Press)

KAPSTEIN, ISRAEL J.   TRANSLATOR
and William G. Braude, *Pesikta De-Rab Kahana: R. Kahana's Compilation of Discourses for Sabbaths and Festal Days,* 1975
and William G. Braude, *Tanna Debe Eliyyahu: The Lore of the School of Elijah,* 1981

KARP, ABRAHAM J.   EDITOR
Beginnings: Early American Judaica, 1975

KARPELES, GUSTAV
Jewish Literature and Other Essays, translated by Harriet Lieber Cohen and Henrietta Szold, 1895
A Sketch of Jewish History, translated by Henrietta Szold,
Jews and Judaism in the Nineteenth Century, translated by Henrietta Szold and Adele Szold, 1905

KATZ, JACOB
Jewish Emancipation and Self-Emancipation, 1986

KAYSER, STEPHEN S.   CO-EDITOR
with Guido Schoenberger, *Jewish Ceremonial Art,* 1955; limited paperback edition, *Art of the Hebrew Tradition,* 1955

KELLER, MATHILDE   ILLUSTRATOR
Pilgrims to Palestine, by Elma Ehrlich Levinger, 1940
The Fire Eater, by Henry J. Berkowitz, 1941
What the Moon Brought, by Sadie Rose Weilerstein, 1942
Little New Angel, by Sadie Rose Weilerstein, 1947

KIMMEL, ERIC A.
Nicanor's Gate, illustrated by Jerry Joyner, 1980
Hershel of Ostropol, illustrated by Arthur Friedman, 1982

KLAGSBRUN, FRANCINE
The Best of K'tonton, by Sadie Rose Weilerstein, illustrated by Marilyn Hirsh, 1980 (introduction)
Voices of Wisdom: Jewish Ideals and Ethics for Everyday Living, 1980 (with Pantheon Books)

KLAPERMAN, LIBBY M.
The Fighter Scholar: Saadia Gaon, 1961

KLEIN, AARON   TRANSLATOR
and Jenny Machlowitz-Klein, *Tales in Praise of the Ari,* illustrated by Moshe Raviv, 1970
See Ashtor, Eliyahu; Mahler, Raphael

KLEIN, ABRAHAM M.
Poems, 1944

KLEIN, MORDELL   EDITOR
Passover, 1974 (with Keter Publishing House)

KNOX, ISRAEL   EDITOR
with Jacob Glatstein and Samuel Margoshes, *Anthology of Holocaust Literature,* 1969

KOBER, ADOLPH
Cologne, translated by Solomon Grayzel, 1940

KOBLER, FRANZ   EDITOR
A Treasury of Jewish Letters, volumes 1 and 2, 1953 (with the East West Library)
Letters of Jews through the Ages, 1978 (with Hebrew Publishing Co.)

KOHLER, KAUFMANN   TRANSLATOR
The Book of Psalms, 1903
The Holy Scriptures, 1917 (editor)

KOHLER, MAX J.
Jewish Rights at International Congress, 1917 (reprint from the *American Jewish Year Book,*
5678 / 1917)

KOLB, LEON   EDITOR
The Woodcuts of Jakob Steinhardt, 1962

KONECKY, EDITH
Allegra Maud Goldman, 1987 (paperback, Gems of American Jewish Literature series)

KOPPMAN, LIONEL
and Bernard Postal, *A Jewish Tourist's Guide to the United States,* with a foreword by Jacob
R. Marcus, 1954

KORN, BERTRAM WALLACE
American Jewry and the Civil War, 1951 (with an introduction by Allan Nevins); paperback
reprint, 1961 (with Meridian Books)
Incidents of Travel and Adventure in the Far West, by Solomon Nunes Carvalho, 1954
(introduction)

KRACAUER, F.
and Aron Freimann, *Frankfort,* translated by Bertha Szold Levin, 1929

KRAFT, IRMA
*The Power of Purim and Other Plays: A Series of One Act Plays Designed for Jewish Religious
Schools,* 1915

KRALL, HANNA
*Shielding the Flame: An Intimate Conversation with Dr. Marek Edelman, the Last Surviving
Leader of the Warsaw Ghetto Uprising,* translated by Joanna Stasinska and Lawrence
Weschler, 1986 (with Henry Holt and Co.)

KUBIE, NORA BENJAMIN
Joel: A Novel of Young America, 1952 (with Harper and Brothers)

KUHN, LOUIS HARRIS
The World of Jo Davidson, 1958 (Covenant Book, with Farrar, Straus and Cudahy)

KURZWEIL, ARTHUR   CO-EDITOR
with Sharon Strassfeld, *Behold a Great Image: The Contemporary Jewish Experience in Photographs*, 1978

LANDSBERGER, FRANZ
Rembrandt, the Jews, and the Bible, translated by Felix N. Gerson, 1946

LASK, ISRAEL M.   TRANSLATOR
See Bialik and Bin Gorion

LASKER-SCHULER, ELSE
Hebrew Ballads and Other Poems, translated, edited, and with an introduction by Audri Durchslag and Jeanette Litman-Demeestere, preface by Yehuda Amichai, 1981 (JPS Poetry Series)

LAUTERBACH, JACOB Z.   TRANSLATOR
Mekilta de-Rabbi Ishmael, volumes 1 and 2, 1933; volume 3, 1935 (Schiff Library of Jewish Classics); paperback, 1976

LAZARRE, JACOB   (PSEUD.)
Beating Sea and Changeless Bar, 1905

LAZARUS, MORITZ
The Ethics of Judaism, volumes 1 and 2, translated by Henrietta Szold, 1900, 1901

LEARSI, RUFUS   (PSEUD. OF ISRAEL GOLDBERG)
Kasriel the Watchman and Other Stories, illustrated by Reuben Leaf, 1925
See Ash, Sholom (translation of)

LEEMAN, SAUL   BIBLE TRANSLATION COMMITTEE
The Writings: Kethubim, 1980
TANAKH: The Holy Scriptures, 1985

LEON, HARRY J.
The Jews of Ancient Rome, 1961

LEVIN, ALEXANDRA LEE
The Szolds of Lombard Street, 1960
Vision: A Biography of Harry Friedenwald, 1964

LEVIN, MEYER
The Harvest, 1978 (with Simon and Schuster)

LEVIN, SHMARYA
Forward From Exile: The Autobiography of Shmarya Levin, translated and edited by Maurice Samuel, 1967

LEVINGER, ELMA EHRLICH
Playmates in Egypt and Other Stories, 1920
Wonder Tales of Bible Days: Rabbinic Legends Retold for Jewish Children, 1929
Pilgrims to Palestine and Other Stories, 1940

LEVITIN, MIRIAM
Pathways Through the Bible workbooks, 1, 2, and 3, 1956

LEVOY, MYRON
The Hanukkah of Great-Uncle Otto, illustrated by Donna Ruff, 1984

LEWISOHN, LUDWIG
> *Renegade,* 1942
> *Among the Nations: Three Tales and a Play about Jews,* edited with an introduction by, 1948
> *The Island Within,* with an introduction by Stanley F. Chyet, 1968
> See Brod, Max; Buber, Martin; Morgenstern, Soma; Picard, Jacob; Stern, Selma
>> (translator of)

LEWY, HANS   TRANSLATOR
> with Alexander Altmann and Isaak Heinemann, *Three Jewish Philosophers: Philo, Jehudah Halevi, and Saadya Gaon,* 1960

LIBER, MAURICE
> *Rashi,* translated by Adele Szold, 1906

LIBO, KENNETH
> and Irving Howe, *How We Lived: A Documentary History of the Immigrant Jews in America, 1880–1930,* 1979 (with Richard Marek Publishers)

LIEBMAN, CHARLES S.
> *The Ambivalent American Jew: Politics, Religion, and Family in American Jewish Life,* 1973

LINETSKI, ISAAC
> *The Polish Lad,* translated by Moshe Spiegel, 1975

LIPSKY, LOUIS
> *Memoirs in Profile,* 1976, with a foreword by Ben Halpern

LIPTZIN, SOLOMON
> *Germany's Stepchildren,* 1944; paperback, 1961 (with Meridian Books)

LISKOFSKY, SIDNEY   CO-EDITOR
> with David Sidorsky and Jerome J. Shestack, *Essays on Human Rights: Contemporary Issues and Jewish Perspectives,* 1979

LITMAN-DEMEESTERE, JEANETTE   CO-EDITOR AND TRANSLATOR
> with Audri Durchslag, *Hebrew Ballads and Other Poems,* by Else Lasker-Schuler, 1981

LOEWE, HERBERT   CO-EDITOR
> with C.G. Montefiore, *A Rabbinic Anthology,* 1960 (with Meridian Books); paperback, 1963

LOEWY, BELLA
> See Graetz, Heinrich (translator of)

LOWENTHAL, MARVIN
> *The Jews of Germany: A Story of Sixteen Centuries,* 1936

LURIE, HARRY
> *A Heritage Affirmed: The Jewish Federation Movement in America,* 1961

LUZ, EHUD
> *Parallels Meet: Religion and Nationalism in the Early Zionist Movement (1882–1904),* translated by Lenn J. Schramm, 1988

LUZZATTO, MOSES HAYYIM
> *Mesillat Yesharim: The Path of the Upright,* translated by Mordecai M. Kaplan, 1936 (Schiff Library of Jewish Classics); reprinted 1966

MACHLOWITZ-KLEIN, JENNY   TRANSLATOR
> and Aaron Klein, *Tales in Praise of the Ari,* illustrated by Moshe Raviv, 1970
> See Ashtor, Eliyahu; Mahler, Raphael

MAGNUS, LADY KATIE
>*Outlines of Jewish History: From B.C. 586 to C.E. 1890,* revised by Michael Friedlaender, 1890; new edition revised by Solomon Grayzel, 1929

MAHLER RAPHAEL
>*Hasidism and the Jewish Enlightenment,* translated from the Yiddish by Eugene Orenstein, translated from the Hebrew by Aaron Klein and Jenny Machlowitz Klein, 1985

MALAMUD, BERNARD
>*The Magic Barrel and Other Stories,* 1958 (with Farrar, Straus and Cudahy)

MALIN, IRVING   CO-EDITOR
>with Irwin Stark, *Breakthrough: A Treasury of Contemporary American-Jewish Literature,* 1964 (with McGraw-Hill Book Co.)

MALLER, JULIUS B.   CO-EDITOR
>*American Jewish Year Book,* 5706 / 1945

MALTER, HENRY
>*Saadia Gaon: His Life and Works,* 1921
>*The Treatise Ta'anit of the Babylonian Talmud,* 1928; paperback, 1978 (translator) (Schiff Library of Jewish Classics)

MANDELBAUM, ALLEN
>*Chelmaxioms: The Maxims/Axioms/Maxioms of Chelm,* 1978 (with David R. Godine)
>JPS Poetry Series, co-editor with Yehuda Amichai, 1979–

MARCUS, JACOB RADER
>*Early American Jewry,* volume 1, 1951; volume 2, 1953
>*Memoirs of American Jews,* volumes 1 and 2, 1955; volume 3, 1956
>*The Jew in the Medieval World,* 1960 (paperback reprint with Meridian Books)

MARGOLIS, MAX L.
>*Micah,* 1908
>*The Story of Bible Translations,* 1917
>*The New English Translation of the Bible* (revised from the *American Jewish Year Book,* 5678 / 1917)
>*The Holy Scriptures According to the Masoretic Text* (translator/editor-in-chief), 1917
>*The Hebrew Scriptures in the Making,* 1922
>and Alexander Marx, *A History of the Jewish People,* 1927; reprint, 1958
>*Introduction to the Talmud and Midrash,* by Hermann L. Strack, 1931 (translator)

MARGOSHES, SAMUEL   EDITOR
>with Jacob Glatstein and Israel Knox, *Anthology of Holocaust Literature,* 1969

MARRUS, MICHAEL R.
>and Robert O. Paxton, *Vichy France and the Jews,* 1981

MARX, ALEXANDER
>and Max L. Margolis, *A History of the Jewish People,* 1927; reprint, 1958
>*Essays in Jewish Biography,* 1947

MATERASSI, MARIO   EDITOR
>*Shifting Landscape,* by Henry Roth, 1987

MEIR, MIRA
>*Alina: A Russian Girl Comes to Israel,* translated by Zeva Shapiro; photographs by Yael Rozen, 1982

MELTZER, MILTON
>*The Jews in America: A Picture Album,* 1986 (with photographs)

MENDELSOHN, S. FELIX
  Let Laughter Ring, 1941

MERRIAM, EVE
  Liberty's Daughter: Emma Lazarus, 1959 (with Farrar, Straus and Cudahy)

MICHAEL, SAMI
  Refuge: A Novel, translated by Edward Grossman, 1988

MICHENER, JAMES A.   EDITOR
  Firstfruits: A Harvest of New Israeli Writing, 1973

MICHMAN-MELKMAN, JOSEPH   CO-EDITOR
  with Gila Ramras-Rauch, *Facing the Holocaust: Selected Israeli Fiction,* 1986

MILGRIM, SHIRLEY
  Haym Salomon: Liberty's Son, 1975 (Covenant Book); paperback, 1985.

MILLER, SARA
  Under the Eagle's Wing, 1899

MILLGRAM, ABRAHAM E.
  Sabbath: The Day of Delight, 1944
  Jewish Worship, 1971

MISCH, MARION L.   EDITOR
  Selections for Homes and Schools, 1911

MITCHELL, STEPHEN   TRANSLATOR
  See Pagis, Dan

MODDER, MONTAGU FRANK
  The Jew in the Literature of England to the End of the 19th Century, 1939; paperback reprint, 1960 (with Meridian Books)

MONTEFIORE, CLAUDE G.   CO-EDITOR
  with H. Loewe, *A Rabbinic Anthology,* 1960 (with Meridian Books); paperback reprint, 1963

MOORE, DONALD J.
  Martin Buber: Prophet of Religious Secularism, 1975

MORGENSTERN, JULIUS
  As a Mighty Stream: The Progress of Judaism Through History, 1949

MORGENSTERN, SOMA
  The Son of the Lost Son, translated by Joseph Leftwich and Peter Gross, 1946
  In My Father's Pastures, translated by Ludwig Lewisohn, 1947
  Testament of the Lost Son, translated by Jacob Sloan and Maurice Samuel, 1950
  The Third Pillar, 1955 (with Farrar, Straus and Cudahy)

MORRIS, ROBERT   CO-EDITOR
  with Michael Freund, *Trends and Issues in Jewish Social Welfare in the United States,* 1966

MOSENTHAL, SALOMON H.
  Stories of Jewish Home Life, translated by Adele Szold, 1907

NADICH, JUDAH
  Jewish Legends of the Second Commonwealth, 1983

NATIONAL COUNCIL OF JEWISH WOMEN
  Proceedings, 1897

NEDAVA, JOSEPH
  Trotsky and the Jews, 1972

NEHER, ANDRÉ
  The Exile of the Word: From the Silence of the Bible to the Silence of Auschwitz, translated by
    David Maisel, 1981

NESHAMIT, SARAH
  The Children of Mapu Street, 1970

NETANYAHU, BENJAMIN   EDITOR
  Terrorism: How the West Can Win, 1986 (with Farrar, Straus and Giroux)

NETANYAHU, BENZION
  Don Isaac Abravanel: Statesman and Philosopher, 1953; second edition, 1968; third edition,
    1972; paperback, 1982

NEUMAN, ABRAHAM A.
  Cyrus Adler: A Biographical Sketch, 1942
  The Jews in Spain: Their Social, Political, and Cultural Life During the Middle Ages, volumes
    1 and 2, 1942

NOVITCH, MIRIAM
  with Lucy S. Dawidowicz and Tom L. Freudenheim, *Spiritual Resistance: Art from
    Concentration Camps, 1940–1945,* 1981 (with the Union of American Hebrew
    Congregations)

OFEK, URIEL
  Smoke Over Golan, translated by Israel I. Taslit; illustrated by Lloyd Bloom, 1979

OMER, DVORAH
  Rebirth: The Story of Eliezer Ben-Yehudah and the Modern Hebrew Language, 1972
    (Covenant Book)

OPATOSHU, JOSEPH   (PSEUD. OF JOSEPH OPATOVSKY)
  In Polish Woods, translated by Isaac Goldberg, 1938
  The Last Revolt: The Story of Rabbi Akiba, translated by Moshe Speigel, 1952
  A Day in Regensburg and Other Short Stories, 1968

OPPENHEIM, SAMSON D.   EDITOR
  American Jewish Year Book, 5678 and 5679 / 1917 and 1918

ORLINSKY, HARRY M.   TRANSLATOR AND EDITOR
  The Torah: The Five Books of Moses, 1962
  Genesis: A New Translation, 1966 (paperback with Harper and Row)
  Notes on the New Translation of the Torah, 1970
  The Prophets: Nevi'im, 1978
  TANAKH: The Holy Scriptures, 1985

OZ, AMOS
  In the Land of Israel, translated by Maurie Goldberg-Bartura, 1983 (with Harcourt Brace
    Jovanovich)

OZICK, CYNTHIA
  The Worlds of Maurice Samuel, edited by Milton Hindus, 1977 (introduction)

PAGIS, DAN
>   *Points of Departure,* translated by Stephen Mitchell, 1982 (JPS Poetry Series)

PARKES, JAMES
>   *The Conflict of the Church and the Synagogue,* 1961 (paperback with Meridian Books)

PATAI, RAPHAEL
>   *Israel Between East and West: A Study in Human Relations,* 1953

PAWEL, ERNST
>   *The Nightmare of Reason: A Life of Franz Kafka,* 1984 (with Farrar, Straus and Giroux)

PAXTON, ROBERT O.
>   with Michael R. Marrus, *Vichy France and the Jews,* 1981

PENDLETON, LOUIS B.
>   *Lost Prince Almon,* 1898
>   *In Assyrian Tents: The Story of the Strange Adventures of Uriel,* 1904

PEREZ, ISAAC LOEB
>   *Stories and Pictures,* translated by Helena Frank, 1904

PESSIN, DEBORAH
>   *The Aleph-Bet Story Book,* illustrated by Howard Simon, 1946; paperback and cassette, 1987

PHILIPSON, DAVID
>   *Old European Jewries,* 1894
>   *The Holy Scriptures,* 1917 (editor)
>   *Letters of Rebecca Gratz,* edited with an introduction and notes, 1929

PHILLIPS, JOSHUA
>   *A Will to Survive: Israel: The Faces of Terror 1948/The Faces of Hope Today,* 1977 (with The Dial Press/James Wade)

PICARD, JACOB
>   *The Marked One, The Lottery Ticket, and Eleven Other Stories,* translated with an introduction by Ludwig Lewisohn, 1956

PINSON, KOPPEL S.   EDITOR
>   *Nationalism and History: Essays on Old and New Judaism,* by Simon M. Dubnow, 1958; paperback, 1970 with Atheneum Books

PODWAL, MARK
>   *A Book of Hebrew Letters,* 1974
>   *A Jewish Bestiary,* 1984

POLIAKOV, LEON
>   *Harvest of Hate: The Nazi Program for the Destruction of the Jews of Europe,* foreword by Reinhold Niebuhr, 1954 (with Syracuse University Press)

POLLAK, MICHAEL
>   *Mandarins, Jews, and Missionaries: The Jewish Experience in the Chinese Empire,* 1980; paperback, 1983

POPPEL, STEPHEN M.
>   *Zionism in Germany, 1897–1933: The Shaping of a Jewish Identity,* 1977

POSENER, S.
>   *Adolphe Cremieux: A Biography,* translated by Eugene Golob, 1940

POSTAL, BERNARD
>   and Lionel Koppman, *A Jewish Tourist's Guide to the United States,* with a foreword by Jacob R. Marcus, 1954

POTOK, CHAIM   BIBLE TRANSLATION COMMITTEE
Wanderings: Chaim Potok's History of the Jews, 1978 (with Alfred A. Knopf)
The Writings: Kethubim, 1980
The Book of Lights, 1981 (with Alfred A. Knopf)
TANAKH: The Holy Scriptures, 1985

PREIL, GABRIEL
Sunset Possibilities and Other Poems, translated by Robert Friend, 1986 (JPS Poetry Series)

PROVOST, GARY AND GAIL LEVINE-PROVOST
David and Max, 1988

RABINOVICH, ABRAHAM
The Battle for Jerusalem, June 5–7, 1967, 1972
The Battle for Jerusalem, Revised 20th Anniversary Edition, 1987

RADIN, MAX
The Jews Among the Greeks and Romans, 1915
The Life of the People in Biblical Times, 1929

RAISIN, JACOB S.
The Haskalah Movement in Russia, 1913

RAMRAS-RAUCH, GILA   CO-EDITOR
with Joseph Michman-Melkman, *Facing the Holocaust: Selected Israeli Fiction,* 1986

RASKIN, PHILIP M.
Songs of a Wanderer, 1917

RAVIV, MOSHE   ILLUSTRATOR
Tales in Praise of the Ari, translated by Aaron Klein and Jenny Machlowitz-Klein, 1970

RAWIDOWICZ, SIMON
Studies in Jewish Thought, 1975

RAY, DEBORAH KOGAN   ILLUSTRATOR
The Seven Good Years and Other Stories by I.L. Peretz, by Esther Hautzig, 1984

REIDER, JOSEPH
Deuteronomy, with commentary, 1937

REIMER, JACK
Jewish Reflections on Death, 1975 (with Schocken Books)

REZNIKOFF, CHARLES
The Lionhearted: A Story About the Jews in Medieval England, 1944
and Uriah Z. Engelman, *The Jews of Charleston: A History of an American Jewish Community,* 1950
Louis Marshall: Champion of Liberty, volumes 1 and 2, with a biographical introduction by Oscar Handlin, 1957 (editor)
See Benjamin, I.J.; Cohn, Emil

RHINE, ABRAHAM BENEDICT
Leon Gordon: An Appreciation, 1910

RIBALOW, HAROLD
The Fighter from Whitechapel: Daniel Mendoza, 1962
Autobiographies of American Jews, 1965

RIEGER, SHAY   ILLUSTRATOR
The Secret of the Sabbath Fish, by Ben Aronin, 1979
Honi and His Magic Circle, by Phillis Gershator, 1980

RIEMER, JACK   EDITOR
Jewish Reflections on Death, 1975 (with Schocken Books)

ROBINSON, IRA   EDITOR
Cyrus Adler: Selected Letters, 2 volumes, 1985 (with the Jewish Theological Seminary of
   America)

ROBINSON, JACOB
And the Crooked Shall Be Made Straight, 1965 (with Macmillan Co.)

ROGOW, SALLY
Lillian Wald: The Nurse in Blue, illustrated by Itzhak Sankowsky, 1966 (Covenant Book)

ROSEN, ANNE, JONATHAN, AND NORMA
A Family Passover, photographs by Laurence Salzmann, 1980

ROSENAK, MICHAEL
Commandments and Concerns: Jewish Religious Education in Secular Society, 1987

ROSENBAUM, JEANETTE W.
Myer Myers: Goldsmith, 1723–1795, 1954

ROSENBERRY, VERA   ILLUSTRATOR
Esther, by Miriam Chaikin, 1987
Anne Frank: Life in Hiding, by Johanna Hurwitz, 1988

ROSENBLOOM, NOAH H.
Tradition in an Age of Reform, 1976

ROSKIES, DAVID G.
The Literature of Destruction: Jewish Responses to Catastrophe, 1989

ROTH, CECIL
Venice, 1930 (Jewish Communities Series)
A History of the Marranos, 1932
A Life of Menasseh Ben Israel: Rabbi, Printer, and Diplomat, 1934
The History of the Jews of Italy, 1946
The House of Nasi: Doña Gracia, 1947; 1978 paperback edition, *Doña Gracia of the House
   of Nasi*
The House of Nasi: The Duke of Naxos, 1948
Personalities and Events in Jewish History: A Collection of Essays, 1953
The Jews in the Renaissance, 1959
Essays and Portraits in Anglo-Jewish History, 1963

ROTH, HENRY
Shifting Landscape, edited by Mario Materassi, 1987 (Philip and Muriel Berman edition)

ROTHCHILD, SYLVIA
Keys to a Magic Door: A Biography of I.L. Peretz, 1959 (with Farrar, Straus and Cudahy)

ROTHGIESSER, RUBEN
The Ship of Hope, translated by Felix N. Gerson, 1939
The Well of Gerar, translated by Harry Schneiderman, 1953

ROTHKOFF, AARON
Bernard Revel: Builder of American Orthodox Jewry, 1972

ROZEN, YAEL   PHOTOGRAPHER
   Alina: A Russian Girl Comes to Israel, by Mira Meir, translated by Zeva Shapiro, 1982

ROZENBERG, MARTIN S.   BIBLE TRANSLATION COMMITTEE
   The Writings: Kethubim, 1980
   TANAKH: The Holy Scriptures, 1985

RUBIN, RUTH
   Voices of a People: The Story of Yiddish Folksong, 1979

RUFF, DONNA   ILLUSTRATOR
   The Hanukkah of Great-Uncle Otto, by Myron Levoy, 1984
   Hannah Szenes: A Song of Light, by Maxine Schur, 1986

RUSKAY, ESTHER J.
   Hearth and Home Essays, 1902

RUSSO-JEWISH COMMITTEE OF LONDON
   The Persecution of the Jews in Russia, with a map of Russia, showing the Pale of Jewish
      Settlement, 1891 (edited by Joseph Jacobs)

SACHAR, HOWARD M.
   A History of Israel, 1976 (with Alfred A. Knopf)
   Zionism at the U.N.: A Diary of the First Days, by Eliahu Elath, translated by Michael
      Ben-Yitzhak, 1976 (foreword)

SACHS, ABRAHAM
   Worlds that Passed, Translated by Harold Berman, 1928

SACHS, NELLY
   O the Chimneys: Selected Poems, Including Eli, A Verse Play, translated by M. Hamburger,
      Ruth and Matthew Mead, and Michael Roloff, 1968 (with Farrar, Straus and Giroux)

SALAMAN, NINA
   See Davis, Nina
   Selected Poems of Jehudah Halevi, edited by Heinrich Brody, 1924 (Schiff Library of
      Jewish Classics)

SALZMANN, LAURENCE   PHOTOGRAPHER
   A Family Passover, by Anne, Jonathan, and Norma Rosen, 1980

SAMPTER, JESSIE
   Brand Plucked from the Fire, illustrated by Maxim B. Gottlieb, 1937

SAMUEL, MAURICE
   Harvest in the Desert, 1944
   Prince of the Ghetto, 1948
   Blood Accusation: The Strange History of the Beiliss Case, 1966 (with Alfred A. Knopf)
   Forward from Exile: The Autobiography of Shmarya Levin, 1967 (translator and editor)
   The Worlds of Maurice Samuel, edited by Milton Hindus, 1977
   See Bein, Alex; Morgenstern, Soma (translator of)

SANDROW, NAHMA
   Vagabond Stars: A World History of the Yiddish Theater, 1977 (with Harper and Row)

SANKOWSKY, ITZHAK   ILLUSTRATOR
   Lillian Wald: Nurse in Blue, by Sally Rogow, 1966

SARNA, JONATHAN D.
JPS: The Americanization of Jewish Culture, 1989 (Philip and Muriel Berman edition)

SARNA, NAHUM M.   BIBLE TRANSLATION COMMITTEE
with Moshe Greenberg and Jonas C. Greenfield, *The Book of Psalms: A New Translation,* 1972
The Writings: Kethubim, 1979
with Moshe Greenberg and Jonas C. Greenfield, *The Book of Job: A New Translation According to the Traditional Hebrew Text,* 1980 (introduction)
TANAKH: The Holy Scriptures, 1985

SCHECHTER, SOLOMON
Studies in Judaism, 1896 (with Macmillan)
Studies in Judaism: Second Series, 1908
The Holy Scriptures, 1917 (editor)
Studies in Judaism: Third Series, 1924

SCHEINDLIN, RAYMOND P.
Wine, Women, and Death: Medieval Hebrew Poems on the Good Life, 1986

SCHIMMEL, HAROLD   TRANSLATOR
See Yeshurun, Avoth

SCHNABEL, LOUIS
Voegelle's Marriage and Other Tales, 1892

SCHNEID, HAYYIM   EDITOR
The Family, 1974 (with Keter Publishing House)

SCHNEIDERMAN, HARRY   EDITOR
American Jewish Year Book, volumes 21 to 50 / 1919–1948 (with the American Jewish Committee)

SCHOENBERGER, GUIDO   CO-EDITOR
with Stephen S. Kayser, *Jewish Ceremonial Art,* 1955; limited paperback edition, *Art of the Hebrew Tradition,* 1955

SCHOFFMAN, LOUIS   TRANSLATOR
A History of the Jews in Christian Spain, by Yitzhak Baer, volume 1, 1961; volume 2, 1966; paperback reprint, 1978

SCHOLEM, GERSHOM S.
Kabbalah, 1974 (with Keter Publishing House)
Sabbatai Sevi: The Mystical Messiah, translated by R.J. Zwi Werblowsky, 1975 (with Princeton University Press)
Walter Benjamin: The Story of a Friendship, translated by Harry Zohn, 1982
Origins of the Kabbalah, translated by Allan Arkush, edited by R.J. Zwi Werblowsky, 1987 (with Princeton University Press)

SCHORSCH, ISMAR
Organized Jewish Reactions to Anti-Semitism Before the First World War, 1972 (with Columbia University Press)

SCHRAMM, LENN J.   TRANSLATOR
Parallels Meet: Religion and Nationalism in the Early Zionist Movement (1882–1904), by Ehud Luz, 1988

SCHULMAN, GRACE   TRANSLATOR
At the Stone of Losses, by T. Carmi, 1984 (with University of California Press)

SCHULMAN, SAMUEL
> *The Holy Scriptures,* 1917 (editor)
> *Rosh Ha-Shanah and Yom Kippur,* 1920

SCHUR, MAXINE
> *Hannah Szenes: A Song of Light,* illustrated by Donna Ruff, 1986

SCHWARTZ, AMY
> *Mrs. Moskowitz and the Sabbath Candlesticks,* 1984
> *Yossel Zissel and the Wisdom of Chelm,* 1986

SCHWARTZ, HOWARD
> *Elijah's Violin and Other Jewish Fairy Tales,* illustrated by Linda Heller, 1983 (with Harper and Row)

SCHWARZ, LEO W.
> *Memoirs of My People Through a Thousand Years,* 1943 (editor)
> *The Menorah Treasury,* 1964 (editor)
> *Wolfson of Harvard: Portrait of a Scholar,* 1978

SCHWEID, ELIEZER
> *Israel at the Crossroads,* 1973

SEGAL, DAVID   TRANSLATOR
> See Bartov, Hanoch

SEGAL, NELLY   TRANSLATOR
> See Deem, Ariella

SEID, RUTH
> See Sinclair, Jo

SELDIN, RUTH   ASSOCIATE EDITOR
> *American Jewish Year Book,* volumes 86 and 87, 1986–1987 (with the American Jewish Committee)

SELTZER, ADELE SZOLD
> See Frank, Ulrich; Karpeles, Gustav; Liber, Maurice; Mosenthal, Salomon H. (translator of)

SHABTAI, YAAKOV
> *Past Continuous,* translated by Dalya Bilu, 1985

SHAHAM, NATHAN
> *The Other Side of the Wall,* translated by Leonard Gold, 1983

SHAKED, GERSHON
> *The Shadows Within: Essays on Contemporary Jewish Writers,* 1987

SHAMIR, ILANA   CO-EDITOR
> with Shlomo Shavit, *Young Reader's Encyclopedia of Jewish History,* 1987 (with Viking Kestrel)

SHAPIRO, DAVID   BIBLE TRANSLATION COMMITTEE
> *The Writings: Kethubim,* 1980
> *TANAKH: The Holy Scriptures,* 1985

SHAVIT, SHLOMO   CO-EDITOR
> See Shamir, Ilana

SHAZAR, ZALMAN
> *Morning Stars,* translated by Sulamith Nardi, 1967

SHERMAN, EILEEN BLUESTONE
Monday in Odessa, 1986

SHESTACK, JEROME J.   CO-EDITOR
with David Sidorsky and Sidney Liskofsky, *Essays on Human Rights: Contemporary Issues and Jewish Perspectives,* 1979

SICHROVSKY, PETER
Strangers in Their Own Land, 1986 (with Basic Books)

SIDORSKY, DAVID   CO-EDITOR
with Jerome J. Shestack, and Sidney Liskofsky, *Essays on Human Rights: Contemporary Issues and Jewish Perspectives,* 1979

SIEGEL, RICHARD   EDITOR
with Sharon and Michael Strassfeld, *The Jewish Catalog: A Do-It-Yourself Kit,* 1973

SIGBERMAN, RICHARD   ILLUSTRATOR
In the Shade of the Chestnut Tree, by Benjamin Tene, translated by Reuben Ben-Joseph, 1981

SILVER, ABBA HILLEL
Where Judaism Differed, 1957 (with Macmillan Co.)

SILVER, KENNETH E.
and Romy Golan, *The Circle of Montparnasse: Jewish Artists in Paris, 1905–1945,* 1985 (with Universe Books)

SIMON, HOWARD   ILLUSTRATOR
The Aleph-Bet Story Book, by Deborah Pessin, 1946; paperback and cassette, 1987

SIMON, LEON   EDITOR AND TRANSLATOR
Selected Essays, by Ahad Ha'Am (pseud. of Asher Ginzberg), 1912; new edition, 1936; 1962, paperback (with Meridian Books)

SIMON, SOLOMON
My Jewish Roots, translated by Shlomo Katz, 1956
In the Thicket, 1963

SINCLAIR, JO   (PSEUD. OF RUTH SEID)
Wasteland, 1987 (paperback, Gems of American Jewish Literature series)

SINGER, DAVID   ASSOCIATE EDITOR, EDITOR
American Jewish Year Book, volumes 79 to 88 / 1978-1988, etc. (with the American Jewish Committee)

SINGER, ISAAC BASHEVIS
The Spinoza of Market Street, 1962 (with Farrar, Straus and Co.)
Short Friday and Other Stories, 1965 (with Farrar, Straus and Giroux)
In My Father's Court, 1966 (with Farrar, Straus and Giroux)
The Manor, 1968 (with Farrar, Straus and Giroux)
Tully Filmus: Selected Drawings, 1971 (introduction)
Naftali the Storyteller and His Horse, Sus, illustrated by Margot Zemach, 1976 (with Farrar, Straus and Giroux)
Gifts, 1985 (Philip and Muriel Berman edition)

SLOUSCHZ, NAHUM
The Renascence of Hebrew Literature (1743–1885), translated by Henrietta Szold, 1909
Travels in North Africa, translated by Amy E. Schechter, 1927; 1944 edition, *The Jews of North Africa*

SOCIETY FOR THE HISTORY OF CZECHOSLOVAK JEWS
   The Jews of Czechoslovakia, volumes 1 and 2, 1968
   The Jews of Czechoslovakia, volume 3; Avigdor Dagan, editor-in-chief, Gertrude Hirschler
      and Lewis Weiner, associate editors, 1984

SOLIS-COHEN, JR., EMILY
   David the Giant Killer and Other Tales of Grandma Lopez, illustrated by Alfred Feinberg,
      1908
   The Breakfast of the Birds and Other Stories from the Hebrew of Judah Steinberg, illustrated
      by Alfred Feinberg and Edith Rudin, 1917
   The Holy Scriptures: An Abridgment for Use in the Jewish School and Home, 1931 (editor)
   Hanukkah: The Feast of Lights, 1937 (editor)

SOLIS-COHEN, SOLOMON   TRANSLATOR
   Selected Poems of Moses Ibn Ezra, edited by Heinrich Brody, 1934 (Schiff Library of Jewish
      Classics)

SOLOVEITCHIK, JOSEPH B.
   Halakhic Man, translated by Lawrence Kaplan, 1984

SPECTOR, BARBARA
   The Great Jewish Quiz Book, 1986

SPIEGEL, SHALOM
   Legends of the Bible, by Louis Ginzberg, 1956 (with Simon and Schuster, Inc.)
      (introduction)
   Hebrew Reborn, 1962, paperback (with Meridian Books)
   *The Last Trial: On the Legends and Lore of the Command of Abraham to Offer Isaac as a
      Sacrifice: The Akedah,* translated by Judah Goldin, 1968 (with Pantheon Books)

SPEISER, EPHRAIM A.   BIBLE TRANSLATION COMMITTEE
   The Torah: The Five Books of Moses, 1962
   The Prophets: Nevi'im, 1978
   TANAKH: The Holy Scriptures, 1985

STANISLAWSKI, MICHAEL
   Tsar Nicholas I and the Jews: The Transformation of Jewish Society in Russia, 1825–1855, 1983

STAVROULAKIS, NIKOS   ILLUSTRATOR
   The Book of Jeremiah: A New Translation, 1974

STEHLE, BERNARD F.
   Another Kind of Witness, foreword by Geoffrey Hartman, afterword by Sister Gloria
      Coleman, 1988 (Philip and Muriel Berman edition)

STEINBERG, FANNIE
   Birthday in Kishinev, illustrated by Luba Hanuschak, 1979

STEINBERG, JEHUDAH
   In Those Days: The Story of an Old Man, translated by George Jeshurun, 1915
   The Breakfast of the Birds and Other Stories from the Hebrew of Judah Steinberg, translated
      by Emily Solis-Cohen, illustrated by Alfred Feinberg and Edith Rudin, 1917

STEINER, CONNIE COLKER
   On Eagles' Wings and Other Things, 1987

STEINHARDT, JACOB   ILLUSTRATOR
   The Book of Jonah, hand-lettered Hebrew and English text by Franzisca Baruch, 1953
      (woodcut illustrations)
   The Book of Ruth, hand-lettered Hebrew and English text by Franzisca Baruch, 1957
      (woodcut illustrations)

STERN, ELLEN NORMAN
   Embattled Justice, 1971 (Covenant Book)

STERN, HORACE
   The Spiritual Values of Life, 1953

STERN, SELMA
   The Spirit Returneth: A Novel, translated by Ludwig Lewisohn, 1946
   The Court Jew: A Contribution to the History of the Period of Absolutism in Central Europe,
      translated by Ralph Weiman, 1950
   Yossel of Rosheim, 1965

STILL, PETER
   The Kidnapped and the Ransomed, introduction by Maxwell Whiteman, 1970

STILLMAN, NORMAN A.
   The Jews of Arab Lands: A History and Source Book, 1980

STRACK, HERMANN L.
   Introduction to the Talmud and Midrash, translated by Max L. Margolis, 1931

STRASSFELD, SHARON   CO-EDITOR
   with Arthur Kurzweil, *Behold a Great Image: The Contemporary Jewish Experience in
      Photographs,* 1978

STRASSFELD, SHARON AND MICHAEL   EDITORS
   with Richard Siegel, *The Jewish Catalog: A Do-It-Yourself Kit,* illustrated by Stuart
      Copans, 1973
   The Second Jewish Catalog: Sources and Resources, illustrated by Stuart Copans, 1976
   The Third Jewish Catalog: Creating Community, illustrated by Stuart Copans, 1980

STRAUS, RAPHAEL
   Regensburg and Augsburg, translated by Felix N. Gerson, 1939 (Jewish Communities
      Series)

STRAUSS, LEO
   Philosophy and Law: Essays Toward the Understanding of Maimonides and His Predecessors,
      translated by Fred Baumann; foreword by Ralph Lerner, 1987

SWICHKOW, LOUIS J.
   and Lloyd P. Gartner, *The History of the Jews of Milwaukee,* 1963

SYRKIN, MARIE
   Blessed is the Match: The Story of Jewish Resistance, 1947; paperback, 1976

SZOLD, ADELE
   See Seltzer, Adele Szold

SZOLD, HENRIETTA
   History of the Jews, by Heinrich Graetz, index volume, 1898
   American Jewish Year Book, 5665 / 1904-1905 (co-editor with Cyrus Adler) 1904
   American Jewish Year Book, 5666 / 1905-1906 (co-editor with Cyrus Adler) 1905
   American Jewish Year Book, 5667 / 1906-1907 (editor), 1906
   American Jewish Year Book, 5668 / 1907-1908 (editor), 1907
   See Darmesteter, Arsène; Dubnow, Simon; Ginzberg, Louis; Karpeles, Gustav; Lazarus,
      Moritz; Slouschz, Nahum (translator of)

SZYK, ARTHUR   ILLUSTRATOR
   Pathways Through the Bible, by Mortimer J. Cohen, 1946; paperback, 1987

TAGER, ALEXANDER S.
The Decay of Czarism, 1935

TCHERIKOVER, VICTOR
Hellenistic Civilization and the Jews, translated by S. Applebaum, 1959

TENE, BENJAMIN
In the Shade of the Chestnut Tree, translated by Reuben Ben-Joseph; illustrated by Richard Sigberman, 1981

TRACHTENBERG, JOSHUA
The Devil and the Jews, 1961, paperback (with Meridian Books); with a new foreword by Marc Saperstein, 1983
Jewish Magic and Superstition, 1963, paperback (with Meridian Books)

TWERSKY, ISADORE
Rabad of Posquieres: A Twelfth-Century Talmudist, 1980

USQUE, SAMUEL
Consolation for the Tribulations of Israel, translated by Martin A. Cohen, 1964; paperback 1977

VILNAY, ZEV
Legends of Palestine, 1932
Legends of Jerusalem, 1973
Legends of Judea and Samaria, 1975
Legends of Galilee, Jordan, and Sinai, 1979

VOGELSTEIN, HERMANN
Rome, translated by Moses Hadas, 1940 (Jewish Communities Series)

VOSS, CARL HERMANN   EDITOR
Stephen S. Wise: Servant of the People, 1969

WEIHS, ERIKA   ILLUSTRATOR
Theodor Herzl: The Road to Israel, by Miriam Gurko, 1988

WEILERSTEIN, SADIE ROSE
What the Moon Brought, illustrated by Mathilda Keller, 1942
Little New Angel, illustrated by Mathilda Keller, 1947
K'tonton on an Island in the Sea, illustrated by Michael Berenstain, 1976
The Best of K'tonton, illustrated by Marilyn Hirsh; with an introduction by Francine Klagsbrun, 1980
K'tonton in the Circus: A Hanukkah Adventure, illustrated by Marilyn Hirsh, 1981
Ten and a Kid, illustrated by Janina Domanska Laskowski, 1961

WEINER, LOUIS   EDITOR
See Society for the History of Czechoslovak Jews

WEINER, MAX   EDITOR
Abraham Geiger and Liberal Judaism, translated by Ernst Schlochauer, 1962

WEINRYB, BERNARD
The Jews of Poland, 1973

WEISBORD, ROBERT G.
African Zion, 1968

WEISBROT, ROBERT
The Jews of Argentina: From the Inquisition to Peron, 1979

WEIZMANN, CHAIM
Trial and Error: The Autobiography of Chaim Weizmann, volumes 1 and 2, 1949 (with Harper and Brothers)

WERBLOWSKY, R.J. ZWI
Joseph Karo: Lawyer and Mystic, 1977, paperback
Origins of the Kabbalah, by Gershom Scholem, translated by Allan Arkush, 1987 (with Princeton University Press) (editor)

WHITEMAN, MAXWELL
and Edwin Wolf 2nd, *The History of the Jews of Philadelphia from Colonial Times to the Age of Jackson,* 1956; Bicentennial Edition, 1975
The Kidnapped and the Ransomed, by Peter Still, 1970 (introduction)

WIENER, HERBERT
The Wild Goats of Ein Gedi, 1963; paperback reprint (with Meridian Books)

WIESEL, ELIE
Jews of Silence, 1967 (with Holt, Rinehart and Winston)

WINCELBERG, SHIMON AND ANITA
The Samurai of Vishogrod: The Notebooks of Jacob Marateck, 1976

WINEMAN, ARYEH
Beyond Appearances: Stories from the Kabbalistic Ethical Writings, 1988

WISCHNITZER, MARK
To Dwell in Safety: The Story of Jewish Migration since 1800, 1948

WISCHNITZER, RACHEL
Synagogue Architecture in the U.S.: An Interpretation, 1955
The Architecture of the European Synagogue, 1964

WISE, GEORGE S.   CO-EDITOR
with Salo W. Baron, *Violence and Defense in the Jewish Experience,* 1977

WISE, STEPHEN S.
See Voss, Carl H.

WISE, WILLIAM
Silversmith of Old New York: Myer Myers, 1958 (with Farrar, Straus and Cudahy) (Covenant Book)
Albert Einstein: Citizen of the World, 1960 (with Farrar, Straus and Cudahy) (Covenant Book)

WISSE, RUTH R.   EDITOR
with Irving Howe, *The Best of Sholom Aleichem,* 1979 (with New Republic Books)

WOLF 2ND, EDWIN
and Maxwell Whiteman, *The History of the Jews in Philadelphia From Colonial Times to the Age of Jackson,* 1956; Bicentennial Edition, 1975

WOLFENSTEIN, MARTHA
    Idyls of the Gass, 1901
    A Renegade: And Other Tales, 1905

WOLFF, ULLA
    See Frank, Ulrich

YAHIL, LENI
    The Rescue of Danish Jewry, 1969

YEHOASH
    See Bloomgarden, Solomon

YELLIN, DAVID
    and Israel Abrahams, *Maimonides*, 1903

YERUSHALMI, YOSEF HAYIM
    Haggadah and History, 1975
    Zakhor: Jewish History and Jewish Memory, 1982 (with University of Washington Press)

YESHURUN, AVOTH
    The Syrian-African Rift and Other Poems, translated and with a foreword by Harold
        Schimmel, 1981 (JPS Poetry Series)

ZANGWILL, ISRAEL
    Children of the Ghetto: Being Pictures of a Peculiar People, volumes 1 and 2, 1892
    Dreamers of the Ghetto, 1898 (with Harper and Brothers)
    They That Walk in Darkness: Ghetto Tragedies, 1899
    Selected Religious Poems of Solomon Ibn Gabirol, edited by Israel Davidson, 1923 (Schiff
        Library of Jewish Classics) (translator)
    Selected Works of Israel Zangwill, 1938

ZANGWILL, MARK   ILLUSTRATOR
    Sons of the Covenant: A Tale of London Jewry, by Samuel Gordon, 1900

ZAR, ROSE
    assisted by Eric A. Kimmel, *In the Mouth of the Wolf*, 1984

ZEITLIN, SOLOMON
    The Rise and Fall of the Judaean State, volume 1, 1962; volume 2, 1967; volume 3, 1978

ZEMACH, MARGOT   ILLUSTRATOR
    Naftali the Storyteller and His Horse, Sus, by Isaac Bashevis Singer, 1976 (with Farrar,
        Straus and Giroux)

ZIRNDORFF, HENRY
    Some Jewish Women, translated by Sylvan Drey, 1892

ZOHN, HARRY   TRANSLATOR
    See Scholem, Gershom

INDEX

CPSIA information can be obtained
at www.ICGtesting.com
Printed in the USA
LVHW061915140223
739490LV00005B/284

9 780827 615